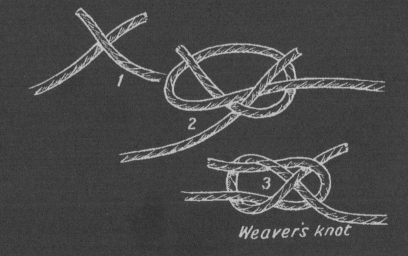

Weaver's knot

1066   1160   1210   1240   1300   1340   1360

1430   1440   1450   1460   1480   1485

1555   1560   1565   1570   1580   1585

Here are 38 illustrations showing how armour developed during the six centuries between 1066 and 1650. The metal armour of the Normans and Anglo-Saxons consisted of a tunic of what is commonly called "mail." It was composed first of all of iron rings, sewn on a foundation

of cloth or leather, and subsequently of rings interlinked with one another. This was called "chaain mail." As time went on additions were made to the mail armour, til the whole body from head to heel, and to the very tips of the fingers, was encased in iron or steel. Armour reached its

L.M.S. "Coronation" and the Train it Draws

The steam passes through the steam pipe to the superheater in front, where it re-enters the boiler in small tubes placed inside larger ones, and returns superheated to pass to the cylinders, where it is admitted on each side of the piston alternately by the slide valves. The exhaust steam passes to a central blast pipe, and thence to the atmosphere, by way of the chimney, which is streamlined. The valve-gear is of the Walschaert type, placed outside the frames, and consisting of rods and links actuated by a crank. The position of the links is moved by the driver when reversing. The whole engine is enclosed in a streamlined casing to minimise wind resistance.

The coaches of the train are luxuriously appointed inside, and are finished in panels of Empire woods. The exterior painting is in blue, with four bands of silver running the whole length of the train. The locomotive shown in the illustration set up on June 29th, 1937, a British Empire speed record of 114 miles per hour during the course of a trial run from Euston to Crewe. On the return journey it established a further record by covering the 158·1 miles from Crewe to Euston in 119 minutes, start to stop, at an average speed of 79·7 miles per hour. It is more than likely that this type of engine will be the normal express locomotive of the near future

How Does That Locomotive Work? The L

In this drawing is shown the magnificent train of the London, Midland & Scottish Railway called " The Coronation Scot," hauled by one of the engines of the Coronation class. In addition to the " Coronation," shown above, there are four sister engines, called " Queen Elizabeth," " Queen Mary," " Princess Alice," and " Princess Alexandra." All are of the 4–6–2 or Pacific type, and are painted in a pleasing combination of blue with silver striping. These engines do the journey between Euston and Glasgow, including one stop in each direction at Carlisle, a distance of 401½ miles, in 6½ hours—that is, at an average speed of nearly 62 miles per hour.

The total weight of the train, exclusive of locomotive and tender, is 297 tons. These engines have four cylinders, two outside ones driving the second axle, and the inside two driving the first axle. In the drawing only one outside cylinder is shown. The tender carries ten tons of coal and four thousand gallons of water. Steam is raised in the boiler to a pressure up to 250 pounds per square inch, from water supplied through the feed or clack valves behind the chimney. The steam is admitted through a regulating valve by the driver, whose position is normally on the left-hand side of the cab, although in the drawing, for clearness, we show him on the right.

Plate II

t? Armour Through Six Centuries

1385 1395 1400 1405 1415 1420

1490 1495 1500 1520 1530 1540 1550

1600 1610 1615 1630 1640 1650

ghest state of perfection in the 15th and 16th centries, and many of the suits made for princes and nobles ere very beautiful works of art, the iron or steel being amascened with gold and magnificently engraved. It was e use of firearms that led to the discarding of armour.

Life guards and Horse Guards wear armour for decorative purposes. Most suits of armour later than 1560 were made for tournaments, rather than battlefields, and some of these are shown on the bottom row. The figures dated from 1600 onwards are wearing actual fighting suits

Plate I

EVERYBODY'S BOOK *of* KNOWLEDGE

A Giant Compendium of Yesteryear's Facts

Edited by Charles Ray

PRION

ACKNOWLEDGEMENTS

The publishers would like to thank the team at IPC Media Ltd
for all their help in compiling this book,
particularly David Abbott and Mark Winterton.

Every effort has been made to acknowledge correctly and contact the source
and /or copyright holder of each picture and Carlton Books Limited
apologises for any unintentional errors or omissions that will be corrected
in future editions of this book.

THIS IS A PRION BOOK

This edition published in Great Britain in 2012 by Prion
An imprint of the Carlton Publishing Group
20 Mortimer Street
London W1T 3JW

First published as *Every Boy's Book of Knowledge* in 2007

ISBN: 978-1-85375-880-5

Editorial Director: Piers Murray Hill
Project Editor: Lara Maiklem

Art Director: Lucy Coley
Design: Chris Francis
Production: Janette Burgin

Printed in Dubai

Knowledge is power. Whether it's during a discussion around the water cooler at work, at the Sunday evening pub quiz, in a lull at a dinner party or at the back of the school bus, knowing if a sloth eats upside down, why onions make us cry, and how to tie a sheepshank is essential stuff. Having the right fact to hand at the right moment will never fail to impress your chums, and *Everybody's Book of Knowledge* is here to help you prepare for those awkward moments, when the golden wheat of facts needs to be separated from the chaff of stuff and nonsense.

The nuggets of knowledge and wonderful illustrations selected for this book were originally found in a two-volume 1930s encyclopedia called *Everybody's Enquire Within*. 'Enquire Within' books were common in households from the Victorian times onwards, dispensing household tips, etiquette, and educating youngsters and grown-ups alike on the mysteries and machinations of the world around them. They were, in effect, the 'Google' of their day. In fact, when Tim Berners-Lee was developing what eventually became the World Wide Web, he began by calling it 'ENQUIRE', recalling nights he had spent as a child with his head lost in a dusty volume.

Our interests may have changed over the years, and in many ways the world has become a much smaller place, but the answers to all the pithy questions posed here (a few of which might be debatable 70 years on!) still have the power to fascinate and instill the wonder of knowledge.

Roddy Lumsden, 2007

INTRODUCTION

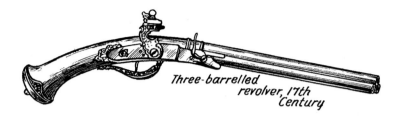

Three-barrelled revolver, 17th Century

This book, as its title implies, is a work that will answer all sort of questions and supply all kind of information to those who consult it. In our reading we are constantly coming across names and references that are unknown to us, and when we consult ordinary books of reference, such as encyclopedias and dictionaries, we are unable to get help. Where, for instance, shall we turn to discover who were the White-eyed Kaffir, the Mad Mullah, or the Hanging Judge? The terms are not in the books of reference generally available.

Then questions often arise in conversation to which it is difficult to find answers. Take for example, such a point as whether mad dogs dislike water. This cropped up in a group of which the Editor formed a member, and when encyclopedias and even medical textbooks on rabies were consulted no answer could be found. The fact is that mad dogs do not dislike water, though people bitten by them do.

It is useful information of this kind that the present book supplies, and a glance at its pages will show the immense variety of subjects with which it deals. Are diamonds always white? What is a magic square? Must the Riot Act be read before soldiers can fire? Did the "Titanic" sink to the bottom of the sea? Can an egg be balanced on end? What is rice paper? Is the number 13 unlucky? What is the Jolly Roger? Is a high forehead a sign of intelligence? Is a scare a cure for hiccoughs? What is a Nordic? Does ivy damage a wall? What is a singing mouse? Does it rain on the Sahara? Was St. George a Briton? These are a few typical questions answered in the book. Every department of knowledge has been drawn upon to supply answers to the questions that are asked, and a vast amount of expert knowledge enlisted to ensure that the facts given shall be accurate and based on the latest information available. The book contains all kinds of out-of-the-way information about people and animals and plants and places. It gives thousands of scientific facts, embodying the most recent discoveries.

Barque

Hopper bucket dredger

Coal barrow

Slinging a cask

Students, old and young, will find the work of the greatest use to them in preparing for examinations, where general knowledge papers are an important feature, and those of maturer years who read or consult the book will find that they have, in the pleasantest manner, added enormously to their stock of knowledge, no matter how well stored their minds may previously have been. Here, brought within the covers of a single work, is given a mass of facts unparalleled in any other book.

An outstanding feature of the work is the vast mass of illustrations specially prepared with the greatest care by a staff of experts – photographs gathered from all over the world, and drawings by artist of technical knowledge and high ability. The full-page drawings are particularly valuable and their comprehensiveness is unique.

A word must be said about the arrangement of the letterpress. No advantage would have been gained by given the matter in alphabetical order, or arranging it in groups according to subjects, for, as it is, any fact or illustration in the book can be turned up in a moment by reference to the large and carefully prepared index at the end of the work. By arranging the matter in the way that has been done, the book becomes not only a valuable work of reference, but a fascinating book of reading, as entertaining as any novel.

Malabar Sword

Charles Ray, 1938

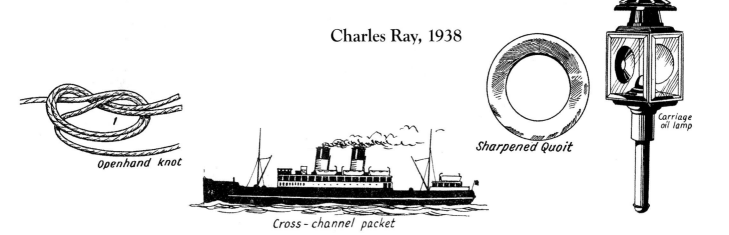

Openhand knot

Cross-channel packet

Sharpened Quoit

Carriage oil lamp

Of What Use Are a Cat's Whiskers?

THE domesticated cat is descended from the wild cat, and this animal, like its relations the lion, tiger and leopard, dwells in country covered with long grass and undergrowth.

The long whiskers of the domesticated cat

It seeks its prey at night, and prowling in the dark the whiskers form a very useful guide. They act almost like a pair of hands reached out to feel the way. They tell the animal where the route is clear, being very sensitive to the touch of obstacles.

The domesticated cat has inherited its whiskers from its wild ancestors, and though they are not needed so much as they were in old days, they are still very useful to the animal, which loves to prowl in out-of-the-way places indoors or out, in search of mice and birds.

Are Diamonds Always White?

ALTHOUGH most diamonds are colourless, these gems are also found in blue, green, pink or rose, yellow, brown, and black, the colours being due to impurities in the carbon of which the diamonds are composed. The yellow diamond, for example, is a compound of carbon and the fluoride of aluminium.

The blue "Hope" diamond

A green diamond is the rarest of all gems and far eclipses the emerald in sparkling brilliance. Pale blue and rose-coloured diamonds are frequently found, but the really dark blue are rare.

The most famous of all coloured diamonds is the blue Hope diamond of $44\frac{1}{4}$ carats, which is believed to be the Tavernier blue diamond of the old French regalia cut down. Black diamonds of great beauty are occasionally found in Borneo. They are so hard that ordinary diamond dust makes no impression upon them and they can be ground and polished only by using their own dust for the purpose.

Although there are many rose-coloured diamonds, only one really ruby red specimen has been found. Many coloured diamonds are not truly transparent, but are more or less opalescent. It is, of course, the transparent ones which are valuable.

How Does a Ship's Siren Work?

IN the ordinary ship's siren, compressed air is blown through holes in the lid of a box against a flat metal disc with corresponding holes. The air rotates the disc, and as each pair of holes coincides the air passes out world. Their sound can be heard five miles away, and yet it is not distressing to passengers on board.

The sirens are worked by steam, which enters a circular chamber and goes round to a valve, where it passes

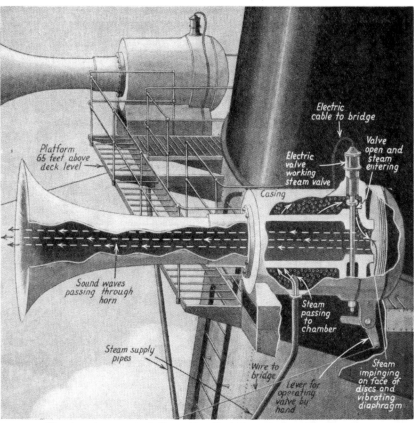

The giant sirens on the "Queen Mary" which can be heard for five miles

and sets up waves that cause the sounds that are heard. These rise in pitch as the disc revolves more and more rapidly.

The latest type of steamship siren, however, is that used on the *Queen Mary*. There are three huge sirens, two on the fore funnel and one on the midships funnel. They are seven feet long, the largest ship's sirens in the

out and impinges on four discs, vibrating diaphragm plates and producing the note which passes out through the horn. The steam valves are operated electrically by push-buttons on the bridge, or by a hand wire and lever.

The electric horn on a motor-car is worked quite differently, as shown in the drawing on the next page. A small electric motor is driven by a battery and operated by a switch on the steering-wheel. This motor revolves at high speed and drives a notched wheel. The notches strike a steel stud fixed in a diaphragm, vibrate the dia-

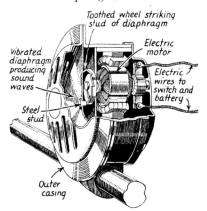

Toothed wheel striking stud of diaphragm

Electric motor

Vibrated diaphragm producing sound waves

Electric wires to switch and battery

Steel stud

Outer casing

The electric horn of a motor-car

phragm and produce the sound waves which we hear. This type of horn is generally fixed on the front cross-bar.

Which is the Tallest Building in the World?

Iᴛ is the Empire State Building in New York, 1,248 feet high. It has 102 storeys above the street, and two below, and can accommodate 80,000 people. It would take two hours to walk from the front door to the top of the building, but there are 63 passenger lifts and four goods lifts. Express elevators go to the 80th floor

The Empire State Building, New York

in less than one minute. With a lightning conductor on top it protects not only itself from lightning, but the buildings all round in a circular area of more than 2,000 feet diameter.

What is a Brass Rubbing?

Iᴛ is an impression of a memorial brass, of which about 4,000 exist in old English churches. These brasses, each consisting of flat plates engraved with a figure or device, were set up in churches in memory of the dead, and they are found chiefly in those districts where stone was scarce. The counties of Norfolk, Suffolk, Essex, Middlesex, Kent and Surrey are rich in them, but they are rare in the north and west.

It is from these brasses that we obtain much of our information about costume in olden times, for most of them have representations of knights, ladies or ecclesiastics in full dress. In some cases brasses originally laid down to the memory of one individual have been taken up, re-engraved, and then used to commemorate someone else.

The brass rubbings are made by first brushing the brass clean with a nail-brush, and then placing a paper over the brass, with a good margin top and bottom, so that heavy objects such as books or hassocks can be placed on top to hold the paper down. The outline of the figure or design, which can be felt through the paper, is then traced with a pencil, and the paper is next rubbed over with heel-ball, a black waxy substance, until the impression is quite black, with the incised lines of the brass standing out clearly in white. To make a rubbing of a large brass is a very hard and tiring job. When the heel-balling is finished it is usual to rub over the impression with a clean flannel to give it a polished appearance.

What is Afrikaans?

Tʜɪs is the name now given to a patois or dialect of Dutch spoken by the descendants of the Dutch settlers in South Africa. The word means African. It was formerly called Taal, which means language or tongue.

Was St. George an Englishman?

Nᴏ, he was a native of Cappadocia in Asia Minor, and suffered as a Christian martyr under the Emperor Diocletian in Nicomedia, where he was military tribune. Practically nothing is known of his life, and even his existence has been doubted.

He became known to Englishmen through the Crusades, and in the fourteenth century Edward III adopted him as the patron saint of England. He was martyred in 303, but the Crusaders declared that he had come to their aid against the Saracens at the siege of Antioch in 1089. Many legends have gathered round his name, the most famous of which is the story of his conquest of the dragon.

Is Our Skin Waterproof?

Tʜᴇ skin is one of the most wonderful substances in the world, for while it is waterproof in the sense that

On the left is the brass of Sir John D'Aubernon, the oldest in England, and on the right a rubbing of it

it will not ordinarily let in moisture from the outside, yet it is not waterproof from the inside, and so we are able to perspire or give off as sweat the moisture we take in through our mouths. No matter how long we may lie in a bath of water, none of the liquid gets through our skins.

It is believed that this is due to the fact that in the tiny tubes through which we perspire the sweat comes out with such a forward pressure that it prevents any water entering from outside. We can, however, make some substances, such as oil, enter the sweat-glands if we rub them into the skin very hard. By means of electricity also liquids can be made to pass through the skin from the outside.

What is a Fuehrer?

Tʜɪs is simply the German word for "leader" or "guide," and is the title given to Herr Hitler, the German Chancellor. As applied to him it has become almost a sacred word, just as the familiar word "saviour" has become when applied to Jesus, or the word "prophet" when applied to Mohammed.

Herr Hitler, "The Fuehrer"

Other men may be fuehrers, but Hitler is to Germans "The Fuehrer." It counts for much more in Germany than his official title of Chancellor.

What Is Beating the Bounds?

THIS term is used for an old custom still carried out in London and other places when the clergyman of the parish, accompanied by parochial officers and other parishioners, and followed by the boys of the parish school and their masters, go in procession to the ancient parish boundaries. The boys carry peeled willow wands in their hands and at various points strike the boundaries.

This used to be done in the old days to preserve the rightful boundaries of the parish and prevent any dispute as to where they were. Sometimes the boys were whipped " to make them remember," and in other parishes boys would be turned upside-down and have their heads bumped on the ground so that they might have an experience which would prevent them from forgetting where the parish boundaries were. This bumping is still carried out at St. Clement Danes in London.

Before the Reformation the beating of the bounds was carried out with great ceremony. The lord of the manor, priests with crosses, and other persons with hand-bells, banners and staves, followed by most of the parishioners, walked in procession round the parish, stopping at the crosses, and drawing crosses on the ground. But at the Reformation most of the religious side of the ceremony was abolished, though prayers were offered in church, and passages of scripture were recited, such as " Cursed be he that removeth his neighbour's landmark."

The beating of the bounds, or parochial perambulation as it is called, is always carried out on Holy Thursday —that is, the Thursday before Good Friday—or on Ascension Day. As a ceremony it somewhat resembles the old Roman terminalia, celebrated every year on February 23rd, the last month of the year, when the boundary stones were visited and decorated with garlands. An altar was set up at each and sacrifices offered to Terminus, the god of boundaries.

What is a Nordic?

THIS name, from the Scandinavian word for North, is used to describe the type of man inhabiting north-western Europe and includes the English, German, Scandinavian and Dutch peoples. The type is characterized by blond hair, blue eyes, elongated head and tall stature. Nowadays it is the fashion for the Germans to attribute superiority to the Nordics over every other race in practically all departments of life.

Bumping a boy in the Temple, London, to make him remember the parish boundary

Boys beating the bounds with willow wands at the Tower of London

Is the Number 13 Unlucky?

No more than any other number. It has been stated that where 13 people have sat down to a meal one of them has died soon afterwards, and no doubt this is true, just as people have died in houses numbered 13.

But they have also died where two, three, four, five, six, seven, and, indeed, any number have sat down to a meal, and people have also died in every house in a road. Any other number might equally well be described as unlucky, if unfortunate incidents that have happened in connection with it were selected and the fortunate instances were ignored. It is because events connected with 13 are always selected that this number is regarded as unlucky.

Schoolboys beating the bounds at the Temple Steps, London, a parish boundary on the Thames

How is the Semaphore Worked?

THE semaphore, which means "I bear a sign," is an instrument used for signalling between warships and consists of an upright post with two movable arms fixed at the top. By means of handles these arms can be swung into different positions, each combination representing a letter, and so a message is spelled out. The whole alphabet with various other signs is given in the drawing on this page. A similar form of signalling was in use for sending messages between London and Portsmouth before the invention of the electric telegraph. Semaphores were erected on several hills between the two places to form relay stations for passing the message on.

The semaphore was invented by Richard Lovell Edgeworth in 1767, but was first regularly employed by the French in 1794 for sending messages from Paris to the armies on the frontier. In the following year it was used in England. The earliest semaphore consisted of a series of shutters like Venetian blinds, but in 1816 Sir Hope Popham substituted a mast with arms as used today. The ordinary railway signals are a form of semaphore.

Who is the "King of Kingdoms"?

THIS fine title was coined by General Smuts, of South Africa, for King George VI in a speech which the general delivered at Cape Town on Coronation Day in 1937. Seeing that King George is king of each separate Dominion in the British Commonwealth of Nations, it is certainly a very accurate and expressive title.

Who Was Spring-Heeled Jack?

ON January 10th, 1838, at the Mansion House police-court in London, the Lord Mayor announced that he had received many letters relating to an individual who was going about the suburbs frightening women, so that they were afraid to go out after dark. It was said that they were met by a man who assumed various disguises, and who would suddenly appear before them with great leaps, and just as suddenly disappear. It was this mode of approach and departure that led to his being named Spring-Heeled Jack. Robbery played no part in his pranks, and apparently he simply wished to frighten women.

His first appearance was at Barnes in December, 1837, when he was said to have appeared as a large white bull. Next he was seen at East Sheen as "a white bear," and later at Kingston, Richmond and Hampton, "clad in brass armour, with large, claw-like gloves."

Then, as he came nearer London he was said to have taken the form of a huge baboon. He then began to attack women, tearing their clothes, and a public subscription was raised to organise means of capturing Spring-Heeled Jack.

For five months he kept the female population of London in a state of terror. Then his escapades ceased and no more was heard of him. Who the man was never became known.

How Long Has Lipstick Been Used?

THE modern girl may think she is original and up-to-date when she uses lipstick, but actually she is only imitating her ancestors, who, thousands of years ago, used this artificial aid to beauty.

In some ancient graves found during excavations for harbour improvements at Lambay Island, off the Irish coast, near Dublin, and supposed to be 2,500 years old, have been found small sticks of a pink, wax-like substance very similar in composition to our modern lipstick, together with stone rings, bronze bracelets and an iron hand-mirror. It is well known that the Ancient Egyptians, Greeks and Romans were well-versed in the art of make-up. The use of cosmetics occurs in cycles, and after a period of general use there occurs a reaction, when they are regarded as taboo for a time.

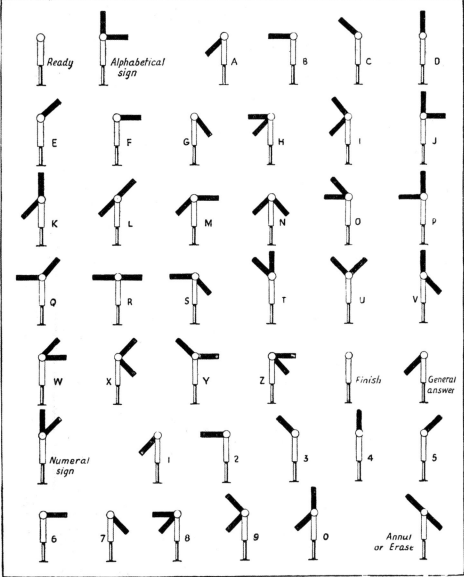

The various positions of the semaphore arms for signalling letters and figures when sending a message. The arms are moved to and fro to attract attention, and then placed at the ready, after which the alphabetical sign is given before starting to spell out words. There is also a numerical sign before numbering. At the end of a message the arms are put to rest. Each word is acknowledged by the general answer signal, and the annul signal is used for cancelling a message that has been sent

Is That Bird a Rook or a Crow?

People often mistake rooks for crows, for the birds are much alike. On this page are drawings showing the various members of the crow family found wild in England. The raven is the largest of the group, but it is now rare, nesting only in a few places on the south coast, in North Devon and Somerset, the Isle of Man and Wales. The hooded crow, called also the grey crow and the Royston crow, is about 20 inches long. Its head, throat, wings and tail are glossy bluish-black with green and purple reflections, while the remainder is ashy grey. The bill and legs are black. The carrion crow is 18 inches long, and the whole plumage is black, with purple and green reflections. The rook, 19 inches long, black glossed with purple and blue, is distinguished from the carrion crow by having at the base of the bill a bare greyish patch. The chough, now becoming rare, is 16 inches long, a uniform glossy purple-black, with bill and legs a bright coral red. The jackdaw and magpie are well known, and the jay is beautifully coloured

Can a Candle be Shot Through a Door?

YES, motion adds hardness and stiffness to a soft and flexible material and when a soft wax candle

A soft wax candle passing through a hard wooden door without damage to itself

is given a tremendous speed by means of the explosive in a rifle, the motion makes the soft wax so hard that it will go clean through the timber of the door, instead of being flattened against it, as would be the case if it were pressed slowly against the wood.

It is this fact of the hardening of the material by motion that gives the projectiles shot from modern guns by high explosives such penetrating power.

Is It Bad to Drink Melted Snow?

THERE is a popular idea that the complaint of goitre, common in Alpine valleys and other high mountains, is caused by the drinking of water from melted snow. This, however, is not the case. Snow water has nothing whatever to do with goitre, for the disease exists in places like Derbyshire and Cambridgeshire, and in the island of Sumatra, where there is no snow water, while it does not exist in countries like Greenland and Lapland, where snow water is constantly drunk.

At the same time, medical authorities believe that the disease is due to some impurity in hard drinking-water, quite independent of the proximity of snow. The water can be rendered innocuous, however, by boiling.

What is Australasia?

THIS term is generally used for that part of Oceania which comprises Australia, Tasmania, New Zealand, Papua, New Caledonia, the New Britain Archipelago, and a few smaller islands. The term, however, is rather elastic, sometimes being confined to Australia, Tasmania, New Zealand and Fiji, and sometimes being regarded as equivalent to Oceania as a whole.

Which is the Biggest River?

IF by the term "biggest river" we mean the one containing most water or draining the largest area, it is the Amazon in South America, which with its tributaries contains about a quarter of the fresh water of

the world. It drains an area of over two and a half million square miles, and flows for about 4,000 miles through Peru and Brazil into the Atlantic. It is navigable for ocean steamers up to Iquitos, 2,300 miles from the mouth. The outflow of fresh water from the

Amazon is over a million cubic feet a second, and this is found on the surface of the sea as far as 200 miles from the estuary. The Amazon has well been

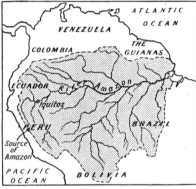

The vast basin of the Amazon River

called the Mediterranean of South America. Tides are felt as far up as Obydos, 400 miles from the sea.

How Many Times Do We Breathe in a Minute?

THIS varies according to age. A new-born baby breathes at the rate of between 62 and 68 times a minute. At one year the normal breathing is 44 times a minute, at five years, 26 ; between the ages of 15 and 20, 20 times, between 20 and 25 years, 18.7, between 25 and 30 years, 16 ; and between 30 and 50 years, 18.1.

The rate of respiration, however, varies according to what we are doing. An adult lying down breathes only about 13 times a minute, but running he may draw 50 breaths a minute. The less the body works the less it needs to breathe, because the smaller the quantity of oxygen that is being used up and the less need for renewal.

Who Was Frankenstein?

HE was not, as some people suppose, a monster, but the hero of Mrs. Shelley's romance, "Frankenstein." He was a young student who built up a monstrous being from materials gathered in the tomb and dissecting-room. When it was completed it became alive and committed a number of crimes, finally coming to an end somewhere in the northern seas.

What is a Strad?

A STRAD is the name given to a violin made at Cremona by the famous Italian Antonius Stradivarius, who was born in 1644 and died in 1737. His renown as a violin-maker exceeded all others, and his praise has been sung by poet and musician. He was a pupil of another famous violin-maker, Nicolo Amati, and his best violins were made between 1700 and 1725. On the rare occasions when a genuine Strad comes up for sale at the auction-rooms it realises many thousands of pounds, but, of course, there are hundreds of forgeries in existence bearing the name of Stradivarius.

Mr. Albert Sandler, the popular violinist, playing on his Strad violin

What Kind of Engine Is That?

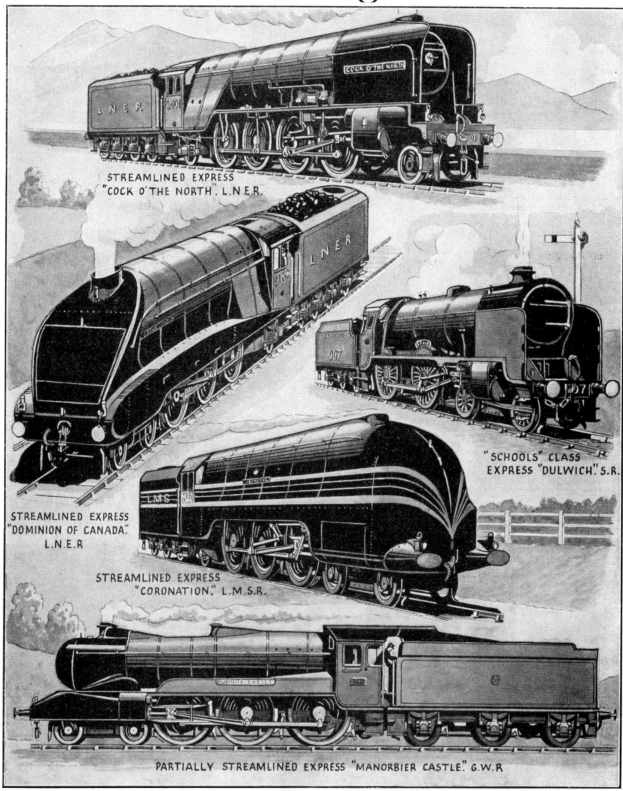

STREAMLINED EXPRESS "COCK O' THE NORTH". L.N.E.R.

STREAMLINED EXPRESS "DOMINION OF CANADA." L.N.E.R.

"SCHOOLS" CLASS EXPRESS "DULWICH". S.R.

STREAMLINED EXPRESS "CORONATION." L.M.S.R.

PARTIALLY STREAMLINED EXPRESS "MANORBIER CASTLE". G.W.R.

On these pages are shown the latest types of passenger locomotives on the four great British railways. This page gives the British express locomotives, and the opposite page shows the tank engines used for local traffic. The engine at the top of this page, the L.N.E.R's "Cock o' the North," was the first "Mikado" or 2–8–2 engine to be built in Great Britain for the express passenger service. This class works the Flying Scotsman expresses between Edinburgh and Aberdeen, and is streamlined. On the left is the first of the five streamlined locomotives built for the London-Edinburgh Coronation Express service. They are known as the Pacific type 4–6–2, and do the journey between London and Edinburgh, 393 miles, at an average speed of 65½ miles an hour. They are painted a bright blue, as is the whole train they draw, and they are named after the great British Dominions. In the middle of the page is shown the very latest example of streamlining on the L.M.S. Railway. This engine is a Pacific, 4–6–2, engine, is called "Coronation," and is painted in blue and silver. It draws the famous Royal Scot trains between London and Glasgow. On its right is shown the new "Schools" class of engines of the Southern Railway. These are the most powerful engines

Types of Passenger Locomotives

"BALTIC" CLASS TANK. L.M.S.R.

SUBURBAN TANK. L.N.E.R.

"RIVER" CLASS TANK. S.R.

"COUNTY" CLASS TANK. G.W.R.

in Europe, and are all named after public schools. They are 4–4–0 engines, and work the London-Hastings expresses. At the bottom of page 16 is the partially streamlined "Manorbier Castle," 4–6–0, of the G.W.R. This and others like it pull the famous Cheltenham Flyer from Cheltenham to London via Swindon in record time. In all these engines the streamlining has proved to be very economical in coal consumption. The locomotives shown on this page are tank engines, carrying fuel and water on their own frames, so that no tender is necessary as on expresses. At the top is a powerful Baltic type 4–6–4 engine of the L.M.S. used for hauling heavy local passenger trains at fast speeds. The L.N.E.R. suburban tanks for the suburban "breadwinners'" trains are very efficient engines. They are 0–6–2, and can carry 1,600 gallons of water and four tons of coal. The River class, 4–6–2, are the latest addition to the Southern Railway's equipment, and do useful work all over the system. They are named after rivers in the southern area. The G.W.R. County tanks, 4–4–2, are very fast and powerful, and are used all over the system for local passenger work. Tank engines can travel equally well backwards or forwards, and this saves time by avoiding the need for turning

Did King John Sign Magna Carta?

As this king could not write it was impossible for him to sign Magna Carta. What he did at Runnymede was to seal it in the presence of his barons There is no evidence that any member of the royal family was able to write his or her name before the

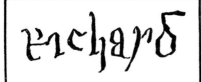

The signature of King Richard II

reign of Edward III. The earliest royal signature is that of the Black Prince in 1370, and even that is not his name, but his motto. Richard II was the first English king who could write his name. His signature is given here.

What is a Fog?

A fog is a collection of myriads of tiny globules of water, each one of which is formed round a minute particle of dust or soot. At a given temperature the atmosphere can only hold a certain quantity of moisture in the form of invisible vapour. As soon as this air becomes cooled, either through striking colder air or cold objects, it must give up a certain amount of its invisible vapour, which becomes transformed into liquid.

But in order that the vapour may be changed into liquid it must have some object upon which to form, and when there is fog the moisture has formed round the tiny particles of dust. Industrial towns are more liable to fog than the country, because there are so many more dust particles in the air round which the moisture can form. When those particles are black soot the fog, instead of being white, is dark, and turns day into night.

Do Mummy Wheat Seeds Grow?

No; despite many plausible stories of wheat seeds obtained from mummy wrappings having grown into plants, it is impossible for these ancient seeds to germinate. All authentic attempts by scientists made at Kew and elsewhere have failed. Sir Wallis Budge, the Egyptologist, writing on this subject, says: "No one will deny that wheat which was brought from Egypt, and even wheat which was taken from sarcophagi and tombs, has germinated, but that wheat was not ancient Egyptian wheat of the Dynastic Period."

When genuine ancient wheat supplied by Sir Wallis was tested in all possible ways, in no case did it sprout. In every instance the grain became mouldy and rotten, without any vestige of germination. Where ancient wheat seeds have been examined under the microscope the grains have always

been either carbonised or the embryo was decayed and dead.

Professor G. Henslow, the botanist, says: "Wheat is particularly short-lived, from four to twelve years being the maximum period which may be allowed; but all stories of 'mummy wheat' extracted from the tombs of Egypt, and supposed to be some thousands of years old, having grown are utterly false."

When Was Jesus Born?

Strange as it may seem, the birth of Jesus is said by scholars to have taken place, not in the year 1 A.D., but in 5 B.C. This date is worked out by comparing references in the Gospels to well-known events with established dates in secular history. It seems paradoxical to speak of Jesus being born 5 years before Jesus was born.

How Does the Elephant Drink?

Many people believe that when an elephant wants to drink it simply places the tip of its trunk in the water and sucks up as much as it requires, the water passing right through the trunk and entering the mouth by the other end. This, however, is not the case. The elephant does suck up water with its trunk, but this water does not pass through into the mouth. When the trunk is full the end is curled up and inserted in the open mouth and the liquid is then squirted into the

throat. The two processes are illustrated in the photographs given here. The elephant's trunk is, indeed, a very wonderful implement and without it the animal would starve or die of thirst. The animal's neck is so short that without some special provision it could not reach its food, but the trunk or proboscis, which is a combination of nose and hand, exercises the functions of touch, taste, suction, expulsion and holding.

It is a prolongation of the upper lip and nose, sometimes reaching a length of seven feet, and it can draw up water because it contains a pair of tubes closed by a valve arrangement. At the end of the Asiatic elephant's trunk there is a small prolongation that acts as a finger, and the African elephant's trunk has two fingers, or, perhaps one might say, a finger and a thumb.

The trunk has about forty thousand muscles and it has been truly said that there is hardly anything that this wonderful implement cannot do, from drawing a cork from a bottle or picking up a pin to hurling a tiger into the air. With its trunk the elephant lifts its driver, pulls over small trees, reaches for its food, takes in water and expels it into its mouth or over its body. An Indian elephant that lost its trunk in an accident had to be fed by hand, all its food and drink being placed inside its mouth.

When an elephant at the Zoo suffers through a chill it is given hot rum and water and drinks this mixture with evident relish. A whole bottle of rum is poured into a bucket containing warm water. The animal first takes a tentative taste and then soon drinks up the lot.

In the upper photograph elephants are seen sucking up water, and below an elephant is squirting water into its mouth

What Was the Great Bottle Hoax?

In 1749 the Duke of Montague, while talking with some friends on the subject of public credulity, declared that if a person advertised that he would creep into a quart bottle he would get a large crowd to pay for the privilege of seeing him do the impossible trick. This was denied by some, and so a wager was made.

The duke inserted the following advertisement in the newspapers : " At the New Theatre in the Haymarket on Monday next, the 16th inst., to be seen a person who performs the several most surprising things following : Namely, first he takes a common walking cane from any of the spectators and thereupon plays the music of every instrument now in use, and likewise sings to surprising perfection.

" Secondly, he presents you with a common wine bottle, which any of the spectators may first examine. This bottle is placed on a table in the middle of the stage, and he (without equivocation) goes into it in sight of all the spectators and sings in it. During his stay in the bottle any person may handle it and see plainly that it does not exceed a common tavern bottle."

The prices for admission were given as 7s. 6d., 5s., 3s. and 2s. It was added that the performance had been seen by most of the crowned heads of Asia, Africa and Europe. The bait was swallowed. The playhouse was crowded with dukes, duchesses, lords, ladies and all ranks. When the performer did not appear there were cat-calls, and then someone in one of the boxes threw a lighted candle on the stage. Thereupon some serious rioting began

a great bonfire in the street, made of property carried from the theatre.

Curiously enough, nobody was hurt, except one young nobleman, who fell from a box and bruised his chin.

Why Are the Trade Winds So Called?

The trade winds are so called because of the regularity with which they blow and follow a steady course. This in the old days of sailing ships was of the greatest value to navigation.

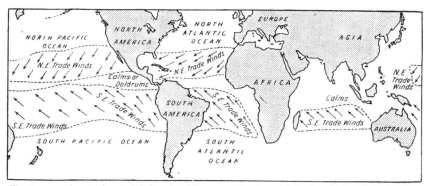

The two regular trade wind belts that blow over the sea and in the old days helped sailing ships on their voyages

Which is the Longest Place Name in Britain?

It is that of a small market town with a railway station in Anglesey, about a mile from the Britannia Bridge. It is noted for a quarry of building stone. The full name of the town and station, which is on the L.M.S. railway, is shown in the photograph on this page. The first twenty letters are sufficient address for the Post Office. The full name, containing 58 letters, means " The Church of St. Mary, in a hollow of white hazel, near to the rapid whirlpool and to

They blow at a rate of from 10 to 30 miles an hour, give fair weather, and are seldom interrupted by storms.

When a sailing vessel entered a trade wind belt it could count on making steady headway. If sailing with the wind, extra sails were often rigged out on the ends of the yards, and thus a broadened stretch of canvas caught as much wind as possible, and enabled the ship to speed along day and night. When planning a journey, a sailing ship always chose, as far as possible, a course which would enable it to take advantage of the trade winds.

The trade winds blow towards the Equator for the reason that the Equator is something like a stove, over which air is heated and rises by convection. Then the cooler winds on each side rush in and take the place of that which has risen. Instead of blowing directly towards the Equator, however, these winds are, by the effect of the Earth's rotation, deflected. North of the Equator they blow towards south-west, and south of the Equator they move towards the north-west.

Trade winds blow over the land as well as over the sea, but there they are much less well developed. They are generally dry, and lowlands over which they blow are made desert by the drying action of their warm air. The African Sahara and the Central Australian desert are thus explained. When trade winds encounter mountain ranges they are forced to rise up the slopes, where the air cools and produces cloud and rain. Then on the other side of the mountains they are dry.

A station in Anglesey on the L.M.S. Railway which has the longest place name in Great Britain. As can be seen, it runs nearly the whole length of the platform

Most of the audience fought its way out of the theatre, many losing a cloak, a hat, a wig or a sword. Those who remained, aided by a mob that broke in, tore up the benches, smashed the scenery and generally dismantled the theatre. The Guards had to be called out, and arrived in time to find

St. Tysillio Church, near to a red cave." There are one or two other long place names in Britain, including Drimtaidhvrickhillichattan, in the Isle of Mull, Argyllshire. The longest English surname is said to be Featherstonehaugh, but many foreign names exceed this, some being nearly double the length.

How Does a Diesel Engine Work?

A DIESEL engine is an internal-combustion engine which instead of using petrol is driven by heavy oil. This has two advantages. In the first place, it is cheaper to run than a petrol-engine of equal power, and, in the second place, there is less danger of fire as the heavy oil is not so inflammable as petrol.

This type of engine was invented in 1895 by a German engineer, Dr. Rudolf Diesel.

The explanatory drawing on this page which shows one of the latest types of Diesel engines used in motor-boats, and as an auxiliary in yachts and fishing vessels, will make clear the principle of the engine. The type shown would develop about 50 horse-power.

There is a four-stroke cycle of working. The first or inlet stroke is shown in the left-hand cylinder, where air is being sucked into the cylinder at atmospheric pressure from the air-intake pipe. It passes by a valve, which is opened at the right time by a cam on the cam-shaft running along the tops of the cylinders. In the next or compression stroke the rising piston compresses the air to a pressure of about 500 or 600 pounds per square inch. This compression raises the temperature of the air to a high degree.

At the third or firing stroke, shown in the third cylinder, a fine spray of oil is timed to enter the cylinder at great pressure, and the heated air immediately ignites it, causing the air to expand and drive the piston downwards. On the fourth or exhaust stroke the rising piston forces the exhaust gases out through the exhaust valve, which is also timed to open by the cam on the cam-shaft, driven from the crank-shaft by gearing. These four strokes happen alternately in the four cylinders, and so there is an ever-turning movement of the crank-shaft, assisted by the heavy flywheel. The crank-shaft is continued to the forward and reverse gear-box on the right, and from there

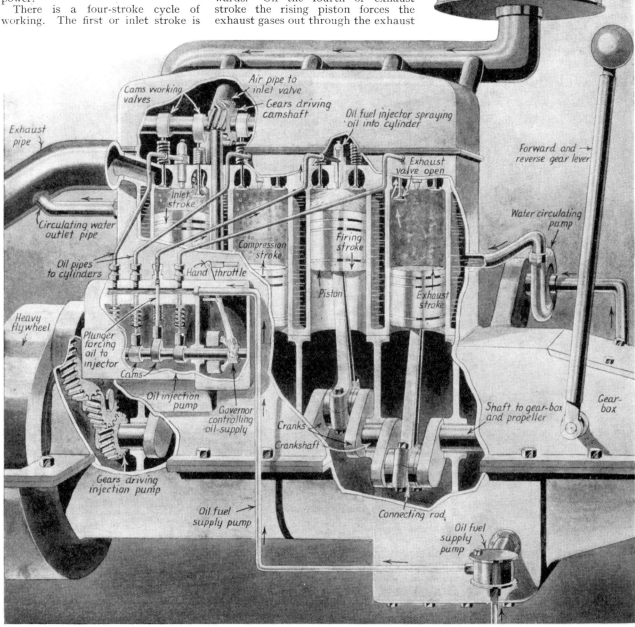

The inside of a Diesel engine showing the four-stroke cycle, a different stage going on in each cylinder as described on this page

What Nation Owns That Aircraft?

Here are the signs painted on the aircraft of the various nations, by which we may know to what particular nation any aircraft flying overhead belongs. These are the official markings of the Air Forces of the nations. The wing marks are shown on the left in each case, and the rudder markings on the right. Some countries, including Great Britain, do not use rudder markings. The British Dominions use the same device as the Mother Country. These drawings have been made from the very latest information available. Russia is given in this alphabetical list as U.S.S.R.

Plate III

What Old-Time Uniform Is That?

Chapel Royal Choirboy — Castle Rising Sister — Doggett's Coat & Badge — Yeoman of the Guard — Lord Mayor's Footman — Royal Page — Royal Scottish Archer — Christ's Hospital Scholar

Tower of London Warder — Royal Postillion — Chelsea Pensioner — Lord Mayor's Coachman — Foundling Hospital Girl — Royal Footman — Royal Marshalman — Royal Exchange Beadle

Royal Waterman — Lord Mayor's Postillion — Bank of England Beadle — Lord Mayor's Swordbearer — Gentleman-at-Arms — Garter King-of-Arms — High Court Judge — Westminster Abbey Choir Boy — Lord Mayor of London

Quite a number of uniforms dating back several centuries are still in use, and many of these are given on this page. The Yeoman of the Guard and the Tower Warder wear dress of the 16th century. Many other uniforms shown here are of the 18th century. Most of them may be seen in London

Plate IV

a shaft runs to the propeller Water is circulated through the engine by a centrifugal pump for cooling purposes, and passes out into the exhaust pipe. The crank-shaft also drives the oil fuel injection pump, where a series of cams, acting on plungers, forces the oil to the right cylinder at the right time. Oil is pumped to this injection pump from the supply tank. The governing mechanism controls the flow of oil for different engine speeds, as does the hand-controlled throttle lever.

The Diesel engine is the only serious competitor of the steam turbine. It is used on many large liners now, and is also used for generating electricity on self-contained streamlined electric locomotives.

It will probably be the middle-powered engine of the future. For low-powered units the petrol engine will probably hold its own, and for very large installations the Diesel engine is not likely to supplant the steam turbine. The efficiency of the Diesel engine is very great

Does Snow Fall in Palestine?

THE popular idea that snow rarely falls in Palestine is quite erroneous. Dr. Cunningham Geikie says that snow covers the streets of Jerusalem at some period in two winters out of three. " But it generally comes," he writes, " in small quantities and soon disappears. Yet there are sometimes very snowy winters. That of 1879, for example, left behind it seventeen inches of snow, even where there was no drift, and the strange spectacle of snow lying unmelted for two or three weeks was seen in the hollows on the hillsides."

There are references in the Bible to snow in Palestine, as where Benaiah, one of David's mighty men, is de-

Jerusalem on one of the rare occasions when there has been a heavy fall of snow

scribed as slaying a lion " in the midst of a pit, in time of snow," and one of the virtues of a good wife is mentioned in the book of Proverbs as

being that " she is not afraid of the snow for her household."

What Do the Letters S.P.Q.R. Mean?

THESE letters, often seen in Ancient Rome and on the standards of the Roman Armies, are the initials of the words Senatus Populusque Romanus and mean the Roman Senate and People. The que is a suffix meaning "and," joined on to the word for people " Populus." All public property bore the initials as an indication that it belonged to the people or existed by their act.

The military ensigns or standards among the Romans were of various kinds. The aquila or eagle was the general ensign of the entire legion, but each division of a legion—that is, each separate maniple and cohort—carried its own ensign, and each had its own particular name. The standard of the cavalry, for example, was called the vexillum, and was a square piece of cloth extended upon a cross, and surmounted by some figure. After the Roman Empire became nominally Christian in the time of Constantine the imperial standard, called a labarum, bore a figure or emblem of Christ

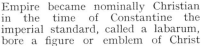

A Roman standard

woven in gold upon purple cloth. This was substituted for the head of the Emperor that had previously been used.

What Is The Origin of the Bowie Knife?

THIS heavy sheath-knife, much used in America in the early part of the nineteenth century, was invented by James Bowie, a notorious frontiersman and slave-dealer born in Kentucky.

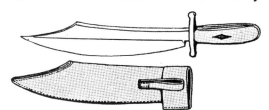

A typical bowie knife and its leather sheath

Being involved in constant brawls, he thought out the most effective and convenient type of knife to use as a weapon and whittled a model in wood. Then he had one made in steel, together with a spring sheath, and wore it regularly in his belt. A little later a Spaniard who was the terror of his neighbourhood insulted Bowie and an immediate duel was arranged. The fight was to be with knives, the men sitting facing one another on a trestle naked from the waist up. The Spaniard with his long knife jeered at Bowie's weapon, but when on the agreed signal being given the Spaniard drew back his arm to strike, Bowie thrust his knife forward and disembowelled the Spaniard before his arm could descend.

Henceforward the bowie knife became very popular in the frontier lands of America. The blade is nine or ten inches long with one sharp edge, the back being straight for three-quarters of its length and then curved in concave fashion towards the point. The guard is small and the tongue the full width of the hilt or grip, which is formed of two rounded pieces of wood or bone. Nowadays, the term is used for almost any kind of large sheath-knife. Most of the early bowie knives were made by frontier blacksmiths out of old files or rasps and varied a good deal in shape. Bowie died in 1836.

How Did Big Ben Get Its Name?

WHEN this famous bell, probably the best known in the world, was cast it was christened St. Stephen, but when, in September, 1856, the question of the name was discussed in Parliament, a member shouted : " Why not call it Big Ben ? " There were roars of laughter, for the name was an allusion to Sir Benjamin Hall, Chief Commissioner of Works, who was a very tall and stout man, and whose popular nickname was Big Ben. From that time on the bell has always been known as Big Ben.

This bell is the second of the name, for the first Big Ben, after being struck for several weeks, cracked badly and had to be recast. The present bell also is cracked.

Is the World Getting Noisier?

WITH pneumatic drills breaking up the roads, with the shrill sound of motor horns as vehicles rush by in town and country, and with the droning of aeroplane engines overhead, people are inclined to think that the world is far noisier than it was in olden times.

But there was always a terrible din in city streets, especially when they were paved with granite blocks or cobble-stones. No motor-car could make more noise in the streets than did those heavy old wagons with broad-brimmed wheels, often 16 inches wide at the tire, lurching and bumping over the cobble-stones with a clatter that must have been appalling.

The butcher killed his beasts in the street outside his shop, and the squeals and bellowings of the poor animals must have been deafening to passers-by and dwellers in the neighbourhood. The smith banged his metal and the wheelwright hammered his tires from morning to night, and the din beat anything that we get in a city street today. Tradesmen and apprentices all cried their wares outside their shops, each trying to drown the voices of his neighbours, and beggars with clack-dishes tried to outvie one another so as to attract attention to themselves.

Perhaps the country roads were quieter before the coming of the motor-car and aeroplane, but towns and cities must have been noisier.

What is Bright's Disease?

THIS complaint, named after Dr. Richard Bright of London, who in 1827 was the first to describe it, is a malady of the kidneys, a degeneration of the tissues into fat with inflammation. The sufferer has a bloodless appearance and is easily fatigued.

A penny-farthing bicycle being ridden over a wet road. As can be seen, there is a very remarkable reflection

What is a 'Penny-Farthing'?

THIS is the popular name given to the type of bicycle which came into use about 1870, and was very popular in the 1880's, in which the front wheel was very much larger than the back wheel. The term was not used in the days when the bicycle was common, for it was then called an "ordinary." It was sometimes described as a "roadster." The name "penny-farthing," given in recent years, long after this type of bicycle had gone out of use, is, of course, due to the fancied resemblance in size of the two wheels to a penny and a farthing.

Who Was Jumbo?

HE was a big African elephant acquired by the London Zoo in 1865, and became very popular with children, who used to ride on his back. But after sixteen years he became dangerous and was sold to Barnum the showman for £2,000 and shipped to America. Some time later he was run into by an engine and killed while crossing a railway track at an Ontario junction.

So popular was this elephant in England that when the Zoo announced his sale there was a great agitation to keep him in London, and when for some days it was found impossible to persuade the beast to enter the wagon prepared for his transport to the docks this was declared to be an indication that the elephant himself wanted to stay in England. Never has any animal been so much in the news as was Jumbo in 1882.

Is the Heart on the Left Side?

IT is a popular belief that the heart of a human being is on the left side of his body, but this is not strictly correct. The most muscular part of the heart, namely, the left ventricle, lies over to the left side, and the largest artery, called the aorta, arches to the left. The point or apex of the heart, also, is to the left, and because

of these facts the beating of the heart —that is, the pulsating as the blood is pumped through the blood-vessels—is felt more on the left side than on the right. But if the heart as it rests in the body were evenly divided, it would be found that no more is on the left-hand side than on the right. The actual position of the heart when seen

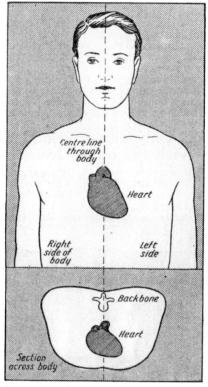

The position of the heart as viewed from the front, and, in the lower drawing, looking down upon it from above

looking at the front of a person, and when seen in a horizontal section through the body, is indicated in the accompanying drawing.

What Are The Two Sides of a Coin Called?

THE obverse side is that which bears the principal device, such as the portrait of the sovereign. The

A penny, showing the obverse or head side and reverse or less important side

other side is called the reverse side. The obverse side is so called because it is that which faces or fronts the observer, in contrast to the reversed or less important side.

Which Fresh-Water Fish is That?

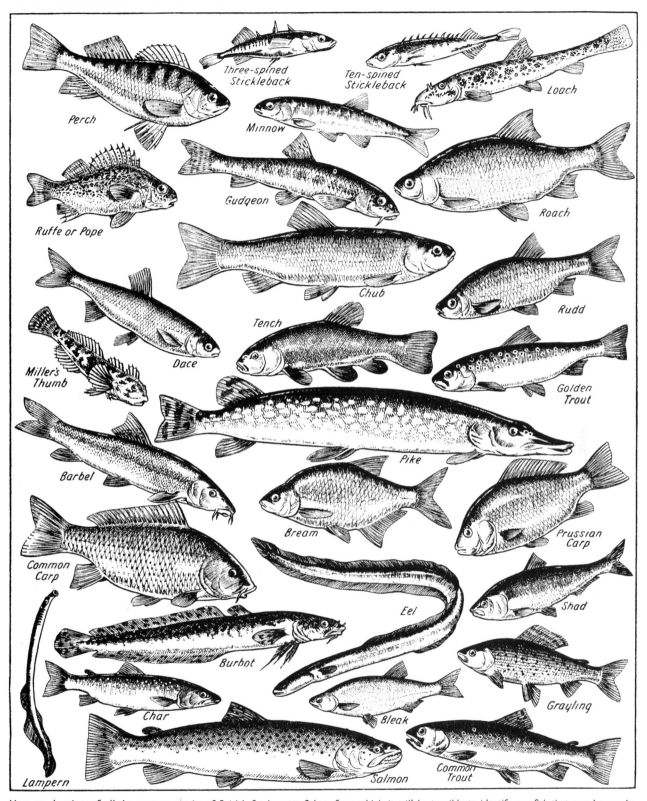

Perch

Three-spined Stickleback

Ten-spined Stickleback

Loach

Minnow

Ruffe or Pope

Gudgeon

Roach

Miller's Thumb

Dace

Tench

Chub

Rudd

Golden Trout

Barbel

Pike

Bream

Prussian Carp

Common Carp

Eel

Shad

Lampern

Burbot

Char

Bleak

Grayling

Salmon

Common Trout

Here are drawings of all the common species of British fresh-water fishes, from which it will be possible to identify any fish that may be caught. They are not, of course, all drawn to scale, as this is impossible owing to the great differences in size between the pike, which is sometimes over 4 feet and weighs 50 pounds, and the minnow, which rarely exceeds 4 inches, or the stickleback, less than 3 inches. Most fresh-water fish are the usual shape, but the eel is quite unlike the others, and though it lives most of its adult life in fresh-water streams and ponds it is born far away in the Atlantic, and the females return there to spawn. The eel does not appear to have scales, but actually there are scales buried in the smooth slippery skin. This arrangement, with the snake-like form, enables the eel to worm its way through reeds and grass and in the mud of river or pond. The lampern, 6 or 8 inches long, looks like a worm, but Frank Buckland says that though it is not much used as food there is no finer dish

What is a Billion?

UNFORTUNATELY this term is ambiguous, for it has different meanings in different countries. In Great Britain when we speak of a billion we mean a million million—that is, 1 followed by twelve o's. But in France, America and other countries a billion is only a thousand millions—that is, 1 followed by nine o's. It is better, therefore, to avoid the term, and to speak of a thousand millions or a million millions.

A billion has been humorously referred to as the only instance of something being bigger in the Old Country than it is in the New.

The word billion is not a very long one and the number it represents may not seem exceedingly great. But let us see if we can get some idea of how great it is. If we started counting a billion (in the English sense) and counted 200 a minute, day in and day out, year after year without a single moment's rest, it would take us more than 9,500 years to count the billion. Since the birth of Jesus in 4 B.C. less than one-sixteenth of a billion seconds have passed. It is when dealing with the infinitely little and infinitely great that we talk in billions. The speeds of Gamma rays are given in billionths of an inch and star distances in billions of miles.

Two examples of the strange reflections given by magic or irregular mirrors

What is the Broad Arrow on Government Property?

THIS mark placed on all naval and military stores, the clothing of convicts, and other property owned by the Government in the United

The broad arrow which marks Government property, and dates back to a private crest of the 17th century

Kingdom, was originally the crest of Henry Sidney, Earl of Romney, who in the 17th century was Master General of the Ordnance. He used this mark as a convenient way of making Government property recognisable, and by an Act of Parliament of 1698 all unauthorised persons in possession of goods marked with the broad arrow were made liable to heavy penalties. The use of the broad arrow has continued to the present day.

Who Was Mrs. Bloomer?

SHE was an American of New York, Amelia Bloomer, who in 1849 tried to introduce reformed dress in the shape of a short skirt and loose trousers, gathered closely round the ankles. The time for such attire was not ripe, and Mrs. Bloomer was greatly ridiculed, but she gave a new word " bloomers" to the English language. She would be gratified and probably surprised if she could see women's dress today. Her campaign for reform was known popularly as bloomerism.

What is a Magic Mirror?

THIS is the name often given to strange forms of looking-glasses exhibited at fairs and similar fêtes. When a person stands in front of such a mirror he sees a grossly distorted image of himself. Sometimes the head is lengthened and the legs shortened, at other times the whole body will be enormously out of proportion.

These different effects are brought about through the mirror having irregularities of surface, instead of a plane surface, as in an ordinary looking-glass. Any curvature will cause distortion, the reason being that the rays of light, instead of being reflected regularly, as they are from a level mirror, are thrown off at various angles, giving an abnormal image as illustrated on this page.

Has the World Ever Been Sold?

THE world has been put up to auction once and once only, and it was sold for a sum equal to about a million pounds. After the Roman Emperor Pertinax, who lived in the second century, had been murdered by the Pretorian Guard, they put up the Empire for sale to the highest bidder. The sale took place on March 28th, A.D. 193, and the world, or all that was known of it at the time, was knocked down to a wealthy Roman merchant, Didius Salvius Julianus, who paid 25,000 sestertii to each of the Pretorian Guards, a total amounting to about a million pounds sterling of our money.

Some outlying regiments, disgusted at the transaction, revolted and marched on Rome, and Didius, abandoned by the Pretorians, was seized and executed. He had "enjoyed" the strange purchase for only two months.

Painted Lady butterflies crossing the English Channel from France to England

Do Butterflies Migrate?

YES, numbers of Red Admiral and Painted Lady butterflies fly across the English Channel every year from the Continent. They arrive about the end of May, and just as students of bird life mark the birds so that they may know from what parts the migrants come, so butterflies are being marked.

This is done by attaching a small paper label bearing a letter and number to their bodies. A number of butterflies, for example, have been marked at St. Jean de Luz with the letter M, and a number of those at Marseilles with a V.

In order to find out the extent to which white butterflies in Great Britain itself travel, numbers of these are marked with an identification number on their right forewing, the figures being marked in magenta dye.

It is not yet known definitely whether butterflies migrate intentionally, as is the case with birds, or whether they are merely blown across the sea by strong winds. Darwin saw clouds of butterflies far out over the sea, having flown from the South American coast, and mariners have seen butterflies flying over the sea 1,200 miles from the nearest possible land, which was Africa. The study of butterfly migration is only in its infancy.

Where Does the Mud Come From?

TO many people the mud in our towns and cities, which are well paved, is a considerable mystery. We can understand mud in country lanes and fields, where the rain mixes with clay or other earth, but in the clean streets where the refuse is regularly swept up it might seem impossible for mud to occur.

Of course, a certain amount of the roadway is pounded into dust by the feet of pedestrians and the wheels of traffic, but this accounts for a very small part of the mud. Most of the solid matter of the mud which we find in the streets of towns and cities has gone up as smoke from the chimneys of factories and houses. Smoke consists of fragments of unburned fuel, and when it rains the rain brings down these fragments and forms the mud. The mud is thus not only a nuisance, needing the expenditure of much money to remove it, but there is a double waste, as it represents so much unburned fuel.

The measures taken in recent years to bring about an abatement of the smoke nuisance have undoubtedly led to a reduction in the quantity of mud in the streets.

Who Fastened a Broom to His Ship's Mast?

IT is said that after he had defeated the English admiral, Blake, in the battle of the Downs in 1652, the Dutch Admiral Van Tromp hoisted a broom

The broom fastened to Admiral Van Tromp's masthead as an indication that he had swept the English from the seas

to his masthead as a sign that he had swept the English from the seas. This is referred to in the song:

"I've a broom at the mast," said he,
"For a broom is the sign for me,
That wherever I go, the world may know,
I sweep the mighty sea."

Blake at once retaliated by fixing a horsewhip to the mast of his flagship as a symbol that he would flog the Dutchman out of the narrow seas:

"I've a whip at the fore, you see!
For a whip is the sign for me,
That the world may know,
wherever we go,
We ride and rule the sea."

At this period there was not much to choose between the British and the Dutch navies. Both were daring and good fighters, and victory sometimes went to one side and sometimes to the other.

Clouds of smoke rising from a South Wales industrial area. These sooty particles will later be brought down by falling rain and form the mud in the streets

Are There Still Undiscovered Animals?

OF course, there must be many smaller creatures, such as insects and sea animals, still to be discovered. Many new ones are found and added to the lists every year. But it is quite possible that there are also large animals which are not yet known to civilisation. It will be remembered that within the memory of middle-aged people still living, the okapi and the Komodo dragon have been found.

Not long ago a well-known South African hunter, who had been into the interior, told of a weird monster, supposed to live in the swamps of Angola, and known to the natives as chepekwe. It is supposed to be a monster weighing about four tons, and has the head and tail of a lizard. It is said to attack the rhinoceros, hippopotamus and elephant. If this monster exists it will probably be caught or killed one day.

Another traveller's tale is of a monster seen at Lake Edward by an explorer who went up from Cape Town. He stated that he had seen it tearing its way through the reeds of a swamp, and described it as much bigger than an elephant, and having the appearance of a brontosaurus.

Then there is a scaly rhinoceros, stated to live in Java, and about forty years ago the remains of a large animal were found in Patagonia, which Sir Ray Lankester declared must have come from an animal living until quite recent times. These appeared to be the remains of a giant sloth, and Sir Ray Lankester believed that a few specimens of this creature weighing many tons might still be living in the unexplored regions of South America.

It must be remembered that the stories about the okapi and the dragons of Komodo were believed to be merely travellers' tales, till the animals were actually caught alive.

What is Swan-Upping?

THIS is the name given to the annual marking of the cygnets, or young swans, on the Thames, which is done in July and occupies about a week.

From Norman times swans have been regarded as Royal birds, and the privilege of owning and using a private swan mark was granted only by the King.

The swan-upping which has been carried out annually for centuries is performed by the swan masters to the King and the Vintners' and the Dyers' livery companies of the City of London who among them own and care for all the swans on the Thames.

Nowadays swans belonging to the King go unmarked, but those of the Vintners' Company are distinguished by a nick made by a penknife on each side of the bill, and the Dyers' swans have a nick on the right side only. Ownership of the cygnets is determined by that of the parent birds, and where the parents belong to different owners the young brood is divided equally, any odd cygnet going to the King.

The King's swans used to be marked with a diamond mark on their bills, but Queen Alexandra caused this custom to be discontinued. That is why they are now left unmarked.

The first marking of the Thames swans in the reign of King George VI. The photograph was taken at Teddington, and the King's Swanmaster is directing the operations

What Was the Woolwich Infant?

THIS was the popular name given to a British 35-ton rifled, muzzle-loading gun constructed in 1870. At the time it was supposed to be the finest gun of its type

The tree of Jesse in Rouen Cathedral

What is a Jesse Window?

IT is a window of painted glass seen in various churches, representing the descent of Jesus from Jesse. Jesse is shown lying down, with a tree springing from his body, and on the branches are the figures or names of his descendants. Most of these Jesse windows date from the fourteenth century.

Which Furs Wear Best?

A TABLE of durability of dressed furs has been worked out, and according to this, reckoning otter fur, the most durable, as 100, the following shows the degrees of durability:

Otter	100	Civet cat	40
Sea otter	100	Fox	40
Wolverine	100	Genet	35
Bear	94	Russian pony	35
Beaver	90	Ermine	25
Seal	80	Kolinsky	25
Leopard	75	Lynx	25
Mink	70	Nutria	25
Persian lamb	65	Grey squirrel	20–25
Marten	65	Cony	20
Raccoon	65	Chinchilla	15
Sable	60	Goat	15
Wolf	50	Astrakhan	10
Skunk	50	Mole	7
Musk rat	45	Rabbit	5
Opposum	40	Hare	5

The figures given refer to dressed furs, but where these are dyed the durability is considerably reduced. The age of the animal and the season when it was caught also cause much variation in the quality.

What Is the Name of That Sail?

Here are all the principal sails used on big sailing ships. With the exception of the two lower rows, the sails may all be regarded as primary sails, because they supply the main motive power to the vessel. The bottom rows can be called secondary sails, as they are generally used in conjunction with the primary sails. A ship with square sails like those shown in the first six drawings is called a square-rigged ship, and a vessel with gaff-sails is stated to be fore-and-aft rigged. A full-rigged ship will have all the square sails on each of her three masts, which are called the foremast, the mainmast and the mizzen-mast, as well as the secondary sails called the jibs and staysail, and also the spanker at the stern. Often the ship carries also a studding-sail to get all the wind available. The other sails shown are used on smaller ships. Practically every kind of sail is shown here, but without their various combinations, which are illustrated on other pages of this book showing the different kinds of sailing ships

Do Grown Men Play Marbles?

Yes; this pastime, which was played in ancient Egypt thousands of years ago, is still played, not

A game of marbles played by men at Tinsley Green, Sussex, where marble championships have been played for over 300 years

only by boys, but by men. There are regular marble clubs and championships, and in the photograph we see a number of men playing at Tinsley Green, Sussex. The old man with the beard, who is 75, won the championship fifty years ago. The championship match takes place at Tinsley every Good Friday, and the game has been played there for three centuries. There are championships for teams as well as for individual players.

Fifty years and more ago marbles was a much more popular game among schoolboys than it is now and at a certain season of the year all boys played marbles.

How Many Words Do You Use?

Nearly eighty years ago Professor Max Müller of Oxford said in one of his lectures that certain farmers of an English parish used not more than 300 words. Nowadays, however, a farm labourer would use far more than this, for since the Great War many new words have come into general use, and the cinema has added greatly to the vocabulary of ordinary people. Millions go to the pictures every week and are constantly learning new words, though not always words of the best kind.

Some years ago an American lady, Mrs. Winfield S. Hall, wrote down every word that her young son uttered from the first time that he began to speak. At 17 months he had used 232 different words, and by the age

of six the number had increased to 2,688. Possibly the number was greater, for it is unlikely that Mrs. Hall had been able to catch and write down every word that her child used.

A German philologist, Herr Windt, found that a two-year-old girl used 489 words, while another girl of the same age used as many as 1,128. Probably, however, these were exceptionally intelligent children. Experiments have proved that the majority of university students know and use

from time to time about 60,000 words, and even people without college education, who are regular readers of newspapers and books, know a total of from 25,000 to 50,000 words. Using words regularly in conversation, however, is quite a different thing from knowing the words. Before the Great War ordinary people used regularly only about 800 different words, but now their vocabulary has been enlarged into several thousands. Even primitive peoples have a much larger vocabulary at their command than we should think.

What Is Reinforced Concrete?

Concrete, which is a mixture of broken stone, gravel or similar material, held together by cement, is a very valuable building substance. It has long been used for making pavements and roadways, but its use in building has been made possible by the principle of reinforcement.

A framework of steel rods and bars is interwoven, and the liquid concrete is poured over and round this. The concrete preserves the steel from corrosion, while the steel bars bind the concrete together, and thus each substance strengthens the other. It is fortunate that changes of temperature affect both substances equally, and so they expand together under heat and contract together in cold weather. When the steel framework is ready a mould is constructed of wood around the steel, into which the concrete is poured.

Reinforced concrete pillars are made in the same way, and they are stronger than stone pillars of equal size.

The steel reinforcement being placed in position for the building of a concrete coal bunker, 90 feet high, which will hold 150 tons of coal

Why is Moses Shown with Horns?

THE Hebrew word for shine is *qaran*, which means literally to emit rays, and for a horn the word is *qeren*. Early translators of the Bible confused the two words and rendered the passage in Exodus XXXIV. 29, 30 which in the Authorised Version reads "the skin of his face shone," "his

The horned Moses, from Michelangelo's statue

face was horned." Artists therefore represented Moses with a horn or a pair of horns. What made this seem suitable was the fact that the ancient Hebrews regarded horns as symbols of power. We find this referred to in Habakkuk III, 4 : "He had horns coming out of his hand: and there was the hiding of his power."

Is There a Pigmy Hippopotamus?

YES, in Western Africa there is a species of hippopotamus which is much smaller than the more familiar species. It is, indeed, not much bigger than a pig and when full-grown weighs only about 400 pounds, or less than four hundredweights. The back of this little animal is slaty black, while its under parts are a dirty greyish-white and the sides greenish slaty grey.

The height of the pigmy hippopotamus at the shoulders is about 2½ feet and the total length 6 feet. Of

A pigmy hippopotamus at the Whipsnade Zoo

this measurement about seven inches consists of tail.

The habits of the animal are said to resemble those of the wild swine much more than those of its huge relative. It wanders for miles in the woods and is never seen in troops like the larger species. Its movements in its native forests are described as ghost-like ; it is a difficult animal to trap, but the London Zoo has a specimen.

Travellers tell us that small hippopotamuses begin their wanderings about dusk, although individually may be seen in broad daylight. Whenever possible the animal takes a mud bath, and any muddy spot will have nightly visitants.

What is Hobson's Choice?

THE phrase is used when there is no choice or alternative, and it is derived from the practice of a 17th-century Cambridge jobmaster, Thomas Hobson, who when anyone wanted to hire a horse, compelled him to take the next animal in rotation—that is, the one nearest the stable door. So emphatic was he about this, that Hobson's Choice became a proverbial phrase. Hobson was something of a public benefactor for he brought a supply of good drinking water into the town, and Hobson's conduit still exists, though there is now another supply.

What are "Bulls" and "Bears"?

THESE are Stock Exchange terms. Bulls are those persons who buy shares hoping to sell them for a higher price before settling day comes round. They buy to bring about an advance in the price. Bears, on the other hand, are persons who sell shares hoping that on settling day the shares will be lower in price than when they sold them, so that they can buy shares back again. Bears sell to bring about a fall in price.

Bear was originally bearskin jobber, an allusion to the proverb, "To sell the bearskin before one has caught the bear." The bear's habit is to pull down, the bull's to toss up.

Who Are the Military Knights of Windsor?

THEY are a body of retired military officers who form part of the Order of the Garter. They date back to 1349

Military Knights of Windsor at Windsor Castle

when Edward III instituted the Order. He included in it a number of veterans who were known as Poor Knights, because owing to wounds or other misfortunes they could not support themselves, and he endowed them with an annual income and gave them quarters in Windsor Castle.

Their number is in future to be confined to thirteen, and appointments are made by the sovereign. One of them, who is given the rank of major-general, is made governor of the rest, and they are all under the orders of the Governor of Windsor Castle. They are the oldest military brotherhood in existence, and are the only military body in England entitled to wear the badge of St. George.

What is Charles's Wain?

CHARLES'S WAIN—that is, Charlemagne's Waggon—is the name given to the part of the Constellation

The Plough or Charles's Wain, part of the Constellation of the Great Bear

of the Great Bear which is alternatively called the Plough and the Dipper. Some think Charles is a corruption of Churl, and that the name is really Churl's Waggon.

What Is That Kind of Saw Used For?

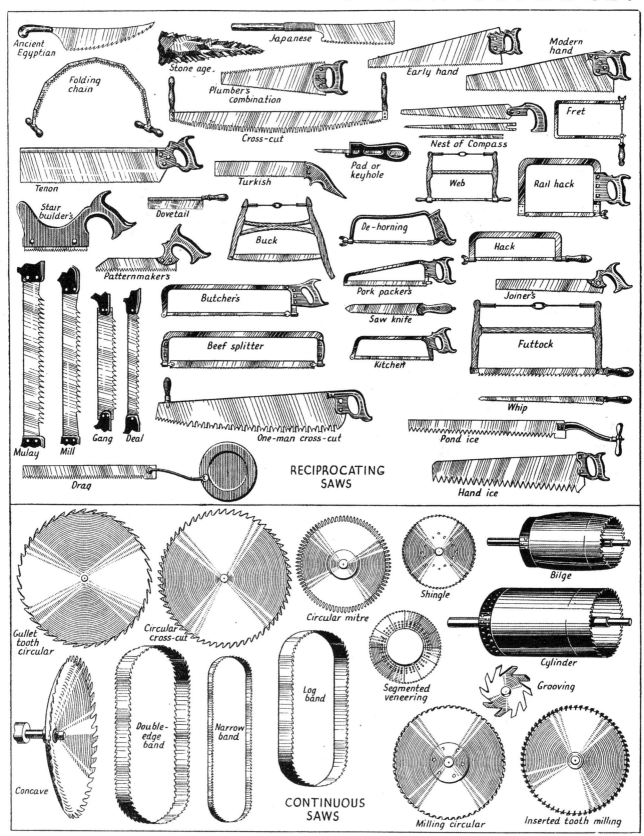

Ancient Egyptian
Japanese
Stone age.
Plumber's combination
Early hand
Modern hand
Folding chain
Cross-cut
Fret
Nest of Compass
Tenon
Turkish
Pad or keyhole
Web
Rail hack
Stair builder's
Dovetail
Buck
De-horning
Hack
Patternmakers
Pork packers
Joiner's
Butcher's
Saw knife
Beef splitter
Futtock
Kitchen
Whip
Mulay
Mill
Gang
Deal
One-man cross-cut
Pond ice
Drag
RECIPROCATING SAWS
Hand ice

Gullet tooth circular
Circular cross-cut
Circular mitre
Shingle
Bilge
Cylinder
Concave
Double-edge band
Narrow band
Log band
Segmented veneering
Grooving
Milling circular
Inserted tooth milling
CONTINUOUS SAWS

There are many kinds of saws, as can be seen by the drawings on this page. Saws are classified under two main heads, namely, reciprocating saws, which work to and fro, and continuous or circular saws, which go round and round. The saw as a tool is as old as the Stone Age, and the Ancient Egyptians used handsaws remarkably like ours today. But the teeth were inclined towards the handle, and so cut on the pull instead of on the push. Japanese saws cut in the same way. Many saws, as can be seen, are adapted to particular trades. A futtock saw is used in shipbuilding. Bilge and cylinder saws are used for making barrels. Milling saws are for cutting steel and iron bars, and sometimes have removable teeth

Do Bees Ventilate Their Hives?

IF we look at a beehive on a warm day, we shall see round the entrance a number of bees that remain more or less in the same position and continue flapping their wings vigorously, their heads pointing to the door. Their wings are moved

Bees fanning their wings at the entrance to the hive to keep it cool

so rapidly that they are almost invisible, like the propeller of an aeroplane when it is rotating rapidly. These bees are ventilating the hive and preventing the inside from getting too warm for the health of the inmates.

Inside the hive there are other bees also moving their wings, with their heads towards the opening. As the Sun gets higher and the weather warmer, more and more bees take up this task of ventilation. After a time some of the bees get exhausted. They then stand aside, and other bees take their place and carry on the good work. If the summer nights are very hot, the fanning goes on at night as well as by day. The draught created is often so strong that if a lighted candle be placed near the entrance, the flame will be blown out.

Do Some People Have Double Joints?

SOME people's joints are so flexible that they can do many things with their limbs, fingers and toes which ordinary people cannot do. But they are not "double-jointed." Their unusual powers are merely due to the fact that the ligaments which hold the ends of two adjacent bones are rather looser than in ordinary people, and so give greater play to the bones.

What is the Treacle Bible?

THIS is a popular name given to both Coverdale's Bible of 1535 and the Bishop's Bible of 1568, because the passage in Jeremiah VIII, 22, is translated "Is there not treacle at Gilead?" instead of, as in our Authorized Version, "Is there no balm in Gilead?"

Which is the Largest Flower?

IT is difficult to give a direct answer to the question in this form, because of the varied shapes of flowers. The blossom of the rafflesia, which grows in the forests of Sumatra and is a parasite upon the roots of climbing plants, has no petals, but a calyx of five spreading fleshy lobes. The flower when opened is three feet across, of a reddish tint, and gives out a smell like carrion, which attracts flies and causes them to fertilise it. The rafflesia has neither leaves nor stems. The blossom weighs about 15 pounds, and the central cavity would hold about a gallon and a half. This is the largest spreading flower.

A huge blossom of another kind is that of a plant called by botanists *Amorphophallus titanum* (it has no popular name). This also grows in Sumatra, and it belongs to the arum family, to which our familiar cuckoo-pint belongs. Indeed, the plant is like a gigantic cuckoo-pint, with a spathe and spadix. It reaches a height of 17 feet in its native jungle, and the spadix or spike is six inches in diameter and over six feet high. The whole blossom is about 13 feet in circumference.

It is an amazing flower, for it opens so rapidly that from the time it begins to unfold to the time it is fully developed is only an hour and a half. The flower gives out an odour like stale fish.

It is yellow and green outside, and maroon inside, while the spadix is

yellow and the stem dark blue and green with yellow spots. The *Amorphophallus* was first discovered in 1878 by Dr. Beccari, and to transport a flower this was lashed to a long pole and carried by two men on their shoulders.

The rafflesia was first discovered by Dr. Arnold and Sir Stamford Raffles (after whom it is named) in 1818. Dr.

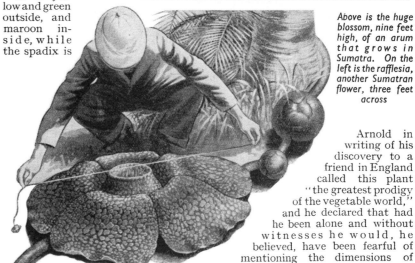

Above is the huge blossom, nine feet high, of an arum that grows in Sumatra. On the left is the rafflesia, another Sumatran flower, three feet across

Arnold in writing of his discovery to a friend in England called this plant "the greatest prodigy of the vegetable world," and he declared that had he been alone and without witnesses he would, he believed, have been fearful of mentioning the dimensions of the flower.

Where is the Biggest Bell in the World?

IT stands in the middle of a square in Moscow, and was formerly known as the Tsar Bell. Up to the Revolution

The Great Bell of Moscow, which weighs nearly 200 tons—the biggest bell in the world

it was used as a chapel. It was cast in 1733, and weighs 440,000 pounds, or over 196 tons. The bell stands 19¼ feet high, is 22 feet 8 inches in diameter, and the metal is 3 feet thick. The tongue is 14 feet long and 6 feet in circumference at the thickest part.

When an attempt was made to hang the bell for ringing it broke from its support and fell, a piece being broken out of it. It lay where it fell for over a century, and then, in 1836, the Tsar Nicholas set it up as a church, the broken part serving as a door.

This bell was made from the metal of an earlier bell cast in 1654 which weighed 228,000 pounds, or nearly 102 tons. After it had been damaged by fire in 1701 the Empress Anne added another 72,000 pounds of metal for the making of a new bell.

The largest bell in use hangs in a great Buddhist monastery near Canton. It is 18 feet high and 45 feet in diameter, being made of bronze. It was cast in 1400, and eight men lost their lives in the casting. The biggest bell in Great Britain is Great Paul, of St. Paul's Cathedral in London, which is 9 feet 6¾ inches in diameter, 8 feet 10 inches high, and weighs 16 tons 14½ cwts. The tongue weighs 4¼ cwts. The great bell of St. Peter's at Rome is only 8 tons, but the Kaiser Bell at Cologne weighs 25 tons.

What Exactly is Manna?

THIS is the name given to the food with which the Israelites were miraculously fed during their exodus from Egypt to Palestine as described in the Book of Exodus, Chapter XVI What that material was no one can say definitely. Various explanations have been given, but there are a number of foods to which the name manna is still given.

First of all there is a sweet sap which hardens into small lumps of sugary substance exuded by a small tree growing in Hungary, Italy and Sicily. It is called the manna ash, and the sap, which is obtained by tapping in the same way as maple sugar is obtained in America, is called manna. The hardened sap is gathered in pieces shaped something like stalactites. The botanical name of the manna ash is *Fraxinus ornus*.

There is a lichen found growing over a wide area in Asia and Africa which bears many points of resemblance to the manna described in the Bible. It appears on fragments of stone as a greyish yellow crust, dry and wrinkled. The winds uproot it and whirl it into the air, and it falls sometimes in such quantities as to be on the ground several inches deep. It is known as manna, but its botanical name is *Lecanora esculenta*. It can be made into bread.

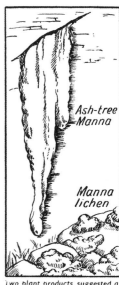

Two plant products suggested as the manna of the Bible

Why Do We Screw Up Our Eyes?

WE do this when looking towards a bright light or up towards the sky, and the screwing up of the eyes is for the purpose of shutting off some of the light from entering the iris. Of course, the iris or pupil itself, through which the light enters the eye, closes a good deal when we are looking at a light, but when

that is not sufficient, then we instinctively bring the lids together to shut out still more light.

There is another reason why some people screw up their eyes, and that is because they are short-sighted. They do this in order to see better. The bringing together of the eyelids has a slight effect in bending the rays of light as they enter the iris, thereby causing them to focus better on the retina.

Children screwing up their eyes as they look upward at a Punch and Judy show

How Much Air is Moved in a Year?

METEOROLOGISTS tell us that every year 10,000 million tons of air shift from hemisphere to hemisphere. It is this movement of the air which is largely responsible for the weather we experience, and the only way to understand the weather is to investigate the conditions in the Arctic. The Russian scientists made a beginning by establishing a research station practically at the Pole.

What Are Panama Hats Made From?

THESE hats are made from the young leaves of a palm known to botanists as *Carludovica palmata*, which grows in Central America. Formerly these hats were made only in Ecuador and Colombia, but now the leaves are imported into Europe and Panama hats are made there.

Why Does a Fire Twist Massive Girders?

HEAT is a form of energy, and the enormous energy exerted by intense heat is seen by the results of a great fire in a building. When the fire is extinguished we see the massive steel girders all twisted and bent.

To realise the amount of energy exerted we have only to imagine the time and power that would be needed to bend up the girders in this way in a modern factory. The heat sets

The tangled mass of steel girders after a fire. The intense heat has caused them to warp

the molecules or particles of which the girders are made up in rapid motion, and the faster they move, as the steel or iron gets hotter, the less powerful is the cohesion between the particles. The result is that the metal becomes soft and can be bent by any pressure.

Are Cactus Plants Useful?

OWING to their prickles they have not been used very much, although Luther Burbank, the plant wizard of America, bred a prickly pear cactus without spines, and it could then be used as food for cattle. It is nourishing and stores up water, and with its aid large arid tracts in the United States where no animals could live are now able to support numbers of cattle.

A young porcupine with its quills erect

Scientists have also discovered how to make other forms of cactus useful. They have devised means of producing from these strange plants drugs, soap, cleaners, water-softeners and a boiler compound. One gallon of cactus juice placed in 10,000 gallons of water will purify an iron heating system and prevent it from being clogged by scale and corrosion. The cactus solution can also be used for cleaning rust from exposed casings, and removing harmful products from steam when it is used in the manufacture of food preparations.

Does a Porcupine Shoot Out Its Quills?

THE popular notion that a porcupine when attacked by an enemy shoots out its pointed quills like arrows fired from a bow is quite erroneous. It is true that though normally the quills lie down smoothly, and are directed backwards, the animal when excited can by means of muscles under the skin erect the quills, very much in the same way as a hedgehog erects its spines. At the same time the hollow quills at the tip of the tail are rattled, making a sound something like the rattle of a rattlesnake.

If attacked by dogs or other four-footed foes the porcupine often rushes backwards, and inflicts severe wounds with the long quills at the back. These are easily detachable, and often come out in such a contest, and it is this fact that has given rise to the idea that the porcupine will fire quills at its foe.

The number varies from 25,000 to over 30,000. Ernest Thompson Seton, the famous naturalist, counted 36,450 quills on a specimen which he examined. Porcupines are found in both the Old and New Worlds. In North America they live mostly in clefts of rocks and hollow trees, while in South America they live among the branches of the trees. Porcupines of the Old World dwell in burrows, which they dig themselves, or in hollows among the rocks. The porcupines are rodents, and live on vegetable food.

Is Red Flannel Warmer than White?

THERE is no ground whatever for such a belief. Probably the idea arose owing to the fact that a fire is hot and red, while snow and ice are white and cold. Of course, when the outer garments are white, they reflect some of the Sun's rays falling upon them, while red clothing absorbs more of these rays. But when red or white flannel is worn as part of the under-clothing, this does not apply.

Does the First or Last Stroke of Big Ben Mark the Hour?

THE first blow on Big Ben denotes the exact hour, and it takes a fifth of a second for the sound of the bell to reach the bottom of the tower

A tank mounting a steep incline

One of the original conditions when the clock was being ordered was that the first blow of the hour should always be struck within a second of the real time. In order that this may happen the hammer has to fall exactly when the clock reaches the 60th second of the last minute of the hour. Big Ben is wound up by an electric motor, and is lighted by electric lamps.

What is Iambic Verse?

IT is verse in which each foot is an iambus, or foot of two syllables. The first is short or unaccented, and the second long or accented. It is the form used in Greek tragedy, and the most usual kind of verse in English literature.

Is a Hornet the Same as a Wasp?

NO; it is another species of the same genus, being distinguished by its greater size and the red markings on the head and body. The hornet is known to scientists as *Vespa crabro*, while the common wasp that builds its

The comparative sizes of the hornet and the wasp. The drawing shows these insects rather more than half their natural size

nest in the ground is *Vespa vulgaris*. The tree wasp, whose nests hang in trees, is *Vespa arborea*.

What Are Buchan's Cold and Warm Periods?

ALEXANDER BUCHAN was a Scottish meteorologist, born in 1829, who studied the weather over a course of years, and came to the conclusion that there are certain periods, more or less well defined, when definitely cold or warm weather may be anticipated. According to Buchan, there are six cold and three warm periods of this kind, as follows:

1st cold period, February 7th to 10th.

2nd cold period, April 11th to 14th.

3rd cold period,

A tank in a perpendicular position about to surmount a wall

May 9th to 14th.

4th cold period, June 29th to July 4th.

1st warm period, July 12th to 15th.

5th cold period, August 6th to 11th.

2nd warm period, August 12th to 15th.

6th cold period, Nov. 6th to 12th.

3rd warm period, December 3rd to 9th.

That there is some truth in Buchan's observations is suggested by the fact that he is often right, though he never suggested that the periods must invariably occur every year.

Why Can Tanks Travel Anywhere?

TANKS can travel over almost any kind of country, except that which is boggy, and even on muddy or soft ground they can make headway when wooden blocks called spuds are bolted to the tractor plates.

Tanks were invented in 1914, and first appeared in action with the British Army on September 15th, 1916, on the Somme. The early tanks were very slow-moving, but they have been gradually improved, till now they can rush across rough country at the rate of about 30 miles an hour.

They are able to cross ditches and trenches because of their peculiar shape, the position of their centre of gravity, and the tractor-belts, working over sprocket wheels. These tractor-belts, working along the whole length of the tank and up the front and back, enable the vehicle to get a grip even on the most inclined plane.

The photographs on this page will show the possibilities of the latest types of tanks. Not only can they go up and down hill and over trenches, but they can cross walls as the tank is doing in the middle photograph, rising perpendicularly to do so. When going at full speed they can even leap a low wall, as shown in the bottom photograph.

Who Was the Scourge of God?

THIS is a name given to Attila, King of the Huns, who with his hordes invaded the Roman Empire in the fifth century. He was born about 406, and he and his brother became joint kings of countless hordes scattered over the country between the Caspian and the Danube. In 447 he devastated all the country lying between the Black Sea and the Mediterranean. Later

An acrobatic manoeuvre by a fast-moving tank

he invaded Gaul, but he was defeated by Theodoric, King of the Visigoths, at the battle of Orleans. Attila retreated, but afterwards invaded Italy, and he died in 453 in Pannonia.

Where is Ultima Thule?

THULE is a name mentioned by Pytheas, a Greek navigator and astronomer of Marseilles, who lived in the second half of the fourth century B.C. He visited the coasts of Britain, but

The region of northern Europe in which Ultima Thule was situated

exactly where his Thule was situated has been a matter of dispute for more than 2,000 years. According to some it was the Shetland Islands, but others think it must have been Iceland, while still others believe it was Lapland. The Romans generally added the word ultima, and spoke of Ultima Thule, which means the Farthest Thule. Poets have always used the name to designate some unknown far distant northern or purely mythical region.

Who Invented the Police Whistle?

THIS useful instrument was invented in 1884 by Mr. Joseph Hudson, a whistle-maker, of Birmingham. His first contract was an order for 21,000 police whistles, and his firm afterwards made as many as a million whistles a year.

Sir H. M. Stanley, the great explorer, took one of Hudson's early police whistles with him to Africa, and found it exceedingly useful in calling his native servants. Before the advent of the police whistle constables used to carry wooden rattles. Two advantages of the whistle over the rattle are that the instrument is very small and portable, and the policeman can go on whistling while keeping his hands free to hold a prisoner or defend himself. The rattle, of course, needed one hand to swing it.

How Many Hairs Has Your Head?

THE number of hairs on the head of an ordinary person is said to be about 100,000. Each hair is about one-400th of an inch in diameter, but

hair is very strong, four average human hairs being capable of supporting a weight of a pound. The loss of hair resulting in baldness comes about owing to the decay of the hair follicles —that is, the little solid masses of cells in the skin out of which the hair grows. The turning of the hair grey late in life is due to a deficiency in the formation of pigment in the skin. The silvery lustre of white hair is further increased by the development of many air bubbles which reflect the light.

Why is an Umbrella Called a Gamp?

THIS name has been given to a large umbrella ever since the publication of Charles Dickens' novel "Martin Chuzzlewit." In that book an umbrella formed part of the belongings of Mrs. Sairey Gamp, a nurse celebrated for her constant references to an imaginary friend, Mrs. Harris, and for her fondness for alcoholic liquor.

Does a Fish Diet Help the Brain?

IT is quite a mistake to suppose that fish is a specially valuable food for the brain. This error arose in two ways. A scientist, Dr. Buchner, once declared that "Without phosphorus there is no thought." But this statement is true only in the sense that the brain contains phosphorus, and without the brain there can be no thinking.

Dr. Robert Hutchison, the great expert on food and dietetics, tells us that it has never been shown that an increased supply of phosphorus in the food is specially favourable to mental effort.

The second error is to suppose that fish is specially rich in phosphorus. The Swiss naturalist, Agassiz, was responsible for this statement, but there is no justification for it whatever. Fish is, of course, a good food, but not specially for the brain.

Is Wassailing Still Carried Out?

YES, the ancient ceremony of wassailing is still observed on Twelfth Night in some parts of England, as in Somersetshire and Herefordshire.

The farmers and villagers go out into the apple orchards with a large pitcher of cider and there among the trees drink the following toast :

Here's to thee, old apple-tree,
Whence thou mayest bud, and whence
    thou mayest blow,
And whence thou mayest bear apples
    enow.

Hats full, caps full,
Bushel, bushel, sacks full,
And my pockets full too, hurrah !

The song having been sung to weave a spell round the trees, a great hubbub is then made, guns being fired through the branches to drive away the imps and evil spirits. In the old days people feared that if they did not wassail the apple-trees, these would bear no fruit.

Wassail is an old English word meaning to be whole, and to wassail a person was to wish him health.

The ancient ceremony of wassailing the apple-trees in the cider orchards of Somerset

Can Monkeys Be Taught To Work?

UNDOUBTEDLY, and the higher apes, especially the chimpanzee, show remarkable intelligence in learning and doing things. The orangutan can be trained to become a servant, waiting at table and performing other domestic service. The chimpanzee also has been trained to perform domestic duties. He has, says Dr. Lander Lindsay, been taught to feed and attend a baker's oven-fire on board ship, and to act as galley fireman, regulating the temperature.

These workmanlike apes become accustomed to wear clothes, drink out of glasses, use a spoon and fork, uncork bottles, clean boots and brush clothes and have been employed in various tasks in house and field.

On shipboard, says Dr. Lindsay, they help to reef and furl the sails. They make themselves a bed with a raised pillow, light a fire and cook food, dust furniture, clean the floor. Bastian, the scientist, saw in an English man-of-war an ape sitting among the sailors sewing as zealously as they.

One of the most intelligent animals of which we have any record is the pet chimpanzee of Mr. Cherry Kearton, the well-known naturalist. His name was Toto, and Mr. Kearton says, " He would fetch and carry for the other inmates of the house, he would watch the operations of cooking with the greatest interest, and he learnt to help at washing plates and dishes. He played with the dog. Children came to see him and play with him, and he made many lasting friendships. Everyone adored him, and I most of all."

This remarkable animal was not taught to any great extent. He taught himself by watching human beings. In this way he learned to wash himself regularly and even to clean his teeth with a tooth-brush.

" One day," says Mr. Kearton, " we saw a group of native boys sitting on the ground, washing clothes. Taking his place in the circle, accepted apparently without question as an additional helper and hard at work, sat Toto. He was entirely absorbed in his task, washing a cloth with soap in a bowl of water, wringing it out in exact imitation of the way the natives worked, then wetting it with a cupful of clean water and wringing it out again."

The intelligence of this monkey was really remarkable. Toto was fond of preserved cherries, and a friend of Mr. Kearton gave him a bottle with a cherry inside which was too big to be shaken out. " Toto was faced with the problem of how to secure it. First he tried passing one of his long fingers into the neck of the bottle. But the fruit was slippery and he could not keep hold of it.

" Then he set the bottle down on the table in front of him and considered it. He quickly made up his mind, and looked round the room for what he wanted. On the sideboard stood the remains of a cold fowl. Toto went to it at once, helped himself to a long, thin bone, and put this like a spoon into the bottle. Then he held the bottle upside-down and slowly drew out the cherry, balanced on the end of the bone.

" It was one of the cleverest things I ever saw him do," adds Mr. Kearton. " My host declared that there was not a native in Central Africa who would have had the intelligence to do it ; and for my part I doubt whether many white men would have solved the problem so quickly and so effectively. As I have said, Toto was a genius among apes."

A chimpanzee threading a needle. These monkeys can be taught to sew quite well

What is a Daguerreotype?

IT is the earliest form of photograph, and is named after its inventor, Monsieur Louis Daguerre, who was born in 1789 and died in 1851. He was first of all a Civil Servant, then became

A good example of a daguerreotype photograph

a scene painter, and afterwards studied the problem of making pictures by the action of sunlight. He perfected his process in about 1839. The process of making daguerreotypes consisted of exposing silver plates to the vapour of iodine. These were then placed in the camera, or, as it was called at that time, the camera obscura, and after sufficient exposure the light acted upon the iodised surface of the plates, which were then exposed to the vapour of mercury. This led to the latent image being developed. The iodide of silver was then washed off by a solution of the hyposulphite of soda, and the further action of the light was stayed, the image already on the plate being rendered permanent.

What is Aldgate Pump?

IT is an old pump, now out of use, at the junction of Leadenhall Street and Fenchurch Street at the east end of the City of London. It is mentioned by Stowe and referred to in Fielding's works. For a long time the water from Aldgate Pump enjoyed great local celebrity, but when, in 1876, the water was found on analysis to be impure, the pump was closed.

Aldgate pump as it is today

What Kind of Bridge is That?

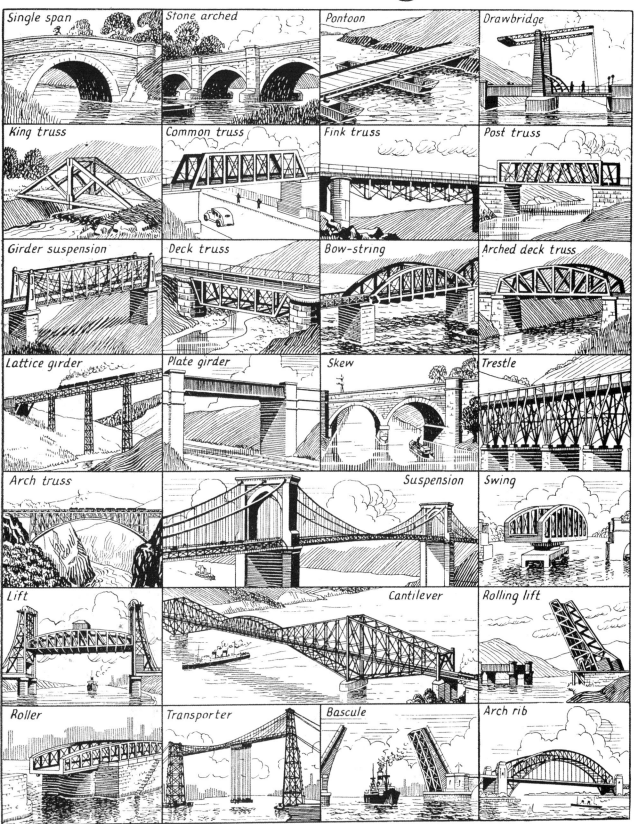

Single span · Stone arched · Pontoon · Drawbridge

King truss · Common truss · Fink truss · Post truss

Girder suspension · Deck truss · Bow-string · Arched deck truss

Lattice girder · Plate girder · Skew · Trestle

Arch truss · Suspension · Swing

Lift · Cantilever · Rolling lift

Roller · Transporter · Bascule · Arch rib

Here are 26 drawings showing the various types of bridges which are built today. The stone bridge is fast giving place to steel and concrete structures. Each type has some feature which makes it peculiarly suitable for the situation in which it is placed. The cantilever principle, for example, is generally used for long spans, and truss bridges for railways. Roller bridges and rolling lift bridges are used where a passage through a bridge has to be opened from time to time to allow ships to pass. Where a wider space is needed a double bascule bridge is often used. A famous example is the Tower Bridge in London. In a transporter bridge a platform suspended from an overhead structure is moved to and fro across the river

Why Were Aqueducts Built?

THE Romans and other ancient people built these artificial canals for conveying water from one point to another on the same level. They took pleasure in making them works of great architectural beauty, and many examples remain today, like the Pont-du-Gard at Nismes in France. The reason these great structures were erected was not because the Romans did not understand that water found its own level. Their difficulty consisted in making pipes sufficiently strong to carry large volumes of water.

What is it to Sell by the Candle?

THIS is a curious form of auction in which a pin is stuck through a candle about an inch from the top and bidding goes on till the candle is burnt down to the pin, the last bid as the pin drops into the candlestick being accepted. Such an auction was held at Aldermaston, the little Berkshire village near Reading, as recently as the year 1893.

Does Gutta-Percha Differ From India-Rubber?

THE substances are much alike, both being juices exuded by trees which solidify in the atmosphere.

Brazilian Rubber tree   *Taban tree yielding gutta-percha*

The leaves and flowers of the trees that produce india-rubber and gutta-percha

What is Hock Tide?

HOCK TIDE is an ancient ceremony carried out on the Tuesday following the second Sunday after Easter. On this day the women went into the streets with cords and stopped and bound any of the opposite sex whom they met, holding them till they purchased their release by a small money contribution. At one period the men behaved in the same way towards the women, choosing the previous day for their part of the ceremony.

At some places, as at Coventry, there was a hock-tide play, and in 1575 this was performed before Queen Elizabeth during her visit to Kenilworth. In many of the old parish registers there are entries of money collected by the women at Hock Tide. At one time the ceremony was performed all over England, but in 1450 the Bishop of Worcester prohibited it on the ground that it led to much dissipation.

Gradually it died out, but it still survives at Hungerford in Berkshire. There officials known as tutti-men go round the town demanding a coin of the realm from every male over the age of twelve and a kiss from every woman. An " Orangeman " goes with them distributing oranges. A lunch is held and then the tutti-men give away the pennies to the children. The meaning of the word hock is unknown.

Gutta-percha comes as a white juice from several Malayan trees, especially *Palaquium gutta*. It becomes soft and impressible at the temperature of boiling water, and in composition and many of its properties closely resembles india-rubber. It is used for insulation, being an even poorer conductor than rubber.

India-rubber is a white milky juice obtained from many tropical trees which is soluble in chloroform and some oils, but not in water or alcohol. It is used for waterproofing and also for insulation and a great variety of other purposes. It is sometimes called caoutchouc, pronounced koochook.

In both cases the juice is obtained by cutting the bark of the tree.

Do Monkeys Hunt for Fleas?

IT certainly looks as though they were doing so, if we watch the monkeys at the Zoo. But actually monkeys rarely have fleas. When a monkey is seen searching in the fur of another monkey, he is really hunting not for fleas, but for small masses of a salty secretion which exudes from the pores of the skin.

What is Jingoism?

IT is a blustering, vulgar and vehement form of patriotism whose advocates are known as jingoes. It was in general vogue between the years 1874 and 1880, when Lord Beaconsfield took up a strong attitude about the Russo-Turkish war. The word became popular as the result of a music-hall song sung by " The Great Macdermot " in 1878, the refrain of which ran : " We don't want to fight, but by jingo if we do, we've got the ships, we've got the men, we've got the money too." Jingo is said to be a corruption of the name of St. Gengulphus, a Burgundian saint of the eighth century.

Tutti-men and the orangeman at the ancient Hock Tide festival at Hungerford

What is a Protocol ?

THIS was originally a small slip or tab glued to the top edge of a roll of manuscript, especially of an official document, and on it was written the date, name of the author and other similar particulars. Now it is used to denote a first draft or the original copy of a Government document or treaty forming the basis of a final treaty.

Has Anyone Crossed Niagara on Stilts ?

YES, Blondin, the tightrope-walker, after crossing the falls walking on a tightrope on June 30th, 1859, decided to make a more sensational journey. He had walked over on the rope in the presence of 25,000 people in five minutes. Four days later he crossed again, blindfolded and pushing a wheelbarrow. Then on August 19th of the same year he went over carrying a man on his back. And on September 14th, 1860, he crossed on a tightrope on stilts in the presence of the Prince of Wales, afterwards King Edward VII. Blondin offered to carry the Prince across on his back, but the invitation was courteously declined.

What Was the Calves' Head Club ?

IT was a club said to have been instituted in Charles II's reign in ridicule of Charles I. It had an annual banquet on January 30th, the anniversary of the king's execution, at which a cod's head represented Charles, a pike with little ones in its mouth was regarded as an emblem of tyranny, and a boar's head with an apple in its mouth represented the king preying on his subjects. A dish of calves' heads represented the king and his friends, and an axe was treated as a symbol for reverence. In early years the club met in secret, but in 1734 it ended.

What is the "Roaring Game" ?

THIS is the name given to curling, the winter sport of Scotland which has been played in one form or another for about four centuries.

Preparing stones for curling, which is known in Scotland as " the roaring game" and is played on the ice

Originally confined to Scotland, it has now spread to England, America, New Zealand and Switzerland.

Curling takes place on the ice and consists in hurling along the surface circular stones fitted with handles on top. These stones weigh about 34 or 38 pounds, but at one time they weighed as much as 50 pounds each; and the earliest curling-stones were merely natural boulders, termed loofies. These had no handles, but holes were cut in them for finger and thumb.

Curling is played on a rink from 32 to 42 yards long. At each end is a "diagram" consisting of three concentric circles with radii of 7 feet, 4 feet and 2½ feet respectively, and the game, which is something like bowls, is to get the stones as near as possible to a "tee" in the centre of the circles. Brooms are used for sweeping the ice clear in front of the stones.

Curling is now independent of natural ice and can be played in artificial ice under cover. The game is controlled by the Royal Caledonian Curling Club.

Is Any London Borough on Both Sides of the Thames ?

YES, there is one such borough, and that is Woolwich. The greater part is in Kent, on the south side of the river, but there is a portion on the other side of the river in Essex, and the two parts are connected by a tunnel under the river for foot-passengers and a ferry service across the water for vehicles and passengers.

This free ferry was established by the London County Council in 1889, and was opened by Lord Rosebery on March 23rd of that year. The ferry-boats, of which there are three, are driven by steam and are very broad, and vehicles drive on to the upper deck. There is a lower deck for the use of ordinary foot-passengers.

Can Ants be Kept Out of a House ?

IT is unpleasant to have ants overrunning a house, although they may do little harm. The best way to keep them out is to sprinkle flowers of sulphur or powdered borax in the places they haunt. If their entrance from the garden can be found it is good to paint this with some sticky substance, or the doorsteps and window-sills they cross may be painted with ordinary paraffin. Any of these methods seems to be effective in keeping down the pest.

One of the huge ferry-boats which cross the Thames between North and South Woolwich

Which British Owl is That?

Tawny, or Brown Owl

Eagle Owl

Tengmalm's Owl

Scops Owl

Barn Owl

Little Owl

Hawk Owl

Short-eared Owl

Long-eared Owl

Snowy Owl

Ten owls are found wild in England, and by means of these drawings it will be possible to identify any owl that may be seen. The commonest owls are, of course, the white or barn owl, seen all over the country in the neighbourhood of church towers and barns ; the tawny or brown owl, common in wooded districts, and the long-eared owl, also found in woodland districts. The short-eared owl is resident only in northern counties, but in autumn and winter migrates all over the country. It is seen in moorland and marshy districts. The other owls are rarer. Scops owl is the smallest in the British Isles, and is only a summer visitor. The eagle owl and hawk owl are recorded only from time to time, and the snowy owl is an annual visitor to the Orkneys and Shetlands. The little owl is becoming more common than it used to be and is now found in many wooded areas

When Was the First Terrestrial Globe Made?

A GLOBE is the only surface on which the Earth can be correctly portrayed. Any flat map must be more or less inaccurate, because the world is a sphere and the surface

The globe made at Nuremberg in 1490 by Martin Behaim, believed to be the first terrestrial globe ever constructed

of a sphere cannot be spread out flat. But globes though very accurate as representations of the Earth, are inconvenient to carry about, hence the use of flat maps as a second best.

The first terrestrial globe is said to have been made in 1490 by Martin Behaim of Nuremberg, a celebrated navigator and cosmographer, who died at Lisbon in 1506. This globe is in the Germanic Museum at Nuremberg and is shown in the photograph above.

The earliest globe made in England was that constructed by William Molyneux in 1592. It is preserved in the Middle Temple, London.

Collapsible terrestrial globes have been made in recent years of india-rubber and gutta-percha and also of thin paper which can be folded up and inflated when required for use.

What is a Parliamentary Whip?

THE term stands for both a person and a document. A Whip is an official appointed by a political party in Parliament to enforce discipline among its members, seeing that they attend the House and are ready to go into the lobbies at division times. The Whip issues a whip to all members of the party in the House of Commons, which is a document urging them to attend on important occasions and when a division is likely. If the occasion is one of very great importance he sends to members a three-line whip—that is, one in which the summons to attend is underlined three times as a sign of urgency. The word whip is used because it is regarded as a lash to keep members up to their duties.

What is a Legal Refresher?

BESIDES the retaining-fee paid to counsel upon his acceptance of a brief, it is usual for him to receive additional payment for each day's hearing in the Court if the trial lasts over the first day and for more than five hours. The additional fee is also paid where a case is adjourned from one term or sittings to another. These refreshers often amount to large sums, varying with the reputation of the counsel. The word implies that the counsel is expected to refresh his memory from time to time as to the facts of the case.

Where is the Devil's Dyke?

IT is a ravine in the South Downs at Brighton. According to an old legend, St. Cuthman, walking on the downs, was congratulating himself on having Christianised the surrounding country and built a nunnery, when the devil appeared and told him all his work was vain, for he would swamp all the country before morning. St. Cuthman told the abbess and her nuns to pray till after midnight and to illuminate all their windows.

At sunset the devil arrived with mattock and spade, and began to cut a dyke through which to let in the sea to flood the country. But he was seized with rheumatic pains and had to throw down his tools. Then the cocks, mistaking the lighted windows for sunrise, began to crow, and at once the devil fled, leaving his work only half done. That is the dyke as we know it today. Thousands of people on holiday at Brighton visit it every summer

When Was a Man Last Placed in the Stocks?

A MAN named John Foster was placed in the stocks in the town of Newcastle Emlyn on January 19th, 1872, and was kept seated there for three hours with both legs fast, and then he was kept for another three hours standing, with both hands fast to the posts of the stocks. This is believed to be the last case in which a person was officially placed in the stocks. Six years before a prisoner had been placed in the stocks at Rugby, and a photograph is in existence showing him with a policeman by his side, the constable wearing a tall hat.

How Are Firework Boxers Arranged?

ONE of the most ingenious and realistic forms of firework displays is two boxers outlined in fire who actually box like real men in the ring. This is not done by means of some clever mechanism, but behind the fiery boxers are a pair of real boxers.

These men are dressed in suits of asbestos which have attached to them jointed wooden frames and on these frames the fireworks are fixed. When the fireworks are touched off the men spar and box and their movements

Men dressed in asbestos suits, with fireworks attached. It is in this way that a boxing match outlined in fire is seen during a firework display

are communicated to the framework representations, so that the spectators see two fiery fighters.

Do Moths Eat Clothes?

No, the moths we see flying about do not make the holes in our garments. It is another stage in the lives of these creatures which is responsible for the damage done. The

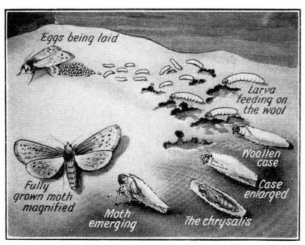

The life story of the pestilent clothes-moth

moths we see flying about lay eggs on flannel or woollen clothes packed away in some quiet or dark spot. These eggs hatch out into grubs or larvae, and it is the grubs that eat our clothes, feeding upon the wool. Not only so, but from the wool they make a case inside which they can live and grow. Then they change into a pupa or chrysalis, and finally emerge as winged insects. The winged clothes-moths should always be killed when seen flying, so that they may not lay their eggs, and blankets and other clothes packed away should be carefully examined at frequent intervals to see that no moth has found access to them.

The damage done by clothes-moths in a year is immense. It has been estimated that this amounts to at least £1,000,000 in England, and in America to about £40,000,000.

What is the Game of Conkers?

Conkers is a corruption of the word conquerors, and it is a game that has for centuries been played by boys with horse-chestnuts threaded on strings. In recent years, like so many other games that were played regularly at certain seasons of the year by schoolboys, such as marbles and peg-top and whipping-top, conkers have lost in popularity.

Two boys face each other and while one holds his conker or chestnut suspended, the other strikes it with his nut in the effort to smash it. It is considered bad play for the string to be struck; the nut only should be hit. Three tries are generally allowed, and then the positions of attacker and defender are reversed. A conker that has several victories to its credit is regarded with pride by its owner. The name conker given to the game

is also given to the horse-chestnuts. In some parts of the country a doggerel rhyme was recited while the nut was being struck, thus in London :

Cobbly co !
My first blow !

In Worcestershire the rhyme was :

Hobley, hobley, honcor,
my first conker ;
Hobley, hobley, ho, my
first go ;
Hobley, hobley, ack,
my first crack.

An older form of the game was for one conker to be laid on a log or on the ground, the attacking player striking it with his chestnut. The players struck alternately till one chestnut split the other. The nuts were often artificially hardened by being placed up the chimney.

What is An Accessory After the Fact?

This is a law term for an accomplice who, while he did not actually take part in a crime, learnt about it afterwards and did not inform the police. Every citizen is compelled by law to notify the police when he comes

Schoolboys playing the ancient game of conkers

into any knowledge about a crime. One who, knowing of a crime, in any way helps the criminal to escape justice is an accessory after the fact.

What Famous Surgeon was Buried Twice?

John Hunter, who is described as the Father of Modern Surgery, was buried first in the vaults of St. Martin's-in-the-Fields Church, London, on October 22nd, 1793, and fifty years later his body was exhumed and removed to Westminster Abbey.

Dr. John Hunter

What is Shagreen?

It is a kind of untanned grained leather prepared in Russia and the East from the skins of horses, asses and camels. It is covered with small granulations by pressing seeds into the grain or hair side when moist, and when dry scraping off the roughness. The skin is then soaked, which causes the indented portions to swell up into relief.

Another kind of shagreen is also made from the rough skin of sharks and rays, but this is really only an imitation of the real thing. It is used chiefly for polishing wood and, when dyed green, for sword handles.

The word " shagreen " is from the Persian name for this leather, and " chagrin," the Anglicised French word meaning " ill-humour " or " disap-pointment," is really the same word. From being used to polish wood it came to be used as a type of grinding or gnawing care.

Where Are England's Most Extensive Sidings?

THE most extensive railway sidings in England are said to be those on the London, Midland & Scottish railway at Toton, six miles south-west of Nottingham. These form the largest mineral marshalling centre in the world and have 58 miles of sidings, dealing with over 9,000 coal wagons a day.

What Does Selah Mean?

THIS is a Hebrew musical term which occurs 71 times in the Psalms, and only one other time in the Bible, namely, in the third chapter of Habakkuk, verse 13. Its meaning is not definitely known, but it is believed to be a sign of repetition, or the indication of a pause in the singing to be filled up with instrumental music.

What is the Meaning of Taboo?

THE term is a corruption of a Polynesian word tapu, and that describes a custom of setting apart certain persons or objects as either sacred or accursed. Such persons or things may not be touched, nor may their names be mentioned. The term has been adopted by Europeans to describe certain social or religious prohibitions and restraints. If, for example, a man greatly disgraces himself he is taboo among those of his social or religious class.

Who Were the Young Turks?

THIS name was given before the Great War to a party of reformers, mostly made up of younger officials, who set out to introduce modern methods into the administration of the Turkish empire. They started out with high ideals, gained power, but did not maintain their lofty aspirations, and after the War were superseded by Kemal Pasha, who really reformed the old Empire and put down corruption.

The departure roads at Toton Sidings, near Nottingham, on the London, Midland & Scottish Railway, the largest mineral marshalling centre in the world

Which is the "Mother of Cities"?

THIS is the name given to Balkh, the chief city of a desert region in Central Asia belonging to Afghanistan. The city, associated with the history of Zoroaster, the founder of the Parsee religion, was destroyed by Jenghiz Khan in 1220, and after being rebuilt was again destroyed by Timur. It was at one time of great importance.

What is the Succession to the British Throne

THE next heir to the throne after King George VI is Princess Elizabeth, and following her Princess Margaret. Then comes the Duke of Gloucester and any children his wife may bear him ; then the Duke of Kent and his children in order of age, and next the Princess Royal and her sons in the order of their age.

What Are Fabian Tactics?

THEY indicate a policy of patient and dogged resistance as opposed to violent and decisive attack. The reference is to the methods of the Roman General Quintus Fabius, one of the commanders against Hannibal in the second Punic War. Hannibal entered Italy and defeated the Romans in a number of pitched battles ; but Fabius eventually wore him out by cautious, guerrilla fighting without definite battles.

Do Flying Fish Have Wings?

NO, all they have are extended fins, and these are used like the wings of a glider to sustain them in the air for a time when they leap out of the

Are Fortunes Found in Dustbins?

MOST large municipalities have the dust collected from houses and factories examined, and it is true to say that there is a fortune in the dustbin ; for much of the matter thrown away is valuable. Professor A. M. Low estimates that in England there is an annual preventable waste of anything up to £400,000,000. That, of course, includes waste of all kinds, but much of this waste is in the dustbin. Here is an analysis of London refuse, taken some time ago :

Coal .. .. 0·35	Rags .. .. 0·40
Coke .. .. 0·15	Bones .. .. 0·37
Cinders .. 23·55	Bottles .. 0·48
Ash .. .. 47·00	Glass .. .. 0·37
Dust .. .. 9·75	Crockery .. 1·72
Paper and	Metals.. .. 0·68
vegetable	
matter .. 13·15	

An analysis taken in Sheffield was rather different :

Dust .. .. 31·3	Rags .. .. 0·4
Cinders .. 45·6	Paper .. .. 3·0
Stone and	Vegetable
hard debris 14·37	matter .. 3·73

In handling the refuse at many places dust is disposed of to agriculturalists for fertiliser, the cinder is made into brickettes, from the tins the solder and tin are recovered, rags and paper are sent to paper mills for pulping ; bones, bottles and jars are sold for various purposes, and clinker is used in road-making. Of course, sometimes real treasures are found in a dustbin—jewellery, money and other articles which have got into the bin by accident.

The flying fish gliding in the air after its leap from the water

sea. It is sometimes stated that they flap their fins like wings, but this is quite incorrect. The fins are motionless from the time the fish leaps out of the sea till it drops back again.

Are Twins Always Alike?

No; there are two different kinds of twins. In one case both children are of the same sex and are almost identical in form and face. In the other kind of twins the children may be of different sexes and have no more resemblance to one another than ordinary brothers and sisters of different births.

Two sets of identical twins, both, as will be noticed, of the same sex

The cause of twins is different in the two cases. The human being, like all animals, comes from a fertilised egg, and in the case of the twins of different sexes and different in appearance, the children have resulted from two different ova or eggs. In the case of the identical twins, which are always of the same sex, not two eggs have been fertilised, but only one, and this has developed simultaneously into two embryos, or, as Mr. Julian Huxley puts it, "a single early embryo has divided into two halves and each has grown into a complete child."

The same facts apply also to triplets, quadruplets and quintuplets. Everyone knows that the famous Canadian quintuplets are all girls, so that in that case the ovum or egg produced an embryo that divided into five.

It will be noticed that the striking photographs of twins, triplets and quadruplets which are given on this page are all girls and the extraordinary similarity in face and form indicates clearly that these are of the identical type coming from the one ovum in each case.

There seems to be also a remarkable similarity of tastes among identical twins and triplets, and also a strange sympathy, so that when one is unwell the other knows or senses it though he or she may be a considerable distance away.

Should Flowers Be Kept in a Bedroom?

Many people think that flowers in a bedroom are harmful, especially at night, and it is quite a common practice when evening falls to carry all the flowers out of a sick patient's room. But this is an erroneous idea, provided, of course, that the flowers are fresh and that the water in which they stand is changed from time to time, so as not to become stale.

Human beings breathe out carbon dioxide gas, and the green colouring matter of the plant, called chlorophyll, under the action of sunlight breaks up the carbon dioxide, using the carbon and releasing the oxygen, which is vital to human beings and all animals. Flowers with green leaves, therefore, so far from being harmful are beneficial in a room during the daylight hours.

But plants also give off carbon dioxide gas, though in the day-time the quantity is very small compared with the oxygen which they release.

Triplets living at Leytonstone, Essex, who are so much alike that they have to have their initials embroidered on their dresses

At night, while the carbon dioxide is still produced, the oxygen is not released as in the day-time. But the quantity of carbon dioxide is very slight, and does no real harm. It has been said that an ordinary gas-burner or a lamp flame produces more carbon dioxide than a good-sized oak tree.

Who Was Amadis of Gaul?

He was the hero of a romance in prose of the same title originally written, it is believed, in Portuguese, though some have supposed there may have been an earlier French version. The Portuguese original is lost, but the work is known by a Spanish translation.

Amadis is the oldest of the heroes of chivalry. He is described as the son of Perion, King of Gaul, and Elisena, Princess of Brittany. His mother exposed him in a cradle on the sea soon after birth, but he was picked up by a Scottish knight and, after being educated at the Scottish king's court, fell in love with Oriana, daughter of Lisuarte, King of England, whom he married. After being knighted he returned to Gaul, and there performed many wondrous exploits. A supplement added later to the work records the deeds of Amadis of Greece.

Amadis is described as a tall man of fair complexion, with a black beard. He was a person of few words and his aspect was between mild and severe.

Quadruplets at Lansing, Michigan, who, like the triplets above, have to have their initials embroidered on their dresses so that their school-teacher can identify them

What Was That Bygone Used For?

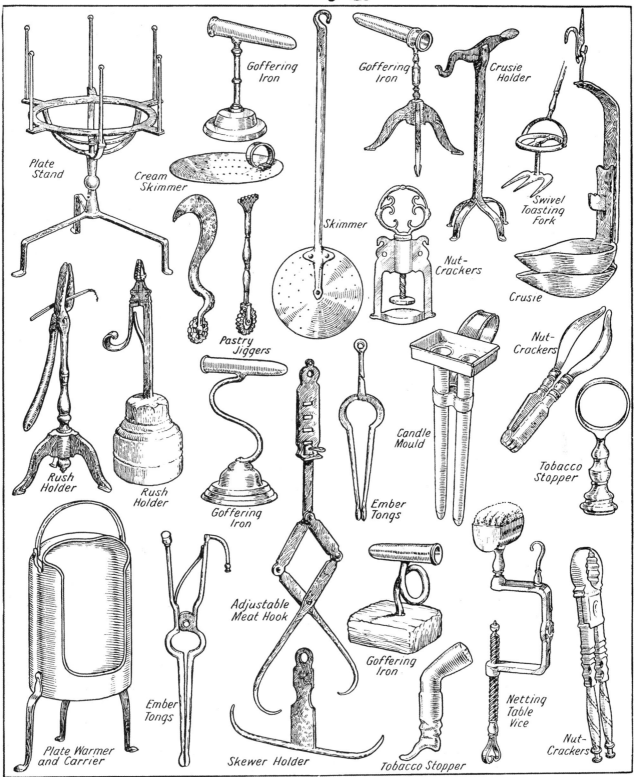

Plate Stand

Cream Skimmer

Goffering Iron

Goffering Iron

Crusie Holder

Swivel Toasting Fork

Skimmer

Nut-Crackers

Crusie

Pastry Jiggers

Rush Holder

Rush Holder

Goffering Iron

Candle Mould

Nut-Crackers

Tobacco Stopper

Ember Tongs

Adjustable Meat Hook

Goffering Iron

Ember Tongs

Plate Warmer and Carrier

Skewer Holder

Tobacco Stopper

Netting Table Vice

Nut-Crackers

Domestic bygones are greatly sought after in these days, and they certainly make a very interesting collection of antiques, for they tell us so much of the kind of life our ancestors lived, and the things they did. Yet many people when they come upon such objects in dark cupboards and lofts of old houses very often throw them away, not knowing what they are. Here are 26 domestic objects with their names. The goffering irons were used for crimping or fluting the edges of ladies' caps, aprons and collars. They were sometimes of iron and sometimes of brass. An iron was heated in the fire and when red-hot was inserted in the goffering iron, and the cap was then worked into flutes over the end of the iron. A crusie was an old lamp with a floating wick, much used in Scotland, and it could be hung on a nail or on a crusie holder. Pastry jiggers were for decorating pie-crusts. Ember tongs were for lighting tobacco pipes by taking a small ember from the fire. This was in the days before matches. A rush holder supported the rushlight used by poorer people. A netting vice was screwed to the edge of the table and used for holding pins, needles and threads

41

What is a Bucket-Shop?

THIS is the curious name given to the office of an outside broker—that is, a stockbroker who is not a member of the Stock Exchange. Such a broker endeavours to secure business by sending out circulars to prospective clients, and he gets his business done by members of the Stock Exchange. The origin of the term is not certain. It may be from a slang term " bucket," meaning to swindle, or it may refer to the " bucket " into which falls the recording tape of the tape machine, on which are printed the telegraphed prices. Still another explanation makes the Pit or wheat market in Chicago responsible for the term. There in the 1880's no deal was allowed in options of less than 5,000 bushels. To catch men of small means an outside market was started under the offices of the official Board. When business inside the Exchange was slack members would say, " I'll send down and get a bucketful," referring to the business done by the street speculators. From Chicago, it is said, the term spread to all transactions of the kind.

What is a Gyro-Wheel?

IT is an apparatus which is being used in Germany for a new form of sport or exercise. It consists of a double wheel nearly 6 feet in diameter with handles and stirrups for the feet. The player places his feet in the stirrups, grasps the handles on the opposite side of the rim and then by swaying the body sets the wheel rolling. Considerable speed can be obtained with this apparatus, and the changing tensions as the wheel goes round and round give the body some splendid exercise. The principal cause that is likely to militate against a widespread use of the gyro-wheel by ordinary people is the cost of the apparatus and the difficulty of housing it.

What Were Banyan Days?

IN the old days of the British Navy these were Monday, Wednesday and Friday, and meant the days on which no meat ration was issued, plum-duff being served instead. The name is taken from the *banians*, a class of Hindu merchants who abstain from the use of meat. We are told that the meat served out was so bad that the banyan days were looked forward to and regarded as occasions of feasting. The term still exists in the bluejacket's vocabulary, a banyan day being a gala day.

When is a Case Sub Judice?

SUB JUDICE is Latin and means " under the judge "—that is, awaiting his decision. The term is used in reference to a case or matter in which evidence has been heard, but on which the judge's decision has not yet been given. Newspapers are not allowed to make comments on cases that are sub judice.

How Many Muscles Move Your Eyeball?

SIX muscles are used in moving the eyeball. Four of them, the superior, inferior, internal and external

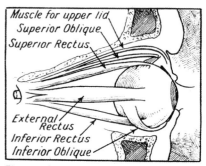

The muscles that enable us to turn our eyeballs in various directions

recti, move it upwards, downwards, inwards and outwards respectively, while the other two, the superior and inferior oblique, in combination with the others, roll it at any angle between the four directions named. In the diagram given above, the internal rectus muscle cannot be seen as it is hidden behind the external.

Are Cork Legs Made of Cork?

NO. Mr. E. Muirhead Little, the distinguished orthopaedic surgeon, has declared that after making exhaustive inquiries he has not been able to find that artificial legs were ever made of cork. Actually they are made of wood, with metal and leather or canvas. Willow wood is that generally used. It has been stated that the name " cork leg " arose from the fact that artificial limbs were made largely in Cork Street, London.

Two examples of how the gyro-wheel is used for open-air exercise. This appliance is becoming very popular in Germany, but the apparatus needs a good deal of space both for housing and for use

Did John the Baptist Eat Locusts ?

UNDOUBTEDLY, for the word used in the original for locusts, where we are told he lived on locusts and wild honey, really means the locust insect and not the pods of the locust tree.

According to the Mosaic Law the locust was one of the clean insects

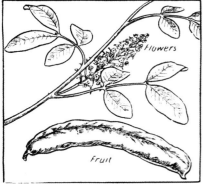

The leaves, flowers and fruit pod of the carob or locust tree, which some erroneously suppose was John the Baptist's locust food

which the Jews were allowed to use as food (see Leviticus XI, 22). Locusts are still largely eaten in Africa. The Bedouins string them together and eat them on their journeys, with un-leavened bread and butter. Dr. Livingstone speaks highly of them, declaring them superior to shrimps ; and another traveller, Mr. J. T. Bent,

tells how he found the Mashonas and Matabele busily engaged in cooking locusts. Honey is still eaten with locusts wherever it can be obtained.

Should a Cobweb be Used to Stop Bleeding?

SHAKESPEARE enjoined the practice, but it is very dangerous. The bleeding may certainly be stopped, but it would be difficult to find any-thing more likely to contain dirt and germs than a cobweb. Cobwebs collect all the dust that may be flying about in their neighbourhood, and the germs might easily cause such blood poisoning as would necessitate amputa-tion. Cases have been known where lockjaw has resulted from the applica-tion of cobweb to a cut on the finger.

How Many Okapis Have There Been in the Zoo?

ONLY two okapis have been seen at the London Zoo. The first one died, and a second one was acquired by the Zoo in July, 1937, by the gener-osity of King Leopold of the Belgians.

The first specimen was presented by the Belgian King in 1935 to King Edward VIII when he was Prince of Wales, and he in turn presented it to the Zoo, but it died after a few months' captivity. The second specimen was given to King George VI, who pre-sented it to the Zoo. The okapi was only discovered in 1900, and it had never been seen alive in England till 1935, when the first one arrived.

How Are the Sunshine Records Made?

THEY are made by means of instruments of which there are several different types. A kind which is much used in Great Britain is known as the burnt-paper recorder. The rays of the Sun are focused by a sphere of glass upon a strip of paper

The instrument with a globe of crystal by means of which the duration of sunshine is measured day by day

arranged in a curved framework. The instrument is placed at an angle facing south, and it is so arranged that any sunshine at all that may occur between sunrise and sunset will be recorded. As the Sun shines through the glass bulb it is focused on the paper, which becomes charred, but directly the Sun gets behind a cloud the charring ceases. Thus the sunshine itself makes the complete record, indicating the time it has been shining.

Another form of instrument is the photographic sunshine recorder, which consists of a cylindrical box with a small opening, but otherwise light-tight. Inside the box there is a piece of sensitized photographic paper, so ar-ranged that when the Sun is shining the rays pass through the opening in the box and shine on the paper, which is thus made dark. If the sunshine is interrupted the dark track on the sensitized paper ceases, and so a complete record is made for the day.

Another sunshine recorder is the electrical contact recorder in which a black bulb thermometer is enclosed in a glass chamber from which all air has been extracted. Two wires are carried into the stem of the thermo-meter. When the Sun shines the black bulb quickly absorbs the heat. The mercury rises in the tube and the two wires are connected, completing an electrical circuit. The recorder may be placed on the roof of a building and the wires carried into an office below, where they operate a pen that makes a graph on the paper of a revolving drum. Directly the Sun ceases to shine the mercury drops, contact is broken and the line becomes straight.

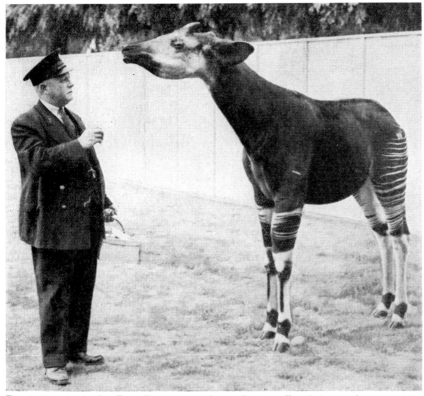

The okapi at the London Zoo. This nearest relation of the giraffe only became known to civili-sation in the closing years of the last century

When Was Dartmoor's First Mutiny?

DARTMOOR was originally built to confine the prisoners captured during the Napoleonic War. The last of the war prisoners left in February, 1816, and Dartmoor remained empty until 1850, when it was reopened as a convict prison.

The first mutiny there occurred in 1815 among a number of American war prisoners. The Treaty of Ghent between England and America was signed on March 14th, 1814, and the prisoners expected a speedy release. But as the days went by and no news of freedom arrived, the American prisoners became exasperated and began to bait their guards.

There were no separate cells, and the inmates of the prison lived together in large halls. This enabled a considerable number to concentrate in one place. The Americans began to dig a subterranean passage to the outside of the prison, but when this was nearly completed it was discovered by the authorities and the prisoners removed to another part of the gaol. There they planned a second tunnel and a number of daggers were forged by blacksmiths working in the prison. These they were to use to defend themselves.

But the plot was discovered and when the prisoners began to abuse the guard a man was knocked down with a musket butt. The prisoners replied with a volley of stones.

Something went wrong with the supply of bread, and the prisoners gathered together yelling "Give us our bread!" Then the whole body of men flung themselves on the gate, brought it crashing down and rushed the storehouses. They were given food and quieted down.

Later the officer in charge, who had been away, rang the alarm bell. At this the prisoners swarmed through the smashed gate, whereupon the military lowered their bayonets and charged. The prisoners replied by a counter-rush and shower of stones. In three minutes the affair was over, but seven men lay dead, two mortally wounded, and 54 others more or less injured. This first mutiny at Dartmoor occurred on April 16th, 1815.

A few years ago a serious mutiny took place among the convicts at Dartmoor, the warders being attacked, and a number of prisoners were punished and others removed to prisons in other parts of the country.

How Deep Are Pillar-Boxes?

AS can be seen by the pillar-boxes in the photograph which are waiting to be fixed in position, a very considerable proportion of the structure is buried in the ground. This is done to give the pillar-box security, so that even if a vehicle collides with it, it is not likely to be knocked over, and it cannot be removed bodily by mischievous or malicious persons. The danger of being run into is not inconsiderable, especially in these days of fast-driven motor-vehicles.

Pillar-boxes as they appear before being placed in position with their foundations buried in the ground

Can Zebra Mules Be Produced?

THE word mule means a he-ass, and the term is generally used for the offspring of a male ass and a mare.

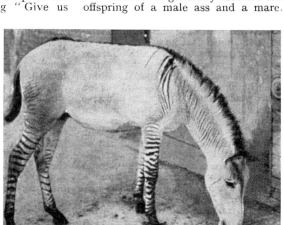
A hybrid between a zebra and a donkey at the London Zoo

The name of the offspring of a she-ass and a male horse is hinny. But just as horses and asses will breed together to produce mules, so will zebras and asses. Indeed, in all cases where experimental breeding has been tried it has been found possible, Mr. Richard Lydekker, the zoologist, declares, to produce hybrids between different species of Equidae—that is, the family to which horses, asses and zebras all belong.

While mules produced by horses and asses are generally unable to propagate their species, a male hybrid bred between an African wild ass and a mountain zebra has proved perfectly fertile, and had young when paired with a bay pony mare.

What is a Horse Mushroom?

IT is a variety of the common mushroom which grows to a greater size. It is usually six or eight inches across, though some specimens reach twelve inches. It is quite common in

A large specimen of horse mushroom

summer and autumn in pastures and under scattered trees. The flesh, unlike that of the common mushroom, does not become brown when cut, and the gills remain dry when old.

What Kind of Crane is That?

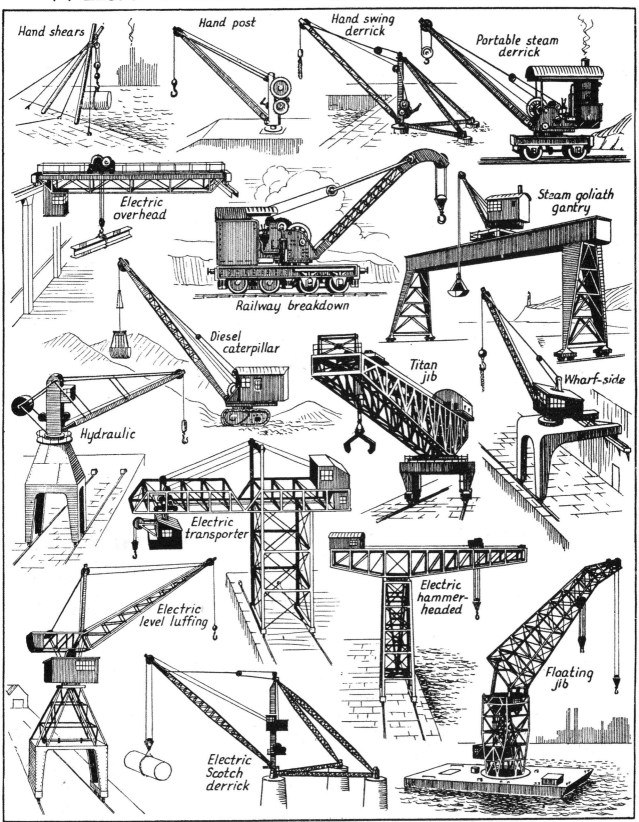

Hand shears

Hand post

Hand swing derrick

Portable steam derrick

Electric overhead

Steam goliath gantry

Railway breakdown

Diesel caterpillar

Titan jib

Wharf-side

Hydraulic

Electric transporter

Electric level luffing

Electric hammer-headed

Floating jib

Electric Scotch derrick

The drawings on this page show the various types of cranes which are used in industry today, with their names. In the top line are hand cranes, and a steam crane often seen on railways, at wharves, and in factory yards. The electric overhead crane is much used in large workshops. The railway breakdown crane is used on the track for raising coaches, trucks or engines that have run off the line, or for removing debris after an accident. The Titan jib and steam Goliath gantry cranes are much used in harbour and breakwater construction. The Diesel-engine driven caterpillar crane can move about easily on big excavating jobs. The remaining types are seen at docks, and vary much in detail and the class of work they do. The drawings, however, show the various family types. The huge floating jib is sometimes moved by an auxiliary engine of its own

How Are Railway Tickets Prepared?

THEY are printed in sheets and are then run through a machine which cuts them into strips, and afterwards the strips are cut up into individual tickets.

In the very early days of railways there were no tickets. Each passenger went to the railway station and booked a passage on a train. He was then given a pass on which was written the number of the receipt, the date, the name of the intending passenger, sometimes his address, his destination, the date up to which the pass would be available, and the name of a railway official. As a survival of this very clumsy system we still use the term "booking-office" for the place where railway tickets are sold.

The earliest season tickets were of pasteboard 3½ inches wide by 2½ inches deep, and later smaller oval metal "seasons" were issued to regular travellers.

The modern railway ticket, whose standard size is 2¼ inches by 1 3/16 inches, was the invention of Thomas Edmondson, a Lancashire Quaker, born in 1792. After being a cabinet-maker and grocer, he became station-master at Milton (now Brampton) on the Newcastle and Carlisle Railway, and, realising the inconvenience of the booking system, he in 1836 introduced tickets and invented a dating machine. Gradually Edmondson's system was adopted by all other booking-offices.

The standard size of our railway tickets is that fixed by Edmondson, and most countries have adopted it. Dog tickets were first introduced on the Manifold Valley Light Railway. The platform ticket was an idea that originated on the Continent.

Why Are Birds Not Electrocuted on Lines?

WE often see numbers of small birds perching on the telegraph or telephone wires, and even on the high-tension wires that form the transmission lines of the grid system. The electric current is passing

Starlings resting in safety on the telegraph wires

through these wires and some people wonder why it is the birds are not electrocuted.

Well, in the first place, if the current is to pass through the bird, the only way in which it could be injured or killed, it must cause a short circuit, as, for example, by joining up two wires with its body—that is, by resting on one wire and touching another. But even if it did this in the case of the

telephone or telegraph wires it is doubtful if the bird would be seriously hurt owing to the low voltage of the current.

Birds are often seen lying dead under the wires, but they have not been electrocuted. What has happened is that in flying they have struck the wires and been killed by the blow just as they might be killed if they dashed themselves against a brick wall. To prevent the birds thus destroying themselves small tablets are sometimes hung on the wires to render them easily visible.

In the case of the high-tension transmission lines birds are sometimes electrocuted. This is when they perch on the cross-bars of the wooden posts that carry the line across fields. The bar is earthed and sometimes a bird resting on it flaps its wings, which touch the wire, causing a short circuit, and the result is the death of the bird by electrocution.

This, however, only happens with the older wooden posts in fields. The more modern posts are so constructed that this cannot happen. A bird resting on a single wire, of course, feels nothing of the current, no matter how high the voltage.

Does Freezing Kill Bacteria?

THE majority of bacteria are not killed by a freezing temperature, although, of course, such perishable foods as meat and milk, which go bad very soon in hot weather, can be kept indefinitely if frozen. The reason is not that bacteria are destroyed by the cold, but that they are rendered inactive. As Dr. Carnegie Dickson says, "Even prolonged exposure to temperatures far below 0° Cen. has little effect on their vitality." The bacillus of bubonic plague, he adds, is very resistant to cold, and is not killed by prolonged freezing, though it is easily killed by heat and antiseptics.

Railway tickets printed in large sheets being cut into strips

Do Snakes Like Music ?

THAT snakes are sensitive to noise seems to be a fact beyond doubt, and the proverbial phrase "deaf as an adder" has no basis of truth to justify it. But there seems no evidence that snakes experience or exhibit any pleasurable emotion at the sound of music as we understand it. As Miss Catherine Hopley says, " Music, properly so called, is certainly very far removed from the gourd-rapping and tum-tumming of the Oriental jugglers ; yet the snakes display a consciousness of these uncouth sounds."

Miss Hopley quotes one owner of a pet boa which, according to his statement, manifested undoubted feeling or, at any rate, consciousness, when the piano was being played. On the other hand, Dr. Arthur Stradling tells us that his own snakes, though almost always within hearing of a piano, never showed the slightest emotion at the sound.

"My idea," says Miss Hopley, an authority on the subject, " is that it is the jarring or vibration through solids, and not the mere sound, that thus affects the snakes. Since first venturing to express this idea I have continued to observe the effect on snakes of what may be called disturbing noises. At the Gardens, where they become accustomed to noises of all kinds, it is less easy to arouse them ; but when the place is unusually quiet, the experiment may be tried.

" The snake men of the East, whose trade it is to hunt out snakes by means of sound, effect this by rapping on the frighten the snakes out of the path. The jingling music here is disturbing, not alluring, but as regards the knocking it proves sensitiveness to vibration conveyed by the ground. . . . As to tune, any sharp sound will answer, and

A trained sow at Périgord in France helping a human gatherer to find truffles below the surface of the ground

as to time, it is not the music, but as we have already hinted, the waving hand or knee, or bright colours used by the charmers, to which the movements of the serpents respond."

On the other hand, in 1937 a remarkable incident was reported from Masai, in Johore State, where a coolie, surprised by a hamadryad or king cobra, apparently saved his life by singing desperately to the snake for an hour. When the snake was about to attack him the coolie climbed a tree, but the cobra showed every intention of following. With much presence of mind the coolie began to sing and the snake stopped, apparently to listen.

The British manager of the estate where the incident happened saw the man's plight and ran off for a gun. He had to go two miles, but on returning found the man still singing desperately and the cobra in the same position. Fortunately a well-aimed bullet killed the cobra and saved the coolie's life.

It is curious that though snakes have no external aperture of the ear, the Psalmist speaks of " the deaf adder that stoppeth her ear ; which will not hearken to the voice of charmers, charming never so wisely."—Psalm LVIII, 4–5.

Where Are Pigs Trained to Hunt?

IN the French district of Périgord pigs are trained to detect the presence of the hidden truffles, which grow under the soil. The pig is very fond of truffles, and it soon directs its owners to spots where these delicacies are to be found, chiefly in wooded places. The truffles are then dug up and placed in a basket. Dogs are also trained to find these edible fungi.

Who First Thought of the Adhesive Postage Stamp?

THE idea of this useful device is generally attributed to Sir Rowland Hill, the founder of the modern postal system. But it is now generally agreed that the idea in Great Britain first came from a Scotsman, James Chalmers of Dundee, who wrote to Hill suggesting his plan. Hill adopted this without giving credit to Chalmers.

Curiously enough, however, there is evidence that small adhesive labels were used in Greece nine years earlier than stamps were used in England. They were printed with ordinary printer's type and were used for franking letters.

A snake-charmer in Jaipur, India, playing on his pipe while the cobra rises

wall or ceiling, or by making loud clucking noises with their tongue, as much as by their so-called music. A custom is prevalent in Ceylon, we are told, of using a jingling stick in the dark to strike the ground in order to

How Does the Telephone Work?

IT is a very wonderful thing that we can speak into a mouthpiece and be heard hundreds, and even thousands, of miles away. Two or three centuries ago it would have been regarded as magic for two people to carry on a conversation even from one side of a city to the other. Yet the telephone, invented in the second half of the 19th century—that is, within the memory of people living today—makes this marvel possible.

How exactly does the telephone work? Well, the drawing on this page will make the matter clear. When we lift the receiver of the telephone from its stand a spring is released and an electrical contact is made which completes a circuit and lights a red lamp at the exchange. The operator asks the number of the subscriber we wish to speak to, and, having received it, puts a plug in a hole which completes an electrical circuit and links up his telephone with ours across the intervening miles.

The connection being made, we can begin to talk. As we speak into the mouthpiece we set up waves in the air, and these strike upon a diaphragm, or drum, which at once begins to vibrate. The vibrations vary in strength according to the sounds we emit.

As the diaphragm vibrates it shakes a number of carbon grains inside a microphone, through which an electric current is flowing. The vibration of the grains causes this current to fluctuate, and so as it passes to the wire and thence to the receiver, which our friend at the other end of the wire is holding to his ear, the current is constantly interrupted.

In the receiver there is a U-shaped magnet with induction coils at the end. When the electric circuit is completed the current flows into the induction coils, and the U-shaped bar of iron, being thereby magnetised, attracts the diaphragm.

But the current being fluctuating, the diaphragm is not held still, but is drawn to and fro rapidly as the U-shaped iron becomes magnetised and demagnetised by the fluctuating current. The diaphragm sets up waves in the air corresponding with those which we at the other end of the line are making as we speak, and these, entering the listener's ear, strike on its drum and send a message to the brain. When we telephone by wireless, the fluctuating current is carried by the ether of the air instead of by a wire.

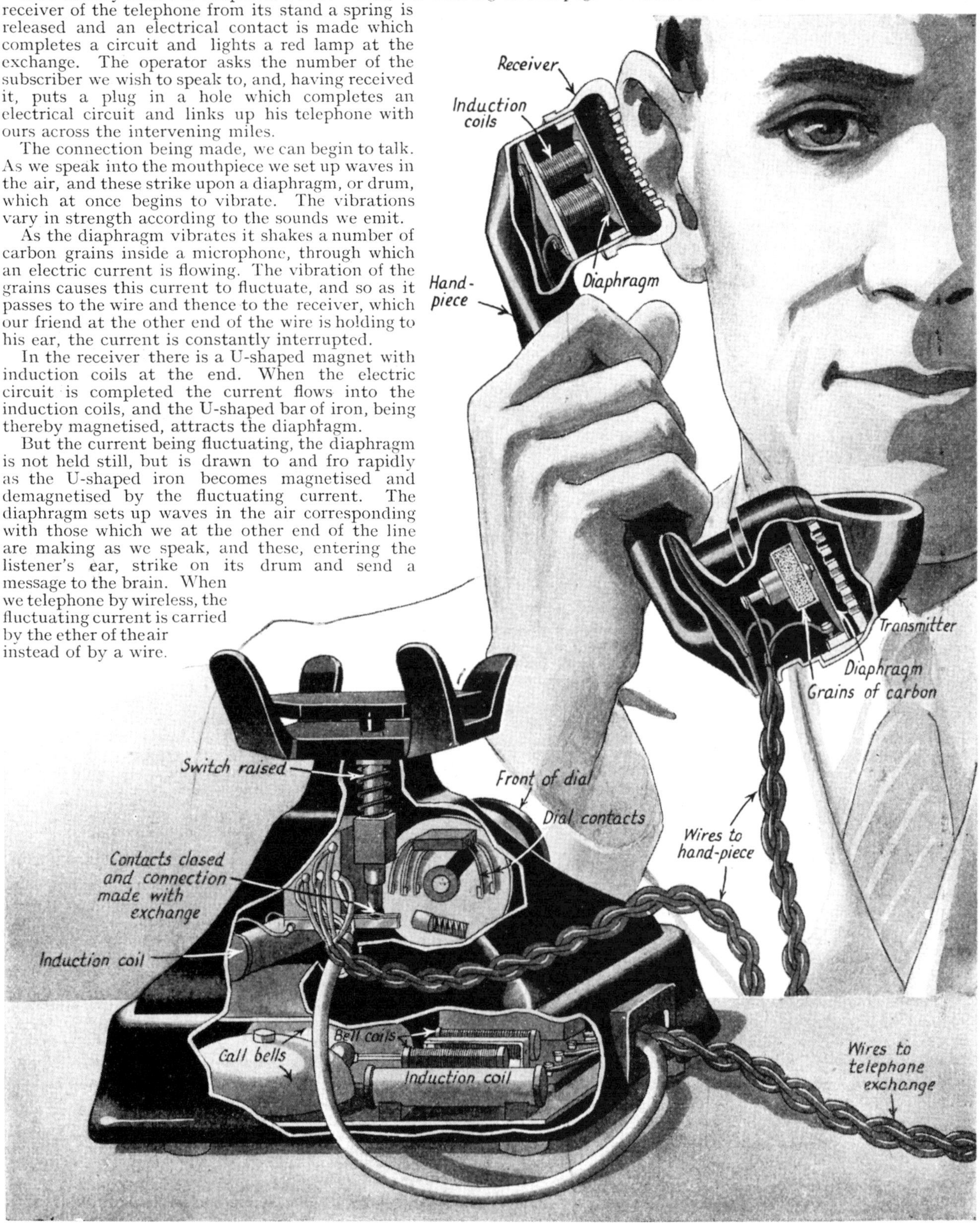

This diagram shows how the telephone, by means of an electric current, will carry a human voice across thousands of miles of space

What Are Those Parts Called?

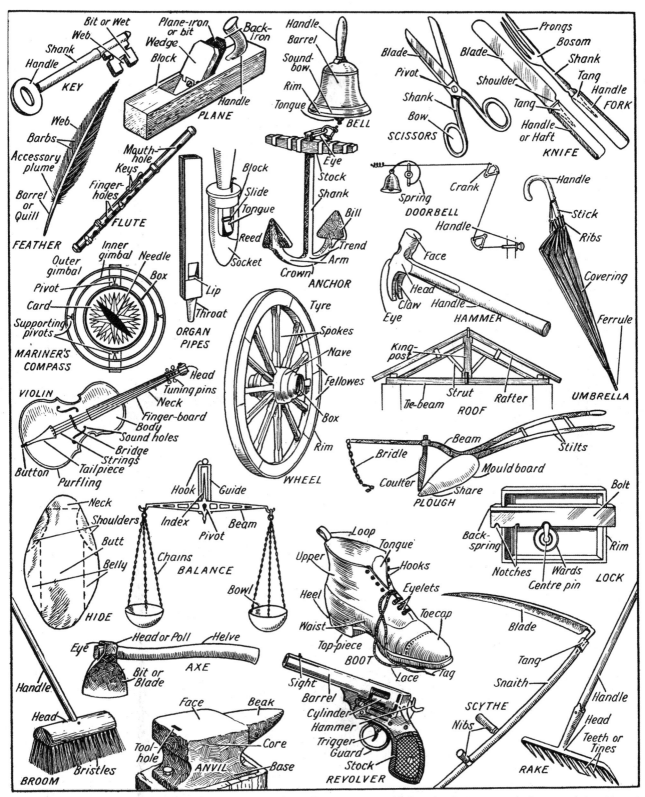

The common objects which we see around us everywhere are made up of various parts, and it is curious how many people there are who are ignorant of the names of these various parts. Take, for example, such a familiar object as a pair of scissors or a door key. The parts of these have special names, and it is well that we should know them. On this page are given 29 common objects with the names of their various parts. Probably more people know these names now than was the case ten years ago, for the practice of solving crossword puzzles has added enormously to their vocabulary. A violin is an interesting example of a comparatively small object being built up of many parts. There are, indeed, 70 different parts, all of them, except the strings and the loop that holds the tailpiece to which the strings are fastened, being of wood, though the wood is not all of one kind. Even in knives and forks there are many parts with individual names. How many people know the names of the parts of a wheel?

x

49

How Old Are Noah's Ark Toys?

WE might suppose that the Noah's Ark, with its pairs of wooden animals painted in more or less natural colours, was a very ancient toy, but, as a matter of fact, the earliest reference given to it by the

It is to be feared that this interesting and educational toy has now largely lost its popularity.

Curiously enough, even the most pious parents did not seem to object to the Noah's Arks that housed the

A Noah's Ark with 200 pairs of animals, said to have been made in 1810, and now preserved in the Public Library at Wallington, Surrey

great Oxford Dictionary is in 1846, when Charles Dickens in his " Cricket on the Hearth " referred to the toys as " Noah's Arks in which birds and beasts were an uncommonly tight fit."

But there seems no doubt that Noah's Arks as toys were in existence before this, for in the new library building at Wallington, Surrey, there is a remarkable Noah's Ark with two hundred pairs of animals which is said to have been made in 1810. The animals, which vary from grasshoppers to elephants, are beautifully formed and brilliantly coloured, and their freshness remains today. They can be seen with the Noah's Ark in the photograph.

If it did not originate then, the Noah's Ark as a toy for children undoubtedly reached the height of its popularity during the evangelical revival, when religious people felt it was wrong for their children to play

model animals being very different from the description given in the Bible. There the Ark has only one window, whereas the toy Arks were gay with windows all round, as can be seen in the one in the photograph here.

How Does a Snake Travel?

SNAKES always move over the ground by horizontal oscillations, and pictures showing them moving by vertical contortions are quite incorrect. As to how they can make progress, Mr. Richard Lydekker says: " A special feature is the presence of large transverse scales or shields, extending right across the lower surface of the body, but on the tail frequently divided into a double series. Each scale corresponds to a pair of ribs ; and in gliding a snake advances the fore-part of its body, when the scales on the lower surface are partially erected and take hold of the ground or other surface in such a manner that the rest of the body may be drawn forwards. As the

The upper drawing shows how the snake travels by wriggling horizontally. The lower drawing is incorrect. Snakes never move over the ground in this way

with ordinary toys like tops and dolls and soldiers on Sunday. The Noah's Ark, however, was regarded as being in a different class and enabling children to add to their Bible knowledge.

ribs are the active agents in this peculiar mode of progression, snakes may be appropriately called ribwalkers." Snakes can, of course, move very rapidly.

How Did the Stone Age Men See to Paint?

ON the walls of many of the dark caves where the men of the Stone Age took shelter there are painted remarkably good pictures of animals and men, and the question is often asked how in the darkness of these underground chambers the artists could see to draw and paint.

It has been suggested that they arranged a series of mirrors at angles so as to reflect the sunlight from outside into the caves. But where could those primitive men have obtained mirrors that could reflect light so well as to direct it from surface to surface until it shone upon the wall to be painted ? It would not be easy even in the 20th century, with the efficient and highly polished mirrors we have today, to do such a thing.

Expert archaeologists think it far more likely that the Stone Age artists painted by the light of tiny oil lamps with floating wicks. Hollowed-out stones have been found in the caves which might have been used as primitive lamps, but even then it is still somewhat of a problem to know how these could have given sufficient light to enable the artists to draw and use colour so effectively in the caves. It is well known that a modern artist must have a good light if he is to do his best work, and certainly these primitive artists did excellent work, even by modern standards. The problem still remains something of a mystery.

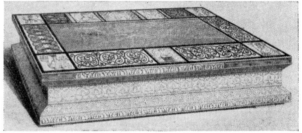

A super-altar made of jasper and silver in the 13th century

What is a Super-Altar?

IT is a portable altar-stone placed above the altar and let into a wooden altar-frame. This was the general construction of English altars in the 13th and 14th centuries. The super-altar was often of very costly marble or jasper, sometimes richly jewelled, and it was placed on the altar for purposes of magnificence and devotion. One of ivory was given to Exeter in 1050. The slab usually had a hollow, called a sepulchrum, in which relics could be placed.

The super-altar shown in the drawing consists of a slab of jasper on a base of wood, the whole mounted in silver and richly ornamented in niello— that is, inlaid with a deep-black metallic amalgam. It is of the thirteenth century and is a very good example of this form of church furniture.

How Can a Speaking-Tube Carry a Voice?

IN the days before telephones large office buildings usually had their various rooms linked up with one another and with the manager's office

A speaker starting the sound-waves

by means of speaking-tubes. When a person wanted to speak to another part of the building, he removed a whistle from the tube, blew so as to sound a whistle at the other end, and then when a reply came through he would talk, replacing the whistle after he had finished.

Many of these tubes went for quite considerable distances, and a voice at one end could be heard quite distinctly at the other. The reason the voice was transmitted so clearly was that the waves set up in the air of the tube were unable to dissipate themselves, being concentrated by the walls of the tube. As the sound-waves passed they were reflected from one side to another of the tube and at angles where the tube turned a corner, and so the message was passed on till it reached the recipient's ear.

Where is the Roof of the World?

THIS name is generally given to the Pamirs, an extensive plateau region in Central Asia, north-east of Afghanistan. The name is Russian and

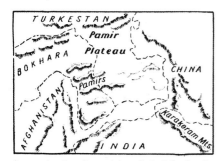

A map showing the position of the lofty Pamir plateau, known as the " Roof of the World "

means " on the world "—that is, on top of the world. The Pamir plateau is about 13,000 feet above sea-level, but the Chang plateau, lying north of and running nearly parallel to the headwaters of the Western Brahmaputra, is believed to be higher and to have a better claim to the title " roof of the world."

Is Rice Paper Really Made From Rice?

RICE paper is a snowy-white paper used in China chiefly by native artists, who paint on it brilliantly coloured pictures. But rice has nothing to do with its manufacture. The paper is made from layers of the pith of a plant called by botanists *Aralia papyrifera*. This grows wild in Formosa. It is very brittle, but is nevertheless used by the Chinese for making artificial flowers and certain toys. The plant from which it is made grows about five feet high. With a sharp knife the pith is pared into cylinders of uniform thickness, which are then unrolled and pressed out.

The so-called " rice paper " used in

The sound-waves received at the other end of the tube after being reflected to and fro

making cigarettes is quite a different product and this also has nothing to do with rice. It is made from new trimmings of linen.

Has the Tartan Ever Been Forbidden?

YES, after the Scottish rebellion o. 1745 led by Prince Charles Edward, the Young Pretender, an Act of Parliament was passed forbidding the wearing of a tartan as any part of a Highland dress, under penalty of six months' imprisonment for the first offence and transportation overseas for seven years for the second offence.

No Highlander could receive the benefit of the Act of Indemnity without first taking the following dreadful oath : " I, A. B., do swear, and, as I shall answer to God at the great day of judgment, I have not, nor shall have in my possession any gun, sword, pistol or arm whatsoever, and never use tartan, plaid, or any part of the Highland garb ; and if I do so, may I be cursed in my undertakings, family and property, may I never see my wife and children, father, mother or relations, may I be killed in battle as a

coward, and lie without Christian burial in a strange land, far from the graves of my forefathers and kindred ; may all this come across me if I break my oath."

This extraordinary and severe Act remained in force till 1782, when, owing to the discontent it caused, it was repealed.

What is a Rodomontade?

THIS is the name given to a boastful, bragging speech full of bombast. It comes from Rodomont, a character in Ariosto's poem " Orlando Furioso," which deals with the times of Charlemagne. Rodomont is there portrayed as a fierce knight much addicted to boasting and blustering.

What is the Sacred Bo-Tree?

THE name Bo means enlightenment, and the bo-tree is the pipul or sacred fig-tree of India, being the tree under which Gautama, the Buddha, was sitting in meditation when enlightenment came to him. This tree still stands at Gaya and, with its daughter bo-tree, grown from the branch of the parent tree and sent by King Asoka in the third century B.C. to Ceylon, receive the worship of pilgrims who go by thousands to these trees and offer prayer before them.

The Buddh-Gaya, the famous Buddhist temple at Gaya, in India, with the remains of the sacred bo-tree in front of the entrance. This is the tree under which Gautama, the Buddha, sat when enlightenment came to him. On the right is a daughter tree of the original plant

Where Was That Battle-Axe Used?

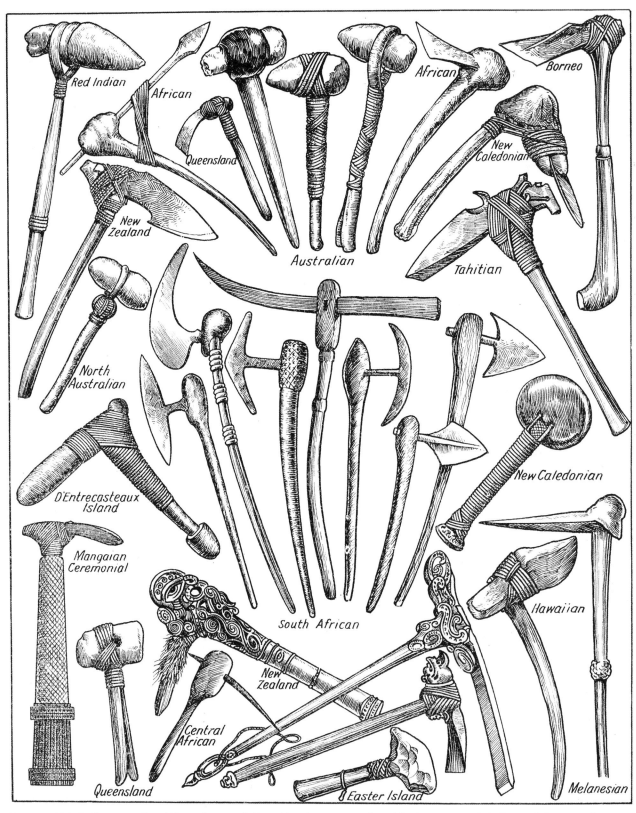

Red Indian

African

Queensland

New Zealand

Australian

African

Borneo

New Caledonian

Tahitian

North Australian

New Caledonian

D'Entrecasteaux Island

Mangaian Ceremonial

South African

Hawaiian

Queensland

Central African

New Zealand

Easter Island

Melanesian

Here are thirty battle-axes gathered from all parts of the world and we can see that while they vary greatly in form and character, they nevertheless all embody the same idea or principle. There is a handle, varying in length, for the user to hold when wielding the weapon, and there is a blade with which a wound can be inflicted. In some cases the battle-axes are very crude. This is particularly the case in the Australian weapons, the " blacks " of the island continent who made them being at a very elementary stage of culture. On the other hand the New Zealand weapons, made by the Maoris, are well formed and are artistically decorated. Some of the South African axes are curious with their blades projecting a considerable distance from the handles. In many cases the Pacific Islanders are ingenious in their methods of affixing the blade to the handle

Is the Steeplejack's Calling Dangerous?

YES: it is more than risky, for many steeplejacks fall and are killed. Mr. William Larkins, the most famous of all steeplejacks, whose father, a steeplejack before him, was killed in his fourth serious accident, says:

Steeplejacks at their dangerous work on a church spire at Bethnal Green, London

"The fact remains that, apart from the strenuous and exciting nature of his work, the steeplejack's life is one of constant peril. A rotten coping, a puff of wind coming up unexpectedly from nowhere in particular, a loose brick or a piece of decayed ironwork, any of these may easily spell death for the men who earn their living by climbing."

Mr. Larkins has had many narrow escapes, but he has only suffered a few bruises. "Steeplejacks are not made, but born," he says, "and if a man does not possess the instinct for climbing, no amount of teaching will ever make him a steeplejack. Given an inborn taste for the work, he will soon overcome its initial difficulties; and although death may await him in any of his adventures, it is remarkable how soon familiarity breeds contempt."

Once when working with two assistants on top of a 150-ft. chimney in London, Mr. Larkins saw one of the assistants suddenly throw down his tools and in a fit of madness prepare to dive down the inside of the chimney, out of which smoke and hot fumes were pouring. Larkins and the other assistant just managed to clutch the man's legs in time and drag him back on to the parapet.

"A terrific struggle ensued before we were able to drag him into safety," says Mr. Larkins, "and that battle in mid-air will haunt me to my dying day. Mad persons when engaged in a scuffle with others are generally known to be possessed of extraordinary strength. It was so with this man. He fought like a wild-cat to carry out his maniacal act, and it was fortunate indeed that he was at length overcome by the fumes.

"Backwards and forwards we swayed on the narrow ledge, every minute expecting to be hurled to death, striving with might and main to rescue our maddened comrade. We only saved him in the nick of time. By the time we caught hold of his legs, his head and shoulders had disappeared in the mouth of the shaft. It was this fact that undoubtedly saved his life. Caught as he was in this position he was unable to put up the fight that he might have done had his limbs been entirely free.

"When at length he was overpowered, an eventuality not so much due to our efforts as to the poisonous fumes rising from the chimney's mouth, we dragged him out of his perilous position as quickly as possible, and laid him flat and gasping on the narrow coping.

"Even then he flapped and floundered like a fish newly removed from the water; but by this time we were not taking any more chances. For his own sake, we bound him hand and foot with a ladder rope, and before he had properly returned to his senses, lowered him with the aid of others who had watched the desperate fight from the ground. We lowered him by means of a rope. He gave no more trouble. Doctors were called to the scene as hastily as possible. They diagnosed his trouble as a temporary affection of the brain due to sunstroke and the heat from the shaft."

Mr. Larkins' experience on this occasion was not unique. Other cases where steeplejacks have had to deal up aloft with men who were mad have occurred. There seems no doubt that when one takes into consideration all the risks, the steeplejack's calling is the most dangerous in the world, after that of the soldier or sailor in wartime. The wind, a faulty rope, a slip—any of these may send him hurtling below.

In 1937 an English steeplejack, William Parkinson, fell from an 85-ft. chimney at Spalding and was killed. A few months before an American steeplejack fell from the top of a 200-ft. chimney at Granite City, Illinois, and was miraculously saved by being caught 120 feet from the ground by a guy wire attached to the chimney on which he was working.

How Strong is Snake Poison?

IT varies enormously in different species of snakes. The English adder, for example, though venomous, rarely kills a person, whereas snakes like the puff-adder of South Africa and the Russell's viper of India will kill a person with a single bite in a very short time.

The Russell's viper, called by scientists *Tic polonga*, is responsible for hundreds, if not thousands, of deaths in India every year. It is far more deadly than the cobra. Such is the power of its venom that if it be diluted a million million million times it can still exert a retarding effect upon the normal blood-flow of a human being. "Expressed more picturesquely," says Mr. E. G. Boulenger, the distinguished zoologist, "a piece of dried Russell's viper venom no bigger than a pea would make itself 'felt' in the waters of the English Channel."

What is a Puisne Judge?

THE word puisne, pronounced "puny," is an old French word meaning junior, and applied to a judge it means one who is junior or of lower rank. It is applied to all the judges of the High Court of Judicature except the Lord Chancellor, the Lord Chief Justice, the Master of the Rolls, and the President of the Admiralty, Probate and Divorce Court.

Is the Coney of the Bible the Rabbit?

NO; the animal mentioned in Psalm CIV, verse 18, "The high hills are a refuge for the wild goats; and the rocks for the conies," is the Syrian hyrax, a small hoofed mammal whose cousin at the Cape of Good Hope, the Cape hyrax, is sometimes miscalled the rock badger.

The little coney or hyrax, which is the nearest relative of the elephant

The hyrax, which looks something like a guinea-pig, is really a very interesting animal, for it is the nearest living relative of the mighty elephant, though in size and appearance it is so different. It is descended from the same remote ancestors as the elephant, and provides a striking example of the extremes to which evolution can lead.

The coney of the fur trade is the rabbit, and the skin called coney seal is only rabbit skin with a high-sounding title given for selling purposes.

How Are Eggs Graded?

THE testing and grading of eggs has been brought to a fine art, and where large quantities are handled the grading is done by an ingenious machine. The eggs are taken by a conveyer to a rotating device which receives them on little platforms according to size, and then as it goes round sends them off into different compartments, all the eggs in any particular division being practically of the same size.

To test the eggs for quality a girl holds each one up in turn before a powerful electric light, and this reveals the inside. When the egg is new-laid, no air space is seen at the end, but if the egg is stale then an air space has been formed and can be seen by means of the transmitted light. If the egg is very stale it shows a more or less mottled appearance.

How is Snowfall Measured?

THE amount of snow that has fallen is measured in quite a different way from the rainfall. In the latter case a rain-gauge is used, but in finding the quantity of snow two measurements are taken. The actual depth of snow is taken by means of a measuring rod in places where there has been no drifting. Three or four such places are measured, and the average taken. Then the snow collected in a rain-gauge from which the funnel and inner cylinder have been removed is melted down, and the depth of the resulting water is measured.

But sometimes when a strong wind has been blowing too much snow may have been blown into the rain-gauge. Another method is then used. A sample is taken by inverting the can and pressing it down in the snow at a place where there has been no drifting. A sheet of tin is then passed under the can and the whole is then lifted up with the snow in it. This is then melted down. The number of inches of snowfall corresponding to an inch of water varies a great deal. Six inches of

snow of close texture may make an inch of water, but, on the other hand, where the snow is loose and of large flakes it may take 30 inches of snow to make an inch of water. The larger the flakes, the looser is the snow's texture.

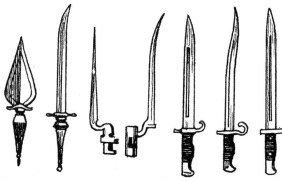

Here are various types of bayonets. The first two are English 17th century, the third a bayonet with ring and socket, the fourth a triangular bayonet, the fifth and seventh British sword bayonets, and the sixth a French bayonet

How Long Have Bayonets Been Used?

BAYONETS were in use in the French army about 1647, and in the English army in 1663. They were being made at Bayonne at the end of the 17th century and it is from that town that they take their name.

Their origin is said to be due to the Basques, a regiment of whom was hard pressed on a mountain ridge near Bayonne. Their ammunition being exhausted, the men fixed their knives in the barrels of their muskets, and, charging the enemy, won a victory. The bayonet finally supplanted the pike early in the 18th century. In 1856, Sir Charles Napier called it the queen of weapons. The Great War restored the bayonet to the place it held in the days of the muzzle-loading musket, when tactics consisted of a volley and a charge.

Why Do Sailors Wear Blue?

THE earliest notice we have of seamen wearing blue clothes comes to us from the times of the Roman invasion of Britain. We learn that the Venetii put to sea in longboats, and that the sails and clothing of the crew were dyed a light blue. It is supposed that this was to lessen the chance of being seen, an early example of camouflage.

When the Danes arrived in Britain they mostly wore black, but blue was worn by the Saxon seamen at the time of the Norman Conquest. In the Middle Ages seamen wore the same clothing as ordinary people. For centuries any colours almost could be worn. It was only in 1748 that a regular uniform for naval officers was introduced, and the coat was blue, with white cuffs and gold facings. Not till 1857 was a uniform dress ordered for the men. This consisted of a blue cloth jacket, blue cloth trousers, a duck frock, duck trousers, a serge frock, a pea-jacket, and black and white hats.

Above is the machine which automatically grades hens' eggs according to size, and below a girl is seen examining eggs before a powerful electric light

What Was That Fire-Lighter Called?

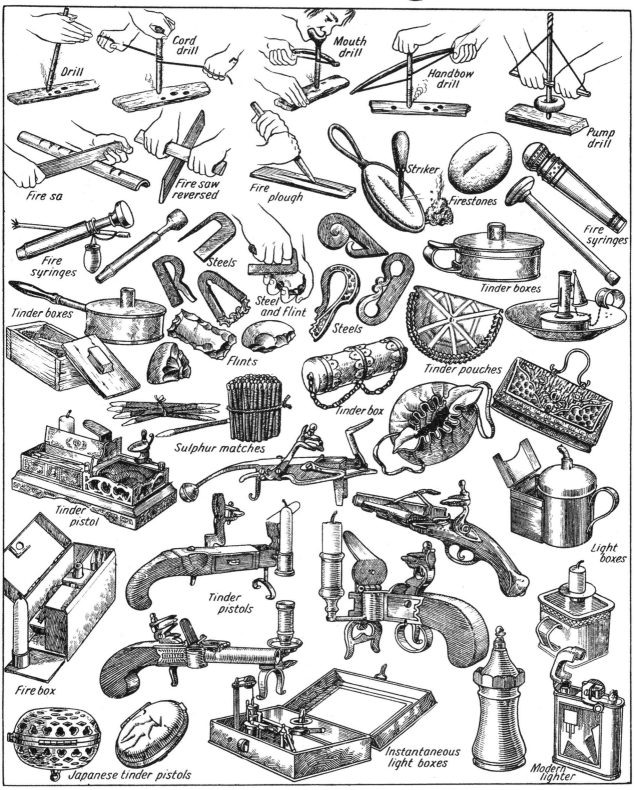

Very early in his history man learned to produce fire, and through the ages he has done this in a great variety of ways. At first his methods were very primitive, as can be seen in the upper drawings. A stick was rotated on another piece of wood, and later flint and iron or steel were used. The spark produced by striking the steel on the flint set light to some tinder, which was a finely divided powder, and then by blowing on this enough heat was produced to light a sulphur match. This was the method in use for many centuries. In the 18th century it was improved by using a kind of pistol with a trigger for producing the spark. Sometimes a candlestick was attached to the tinder pistol. In various types of fire and light boxes the heat was produced by chemical means. The invention of the modern lucifer match, however, made these various means of obtaining light obsolete, but curiously enough, in recent years, the friction method has been revived in the modern cigarette lighter, as shown in the bottom corner

What is the Name of That Knot or

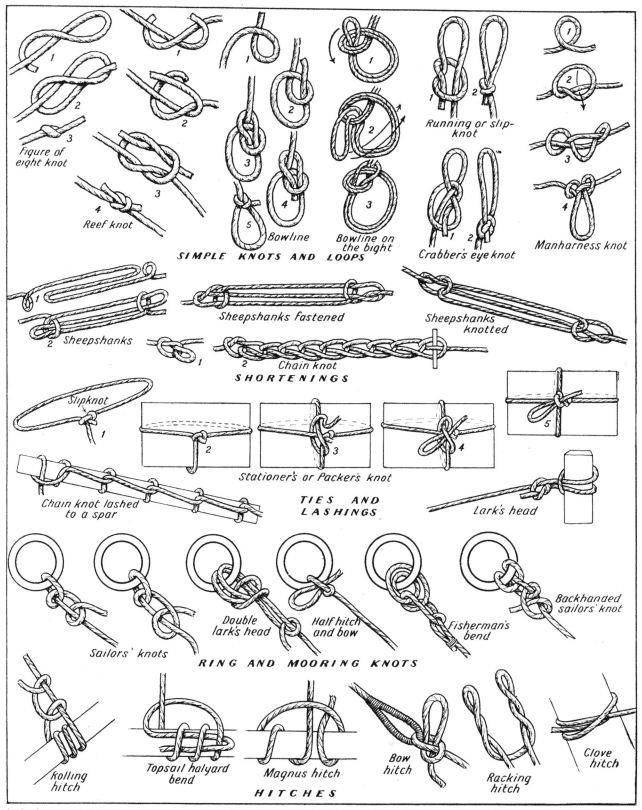

Figure of eight knot

Reef knot

SIMPLE KNOTS AND LOOPS

Bowline

Bowline on the bight

Running or slip-knot

Crabber's eye knot

Manharness knot

Sheepshanks

Sheepshanks fastened

Sheepshanks knotted

Chain knot

SHORTENINGS

Slipknot

Stationer's or Packers knot

TIES AND LASHINGS

Chain knot lashed to a spar

Lark's head

Sailors' knots

Double lark's head

Half hitch and bow

Fisherman's bend

Backhanded sailors' knot

RING AND MOORING KNOTS

Rolling hitch

Topsail halyard bend

Magnus hitch

Bow hitch

Racking hitch

Clove hitch

HITCHES

In the drawings on this page and the next are shown all the principal kinds of knots, loops, and hitches, and by carefully examining the drawings we shall be able to tie any particular knot or hitch. Starting with the simplest of all knots, the figure of eight and the reef knot, we go on to more complicated varieties, and in many cases different stages in the making of the knot or hitch are shown, for the sake of clearness. The security of a knot depends upon friction, just as does the holding together of the strands that form the rope. The tighter a knot is pulled the safer it becomes, because the friction is increased. The commonest kind of knot for joining the ends of two ropes is the reef or sailor's knot, and when the rope is pulled taut the knot holds. The bowline is a very usual knot when we want to make a loop, and a variation of this is known as the bowline on the

Hitch, and How Can it be Made?

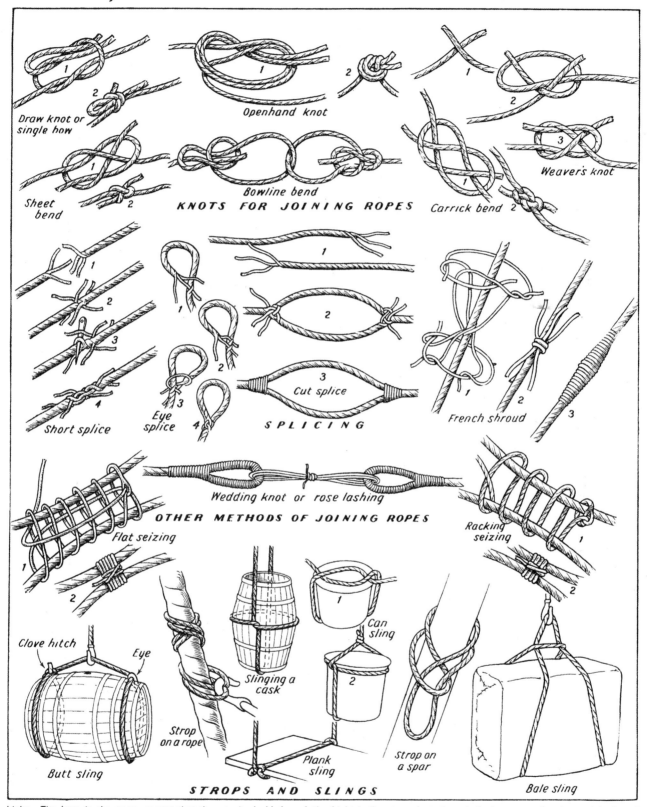

Draw knot or single bow

Openhand knot

Weaver's knot

Sheet bend

Bowline bend

KNOTS FOR JOINING ROPES

Carrick bend

Short splice

Eye splice

Cut splice

SPLICING

French shroud

Wedding knot or rose lashing

OTHER METHODS OF JOINING ROPES

Flat seizing

Racking seizing

Clove hitch

Eye

Slinging a cask

Can sling

Strop on a rope

Strop on a spar

Butt sling

Plank sling

Bale sling

STROPS AND SLINGS

bight. The knot is the same, except that the rope is doubled, and the bight is then passed up through the loop, opened and turned backward over the rest of the knot. The manharness knot is a simple loop which gets its name from the fact that it is used to harness men to a tow-line or to drag ropes. There are various ingenious ways of shortening a rope, and the chief of these are shown in the middle of the previous page. The ties and lashings, the ring and mooring knots and the hitches are all well worth studying, and each has its use in different circumstances. Various knots for joining ropes are shown, and also the way of splicing two ropes so that they form one. Strops and slings are used for lifting various objects, one of the simplest and quickest to tie being the can sling seen near the bottom of the page

What is the Thin Red Line?

THIS is a phrase originally used during the Crimean War by Dr. Howard Russell, the war correspondent, to describe the men of the 93rd Highlanders, under Sir Colin Campbell, when in 1854 they stood two deep and repulsed the attack of the Russian cavalry. When attacked at Balaclava Sir Colin did not think it "worth while" to form his men into a square. They stood in a "thin red line" and repulsed the Russians with deadly loss to the latter and little loss to themselves. The correspondent's phrase has now become proverbial.

What is a Kimono?

THIS is the name given to a loose style of dressing-gown worn by European women. It is really an adaptation of the Japanese kimono, which is the chief outer garment of Japanese women. It is a loose robe

it up, a sort of pannier or "improver" is placed underneath, while a handsome string keeps it in position above. The obi costs much more than the kimono.

Men when dressed in Japanese national costume also wear the kimono as an outside gown, but their obi or sash is much narrower than the women's, and is not an article of adornment. A gentleman's native costume will cost much less than his wife's.

What Famous Astronomer Lost His Nose?

IT was Tycho Brahe, the Swedish astronomer, who was a nobleman born in 1546, when Sweden was under the Danish crown. Sent to various universities to study law, Tycho Brahe was interested in nothing but science, and with no other instrument than a pair of compasses, he studied the stars through his bedroom window, correcting many errors in the calculations of previous astronomers.

Then two or three days after Christmas in 1566 he fought a duel with another young nobleman, with whom he had quarrelled about some mathematical proposition. They fought with swords in total darkness, and at

the first blow the front of Tycho's nose was sliced off. This ended the duel, and the young men settled their squabble.

Tycho Brahe, the great Swedish astronomer, who always wore a false nose

Tycho repaired the loss of his nose by cementing on his face an artificial nose of gold and silver, which he coloured so that it formed a good imitation of the lost organ, and with this he went through life. Tycho Brahe seems to have been of a quarrelsome nature for in his later life he was often involved in disputes.

What is Goldbeater's Skin?

IT is a very thin but very tough membrane prepared from the outer coat of the great intestine of the ox. After being immersed in a weak solution of potash the intestine is scraped with a knife, beaten, soaked in water, and then carefully stretched. It is then treated by a complicated process with alum water, isinglass and white of egg. The membrane is then cut into squares and placed between the thin leaves of beaten gold to keep them separate, hence the name. Goldbeater's skin is also used for the dressing of slight wounds.

Were Mummies Ever Sold for Medicine?

YES, objectionable as this may seem, it was actually a fact. Sir E. A. Wallis Budge, the distinguished Egyptologist, says: "About three or four hundred years ago Egyptian 'mummy' formed one of the ordinary drugs in apothecaries' shops.

"The trade in mummy was carried on chiefly by Jews, and as early as the 12th century a physician called El-Magar was in the habit of prescribing mummy to his patients. It was said to be good for bruises and wounds. After a time, for various reasons the supply of genuine mummies ran short and the Jews were obliged to manufacture them.

"They procured the bodies of all the criminals that were executed in gaols, and of people who had died in

hospitals, Christians and others. They filled the bodies with bitumen and stuffed the limbs with the same substance; this done, they bound them up tightly and exposed them to the heat of the Sun. By this means they made them look like old mummies.

"In the year 1564 a physician called Guy de la Fontaine made an attempt to see the stock of the mummies of the chief merchant in mummies at Alexandria, and he discovered that they were made from the bodies of slaves and others who had died of the most loathsome diseases.

"The traffic in mummies as a drug was stopped in a curious manner. A Jew at Damietta who traded in mummies had a Christian slave who was treated with great harshness by him because he would not consent to become a Jew. Finally, when the ill-treatment became so severe that he could bear it no longer the slave went to the pasha and informed him what his master's business was. The Jew was speedily thrown into prison, and only obtained his liberty by payment of 300 pieces of gold. Every Jewish trader in mummy was seized by the local government of the place where he lived, and money was extorted from him. The trade in mummy, being hampered by this arbitrary tax, soon languished, and finally died out entirely."

Japanese girls wearing the kimono, and the obi or decorative sash

with short, very wide sleeves, and is made of silk, artificial silk or cotton. It generally has a flowered pattern in bright colours. The kimono is kept in position by a thin belt, over which is bound a large sash called an obi, which is the chief article of feminine adornment in Japan. In order to hold

What is That Weighing Machine?

Family scales

Spring pocket balance

Baby weigher

Tradesmen's counter scales

Parcels balance

Bathroom scales

Kitchen scales

Silver weigher

Tradesmen's circular balance

Counter platform scales

Letter balance

Platform scales

Money scales

Steelyard

Coal weigher

Yarn weigher

Automatic counter scales

Crane scales

Automatic platform scales

Electric counter scales

Personal scales

Weigh-bridge

Here are more than twenty of the scales and weighing machines that are in everyday use. The tradesmen's counter scales, and the balance such as is now used for weighing money, are among the simplest of these weighing devices, but the steelyard is exceedingly ancient. Roman steelyards are often found. Different types of weighing machines are used for different purposes, and work on different principles. Thus, the family scale, like the parcels balance, the letter balance, the tradesmen's circular balance, and others, is a spring device. The pressure of the weight in the pan forces down a spring, and this turns the hand on a dial and indicates the weight. The bathroom scales enable a person to weigh himself day by day. Crane scales are for attaching to a crane, so that heavy goods can be weighed as they are lifted. The weigh-bridge we see at railway stations and elsewhere. The yarn weigher is for weighing wool, and electric counter scales have a device by which the figures are lighted up electrically as the goods press down, thus indicating the weight. The coal weigher is, of course, a very massively built balance capable of dealing with heavy weights

Is Edinburgh or London Nearer to America?

ANOTHER way of putting the question might be "Is Edinburgh east or west of London?" Most people speaking off-hand would probably say that Edinburgh had almost the same

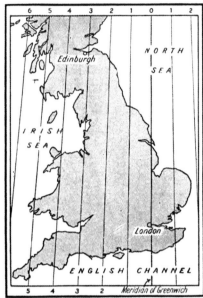

A map showing that Edinburgh is far west of London

longitude as London, but actually it is in longitude 3° 11′ west of London. In other words, Edinburgh is more than 120 miles west of London, and to that extent nearer America than is London.

Where Do Cranberries Grow?

CRANBERRIES are the fruits of a creeping evergreen plant which grows wild in many parts of Britain, though it is not so common as it used to be before the drainage and enclosure of waste lands. It is found in peat bogs in northern Europe, Asia and America, and is a low plant with slender, straggling, wiry prostrate stems that root at intervals. The evergreen leaves are egg-shaped and the berries red.

Most of the cranberries sold in the fruit shops and greengrocers' come from America and are of a different species from the European cranberry.

Who Were the Lake Poets?

THEY were Wordsworth, Coleridge and Southey, who resided in the Lake District of Cumberland and Westmorland, and they were first given this name in derision by the "Edinburgh Review." The characteristic of the Lake Poets was that they sought inspiration in the simplicity of Nature. The term has since come to be one of honour.

What is a Hooligan?

HE is a lively rough who indulges in dangerous horseplay, though he may not necessarily be a criminal.

Nevertheless, gangs of hooligans are great pests to the community at large. The term is used only of the poorer classes, but the rags of Oxford and Cambridge undergraduates frequently develop into hooliganism, though they are not called by that term.

The origin of the name is not certain. Some derive it from the Hooley Gang, a name given by the police in Islington, London, to a gang of roughs led by one Hooley. Others think it is named after an Irish family, the Houlihans, who lived in the Borough district of London in the 1890's.

What is the Origin of A 1?

THE expression means first-rate in every respect, and is derived from the classification of ships in Lloyd's Register. The quality of a ship's hull is there described by a letter and that of the stores by a figure. A 1 means a ship of first-class condition as to both hull and equipment.

How Does a Ventriloquist Talk?

THE word means "one who speaks from the belly," but it is a mistake to suppose that when a ventriloquist is talking without moving his mouth his voice is proceeding from the lower part of his body. Some contraction of the stomach muscles, however, does take place when the person speaks with closed lips.

Ventriloquism is, of course, the art of making the human voice appear to come from a distance or from some person or object other than the speaker himself. Its success depends not on any peculiar structure of the organs of voice, but in practice and dexterity.

The ventriloquist takes a deep breath and then allows the air to escape slowly, the sounds of the voice being modified and muffled by means of the muscles of the upper part of the throat and palate.

Though much skill and practice are needed before a person can become a successful ventriloquist, much of the illusion is brought about by suggestion, the performer indicating by subtle means, gestures, looks, and so on, the direction whence the voice is supposed to proceed. Ventriloquism is a very ancient art; the Greeks practised it, and ascribed it to demons.

What is the Meaning of Ex Cathedra?

THE words mean "from the teacher's chair," and the phrase is used to describe any statement made with authority that cannot be questioned. It is particularly used of any judgment pronounced on questions of faith or morals by the Pope and regarded by the faithful as infallible. He is said to speak "ex cathedra."

How Does the Electric Eel Give a Shock?

THE electric eel is a strange fish found in the rivers of Brazil and the Guianas. It is able to give an electric shock so powerful that it can stun a horse crossing a river. The drawing given on this page of a section through the eel shows how the electric organ consists of two pairs of longitudinal bodies situated immediately beneath the skin and above the muscles. One pair is on the back of the tail and another along the anal fin, and the direction of the current is from head to tail, as indicated in the upper drawing of a complete eel

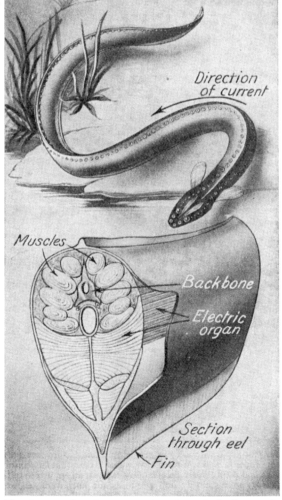

The electric eel, with a section through the body showing the organs that give a shock to those who touch the eel

Do Slugs Multiply Rapidly?

YES; a pair of common black slugs was kept under observation and it was found that one laid 396 eggs in five separate batches, with an interval of only about a week between the batches, while the other laid 477 eggs in four batches. The slug, like the snail, it should be explained, is hermaphrodite—that is, both sexes are found in the same individual. The eggs hatch about sixty days after being deposited, and the young slugs bury themselves in the ground for four or five days without feeding, and then emerge nearly double their original size. In the second year they become full-grown and live for only two seasons. Slugs lurk under stones and boards during the day, but at night they come out in search of food and do great damage to garden plants. In winter they contract their bodies, cover them with slime, and hibernate, each in a separate little hole excavated in the ground.

What is Japanese Isinglass?

THIS substance, also called agaragar, after its Malay name, is a gelatinous product extracted from several kinds of seaweed found in East Indian waters. It is prepared by boiling the seaweed in water and then evaporating the moisture. In China and Japan it is used as a food, chiefly in soup form. It is imported into Europe and used for culinary purposes and by jam manufacturers to assist the jellifying of the cooked fruit. It is also used for dressing textile fabrics and paper.

Have English Officers Carried Umbrellas in War?

YES; Captain Gronow, of the First Foot Guards, in his "Anecdotes of Celebrities of London and Paris," says: "During the action of the 10th of December, 1813, commonly known as that of the Mayor's House in the neighbourhood of Bayonne, the Grenadier Guards, under the command of Colonel Tynling, occupied an unfinished redoubt on the right of the high-road. The Duke of Wellington happened to pass with Freemantle and Lord A. Hill, on his return to headquarters, having satisfied himself that the fighting was merely a feint on the part of Soult (the French marshal). His Grace on looking round saw, to his surprise, a great many umbrellas, with which the officers protected themselves from the rain that was then falling.

"Arthur Hill came galloping up to us saying, 'Lord Wellington does not approve of the use of umbrellas during the enemy's firing and will not allow the gentlemen's sons to make themselves ridiculous in the eyes of the army.' Colonel Tynling a few days afterwards received a wigging from Lord Wellington for suffering his officers to carry umbrellas in the face of the enemy, his lordship observing, 'The Guards may in uniform, when on duty at St. James's, carry them if they please; but in the field it is not only ridiculous but unmilitary.'"

One can hardly imagine officers in the Great War of 1914–18 carrying umbrellas to protect them from the rain that fell in such torrents.

What is Fan Tracery?

IT is a kind of vaulting used in England in the late Perpendicular period. All the ribs that rise from the springing of the vault have the same curve, and develop equally in all directions. The resulting effect is something like that of the bones of a fan, hence the name. This kind of vaulting admits of considerable variety in the subordinate parts, but the general effect of the leading features is very uniform. Fine examples of it are to be seen in Henry VII's Chapel at Westminster Abbey, King's College Chapel at Cambridge, and St. George's Chapel at Windsor Castle. Fan tracery, which is peculiar to English Gothic, is frequently used over tombs, chantry chapels and other small erections.

What is a Lotus Eater?

IT is a term used to describe one who abandons all ambition and activity and lives in a world of dreams. The idea is taken from Homer's "Odyssey," which describes the Lotophagii, a peaceful nation on the coast of Cyrenaica, who were supposed as a result of eating the fruit of the lotus to fall into a state of indolent enjoyment. When Odysseus reached this country his sailors lost all desire to continue their journey home after tasting the lotus.

Who Are the Submerged Tenth?

THE completely destitute and hopelessly poor class, who are the very dregs of society. They were referred to in "Darkest England," the notable book by the first General Booth of the Salvation Army, who estimated their number as one-tenth of the total population of Great Britain. As a result of the work of the Salvation Army, much has been done to help this class.

The cloisters at Gloucester Cathedral, a fine example of fan tracery

What is King John's Cup?

It is a silver-gilt cup decorated with enamel belonging to the Corporation of King's Lynn and said to have been presented to the town by King John, hence the name. The character of the cup, however, shows that this cannot be a fact; its date is probably somewhere in the 14th century and it has been suggested that it was King John of France and not the English John who presented it. John of France was a prisoner in England, but there is no record that he ever visited King's Lynn. The costumes of the figures with which the cup is adorned are evidently of the 14th century.

What is a Bohemian?

The name is, of course, used for a native of Bohemia, part of Czechoslovakia. But it is also a term applied to a person in Britain or elsewhere who lives a free and easy, unconventional life and is not bound by the ordinary rules of social life as to dress, meals, and so on. Some famous men like Dr. Samuel Johnson can be described as Bohemian. The term is derived from the name of Bohemia, the land from which the roving, unconventional gipsies are originally said to have come.

What is an Indian Summer?

It is the term used to describe a short spell of warm, dry weather in the autumn with a hazy atmosphere. The name came from America and is derived from the custom among the Red Indians of harvesting their corn at this season. The expression St. Martin's Summer is often used in England for the same kind of weather occurring about November 11th, St. Martin's day.

Why Does the Sun Bleach Linen?

Linen manufacturers often place their linen out in the Sun to bleach, just as the straw hat makers place their hats in the Sun for the same purpose. The process is the same in each case. There are brownish impurities in the material, consisting mostly of a substance known as lignin. These under the action of the Sun's rays become oxidised, and are changed into colourless compounds. The sunlight causes the formation of hydrogen peroxide, which is an oxidising agent. The Sun method of bleaching is more efficient than an artificial process which is sometimes followed. In this the fabric is soaked in a solution of bleaching powder made

King John's Cup, sometimes known as the Lynn Cup, which is in the possession of the Corporation of King's Lynn

from chlorine and slaked lime, and is then placed in weak sulphuric acid. A substance is released that oxidises the colouring matter in the fabric, just as the peroxide produced by the Sun does.

How Many Worms Are There in an Acre of Ground?

A famous scientist has calculated that there are at least 50,000 worms to a single acre of garden soil. These would weigh altogether about three hundredweights. He found in an acre which he tested a quarter of a million burrows. In a field the number is less. Charles Darwin found the worms in an acre of meadow land to be about half that in a garden.

Is Land Worth More in London or New York?

Land near the Bank of England in the heart of the City of London is worth more than £100 a square foot. The value of land in Wall Street, New York, however, is greater than this. The reason is that owing to its situation on an island, businesses cannot so easily overflow into adjoining districts, and there is thus a greater demand to have offices actually in New York.

Who Was Master Tyll Owlglass?

A German of this name lived in the 14th century and was probably born at Kneitlingen near Brunswick. He was buried at Moellan, where his tomb is shown. A life of him was written in 1483 and his name has since become a centre around which have been grouped popular tales describing all kinds of merry and impudent pranks.

Only a small portion of the deeds attributed to Owlglass are likely to have been actually his own. The book holds somewhat the place in German story that the tales of Robin Hood and his merry men do in English. "The Marvellous Adventures and Rare Conceits of Master Tyll Owlglass" have been translated into English and many other languages. There are altogether 111 adventures, each recorded in a short chapter.

A typical story is that which tells how at Nuremberg, when his master, a physician, went away for a time, he donned the doctor's wig, gown and glasses and, posing as the physician, cured all the wealthy citizens who came to him. Their failing was really that they ate too much, and so Owlglass, looking wise, told them to be blooded and drink only warm water. Strange to say, they all speedily grew well. His German name is Till Eulenspiegel.

Linen bleaching in the Sun at Banbridge, County Down

Where is That Pipe Used?

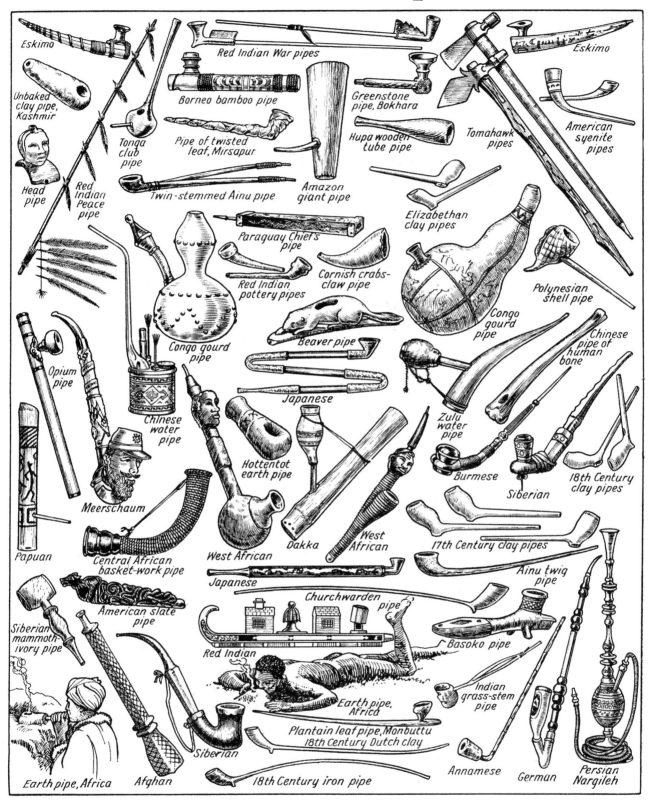

Eskimo

Unbaked clay pipe, Kashmir

Head pipe

Red Indian Peace pipe

Tonga club pipe

Red Indian War pipes

Borneo bamboo pipe

Pipe of twisted leaf, Mirsapur

Twin-stemmed Ainu pipe

Amazon giant pipe

Greenstone pipe, Bokhara

Hupa wooden tube pipe

Tomahawk pipes

Eskimo

American syenite pipes

Elizabethan clay pipes

Paraguay Chief's pipe

Red Indian pottery pipes

Cornish crabs-claw pipe

Polynesian shell pipe

Congo gourd pipe

Chinese pipe of human bone

Congo gourd pipe

Beaver pipe

Japanese

Zulu water pipe

Burmese

Siberian

18th Century clay pipes

Opium pipe

Chinese water pipe

Hottentot earth pipe

Dakka

West African

17th Century clay pipes

Papuan

Meerschaum

Central African basket-work pipe

West African

Japanese

Ainu twig pipe

Siberian mammoth ivory pipe

American slate pipe

Red Indian

Churchwarden pipe

Basoko pipe

Indian grass-stem pipe

Earth pipe, Africa

Afghan

Siberian

Earth pipe, Africa

Plantain leaf pipe, Monbuttu
18th Century Dutch clay

18th Century iron pipe

Annamese

German

Persian Nargileh

Smoking is now an almost universal habit, and while in Great Britain and North America tobacco is used largely in the form of cigarettes and cigars, in Africa, Asia and the native parts of America it is the pipe that is mostly used for smoking tobacco. On this page are given many examples of pipes, taken from all over the world. They vary enormously in form and artistic decoration. Meerschaum pipes were at one time popular in England, and in Germany the typical long pipe, with a coloured porcelain bowl, is still in use. Clay pipes have always been used by working men in England, and many exist that were used in the 17th and 18th centuries. In Africa the natives sometimes make a hole in a little hillock and use that as a pipe. Such is called an earth pipe and two examples of it are given above. Even a crab's claw has been used as a pipe in Cornwall.

Why Was Larboard Changed to Port?

LARBOARD was the term formerly used for the opposite side of a ship to starboard, but there were so many mistakes owing to the words being confused because of their similar

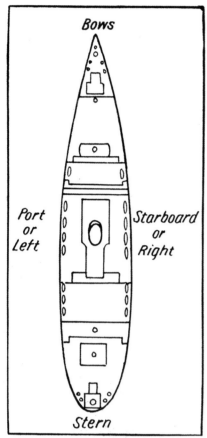

This diagram shows clearly which is the port and which the starboard side of a ship. The bows are, of course, the front, and the stern the back

sounds that "larboard" was dropped and "port" used in its place. "Starboard" is a corruption of "steer board," while "larboard" was so called from the load board or loading plank that was placed on that side. The word "port" as a substitute for "larboard" was in use as far back as the year 1580.

What is the Anglic Language?

IT is a simplified form of English spelt more or less phonetically, invented by the late Dr. R. Eugene Zachrisson, professor of English at Upsala University in Sweden. Professor Zachrisson pointed out that there are more than 500 ways of spelling sounds numbering about 40 that occur in English words in current use. Anglic has 50 letters or letter combinations to represent these sounds.

English, according to the professor, has the greatest prospect of becoming a universal secondary language for other nations. More than 500,000 people, he says, have already adopted it as the common international language of sea and commerce, but spelling is its great obstacle. Courses in Anglic have been given in Stockholm and Upsala, and many educationists have expressed approval of this world English as a means of teaching English to foreigners.

What Was the Cock Lane Ghost?

THIS was a noted imposture practised in a house in Cock Lane, Smithfield, London, in 1762 by a girl aged eleven with the encouragement and connivance of her father, a man named Parsons. Certain knockings were heard and Parsons declared that these proceeded from the ghost of Fanny Kent, who had died suddenly, and whom Parsons wished to suggest had been murdered by her husband.

All London was agog with the story, and the Cock Lane Ghost was visited by many notable people, including Dr. Samuel Johnson. Eventually it was found out that the knockings were produced by Parsons' daughter rapping on a board which she took to bed with her, and Parsons for the fraud was condemned to stand in the pillory

Who Were the Biddenden Maids?

THEY are said to have been two maidens, born at Biddenden in Kent in 1100, who were joined together at the hips and shoulders, very much in the same way as the famous Siamese twins of later days. Their names are sometimes given as Preston, and at other times as Elizabeth and Mary Chulkhurst. They are said to have lived together in this state for 34 years, when one of them died and the other, refusing to be separated from her twin sister, succumbed a few hours later.

At Easter each year at Biddenden small cakes bearing impressed upon them an image of the two maids are distributed freely, the expense being defrayed from a fund derived from 20 acres of land. The benefaction is of unknown date.

Halstead, in his "History of Kent," rejects the story of the joined twins, saying that the lands were left by two maiden ladies named Preston, and that the impression on the cakes is intended to represent merely two widows as general objects of charity.

What is Bee Wine?

THIS is a drink made from a fungus that grows in Palestine and also in British Columbia. The fungus is a white, spongy substance, and a small piece is placed in a large, open glass vessel, and hot though not boiling water is poured upon it. Two tablespoonfuls of sugar are added, and the next day two tablespoonfuls of syrup, then the next day two more tablespoonfuls of sugar, and so on alternately, sugar and syrup, for three weeks. The liquid is then poured off into bottles and tightly corked. In about a month it is ready for use, and provides a cooling drink for hot weather.

How is Papier Maché Made?

THIS material, composed of paper pulp, is made by pressing the pulp, or by pasting together different thicknesses of paper to the hardness and consistency of wood. Often some earthy material and glue or resinous matter are added to bind the material. The composition is rolled into thick sheets, which are moulded and pressed to the requisite shape and are then dried. The article is then decorated with enamel, paint, gilding and bronzing, and sometimes with inlaying of pearl and precious stones. It was invented in the 18th century, and appears to have been first made at Paris about 1740. The first objects made of papier maché were snuffboxes. Then trays were made and eventually the material was used in the making of the smaller articles of furniture such as work-tables.

A signpost at Biddenden in Kent, which has a representation of the Biddenden Maids

What is That Variety of Lamp?

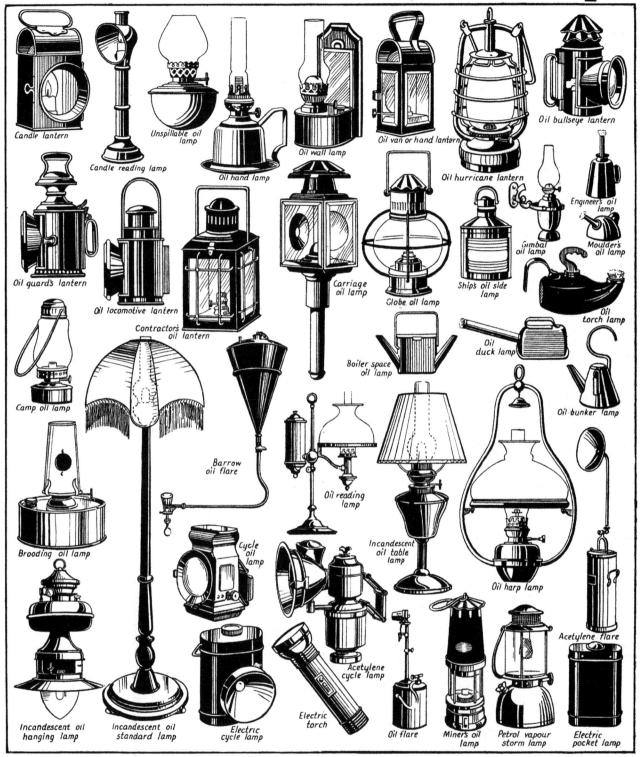

Candle lantern

Candle reading lamp

Unspillable oil lamp

Oil hand lamp

Oil wall lamp

Oil van or hand lantern

Oil bullseye lantern

Oil hurricane lantern

Engineer's oil lamp

Moulder's oil lamp

Gimbal oil lamp

Oil quard's lantern

Oil locomotive lantern

Contractor's oil lantern

Carriage oil lamp

Globe oil lamp

Ship's oil side lamp

Oil torch lamp

Camp oil lamp

Boiler space oil lamp

Oil duck lamp

Oil bunker lamp

Brooding oil lamp

Barrow oil flare

Oil reading lamp

Incandescent oil table lamp

Oil harp lamp

Cycle oil lamp

Acetylene cycle lamp

Acetylene flare

Incandescent oil hanging lamp

Incandescent oil standard lamp

Electric cycle lamp

Electric torch

Oil flare

Miners oil lamp

Petrol vapour storm lamp

Electric pocket lamp

Portable lamps are now made in many forms, and while some burn paraffin or other oil, others produce their own gas, as in the case of acetylene lamps, and others are electrical. On this page are given 38 varieties of lamps, which can be moved from place to place. Some are standard lamps, others hanging, and still others for carrying. Candle lamps are, of course, used where other means of illumination are not available, and are very useful in their way. The candle reading lamp has a brilliant reflector, which is slanted so as to throw the light down upon the book. The unspillable oil lamp is weighted at the bottom, so that if it gets a slight knock it will not go over, but right itself. The oil hurricane lantern is used on farms and other places for outdoor work, the flame being very carefully protected, so that it cannot be blown out. The oil bull's-eye lantern was formerly carried by the London and other police, but this has now given place to the electric lamp. The acetylene flare is used in the streets of large cities when fog suddenly descends, or to give light for night work on road-making. The various electric hand-lamps, which are a development of recent years, are exceedingly convenient. The miner's oil lamp, which in many mines is giving place to the electric lamp, was a very valuable invention. It was invented simultaneously by Sir Humphry Davy, the great scientist, and George Stephenson, the father of the railway

What Kind of Trap is That?

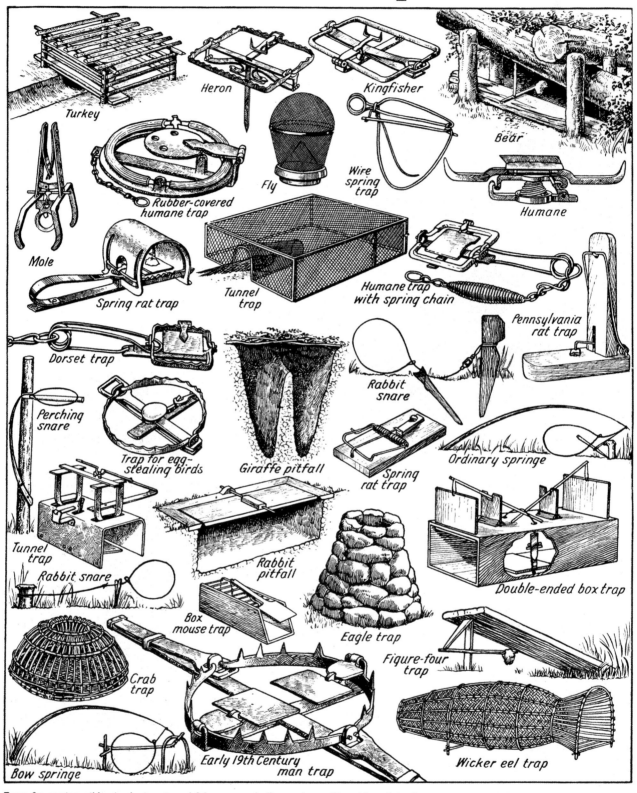

Turkey

Heron

Kingfisher

Bear

Rubber-covered humane trap

Fly

Wire spring trap

Humane

Mole

Spring rat trap

Tunnel trap

Humane trap with spring chain

Pennsylvania rat trap

Dorset trap

Rabbit snare

Perching snare

Trap for egg-stealing birds

Giraffe pitfall

Spring rat trap

Ordinary springe

Tunnel trap

Rabbit snare

Rabbit pitfall

Box mouse trap

Eagle trap

Double-ended box trap

Crab trap

Figure-four trap

Bow springe

Early 19th Century man trap

Wicker eel trap

Traps for snaring wild animals, insects and fishes are used all over the world, and have been for many centuries. Some have been cruel in their operation, but the tendency today in civilized countries is to insure that traps should be of such a character that the animal shall suffer as little as possible ; in other words, that it shall either be captured without injury or killed instantly. In the bear trap the bait when taken releases a stick, and a heavy log falls upon the bear, killing it. In the native African giraffe trap a pit is dug and covered with brushwood, and the giraffe, falling into the pit, is trapped with its front legs on one side and the hind legs on the other side of a division. The eagle trap consists of a circular tower built roughly of stones. It is about four feet high, and the same diameter at the bottom, narrowing at the top. A bait is put at the bottom, the eagle enters and is unable to leave. He cannot open his wings to fly out, and the hop to the top of the enclosure is too great

What High Official Wears a Golden Key?

H<small>E</small> is the Vice-Chamberlain of the Household, who is a Member of Parliament and conveys to the King

Mr. Ronald Cross, M.P., the Vice-Chamberlain of the Royal Household wearing the large gold key, which he carries

the House of Commons' loyal address in response to His Majesty's speech from the throne. He wears a golden key attached to his sash as a symbol.

What Were Nelson's Last Words?

T<small>HE</small> last words whispered by the victor of Trafalgar, who lost his life in the moment of triumph, were " Thank God I have done my duty."

Not long before Nelson had said to his Captain, " Kiss me, Hardy ! " and the officer knelt down and pressed his lips to the Admiral's cheek. " Now I am satisfied," said Nelson, " thank God I have done my duty." Hardy stood silent for a few moments, and then, kneeling, again kissed his chief's forehead. Nelson asked, " Who is that ? " and the Captain answered " It is Hardy." " God bless you, Hardy," said Nelson. The Captain then went on deck. Nelson became speechless a little before four o'clock in the afternoon. Almost the last words he said to his Chaplain, Scott, were, " Doctor, I have not been a great sinner," and his very latest utterance was as set forth above.

It has been stated that what Nelson said to his Captain in his dying moments was not, " Kiss me, Hardy," but " Kismet, Hardy." Kismet, meaning fate or destiny, is the word Mohammedans use to signify resignation to the will of Allah.

But there is no reason to think there is any truth in this. Mrs. Joyce Cruickshank some time ago wrote to " The Times," " My great grandfather, Richard Didham, served under Hardy in H.M.S. *Creole* in South American waters during 1821. On his return home he related to his family how the midshipmen of the *Creole* used to sing in chorus, ' Kiss me, Hardy ; kiss me, Hardy.' The gunroom was sufficiently near to Sir Thomas Hardy's quarters for him to hear ; he was obliged to take notice of it, and represented to them how thoughtless and callous was their conduct. Had Nelson's last word been ' Kismet,' there would have been no point in this story."

How Many Words Has the Oxford Dictionary?

T<small>HIS</small> greatest of all English dictionaries has 414,825 words, 240,165 of which are main words, 67,105 subordinate words, 47,800 special combinations, and 59,755 are obvious combinations. There are about half a million definitions and 1,827,306 illustrative quotations. These quotations were collected from probably about ten millions sent in. The work contains 46,464 columns, which, if placed end to end, would reach over nine miles. There are 178 miles of type, containing approximately 50 million words and 227,779,589 letters and figures, not counting punctuation marks. The letter S yields the most words, no fewer than 57,428, P coming next with 37,689, and C third with 29,295. Under X, Y, Z there are 4,746 words.

The Fat Boy of Cock Lane, set up after the Fire of London as a warning against gluttony

Who is the Fat Boy of Cock Lane?

H<small>E</small> is a carved wooden figure representing an uncommonly fat boy, which formerly rested on the wall of the Fortune of War tavern at the corner of Cock Lane, and bore an inscription which said : " This boy is in memory put up for the late Fire of London occasioned by the Sin of Gluttony, 1666." According to an old story, a greedy baker's boy, while stealing his master's pies one evening, knocked over a lamp and so started the Great Fire.

Various accounts of the origin of the fire are given, and Mr. Walter G. Bell, the historian of the Great Fire, says that as an explanation of the fire this is as good as some others.

The Fortune of War was pulled down and a new building erected in its place,

and the fat boy, gilded, has been set up on the wall of this building. The inscription is not now there.

A preacher in his sermon on the anniversary of the Great Fire asserted that " the calamity could not have been occasioned by the sin of blasphemy, for in that case it would have begun in Billingsgate ; not lewdness, for then Drury Lane would have been first on fire ; nor lying, for then the flames had reached the City from Westminster Hall. No, my beloved, it was occasioned by the sin of gluttony, for it began at Pudding Lane and ended at Pie Corner."

But with regard to this latter statement, Mr. Bell says, the fire continued to spread about Cripplegate 20 hours after Pie Corner had been razed.

What is a Martello Tower?

A MARTELLO tower is a round tower about 40 feet high built for coast defence. Many such towers were erected on the southern and eastern coasts of England during the period of the Napoleonic Wars when invasion was threatened, but they are now quite obsolete. Numbers have been demolished, but others have been turned into dwelling-houses.

The name Martello is a corruption of Mortella, and the towers are named after a tower on Cape Mortella in Corsica, which a British squadron, under Lord Hood, bombarded unsuccessfully in 1794. The British warships cannonaded the fort for three hours, yet although the fort had only two 18-pounders and one 6-pounder, and was manned by only 33 men, it resisted the attack and sustained no damage.

As a result of this the Duke of Richmond proposed the erection of Martello towers round the south, south-east and east coasts of England, and a line of them was built extending from Hythe in Kent to Seaford in Sussex, as well as elsewhere. There were about 74 altogether. They were built of solid masonry with very thick walls, and rooms for a garrison of about 30 men. The only entrance was placed some 20 feet above the ground and was reached by a ladder When the tower was sur-

rounded by a moat there was a drawbridge for access to the ladder.

A platform on top had one big gun which could be turned for firing in all directions. The cost of erecting the towers was enormous, but they never had to be used.

Though the Martello towers derived their name from the Mortella Tower in Corsica, that was not the first defence of its kind. Robertson in his life of the Emperor Charles V tells us that the Spaniards in the 16th century were compelled to erect watch-towers at regular distances along the coast, and to keep guards continually on the alert to protect the population from the attacks of Barbary corsairs.

In the converted Martello towers on the south coast of England windows now pierce the walls, and the flat top has been turned into a roof garden.

Martello towers, with their massive walls of masonry, were an excellent defence against the artillery of the late 18th century. But, of course, against modern armaments, with high-explosive shells, they would be quite useless. The " pill-boxes " erected during the War and armed with machine-guns, were a kind of miniature Martello tower.

Did the Ancient Egyptians Wear Wigs?

YES; both men and women wore them. The men kept their heads shaved, and put on wigs for all

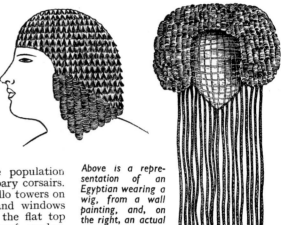

Above is a representation of an Egyptian wearing a wig, from a wall painting, and, on the right, an actual wig found in a tomb, and now in the Berlin Museum

full-dress occasions. There were short wigs imitating curly hair, and also long wigs. The wigs worn by women were always long, and were made of human hair mixed with sheep's wool.

Two Martello towers on the English coast at Hythe in Kent. The one on the right has been adapted to be used as a dwelling-house. The one above appears very much as it did in Napoleon's time. These towers were erected to protect England from a French invasion

Did Cleopatra Drink a Dissolved Pearl?

THE story is told that at a banquet when Mark Antony expressed surprise at so much magnificence, Cleopatra took a pearl from her ear-ring and, dissolving it in vinegar, drank to the health of the Roman general. But there can be no truth in the story for vinegar, experts say, would not dissolve a pearl, and any stronger acid would be unfit to drink.

As against this opinion, however, we may quote the following statement by Professor Louis Dieulafait, a French scientist. " This experiment may possibly

have been tried upon real pearls without success, but then probably the action of the acid did not last long enough. The pearl, as we have seen, is formed of carbonate of lime and an organic substance. The vinegar easily effects a soluble combination with the carbonate of lime; but as soon as the lime of the first layer is consumed, the organic matter of a gelatinous consistence continues to envelope the pearl; and as this matter is not soluble in vinegar, nor can be attacked by it, a protection is formed around the interior layers, so that they are not reached by the corrosive liquid. But by persistence, in the end even this is penetrated, and the pearl is completely dissolved."

The story is probably fabulous, in part at any rate, for even if Cleopatra placed the pearl in the vinegar, the dissolving of it would have taken too long.

Where Are There Blind Fish?

THERE are several species in the Mammoth Cave of Kentucky, the largest known cave in the world. But that is not the only place where blind fish exist. They are found in several other large caverns, including a cave in the Belgian Congo. Here they are three and a half inches long, with creamy white bodies. These fish, like those of the Kentucky Cave and other underground rivers and lakes, have through long centuries lost the use of their eyes, because the darkness made sight unnecessary.

How is That Barrow Used?

Coal barrow

Wood garden barrow

Tilting barrow

Foundry barrow

Sack truck

Pig metal barrow

Iron garden barrow

Caterpillar lawn barrow

Navvy barrow

Dock truck

Street truck

Luggage truck

Laundry truck

Linoleum truck

Warehouse truck

Cask truck

Bar truck

Revolving trolley

Warehouse or luggage trolley

Here are various types of barrows and trucks which are used for a variety of purposes. The work for which they are intended is in most cases indicated by the name, as, for example, the coal barrow, the navvy barrow and the laundry truck. The tilting barrow can, of course, be released and tilted to empty out the contents easily. The pig metal barrow is used for carrying the pigs of iron in an iron foundry, and the foundry barrow is also used for hot material in a foundry. The upright trucks, sometimes called trolleys, are generally used for moving heavy weights short distances. They vary in shape according to the goods they are to carry. The cask truck, for example, is rounded, so that the cask may not roll off. The bar truck is for heavy bars of metal, and the linoleum truck is for moving rolls of linoleum in a shop. The revolving trolley can be rotated on its central wheel

Are Rams Good Fighters ?

YES ; a ram of a domesticated species of sheep is able to fight a bull. It takes advantage of its far greater agility, and keeps butting the foe with its strongly-armed forehead. So strong is a powerful ram that one has been known to throw a bull on the ground at the first onset, and a ram is always ready to defend himself and his companions against a dog. Many rams exhibit great pugnacity, and a ram in a field has knocked a woman down again and again, running and butting her every time she tried to rise, for over an hour, till some men arrived with sticks and drove the ram away.

" Sheep," says Mr. James Macdonald, " differ from goats in their mode of fighting ; goats rear themselves on their hind legs and throw themselves sideways on their adversary, to bring the points of their horns to bear ; whereas sheep rush straight at each other, a mode which better suits the different style of armature of the head.

" Rams of the black-faced variety are especially powerful with their heads, and often at the rutting season kill each other. Their naturally strong skull is further protected in battle by heavy arched horns. A thorough ram fight is a terrifying sight. The two warriors go backwards each some fifteen or twenty yards, and then meet each other with great violence, their heads cracking loudly, and their beam-ends rising in response to the collision of heads. Ewes of this breed

breeds only the males, and in other breeds, like the Southdowns, horns are absent in both sexes. In some breeds there is a tendency to produce additional pairs of horns, so that there are four-horned and even eight-horned sheep. In the Wallachian breed the horns of the ram spring almost perpendicularly from the frontal bone, and then take a spiral, corkscrew form.

Hoar-frost covering the ground and bushes

What Exactly is Hoar Frost ?

THOUGH it is not exactly frozen dew, it is formed in the same way as dew. As we know, dew is caused by the precipitation as tiny drops of water of the invisible moisture in the air, when the air is cooled to what is known as dew point. For the deposit of dew the air must be still and there must be no blanket of clouds overhead to keep the earth warm. On a clear, still night the Earth's surface radiates its heat, and the layer of moist air in contact with the ground, being cooled, is unable to hold as much water vapour as it was doing and so deposits some of this as dew.

Now, when the air is so dry that the dew point—that is, the temperature at which the air must deposit some of its moisture—is at or below 32° Fah. or 0° Cen. the moisture condenses not as drops of liquid water but in the solid form as delicate ice crystals. Hoarfrost is not dew that has been frozen after it was formed, but moisture precipitated directly in a solid form from the atmosphere. The white, glistening appearance of hoar-frost is due to the reflection of the light by the facets of the many tiny crystals.

Are Worms Found on Mountains ?

WORMS are found in most parts of the world, and even on mountains up to a height of over 15,000 feet, or nearly three miles. They are not found in deserts, however, for there must be a certain amount of moisture in the soil if they are to thrive and be able to make their burrows. Of course, they are not found in the Polar regions. There are many worms high up in the Alps, and they are found in the Andes at a height of 15,870 feet above sealevel. They are also found on the Nilgiri mountains in South India, and on the Himalayas.

A Dorset ewe charging a sheep-dog to protect her young

fight also. Sheep without horns are not usually so pugnacious as the mountain breeds."

Domestic sheep vary much in the character of their horns. In the Dorset breed both sexes have horns, in other

More remarkable still are the so-called unicorn sheep of Nepal, in which the horns of the rams grow together to form a large single horn.

Ewes with lambs are ready to fight fiercely in defence of their young.

What is the Nansen Passport?

AFTER the Great War, when nationalism became so strong, and many people, because of political changes, were refugees from their native countries, there were more than a million of these who, because they could not get passports from their former lands, were practically outcasts. Without passports they had no right to go anywhere, and their plight, herded together in certain places without the power or right to go elsewhere, was pitiable.

Dr. Fridtjof Nansen, the distinguished Arctic explorer, who was also a great humanitarian, devised a plan by which a special kind of passport, afterwards called the " Nansen passport," was granted to these refugees, giving them a limited freedom of movement. Most governments recognised this passport, and as small loans were advanced to the refugees and they were granted reductions in railway fares, Nansen's scheme proved an untold blessing to hundreds of thousands of people.

Where is the Knee of a Horse?

IT is not where most people think it, but is high up near the body, as can be seen in the accompanying diagram. It is interesting to compare the knees, elbows, ankles and wrists of a horse with those of a man. In a dog the various bones are in much the same relative positions as in the horse given here. The elbow and knee are close to the trunk, but the ankle and wrist are a good deal lower down than they are in the horse.

Where is There a Kicking Machine?

AS we might suppose, it is in the United States that a kicking machine has been set up. It was erected in 1937 in the main square of a small town in South Carolina and was installed by the mayor's orders. Realising how many men, after some unwise or foolish action, use the expression, " I could have kicked myself," but take no further steps to carry out their expressed desire, the mayor, with a ready wit, decided to make it easy for them to administer the kick to themselves mechanically.

The penitent, we are told, has to seat himself on a parallel bar arrangement and then turn a handle, when a device like the sails of a windmill, with four boots at the ends, begins to rotate and lifts the man sufficiently in the air to allow the boots to pass. By a mechanical arrangement quite a light turn of the handle administers a powerful kick.

What Was the Boston Tea Party?

IT may almost be regarded as the beginning of the American Revolution, which ended in the United States

Some of the barrels now in London that contained the tea shipped to Boston and later thrown into the sea during the Boston Tea Party

becoming independent of Great Britain. When the English Parliament imposed taxes on tea entering the American colonies, the colonists determined that none of the taxed tea should be allowed to land at any American port.

When they could not obtain sanction to send the tea away in the ships that brought it, they decided that the only way to get rid of the tea was to throw it overboard.

So, late on a December afternoon in 1773, just as dusk was falling, a body of forty or fifty men disguised as Red Indians, with feathers and choppers complete, went down to the wharf at Boston where the tea-ships were lying and, going aboard, broke open the chests one after another and poured their contents into the harbour. In about three hours 340 chests of tea had been emptied into the water. Then the men retired and Boston became quiet once more. But the rebellion against the Mother Country had begun. Eighteen months later an American force surrounded Boston, and the famous battle of Bunker Hill took place between them and the British troops, the first battle of the War of American Independence.

It is interesting to note that the London firm responsible for the shipping of the tea to Boston is still in existence and carrying on business. It still possesses some of the large barrels that contained the tea later shipped to Boston. The firm carries on business at the " Crown and Three Sugar Loaves," in Creechurch Lane, in the City of London, and is one of the oldest tea-importers in London.

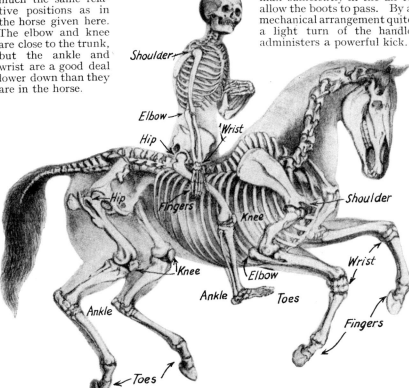

A comparison of the skeletons of a man and a horse

What is the Line of Beauty?

THIS term is used for a supposed ideal line, curved and undulating, outside which it is said there is no line really beautiful and worthy of admiration. Hogarth in his "Analysis of Beauty" was the first to formulate the theory of the line of beauty. He placed his line of beauty on a palette underneath his own portrait, now in the National Gallery. Different artists have since given it different forms, but Hogarth's is the most familiar.

Hogarth's line of beauty

What is Holystone?

IT is a soft sandstone used in the Navy for scrubbing decks, and it obtained its name because the men using it went down on their knees in an attitude of prayer. The large holystones are called "hand Bibles," and smaller ones are called "prayer-books."

Are Sleds Used Only on Snow?

NO; in some places they are used for travel over cobblestones and other roads of a similar kind, as in Madeira, where the "taxis" of the island are in the form of sleds with basket-work seats and a roof and curtains, something like those of a four-

Did Dick Turpin Really Live?

YES, he was a notorious highwayman who was hanged at York in April, 1739, for stealing a black mare and foal at Welton. He was the son of an innkeeper at Hempstead in Essex and, after joining a gang of robbers, entered into partnership with the highwayman Tom King on the Cambridge Road in 1735. He shot King by accident and fled to Yorkshire, where he was arrested for horse-stealing as described. His fetters, weighing 28 pounds, are still shown at York Museum.

Many legends have grown up round his name, the best known of which is his famous ride to York on his mare "Black Bess," which fell dead on reaching that city. The spot where this happened is pointed out today, but the story is apocryphal as are most of the spots associated with Turpin's name. There was nothing heroic about Turpin. Harrison Ainsworth, the novelist, idealised him in "Rookwood."

Where is a Police-Station in a Lamp-Post?

A LAMP-POST may seem a strange place for a police-station, but nevertheless one of the lamp-pillars

The pedestal of a lamp-post in Trafalgar Square, London, which has been fitted up as a police-station

in Trafalgar Square is really a police-station. These pillars, with lamps on them, were put up in 1927, and it was believed that they would give much more light than ordinary lamp-posts, but they did not fulfil expectations in this respect. One of the pillars is hollow and contains a telephone, which would prove useful in case of disturbances in Trafalgar Square. It is registered as a police-station.

What Are the Diamond Sculls?

A TROPHY rowed for at Henley Regatta each year. Established in 1844, it consists of a pair of crossed silver sculls, not quite a foot in length, surmounted by a representation of a laurel wreath and having a pendant of diamonds. It rests in a box lined with velvet, which bears the names of all the winners. The trophy passes from winner to winner, but each successful rower receives a silver cup which becomes his own property.

What is a Dog-Whipper?

THIS was the title given to an official who in the old days used to carry a long-handled whip to drive all dogs from the precincts of a church. So recently as 1856 a Mr. John Pickard was appointed dog-whipper in Exeter Cathedral.

A sled drawn by bullocks used as a public vehicle in the streets of Madeira

poster bedstead. The sleds are drawn by cattle yoked to the vehicle, which move in leisurely fashion through the streets and up and down the hills.

Are Polar Bears Good Swimmers?

ALTHOUGH among the largest of the bears and weighing sometimes as much as six or seven hundred pounds, or nearly a third of a ton, Polar bears are able to swim with much

A Polar bear floating in the water

swiftness and endurance. As they live largely on fish, seals and white whales, it is, of course, necessary that they should be good swimmers. Mr. M'Tavish gives the following account of the way in which Polar bears capture their prey : " The bear having discovered a seal asleep on an ice-floe immediately slips into the water if he himself be on another ice-floe. Diving, he swims under water for a distance, then reappears and takes observations. Alternately diving and swimming, he approaches close to his victim. Before his final disappearance he seems to measure the intervening distance, and when he next appears it is alongside of the seal. Then, either getting on the ice, or pouncing upon the seal as it tries to escape, he secures it. Both seals and porpoises are not infrequently met with bearing the marks of a bear's claws upon their backs."

Bears are often carried away from the mainland on ice-floes, and then they feed by diving and swimming from time to time in order to catch fish. As they are able to float as well as swim, they can remain in the water for a long time.

Even other bears, like the black and brown, do not mind the water, and will often go into deep water in large streams to catch fish.

What Was the Tragedy of Mayerling?

IT was in his hunting-box at this place near Vienna that the Crown Prince Rudolf, heir to the Austro-Hungarian throne, committed suicide after killing his woman friend, Baroness Vetsera. The tragedy happened on January 30th, 1889, and the next day a bulletin issued by the Ministry of the Interior at Vienna declared that the Crown Prince had died suddenly of apoplexy. Almost at once Vienna was seething with rumours. One stated that a huntsman had surprised the Crown Prince with his wife and slain him in a fit of jealousy. Another declared that the Archduke had been killed in the course of a quarrel after a drinking bout. Still another rumour said he had been assassinated by " one who desired to occupy the throne," without specifying the name of the person.

But before long it became known that the baroness had been found dead with the Archduke, and then opinion was divided between those who regarded the tragedy as a romantic love affair and those who suggested a sinister political background and maintained that the Crown Prince's father, the old Emperor Francis Joseph, had told his son in the course of a violent altercation on the previous day that there was " only one way out."

During nearly half a century since the Crown Prince's death many books have been published professing to give all sorts of supposed " revelations." But forty-eight years after the tragedy the Archduke's widow, Princess Stephanie of Belgium, who, by the way, found happiness in a second marriage with the Hungarian Prince Elmer Lonyay, published a book with the Crown Prince's letters to her, including the last letter written within a few minutes of the tragedy. These all appear to be the letters of a perfectly sane man. Princess Stephanie's account seems to make it clear that the Archduke's suicide was a deliberate and premeditated action and that it was due to the miscarriage of a political conspiracy. Beyond this the mystery of Mayerling is still a mystery.

Why is a Cooper Rolled in a Barrel?

IT has long been the custom for an apprentice cooper, when he has finished his time, to be initiated as a journeyman cooper—that is, a regular workman who has learned his craft—by being rolled in a barrel or cask which he has made with his own hands.

When the barrel is completed the cooper's workmates put him inside and then roll the barrel and its contents round the shop, while they cheer. Sometimes crackers are let off, and

A cooper, just out of his apprenticeship, being rolled, according to ancient custom, in the first barrel he has made as a journeyman

always the ex-apprentice is " rung out of his time." This means that his fellow coopers strike their adzes and axes with hammers, making as loud a clanging as they can.

Can Parachuting Be Learnt Without Aircraft?

In Russia young would-be aeronauts are taught parachute - jumping without going into aircraft. They go to the top of a high girder-built tower, so constructed that one can jump with a parachute from an open platform. In this way the sensation of descending can be mastered before actual jumping from an aeroplane is attempted.

At the Paris Exhibition of 1937 a similar tower was built and visitors were able to make parachute jumps in perfect safety. The tower was over a hundred feet high and the parachutist was taken to the top in a lift. Then after the harness of the parachute was adjusted he stepped off the platform with the open parachute above him and glided gently to the ground. A steel wire was attached to the top of the parachute, and the weight of the latter was counterbalanced to prevent a too speedy descent. See picture below.

Why Are Horseshoes Considered Lucky?

Two theories are given to account for the practice of hanging a horseshoe up over the door for luck.

A novice in parachuting descending from the platform of the parachute tower at the 1937 Paris Exhibition

According to an old legend, the devil one day asked St. Dunstan, who was noted for his skill in shoeing horses, to shoe his hoof. Dunstan, knowing who his customer was, tied him tightly to the wall and then, proceeding with his job, put the devil to so much pain that he roared for mercy. Dunstan at last consented to release his captive on condition that he should never again enter a place where he saw a horseshoe displayed.

At one time many houses in the West End of London used to have a horseshoe hanging over the threshold as a protection against witches and the devil. As late as 1813 seventeen horseshoes were counted in Monmouth Street.

Another theory to account for the practice, still often carried out by foolish and superstitious people, is that it dates back much earlier than St. Dunstan, that it is, in fact, a remnant of the worship of the goddess Astarte or Ashtaroth, whose symbol was the crescent moon. The horseshoe is the most easily obtained representation of this heavenly body, and animals left out in the fields at night used to wear the symbol to ensure the protection of Astarte. In the book of Judges in the Bible, chapter VIII, verse 21, there is a reference to ornaments on the camels' necks, and the marginal translation of this is " ornaments like the moon."

In this connection it is interesting to remember that many of the brass ornaments worn by cart-horses down to the present time are crescents.

The curious fruits of the sausage tree that grows in Africa. These are two and a half feet long

What is the Sausage Tree?

This is the name given to a tree that grows in the tropical and subtropical parts of Africa on account of the curious form of its fruits, which are something like large sausages. The tree is called by botanists *Kigelkia pinnata*, the first word being the native name for the plant on the coast of Mozambique, and the latter word meaning feather-like, a reference to the leaves. Americans call the tree the hot-dog tree, hot-dog being a slang term for sausage.

The kigelkia is a large tree with white bark and spreading branches. It grows to a height of 50 feet or more. The leaves, as already stated, are pinnate, and the flowers hang in long, loose clusters. The fruit is often two and a half feet long. It has a corky rind, and inside consists of pulp with many round seeds. In Nubia the tree is regarded as sacred, and religious ceremonies take place by moonlight under its branches. The fruit is used as an external application for the cure of rheumatism.

How Long Has Christmas Pudding Been Eaten?

CHRISTMAS pudding, which is now such an indispensable feature of the Christmas festivities, is not a very ancient institution. It gradually came into the Christmas fare in the early years of the 18th century, and according to the Oxford Dictionary the very earliest reference to plum-pudding is in 1711.

It developed from the plum-porridge which used to be eaten at Christmas in earlier days, and continued as late as the beginning of the 19th century. " Plum-porridge," says one account, " was made of a very strong broth of shin of beef, to which was added crumb of bread, cloves, nutmeg, cinnamon, mace, currants, raisins and dates. It was boiled gently, and then further strengthened with a quart of canary and one of red port ; and when served up, a little grape verjuice or juice of orange was popped in as a zest."

Still earlier Christmas pie used to be a feature of the Christmas feasting, and here is a recipe from a manuscript of 1394 : " Take a pheasant, a hare, a capon, two partridges, two pigeons and two conies ; chop them up, take out as many bones as you can, and add the livers and hearts, two kidneys of sheep, forcemeal made into balls with eggs, pickled mushrooms, salt, pepper, spice and vinegar. Boil the bones in a pot to make good broth ; put the meat into a crust of good paste made craftily into the likeness of a bird's body ; pour in the liquor, close it up and bake it well ; and so serve it forth with the head of one of the birds at one end and a great tail at the other, and divers of his large feathers set cunningly all about him."

Plum-pudding is essentially an English dish, and foreigners rarely know how to make it properly. Here is a recipe copied from the German " Kreuz Zeitung " in 1890 for making Christmas plum-pudding : " The cook is to take dough, beer in the course of fermentation, milk, brandy, whisky and gin in equal parts ; bread, citronate, large and small raisins in profusion. This must be stirred by the whole family for at least three days, and it is then to be hung up in a linen bag for six weeks in order thoroughly to ferment." It would be interesting to watch an Englishman's face when he tasted this concoction.

A good plum-pudding story is told of Lord Macartney, British Ambassador to China, who wanted to give gratification to a distinguished mandarin by inviting him to eat real English plum-pudding. He gave instructions to his Chinese chef, and no doubt they were carried out most conscientiously, but the pudding came to table in a soup tureen, for the Ambassador had forgotten to tell the chef anything about the cloth.

It is said that at one time at Paignton, Devon, a plum-pudding of huge dimensions was drawn through the town amid great rejoicings. It contained 400 lb. of flour, 170 lb. of beef suet, 140 lb. of raisins, and 240 eggs. It was boiled from Saturday morning till the following Tuesday evening.

The diplodocus of a former geological age, with an African elephant drawn to the same scale

What is the Biggest Animal That Has Lived on Land?

TODAY the biggest land animal is the African elephant, exceptional specimens of which may weigh as much as six tons and stand 12 feet high. But millions of years ago, in the Jurassic Age, in what is now North America, there lived an animal that was over 80 feet long, though lightly built. It was a herbivorous dinosaur called the diplodocus, a word that means " double beam." It was so named by the scientists because each bone covering and protecting the blood-vessels on the lower face of the tail consists of two separate bars slung in the middle. This creature probably lived partly in the water, and is believed to have fed mostly on sea-weed.

Of course, none of these animals can for size and weight compare with the whale. Some rorquals measure over 100 feet in length and weigh 200 tons. (See the picture on page 388.)

What is an Infant in Law?

IT is a person under the age of twenty-one years, the age at which persons are regarded as competent for all that the law requires them to do. They are then said to be of full age, and this age is gained on the day preceding the twenty-first anniversary of a person's birth. An infant is sometimes called a minor, but in probate for the purpose of a grant of administration a minor means a person above seven and under twenty-one, while a person under seven is called an infant.

While a person under twenty-one cannot bind himself by contract except for necessaries, or make a will, and cannot after attaining his majority ratify contracts made previously, yet he is bound by certain contracts set forth in law, such as apprenticeship and marriage.

Lady Twyford, Lady Mayoress of London, helping to stir the Christmas pudding at the Mansion House

What is the Name of That Beetle?

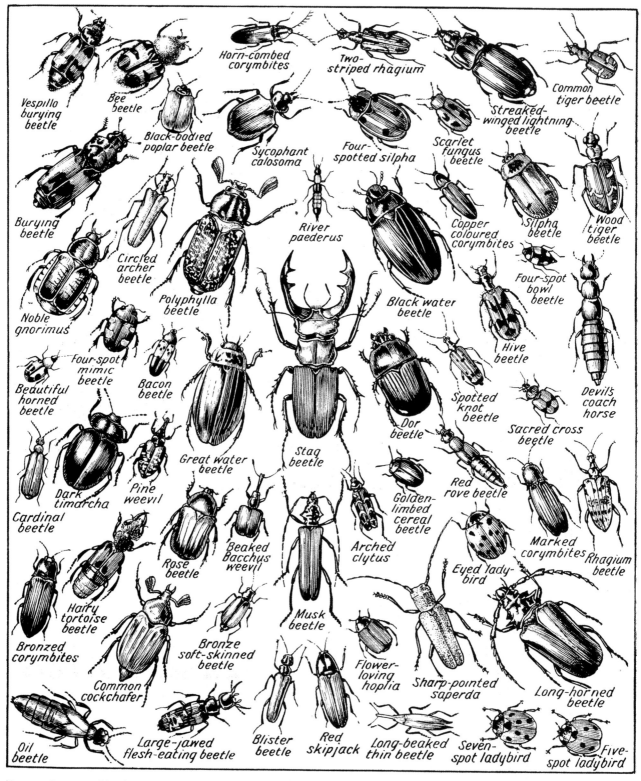

Vespillo burying beetle

Bee beetle

Black-bodied poplar beetle

Horn-combed corymbites

Two-striped rhagium

Common tiger beetle

Streaked-winged lightning beetle

Sycophant calosoma

Four-spotted silpha

Scarlet fungus beetle

Burying beetle

River paederus

Copper coloured corymbites

Silpha beetle

Wood tiger beetle

Circled archer beetle

Polyphylla beetle

Black water beetle

Four-spot bowl beetle

Noble gnorimus

Hive beetle

Four-spot mimic beetle

Bacon beetle

Devil's coach horse

Beautiful horned beetle

Spotted knot beetle

Sacred cross beetle

Dor beetle

Dark timarcha

Pine weevil

Great water beetle

Stag beetle

Red rove beetle

Marked corymbites

Cardinal beetle

Golden-limbed cereal beetle

Rhagium beetle

Rose beetle

Beaked Bacchus weevil

Arched clytus

Eyed lady-bird

Hairy tortoise beetle

Musk beetle

Bronzed corymbites

Bronze soft-skinned beetle

Flower-loving hoplia

Sharp-pointed saperda

Long-horned beetle

Common cockchafer

Oil beetle

Large-jawed flesh-eating beetle

Blister beetle

Red skipjack

Long-beaked thin beetle

Seven-spot ladybird

Five-spot ladybird

Here are the principal beetles that we see in Great Britain. Of course, there are many more, but these are the ones we notice most often. The largest of all the British beetles is the stag beetle, the male of which is shown in the centre of the page. This beetle gets its name from the huge jaws of the male, which are something like the horns of a stag. In the female the jaws are small, curved and sharply pointed. The head is smaller than that of the male. This beetle sometimes reaches a length of three inches. The males always fight for the possession of the females, and so only the largest and strongest have a chance of obtaining a mate. The great water beetle has powerful jaws and can give a nasty wound to the hand. Its voracity is astonishing. It will eat almost any kind of insect, any kind of meat, raw or cooked, and will even attack goldfish and frogs. At night it often takes to its wings and flies off in search of more food. Beetles belong to the order of insects known as Coleoptera, which means "sheath-winged," because the flying wings are protected by sheaths. It is one of the largest orders, and includes more than 150,000 species.

Why Can a Heavy Warship Float?

SOME battleships weigh over 30,000 tons and yet they float as easily as a paper boat. Steel is about eight times as heavy as water. What is the explanation, then, that such a great mass of steel can float?

Well, of course, if the steel were all pressed together to form a solid lump it would sink to the bottom at once, but in the ship it is spread out with thousands of cubic feet of air inside and the total weight of the ship with all its compartments filled with air is less than that of a similar bulk of water.

A ship floated in the water displaces a quantity of water equal to its own weight. The weight of a ship and everything on board is always equal to the weight of water that the submerged part displaces. That is why it floats.

Sometimes a derelict ship with a timber cargo becomes waterlogged and floats with its deck at the surface of the sea. In this position it displaces its own weight of water.

Why Cannot We See Round a Corner?

IT may seem strange that though we can hear round a corner we cannot see. The reason is that while sound comes to us in waves of air and so can reach our ears round a corner because air or wind can blow round a corner, light waves are in the ether and travel only in straight lines. We see that light travels in straight lines if we watch a searchlight shining up into the sky or across a distance.

But, of course, if we use mirrors to change the direction of the light ray, then it is possible to see round a corner. The modern underground strong rooms of some big banks have space left all round them, and mirrors are placed at angles so that a guard passing along the front of the strong room can see by looking up the side whether there is anybody lurking at the back. The mirrors help him to see round a corner. Light rays are bent by passing from one medium into another, as from air into water.

What is the Story of Psyche and Cupid?

PSYCHE, according to the classical mythology, was the youngest of the three daughters of a king. Venus was jealous of her beauty, and ordered Cupid to inspire Psyche with a love for the most contemptible of men. Cupid however himself fell in love with her, and took her to an unknown spot, where he visited her regularly. Her jealous sisters

Psyche, from an ancient gem

told her that in the darkness she embraced a hideous monster, and once while Cupid was asleep Psyche approached him with a lamp, when to her astonishment she saw the handsomest of all the gods. In her excitement she let a drop of hot oil fall from her lamp upon Cupid's shoulder, and this woke him up. He censured her for her mistrust, and fled. Psyche in her unhappiness wandered from temple to temple, inquiring for her lover. On her arrival at the palace of Venus that goddess kept her as a slave, and gave her the hardest and worst tasks to perform. She would have perished had not Cupid, who still loved her, invisibly assisted her in her toils. At last with his aid she overcame the jealousy of Venus, became immortal, and was united to Cupid for ever. Psyche is regarded as representing the human soul, which is purified by misfortune and so prepared for the enjoyment of true happiness. In art Psyche is generally represented as a maiden with the wings of a butterfly.

Is an Octopus Dangerous?

CERTAINLY an octopus of any size is dangerous, especially to a diver who may encounter one on the sea-bed, where the octopus spends most of its time.

Some years ago a British diver was destroyed at Gibraltar by an octopus, and another diver who went down to his rescue was also attacked. The second diver lashed out at the long tentacles as they darted in and out all round him, and frequently he could feel them fasten on his hands; but he used his axe so effectively that soon the water all round was stained with blood. At last the diver slipped and fell right into the writhing arms of the octopus.

" I gave myself up for lost," he says, " but continued to wield my axe right and left. More than once I felt the evil tentacles close in on me, but the beast must have been by this time deprived of some of its power through injury and loss of blood."

Eventually the diver managed to escape up the rope-ladder.

A battleship of nearly 30,000 tons, H.M.S. " Royal Oak," floating in a rough sea

Can Pigs Be Trained?

Dʀ. W. Lander Lindsay, the great authority on mind in the lower animals, says that the pig has a native intelligence that can be developed by education to such a degree that there have been learned pigs, just as there are and have been

upon a railway line as a train approached. Instead of scattering themselves in a stampede as sheep, horses, deer, cattle, buffaloes, and other animals do, they remained in line and stood perfectly still till the train had actually passed over them and not one

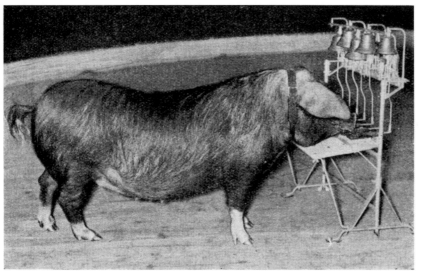

A trained pig which is able to ring peals of bells

learned dogs; pigs able, for instance, to form words from or with letters.

" Where it lives on terms of intimacy with its master," he says, " as in Ireland or among the New Zealand Maoris, when it is treated and trained as a pet or companion, it assumes the position of the dog, becoming thoroughly tame by following its master as the dog does. Not only has it been taught to spell, but also to point, to find and to retrieve like a dog, and to hunt for truffles, and in other ways it has been and may be rendered useful, by reason of its trained intelligence, to man."

Some people regard the pig as perverse, obstinate and dirty, but all these qualities can be eliminated by proper treatment and training. Dr. Lindsay says the pig " profits by experience to the extent of becoming artful, as well as sagacious, while certain authors attribute to it much talent, natural and acquired. So-called sporting pigs are as fond of sport as dogs are, and in the same way solicit to be taken out for the purpose of enjoying it. Other pigs show great affection for their young, conjugal fidelity, and attachment to persons, recognising friends and protectors They defend each other resolutely Their capacity for education and their tractability lead to their becoming useful to man in many ways—for instance, as beasts of burden."

Pigs often show themselves to be anything but stupid. Edward Jesse gives the following instance of presence of mind, of nerve, and of the soundest good sense in sudden and serious danger. Fifteen young pigs had got

was hurt. They appeared to be sensible of the escape they had had by running back to the field, squeaking and capering with satisfaction.

An old pig has been known to work a pump handle with its mouth in order to obtain a supply of whey, and, as shown in the photograph above, the pig can be taught to ring a peal of bells. It does this, of course, mechanically and not by ear.

Has Bamboo Many Uses?

Bᴀᴍʙᴏᴏ is one of the most useful of plants, especially in countries like China, where it grows to a great size. The young shoots and seeds are used as food and the hard woody stems are excellent for building houses, making furniture, or constructing carts and agricultural implements. The tall stems also make excellent masts for sailing boats and the fibrous matter is used for constructing the walls of native houses. It is also woven into mats, screens, baskets, hats, clothes, and other utensils, and is plaited into ropes. The fibre is also used for the wicks of candles.

The sails of Chinese junks and the rigging are often made of bamboo, and the Chinese make paper from bamboo by hand processes. Attempts are now being made by European scientists to find some method of making paper on a large scale by machinery from bamboo. This would solve the prospective paper famine, for bamboo grows so rapidly that there would be no lack of material. Sections of the stem make vases and umbrella stands.

The difficulty is that when the stems become dry they often split. Bamboo stems are also used as water-pipes and for making bows and arrows.

Who Was Calamity Jane?

Cᴀʟᴀᴍɪᴛʏ Jᴀɴᴇ is a nickname that is often given to women out in the Far West of America who do something daring. The real name of the original Calamity Jane was Mary Burke, a kind but determined woman, absolutely fearless, a clever horse-woman and a dead shot. She became famous for her daring, and in the photograph on this page she is seen driving her own team of oxen in Texas.

Mary Burke, known as Calamity Jane, driving her ox team in Texas

What Makes Our Blood Red?

IN the liquid part of our blood, which is called plasma, there float hundreds of thousands of little discs called red corpuscles. Actually they are a deep yellow, but owing to their numbers they give the impression to the eye of redness.

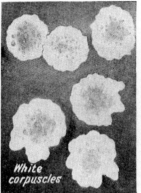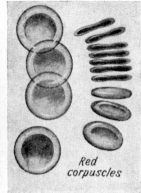

White and red blood corpuscles, greatly magnified

A red corpuscle is only one 3,200th of an inch in diameter, and about a third of that in thickness. It would take 10,000 of them piled one on another to make an inch, and at least 10,000,000 would be needed to cover a square inch. Half the weight of our blood consists of these red corpuscles.

Now each red corpuscle is a framework of protein, in the meshes of which is a colouring matter known as haemoglobin, and it is this that gives the red colour to the blood. It is a wonderful substance, for it is able to unite with oxygen gas and thus enable the red corpuscles to carry this vital gas from the lungs to the tissues in all parts of the body.

Does Lightning Ever Strike a Mine?

YES, a number of instances are on record where lightning has done damage to a mine. In December, 1913, eight native workers were killed in a Rand mine in South Africa when lightning struck a bell wire on the head-gear of the central shaft and, travelling down, detonated eleven dynamite cartridges 4,000 feet underground. Four other miners were badly injured.

On June 5th, 1855, a number of workers were occupied in the mines of Himmelsfurth in Austria. The labourers were dispersed along a load of ore when suddenly they all received violent shocks, distributed among them in the most curious and irregular manner. Some felt a blow upon the back, while their neighbours were struck about the arms or legs. It appeared as if they were roughly shaken by an invisible mysterious hand which at one instant came out of the ground and at another from the sides or roof of the gallery. One of the miners was thrown with force

against the wall; two others, whose backs were turned to each other, came suddenly together face to face. Each supposed that he had received a blow from the other in his back. What had happened was that a flash of lightning during a storm above had penetrated down the shaft a thousand feet underground.

On May 25th, 1845, a mine was struck at Freiberg in Saxony. An iron wire rope descended from the mouth to the level of the lowest gallery. A guard stood near each extremity, and the one above saw lightning strike the rope and pass down the mine. The guard below saw at the same instant a clear, vivid and sudden flame emanate from the other extremity of the wire rope. The light seemed to spread over the interior of the mine without injuring anyone with the slightest shock. The wire rope was about 1,500 feet long.

Is a Pound of Cork Heavier Than a Pound of Lead?

THIS may sound a foolish question, but actually the cork is heavier, because when they are weighed in air, the cork, being so bulky, is buoyed up much more than the dense pieces of lead. If a pound of cork and a pound of lead were counterpoised at opposite ends of a small balance in air, and the balance were then placed in a vacuum, the cork would weigh down its end of the balance.

Did Napoleon Smoke?

No, he disliked smoking. Once during his Egyptian campaign he tried to smoke, thinking this would be a preservative against the plague, but the tobacco made him cough a great deal, and he never smoked again. He was, however, an enthusiastic snuff-taker, and collected snuff-boxes.

How is Air Liquefied?

THE apparatus which turns air into a liquid is based upon the principle that when a gas is compressed its temperature rises and when it expands the temperature falls. During expansion the gas is really working and giving off energy in the form of heat.

A pump is connected with a coil of pipe surrounded by cold water. The pump forces the air at a pressure of about 200 atmospheres into the coil, where the temperature, which has risen owing to the pressure, is reduced by the coldness of the water outside the coil. The compressed air then passes up into a small pipe which runs inside a larger pipe through which cold water is circulating. Here it is cooled and, entering a chamber, expands, giving up more heat. The process is repeated several times, and at last the air is so cold that it becomes a liquid and drips from the small pipe as shown in the diagram. Any air not liquefied returns cold up the outer pipe to the pump. The liquid air is drawn off.

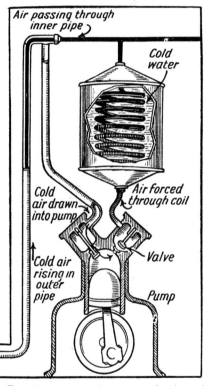

This diagram shows how air can be changed into a liquid

Does Any Bible Verse Contain Every Letter?

No; but the 21st verse of the 7th chapter of Ezra contains every letter of the alphabet except j. Here is the verse: " And I, even I, Artaxerxes the king, do make a decree to all the treasurers which are beyond the river, that whatsoever Ezra the priest, the scribe of the law of the god of heaven, shall require of you, it be done speedily." It is remarkable that all but one letter should be in one verse.

What is the Name of That Duck?

Here are examples of all the species of British wild ducks. The mallard is the commonest of these, and is found throughout Great Britain The gadwall is only a rare visitor, from autumn to spring. All the others are winter migrants, except the garganey, which comes to us in spring, and the pochard and tufted duck, which are partial residents, though the majority come to us in winter. The velvet-scoter and the ferruginous or white-eyed duck are rare winter visitors. A number of these ducks are nowadays to be found semi-tame on the lakes in public parks

A Hundred Familiar Varieties

Plate V

What is That Butterfly Called?

Here are coloured drawings of all the species of butterflies native to Great Britain. The Large Copper, formerly common in Britain, is now extinct, and some others are rare. Many Camberwell Beauties, for example, are not produced here, but are blown across from the Continent. The upper sides of the butterflies are shown, except in the Green Hairstreak. Here the underside is seen,

because that side has the green colouring that gives the butterfly its name. The upper side of the wings is brown, with a golden tinge above. The Mountain Ringlet is of local occurrence, being found during June and July in the Lake District, Scotland, and the west of Ireland. Of course, individuals of any species may vary in tint and markings. Here are the names of the butterflies:

Plate VI

All the Species Found in Britain

1. Purple Emperor. 2. Marbled White. 3. Chalk Hill Blue. 4. Adonis Blue. 5. Peacock. 6. Large Blue. 7. Holly Blue. 8. Large White. 9. White Admiral. 10. Brown Hairstreak. 11. Green Hairstreak. 12. Black-veined White. 13. Silver-studded Blue. 14. Small Blue. 15. Common Blue. 16. Small White. 17. Meadow Brown. 18. Gatekeeper. 19. White Letter Hairstreak. 20. Purple Hairstreak. 21. Black Hairstreak. 22. Green-veined White. 23. Painted Lady. 24. Wood White. 25. Speckled Wood. 26. Small Copper. 27. Grayling. 28. Camberwell Beauty. 29. Large Heath. 30. Scotch Argus. 31. Small Heath. 32. Orange Tip. 33. Swallow Tail. 34. Mountain Ringlet. 35. Ringlet. 36. Wall. 37. Dingy Skipper. 38. Large Tortoiseshell. 39. Comma. 40. Marsh Fritillary. 41. Brown Argus. 42. Pale Clouded Yellow. 43. Lulworth Skipper. 44. Brimstone. 45. Chequered Skipper. 46. Clouded Yellow. 47. Large Skipper. 48. Grizzled Skipper. 49. Essex Skipper. 50. Small Tortoiseshell. 51. Duke of Burgundy Fritillary. 52. Silver-washed Fritillary. 53. Queen of Spain Fritillary. 54. Small Pearl-bordered Fritillary. 55. Silver-spotted Skipper. 56. Pearl-bordered Fritillary. 57. Red Admiral. 58. Small Skipper. 59. Heath Fritillary. 60. High Brown Fritillary 61. Glanville Fritillary. 62. Dark Green Fritillary. Some of these are rare

What is That British Caterpillar?

Here are a hundred British caterpillars, some of butterflies and others of moths, in their natural colours. Except where "butterfly" is mentioned, the caterpillars are those of moths. Their names are : 1. Poplar Hawk. 2. Water Betony Shark. 3. Lettuce Shark. 4. Silver-washed Fritillary Butterfly. 5. Great Prominent. 6. Dark Green Fritillary Butterfly. 7. Clifden Nonpareil. 8. Emperor. 9. Lunar Marbled Brown. 10. Kentish Glory. 11. Lackey. 12. Heath Fritillary Butterfly. 13. Wood White Butterfly. 14. Pebble Prominent. 15. Iron Prominent. 16. Sprawler. 17. Death's Head. 18. White Satin. 19. Dark Tussock. 20. Common Wainscot. 21. Great Oak Beauty. 22. Painted Lady Butterfly. 23. Pale Tussock. 24. Camberwell Beauty Butterfly. 25. Old Lady. 26. Poplar Kitten. 27. Vapourer. 28. Broad-bordered Yellow Underwing. 29. Sword Grass.

30. Spurge Hawk. 31. Cinnabar. 32. Pale Brindled B[eauty] Hawk. 35. Gold Tail. 36. Common Magpie. 37. Merve[ille] and Salt. 40. Copper Underwing. 41. Small Coppe[r] 43. Ground Lackey. 44. Comma Butterfly. 45. Cloude[d] 48. Clifden Blue Butterfly. 49. Eyed Hawk. 50. Lesser [——] fly 52. Grass Eggar. 53. Goat. 54. Scarce Lappet. [——] Leopard. 58. Red Admiral Butterfly. 59. Grey Dagg[er] 62. Puss. 63 Glanville Fritillary Butterfly 64 G[——]

A.S.N.

What is a Hedger and Ditcher ?

THE hedger and ditcher is an agricultural labourer who makes, trims and repairs hedges, and digs ditches and keeps them free from

A Shropshire hedger at work, trimming back the bushes

undergrowth so that the water can run away and thus serve for the proper drainage of the fields.

This is really very important work, though when agriculture is suffering badly from depressed prices it is not carried out as extensively as it should be owing to the farmer's lack of means.

In the old days of open common fields, the absence of hedges was bad for the crops, for there was nothing to give shelter from the drying and scorching winds, and in the open wastes and meadows the live stock sadly needed shelter and shade. The enclosure of the land led to the formation of hedges and the digging of more ditches for drainage. Old writers on agriculture like Thomas Tusser in his " Five Hundred Points of Good Husbandrie " emphasize the importance of keeping the hedges in a good state of repair.

> Let pasture be stored and fenced about, and tillage set forward, as needeth without ;
> Before ye do open your purse to begin, with anything doing for fancy within.

And again, " Keep safely and warely thine uttermost fence."

Milton also refers to the hedger in his " Comus " :

> What time the labour'd ox
> In his loose traces from the furrow came
> And the swink'd hedger at his supper sat.

Swinked is an old English word meaning fatigued or overtired.

Why Did the Flagellants Whip Themselves ?

THE Flagellants were a body of fanatics who in the Middle Ages believed that by whipping themselves they could appease the divine wrath

An association of flagellants, founded about 1260, spread all over Europe, and its members used to march about in long procession publicly lashing one another on the bare back till the blood ran. Hecker regards the movement as one of the strange epidemics of the Middle Ages.

Like many other fanatical movements, disorders resulted, and the movement was suppressed ; but in 1348 and subsequent years it was revived with demoralising results.

What is a Caveat ?

THIS is a legal term meaning " let him beware." It is an intimation to the proper officer of a court of justice that he is to prevent the taking of any step, such, for example. as the granting of probate, without notice being given to the person interested, who is known as the caveator, so that he may appear and make an objection if he wishes.

Where Are There Springs of Bubbling Paint ?

ON the edge of the Salton Sea, a lake in Southern California, there is a strange volcanic region where geysers spout, not boiling water, but a thick liquid of varied colours, which has proved a useful substitute for paint. The region is pitted with scores of geysers, but few travellers go there, because of the many deadly quicksands and the intense heat. The region is known popularly as " Hell's Kitchen," and that also is the name given to a store and eating-house, the only permanent habitation in the area.

The pigment geysers are weird-looking hollows or basins three feet or more in diameter, and in them can be seen the liquid, which has the consistency of thick mud, bubbling as the steam rises through it from beneath. Different geysers have different colours, varying from a dirty white to a dark brown. Geologists are not quite clear as to the reason for the colours.

The store in " Hell's Kitchen " is painted with pigment supplied by the geysers. Quantities of this are also supplied to builders and oil-and-colour-men in the Imperial Valley close by. It is said to be equal in body, colour and durability to any paint on the market. There is some talk of packing it in tins for the market, instead of allowing it to run to waste as it does now

The strange geysers of the Salton Sea district in Southern California, which yield a natural paint

How is Jack Frost Fought in the Orchards?

IN California frosts are rare, but if one occurs suddenly it may ruin a whole crop of citrous fruits, like oranges and grape-fruit, worth thousands of pounds. To fight Jack Frost

How the temperature of the Californian orchards is raised by means of a scientific windmill, which pours out heated air that prevents the frost from reaching the plants

the orchard keepers place oil burners at intervals in the avenues between the trees. Directly the thermometer shows that the danger point has been reached the flares are lighted and they give sufficient heat to keep the temperature in the orchard just above freezing-point. The wind disperses the heat, so that all the trees are reached by the warmth.

So effective has this method of fighting the frost proved that a new device has recently been invented for use in the orchards, which does away with the necessity for smudge-pots, as the oil burners are called. This new device is known as a "scientific windmill." The apparatus contains a built-in air-heater and an oscillating motor-driven blower which disperses the heat. The windmill is built on a concrete foundation, and a number of the devices are set up in different parts of the orchard. Then, according to the direction of the wind, any windmill can be set working and the wind is made the channel for conveying the heat to the trees.

Are We Moving When in Bed?

WE may appear to be lying very still, and except for the movement of our breathing we may appear to be quite still. Nevertheless, we are really moving very rapidly, but, of course, the movement is not relative to the bedroom or the street in which we live. We are travelling with the Earth in many different directions.

First of all the Earth is rushing round on its axis, and at the Equator the rate is over a thousand miles an hour. Then the Earth is rushing round the Sun in its orbit at the rate of 18½ miles a second or 66,000 miles an hour. In addition, the Sun with the Earth and the rest of the planets is tearing through Space in the direction of the star Vega at about 40,000 miles an hour.

In every case we are travelling with the Earth, so that when we appear to be so stationary we are actually being whirled along in various directions at speeds that make an express train, or even a fast aeroplane, look almost stationary. In one direction alone—that is, moving with the Earth in its orbit round the Sun—even a bed-ridden person travels about 145 million miles in three months.

Are Alligators Kept as Pets?

SMALL alligators have long been kept as pets, but about 1937 it became more and more fashionable to keep baby alligators and large numbers were imported into England from Florida. Of course, when very young they are harmless, but as they grow they become rather dangerous pets to harbour, and are often then sent by their owners to zoos and menageries.

The female alligator makes a nest among the bushes or reeds fifty or sixty yards from the water's edge, and lays anything up to a hundred white eggs about the size of a hen's egg but a little longer and more elliptical in shape. These eggs are covered with leaves and other vegetable matter, and the heat caused by the decomposition of this vegetation in a hot and sunny land like Florida is sufficient to cause the young alligators to hatch out. When they emerge they are led to the water by their mother, who has all the time been watching and guarding the eggs. The young alligators are then collected and sent to different parts to be sold as pets.

A group of young alligators after their arrival in England to be sold as pets

How is That Ladder Used?

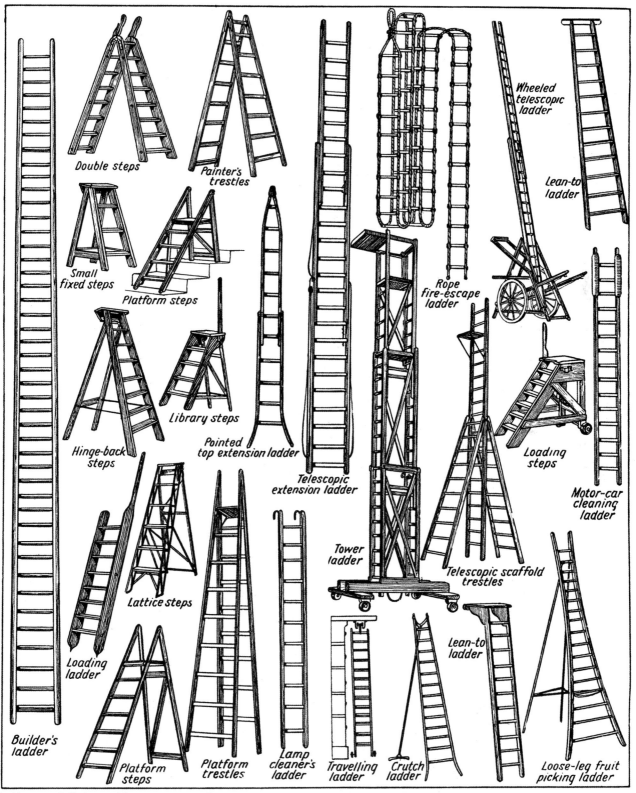

Double steps

Painter's trestles

Small fixed steps

Platform steps

Library steps

Hinge-back steps

Pointed top extension ladder

Telescopic extension ladder

Wheeled telescopic ladder

Lean-to ladder

Rope fire-escape ladder

Loading steps

Motor-car cleaning ladder

Lattice steps

Loading ladder

Tower ladder

Telescopic scaffold trestles

Lean-to ladder

Builder's ladder

Platform steps

Platform trestles

Lamp cleaner's ladder

Travelling ladder

Crutch ladder

Loose-leg fruit picking ladder

Ladders are of all sizes and forms, their particular construction depending upon the purpose for which they are to be used. The ordinary builder's ladder is shown on the left, but sometimes a lean-to ladder has a board across the top, enabling it to be placed against an uneven surface. It may even have a platform at the top for holding a paint-pot or pail. It is also sometimes wider at the foot. Ladders are sometimes made to extend, to increase their length in use, but to enable them to be stored away compactly. A lamp-cleaner's ladder has hooks at the top to rest over the bar projecting from the lamp-post. Sometimes extension ladders come to a point at the top, enabling them to be rested against a very small surface. Motor-car cleaning ladders have adjustable pads, so that they shall not damage the surface of the car. A loading ladder has a handle at the top, by which the man can steady himself while turning off his load. A travelling ladder works on a rail and can be moved along the ground. Tower ladders are for repairing overhead electric lights. Lattice steps, being very light, are now used for domestic purposes. The other examples explain themselves

What is a Doss-House?

THIS is a slang term for a cheap lodging-house, so called because to go to sleep is to doss. Probably the word doss is a corruption of dorse, meaning the back, a reference to sleeping or lying on the back when resting. Dr. Brewer derives it from doss, a hassock stuffed with straw or a straw bed. Dossel is an old word for a bundle of straw or hay.

What is the Swede?

THE swede is the most valued member of the turnip family. It gets its name from the fact that it was originally called the Swedish turnip. It is more valuable than the turnip because it is not only more nutritious, but is also more hardy. It is distinguished from other turnips by having smoother leaves, which are of a bluish colour.

Another distinction is that the swede has at the crown of the root a " neck," from which the leaves spring and which is absent from the other kinds of turnips. Swedes also keep much better through the winter, and are able to resist frost to a much greater extent. In the rotation of crops swedes are generally grown following the wheat crop.

Of course, like most other root crops, the swede is composed chiefly of water. No less than 89·23 per cent. consists of water, about 1 per cent. albuminous compounds containing nitrogen, and 5·54 per cent. consists of sugar. For the feeding of stock the swede is a very useful plant, and it has been enormously improved in modern times. Swedes are now grown three or four times as big as a man's head. It is the development of root crops in modern times that has enabled cattle and other live stock to be kept healthily through the winters.

A group of huge swedes exhibited at an agricultural show in South Wales

What is Brandy Made From ?

BRANDY is a spirit distilled from fermented grape juice. The best qualities are distilled from white wines and the inferior qualities from red wines. When first distilled the brandy is colourless and remains so if kept in glass vessels. But when it is stored in casks the spirit dissolves the colouring matter of the wood and becomes yellowish. Dark coloured brandies have had caramel, or burnt sugar, added to them.

The peculiar aroma, or *goût*, as it is called, is caused by the presence in the brandy of small quantities of various ethers. The largest quantities of brandy are manufactured in the South of France, and the best qualities in the Cognac district, hence their name " Cognac." In England brandy is made from grain spirit and flavoured with oil to imitate Cognac.

What is Berserk Rage ?

IT is war-like fierceness, and is so called after the Berserkers, wild warriors of the old Norse folklore. They were supposed to be able to assume animal shapes, especially those of the bear and wolf. They wore the skins of these animals, and then in fierce rage they howled and growled.

How Long Are Star Photographs Exposed ?

WE should not know how vast is the number of stars in the heavens, if we had to rely upon our eyesight, even with the aid of powerful telescopes. Something more than the big

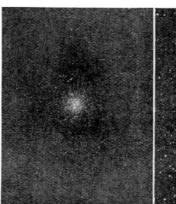

Two photographs of a star cluster in the constellation Hercules. The first one had a six-minute exposure, and the second one a 94-minute exposure

telescope is needed to see what exists in distant space and that is the camera. The camera with a sensitive plate can pick out far more stars than could ever be detected with the astronomer's eye looking through the telescope.

By increasing the time of exposure smaller and smaller stars are recorded on the photographic plate, and as telescopes, cameras and plates are all becoming more efficient there would seem to be eventually hardly any limit to the faintness of the stars that can be photographed. There is already a 100-inch reflector telescope and soon there will be a 200-inch reflector. What wonders that, in conjunction with the camera, will reveal none can say at present.

The reason stars too faint to be seen by the human eye can be photographed is that by a long exposure the photographic plate can store up light till the star appears on it. Plates are often exposed for four or five hours and sometimes for longer periods. The two photographs given here show how many more stars will appear with an extra hour and a half's exposure.

There is no doubt that in searching the depths of space we owe quite as much to the camera and the sensitive plate as we do to the telescope.

What Are Aqua-Fortis and Aqua-Regia?

THE former is the commercial name of dilute nitric acid. The words mean " strong water," and are given because of the corrosive action of the fluid. Aqua-regia, meaning " royal water," is a mixture of nitric acid and hydrochloric acid in the proportions of one of the former to two of the latter. The name was given because it alone would dissolve gold, regarded as the king of metals.

Who Uses That Musical Instrument?

Siamese Gong

African Wooden Gong

Chinese Cymbals

West African War Bell

African girl's dancing belt

African Bamboo Gong

Snake charmer's Pipe

Egyptian Pan's Pipes

Javanese Bamboo Bells

African Lyre

Burmese Harp

Egyptian Lyre

Malay Metal Drum

Dahomeyan War Drum

South African Drum

Syrian Bagpipe

Siamese Drum

Siamese Metal Drum

Sandwich Island Drum

Haitian Drum

Moorish Pottery Drum

West African Drum

Syrian Pottery Drum

British Columbian carved Rattles

Cingalese Double Kettle-drum

Alaskan Shell Rattle

Korean Drum

African Sansa

African Zanse

Phillipine Bamboo Clapper

Alaskan Goat-hoof Rattle

Alaskan Clapper

Chinese Balloon Guitar

On this page are given a large number of native musical instruments used by primitive peoples in different parts of the world, and in addition are given some instruments used by such people as the Chinese, Japanese and Siamese. The drums, as can be seen, are of all shapes and forms, though the principle is the same in all cases. The African dancing belt is, of course, worn round the waist, and the small bells attached to the girdle ring as the dancer goes through her evolutions. In the African sansa and zanse a number of bent metal strips are arranged on a board and are played by plucking. Some of the instruments, like the Burmese harp, are of highly artistic form. As can be seen, gongs are made not only of metal but also of wood and bamboo. The drumsticks for the Cingalese double kettledrum are of curious form, having flat rings instead of knobs

Who Was Phaethon?

THE name means " the shining one," and was used as a surname of Helios or the Sun. The same name was also given to a son of Helios, whose mother was Clymene. Being so pre-

Phaethon trying to drive the chariot of the Sun, from an old sculpture

sumptuous as to ask his father to allow him to drive the chariot of the Sun across the heavens for a day, he was allowed to do so, but found himself too weak to check the horses. They rushed off their usual course, and came so near to the Earth as almost to set it on fire. For this Zeus killed him with a flash of lightning, and hurled him down the river Eridanus. Phaethon's sisters, who had yoked the horses to the chariot, were changed into poplar trees, and their tears into amber.

How Far Apart Are the Stars?

ALTHOUGH, as we look up, the stars seem to be very close together, they are, as a matter of fact, hundreds of millions of miles apart, and that is why they do not come into collision.

Sir James Jeans has told us that Space is so vast that it is emptier than anything we can imagine. If only three wasps were left alive in the whole of Europe, he says, the area of Europe would be more crowded with wasps than Space is with stars. That will give us some idea of how far apart the stars are.

How Big Are the Tusks of a Hippopotamus?

THE huge head of the hippopotamus appears as if it were too big for the body, and, indeed, the animal may often be seen resting its muzzle on the ground as though to relieve the neck from the strain of its weight.

The gigantic mouth when opened to the widest is described by Mr. R. Lydekker as " one of the ugliest sights in Nature, looking like a huge red cavern." From the edges project the enormous tusks and incisor or cutting teeth. The tusks or canines are by far the largest of the teeth in the animal's jaws and are curved backward in a bold sweep, with their extremities bevelled off obliquely by mutual wear. These tusks grow throughout the animal's life. There

are never more than two pairs, those of the upper jaw being directed downward, while the lower ones project forward in advance of the jaw. One of the largest recorded pairs of lower tusks has a total length of $31\frac{1}{2}$ inches each along the curve and a circumference at the base of over 9 inches. The sides of the animal's jaws are provided with seven pairs of cheek teeth.

The hippopotamus is, next to the elephant, the bulkiest of existing land mammals. A male which lived for many years in the London Zoo measured 12 feet from the tip of the snout to the root of the tail, the length of the latter being 22 inches. The weight of this animal was about 4 tons.

Sir Samuel Baker, the famous African traveller and hunter, tells of an old male, measured by himself, the length of which was $14\frac{1}{4}$ feet from the snout to the end of the tail, the latter being only 9 inches. The hide alone, when removed from the body, weighed a quarter of a ton.

In an earlier age the hippopotamus was common in England and ranged as far north as what is now Yorkshire.

The hippopotamus at the London Zoo, with its mouth open, showing the tusks. This animal is given many pounds of onions as a preventive against catching colds

Hippopotamus tusks have often been carved by the natives of Africa, and some of them date back several centuries and show a good deal of artistic merit. They are much sought after.

How Long Have Toothpicks Been Used?

WHILE the toothbrush is only as old as the end of the 18th century, the toothpick is a very ancient device. It has been used by civilised people right through the ages. Agathocles was poisoned by means of a medicated quill handed to him after dinner in 289 B.C., and Martial, the Roman author, mentions toothpicks in his Epigrams.

What is the Annus Mirabilis?

THESE Latin words mean " wonderful year " and are used to denote a year marked out by remarkable events. They are specifically applied in English history to the year 1666, memorable for the Great Fire of London and the important naval battles, those of the North Foreland and the Goodwins, in which the English defeated the Dutch. Dryden commemorated these events in his poem " Annus Mirabilis."

Whose Dog Was Called Diamond?

THIS was Sir Isaac Newton's favourite little dog. One winter morning, while Newton was attending early service in Trinity College Chapel, Cambridge, he left Diamond shut up in his room. On returning he found that the dog had upset a candle on his desk and destroyed some papers which bore the results of years of experiment. On seeing this irreparable loss, Newton merely exclaimed, " Oh, Diamond, Diamond, thou little knowest the mischief thou hast done ! "

Which British Lighthouse Is That?

Bishop Rock. Scilly Isles — Round Island. Scilly Isles — Wolf Rock. English Channel — The Longships. Lands End — Lizard Head. Cornwall — St. Anthony's. Falmouth

Eddystone. English Channel — The Needles. Isle of Wight — Hurst. Isle of Wight — Beachy Head. Sussex — North Foreland. Kent — The Chapman. Thames Estuary

Maplin Sands. North Sea — Flamborough Head. Yorkshire — Bell Rock. Scotland — Rattray Head. Scotland — North Unst. Shetland Islands — Flannan Islands. Outer Hebrides

Skerryvore. Scotland — Dhu-Heartach. Scotland — Point of Ayre. Isle of Man — Douglas Head. Isle of Man — Chicken Rock. Isle of Man — South Stack. Holyhead

St Ann's Head. Milford Haven — The Smalls. Bristol Channel — Hartland Point. Devonshire — Trevose Head. Cornwall — Godrevy. St. Ives — Fastnet. S. Ireland

Here are thirty of the most famous lighthouses round the British coasts, most of which will be familiar to those who go to the seaside or travel in coasting steamers. As can be seen, those that stand in exposed situations on rocks all follow one main design, that of the trunk of a tree. With a broad base keyed into the solid rock, and tapering towards the top, this shape has been found to resist wind and wave most securely. For many feet up a lighthouse of this type is solid stone, and it is all so keyed together and to the rock that it becomes an actual part of the rock. The lighthouses are given roughly in the order in which we should see them if we travelled round the coast starting at the Scilly Isles and proceeding via the English Channel to Scotland. Some of the lighthouses are known as iron pile lighthouses because they are based on a network structure of iron girders

Why Can We Skate on Ice But Not on Glass?

Skating—that is, moving rapidly over the surface of ice—is possible because the smoothness of the ice and the smoothness of the shiny metal skate blade reduce the friction between the two surfaces almost to

nothing. At the same time, skating must be learned, because on a surface where it is easy to slip about in all directions it is not easy to keep one's balance. But once the art of preserving one's balance on the ice is acquired, enormous speeds and astonishing evolutions are possible on skates.

When we are standing or walking on ordinary ground, we do not slip and fall, because the friction between our shoe soles and the ground prevents the one slipping easily over the other.

We may perhaps wonder why it is that if we can skate so easily over an ice surface, we cannot equally well skate over glass, for the latter is smooth and looks like ice. When we skate on ice we give ourselves a constant series of pushes forward by sticking the edge of the skate into the ice and pushing backward. The reaction drives us forward. Of course, we stick the blade into the ice only the merest fraction, but it is sufficient to give a grip and enable us to push off.

On glass, however, we cannot get the necessary push. The glass, unlike the ice, is too hard for the blade of the skate to make any impression, and absence of friction merely causes the blade to slip backwards over the glass.

Thus we cannot get the grip which will enable us to give ourselves the little push off.

But even if the skate would make an impression in the glass, the little holes thus made would not fill up, and soon the tiny fragments of glass all over the surface would increase friction and prevent skating. On ice, the slight indentations made by the skaters soon fill up with water and become frozen over again.

The progress of a roller-skater is rather different. Here, instead of overcoming sliding friction, as in the case of the skate's blade on the ice, the rolling friction between the wheels of the skates and the surface over which they run is reduced to a minimum. But, curiously enough, it would be impossible, or at

any rate difficult, to travel over ice on roller skates, for there must be a certain amount of friction between the wheel and the ground to give grip to the rollers to enable them to turn. It is one of the paradoxes of life that, though we try to eliminate friction, we cannot do without it.

A party of children roller-skating on the sea-front at Hove, Sussex

Is There a New Bell Bigger Than Big Ben?

The biggest bell in Great Britain is Great Paul at St. Paul's Cathedral, and till 1938 Big Ben, 13½ tons, was the second in size. But in that year Lord Vestey and his brother Sir Edward Vestey presented a huge bell weighing 14½ tons and costing £6,800 to Liverpool Cathedral. Thus Big Ben, though still the most famous bell in the world, is now only the third in size in Great Britain.

Who Were the Seven Sleepers of Ephesus?

They were seven young Christians who, according to an ancient legend, sought to escape persecution under Decius by hiding in a cave at Ephesus. Their enemies closed the mouth of the cave, but 200 years later, when the cave was discovered and opened, the seven Christians awoke from sleep, youthful and in good health.

How is Oxygen Supplied in Hospitals?

The oxygen is obtained from firms that prepare it and supply it under pressure in strong metal cylinders and it is then carried to any part of the hospital where it may be required. But at the new Westminster Hospital, following the plan carried out in one or two of the larger existing hospitals, an original method of conveying oxygen to the wards and operating theatres has been devised. The gas is supplied through a pipe-line to various points in the wards throughout the hospital and to the theatres. This up-to-date method is both more economical and more efficient than the old method.

Why is a Flat Map Inaccurate?

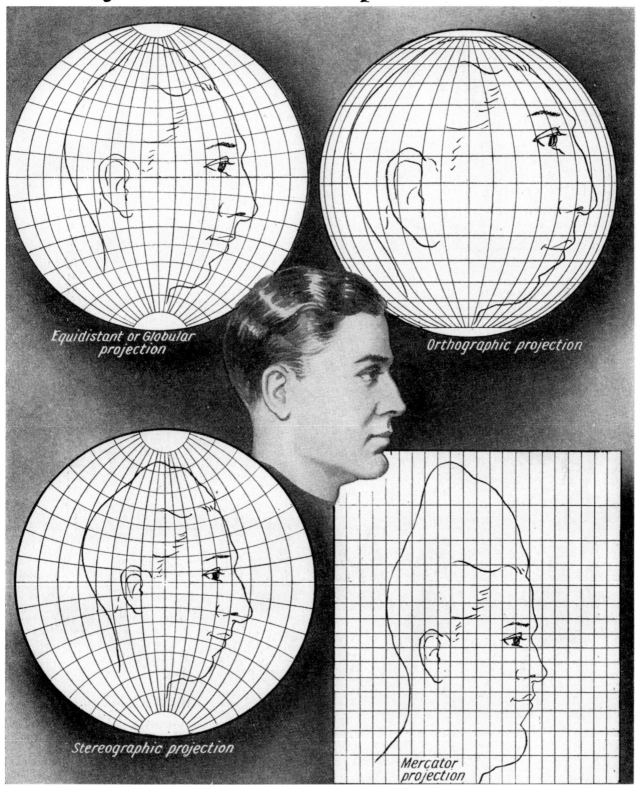

Equidistant or Globular projection

Orthographic projection

Stereographic projection

Mercator projection

The Earth on which we live is a sphere and as no portion of a sphere can be represented properly on a flat surface, all the maps in our atlases are more or less inaccurate. That it is impossible to spread out any part of a sphere flat we can prove for ourselves by taking the peel of an orange and trying to press it flat on the table. If one part is levelled fairly well another part becomes much distorted. The only accurate map of the world is a globe, but as a globe is so inconvenient for carrying about, we must have flat maps. Different methods of representing the Earth or part of its surface on a flat sheet are used and these are known as projections. Each has its particular advantages for certain purposes, and for small areas the flat map may be fairly accurate. It is when we come to large sections of the Earth's surface that the distortion becomes so apparent. The drawings on this page will show very clearly how great, and how varied, is the distortion. In the centre is a portrait of a man's head reproduced by perspective, and in the four corners will be seen the same head drawn according to various map projections. We can see in the last example why a Mercator map shows Greenland and the North so much bigger than they really are, while the orthographic projection greatly distorts the centre portion

Who Was Hecate ?

SHE was one of the Titans, and was honoured by all the immortal gods, being endued with extensive power. She was in later times identified with several other deities—Selene or Luna in Heaven, Artemis or Diana on Earth, and Persephone or Proserpina in the lower world. Because of this she was supposed to send at night demons and phantoms from the

Hecate, one of the Titans, from an ancient statue

lower world, and she taught sorcery and witchcraft. Her approach when she wandered about with the souls of the dead was announced by the whining and howling of dogs.

Does Big Ben Swing ?

THERE was a popular song sung in 1938, part of the refrain of which was "Swing Big Ben Over London Town," followed by a sound resembling the booming of Big Ben. But Big Ben does not swing. It is far too big a bell to be rung by swinging, weighing as it does thirteen and a half tons. This, the best-known bell in the world, is sounded by being struck from the outside by a hammer that weighs four hundredweights.

The huge clock is worked by heavy weights of nearly two and a half tons that are suspended on wire ropes wound round drums. The weights run down nearly the whole depth of the clock tower. As the central drum turns it works a series of toothed and bevelled wheels which turn a shaft, and this again, by means of another series of toothed and bevelled wheels, turns the shafts that work the hands of the clock faces. By an elaborate series of toothed wheels and cams, a lever is operated which pulls a rope and moves the clapper that strikes the great bell.

Was Queen Victoria Ever Hissed By Society ?

YES ; she became very unpopular in her early days owing to a line of action which she took with regard to the ladies of her household on a change of ministry. Lord Melbourne's government was defeated and resigned, and Sir Robert Peel was asked to form a ministry. He was willing, but when, according to custom, he wanted to replace the ladies of the household with his own nominees, Queen Victoria, then young and inexperienced, objected. She had become

attached to the ladies who had served under Lord Melbourne's premiership and insisted that these should be retained in their positions. Of course, Sir Robert Peel could not agree to this, and declined to form a ministry. Thereupon the Queen sent again for Lord Melbourne and he carried on the Government, the female entourage remaining in office.

At Ascot races a week or two later the Queen was hissed by some of the Society persons present, though who these were did not become known. The "Morning Post" of June 25th, 1839, said : "At the last Ascot races we have reason to believe that the Duchess of Montrose and Lady Sarah Ingestre received an intimation that her Majesty was impressed with the idea that they were among the persons who had hissed at a moment when no sounds but those of applause, gratulation and loyalty ought to have been heard. It was, we believe, further intimated to the noble ladies we have mentioned that the royal ear had been abused, to the effect already stated by Lady Lichfield. The ladies, who had reason to think that they had been thus unjustly and ridiculously accused, applied immediately to their supposed accuser, who denied that she had made any such communication."

The matter created a great stir, and on July 5th the "Times" published a denial.

"We are authorised," it said, "to give the most positive denial to a report which has been inserted in most of the public papers that the Countess of Lichfield informed the Queen that the Duchess of Montrose and Lady Sarah Ingestre hissed her Majesty on the racecourse at Ascot. Lady Lichfield never insinuated any such report."

The episode is known in English history as "the Bedchamber Crisis."

How Can Headquarters Know Where a Bus Is ?

THE London Passenger Transport Board has introduced an idea into motor-bus transport which has never been tried anywhere else. Eventually all buses are to carry on their roofs a coil of wire through which an alternating current is passing. At certain points on the bus route wires are sus-

A motor-bus passing under the fixed wire which transmits electric current to a clock in the central office and indicates the bus's position

pended across the roadway and as the bus passes under this wire, the current in the coil on the roof will induce a current in the fixed wire. This will be amplified and transmitted by wire to the central office, where it will record the passing of the bus on a clock face. Thus eventually the movements of all buses will be automatically recorded on dials at headquarters.

The clock on which a bus's position at any particular moment is recorded

Why Has New York So Many Skyscrapers?

NEW YORK is now a great city of 309 square miles, with a population of about seven millions, but the original New York and the central

A striking view of New York, showing the large number of lofty skyscrapers, which are really streets on end. Two American Navy dirigibles can be seen hovering over the city

part of the city today is confined to a long, narrow island called Manhattan. This is the business centre of New York and the difficulties of extending the business area are far greater than in the City of London, for being surrounded by water any access to adjacent districts involves the crossing of a bridge or the passing through a subterranean tunnel.

All important business concerns want to have their headquarters in the very centre of the commercial city, and so, as it is impossible to extend horizontally on Manhattan Island, the business city has grown perpendicularly. There are scores of buildings higher than St. Paul's Cathedral, and two at least higher than the Eiffel Tower. These are really streets set on end, rather than individual buildings. Thousands of workers find employment in each one of these skyscrapers, and when they all pour out at the close of the working day, the terrible congestion in the streets and on the bridges and in the subways can hardly be imagined.

What Was the Largest Cheese Ever Made?

IT is said to have been a great Cheddar cheese presented to Queen Victoria on February 19th, 1841. It was made from the morning's milking of 737 cows, and prepared by the labour of fifty dairymaids at West Pennard, Somerset. The cheese was octagonal in shape and weighed 11 hundredweights. Its upper surface was decorated with the Royal arms, surmounted with a wreath of roses, thistles and shamrocks. It had been made two years before, but was not considered fit to eat for another eighteen months after the presentation.

Cheese is a very old form of food, and was eaten as far back as 1400 B.C. The Greeks and Egyptians made it from the milk of sheep, goats and mares, and in the Middle Ages it was made from deer's milk.

What Causes the Click of the Train?

WHEN we travel by train we are always conscious of a clickety-click sound that goes on all the time and becomes more noticeable as the train slows down. This is caused by the wheels passing over the joints between the rails, and for a long time engineers have been trying to find some way of getting rid of this noise and making railway travelling quieter.

As most people know, a space has always been left between adjacent rails, because it has been supposed that the changes of temperature would vary the length of the rails so much that sometimes in hot weather, when the Sun was pouring down upon them, they would lengthen sufficiently to buckle or bend. Space was therefore left between contiguous rails to allow for expansion.

Strangely enough, however, recent research and experiments have shown that this idea is largely an illusion, and that rails can be made as long as 1,500 feet without any danger. Such experiments have been carried out both in England and the United States, and it is likely that in the future long rails of this kind will be used on railway tracks and we shall have much less noise when we travel. The noise is, of course, greatest in tunnels, where sounds are echoed and re-echoed, thereby being magnified, and on the London underground railways lengths of rail are, at places, being welded together, thus eliminating many of the gaps that cause the trouble. The joints between rails are the weakest parts of a track, and it is therefore a great advantage to cut them down in number as far as possible, by using longer rails.

Railway metals, each 1,500 feet long, ready to be placed in position near New York City

Of What Are Baskets Made?

Baskets are among the most useful of containers, for not only are they light in weight, but they are much stronger than might be supposed from the frail material from which they are woven, and their elasticity enables them to endure a great deal of rough usage, where often a more rigid object would be cracked or broken.

Basket work dates back to the most ancient times, but there is no sign of it becoming obsolete even in these modern times when containers are made of such a vast variety of materials. More baskets of one kind and another are made today than were ever made before and, as can be seen in the photograph on page 288 showing a basket-worker engaged in his trade, the process is still carried out by hand just as it was thousands of years ago. Indeed, it would probably be difficult to find any industry which has changed less in the course of the centuries.

Baskets are made mostly from willow branches, and though these are largely grown in Holland, France and Germany, English willows are still regarded as the finest in the world.

Much attention is paid in England and Scotland to the cultivation of willows for basket-making.

The particular willows used for basket-making are known as osiers. They are of low bushy growth and rarely reach any great height. Their value, of course, depends upon the length and slenderness of their branches, which must also be supple and tough. They are not allowed to grow into trees. For the larger types of baskets the common osier is used, but for the finer kinds other species are better. The branches are cut once a year, those intended for brown baskets being dried and stacked, and those for white baskets being soaked and peeled.

Shopping basket
Pastry basket
Green-grocer's bushel basket
Dog-basket
Hamper
Work-basket
Fruiterer's arm basket
Picnic basket
Butcher's arm-basket
Baker's arm basket
Log basket
Angler's basket
Wastepaper basket
Stone jar basket
Egg display basket
Wheeled laundry basket
Small work-basket
Hooded dog-basket
Laundry basket
Grocer's arm-basket
Baby basket
Strawberry basket
Cutlery basket
Builder's rubbish basket
Umbrella basket
Workman's lunch basket
Bicycle basket
Office letter basket
Jardiniere
Linen basket
Collar basket
Theatrical travelling basket
Flower basket
Washing basket
Bottle basket

Here are the principal types of baskets which are made and sold in Great Britain. Their names explain their various uses

Which Small British Isle is Most Populous?

THE Isle of Wight is the most populous of the smaller islands of the British group, its population at the 1931 census being 88,454. Jersey is next with 50,462 inhabitants, then the Isle of Man with 49,308, and Guernsey fourth with 42,743.

How Did Amen Corner in London Get Its Name?

THIS thoroughfare like the adjacent Paternoster Row, Ave Maria Lane and Creed Lane are all under the shadow of St. Paul's Cathedral, and their names date from the time when the ecclesiastics and priests lived round about, and the text-writers and rosary-makers had their shops there.

What Are Mr., Mrs. and Miss in Other Languages?

BELOW is a list of European countries with the words they use corresponding to the English Mr., Mrs. and Miss. In Irish the words used are nearly equivalent to Esquire, and in addresses are put after the surname of a man and between the Christian and surnames of women. The words used in pre-War Russia corresponded to our Mr., Mrs. and Miss, but those used in Russia today are more like our Citizen. Of course, the Russian alphabet is different from the Roman which is used in England. There are more letters, and the words in Russian appear thus:

Mr.	Mrs.	Miss
ГОСПОДИН	ГОСПОЖА	БАРЫШНЯ
ГРАЖДАНИН	ГРАЖДАНКА	ГРАЖДАНКА

but in the list below they have been printed with their English phonetic equivalents. Eire is the Irish Free State.

COUNTRY	MR.	MRS.	MISS
ALBANIA	Zotni	Zonje	Zonjushe
AUSTRIA	Herr	Frau	Fraulein
BELGIUM	Monsieur	Madame	Mademoiselle
BULGARIA	Gospodin	Gospoja	Gospojitza
CZECHOSLOVAKIA	Pan	Pani	Slecna
DENMARK	Herr	Fru	Froken
EIRE	Uasal	Ban Uasal	Uasal
ESTONIA	Harra	Proua	Preili
FINLAND	Herra	Rouva	Neiti
FRANCE	Monsieur	Madame	Mademoiselle
GERMANY	Herr	Frau	Fraulein
GREECE	Kyrios	Kyria	Thespaenis
HOLLAND	Mijnheer	Mevrouw	Juffrouw
HUNGARY	-Ur	-Ne	-Kisasszony
ITALY	Signor	Signora	Signorina
LATVIA	Kungs	Kundze	Jaunkundze
LITHUANIA	Ponas	Ponia	Panele
NORWAY	Herr	Fru	Froken
POLAND	Pan	Pani	Panna
PORTUGAL	Senhor	Senhora	Senhorita
RUSSIA :			
(Pre-Revolution)	Gospodin	Gospoda	Bapshchnya
(Soviet)	Grashdanin	Grashdanka	Grashdanka
RUMANIA	Domnul	Doamna	Domnisoara
SPAIN	Senor	Senora	Senorita
SWEDEN	Herr	Fru	Froken
YUGOSLAVIA	Gospodin	Gospodja	Gospodjica

How Long Did the Trial of Warren Hastings Last?

THE trial opened on February 13th, 1788, in Westminster Hall, amid great pomp, and with many adjournments the trial went on year after year until at last in the spring of 1795, nearly eight years after Hastings had been brought by the serjeant-at-arms of the Commons to the bar of the Lords, the verdict was given.

Many of the peers who had sat at the opening of the trial were dead, and only 29 peers voted, of whom 23 found Hastings not guilty. He was called to the bar and informed that the Lords had acquitted him, and was then solemnly discharged. Hastings declared that the arraignment had taken place before one generation, and the judgment was pronounced by another. The trial nearly ruined Hastings, costing him £70,000. The East India Company compensated him partly by lending him £50,000 free of interest, and granting him an annuity of £4,000. In later years Hastings was honoured by the Prince Regent, who made him a Privy Councillor, and he received honours also from the City and Parliament.

Why Do Onions Make Our Eyes Water?

EVERY time we blink a tear is squeezed from the lachrymal gland in the corner of the eye and spreads over the eyeball. This keeps the eyeball clean, and the tears escape through a duct into the nose. Thus our eyes may be said to be always watering, though in the ordinary way we do not notice the fact.

If, however, anything irritates the eyes, as when cold wind or dust blows into them, tears form more quickly

A worker in a pickle factory peeling onions. A volatile oil from the onions strikes the eyes and causes tears to flow

for the protection of the eyeball, and as there is too much water to escape into the nose through the usual duct, the water overflows and trickles down our cheeks.

This is what happens when we peel onions. The onion contains a white, acrid, volatile oil which escapes into the air when the onion is peeled or cut, and the particles of the oil, striking upon our eyeballs, make them smart. Then, for their protection, the tears begin to flow profusely. The rapid flow helps to shield the eyeballs from contact with the oil.

What is a Dorcas Society?

IT is a society of ladies who meet from time to time and make garments for the poor, and is named after Dorcas, who, as described in Acts IX 36, was "full of good works and alms-deeds," and made coats and garments for the poor. In these days of higher wages and unemployment benefit there is, of course, less need for such societies than formerly, when they were an important part of the organisation of most town churches.

What Kind of Loaf is That?

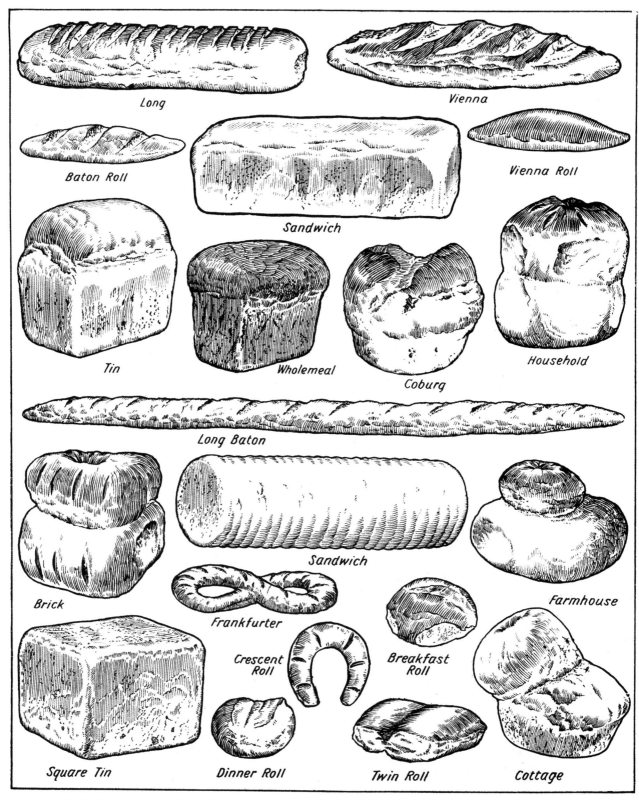

Long

Vienna

Baton Roll

Sandwich

Vienna Roll

Tin

Wholemeal

Coburg

Household

Long Baton

Brick

Sandwich

Frankfurter

Farmhouse

Crescent Roll

Breakfast Roll

Square Tin

Dinner Roll

Twin Roll

Cottage

The earliest kind of bread was made by soaking grain in water, pressing it, and then drying it in the sun or by artificial heat. Later, the grain was pounded in a mortar to make flour, but the greatest step forward was taken when leaven—that is, some kind of material to excite fermentation —was added. Probably the ancient Egyptians were the first to do this. The rising of the gas bubbles due to fermentation makes little pockets in the dough and lightens the loaf, which is always very heavy and compact without fermentation. Yeast is generally used nowadays as the leaven in the loaf. Loaves are made in many shapes, all of which have particular names, and some shapes are confined to particular varieties of bread. In the making of bread in Great Britain, different wheat flours are blended. Good bread requires three ingredients, flour, yeast and salt water. On this page are shown the different kinds of loaves generally sold. Bread, except for French rolls and fancy bread, must be sold by weight only

What Was Diana of the Ephesians?

IT was an image of the goddess Diana kept at Ephesus, and its shrine became a great place of pilgrimage. Quite an industry existed in the city of making little silver replicas of the image, which was popularly supposed to have fallen from Heaven, as described in the New Testament, Acts XIX, 24–38. Some think the original " image " may have been a meteorite, hence the legend, but Pliny tells us that the image was made of ebony.

Is Apple-Bobbing an Ancient Game?

YES; it dates back many centuries and has from far distant times been practised on All-Hallows Eve. Diving for apples floating in a tub of water is a variation of the bobbing

The game of bob-apple, from an ancient illuminated manuscript

game. The apple is suspended by a string from a beam, and the players, without using their hands to help them, have to try to take bites out of the apple while it swings, a very

Modern children playing at bob-apple

difficult feat. There is an amusing illustration of two people apple-bobbing in an ancient illuminated manuscript, and this is reproduced in Strutt's " Sports and Pastimes of the People of England."

What is the Almonry?

THIS was formerly a rookery of houses off Tothill Street, Westminster, where the monastic alms of the adjacent Abbey were distributed. The first printing press in England was set up by William Caxton in the Almonry under the patronage of the Abbot of Westminster.

Nowadays the Almonry is the office in Dean's Yard, whence the Royal alms are distributed at Easter and Christmas. This, known as the Royal Almonry Office, has no connection with the Almonry of Westminster Abbey already referred to.

What Are "Sour Grapes"?

THIS expression refers to some greatly desired object, which when it cannot be obtained is belittled and spoken of as worthless. It is, of course, a reference to Aesop's well-known fable of the Fox and the Grapes. The fox tried hard to reach the grapes, but when he found he could not get them, went away declaring that they were sour and not worth having.

Why Do We Sometimes Lose the Sense of Smell?

WE often lose the sense of smell when we have a cold, because the nasal passages get stopped up, and the minute particles which float in the air from an odoriferous substance cannot reach our olfactory nerves.

But apart from this, the sense of smell is easily tired. If we go on smelling a particular odour continuously for some time we soon cease to notice it, even though it may be unpleasant. People who have to work in factories where there are unpleasant smells, as, for example, in fertiliser factories, soon cease to notice the odours. But though our sense of smell may be fatigued so as to be insensitive to one kind of odour, another kind may excite it at once. Further, though the nerve of smelling is soon exhausted, about one minute's respite will enable the exhausted nerve to recover. The power of smell is impaired by fever and also by certain drugs.

Men of science believe that smell is the oldest of our senses, that in the course of evolution smell came before sight, hearing, feeling or taste. There is no doubt that in the early days of his history man used his sense of smell to a much greater extent than he does now. At the present time smell is the least developed of all our senses, and the least used.

What is the Great Rift in Ophiuchus?

THIS is a black patch which is recorded in photographs taken through the big telescopes of the constellation known as Ophiuchus, or the Serpent Bearer. Formerly it was supposed that this and other similar

The Great Rift in Ophiuchus, a dark nebula or mass of cosmic dust

dark patches were really rifts in the great mass of stars—that is, vast areas where no stars occurred. It is now believed, however, that the patches are really dark nebulae—that is, huge masses of cosmic dust, which act as screens, and shut out our sight of the stars lying behind.

Not all the dark nebulae, however, completely shut off the stars behind. " More often," says Dr. Trumper, " they only dim the light of the stars seen through them."

It has been pointed out that a dark nebula appears, in a photograph, darker than the surrounding part of the sky in the spaces between the stars. Professor Barnard suggests that the sky is filled with a faint luminosity, due to numberless distant stars which cannot be seen as individuals ; the dark nebulae, by obscuring this light, appear darker than their background.

Can Twins Be Born in Different Years?

CERTAINLY they can if the birth takes place at the time when two years join. There has been a number of cases where one of the twins was born in the last hours of December 31st in one year and the other in the opening hours of the succeeding year. At Perth in Western Australia the wife of a coal-miner gave birth to a first twin at the end of 1937 and the second child followed five days later in 1938.

What is That Brush Used For?

Sweeping broom — Winged broom — Wall broom — Picture duster

Winged toy banister — Winged banister — Banister — Turk's head broom

Stage broom — Double banister — Narrow stock

Slipper — Oven flue — Lawn broom — Window

Spoke — Flue — Decanter — Dandy

Bill posting — Bottle — Aphis — Flower pot — Engine oilers

Venetian — Wardrobe — Bed broom — Hearth

Double wing furniture — Dumbell — Billiard table — Nail — Cloth

Shoe — Barrel scrubbing — Butcher's block

Pastry — Churn — Saucepan

Carpet broom — Stove — Street orderly — Deck scrubbing

Scrubbing — Laundry — Can

Sink — Plate — Bass broom

Boot wiper

Brushes are now made in a great variety of forms, the shape and character depending, of course, upon the purpose for which the brush is to be used. On this page are shown 50 brushes and brooms of various kinds, and the names underneath the drawings in most cases explain the use for which the brush is intended. The " wings " at the ends of winged brooms are for sweeping out angles and corners. In some cases the brooms have soft hair, while in other cases stiff bristles are used. We find the latter in carpet brooms, scrubbing brushes, stove brushes, butcher's brushes, and so on. The billiard table brush is specially shaped for brushing the cushions and round the pockets. Dandy brushes are used for cleaning animals

What is the Name of That Cheese?

Here are the principal cheeses seen in the shops or on the table, with their names. Ordinary Cheddar cheese is known to most people, and also Cheshire and Dutch cheeses. Gruyère also is familiar because of the holes through which the bubbles have escaped. Some other cheeses, however are not so well known. Gloucester is milder than Cheshire, and is made of whole milk and cream. Stilton is made by adding the cream of one day to the milk of the next. Gorgonzola is very much like Stilton. Parmesan is made of skimmed cow's milk. Roquefort is a French cheese made from the milk of sheep and goats. The various cream cheeses are not cheese in the true sense, but are merely cream dried sufficiently to be cut

Plate VII

What is the Name of That Parrot?

Red-and-Blue Macaw

Grey Parrot

Yellow-and-Blue Macaw

Hyacinthine Macaw

Cockatiel

Budgerigars

Great White Cockatoo

Purple-capped Lory

Leadbeater's Cockatoo

Greater Sulphur-Crested Cockatoo

Ring-necked Parraquet

There are many parrots found wild in different parts of the world, but only a limited number are kept regularly as pets, and the chief of these are shown in this colour drawing. The common grey parrot (Psittacus erithacus), which is a native of West and Central Africa, is the most familiar of all the parrots, and closely following it are the cockatoos. Leadbeater's cockatoo (P. Leadbeateri), generally affectionate and peaceable, is found wild in South and West Australia. The great white cockatoo (P. leucolophus) is a native of the Eastern Moluccas, while the greater sulphur-crested cockatoo (P. galeritus), first obtained on Captain Cook's voyage, is a native of Eastern Australia and Tasmania. The cockatiel (P. Novae-Hollandiae) is found throughout Australia. The macaws are very handsome birds. The hyacinthine (P. hyacinthinus) is found in Central Brazil, the yellow-and-blue (P. ararauna) and the red-and-blue (P. macao) are natives of northern South America. The purple-capped lory comes from the Dutch East Indies, while the ring-necked parakeet, or parraquet, is found wild in both Asia and Africa. The budgerigars or lovebirds, the prettiest of all the parrots, are natives of Australia. Of course, the most popular parrots are those that can imitate the sounds they hear, such as speaking, whistling and so on

Plate VIII

How Has Motoring Changed the Signposts?

In the old days of carriages, coaches and dogcarts drawn by horses the driver sat high up, and the signposts by the road were tall enough for the

The new type of signpost, with the inscriptions low down so that motorists can read them easily

directions to be on a level with the driver's eye. But with the coming of the motor-car the driver sits much lower, and it is often difficult for him to read the old type of signposts. Because of this, new signposts are being set up by the roadside which are much lower than the old ones and are easily readable from the driver's seat of a modern car.

Who Was the Hanging Judge?

This title has been given to several judges, including Sir Francis Page, a judge of the Common Pleas and afterwards of the King's Bench, who died in 1741. He was satirised by the poet Pope and was assailed by Dr. Johnson and attacked by Richard Savage, the poet, whom he had condemned to death for killing a man in a tavern brawl in 1727, but who was pardoned.

Another "hanging judge" was John Toler, Earl of Norbury, Chief Justice of the Common Pleas in Ireland from 1820 to 1827. He was very cruel when as Attorney-General he prosecuted Irish rebels, and on the bench showed gross partiality, buffoonery and scanty legal knowledge.

At a later date Sir Henry Hawkins, afterwards Baron Brampton, who died in 1907, very unjustly obtained the nickname of "Hanging Hawkins," because of the number of murder cases he happened to try. Actually he was an admirable criminal judge, very patient and thorough. Even the most hardened criminals were ready to acknowledge that he was always scrupulously fair and just.

What is "Shove-Ha'penny"?

It is an old English game that has long been played in inns and public-houses, and it is mentioned by Shakespeare, Ben Jonson and other well-known authors.

The game consists in driving a coin or disk by a blow of the hand along a highly-polished board into compartments marked out at one end of it. The coin most commonly used in the old days was a shilling, especially a shilling of Edward VI, which was, in consequence, called a "shove-groat shilling" or a "shovel-board shilling." Later, pennies and halfpennies were used, but nowadays the game is played not with a coin at all, but with a nickel disk that has milled edges and a hole in the middle. The "coin" must be perfectly smooth and, as it would be illegal to deface a coin of the realm deliberately to smooth its face, a special disk is used.

In "The Merry Wives of Windsor," Act I, Scene I, Slender speaks of "seven groats in mill-sixpences, and two Edward shovel-boards," and in II Henry IV, Act II, Scene 4, Falstaff says, "Quoit him down, Bardolph, like a shove-groat shilling." Ben Jonson in "Every Man in His Humour" says they "made it run as smooth off the tongue as a shove-groat shilling." The easy sliding of the coin over the board is also referred to by Middleton and Dekker in "The Roaring Girle," "Away slid my man like a shovel-board shilling."

For a time the game was in ill repute, but it has recently gained in respectability and is much played in the south of England, where contests are held before large bodies of spectators. Two thousand people once watched a final at Reading, and at the beginning of 1938 the B.B.C. included a shove-ha'penny match in its television programme. Many people then heard of the game for the first time.

Are All Steamship Funnels for Smoke?

No, in some large liners one of the funnels is a dummy, and is used for various purposes. On the *Britannic*, for example, the fore funnel has inside a rest room for the engineers and a place for storing baggage.

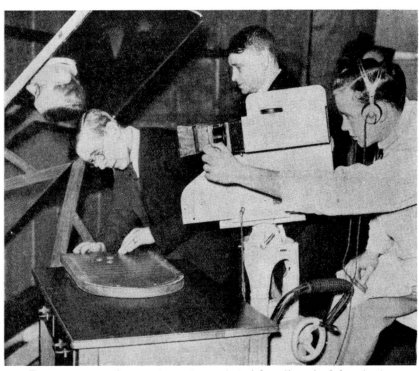

The ancient game of shove-ha'penny being televised from Alexandra Palace, London

What is the Meaning of Those

Athlete (Wolf Cubs)
Swimmer (Wolf Cubs)
Team Player (Wolf Cubs)
First Aider (Wolf Cubs)
Guide (Wolf Cubs)
House Orderly (Wolf Cubs)

Observer (Wolf Cubs)
Collector (Wolf Cubs)
Gardener (Wolf Cubs)
Artist (Wolf Cubs)
Homecraft (Wolf Cubs)
Toymaker (Wolf Cubs)

District Cubmaster
Cubmaster
Assistant Cubmaster
Tenderpad
1st Star
Cub Cap Badge
2nd Star
Cub Instructor
Rover Instructor

Cub Service Stars
Scout Service Stars
Rover Service Stars
Scouter Service Stars
"Cornwell" Scout
Surgeon

Sea Scout Anchor Badge
Metal Tenderfoot Buttonhole Badge
Tenderfoot
Second Class
First Class
King's Scout
Chaplain

Thanks Badge
Old Scout

Wood Badge
Bronze Cross
Silver Cross
Gilt Cross
Silver Wolf
Silver Acorn
Medal of Merit
Rover Scout Hat Badge

Lady Worker
Instructor
Examiner
Local Association Treasurer
Local Association Secretary
County Treasurer
County Secretary
Patrol Leader's Hat Badge

On these pages are given, by courtesy of the Boy Scouts Association, the various badges and decorations worn by Boy Scouts, with their names, which explain their purpose or use. The three crosses, bronze, silver and gilt, are awarded for gallantry, and the Silver Wolf, Silver Acorn and Medal of Merit for long and meritorious service. The coiled braid shown at the top of each ribbon is worn on the right-hand side of the chest, above the pocket. The badges at the top of this page are those of the Wolf Cubs. The badges at the bottom of this page and at the top of page 99 are

Badges Worn by the Boy Scouts?

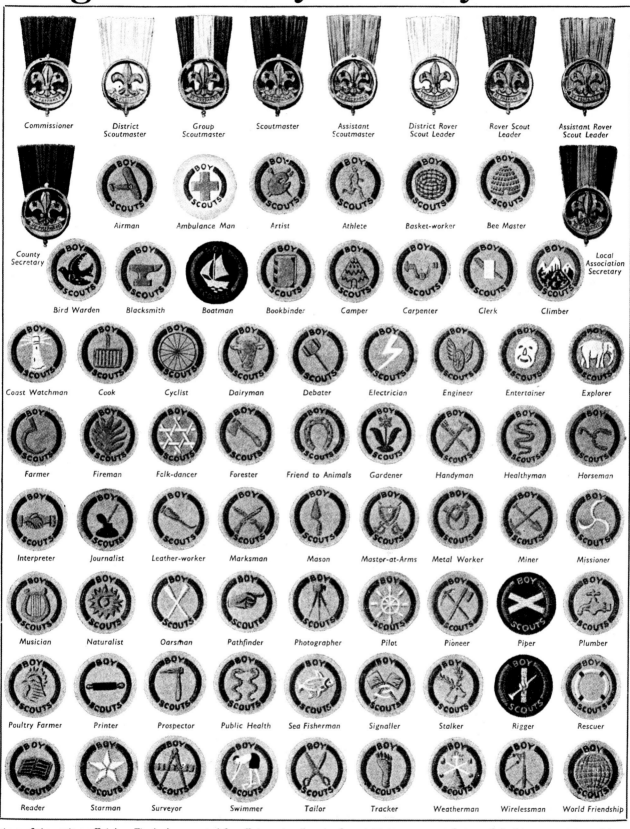

Commissioner · District Scoutmaster · Group Scoutmaster · Scoutmaster · Assistant Scoutmaster · District Rover Scout Leader · Rover Scout Leader · Assistant Rover Scout Leader

County Secretary · Airman · Ambulance Man · Artist · Athlete · Basket-worker · Bee Master · Local Association Secretary

Bird Warden · Blacksmith · Boatman · Bookbinder · Camper · Carpenter · Clerk · Climber

Coast Watchman · Cook · Cyclist · Dairyman · Debater · Electrician · Engineer · Entertainer · Explorer

Farmer · Fireman · Folk-dancer · Forester · Friend to Animals · Gardener · Handyman · Healthyman · Horseman

Interpreter · Journalist · Leather-worker · Marksman · Mason · Master-at-Arms · Metal Worker · Miner · Missioner

Musician · Naturalist · Oarsman · Pathfinder · Photographer · Pilot · Pioneer · Piper · Plumber

Poultry Farmer · Printer · Prospector · Public Health · Sea Fisherman · Signaller · Stalker · Rigger · Rescuer

Reader · Starman · Surveyor · Swimmer · Tailor · Tracker · Weatherman · Wirelessman · World Friendship

those of the various officials. The badges granted for efficiency in all sorts of occupations are a great feature of the Scout movement, and have had much to do in making the rising generation more handy than previous generations. Boy Scouts take a great pride in gaining these badges, which are worn on the right arm. Badges for public service, such as the Rescuer and World Friendship badges, are worn on the left arm.

Is Any Surname Deliberately Misspelt?

YES; in the telephone directory a lady doctor's name is inserted twice, and in one place it is deliberately misspelt for the convenience of would-be patients. She is Dr. Helen Lukis of New Malden, Surrey, but her patients mostly know her as "Dr. Lucas." It is under this spelling that people generally look for her name in the telephone directory when they want her services. Dr. Lukis, therefore, arranged that her name should appear there twice, once correctly spelt and in the proper place, and a second time spelt as Lucas.

For a small charge anyone with an uncommon name can have it inserted in the directory in the place where people will be most likely to look for it, as well as in its regular position. But of over a million telephone subscribers, Dr. Lukis was in 1938 the only one to have her name deliberately misspelt.

Did an English King Knight a Loin of Beef?

THIS story is told of various kings, and is supposed to explain the name of the joint called the sirloin. But there is no evidence that it ever happened. The word "sirloin" is from the French *surlonge*, which means "upon the loin."

Who Invented the Automatic Machine?

THE inventor of this device was probably Ctesibius, who flourished about 200 B.C. The earliest automatic machines are said to have been used in Egyptian temples to supply purifying water to the worshippers, who had to put five drachmae in a slit at the top. These moved a lever and delivered the water.

In modern times the automatic machine was first used in a London coffee-house in 1829. It was in the form of a jar-shaped vessel, and when a penny was inserted a lock was released and a pipeful of tobacco delivered. The modern type of automatic machine was first patented in the United States in 1884.

Who Made the Catacombs?

THE catacombs are the extensive underground burial - places at Rome where the Early Christians took refuge from their persecutors and where they celebrated their services. Catacombs also exist at Syracuse, Palermo, Agrigentum, Naples, and other places. There are also catacombs at Paris.

These extensive passages and chambers were probably originally stone quarries. In the catacombs of Rome have been found a large number of paintings, the earliest examples of Christian art, and from their study much has been learnt of early Christian rites and practices.

What Parrot Preys on Sheep?

IT is a New Zealand parrot called the kea, which formerly lived in remote mountain regions among the snows of South Island, feeding upon fruit, seeds and insect grubs. The seeds of the "vegetable sheep," a species of Raoalia, formed an important item in the kea's diet. This is a bushy plant with dense whitish foliage.

But the bird's ancient habits have been changed since the introduction of sheep into New Zealand. At a time when its natural food was scarce, the kea took to haunting the sheep stations and feeding on the offal of the animals that had been killed for their mutton. It soon began to show a preference for the fat surrounding the kidneys and before long developed into a bird of prey which attacked living sheep. In some way it seems to have learned the exact position of the choice fat, and when it attacks a living sheep it tears off the wool and flesh of the loins and reaches the kidneys.

So remarkable is this fact that when some years ago a conference of naturalists met at Wellington to investigate the charge against the kea, they could not be convinced of its truth. But the bad habit is now too well authenticated to be doubted, and the destruction of sheep on some of the runs by the kea is very great. The bird is such a pest that it is shot on sight. No more remarkable instance can be cited of a complete change of habit on the part of a living creature in a comparatively few years.

Nowadays in summer the kea inhabits the slopes of

Vegetable sheep, a bushy plant that grows in New Zealand, the seeds of which formed an important item in the kea's diet before sheep were introduced to the country

The kea, or mountain parrot of New Zealand, which attacks sheep

the mountains, but in winter it visits the lowlands. Mr. W. P. Pycraft points out that in view of the kea's change of habits, birds may well have played an important part in the past in controlling mammalian life in the world.

Is There Ozone at the Seaside?

THE oft-repeated statement that seaside air contains ozone has no real basis in fact. There is no more ozone at the seaside than elsewhere, and actually there is very little, if any, ozone in the lower atmosphere. In the upper atmosphere, however, there is plenty of ozone, which is formed from oxygen by the ultra-violet rays of the Sun. In the lower atmosphere ozone is formed from time to time by lightning.

This gas is really a form of oxygen, but instead of having two atoms in the molecule, as is the case with oxygen, there are three in a molecule of ozone. Ozone molecules have more energy than those of oxygen, but when they come in contact with dust particles in the lower atmosphere they give up their energy and become oxygen molecules.

Ozone can be prepared artificially by passing an electric discharge through oxygen in an apparatus. Most of the oxygen is changed by the current into ozone. Ozone is used for purifying the air in underground railway tubes and water in reservoirs.

Where Did the Borzoi Originate?

THIS dog, which is also known as the Russian wolfhound, is really a sporting dog, and was used in Russia in the old days to capture and kill wolves. Wolves, however, had become so scarce in the days now grown out of this habit. The borzoi is a very speedy dog, being built very much on the lines of the greyhound. A male borzoi is 28 inches or more in height at the shoulder, the females being a little less.

Where is Palmyra?

THIS was once a celebrated city of Syria, and its splendid ruins, which form a very striking object in the midst of the desert, stand in an oasis. They date from the Roman period.

Palmyra had long been a halting place for caravans between Syria and Mesopotamia, and there King Solomon built a city. He called it by the Hebrew name

Egypt within her sway, and called herself the Queen of the East, she was defeated by Aurelian, taken prisoner and carried to Rome to grace his triumph. Her life was spared, but she lost her kingdom.

After the Roman Empire became Christian Palmyra was made a bishopric. Then the Moslems conquered Syria, and Palmyra submitted, and from the 15th century it began to sink into decay, along with the rest of the Near East. Chief among the magnificent ruins is the great Temple of the Sun, with a colonnade nearly a mile long.

What is the Latest Idea in Fire-Escapes?

THE very latest idea in fire-escapes is to be seen at a cripples' home in New York, the Jewish Memorial Hospital at Brooklyn. Escapes have been built from each floor reaching to the ground, and these are in the form of large pipes or chutes. Inside they are smooth and in case of fire the cripples would be placed in them at the top and would slide down to be received by helpers waiting at the lower ends on the ground. These rigid chutes are much more satisfactory for helpless persons than the canvas chutes that are so often used.

A fine specimen of a borzoi, or Russian hunting dog. This is the champion, "Krown Kossack"

immediately preceding the War that Russian noblemen had their borzois taught to capture a wolf released from a cage but not to kill it. After the wolf had been caught a muzzle would be slipped on the wolf's head, and it would be lifted into a wheeled cage to be carried into captivity once more and released for sport on another day.

It is generally agreed that nowadays the borzoi has not sufficient courage to tackle single-handed a powerful wolf, as it used to do in the old days.

During the present century the borzoi has become exceedingly popular in Great Britain, and Queen Alexandra had some fine specimens, which came from the kennels of the Tsar.

In England the borzoi does not grow such a long coat as it does in Russia, probably because the climate in England is warmer. Here, however, the coat is smoother than in the dog's native land. This type of dog is very affectionate, and is easily managed.

The early borzois kept in England would chase a flock of sheep or a herd of deer at sight, but they have

Tadmor, referred to in the Bible as Tadmor in the Wilderness. The name means "the city of palm trees," and Palmyra is only a Greek translation of this. The city reached its greatest splendour under the Emperor Hadrian and the Antonines.

In the third century of the Christian era it for a short time reached the rank of a capital, its queen being the famous Zenobia. She is said to have assassinated her husband Odenathus. When she tried to include all Syria, Asia and

A useful form of fire-escape, fitted to the upper floors of a home for cripples in Brooklyn, New York

What is That Curious Weapon?

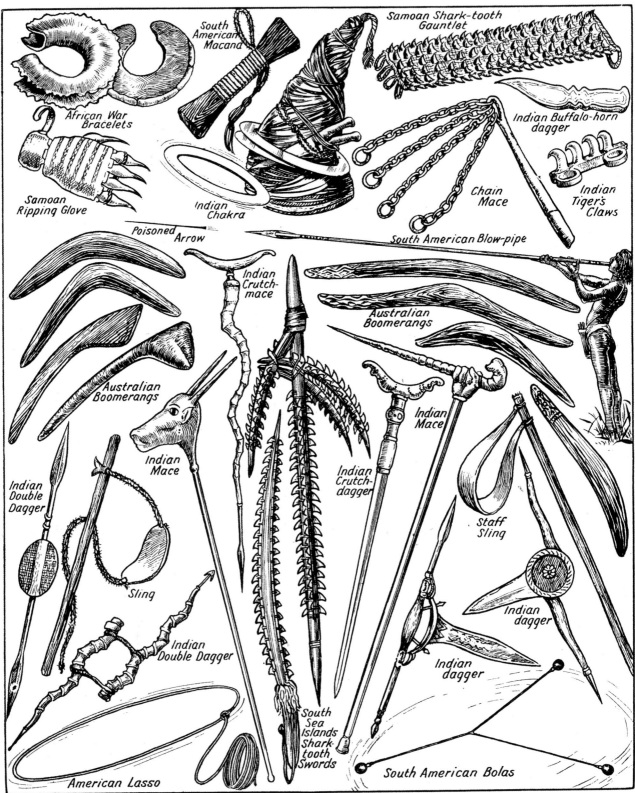

African War Bracelets

South American Macana

Samoan Shark-tooth Gauntlet

Samoan Ripping Glove

Indian Chakra

Indian Buffalo-horn dagger

Chain Mace

Indian Tiger's Claws

Poisoned Arrow

South American Blow-pipe

Australian Boomerangs

Indian Crutch-mace

Australian Boomerangs

Indian Mace

Indian Double Dagger

Sling

Indian Mace

Indian Crutch-dagger

Staff Sling

Indian dagger

Indian Double Dagger

Indian dagger

South Sea Islands Shark-tooth Swords

American Lasso

South American Bolas

Here are a number of curious weapons used by native peoples in various parts of the world. The Samoan ripping glove and the Indian tiger's claws were worn on the hand and used for tearing the body of a naked foe. The Indian chakra was a steel disk sharpened to a keen edge all round, which was hurled at a foe, and in the hand of a dexterous thrower might almost take off the enemy's head. The chakra was worn on the head-dress, as shown. Australian boomerangs and throwing sticks are, of course, well known. The double dagger is made of steel-tipped horns, and is held in the middle. It can be thrust in either direction, and also serves as a shield for warding off sword blows. The bolas was hurled at an enemy's legs to bring him down. The blowpipe is used in South America and in Borneo for shooting poisoned arrows, and the natives are very skilful marksmen

What is a Hearse?

Most people think of a hearse as a carriage specially used for conveying the dead to the cemetery for burial, but this is a modern use of the word. At an earlier date it was a bier or hand-barrow used for the same

A hearse erected over a coffin and covered with a pall

purpose, and Shakespeare refers to this when he makes Lady Anne in "Richard III" say: "Set down, set down your honourable load, If honour may be shrouded in a hearse."

Still earlier the word was used for a grave, tomb or monument, as when Ben Jonson, in his epitaph on the Countess of Pembroke, says: "Underneath this sable hearse Lies the subject of all verse."

Another early meaning of the word was a framework of light wood, metal, iron or brass, bearing wax lights and set up in a church with the coffin of a deceased person underneath, during the funeral ceremonies. The hearse, in the form of a framework of wood or metal, was placed over the coffin or bier or tomb, and covered with a pall. Such hearses were often set up in the streets for noble or royal funerals.

Are Bats and Moles Blind?

We often hear the expression "blind as a bat," or "blind as a mole," but bats, though mostly nocturnal in their habits, are not blind. They can see quite well, but when they come out in the day-time the glare of the light distracts them a good deal.

The mole is proverbially regarded as a blind animal, and the old writers declared that it had no eyes. But though the eyes of a mole are very small, a necessary fact for an animal that burrows through the ground, it has eyes, and they are covered by skin and fur. Tests have shown that their eyes are sensitive to light, but their sight is defective.

What is a Ticket of Leave?

It is a written licence to a convict who has been sentenced to penal servitude to be at large before his sentence has expired. Such a licence is granted under the hand or seal of one of his Majesty's principal Secretaries of State (generally the Home Secretary), and can be revoked for misconduct on the part of its holder.

What is Gastric Juice?

It is the digestive fluid of the stomach, produced by glands at the rate of about two gallons a day in an adult. The function of this fluid, which is of great importance to health, is to convert insoluble proteids into soluble peptones. The fluid is colourless and of sour taste and odour. It consists of 99·3 per cent. water, ·3 per cent. pepsin, ·2 per cent. hydrochloric acid, and ·2 per cent. of salts, chloride and phosphates

What is a Mezzotint?

The word means "middle tint," and it is a particular method of engraving which gives the effect of the old kind of Indian ink drawing. The whole surface of the metal plate is scratched uniformly by means of a tool called a cradle or rocker, so that an impression taken from it in that state would be entirely black.

The rocker is a kind of chisel with a sharp, bevelled edge which is stood on the surface of the copper plate and rocked to and fro, so as to obtain a series of points forming a rough grain. This grain retains the ink and enables the engraver to get a proof of pure black of equal tint. Then the drawing is traced and the lights of the picture are obtained by scraping away the ground, highlights being obtained by means of burnishing.

One advantage of mezzotint engraving is that it is a much more rapid process than that of line engraving and etching, in which the lines have to be ploughed into the copper. Its range of tone, too, is well adapted for the representation of the various textures in a portrait or a landscape.

The method is sometimes said to have been invented by Prince Rupert, who hit upon the plan through seeing a soldier scraping the rust off his musket. But this is not correct. The real inventor of mezzotint was Ludwig von Siegen, who in 1642 published a print of Princess Amelia of Hesse, and ten years later explained his process to Prince Rupert, who introduced it into England. It is in England that the mezzotint was brought to its greatest perfection

How Thin Can Gold Be Beaten Out?

Gold, which is the most malleable of all metals, has been hammered into sheets one 300,000th of an inch in thickness. In other words, it would take 300,000 of these sheets placed one upon another to make a thickness of an inch. The best gold leaf is made from 23-carat gold.

The metal is first rolled from a thin ingot into a leaf one 800th of an inch in thickness. This is then divided into pieces an inch square, and 150 squares with sheets of velium or tough paper between, each four inches square, are piled on top of one another. They are then beaten till the gold has been flattened out as large in area as the vellum or paper.

The gold is then once more cut into inch squares and, after being placed between layers of goldbeater's skin, is again hammered out. Generally the process is continued till the thickness of the gold is only one 282,000th of an inch. Then the leaves are cut and made up into books of 25 leaves

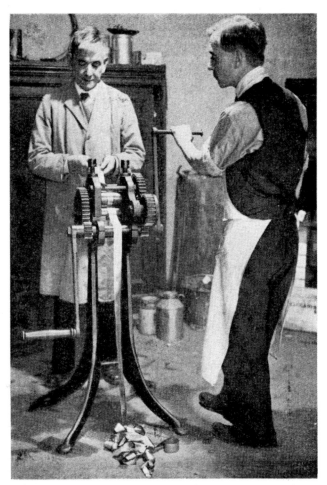

Craftsmen rolling a ribbon of pure gold from a small ingot prior to beating it into gold leaf. A bar of pure gold is rolled into a ribbon six yards long and is then cut into small squares ready for the actual beating. The process of rolling takes half an hour

What is the Food of Lions?

It varies according to the region in which they live. Mr. Richard Lydekker says: "With regard to the ordinary food of lions and the manner variably feast upon any dead animal left by the hunter, from a buffalo to a steinbuck, that they may happen to come across."

When lions grow too old to be able to catch game they take to killing the

A remarkable flashlight photograph, taken in Africa, showing a lion starting upon his midnight meal, which is a zebra he has slain. The flashlight made the lion look up

in which they attack the larger animals on which they prey, in the oak forests of Persia their staple food is furnished by the wild pigs which frequent these woods. In India, lions usually feed on deer, antelope, wild pigs, cattle, horses, donkeys and camels, and formerly a large number of the latter were destroyed by them.

"In Africa lions prey largely upon antelopes, zebras, buffaloes and giraffes, the Hon. W. H. Drummond stating that on the many occasions on which he had seen lions hunting by daylight, he could not recall one when they were not in pursuit of buffaloes, while herds of those animals which he had been hunting during the day were scattered and dispersed by lions at night.

"Lions do not restrict themselves to the flesh of animals that have fallen to their own attacks; and besides eating the flesh of animals recently killed they will also prey upon carcasses in an advanced state of decomposition."

Mr. Selous, the famous hunter, tells us that when elephants have been shot, "lions prey upon the stinking carcasses as they lie festering in the rays of a tropical sun and at last become a seething mass of maggots, returning night after night to the feast until no more meat is left. This occurs in parts of the country abounding in game, where it would give a party of lions but little trouble or exertion to catch a zebra, buffalo or antelope and procure themselves a meal of fresh meat. In the same way, no matter how plentiful game may be, lions will almost in-

villagers' goats, and women and children who fall in their way at night may also become victims. When, however, such decrepit lions live far from human habitations, they are said to catch mice and other small rodents and will even eat grass at times, although this may perhaps be taken merely as a medicine, just as our domestic cats and dogs are often seen eating grass in the garden.

Is Much Milk Wasted in England?

Dr. A. Parker, of the Department of Scientific and Industrial Research, in a paper on "Water Pollution and Trade Effluents," read before the Institutions of Civil Engineers and Chemical Engineers in January, 1938, said that the work of the Water Pollution Research Board proved that the quantities of polluting matter carried away in the wastes from various factories engaged in the milk industries was very extensive. These could be greatly reduced by simple and inexpensive modifications in the operations within the factories to lessen losses of milk, whey, buttermilk and other products and by-products. If adequate drainage trays were installed at all the depots and factories in the country, the total saving of milk would be of the order of three million gallons a year, or £150,000. It seems wrong that so much of this valuable food should be wasted when hundreds of babies need it.

What is "A Bawbee She Kyles"?

This is the name given to an ancient game still played in some parts of Scotland. Kyles is a game of chance of the ninepins type, and Robert Burns refers to it in the lines:

The great Argyle led on his files.
I wat they glanc'd for twenty miles;
They houghd the clans like ninepin kyles.

In the game of "A Bawbee She Kyles" each player places a bawbee or a penny on the ground, and the players then take turns at rolling an iron ball towards a number of holes more than five yards from the place where they stand when bowling. The player who puts the ball in one of the holes wins the bawbees.

The ancient game of "A Bawbee She Kyles" in progress

Which Well-known Poets Kept Strange Pets?

SEVERAL British poets were fond of keeping unusual pets. William Cowper, for instance, kept tame hares, housing them in boxes which he made himself, and he took pride in the fact that in his house, man, dog and hare lived together in harmony. While at Cambridge University Alfred Tennyson bought and tamed a snake, which he kept in his room, and he used to sit smoking and watching " its sinuosities upon the carpet."

As a boy Robert Browning kept in his father's garden a collection of newts, frogs, owls, monkeys, hedgehogs, snakes and an eagle. After Mrs. Browning's death he kept in his London garden lizards, toads, an owl and a pair of geese.

But the strangest of the poets in their taste for unusual pets were Lord Byron and Dante Gabriel Rossetti. The former when at Cambridge kept a tame bear. Shelley visiting him years later in the Guiccioli Palace at Ravenna wrote that " he had many servants, ten horses, eight enormous dogs, three monkeys, five cats, an eagle, a crow and a falcon. I have just met on the grand staircase," continued Shelley,

of animal tamers. In the Cheyne Walk house and garden he had a wombat, a chameleon, a white peacock, white mice, an armadillo, a racoon, a deer, a kangaroo, a woodchuck, a salamander and a zebu—the last dangerous. On social occasions the wombat used to sleep in an epergne in the middle of the table, indifferent to the talk and light. In moments of intense conversation it would suddenly emerge to eat a few cigars. The white peacock eventually died under the sofa. Rossetti one day invited a friend to come and watch his white mice wake from their hibernation ; but they were discovered dead and stinking. He once bought a white bull because its eyes resembled those of a lady he affected. It was tethered in the garden until the neighbours found it dangerous, and it had to be sold."

Does the " Mayflower " Exist Today?

THE ship in which the Pilgrim Fathers sailed to America has long since disappeared, but a barn at Jordans, the famous Quaker shrine at Chalfont St. Giles in Buckinghamshire, is said to be built of timbers taken from the *Mayflower* when it was broken up. The barn is a picturesque structure, as can be seen by the photograph given here, and the timbers may well have come from the historic ship.

The *Mayflower* was a vessel of 180 tons, and when on September 6th, 1620, she set sail from Plymouth for the New World she had on board 41 men and their families, a total of 102 persons in all. Their stormy journey across the Atlantic took 63 days.

Jordans, near which is the barn referred to, is a sacred spot of the Quakers or Society of Friends, for in the little cemetery attached to the meeting-house there lie buried William Penn, the founder of Pennsylvania, with his two wives, as well as other

worthies. This quiet God's acre and the *Mayflower* barn attract hundreds of American visitors to Chalfont St. Giles every year.

A map showing the position of the Golden Gate at San Francisco

Where is the Golden Gate?

IT is the name given to the entrance of the land-locked bay on which San Francisco is situated. It is a strait about two miles wide connecting San Francisco Bay with the Pacific Ocean and the name was given by Sir Francis Drake.

This is also the name given to the entrance of the Golden Horn at Constantinople, an inlet of the Bosporus forming the harbour of the city, and separating Pera and Galata from the main part of Constantinople, called Stamboul.

How Can Boiled and Raw Eggs Be Distinguished?

IF boiled eggs that have become cold are mixed with raw eggs, all look alike, yet they can be sorted out quite easily. We try to spin the eggs one after another, teetotum fashion. Those that are raw will not spin, while the cooked eggs spin quite well. With the raw egg, the time during which the fingers act on the egg is not long enough to impart motion to the contents if they are liquid, but when the contents are solid, the movement of the fingers is imparted to the whole egg from the start, and when let go the entire mass continues to rotate like a top.

Did Cinderella Wear a Glass Slipper?

THIS popular idea is said to have been the result of a mistake on the part of the translator of the story into English. Using the French version of Perrault and Madame d'Aunoy, he misread *vair*, fur, for *verre*, glass, and so what should have been described as a fur slipper is perpetuated as a glass slipper. The story is a very ancient one, probably of Eastern origin, and a similar kind of story has been found in the writings of ancient Egypt.

The barn of Jordans, in Buckinghamshire, believed to have been built of timbers from the Pilgrim Fathers' ship " Mayflower "

" five peacocks, two guinea-hens and an Egyptian crane." All of these creatures except the horses were loose in the house.

" Rossetti," says Mr. Chard Powers Smith, " was of the fantastic variety

Is Dresden China Made at Dresden?

No; it is made at Meissen on the Elbe, 13 miles from Dresden. It is true that the first European hand porcelain was made at Dresden, but the first European manufactory was established at Meissen and it is this factory which produced for centuries the well-known Royal Dresden China.

What is the Soya Bean Used For?

It is one of the most valuable of all the leguminous plants and the quantity produced is growing every year. It is used for human and animal food, but it has in recent years become one of the great sources of vegetable oil. Though grown in China and Japan from time immemorial, it is only in the last twenty years that its cultivation has spread on a large scale to the United States, and to a less degree to Italy, France, Russia, Hawaii, Egypt and South Africa. China produces

Soya beans grown and harvested at Boreham in Essex

5,600,000 tons a year, Manchuria 3,350,000 tons, the United States 1,070,000 tons, and Japan and Korea 770,000 tons. In America this bean is called the soy bean and it is also called the soja bean.

Soya-bean cake, a valuable feeding stuff for cattle, is prepared by compressing the beans after most of the oil has been extracted.

Why Are Cambridge Men Called Cantabs?

The word Cantab is merely a shortened form of Cantabrigian, a word made up from the medieval Latin name of Cambridge, Cantabrigienses. Similarly, Oxford men are called Oxonians, from Oxonia, which is the Latinised form of the name Oxford.

How Far Can a Fly Fly?

Careful investigation with marked flies have been carried out, and it has been found that with a favourable wind flies could reach Florida from Cuba, crossing the sea for a distance of 95 miles. When experiments were carried out in Texas to ascertain how far the flies flew overland, it was found that in two days a housefly could easily cover nine miles. The flies were captured alive in traps, sprinkled with red pigment, and then released. Other traps were set in various places at different distances away, and bait consisting of waste from food-preserving factories was placed to attract the flies.

It was noticed that as soon as the flies were released from the traps they did not all fly with the wind, as might have been expected. Many travelled at right angles to a breeze varying in velocity between 13 and 24 miles an hour. Within 24 hours over 60 per cent. of the released flies had been recaptured within a few miles of their starting-point.

The first 300 yards were covered at a good speed. Flies that went the longest distances had passed over houses, and even over towns, that might have seemed favourable to them for feeding and egg-laying. This fact is supposed to point to a migrating instinct in some flies comparable to that of birds. When we remember the size of a fly five miles is a great distance for the insect to travel.

Flies often pass from the continent of Europe into Kent, when a wind is blowing in the right direction during summer. Wind, indeed, seems to be the chief factor in the distribution of flies.

What is a Fret?

This is the name given to an angular interlaced ornament used in architecture. It is also much used in heraldry and examples of both uses are given in the illustrations on this page. The fret shown in the shield

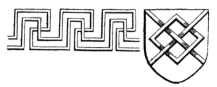

Examples of the fret or angular interlaced ornament in architecture and heraldry

forms the arms of the Harrington family and is popularly known as the Harrington Knot.

In architecture the fret is generally used in borders in Gothic architecture, and it is sometimes very complicated in design. It is also found in textiles and inlaid patterns.

How Many King Herods Were There?

There were four. First of all there was Herod the Great, King of Judea from 47 B.C. to A.D.2. He built the magnificent temple at Jerusalem and kept in with the Roman power by cringing servility. It was he who ordered the massacre of the infants at Bethlehem in the hope of killing Jesus. He died at Jerusalem in great agony of a loathsome disease.

His son Herod Antipas was appointed by his father to succeed to the throne of Judea, but the Romans would only allow him to rule over the tetrarchy of Galilee. It was he who beheaded John the Baptist and was described by Jesus as "that fox."

Herod Agrippa I, born about 11 B.C., was a grandson of Herod the Great and was appointed king over the tetrarchies of north-eastern Palestine in A.D. 37, and in A.D. 41 over Judea also. He was the King Herod who persecuted the Christians as described in the 12th chapter of the Acts of the Apostles and who died a horrible death, referred to in verse 23.

Herod Agrippa II, son of Herod Agrippa I, was born about A.D. 27 and died at Rome in 100. He became king of northern Palestine in 52 and sided with the Romans in the conquest of Jerusalem. He was the King Agrippa before whom Paul pleaded as described in the 26th chapter of the Acts of the Apostles.

What is a Chamfron?

This is the piece of armour, generally made of steel, but sometimes of leather, which protected the front of a war-horse's head from the ears to the nose. It was known to the ancients, but came into common use in Europe in the 15th century. Some chamfrons are very beautiful works of art.

Which Language is Spoken by Most People?

THE language spoken by the most people is Chinese, used by about 450 million men, women and children. But, of course, this is not a single language. There are so many forms of Chinese that all could not understand one another.

The language spoken by the most people which all who use it could understand if they met others who spoke the same language is English. About 225 million people speak this, including Great Britain, the Dominions, the United States and Liberia.

Russian comes next with about 160 millions; then Japanese, 90 millions; German and Spanish, 80 millions each; Hindi, 72 millions; French, 70 millions; Portuguese, 50 millions; Italian, 50 millions; Bengali, 50 millions; Javanese, 42 millions; Arabic, 40 millions; Polish, 32 millions. Other languages are spoken by fewer people than 30 millions.

What Is a Fennec Fox?

IT is a pretty little North African animal, a relation of our English foxes, but much smaller in size. The total length of the body and head together is only about a foot and a quarter, and the tail is another six or seven inches. But the ears are very long in proportion to the rest of the body, being at least three inches in length and sometimes more. They are wide in proportion to their length and give the animal a very strange appearance.

An African fennec fox with its remarkably large ears

The fur of this animal is pale fawn, while the under parts of the body are white. The fennec ranges from Nubia

to Algeria and is found all over the Sahara, being essentially an animal of the desert. Its colour harmonises with that of the sand, so that even in the day-time it is not easily seen. The fennec, however, is nocturnal in its habits and at sunset goes to its drinking place. But it does not travel direct. It goes by way of ravines and hollows, in which it seeks protection from possible enemies. After satisfying its thirst it hunts for food, and this consists of jerboas, small birds, lizards and fruits.

The fennec digs a burrow, generally near a clump of plants, and lines the inside with feathers, fur and vegetable substances. The burrow is kept remarkably clean and during the day the inmate lies curled up with its tail covering its body and only its long, sensitive ears exposed. At the slightest sound it is on the alert, but after whimpering goes off to sleep again.

The burrows are near together for the fennec likes to live in colonies. The young are born in March each year and there are three or four cubs in a litter. The haunts of the fennec can always be detected, for round its drinking places can be seen countless impressions of its feet in the moist earth made as the animals moved about.

What is the Hexapla?

THE word means sixfold and the name is given to an edition of the Old Testament which has six texts or versions in parallel columns. The name was originally given to Origen's Old Testament, which had in the six columns the following versions: Hebrew, Hebrew in Greek characters, the Septuagint, the text of Aquila, that of Theodotian, and that of Symmachos. The book does not exist now : it disappeared in the seventh century.

Hexateuch means six books and is a name given by Biblical critics to the first six books of the Old Testament. Pentateuch, of course, means five books

and the Pentateuch in the Bible includes Genesis, Exodus, Leviticus, Numbers and Deuteronomy.

What Are the Human Figures Used as Pillars?

WHEN the statues used as pillars to support parts of classical buildings are males, they are called Atlantes, Telamones, Perces or Gigantes, though the first name is most common. When the figures are female they are called

An Atlas on the left, and on the right, a Caryatid, male and female figures used as supports for parts of ancient buildings in place of ordinary pillars

Caryatides, and they are very abundant in the remains of ancient architecture. Atlantes is the plural of Atlas.

Caryatides possess much grace and dignity of bearing, despite the servile character of their employment. They are said to have been originally intended to denote the subjection of the people of Caryae in Arcadia, hence the name. The inhabitants of that city having warred, in company with the Persians, against the Greeks, were defeated and the Greeks destroyed the city and the male inhabitants, carrying away the females into slavery. To commemorate this defeat, representations of the women of Caryae were employed as supports to architecture. In the same way the Persians were sculptured as Atlantes or Telamones. These human figures were only used in architecture when ordinary pillars would be too insignificant for the erections. They are suited to a rich style and for supporting a gallery.

Of What is a Human Body Composed?

SCIENTISTS tell us that the body of an average man of 12 stones contains about 96 pounds of oxygen, 52 pounds of carbon, 15 pounds of hydrogen, 4 pounds of the metal calcium, $3\frac{1}{2}$ pounds of nitrogen, $1\frac{1}{4}$ pounds of chlorine, $1\frac{3}{4}$ pounds of phosphorus, $3\frac{1}{2}$ ounces of sulphur, $3\frac{1}{2}$ ounces of fluorine gas, $2\frac{3}{4}$ ounces of potassium, $2\frac{1}{2}$ ounces of sodium, $1\frac{3}{4}$ ounces of magnesium, $1\frac{1}{2}$ ounces of iron, and traces of copper, lead, arsenic, magnesia, aluminium, silicon and bromine. A woman's body appears to be worth rather more than a man's.

What is a Camera Obscura?

THIS is an optical instrument described as far back as 1558 by Baptista Porta. The form in which it is generally seen is that popular at seaside resorts. In the roof of a little hut is arranged a mirror at an angle of 45°. This catches a reflection of the

scene outside, which is thrown down through a lens which magnifies it, and appears upon a white table. The top of the roof can be moved round by a cord, and so the scene all round the hut for a considerable distance can be shown upon the table.

Of course, the room in which the image appears must be in darkness, except for the light reflected by the mirror. The words " camera obscura " mean " dark room." An ordinary camera is a form of camera obscura.

What Was a Faun?

IT was one of a number of beings in the old classical mythology who were described as half men and half goats, and they had horns. They developed in the course of time from the story of the god Faunus, son of Picus and grandson of Saturnus, who was the third in the series of kings of the Laurentes. He was worshipped as the protecting deity of agriculture and shepherds.

A faun, from an ancient carved gem at Florence

After the worship of the Greek god Pan had been introduced into Italy, Faunus came to be identified with Pan and was represented like Pan with horns and goat's feet. As time went on fauns were spoken of in the plural and were of both the male and female sex. Eventually, as Faunus was identified with the Arcadian Pan, so the fauns were identified with the Greek satyrs.

Does the Monument Bear a False Inscription?

YES. It says, " Three short years completed that which was considered the work of an age." This is not true, for London was rebuilt very slowly, and for some years afterwards only isolated houses existed, and owing

to fear of robbers rich merchants were often afraid to occupy these.

The inscription mentioned is not the only false one that the Monument has borne. The Fire of London occurred in fanatical times. On the west side there was formerly an inscription which said, " This pillar was set up in perpetual remembrance of the most dreadful burning of this Protestant city, begun and carried on by the treachery and malice of the Popish faction. In the beginning of September in the year of our Lord MDCLXVI. In order to the effecting of their own horrid plot for the extirpating of the Protestant religion and English liberties and to introduce Popery and slavery."

This was a gross falsehood. This inscription was added in 1681 during the madness of the Popish plot. It was obliterated by James II, but in the reign of William III was cut again. It was finally erased in 1831.

What Happens When a Ball Falls into Water?

A GREAT deal of study has been given by scientists to the behaviour of water when a ball is dropped into it, for from the results can be learned much about the properties of liquids. While the matter has been studied for thirty years or more, it is only in recent times, with the enormous improvements in speed photography and lighting, that the real facts could be understood. The photographs given here, which show what happens when a golf ball is dropped into a pail of water, are the most remarkable of their kind that have ever been taken. The exposure in each case was only one half-millionth of a second and a wonderful electrical device gave intensely rapid flashes of light.

When the ball first enters the water no splash is visible, but instantly a crown-like formation rises, getting higher and throwing out more and more splashes. Then the crown-like formation falls after it has risen to its

These four photographs show four stages of what happens when a golf ball is dropped into a pail of water. The photographs were taken at the Massachusetts Institute of Technology by Professor Edgerton and Mr. K. J. Germeshausen, with exposures of only one half-millionth of a second. They are given here by courtesy of the Institute

greatest height, and is replaced by a sharp spire of water rising in the centre. It rises higher and higher, and then, having reached its maximum, falls back into the pail.

Has a Lion Ever Attacked an Aeroplane?

YES; one of the most extraordinary incidents in the history of flying occurred near Arusa in East Africa in 1930. An aeroplane which formed part of a German film expedition was flying low in order to get photographs of a lion when the animal, angry or alarmed, jumped at the machine and damaged the wing. The pilot succeeded in making a safe landing, and fortunately the lion went off. But the airmen were attacked by a rhinoceros, which as soon as it landed charged the machine and injured one of the men.

Are Any Trains Driven By Electric Batteries?

YES ; the London Passenger Transport Board have a number of locomotives which are driven entirely by batteries carried on the vehicles. These locomotives are used for new works and for track maintenance. They can travel over electric lines when the current from the power station is cut off. They haul the trucks carrying workmen, equipment and material and travel at a speed of three miles an hour. They are so designed that they can be used in conjunction with any main-line type of rolling stock.

A view inside one of the new battery locomotives, showing the large number of batteries required to drive the vehicle

What Musician Discovered a New World?

THE planet Uranus, whose path lies between the orbits of Saturn and Neptune, was discovered on the night of March 13th, 1781, by William Herschel, afterwards knighted, who was at the time Director of Public Concerts at Bath.

He was only an amateur astronomer, but discovered this unknown planet, which at first was supposed to be a comet. The discovery was the turning-point in Herschel's career and transformed him from a music master into a great astronomer.

How Strong is a Gorilla?

HUNTERS tell us that a full-size male gorilla, which is the largest of all the man-like apes, is more than a match in physical strength for ten men. Even a baby specimen needs two or three men to master it. A gorilla shows no fear of anything except man, and it has been known to seize a leopard, maul it to death, and then toss it aside as though it were

a kitten. It can take a rifle and bend the barrel double with its hands.

The gorilla reaches a height of nearly six feet and weighs as much as 30 stones. Its footprint is three times the size of a full-grown man's.

Do Hedgehogs Climb Fruit Trees?

IT is a popular idea that hedgehogs climb fruit trees and carry off the fruit by impaling it on their spines. The animals are then supposed to drop to the ground, the fall being broken by the elasticity of their spines, so that no harm happens.

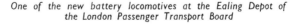

One of the new battery locomotives at the Ealing Depot of the London Passenger Transport Board

But this is simply a fairy tale. Hedgehogs never climb trees for their fruit, and they never eat fruit. The hedgehog is a nocturnal animal that comes out at night, seeking for mice, young rats, and perhaps baby rabbits.

How Much of the Sun's Heat Do We Receive?

THE Sun is pouring out heat in all directions, but of this heat the Earth receives only about one 2,200-millionth. Astronomers reckon that altogether only about a hundred-millionth of the heat radiated by the Sun is caught by the whole of the planets in the Solar System.

How Did Barnum First Attract Crowds?

PHINEAS T. BARNUM was the greatest showman of all time. When he first bought a museum at a knock-down price he realised he must do something out of the way to attract crowds to the show. He therefore, before the museum opened, engaged a man at six shillings a day, gave him some bricks, and told him to walk along the street and place one at the corner of Broadway and Ann Street. Then he was to go on and place another brick at the corner of Broadway and Vesey Street, and so on.

As soon as he had laid four bricks he was to walk round the block to where he had put the first brick, exchange another for the one on the pavement, and then proceed to the next brick and replace that, and so on. He was to speak to nobody. At the end of every hour he was to stop at the museum, walk through the building, and go out at the back exit, continuing his brick work.

Half an hour after he began 500 men and women were watching him. They asked him questions, but he made no reply, merely going on with his brick work. By the end of an hour the streets all round were packed with people, and when the man entered the museum crowds bought tickets and followed him in, hoping to find the solution of the riddle.

The brick-laying went on for several days, till the police interfered, as traffic in the neighbourhood was held up. Barnum's museum had already become a centre of attraction to thousands.

Barnum was always very fertile in ideas. Once, when the people crowded into his show and stayed too long, preventing others from coming in, he put a notice up over a door: "This Way to the Egress." The people went through to see the egress, and found themselves in the street.

What Are Horse Ornaments?

THEY are the small brass disks and crescents which used to be seen on the harness of most cart-horses and are still often seen in the country on the shire horses used on the land. These objects are now collected and the older ones are much sought after

show the kangaroo and emu, were probably made for export to Australia.

Horse ornaments of brass are by no means peculiar to England. They are found on the Continent in most countries. It must be admitted that a well-groomed cart-horse, well decorated

A pair of ploughing horses decorated with brass horse ornaments

by connoisseurs. There are hundreds of fakes about, but they can be generally identified by their appearance. The genuine old horse-ornaments by constant polishing have become very smooth, whereas these replicas and imitations, though the surfaces may have been artificially smoothed, show the roughness of their casting in the grooves and interstices.

Horse brasses, though dating back several centuries, came into common use in England only after the close of the Napoleonic Wars, and the majority of those in existence were made in the second half of the 19th century. The earlier specimens, especially examples dating from the 17th and 18th centuries, are very rare and are much sought after.

Horse ornaments, which vary a great deal in detail of design, can be divided into one or two main groups. The early forms represent the Sun, Crescent Moon, Cross and Heart. Then there are the sporting and agricultural group, which embody representations of the fox, horse, partridge, and even the elephant. Finally, there are those with heraldic designs.

Certain designs were more or less common in particular districts; thus according to Mr. H. S. Richards, the cart-horse, walking or trotting, was common in Sussex, the windmill in Lincolnshire, and the owl near Leeds. Some have religious subjects, such as the flight into Egypt, while others, which

Six typical examples of old brass horse ornaments. The first one shows a crescent Moon, the second one a star, the third represents the Sun, the fourth is heraldic, and the others are familiar types of decoration

with polished brass ornaments, is a fine sight. In some cases, before the advent of the motor-car, large horses would wear as many as eighteen brasses, a weight of over six pounds. Some have traced these objects

back to the amulets that in ancient times were hung on animals to ward off evil spirits, but it is doubtful if they had any other origin than a desire to make the horse with its harness look beautiful.

What is the Barn Dance?

IT is a dance imported into England from America about 1896, and was originally danced to the music of Meyer Lutz's "Pas de Quatre," by which name the dance was at first known. It is a combination of polka steps and waltz movements, but is now almost obsolete.

What is "Corked" Wine?

WINES which have been kept in bottles for a long time sometimes acquire a peculiar flavour, and as this is attributed, though quite erroneously, to the cork, such wine is described as "corked."

What really happens is that a peculiar mould grows from the outside of the cork inwards, and when it reaches the inner surface it imparts its taste to the wine. It would do the same with any other stopper.

A somewhat similar spoiling of the flavour occurs sometimes before the wine is bottled, and then it is said to have "the taste of the cask." This flavour is due to an essential oil which develops during the growth of mould on the surface of the wine. It can be removed by adding olive oil to the wine. This dissolves the unpleasant flavouring matter and carries it to the surface, when it can be removed.

What is a Deep Depression?

IN weather forecasts a cyclone, depression and low pressure are all different names for the same thing. They mean a condition where the mercury stands low in the barometer because the pressure of the atmosphere is light, and such a condition generally means a spell of bad, wet weather. The barometer falls because damp air is less heavy than dry air. A depression may be two or three thousand miles in diameter, and when the area of bad weather is more extensive than usual it is generally spoken of as a " deep depression."

Who Were the Peripatetic Philosophers?

THE word peripatetic means a person given to walking about, and the peripatetic philosophers were followers of Aristotle, who derived their peculiar name from Aristotle's habit of walking with his disciples in the shady groves of the Athenian gymnasium or Lyceum while he discussed with them the problems of philosophy. The chief of these peripatetic philosophers were Theophrastus of Lesbos, Eudemus of Rhodes and Strato of Lampsacus. Their teaching was a modification of that of Aristotle their master.

Which is the Third Largest Bell in England?

THE largest existing bell in 1938 was Great Paul at St. Paul's Cathedral in London. The second was Big Ben at Westminster, and the third was Great George, the bell in the tall tower of Bristol University. This weighs nine and a half tons.

What Exactly is a Bunsen Burner?

THIS burner, which is used not only in the laboratory but in the domestic gas-ring and in the mantle gas-burner, was invented by a German chemist named Robert Bunsen. He was a friend of the English scientist Sir Henry Roscoe, and when Roscoe

Oirat women of Siberia milking mares. The milk is fermented to form a drink known as kumiss

took to Heidelberg, where Bunsen taught, a certain gas-lamp for heating purposes, Bunsen, finding the temperature of the flame often low, said : " Roscoe, I am going to make a lamp in which the mixture of gas and air shall burn without any wire gauze." He carried out many experiments and in 1855 produced his burner, which has proved of such value in many ways.

Where is Mare's Milk Used?

MARE'S milk is used for certain types of invalids in various European countries, but, of course, this is rare. In some parts of Siberia, however, mares are milked regularly, and the milk is then fermented, to form an alcoholic drink known as kumiss. It is said to taste like strong beer.

Why is a Mitre-Joint So Called?

A MITRE-JOINT is a joint formed by pieces of wood that are matched and united upon a line which bisects the angle of junction. The pieces thus joined form a right angle, and the name was probably given because of the rough resemblance of such a joint to a bishop's mitre.

Why is a Peacock's Feather Thought Unlucky?

THE peacock's feather is a very beautiful object, and the colour, being caused not by pigments but by the breaking up of the light into its constituent hues, does not fade. Yet people foolishly regard this lovely object as bringing bad luck. It is not known definitely how this superstition arose. Some think the Crusaders brought back to Europe a tradition of the Devil worshippers of Kurdistan, who believe the Devil created from a dead cock a phantom of a peacock, saying, " Henceforth worship me under this symbol." Curiously enough, the peacock was originally a Christian emblem of the soul.

Another theory is that the superstition comes from the tradition that when the peacock with its hundred eyes was set to guard the entrance to Paradise, it admitted Satan and has been under a curse ever since. Yet this bird, strangely enough, is known to be a deadly foe of another creature under a curse, the serpent.

Great George, the bell in the tower of Bristol University, which is next in size to Big Ben

Which Animal Has the Most Massive Horns?

THE most massive and powerful horns are undoubtedly those of the Cape buffalo, the animal which scientists call *Bos caffer*. These horns, which in old bulls almost meet over the forehead, form an enormous helmet-like mass. Specimens are

weighs 228 pounds, and tusks have even been known twelve feet long and weighing about 300 pounds. The tusks continue to grow throughout the lives of their owners.

But apart from its tusks, the elephant's teeth are very wonderful. The molar teeth are remarkable for their great size and extreme complexity of structure. The crown, of

succeed one another from the front backwards in an arc of a circle ; and as the tooth in front is worn away its place is gradually taken by the one rising from behind, till at length the sixth and last tooth alone remains.'' In other words, each old front tooth as it is worn away is pushed out of place by its successor.

These teeth are of enormous size, sometimes measuring 15 inches in length and weighing 14 pounds. The elephant's tusks, of course, provide the finest ivory in the world, but the molar teeth are worth nothing at all commercially as ivory.

The record African buffalo's head, with horns measuring 56 inches across. This was exhibited at the International Hunting Exhibition held in London in 1938

often shot where the outside measurement of the horns is from 47 to 49 inches, but the world's record buffalo head is shown in the accompanying photograph. Here the horns measured 56 inches.

This animal is the largest member of its kind. It is a ferocious and dangerous creature, and when it charges nothing can stand before it. It charges with its head up, its nose straight out, and with the horns laid back over the shoulders. But just as it strikes it lowers its head, so that the full force of the massive horns, with the thick skull behind, can be used.

The Cape buffalo frequents marshes and rivers, and wades about, eating aquatic plants. Its sense of smell is remarkably keen, and it is also warned of the approach of foes by the buffalo birds, or ox-peckers, that remain near it with untiring vigilance. These birds are really a species of starling.

The African buffalo is regarded as the most dangerous animal a sportsman can meet. Even a lion will rarely attack a buffalo single-handed. If it does so it is generally beaten in the fight.

How Big is an Elephant's Tooth?

THE tusks are, of course, incisor or cutting teeth, remarkably developed, and these often attain an enormous size. One in the British Museum is over ten feet long and

which a great proportion is buried in the socket, with little more than the grinding surface appearing above the gum, is deeply divided into a number of transverse perpendicular plates consisting each of a body of dentine, coated by a layer of enamel, and this again by cement which fills the interspaces of the enamelled plates, binding together the several divisions.

"An elephant," says Mr. Richard Lydekker, " has a total of six cheek teeth on each side of both the upper and lower jaws ; but instead of all being in use at once, in the existing species only two are ever above the gums at any one time, and one of these is only partly protruded ; while in all animals only a single tooth remains on each side of both jaws. . . . The individual teeth

Does the Post Office Make a Profit?

YES ; the British General Post Office, which is run very efficiently, makes a handsome annual profit, which goes towards the relief of taxation. For the year ending March 31st, 1937, the profit was £12,350,000, which, although £189,000 less than the record surplus for 1935–36, was the second highest in the history of the Post Office. The total transactions for the year 1936–37 reached a total of £962,000,000, the highest total yet and £61,000,000 more than 1935–36.

Do Icebergs Damage Submarine Cables?

IN shallow northern waters the shore-ends of submarine cables have to be very heavily armoured to protect them against icebergs, which often ground at the point where the cable lands, and by the grinding action as the water sways them would break the cable. In 1866 the grounding of icebergs at the entrance to Trinity Bay, Newfoundland, caused serious faults in the Atlantic cable.

A single molar tooth from an elephant's head. It weighs over fourteen pounds

What is the Whale-Headed Stork?

THIS is one of the strangest-looking birds in Africa, and it gets its popular name from a fancied resemblance of its big head to a whale's

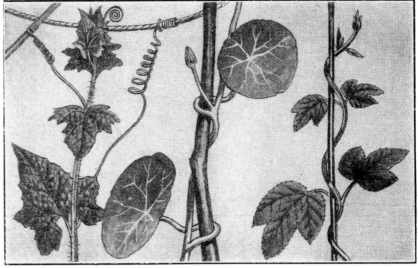

A shoe-bill or whale-headed stork at the London Zoo, having its curious beak brushed by its keeper

head. Another name given to it is the shoe-billed stork, because its bill is something like a shoe in shape, and the Arabs call it by a name which means "father of a shoe."

The bird is big and has long legs, but its most striking feature is its bill, which is broad and in profile is concave. There is a strong ridge down the middle of the upper half of the bill and the tip is extended into a bold hook. The lower half of the beak is covered with a soft leathery skin for the greater part of its length, although it is horny at the tip.

The bird is not very well known for it is confined to the White Nile region and frequents places remote from human habitations, where it is generally seen standing breast-deep in water by the side of the papyrus plant, and often rests on one leg.

When first disturbed by a passing boat it will fly off slowly with a great noise and then soon settle again. But if it is disturbed a second time it will rise high into the air and not return to its former haunt till all danger is past. In flight the heavy, ungainly beak is kept resting on the crop.

Its chief food is fish, and to catch this the bird stands breast deep in the water with its enormous beak lowered to the surface. At times, however, a number of the shoe-billed storks

combine to drive the fish towards the shallows by marching in a semicircle through the water and flapping their wings vigorously.

It is sometimes said that these birds kill and eat snakes, but this is probably an error and may have arisen from the fact that they devour the fish known as the bichir, which the natives sometimes call the water-snake. The stork also feeds on carrion. The birds when taken from the nest young are quite easily tamed.

What is a Barge-Board?

IT is a board, often decorated, under an overhanging gable, and is sometimes called a verge board. The earliest barge-boards known to exist are of the 14th century. After that time they are used abundantly. They are generally either feathered or panelled or pierced with a series of trefoils, or quatrefoils, and the spandrel or triangular space beneath the point of the gable is often carved with foliage.

Barge-boards of the 15th century, though less deeply cut than those of earlier date, have a rich and beautiful effect. Later they have little enrichment beyond plain mouldings.

What is a Black Frost?

IT is a frost occurring when there happens to be a strong breeze or a dry atmosphere, so that there is no deposit of white hoar-frost on ground, roofs and trees. The name was given because at such times the ground appears to have a slightly blackened appearance, owing to the deadening effect of the cold upon the grass and foliage.

There is no ground for the popular belief that black frosts are more severe than white ones. Some of the greatest frosts, like that of February, 1895, have been white frosts.

How Do Plants Climb?

ALL climbing plants do not rise in the same way. Some, like the hop, have twining stems, which twine in a definite direction, and these raise themselves by curling round any support that is handy. The hop and honeysuckle ascend in a right-handed spiral, while the bindweed or convolvulus climbs in a left-handed spiral.

Other plants, like the pea, vine and bryony climb by means of sensitive tendrils, which coil round or fix themselves to any suitable object. They can embrace even slender supports, which are horizontal in position, and are capable of twisting round the support in both a right-handed and a left-handed direction.

Other plants, again, like the nasturtium, climb by means of coiling leafstalks. The ivy ascends by means of numerous aerial roots, which are given off by the stem, and fix the plant to the supporting object. Some plants rise by merely leaning against or scrambling over other plants, while some clamber by the aid of hooks or prickles, as in the case of the bramble.

Climbing plants usually have slender stems, with long stretches between the nodes, where the leaves grow out. When there is no external object up which to climb, a climbing plant may grow prostrate.

On the left is the bryony climbing by means of a tendril; in the centre, the nasturtium, which climbs with a coiling leafstalk, and on the right the hop, which has a twining stem

Why Are Wines Stored in Casks?

SOME wines, like those of the Rhine district, cannot be kept long, because they contain but little alcohol or contain much sugar and little tannic acid. But other wines improve with age, and these are cellared—that is, stored in casks in cellars. The wine then becomes less acid, develops odoriferous substances and improves in flavour.

"Wine," says Mr. John Angell, "is improved by being kept in wooden casks, as water escapes by evaporation and the other constituents are relatively increased. The vinous constituents, being thus concentrated, exert a stronger chemical action upon each other and render the wine not only stronger but better flavoured. The change, however, does not stop here. The loss of water must be replaced by the addition of wine, otherwise the action of the air would turn the wine sour and convert the alcohol into acetic acid ; and the diminution of water which is thus replaced by wine causes a constant increase of tartaric acid. Wines which are poor in sugar may thus soon become too sour, and consequently all wines cannot undergo this process. The popular idea that wine which has grown old in bottles has therefore become richer in alcohol is false."

The phrase often seen at inns and hotels, "Wines from the wood," means that wine can be obtained drawn direct from the cask in which it is kept.

How Are Pearls Formed?

NATURAL pearls are very beautiful objects and form a dainty ornament for a lady's neck. Yet these treasures are really nothing but the tombs of little worms.

The pearl oyster secretes inside its shell a substance known as mother-of-pearl, but if anything gets inside to irritate the oyster it will cover this with mother-of-pearl. In Japan pearl oysters are kept in tanks, and the Japanese insert grains of sand and other objects, and the oysters cover these with mother-of-pearl, thus forming what are partly natural and partly artificial pearls. They are generally spoken of as culture pearls.

But the real natural pearls are due to parasites which slip in through the two valves of the oyster shell and irritate the oyster, which at once begins to coat them with mother-of-pearl, or nacre, as it is also called. The parasites die, and the beautiful pearl which is produced layer by layer is thus a tomb.

Enormous numbers of oyster shells are examined for pearls. In one year in Ceylon, for example, in 38 days over 41,000,000 oysters were taken and examined.

What is Tooth Ornament?

IT is a peculiar form of decoration used extensively in the Early English style of architecture. It consists of a

An example of tooth ornament

series of closely placed small flowers, each consisting of four leaves, which project forward to a central point. These are generally arranged in hollow mouldings. This form of decoration is also called "dog tooth" and "nail head."

How Long is a Lightning Flash?

SCIENTIFIC experts who have studied the lightning tell us that the flashes are quite as long as they look. There is nothing of the optical illusion about them. Often a flash is five miles in length, and its energy is equal to the driving power of a 200-ton train travelling at 50 miles an hour.

Did Napoleon Play Cards?

YES ; but he was not a good player and did not like to be defeated, so that those who played with him did not have a very pleasant time. Mr. W. P. Courtney tells us that "Neither in prosperity nor in exile could he bear that his plans at whist should be thwarted, but he was never happy without his game at cards in the evening." Vingt-et-un was the game he liked best, but he was frequently ready to play whist.

What is a Bumping Race?

IT is a form of boat racing practised at Cambridge and Oxford, where the rivers Cam and Isis are too narrow for boats to race side by side. Instead of rowing abreast, as in an ordinary race, the boats start one behind another from allotted stations about two lengths apart. There may be eighteen or twenty boats in a race, and the object of each is to catch up the one in front and bump into it, at the same time avoiding being bumped by the boat behind. When a bump is made both crews concerned draw to the bank, and for them the race is over for the day.

The races last for several days, and the second day any crew that made a bump the day before starts one place up, and the crew that was bumped goes down one place. In other words, the two boats change places in the line. A crew that rows the whole course without bumping another boat or being bumped is said to have "rowed over" the course.

In these races each boat has a rubber ball fastened to its prow. This has been done since a tragedy occurred at Cambridge in the races of 1888, when the sharp nose of a boat ran into a man in another boat and killed him.

Wine in wooden barrels stored in the vaults at the London docks

What is That Type of Hinge Called?

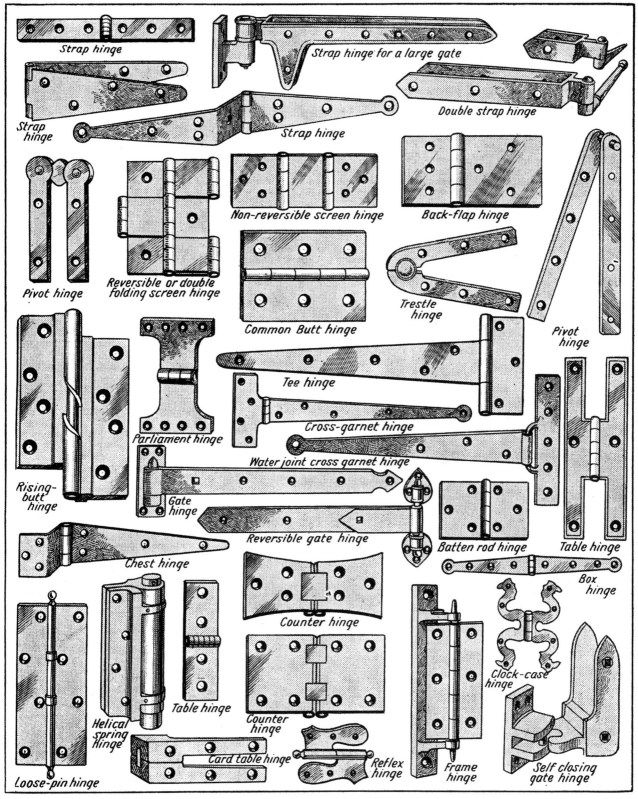

Strap hinge

Strap hinge for a large gate

Double strap hinge

Strap hinge

Strap hinge

Pivot hinge

Reversible or double folding screen hinge

Non-reversible screen hinge

Back-flap hinge

Common Butt hinge

Trestle hinge

Pivot hinge

Parliament hinge

Tee hinge

Cross-garnet hinge

Water joint cross garnet hinge

Rising-butt hinge

Gate hinge

Reversible gate hinge

Batten rod hinge

Table hinge

Chest hinge

Box hinge

Counter hinge

Clock-case hinge

Helical spring Hinge

Table hinge

Counter hinge

Loose-pin hinge

Card table hinge

Reflex hinge

Frame hinge

Self closing gate hinge

Hinges are of all sizes and shapes, and on this page will be found more than 30 different kinds of hinges, which are in common use, with their names. Some get their names from their shapes or styles, others from the use to which they are put, and others from some particular action as they work. The strap hinge, for example, is so called because it is extended in the shape of a leather strap. A rising butt hinge is a convenient type, used for the doors of rooms on the floors of which are thick carpets. The rising butt hinge raises the door as it is opened, so that it will pass easily over the carpet. Some of the hinges, like the Parliament hinge and the cross-garnet hinge, merely have fancy names and are used for the same purpose as some of the other hinges shown. The helical spring hinge is used for doors, and causes the door to close automatically. In preparing this page of drawings the artist has received the courteous help of Messrs. Buck & Hickman, Ltd., the tool merchants of Whitechapel, London

What is a Squirting Cucumber?

THIS is the name given to an interesting plant known to botanists as *Ecballium elaterium*, which when the fruit is ripe has a curious method of distributing the seeds. The fruit resembles a small fleshy cucumber covered with little bristles and borne by a hooked stalk. The end of the stalk projects into the inside of the fruit very much like a stopper. As soon as the seeds are quite ripe the tissue that surrounds them is changed into a gummy mass. At the same time the tissue linking the stalk and the fruit becomes loose.

In the wall of the fruit there is a layer of cells under great tension, which is all the time trying to stretch itself out. So long as the fruit remains unripe any expansion is prevented by the tense tissue close to the stalk, but directly, on the ripening of the fruit, this obstacle is removed the fruit severs itself from the conical end of the stalk and the strained layer of tissue at once expands. The result is that the seeds and mucilage inside the fruit are squirted out with much force through the hole which the stalk previously closed.

This curious plant is a close relation of the common cucumber of our greenhouses and salads.

Who Were the Honveds?

THE word is Hungarian and means "defenders of the Fatherland." They were originally the Landwehr or militia of Hungary, exclusive of the artillery, and in the Hungarian rebellion of 1848–49 the name was first given to ten battalions of volunteers who organised themselves in the defence of house and home. Then after a time the entire revolutionary army was called the Honveds.

What Thickness of Ice Will Support a Man?

AN inch and a half will support the weight of a single average man, four inches a horseman, ten inches a crowd of people, and eighteen inches will support a railway train.

What is a Chopine?

A CHOPINE is a form of high shoe or clog, still used by Asiatic women such as the Japanese, and fashionable in Europe in the 16th century. The European chopine originated in Venice, and from there was introduced into England.

Chopines of the 16th century

But it had only a brief reign among English ladies. Shakespeare refers to it in "Hamlet," where he speaks of "The altitude of a chopine."

Why Has the George VI Farthing a Wren?

THE farthing of the coinage of King George VI's reign bears on its reverse side a representation of a wren, and it is interesting to learn from the Deputy-Master of the Mint how this bird came to appear on the coin.

"During 1936," says Sir Robert Johnson, "in the early stages when the coinage for King Edward was in question, I was made aware that some desire existed for a complete departure

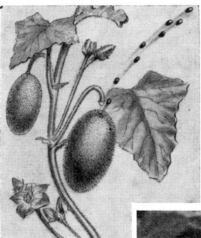

How the squirting cucumber shoots out its seeds

from the heraldic tradition which has been associated for several centuries with our principal coins. Some held the view that heraldry was not 'understanded of the people,' and that persons unversed in the science would prefer simple pictorial devices upon the coins which they used day by day.

"No doubt these ideas have been encouraged by the issue of what I may call, I hope without offence, the 'Zoological' coinages, of which the Irish Free State coins are so charming an example, and in which the new issues for New Zealand and Southern Rhodesia may perhaps be included. There is much to be said for this 'modern' view, but, on the other hand, the traditional school held firmly that heraldry not only affords the best basis for design, but that for one of the few remaining monarchies to abandon it would be little short of disastrous."

Sir Robert Johnson says that he and

his advisers felt that an opportunity should be given to the "modern" school to show what might be done. Twelve artists were invited to submit ideas, but unfortunately there was failure to produce a completely novel series and this was due to the inherent difficulties of the problem. A purely agricultural country or a new country with characteristic fauna or flora could seek motives within itself to proclaim its individuality, but an old

The farthing of George VI with the wren design

country like Great Britain afforded few characteristics eminently peculiar to it.

"Aeroplanes, for example," says Sir Robert, "which were favoured by more than one artist, or steelworks, or mines, or corn, or cattle, are by no means peculiar to Great Britain.

"One artist produced a series of models based on the royal animals, which displayed both originality of thought and delicacy of craftsman-

A photograph of a squirting cucumber with the fruit ripening

ship. One of these, depicting the wren, was regarded as too pleasing to be rejected altogether and now appears upon the farthing." That is how it is we have a bird on our coin of smallest denomination. While heraldic designs on coins give continuity and have an historic value, the new type of design certainly adds something of the picturesque to a coinage.

What is a Snake Farm?

IT is a place where snakes are bred for scientific purposes, as, for example, to provide the virus which is used as an antitoxin against poisonous snake-bite. Such farms are

The Government snake farm at Butantan in the state of Sao Paulo, Brazil, where much of the world's antitoxin against snake-bite is collected. Snakes are picked up on hooked poles

found in North and South America and in South Africa. Snakes are also provided for experiment by scientists. Thousands are bred and used each year in this way and the attendants on the farm become expert in moving the snakes without getting a bite. Proper houses are constructed for the snakes, with a reproduction, so far as possible, of their natural habitat.

What is the "Poor Sinner's Bell"?

THIS is the name given to a bell in the Church of St. Mary Magdalene at Breslau in Germany. The legend which accounts for the name is thus recounted by the Rev. George S. Tyack:

"Some five hundred years ago a founder was employed in constructing a bell to hang in the south tower of the Church of St. Mary Magdalene in that town. The mould had been duly made and the metal was nearly ready for tapping, when the master was called away for a short time ; and in leaving a boy in charge gave him strict injunctions not to interfere with the furnace. Scarcely had he turned his back, however, when the lad, boy-like, began to finger the catch which kept the metal in, and presently to his horror the youngster saw the crimson stream of glowing metal come leaping from the furnace, and flowing in full tide to the pit where lay the mould.

"In terror at what he had done, he rushed from the foundry shouting wildly for his master ; and the latter on entering, seeing, as he thought, his labours all thrown away and his work absolutely ruined, struck the lad a blow which passion rendered so severe that he fell lifeless at his feet.

' In due time the metal cooled, the cope was drawn off and the bell was lifted from the core, when the amazed artificer beheld it smooth and perfect in finish, and found it, on testing, clear and sweet in tone. Overcome with remorse for the fatal consequences of his momentary rage, the master gave himself up to the authorities, accusing himself of the murder of his servant. The law took its course and its full penalty was exacted ; and the first man on whose behalf the bell rang out, calling the faithful to pray for his parting soul, was the skilful maker of the bell itself. St. Mary's bell was the name given to it at its dedication, but from that day forward, even to our own times, the Breslau folk have called it the bell of the ' Poor Sinner.' "

Why Are Modern Trains Streamlined?

THE idea is to reduce air-resistance and enable increased speeds to be obtained at a minimum expenditure of fuel. The faster the train travels, the greater is the effect of air resistance. As an illustration of this Mr. Harry Bentham, a London engineer, in his presidential address to the Society of Engineers in 1938, mentioned that if, as had been proposed, a Channel Tunnel should be made and trains run between London and Paris at an average speed of ninety miles an hour, with a maximum of 120 miles per hour, a passenger by putting his head out of the window at that speed would make a call for fifteen additional horse-power from the locomotive.

Where Are Homework Cubicles Provided?

ONE of the great difficulties of school-children who live in small and crowded homes, where privacy is impossible, has been to find an opportunity of doing their homework properly. In order to meet this difficulty a children's library in Walthamstow, one of the Essex suburbs of London, has carried out an excellent idea which will no doubt be followed elsewhere.

It provides a number of cubicles in which children who wish to do their homework away from home can sit and write in peace and quietness. Cubicles can be reserved by boys and girls for an unlimited time. Daylight lamps are provided and upholstered chairs in which the children can sit comfortably while they work. Such provision for homework is a great boon.

The special cubicles in which children can do their homework in the Walthamstow Library

What is That Firework?

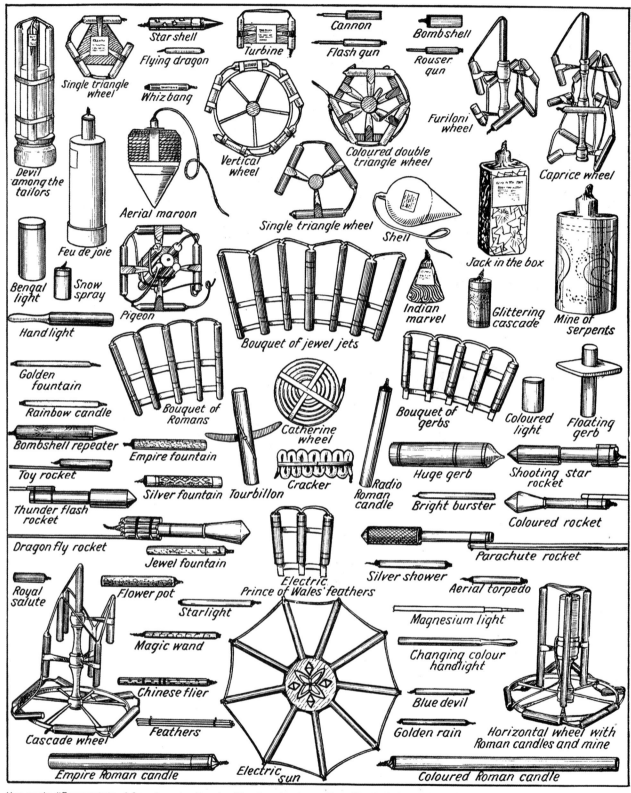

Here are the different varieties of fireworks used on November 5th and at other times. Many, like the Catherine Wheel, Hand Light and Roman Candle, are well known. The Devil Among the Tailors shows a steady fountain of light, surrounded by four Roman Candles. These burn down to a base and throw up crackers as a finale. A Flying Dragon is an erratic stickless rocket, finishing with a bang. In the Turbine the centre-board is fastened to a post, and the firework revolves while the two cases burn. In the Caprice Wheel cases are set at various angles, and burn in succession, the fire they emit changing its direction each time a new case ignites. A Furiloni Wheel is the same, except that the cases are all at the same angle. The Mine of Serpents shoots out a cascade of squibs. A Gerb (pronounced jerb) throws out a wheat-sheaf of fire. An Indian Marvel is a fire fountain. A Tourbillon, meaning whirlwind, has four holes through which fire rushes, whirling the whole thing round, and finally driving it up into the air. A Cascade Wheel is a Caprice Wheel with a fountain. An Electric Sun is a fountain giving dazzling white fire. A Pigeon is arranged on a horizontal wire between two poles, and when lighted the firework revolves and rushes to and fro along the wire. Rockets rise to various heights, a 2-lb. rocket going up 2,000 feet, and a 1-lb. rocket 1,400 feet. These drawings are given here by courtesy of Messrs. C. T. Brock & Co., the well-known fireworks manufacturers

Has the Government Used Picture-Writing?

YES, in the early days of the colonisation of Tasmania, picture-writing was used by Governor Davey to inform the illiterate natives that British rule would be just and impartial. He issued a proclamation entirely in picture form, and this is shown in the illustration on this page.

Governor Davey's picture-writing announcement to the natives of Tasmania in 1816

The idea was to let the natives know that coloured men would receive the same justice as white men. In the upper part of the picture black and white folk are shown in friendly intercourse, and on the next line the governor is shaking hands with a chief, to show his friendship, whites and blacks looking on. In the third line a black is shown killing a white man, and afterwards being executed as punishment for his crime. Finally, in the last line a white man is seen shooting a black, and he also is being hanged for his crime.

What is the Canadian "Dust Bowl"?

IT is an area about 400 miles long and 300 miles wide in Saskatchewan, Canada, consisting of arid plains where formerly were flourishing and productive cornlands. But several years of drought, grasshopper plagues and soil erosion turned what was a garden into a wilderness. Haphazard methods of settlement in the early days assisted the destructive process, for vast areas of prairie grass were ploughed up, and this resulted in an increase of evaporation and a drifting of the soil.

These miles of burnt-up plains were a few years ago prairies covered with waving crops of wheat, as far as the eye could see. Whereas in 1928 Saskatchewan produced 321,215,000 bushels of wheat, in 1937 its output was only about 75,000,000 bushels. Some of the lands are poor, and should never have been settled, but much is rich clay soil, sometimes a hundred feet deep, and the rest is quite fertile land, which only needs irrigation to make it continuously productive.

The "Great Dust Bowl" in the United States is the name given in America to a large area in the middle states, which owing to the cutting down of forests has become arid and lost its soil. The aggregations of trees with their roots hold the soil and the moisture, but when the trees were cut down it became dry and pulverised, and the strong winds which pass over those areas carried away the soil in dust storms.

What is the Height Record for an Aeroplane?

THE official height record for a heavier-than-air machine is 16,440 metres, or 53,937 feet, held for Great Britain by Flight-Lieutenant M. J. Adam, R.A.F., who on June 30th, 1937, rose to this height in a Bristol 138 monoplane with a 490 horse-power engine.

The record height for a balloon is 74,187 feet, or just over 14 miles, made by two United States Army officers in a metal ball 9 feet in diameter attached to a balloon as tall as a thirty-storey building. This was at White Lake, 230 miles east of Rapid City, South Dakota.

Should One Eye Be Shut in Using a Telescope?

MOST people when looking through a telescope or a microscope shut the eye they are not using, but this is never done by expert users of such instruments. Scientists do not screw up one eye when examining objects through the microscope, nor do sailors close one eye when using a

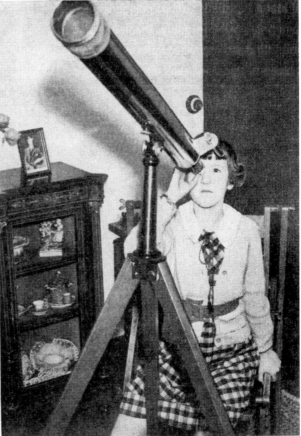

The correct way of looking through a telescope, with both eyes open

telescope. A little practice in keeping both eyes open makes it quite easy to do so when using an instrument of this kind and is much less tiring for the observer.

119

Is the Yak an Ox?

IT is a member of the ox family and forms a link between the group to which domestic cattle belong and the bisons. It is peculiar to the elevated plateau of Tibet and the adjacent regions of China, and its most distinctive feature is the mass of long hair on the flanks, underparts, limbs and tail. On the head the hair is short and nearly smooth. The colour of the hair of the wild yak is blackish brown, but among domesticated yaks the colour may be black and white, brown and white, or pure white.

scientific name of the species, *Bos grunniens*, or grunting ox, is derived. But the wild animals do not utter these grunts.

The domesticated animals are absolutely essential for crossing many parts of Tibet and they are kept not only as beasts of burden, but also for their flesh. The yak has been crossed with ordinary cattle and the half-breeds have the advantage of being able to stand much higher temperatures than the pure-bred yaks. They are used for carrying burdens in the hot valley of the Indus.

The yak has enormous powers of endurance and can traverse glaciers and swim icy torrents without disadvantage. Curiously enough, it will not eat corn and this is a great disadvantage for it frequently necessitates the pushing on of a caravan by forced marches to reach food. In the wild herds, at the prospect of danger the older bulls and cows surround the calves to protect them, and the whole herd gallops away.

The yak of the highlands of Tibet

The yak is a massively built animal with short, stout legs. The average height at the shoulders is about 5½ feet, though some old bulls stand six feet. The horns are very large in the bull and are smooth and nearly cylindrical. They vary in length from 25 to 30 inches, measured along the curve, but a pair has been recorded measuring 40 inches with a girth at the base of 19 inches. The horns of the cows are thinner and smaller. A bull yak weighs about half a ton.

The country in which the wild yak lives is utterly desolate and dreary, and the animals confine themselves to the wildest and most inaccessible parts. They are found only at great heights, ranging in summer from 14,000 to 20,000 feet above sea-level. They delight in cold, but cannot endure heat.

In northern Tibet, where the old bulls are found alone, the herds of cows and younger males number hundreds, and sometimes, it is said, thousands.

The yak has been domesticated for centuries and it is the only beast of burden that can work at the high altitudes of the Central Asian plateau. A peculiarity of the domesticated yak is its grunting voice, from which the

Can There Be a Month Without a New Moon?

YES, sometimes in February there is no new moon, but there are, in that case, two new moons in the January and two in the March following. This happens about once in every twenty-seven years. It occurred in 1911, in 1938, and will occur again in 1961. In the latter case only 23 years will elapse.

Does Drinking Sea-Water Send People Mad?

IT is not the drinking of sea-water that drives people mad, but the exposure to starvation and thirst. The reason it is bad when suffering in this way to drink sea-water is that it aggravates the thirst, and thereby increases the tendency to lose one's reason.

What Famous Actresses Have Played Peter Pan?

THE part of Peter Pan has always been played by an actress, and among the notable performers who have taken the part are Nina Boucicault, Cecilia Loftus, Pauline Chase (who played it eight seasons), Madge Titheradge, Unity More (two seasons), Fay Compton, Faith Celli, Georgette Cohan, Edna Best (two seasons), Joan Maclean, Gladys Cooper (two seasons), Dorothy Dickson (two seasons), Jean Forbes-Robertson (eight seasons), Nova Pilbeam, Elsa Lanchester and Anna Neagle. Miss Zena

Domesticated yaks loaded for a journey over the mountains

What is an Iceland Dog?

IT is the name of a rough, shaggy, white breed of dog that was once a great favourite with ladies. It is mentioned by Shakespeare in his play " King Henry V," Act 2, Scene 1, where Pistol calls Nym " Iceland dog, thou prick-eared cur of Iceland."

Dare played the part at Sheffield in 1906.

Peter Pan had its first performance in London at the Duke of York's Theatre on December 27th, 1904, and it has been revived every year since. About a million playgoers, large and small, have seen the play and it seems as popular now as ever.

What is That Kind of Nail Used For?

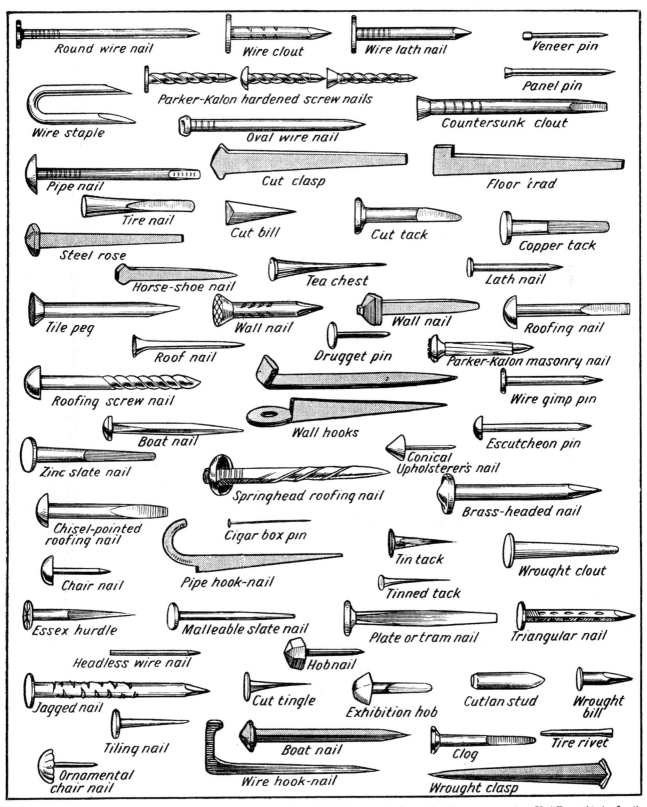

Round wire nail · Wire clout · Wire lath nail · Veneer pin · Panel pin · Parker-Kalon hardened screw nails · Wire staple · Countersunk clout · Oval wire nail · Pipe nail · Cut clasp · Floor brad · Tire nail · Cut bill · Cut tack · Copper tack · Steel rose · Horse-shoe nail · Tea chest · Lath nail · Tile peg · Wall nail · Wall nail · Roofing nail · Roof nail · Drugget pin · Parker-Kalon masonry nail · Roofing screw nail · Wall hooks · Wire gimp pin · Boat nail · Escutcheon pin · Zinc slate nail · Conical Upholsterer's nail · Springhead roofing nail · Brass-headed nail · Chisel-pointed roofing nail · Cigar box pin · Tin tack · Wrought clout · Chair nail · Pipe hook-nail · Tinned tack · Essex hurdle · Malleable slate nail · Plate or tram nail · Triangular nail · Headless wire nail · Hobnail · Jagged nail · Cut tingle · Exhibition hob · Cutlan stud · Wrought bill · Tiling nail · Boat nail · Clog · Tire rivet · Ornamental chair nail · Wire hook-nail · Wrought clasp

There are many different kinds of nails, all adapted to the uses for which they are manufactured. Here are more than 50 different kinds of nails with their names. Many of the names indicate the use to which they are put. Clout nails are wrought iron nails with a large, flat head, and were originally used for fastening clouts or iron plates on axle-trees. Veneer pins are, of course, used for attaching veneer. Wire nails are so called because they are made from thick wire. Hobnails are used for driving into the soles of boots, and are worn where men have to walk or work on rough, hard surfaces. They protect the leather soles. Screw nails of various kinds hold better than smooth ones in soft wood. Some nails are patents, and have proprietary names. Most of these drawings are given by courtesy of Messrs. Buck & Hickman, Limited, of Whitechapel, London

Have a Penguin and Ostrich the Same Neck Bones?

YES, it is a fact that there are the same number of bones in the necks of both these birds, although that of the ostrich seems so very long, while the penguin appears to have no neck at all. The comparison is very much like that of the elephant and the giraffe, both of which have the same number of bones in their necks, namely seven.

Why Was Aristides Called the Just?

THIS famous Athenian of noble family was the great rival of Themistocles, through whose influence the people ostracised or exiled him in 483 B.C. He was still in exile is 480 B.C., when the battle of Salamis took place, and raising and arming a band he did good work by dislodging the enemy.

After this he was recalled from banishment and appointed general in the following year, when he commanded the Athenians at the battle of Plataea. By general consent he was given the task of drawing up the laws

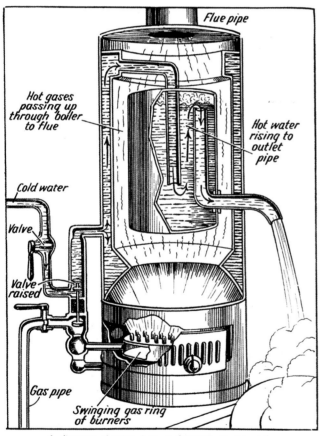

A diagram showing how a domestic geyser works

and fixing the taxes. He died about 468 B.C. so poor that he did not leave enough even to pay for his funeral. His daughters and his son Lysimachus received a grant from the State. It was because of his constant integrity that he was surnamed " the Just."

How Does a Bathroom Geyser Work?

THE drawing given on this page will show how this useful appliance works. When the cold-water tap is turned on, water enters a pipe, and the pressure raises a water-valve at the bottom of a valve stem. Here there is another valve, controlling the gas supply, which has previously been turned on, and this valve is also raised by the pressure of the water.

The gas is now able to flow to the gas-ring, studded with burners, and these when lighted generate great heat. The cold water circulating near the gas-jets becomes immediately hot and rises to a circular tank above. From this tank it descends into a central tank, where it is further heated by the gas flames. It is now very hot and can rise and pass through the outlet pipe to the bath.

The moment the cold water is turned off the dual valve drops, and the gas supply also is cut off, except for a small pilot jet for relighting the burner. When the cold water is turned off the level of the hot water drops in the central tank, and so does not reach the outlet pipe.

The burner is swung out of the geyser for safety in lighting. The hot gas circulates round the inside, and passes up to the flue at the top, and so to the outside atmosphere. Geysers without flues are very dangerous.

What is Cap-a-Pie?

THE words are Old French, and mean " from head to foot." The term was used to describe a knight or other person who was completely armed at all points. The armour and weapons, of course, varied greatly at different periods of history.

Can Fir Cones Be Used as Weather Glasses?

FIR cones are very good hygrometers and respond in a striking manner to the moisture in the atmosphere. When the air is dry and fine conditions are likely, the scales of the cones are opened wide, but when there is much moisture in the air and rain is likely the scales shut up closely. A fir cone barometer may be made amusing by attaching to the

A fir cone used as a weather glass. Above, the scales are closed, indicating rain, and below they are opened, foretelling fine weather

cone a cardboard head and giving it the appearance of a hedgehog. Then in dry weather the hedgehog will open out, as shown in the photograph here, and in wet weather it will close up.

What is the Feast of Purim?

IT is an annual Jewish festival celebrated on the fourteenth and fifteenth days of the month Adar. Its origin is described in the ninth chapter of the Book of Esther in the Old Testament. It is preceded by the Fast of Esther on the thirteenth. The word " purim " means " lots," and it is a mocking reference to the lots by which Haman, the enemy of the Jews, discovered the lucky day, as he thought, for the extermination of that race. The feast celebrates the deliverance of the people from his murderous design by the work of Queen Esther and Mordecai.

On the Feast of Purim the Jews meet in their synagogues, and the Book of Esther is read through. When the names of Haman and his sons are reached, the whole congregation stamp with the feet and hiss, crying out " Let his name be blotted out! Let the name of the wicked perish! " After the service the people indulge in merriment. Formerly an effigy of Haman was carried in procession and then hanged and burned. There is no reference to the Feast of Purim in the New Testament, but some think it may be the feast spoken of in the first verse of the fifth chapter of St. John's Gospel. But Purim was a feast for which it was not necessary to go to Jerusalem.

How Are Terrestrial Globes Made?

As explained on page 89 the only accurate map of the world is that on a globe, and many thousands of globes of all sizes are made for educational purposes every year. Messrs. George Philip and Son, the cartographers, make globes of from one inch to five feet in diameter and for every size there is a corresponding wooden ball which is the foundation of each globe.

The first process is the making of the shell. Coarse, glued paper is damped and applied to the ball whose shape it takes when dry. This paper shell is then cut right round so that it can be removed from the ball in two halves. To the inner edge of one half a circular strip of card is pasted so that it forms a kind of flange. When this has dried the two halves of the shell can be fitted together like the halves of an Easter egg.

Next a steel spindle is thrust through the points which will eventually be the North and South Poles of the finished globe. This is for working purposes at a mounting table, to which the shell is now moved. The table has a semi-circular space cut out of its edge with a sharp metal rim all round. The spindle ends rest on the table and the shell can thus be revolved by a touch of the finger while a special plaster composition is laid upon it in layers. There are usually four or five layers and each one is carefully smoothed by revolving the shell against the sharp metal edge.

This process completed, the map, political or physical, has to be applied to the blank globe. Political maps are litho-printed in four colours in a series of gores or roughly lozenge-shaped strips. These gores are cut out of the printed sheets by hand, glued on to the globe and carefully smoothed down with a bone. Women are employed for this work and great care has to be taken in carrying it out as the

The Sands of Dee, whose dangers are described in Charles Kingsley's poem

paper is liable to stretch when damp. Each gore must be worked by the fingers of an expert at this stage. Besides the gores each globe has two polar caps. The globe is left to dry and then after being varnished is again dried. The spindles are removed and the completed globe having been passed after careful examination by the forewoman, it is finally arranged on a stand with its meridian of metal or wood.

Celestial globes showing the principal stars and constellations are made in the same way.

For school use blackboard globes are prepared which can be written upon with chalk. The process of making these is the same as in the case of ordinary terrestrial globes up to the point when the plaster composition is put on them. Then the whole globe is covered with a black ink preparation. As soon as this has dried the map is painted on the globe by hand in white.

What Are the Sands of Dee?

This is the name given to a vast expanse of sand which is exposed at low tide in the estuary of the River Dee, which flows into the Irish Sea. The river itself meanders in a narrow channel, and when the tide comes in it rushes over the sands with great speed.

This is a source of danger, and is referred to in Charles Kingsley's well-known poem, " The Sands of Dee " :

The western tide crept up along the sand,
　And o'er and o'er the sand,
　And round and round the sand,
　　As far as eye could see.
The rolling mist came down and hid the land ;
　And never home came she.

A photograph of the sands, seen when the tide is out, is given above.

What is Encaustic Painting?

Encaustic is a method of painting used by the ancients. The colours were mixed in melted wax, which was kept hot throughout the process of painting. This form of painting was used in architectural decoration, and in the colouring of statues, for the marble statues of the ancients were not left white, but were painted. The word encaustic means "to burn in."

Girls making terrestrial globes in the factory of Messrs. George Philip & Son, Limited. On the left a blackboard globe is being prepared, and on the right the map sections are being stuck on the globes ready for varnishing

A stray dog found by the Banbury police which was so intelligent that it was trained to assist them in their work

of burglaries, decided to use dogs as aids to the police. Large Labrador retrievers were trained at Newbury in Berkshire to accompany policemen at night on lonely country beats and on the outskirts of London and other large towns. These dogs have been trained to chase and hold suspects and to carry messages to and

What Are the Smallest Screws Used For?

THE smallest screws that are made are used in watches. Some of them are so small that it takes 482,000 of them to weigh a ton. Each screw is only 34 thousandths of an inch in length—that is, about one-30th of an inch—and the diameter at the head 12 thousandths of an inch—that is, about one-83rd. Such a screw has very minute threads at the rate of 360 to the inch.

Do the Police Use Dogs as Aids?

ON the continent of Europe the practice of using dogs as an aid to the police in the detection of crime has long since passed the experimental stage. But in Great Britain only spasmodic attempts in this direction have hitherto been made. As far back as the Jack the Ripper murders in 1888 bloodhounds were tried, and from time to time since these dogs have been used in the effort to track murderers.

In European countries, however, police dogs have long been expected to do more than merely track criminals. They have to assist the police when the latter are attacked, to pursue a fugitive and when he is caught to hold him without biting till the police arrive. They are trained to follow escaping criminals over high fences or up ladders, and afterwards to retrace their steps and retrieve anything the man may have dropped in his flight.

The dog chiefly employed on the Continent is the Alsatian. It is active, courageous and teachable, and some years ago attempts were made in England by the Alsatian League of Great Britain to show how useful this dog might be as an aid to the police. Trials were held, but nothing definite resulted.

The authorities of several dockyards in England have employed Airedales to accompany the night patrols, and excellent work these dogs have done. Their acute senses of hearing and smell have enabled them to detect thieves concealed among bales of goods, who might otherwise have escaped human observation.

In 1938 the Home Office, in a new attempt to reduce the growing number

Above, two pure bloodhounds, and others crossed with otter hounds ; and on the right, a bloodhound during police trials that has found its man after following a trail

from the police headquarters.

Another type of dog is being bred to follow scents hours old. This type has been bred from two American bloodhounds brought to England in 1937 which had proved themselves expert in this kind of work. Their six puppies have been crossed with Scottish otterhounds to give them a better stamina for long and sustained chases. No doubt now that a beginning has been made, dogs will more and more be used as auxiliaries for the police.

Quite recently another German variety of dog, the Rottweiler, has been trained and used as a police dog and has proved very useful.

Are All Giraffes Marked Alike?

No; there are several races of giraffes in Africa and each has distinctive markings. The northern group, of which the Nubian giraffe is the type, has a fawn body marked by a coarse mesh-work of white lines. The legs are white without pattern. Races

From this, comments Mr. Pycraft, it will be apparent that the coloration of the legs, whether white or spotted, may stand in direct relation to the country they inhabit. And the same is true, of course, of the coloration of the animal's body.

Giraffes wandering undisturbed through the Kruger National Park in the Transvaal

approximating to this type extend south of the Equator. One of them, known as Rothschild's giraffe, has a nearly black hide, relieved by a network of white. This is the form found in British East and East Central Africa.

In the southern group the legs are spotted right down to the hoofs. This type is found as far north as the Transvaal. In the Kilimanjaro type the markings are regular, star-like, dark blotches on a fawn ground, but in the more southerly forms the blotches are less regular.

The Somali giraffe, says Mr. W. P. Pycraft, is in a class by itself. Agreeing with the northern types in the matter of its horns, in its coloration it is strikingly different, inasmuch as this takes the form of a large-meshed network of narrow white lines on a liver-coloured background.

That this colouring is a useful camouflage concealing the animals from their enemies seems undoubted. Mr. Vaughan Kirby, a big-game hunter of high repute, says, "There are few sportsmen who have hunted in localities where giraffes are found but have been deceived by their tall motionless figures. They stand perfectly still, not even swishing their tails like wildebeeste, and thus bringing about instant recognition; their mottled or dark colour, great height, and comparatively narrow bodies give them a striking resemblance to the many old vari-coloured relics of the forest, blasted by lightning or by bush fires. . . . And the deception is often the other way, tree stumps being mistaken for giraffes. . . . Few animals are so easily lost sight of, if once the attention is taken from them, their bodies being always concealed behind the thick foliage of the trees, their long legs merely doing duty for tree stumps."

What is a Silver Thaw?

After a period of severe frost there sometimes sets in suddenly a much warmer condition of the atmosphere and rain falls, but on touching the ground, which is still cold, it freezes, and the ground then becomes covered with a sheet of ice, which is very dangerous to pedestrians, because everywhere is so slippery. This is a silver thaw, and the name was given because in such cases the ground, roads and trees all take on a silvery appearance owing to the covering of ice. The slippery nature of the ground makes a silver thaw very dangerous.

What Was the Court of Stannaries?

The Stannaries are the districts in Devon and Cornwall containing the tin mines and are so named from the Latin word for tin, stannum. The Court of Stannaries was established to administer justice among the tin miners and workmen, and its judge was called the vice-warden. By the Stannaries Court Abolition Act of 1896, however, the jurisdiction of the court was transferred to the county courts.

What Was the "Duke of Exeter's Daughter"?

This was the name given in olden times to a rack in the Tower of London, and it is said to have been so called from a minister of Henry VI who introduced this instrument of torture. Prisoners were placed on the rack and had their limbs wrenched out of joint to make them confess what was required, and under the continued agony they generally did so, but confessions on the rack were, of course, worth nothing at all.

What is Burnham Beeches?

Burnham Beeches is the name given to a magnificent tract of forest, 374 acres in extent, with patches of heath-covered common, which was purchased in 1879 by the Corporation of London to serve as a public park. In 1921 another stretch of land, 70 acres in extent, called Fleetwood, was added as a gift from Lord Burnham.

The chief feature of this fine public playground is the large number of venerable and stately beech trees, pollarded, according to tradition, by Cromwell's soldiers.

One of the oldest beech trees at Burnham Beeches

Do Lemurs Gnaw Their Own Tails?

Lemurs, like other animals, have a habit, when anything causes irritation to their tails, of gnawing those extremities. They are therefore protected from themselves in zoos by a

A lemur wearing a wooden collar to prevent it from gnawing its tail

large wooden collar placed round their necks. This prevents them from being able to get at their tails and so any wound they may have is enabled to heal without being further irritated. Horses and cattle when they have a sore on their bodies also lick or bite it, often making it worse. They therefore in many cases are also furnished with a wooden collar to prevent them from being able to reach the injured part with their mouths.

Lemurs at the present time are confined exclusively to Madagascar and the Comoro Islands, half-way between the former and Zanzibar, although their remains have been found in Europe and America. They form a link between the monkeys and the insect-eating mammals like the bats. They are forest-dwellers and are mainly nocturnal in their habits. Animals allied to the lemurs, though not true lemurs, are found in Malaya and on the African Continent.

Who Was Orion?

In the old mythology he was a handsome giant and hunter who, going to Chios, fell in love with Merope, the daughter of Oenopion, son of Bacchus, but treated the maiden so badly that her father, with the assistance of Bacchus, deprived Orion of his sight. By exposing his eyeballs to the rays of the rising sun, he recovered his sight, and then lived as a hunter, often accompanying Artemis or Diana. He is supposed to have been slain by Artemis, or by her brother Apollo. After his death Orion was placed among the stars, where he appears as a giant with a girdle and sword. A constellation bears his name.

What is the Eyeball's Range of Movement?

The eyeball is moved by six muscles, four of which (the superior, inferior, internal and external recti) move it upward, downward, inward and outward ; while the other two, the superior and inferior oblique, in combination with these roll it at any angle between these two directions. The eye muscles are shown in the diagrams on page 156. With the eye able to move from side to side, up and down and with a circular movement, a very large field of vision is ensured.

Sometimes control over the eye muscles is lost and the person suffers from a disease known as nystagmus, which means dullness or drowsiness, though the complaint is not one of drowsiness. The eyes are continually moving in a rhythmical fashion from side to side, or up and down, or with a circular motion. This is caused by disease in the labyrinths or semicircular canals of the ear which, as is now known, control the balance of the body.

What Famous Criminals Were Executed at Tyburn?

Among the famous or notorious criminals who were executed at Tyburn, close by where the Marble Arch now stands in London, were the Holy Maid of Kent, 1534 ; Claude Duval, 1670 ; Jack Sheppard, 1724 ; Jonathan Wild, 1725 ; Earl Ferrers, 1760 ; Mrs. Brownrigg, 1767 ; and Dr. Dodd, 1777. In 1661 the bodies of Oliver Cromwell, Ireton and Bradshaw were exposed at Tyburn for twelve hours after they had been exhumed from Westminster Abbey.

Who Called a Tortoise an Insect?

This was not merely a joke in " Punch " as many people suppose. Frank Buckland, the well-known naturalist and inspector of the Board of Fisheries, was one day taking a railway journey with a pet monkey, when the ticket-collector said he would have to take out a dog's ticket for the animal. Buckland agreed. Then he put his hand into his pocket and produced a tortoise. " Do you want a ticket for this animal ? " he asked, and the collector replied : " Oh no, sir, that's only a hinseck."

An example of how the eyeball can be turned in its socket at will. By means of various muscles it can be rolled round in any direction

What is a Tumble-Bug?

THIS is the popular name given to the scarab or dung beetle, various species of which are found in different parts of the world. The best known is the Egyptian scarab, the sacred beetle of the ancient Egyptians which was often represented by them in stone. Seals in this form were common. Scarab-beetles are also

The South American tumble-bug rolling its ball along the ground

found in America and it is in that country that the name of tumble-bug is used. The beetle is in appearance very much like the dor beetle of Great Britain.

The female beetle forms a ball of dung, in which it lays its eggs. As soon as it discovers the necessary substance, it sinks a deep and perpendicular hole in the ground. Then it returns to the substance, generally cow manure, and separates a sufficient quantity for its purpose. Having laid an egg in it, it forms the mass into a ball and then begins to roll this towards the hole. Generally it is the female alone which does the work, but in some species the male beetle assists in rolling the ball to its destination. While he pushes, his mate pulls.

" Seizing the ball between her hind feet," says the Rev. J. G. Wood, " she begins to roll it about in the hot sunshine, not taking it direct to the shaft which she has sunk, but remaining near the spot. Should rain come on she ceases to roll, or should the ball be made just before sunset, she waits for the morning before recommencing her labour. The consequence of all this curious rolling about is twofold ; it accelerates the hatching of the enclosed egg by the exposure to the sunbeams, and it forms a thin, hard clay-like crust round the soft material in which the egg reposes.

" When the ball is sufficiently rolled, it is taken to the hole, dropped down, and the earth filled in. The egg is very soon hatched and from it proceeds a little white grub, which finds itself at once in the midst of food and begins to eat vigorously. By the time it has devoured the whole of the contents of its cocoon—if the mere empty shell may be so called—it is ready for its change into the pupal form, and there lies in the earth until it again changes its form and becomes a perfect beetle. . . .

" Frequently the beetle is very much puzzled to discover a place wherein it may dig a hole for the reception of the ball, especially where the ground is uniformly hard. The material which it desires is generally to be found plentifully upon roads, but as roads are usually too hard to be penetrated by the beetle's limbs, the unfortunate insects may be seen rolling their pellets with a patient and hopeless industry only to be equalled by that of Sisyphus."

What is "Buller's Thumb"?

UP to the middle of the 19th century the law of England allowed a husband to chastise his wife if he thought she needed it, but he might only beat her with a stick not thicker than a man's thumb. This permission was the result of a decision given by Mr. Justice Buller, and afterwards such a stick used in chastising a wife was known as Buller's Thumb.

What is it to Sue "In Forma Pauperis"?

THIS means to sue in the character of a pauper. Any person who has not the means to sue in the courts in the ordinary way may, on proof that he is not worth £50, excluding clothes, the tools of his trade, and the subject matter of the action, be allowed to take part in legal proceedings as a poor person. In such a case he is exempted from all court, counsel's and solicitor's fees.

Why is the Exchequer So Called?

EXCHEQUER is an old French word meaning a chess-board. In olden times the Chancellor of the Exchequer and other officials who dealt with the nation's finances used to sit round a table covered with a chequered cloth divided into squares like a chess-board. The sheriff read out the sums he had expended in the king's name, and as each sum was passed counters representing the amounts were placed in the various squares, which represented pence, shillings, pounds, tens of pounds, hundreds, and so on. Then a balance was drawn. The practice has long since disappeared, but the name Exchequer remains.

How Are Wax Tapers Made?

THE cotton thread for the wicks of the tapers is wound round large revolving drums, and from these it is unwound slowly and passes through two drums of molten wax. Here it collects the requisite amount of wax and then the thread passes on, the wax hardens and dries, and the waxed threads are then cut up into the required lengths for tapers.

How tapers are made by passing thread from large drums through melted wax

To What Does That Tail Belong?

Most animals and birds have tails, but these vary in form and colour, and the tails are also put to different uses. In fish they are often used for driving the creature through the water, though in some the tail is a weapon. Some animals, like the ox and horse, use their tails in self-defence against irritating insects that settle on their bodies. It is among birds that the most beautiful tails are found, and perhaps the most striking is that of the lyre bird, bearing a remarkable resemblance in shape to the musical instrument after which it is named. The so-called tail of the peacock, with its "eyes" and iridescent colours, is given in the centre of the page, but it is not really a tail at all. These feathers are the tail coverts which the cock bird spreads to make himself look attractive to the pea-hens. Some of the tails are used by human beings. The yak's, for instance, is made into a fly-whisk in the East, and from ox tails soup is made. These examples are not, of course, drawn to scale. They vary much in size

What is the Story of Jenkins's Ear?

CAPTAIN ROBERT JENKINS was master of a sloop trading from Jamaica to Spanish America, and, at a time of great tension between the two nations, he declared that a Spanish coastguard had in a dispute torn off one of his ears and bade him carry it to his king and say that if the king were present he would have been treated the same way. The whole story was probably an invention, but on March 16th, 1738, Jenkins appeared at the bar of the House of Commons and told his story, and was supported by Pitt and others, though Burke declared the incident a mere fable.

However, it raised fierce public indignation in England, and led to a declaration of war with Spain. "It is certain," says Earl Stanhope the historian, "that Jenkins had lost an ear or part of an ear, which he always carried about with him wrapped in cotton to display to his audience, but I find it alleged by no mean authority that he had lost it on another occasion, and perhaps, as seems to be insinuated, in the pillory."

What is the Most Malleable Metal?

IT is gold, which is also the most ductile—that is, it can be drawn out into a thinner thread than any other. Gold can be beaten out into leaves so thin that it takes 300,000, one on top of another, to make the thickness of an inch. Although in the ordinary way the metal looks yellow, when a thin gold leaf is seen by transmitted light it appears a green or bluish colour.

What Snake Skins Are Used For Shoes?

THE skins of several snakes are used for the making of shoes, but the chief of these is the African python, a reptile that is stated sometimes to reach a length of 23 feet. It is rarely, however, that specimens longer than 15 or 20 feet are caught. Such snakes are formidable creatures for they have a girth as large as a man's thigh and can easily kill animals like small deer, full-grown sheep and large dogs.

A python destroys its victim by gradually smothering it by throwing over it coil after coil of its body. In swallowing, writes Dr. A. Günther, pythons "always begin with the head, and as they live entirely on mammals and birds, the hairs and feathers offer a considerable impediment to the passage down the throat. The process of deglutition is, therefore, slow, but it would be much slower except for the great quantity of saliva discharged over the body of the victim.

"During the time of digestion, especially when the prey has been a somewhat large animal, the snake becomes very lazy; it moves itself slowly when disturbed, or defends itself with little vigour when attacked. At any other time the rock-snakes will fiercely defend themselves when they perceive that no retreat is left to them."

Pythons are generally nocturnal in their habits. Since the demand for their

The African python, one of the snakes whose skins are used nowadays for making shoes and ladies' handbags

skins for leather, some attempts have been made to breed them in captivity as a successful commercial proposition.

What is a Chartered Company?

IT is a British public company with shareholders which has received from the Crown a charter granting it power to settle, trade and govern some particular territory within the British sphere of interest. The British South Africa Company was an example of such a chartered company.

What is the Pool of London?

THIS is the name given to that part of the Thames between London Bridge and Limehouse Point, where vessels are anchored or moored. From London Bridge to King's Head Stairs, Rotherhithe, is called the Upper Pool, and from King's Head Stairs to Cuckold's Point opposite Limehouse, the Lower Pool. Navigation in the Pool is under strict regulations.

The Pool was a recognised term for this part of the river as far back as the 13th century. In the Articles of Ancient Usage, collected and promulgated in the reign of Edward I, it is ordered in the article against forestallers—that is, those who bought up goods to raise the price—that "no merchant, denizen or stranger, whatever he may be, shall go to the Pool or any other place in the Thames to meet wines or other merchandise, or go on board of vessels to buy wines or other things, until such time as they shall have come to land."

Part of the Upper Pool of London, with the Tower of London, Tower Bridge, St. Paul's Cathedral and Port of London Authority's building all clearly visible

Can a Paper Star Be Made With One Cut?

It is quite easy to cut out a five-pointed star from a square of paper with only one cut. It is neces-

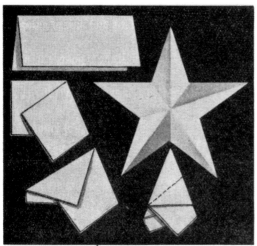

How a five-pointed star may be made with one scissor-cut

sary, however, that the paper should be folded in a certain way, and the diagram on this page will show how the folds must be made. The paper is folded double, then slanting-wise, then across again, and finally across once more, as indicated in the first four drawings. Then, by cutting across the dotted line and opening out the upper or triangular part of the paper, a five-pointed star of perfect shape will be revealed.

What is Pepper's Ghost?

Pepper's Ghost is an optical illusion which was a very popular form of entertainment in the middle of the 19th century. The audience, looking at a stage where actors were going through a scene, suddenly saw a ghost appear and move about. The ghost would pass through tables or chairs, or the actors could pass through the ghost. It was all very realistic, but the method of its production was very simple.

A real person dressed as a ghost went through certain actions below the stage, and was strongly illuminated by a lantern. In front of the stage was a large sheet of glass inclined towards the spectators, but invisible to them. The reflection of the illuminated person was caught by this glass, and though the spectators could not see the glass they could see the reflection of the " ghost," which seemed to be walking about the stage.

Are Railways Increasing Their Speed?

According to the " Railway Gazette's " annual review of world railway speed in 1937, that year saw the most rapid advance in speed in all railway history. The progress made in Great Britain has been the most substantial of any country. A daily total distance of 830 miles run by the various streamlined trains of the London and North Eastern Railway passing through the Hatfield-Doncaster section at an average of almost exactly 75 miles per hour is the highest mileage covered at this speed by steam locomotives anywhere in the world.

Relatively to route-mileage Great Britain leads the world in distance run by mile-a-minute trains. So far as steam propulsion is concerned, it is second only to the United States in high-speed mileage in all ranges from 70 to 60 miles per hour.

Diesel traction still holds the blue riband of speed start-to-stop runs with 82·3 miles per hour by the German Fliegende-Kölner diesel-electric train, and Germany also holds the world start-to-stop steam speed record in the 74·2 miles per hour average of a Berlin-Hamburg express.

From 1935 to 1937 Great Britain and the United States doubled their mile-a-minute mileage—the former from 5,371 to 11,228 and the latter from 19,279 to 37,412. In 1937 a greater aggregate mileage of start-to-stop runs by nearly 2,000 miles was booked at 70 miles per hour and over than was booked at 60 miles per hour and over in 1932. The increase in speed has been so marked in the last five years that the Great Western Railway Cheltenham Flyer, in 1932 the fastest train in the world, at an average speed of 71·4 miles per hour, now takes 67th place and is eighth in the list of steam trains. Much effort is still being expended in all the leading countries to increase railway speeds and out-distance even the high speeds already attained.

Why is the Pitt Press So Called?

The University Press at Cambridge is known as the Pitt Press, and received this name after the erection of its chief building in Cambridge, the Pitt Memorial Building. This is a Gothic edifice designed by Edward Blore, creator of Sir Walter Scott's seat Abbotsford and official architect to William IV and Queen Victoria. The building, we are told, was " erected on such a scale as to be a distinguished ornament to the University and . . . to perpetuate the name and memory of Mr. Pitt "—that is, the younger Pitt.

The University Press at Oxford is known as the Clarendon Press, after the Earl of Clarendon, the distinguished statesman of Charles II.

How Are Barrel Hoops Made?

The making of wooden hoops for barrels is a very ancient craft, and is still carried on by hand in the same way as it has been done for centuries. No machinery has yet been devised that can make wooden hoops

Hoops for barrels being made in Kent by the same methods that have been used there for centuries

satisfactorily. The tool used is a kind of spoke-shave, and the hoop-maker works at a rough hand-made sloping bench as shown in the photograph.

What is That Knife Used For?

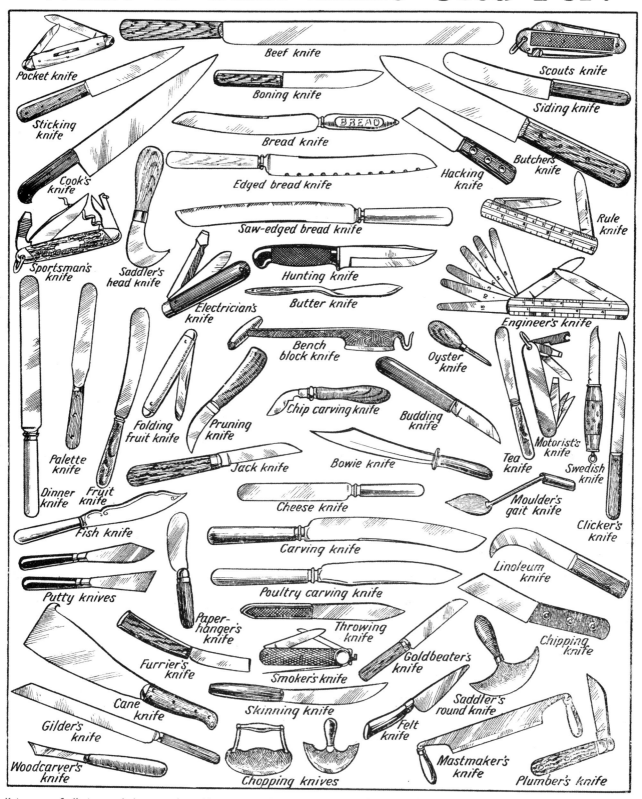

Pocket knife

Beef knife

Scouts knife

Boning knife

Siding knife

Sticking knife

Bread knife

Hacking knife

Butchers knife

Cook's knife

Edged bread knife

Rule knife

Saw-edged bread knife

Sportsman's knife

Saddler's head knife

Hunting knife

Electrician's knife

Butter knife

Engineer's knife

Bench block knife

Oyster knife

Chip carving knife

Budding knife

Folding fruit knife

Pruning knife

Motorist's knife

Palette knife

Jack knife

Bowie knife

Tea knife

Swedish knife

Dinner knife

Fruit knife

Cheese knife

Moulder's gait knife

Clicker's knife

Fish knife

Carving knife

Linoleum knife

Putty knives

Poultry carving knife

Paper-hanger's knife

Throwing knife

Chipping knife

Furrier's knife

Smoker's knife

Goldbeater's knife

Cane knife

Skinning knife

Saddler's round knife

Gilder's knife

Felt knife

Mastmaker's knife

Woodcarver's knife

Chopping knives

Plumber's knife

Knives are of all sizes and shapes, and on this page are given many varieties. There are, of course, many kinds of pocket knives, with various gadgets in addition to the blades. The kind of gadget depends upon the use for which the knife is intended. Several examples are given on this page. Sportsmen's knives may be of almost any size, and contain a great number of tools. A motorist's knife also varies in the folding tools it has. Various kinds of knives are used for carving meat. The poultry carver, for example, has a shorter blade and a longer handle than an ordinary carving knife, and a beef knife, used for cutting up beef in a restaurant or ham-and-beef shop, has a very long blade. Many of the knives are intended for special trades. A clicker's knife, for example, is used by a shoemaker for cutting up the skins from which the uppers of boots and shoes are made. A bench block knife is temporarily fixed to a wooden block. A saddler's knife is curved for cutting thick butt leather

When Was That Machine Made?

Dandy horse 1819

Hobby horse 1840

Boneshaker 1860

Extraordinary 1883

Ordinary 1880

Kangaroo 1883

Adjustable Safety 1884

Rover Safety 1885

Humber Safety 1885

Rear driving Facile 1886

Safety with pneumatic tyres 1890

Safety Roadster 1890

Front driving Safety 1891

Giraffe 1894

Modern Safety

The drawings on these pages show bicycles at various periods during the past 120 years, and by looking at the drawings we can trace the evolution of the bicycle. It started with the dandy horse about 1819. On this instrument the rider rested on the saddle and then ran along the ground—or, rather, kicked the ground—the wheels helping his progress. From this developed the hobby horse, about 1840, in which the back wheel was driven by cranks. The boneshaker, a wooden bicycle, followed about 1860, and was worked by treadles attached to the front wheel. With the coming of the ordinary, popularly known as the penny-farthing, the modern era of cycling really began. The wheels were built with slim spokes, like those of today, but the treadles turned the front wheel directly. If the cyclist ran into a stone on the road, he was often thrown over the front of the machine. During the next few years various attempts were made to make the bicycle more easily worked, and then came the period of the safety

The Evolution of Bicycle & Tricycle

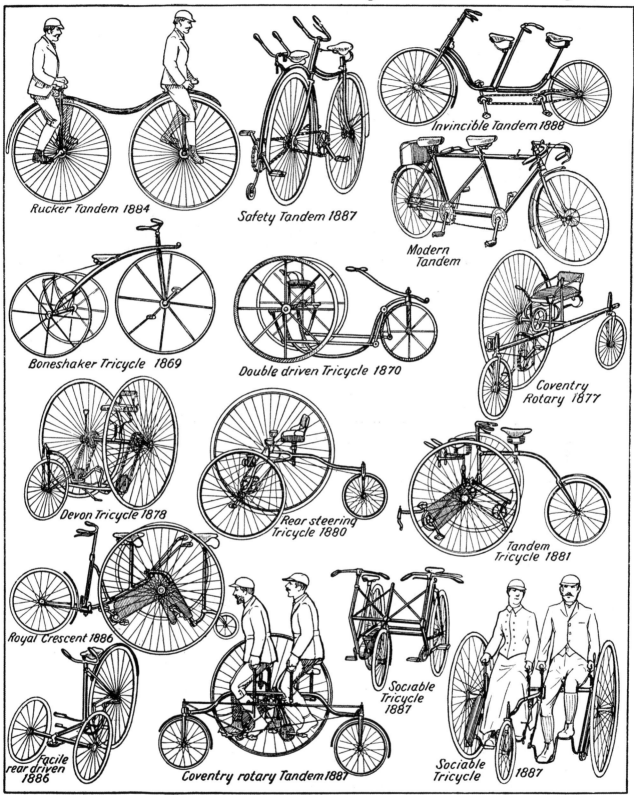

Rucker Tandem 1884

Safety Tandem 1887

Invincible Tandem 1888

Modern Tandem

Boneshaker Tricycle 1869

Double driven Tricycle 1870

Coventry Rotary 1877

Devon Tricycle 1878

Rear steering Tricycle 1880

Tandem Tricycle 1881

Royal Crescent 1886

Sociable Tricycle 1887

Facile rear driven 1886

Coventry rotary Tandem 1887

Sociable Tricycle 1887

machine. Many attempts were made at adjusting the relative sizes of the wheels, till the modern safety was evolved. Sometimes the front wheel was larger than the back, while at other times the front wheel was the smaller. Of course, an enormous advance was made when the invention of the pneumatic tire was accomplished. A patent for this was taken out in the name of Thompson in 1848, but the real inventor was James Dunlop, of Dublin, in 1890. In the drawings above are shown various adaptations of the bicycle. First of all we see different types of tandem machines, and then various forms which the tricycle has taken at succeeding periods. The tricycle was at one time very popular with older people, but with the development of the safety machine the bicycle became less dangerous and was brought more into general use. Tricycles, however, are still seen in such towns as Cambridge and Oxford, where they are ridden by men and women of mature age. Tandem tricycles have disappeared altogether

Are Penguins Good Swimmers?

THEY are so at home in the water that they are often mistaken for dolphins. Their food consists exclusively of fish and this they capture beneath the surface by their remarkable agility in swimming and diving. It is by using their paddle-like wings that they are able to make rapid

A photograph taken from above, showing how penguins swim with their wings that are quite useless as implements for flying

progress in the water. Those wings are, of course, useless for flying.

Professor Moseley tells us that on first approaching Kerguelen Island he was astonished on seeing what appeared to be a shoal of small porpoises or dolphins. "I could not imagine," he says, "what the things could be, unless they were, indeed, some marvellously small cetaceans. They showed black above and white beneath, and came along in a shoal of fifty or more, from seawards towards the shore at a rapid pace, by a series of successive leaps out of the water and splashes into it again, describing short curves in the air, taking headers out of the water and headers into it again : splash, splash went this marvellous shoal of animals, till they went splash through the surf on to the black stony beach, and there struggled and jumped up amongst the boulders and revealed themselves as wet and dripping penguins, for such they were."

Did the Greeks Have a Story of a Flood?

YES, according to the old mythology Zeus or Jupiter resolved to destroy the degenerate race of men, and Deucalion, son of Prometheus, and his wife Pyrrha were on account of their piety the only mortals saved.

Deucalion built a ship in which he

and his wife floated in safety during the nine days' flood which destroyed all the other inhabitants of Hellas. At last the ship rested on Mount Parnassus in Phocis, and Deucalion and his wife then consulted the sanctuary of Themis as to how the race of men could be restored. The goddess told them to cover their heads and throw the bones of their mother behind them. They interpreted this to mean that

they were to throw the stones of the Earth behind them. This they did, and from the stones thrown by Deucalion there sprang up men, while from those thrown by Pyrrha came women. Deucalion and Pyrrha then descended from the mountain. The story has many remarkable resemblances to the story of Noah and the Flood as recorded in the Old Testament.

How Many S O S Messages of the B.B.C. Succeed?

THE total number of police and S O S messages broadcast during the year 1937 from all transmitters was 1,213, or over three a day. One in every two of these messages met with success. Of 823 broadcasts for relatives of persons dangerously ill, 472 or 57·36 per cent. were successful. Of 318 appeals for witnesses of accidents, 121 or 38·05 per cent. succeeded. Of 46 special police messages, 17 or 36·96 per cent. were successful, and of the 26 broadcast messages designed to assist the police in the investigation of crime, 6 or 23·08 per cent. succeeded.

What is Concrete Made Of?

IT consists of a conglomerate or mixture of pebbles, stones, gravel, cinders or blast furnace slag embedded in mortar or cement. It is a substance that in modern life is of very great importance in building, road-laying and so on. Cement consists mainly of lime and silica, combined with a certain amount of alumina and small quantities of potash, soda and magnesia in the form of free salts.

Where is a Tree Trunk Used as a Garage?

ONE of the fallen giants in the Mariposa Grove of big sequoia trees in southern California is used as a garage for motor-cars and tractors. This tree, thousands of years old, has a hollow trunk, and there is ample room inside for a number of tractors.

Some of the sequoia trees still standing in the Mariposa Grove are among the oldest living things. They were thriving before the pyramids of Egypt were built. The tallest of the big trees, which has been named "Columbia," is 285 feet high and has a circumference at the base of over 88 feet.

A fallen redwood tree in California, whose hollow trunk is used as a garage

How Long Has Push-Ball Been Played?

THIS game, in which a ball like a huge Association football is used, was invented by M. G. Crane of Massachusetts in 1894 and was first played in England at the Crystal Palace, London, in 1902. It has,

Push-ball players with the large leather ball used in the game

however, never become a popular game. There are two sides of eleven players each, divided into forwards, right wings, left wings and goalkeeper.

The goalposts used are 18 feet high and 20 feet apart, with a crossbar at a height of 7 feet from the ground. The ball used is 6 feet in diameter and weighs 50 pounds. The ground measures 140 yards by 50 yards.

In the game, pushing the ball under the bar counts five points and eight points are scored if it is thrown over the crossbar. A variety of the game has been played at some of the military tournaments in London, and it is also played by women.

Who Was Monsieur de Paris?

THIS was a nickname given to the executioner in Paris, especially at the time of the French Revolution when so many thousands of victims were slain by the guillotine.

How Does the Death-Watch Beetle Work?

THE death-watch beetle, which does so much damage in riddling old timber, so that roofs become unsafe and have to be repaired or replaced, is a small insect only a little more than a quarter of an inch in length. It is dark brown in colour, and carries on its destructive work out of sight of man.

But its presence can sometimes be detected by a curious ticking sound which it makes. This is its way of attracting a mate, and in the old days the sound was supposed to betoken the forthcoming death of some individual. That is why the insect is known as the death-watch beetle. No doubt instances could be found where people have died after hearing the ticking of the beetle, just as thousands of cases might be cited where people have heard it and not died.

The rhythmic tapping is made by the beetle rising on its front legs and jerking its body forward seven or eight times in rapid succession, striking a blow each time on the surface of the wood with the front of its head. It does this tapping very rapidly, making eight taps in less than a second. When it stops, another beetle within hearing will reply by tapping back.

Evidently the beetle can hear, though the position of its organs of hearing is not known. Some scientists think they are in the feelers. The tapping is sometimes continued for a long time.

Dr. Charles Gahan, Keeper of the Department of Entomology at the British Museum, tells of a female beetle that was captured and placed in a small box, where it lived for ten weeks. At almost any moment throughout that period it was ready to respond by tapping to a sound made outside the box by tapping at the same rate with a pencil.

The death-watch beetle goes through the various stages of life common to insects of its kind. After pairing, the female beetle lays about eighty white, oval eggs in cracks and crevices of old wood. A few weeks later the parent beetles die, but from the eggs hatch out little white grubs that seek a crack in the timber, and thereupon commence boring. All through that summer and during the next two summers they feed on the wood, honeycombing it with tunnels. When the grubs are about half an inch long they are full-grown.

Then in the third summer they tunnel towards the outside of the wood, and when near the surface change into pupa or chrysalis, and in the autumn develop into beetles. They gnaw their way out of the wood in the following spring—that is, some time between April and June. If the building is artificially warmed they emerge earlier.

Death-watch beetles have wings and can fly about. Sometimes they attack old furniture. It is rarely they touch any timber but oak and chestnut, though in one City church in London they riddled a piece of Scots pinewood.

In recent years hundreds of thousands of pounds have had to be expended in England in restoring the damage done by death-watch beetles in cathedrals and other buildings.

In fighting the beetle a liquid made of soap, wax, cedar-wood oil and two powerful chemicals is sprayed upon the affected parts. Not only are the existing grubs destroyed, but an invisible film of poison on the surface kills any fresh beetles trying to enter the crevices.

Why Does Beating a Carpet Drive Out the Dust?

THIS is due to a principle which is called by men of science Inertia. Inertia is the tendency which a body has, if it is still, to remain still; and if it is moving, to go on moving. When a carpet suspended over a line is beaten, a motion forward is given to the loose particles of dust in the fabric, and they start travelling, while the heavy carpet, through inertia, tends to remain still. In this way

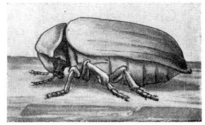

An enlarged view of the death-watch beetle

the light dust particles are thrown out of the stationary carpet.

The same thing happens when a dog, after being in the water, shakes itself. It gives motion to the drops of water which are hurled forward while the dog itself, by inertia, remains stationary.

How Did the Revolver Develop?

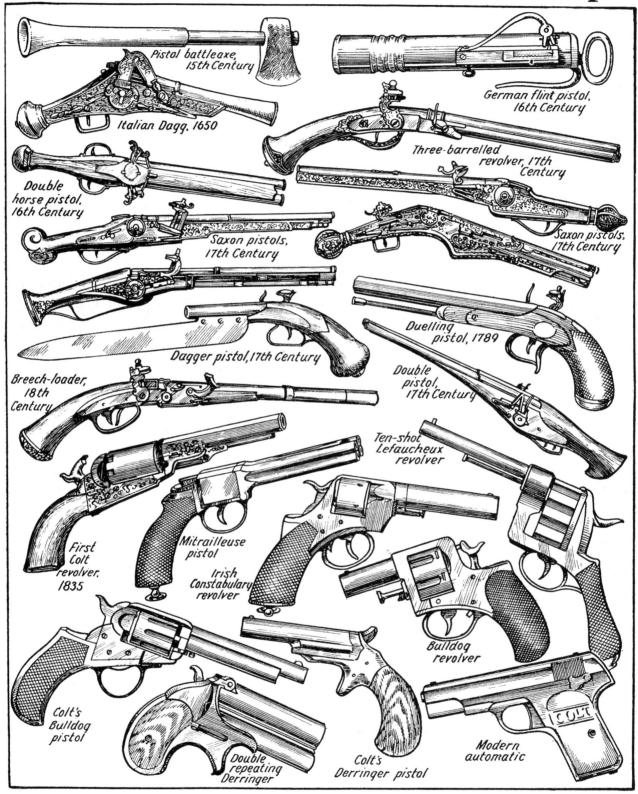

Pistol battleaxe, 15th Century

Italian Dagg, 1650

German flint pistol, 16th Century

Double horse pistol, 16th Century

Three-barrelled revolver, 17th Century

Saxon pistols, 17th Century

Saxon pistols, 17th Century

Dagger pistol, 17th Century

Duelling pistol, 1789

Breech-loader, 18th Century

Double pistol, 17th Century

Ten-shot Lefaucheux revolver

First Colt revolver, 1835

Mitrailleuse pistol

Irish Constabulary revolver

Bulldog revolver

Colt's Bulldog pistol

Double repeating Derringer

Colt's Derringer pistol

Modern automatic

Here are the various stages in the development of the modern revolver and automatic pistol from the simple flint pistols of the early centuries. The very earliest form seems to have been a pistol battle-axe, and then, as the flint-lock musket developed, the need for a smaller and more portable firearm was realised, and the Germans made a flint-lock pistol in the 16th century. During the early centuries pistols were often great works of art, being beautifully damascened or otherwise decorated with gold and silver. During the 18th century duelling pistols sold in pairs were very common, and these are much sought after by collectors today. The need for giving two or more shots in quick succession led to the making of double- and triple-barrelled pistols, and eventually to the invention of the revolver. First of all the barrels were made to revolve, but later only the chamber containing the cartridges. Lastly came the automatic pistol, with its reloading mechanism worked by the recoil, and the magazine in the butt

What is the International Date Line?

It is an imaginary line on the other side of the world, and passes almost everywhere through sea and not through land.

As the Earth turns round on its axis, day and night are caused. But, of course, each day must be reckoned as beginning somewhere on the Earth.

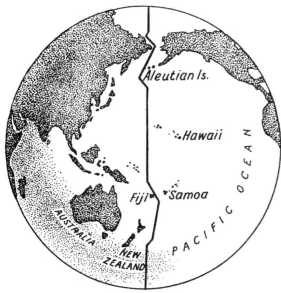

The date line, where every new day and new year begins. The day travels across the world westward

In London the day starts about five hours before it starts in New York. Civilised nations have agreed upon what is known as an International Date Line as being the place where the day begins.

Originally the 180th meridian of longitude was selected because it touched so little land, but the date line is now zigzag in places, the reason being that this enables certain people living close together on islands to have the same day. Thus the line takes a slight turn to the west to include Wrangel Island with Alaska. It turns to the east again to include the East Cape peninsula with Siberia. Then it turns west so that the whole of the Aleutian Islands may be on the same side of the date line as the United States, to which they belong. It afterwards turns back and follows the 180th meridian for many miles, but takes a turn to the eastward to include all the Fiji and Tonga Islands on the west side with New Zealand.

Ships crossing the date line adjust their clocks, as on one side of the date line it is one day and on the other side the next day. Indeed, it would be quite possible for a person lying on the deck of a ship crossing the date line to have his head living in Monday and his feet living in Tuesday. If two vessels start from London, one steaming east and the other west, when they meet at the date line the one going east will be twelve hours in advance of time, while the other will be twelve hours behind.

What Exactly is Sleep?

Sleep, which is described by the poet as "tired Nature's sweet restorer," is a necessity if we are to keep healthy. When animals like young dogs are prevented from sleeping they die in four or five days. But exactly what sleep is no scientist can explain. Our brains are rested when we sleep, yet all the brain does not stop working.

The parts concerned with thinking and willing and balancing and co-ordinating—that is, bringing different actions into relation with one another—all stop working partly or completely during sleep. But that part of the brain which has to do with breathing and the regular pumping of the blood through the body does not, fortunately for us, stop when we are asleep. The heart, however, beats more slowly and the breathing becomes less rapid. Tears and the fluid produced by the nose diminish in amount and so we do not have to wipe our noses when we are asleep.

When we feel sleepy we rub our eyes, because the tear glands, which keep moisture running over our eyeballs, are slowing down, and by rubbing the eyes we stimulate the glands into producing more fluid. We also rub our eyes when we wake up, to set the glands working.

Light stimulates the nerves of the eye, so we close our eyes when we are trying to get to sleep. When we are very tired the eyelids droop, because the nerves and muscles are getting inactive. At such times it needs an effort to keep the eyes open.

When we first go to sleep, the power to make conscious movements is lost, but we can still hear sounds, such as people talking, or the traffic passing. At last we lose consciousness altogether, and even sounds are not heard. The muscles cease to move, and as the body produces less heat, less carbon dioxide is breathed out.

It has been proved by experiment that the deepest sleep is reached about an hour after we fall asleep. If a person does not get sufficient sleep his or her health suffers.

Although consciousness is lost, the nerves still carry messages to the brain, although the brain does not take much notice of them. It has been found that when a loud noise is made that does not wake the sleeper, his pulse quickens somewhat. If the face is tickled, or a fly settles, a message goes to the brain, and though the sleeper does not wake, his hand will be raised to remove the disturber.

Some scientists say that the size of the brain diminishes slightly during sleep, while the feet and hands get a little larger. This is due to the blood leaving the brain and finding its way to the extremities.

The opinion of most scientists is that sleeping and waking are due to variations in the blood-flow through the brain. When we have been awake several hours the nerve centres controlling the blood-vessels that send blood through the brain become tired, and stimulate the vessels less energetically, with the result that the flow is slowed down, and this brings on a feeling of tiredness, which ultimately leads to sleep. After a period of rest the nerves are revived, the blood supply of the brain is increased, and the sleeper wakes.

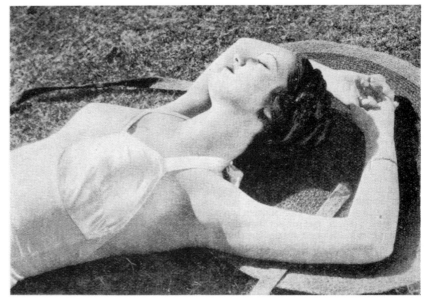

Though we are unconscious in sleep, our brain is still working in certain directions, as for example, in controlling the breathing and the heart

What is the Southern Cross of Pearls?

IT is a curious group of eight pearls arranged in the form of a cross about an inch and a half long, which was found inside a pearl oyster in 1874 by an Australian aborigine at Raeburn

The Southern Cross, a remarkable aggregation of pearls found in the shell of a single oyster in 1874 by an Australian aborigine on the beach at Raeburn, Western Australia

in Western Australia. The man sold the shell for a plug of tobacco, and the purchaser sold it again for £13 to a man who disposed of it for £70. It changed hands several times, and was then sold for many thousands of pounds. This remarkable cross of pearls is perfectly natural, and was given the appropriate name of "The Southern Cross."

What is a Billingsgate Bobbing Hat?

THIS is the name often given to the queer-looking hat of leather worn by porters at Billingsgate Fish Market in London. The hats are made of specially strong and tough leather, which has to be soaked in water for twenty-four hours and is then modelled on a wooden block, adjustable to the size of the customer's head. The crown of the hat is double and has a newspaper filling in between to make the inner leather fit the head closely. The top or working surface is of triple leather to stand wear and is called the "heel." The process of making the hat takes about twelve hours from start to finish, and a quarter of a pound of rivets and 60 feet of waxed thread are used.

Mr. Spink of Love Lane, who has been making the hats for more than forty years, turns out about twenty-five a year, and, once made, the hat lasts its wearer a lifetime. The price is 35s. 6d., and the hat weighs five pounds when new. In the course of time, however, damp and dirt may double this weight.

The hat is worn by the Billingsgate porter as a kind of platform on his head, on which he can carry the boxes of fish. The hat will support a load of from ten to twelve stones of fish—that is, a weight equivalent to that of a well-grown man.

The porters themselves call their strange headgear "leather hats," but the maker gives them the name of bobbing hats. This word is probably connected with the term "bobbing charge," a payment of one penny by a porter in Billingsgate market to give him the privilege of carrying bought parcels of fish for a buyer. A man who stands on a bench by the salesman's side and receives the bobbing charge is known as a bobber.

Who Were the Titans?

THEY were the six sons and six daughters of Uranus (Heaven) and Gaea (the Earth), sometimes increased to thirteen, and in the Greek mythology are demigods of great stature. They are generally spoken of in pairs, namely, Oceanus and Tethys, the sea ; Hyperion and Theia, the Sun and Moon ; Coeus and Phoebe, light or star deities ; Creios and Eurybia, deities of strength ; Cronos and Rhea, heaven and earth ; Themis, mother of the Hours and Fates ; Mnemosyne, mother of the Muses, and Iapetus, who is to produce mankind.

Incited to rebellion by their mother Gaea, they overthrew Uranus and established their youngest brother Cronos as sovereign. He, in turn, was dethroned by his son Zeus, whereupon the majority of the Titans declared for the new ruler, but Iapetus and his family carried on from Mount Othrys a fierce warfare with the gods of Mount Olympus. Finally they were defeated and hurled down into Tartarus, the dark abyss.

Is it True that "One Man's Food is Another's Poison"?

PROFESSOR HENRY C. SHERMAN, an authority on food and health, declares that the cases in which " what is one man's food is another man's poison " are real, but they are rare. " They are, in fact, so rare," he says, " that the quotation tends to mislead. Individual differences and idiosyncrasies actually play a much smaller part than is popularly supposed. If afflicted with a real idiosyncrasy or abnormal sensitivity which causes acute injury to result from eating of what is for other people a staple food, one is then the victim of a rare but recognised disease and should seek medical treatment."

Who Told the Story of Newton and the Apple?

IT was Voltaire, the famous French author, who stated that he had heard the story from Mrs. Carduitt, Newton's niece. According to this, the great philosopher was in the garden at Woolsthorpe, when he saw an apple fall from a tree, and this simple incident led him into the train of thought that resulted in his formulating the laws of gravitation. For many years tradition marked the actual tree and it was shown to Sir David Brewster in 1814. Six years later the tree was felled.

The story of the falling apple has been discredited by some biographers of Newton, though it is difficult to know why, for Voltaire's authority seems satisfactory enough.

There is a great tendency in these days to decry and disbelieve all stories of this kind, without any real reason for scepticism.

Billingsgate porters with their hard leather hats, which enable them to carry great loads of fish boxes on their heads

What is the Vulgate?

THIS is the Latin version of the Scriptures accepted as the authorised version by the Roman Catholic Church. The Douay Bible, which is the English translation read by Roman Catholics, is a translation from the Vulgate. The Vulgate was prepared by Jerome about the close of the fourth century, partly by translation from the original languages and partly by revision of earlier Latin versions. The Anglo-Saxon translations and Wyclif's English version were made from it.

Who Were Gog and Magog?

THESE names are given to two effigies in the Guildhall, London, and are thought to represent Gogmagog and Corineus, two brothers, giants who, according to Geoffrey of Monmouth, held the western part of England in subjection. The original statues stood in the Guildhall in the time of Henry V, but they were burned in the Great Fire of London in 1666. In 1708 the present effigies were made and set up. The older ones were of wickerwork and pasteboard and were carried in the Lord Mayor's procession each year. Children used to be told that when Gog and Magog hear St. Paul's strike midnight they descend from their pedestals.

An old legend states that Gog and Magog were the giant offspring of daughters of the Emperor Diocletian, who murdered their husbands, came to Britain and married demons. All their

What is Habeas Corpus?

THE words are Latin and mean "thou mayest have the body." The Habeas Corpus Act was an Act passed in 1679 for the better securing of the liberty of the subject. It contained

Officials with scientific instruments measuring the noise made by a motor-cycle at Meriden, Warwickshire

no new principle, but gave greater facility for the assertion of the ancient right. Henceforth the Crown ceased to be able to imprison its enemies in defiance of the principles of the security of the person.

A writ of Habeas Corpus commands an officer who has a person in custody to bring him in before the court.

How Are Street Noises Tested?

STREET noises, such as those made by motor-cycles and other vehicles, are tested by a very sensitive instrument, which includes a microphone and a recording apparatus, that gives the relative loudness of the sounds. The instrument is set up by the side of a road, and the vehicles being tested then pass along the road in front of it.

Which is the World's Biggest Horse?

WHAT is believed to be the biggest horse that has ever lived is a Belgian stallion which in 1938 was nine years old and at that time weighed 3,030 pounds, or more than a ton and a third. It is owned by Mr. C. G. Good of Boone, Iowa, who refused an offer of 8,000 dollars or £1,600 for it. The animal was still growing in 1938.

What is an Heir Apparent?

IT is one of the curious rules in law that no one can be the heir of a living person. The heir is called into existence by the death of his ancestor, for no man in his lifetime can legally have an heir.

Because of this the word heir is legally qualified by the addition of an adjective. The heir apparent is the person, who, if he survive the ancestor, must certainly be his heir. Such is an eldest son in the lifetime of his father.

An heir presumptive is a person who would, if the ancestor died immediately, be the heir, though if the ancestor lived for some time longer, might not become the heir on his death. Thus a daughter may be heir presumptive, and if her ancestor died immediately would become heir, but if he went on living he might have a son, who would become heir apparent. That is why Princess Elizabeth, who by present arrangement would succeed King George VI, is called heir presumptive and not heir apparent.

" Brooklyn Supreme," a nine-year-old Belgian stallion, believed to be the biggest horse that has ever lived. It weighs more than a ton and a third

brothers were destroyed, but they were brought in chains to London and acted as porters at the palace that stood on the site of the present Guildhall.

The Gogmagog Hills, just outside Cambridge, are said to be named after one of these giants who, being refused by the nymph Granta, was changed into this rising ground.

Habeas Corpus, although one of the landmarks of English liberty, is less important today as its objects can, by later laws, be obtained in other and simpler ways.

In times of political disturbance the Government of the day has sometimes demanded the temporary suspension of the Habeas Corpus Act.

What is the Name of That Hat?

While men's hats are constantly changing in shape, these changes are very slight. Unlike women, whose fashions in hats vary so completely from season to season, men are conservative, and the most they will tolerate is a very slight change in shape. Thus the silk top-hat, the bowler and the soft felt hat remain very much the same year after year. Sometimes the brim is made broader, and sometimes narrower. At one time it is turned up a good deal, and another time it is kept fairly flat. Here are the types of hats which men wear, with their particular names. The occasions on which many of the hats are worn are indicated by their names, as, for example, in the coxswain's cap, the deerstalker, the motoring hat and the smoking cap. Some of these head-dresses are confined to particular classes or trades, like the meat porter's cap, the chef's caps, the coalman's hat, the scavenger's hat, and the Billingsgate fish porter's hat. Sometimes a new shape is introduced from abroad, like the beret, a very un-British type of headgear, and the Coogan cap, named after the youthful film star. Opera hats can be closed up for convenience at the theatre

Is One Conscious When Falling From a Height?

A GOOD many people have the idea that when a person falls from a height he loses consciousness while he is falling, owing to the pressure of air as he breathes. But this idea is quite incorrect, as those declare who have fallen from buildings, ladders, cliffs and aeroplanes, and have survived.

Here is the testimony of one who has himself fallen and has also had a wide experience in dealing with others who have also fallen from a great height. The authority is Mr. William Larkins, the most famous of all steeplejacks.

" Nobody who has never fallen from a great height can have any conception of the horror of the empty air," says Mr. Larkins. " Speaking as one who has himself been hurtled through space (and what steeplejack has not experienced a fall ?), let me say that it produces a sensation like nothing else on earth. It is difficult to describe. Your heart rises to your mouth. Another feeling he has is that of his legs separating from the rest of his body. The rush of air grips your throat like that of a person about to undergo the penalty of hanging, but one is lucky if at the end of such a drop one is able to record these impressions. When anyone falls from a great height it is not often that his injuries are only of a superficial character.

" ' It was awful,' gasped my workman when I went to his assistance, ' falling through all that space. The horror of the empty air ! I shall never forget it all my life.'

" The marvel was that he was alive to relate his experience. How, indeed, he escaped death will always remain a mystery to me. The incident happened when we were repairing a church spire in Wiltshire. My companion stood on a coping immediately above my head, while I sat in a cradle, working on the masonry underneath. When one is working at such a height it is customary to exchange as few words as possible, but at the time my companion was dashed to earth from his perch it was necessary for us to discuss certain of our operations.

" So that he could address me better, my companion leant over from his position ; then, with an agonising cry that made the blood in me run cold, went hurtling past me to the ground. In speaking to me he had lost his hold. His body passed so close to me that I almost followed suit.

" Fascinated with horror for the instant, I watched his descent, only feeling myself become sick and giddy. I held on like grim death to my cradle. A few minutes elapsed before I was able to pull myself together, and when I had recovered my composure I descended as quickly as possible to his assistance.

" In view of the great height from which he had fallen, I fully expected to find his body reduced to so much pulp. But what was my amazement on reaching earth to discover that he had received only superficial injuries. So

badly shaken was he by the incident that he was a bundle of nerves, however, and after a doctor had carried out an examination of his injuries, I helped to remove him to his home, with the aid of another workman.

" Since the height from which he fell must have been in the region of seventy-five feet, his escape from death was nothing short of miraculous. One of the very worst experiences that

Mr. A. M. Wilkinson and his son, well-known steeplejacks, working on a 150-ft. chimney at the Denaby Main Colliery

can befall any steeplejack is to witness a comrade being hurtled through space, and I am not likely to forget my feelings when the above little incident happened."

But a fall through a slip is not the only danger to which the steeplejack is exposed. He may be asphyxiated by the smoke of a tall chimney on which he is working, and in very cold weather he may be nearly frozen to death. In either case a fall is possible. Once when Mr. Larkins had to repair the Duke of Sutherland's monument, on the top of Ben Vrackie, gale succeeded gale, and the cold was intense. Mr. Larkins had to work on the top of the figure, which was $33\frac{1}{2}$ feet high and stood on a pedestal of 90 feet.

" To allow of my returning at a reasonable time of night," he says, " I had to down tools at two o'clock in the afternoon, and I cannot say which was the more perilous, the daily ascent or descent of this snow-covered, ice-sheathed mountain. The job occupied eight days. I came near to being frozen several times. Often my hands lost all their feeling, and I could clasp them together and strike them against some hard object without experiencing any pain, while in order to support myself on the ladders, at times I had to throw my arms around them, the while I endeavoured to restore my circulation."

The steeplejack was devoutly thankful when the task was done, but worse followed, for no sooner had he finished operations than a terrible blizzard began, with his ladders still up. They were wanted for another job, and so had to be removed.

After struggling to the top of the mountain, the steeplejack and his assistant found that the apparatus had become frozen to the statue. " Fortunately we had prepared ourselves for this contingency, so that with numbed fingers but resolute wills we set to work and chopped the ladders free from the ice with the aid of a hatchet. The only way of getting at them was to cut steps in the ice where we imagined the ladders to be, and climbing as though carving our way up a white precipice, to bring the hatchet down hard and heavy on their icy coating. It was too cold to attempt to untie the knots and loops in the frozen ropes, so these were also cut down, and fell rigid like iron rods."

The job was at last completed, and Mr. Larkins says that as he looks back he often wonders how the feat did not end in a speedy termination of his career.

Mr. Larkins' father, who was also a steeplejack, met his death through falling from a church spire at Dumbarton. He had three times before fallen from greater heights. In the fall that led to his death he missed his footing while ascending a frosty ladder.

Airmen who make delayed jumps with parachutes, of course, confirm the fact that people falling through the air do not become unconscious for they look at their wrist-watches carefully to decide on the moment when the parachute shall be opened.

How Many Rabbits Are Trapped in Great Britain?

THE number of rabbits trapped in Great Britain every year is about 36,000,000. The rabbit is fast becoming a pest in Great Britain, as it is in Australia and New Zealand, and some parts of North America. The number of rabbits varies from year to year, but recently a peak of abundance was reached, though there had been no diminution of trapping. Every year since 1932 the number trapped has increased.

The reduction from time to time in the number of rabbits is probably due to disease, and an increase of those creatures which prey upon them. If history repeats itself, however, it is believed that there will be a new high record in 1943 or 1944. The most efficient method of keeping down rabbits that has been discovered is by fumigating their burrows with cyanide. When this is done the rabbits cannot be sold, although it is stated that the poisoned rabbits are not harmful when eaten by human beings.

Why Are Wet Sands Firm?

WE all know how difficult it is to walk on the dry sands by the seaside. The feet sink into the loose sand at every step, and a walk on such material is exceedingly tiring and calls for much effort. On the other hand, the wet sands where the tide has just ebbed are firm and hard, and we can not only walk easily on such a strand, but can also gallop on horseback along the firm surface of the sands.

grains in the tin. There is no cohesion among the grains, and anything of weight resting upon the surface easily sinks. When, however, the sand is wet, as after the tide has gone out, the liquid coating which covers every grain leads to cohesion among these, so

Riders cantering along the beach at Bishopstone, Sussex, after the tide has gone out

Why should there be such a difference in the texture of the two sections of the beach? Well, the dry sands are like the sugar in the bowl or the rice

that instead of being merely a mass of loose individual particles the sands are bound into one solid body, and the cohesion between the grains is sufficient to support a very considerable weight. So we can walk or gallop over the wet sands as comfortably and easily as along the firm roadway.

Where Are the Largest Suspension Bridges?

THEY are those which span San Francisco Harbour. The Golden Gate bridge, shown in the photograph

A view of the world's largest suspension bridge, crossing the Golden Gate at San Francisco

on this page, has a channel span of 4,200 feet. It cost £7,000,000 and was begun in 1933, being completed in 1937. The towers are 746 feet high and the roadway is 200 feet above high-water level. Eleven lives were lost during its construction.

The other great suspension bridge at San Francisco is the Cross-bay bridge which joins San Francisco and Oakland. There are two suspension spans each 2,310 feet long, three of 1,160 feet, and a cantilever span 1,400 feet long. This bridge cost nearly £16,000,000. During its construction 24 persons were killed and over 1,100 injured.

What is a Diplomatic Illness?

IT is a feigned or exaggerated illness on the part of one who for certain diplomatic reasons is not anxious to appear in public where he can be questioned or be expected to make a statement.

An example of a diplomatic illness is where a Cabinet Minister who is engaged to make a speech, does not, owing to newly arising circumstances, wish to do so, but is anxious not to appear as though he were withdrawing from the engagement. He sends word that owing to indisposition his medical adviser has recommended him to remain indoors and refrain from speaking. To question this would, of course, suggest that the minister was not strictly truthful.

What is That Kind of Tap For?

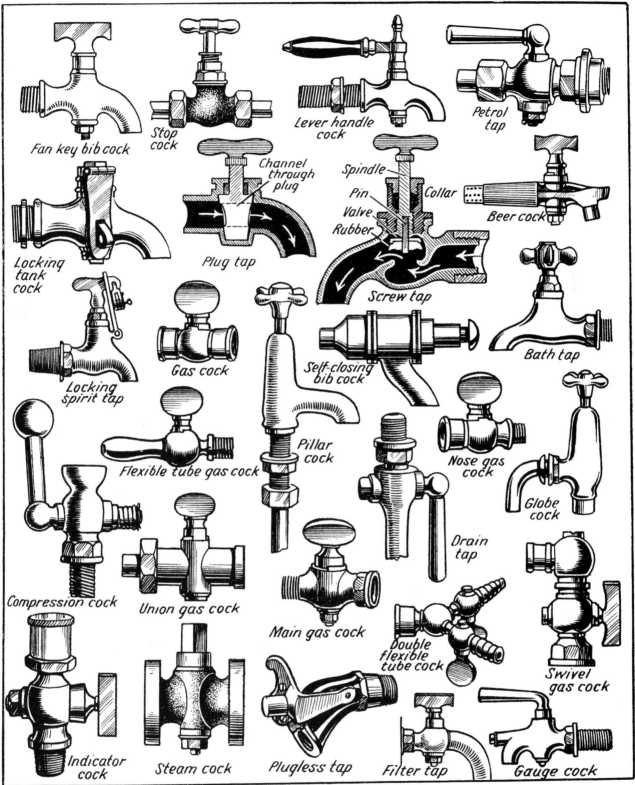

Fan key bib cock

Stop cock

Lever handle cock

Petrol tap

Locking tank cock

Channel through plug

Plug tap

Spindle

Pin

Valve

Rubber

Collar

Screw tap

Beer cock

Locking spirit tap

Gas cock

Self-closing bib cock

Bath tap

Flexible tube gas cock

Pillar cock

Nose gas cock

Globe cock

Compression cock

Union gas cock

Main gas cock

Drain tap

Double flexible tube cock

Swivel gas cock

Indicator cock

Steam cock

Plugless tap

Filter tap

Gauge cock

Taps and cocks are of many different kinds, their form depending upon the purpose for which they are to be used. The ordinary screw tap shown in section near the top is the kind we generally find in our houses for supplying water. The diagram will make it clear how, as the tap is unscrewed, an ever-widening passage is opened for the water to pass. An older form of water-tap, still much used for outdoor purposes, is the plug tap, also shown in section. Here by turning the tap a hole through the cone is brought into line with the pipe, and the water can rush out. Gas taps and cocks are smaller than those used for water. Sometimes two taps are attached to the same connection, so that a rubber gas-pipe can be fixed on either or both. A locking tap is one in which an attachment fits over the top of the tap when it is not in use and prevents it from being turned without first lowering the attachment. A pillar cock is one that is fixed to a stand pipe for the supply of water. In some cases, where the tap is large, there is a longer lever for moving. These drawings are given by courtesy of Messrs. Buck & Hickman, Ltd., of Whitechapel, London

What is That Military Punishment?

In reading history we often come across references to military punishments with curious names. These drawings show what these various punishments were. The whirligig was a circular wooden cage which turned on a pivot. The culprit was put inside, and when the cage was whirled round at great speed he became giddy and sick. The wooden horse was made of planks nailed together so as to form a sharp ridge. The culprit was placed on the horse, and muskets were often tied to his legs to prevent, as was jocularly said, the horse from kicking him off. The horse was then drawn over rough ground. The punishment was very painful. Soldiers when flogged were extended on a wooden triangle. Standing on the picket was a painful punishment. The soldier's right hand was fastened to a hook in a tall post, the arm stretched to its full extent, and he then stood with one foot on a pointed stump fixed in the ground. When a man had to run the gantelope or gauntlet, he was beaten by his fellows, a man with a pike preventing him from running too fast. When a regiment had been guilty of some offence, a certain number were punished, and these were chosen by dice cast on a drum. It is a matter of satisfaction that despite the abolition of brutal punishments discipline in the Army is better than ever

How Are Kerbs Whitened?

In some districts the practice has been introduced of whitening the kerbs of the pavements, so as to make them more conspicuous, especially at

How the Ilford Borough Council whitens its kerbs to make them conspicuous to both pedestrians and motorists

night, and thus to warn pedestrians not to step off them unwarily.

To whiten any extensive length of kerb by hand would be a tedious and expensive process, but the Ilford Borough Council, in Essex, has introduced a mechanical white line marker for the streets. Brushes attached to the wheels of the device whiten the top and side of the kerb simultaneously as the machine is drawn along the side of the road.

What is a County Palatine?

Certain counties ruled over by an earl had royal privileges and rights, and the earl was as supreme in his domain as a king in his realm. These counties were called Counties Palatine, and on the Continent similar domains were known as Palatinates and their rulers Counts Palatine. The name came from the Palatine Hill in Rome on which the Emperor's palace was built. The palatine jurisdiction of Durham remained with the bishop till 1836. That of Lancaster was transferred to the High Court of Justice in 1873.

Are Lifeboats Ever Capsized?

For a modern lifeboat to be capsized in a storm is an almost unheard-of occurrence, yet the seemingly impossible did happen in January, 1938. The St. Ives' motor lifeboat *Caroline Parsons*, which had gone out in a terrific gale to the rescue of the crew of the Italian steamer *Alba*, took the whole of the 23 men off safely. Then their boat was suddenly capsized and five of the rescued men were drowned.

The lifeboat crew and the others were all flung into the water in the sight of hundreds of people watching the rescue from the shore. Fortunately, the lifeboat was of the self-righting type, and after a moment or two regained an even keel. All but five of the swimmers were able to clamber aboard, but the lifeboat was rendered helpless by the terrific Atlantic breakers and it was driven on the rocks and smashed.

A helper from the shore waded through the foaming surf and managed, at the risk of his life, to take a line to the boat by which many of the men were helped ashore. Others jumped into the surf and were assisted ashore by men and women who had gathered on the rocks.

In November, 1928, the Rye lifeboat capsized in a gale and her crew of 17 men were all drowned.

It should never be forgotten that lifeboatmen show quite as great, if not greater, daring and bravery as any soldiers in war, and they do it not to destroy but to save life.

It is the special construction of the lifeboat that makes instances of capsizing so rare. This type of craft is much broader built than any ordinary boat. Then it is fitted with air chambers and other devices to make it exceptionally buoyant so that it can ride easily over high waves. Finally, it has a number of self-acting, non-return valves which enable it to discharge in a few seconds any water that may be washed into it.

The very first lifeboat was invented by a London coach-builder, Lionel Lukin, who bought a Norway yawl and fitted it with projecting gunwales of cork and air compartments running from stem to stern inside and larger air boxes at bow and stern. He gave the boat a heavy iron keel to ballast it.

Lukin took out a patent, and Archdeacon Sharp, the vicar of Bamborough, ordered a lifeboat in 1786 and established it at Bamborough, which thus became the world's first life-saving station. It was the means, during the following years, of saving many lives.

The lifeboat which, after being capsized and righted, was hurled on the rocks at St. Ives Bay, Cornwall, and wrecked at the end of January, 1938

How Long Has the Great Auk Been Extinct?

So far as is known the last living great auk, or gare-fowl as it is also called, was caught in 1844 off Iceland. The bird at one time ranged all over the North Atlantic, from the coast of Canada and the United States in the were in great demand it was slaughtered and became extinct in a few years.

It may seem strange that for a bird that has ceased to exist only little more than a century there should be so few stuffed specimens. There are be-

A year or two ago two young students found on Funk Island, an almost inaccessible rock off the coast of Newfoundland, a complete skeleton of the great auk. It was the first to be discovered for nearly half a century. While the summer plumage of the great auk was chiefly black above and white below, after the autumn moult the throat and foreneck became white.

How Many Milk Bottles Are Used in Britain?

It has been authoritatively estimated that 250,000,000 milk bottles are in use in Great Britain. This seems a very large number, but a more remarkable fact is that over 13,000,000 are lost to their rightful owners every year. The actual number for 1936 was 13,290,742. What happens to them?

Some are stolen, numbers undoubtedly get broken, hundreds of thousands are left about to disfigure the countryside and the beach. In 1936 a million and a half bottles were reclaimed from local authorities after having been deliberately discarded. An equal number was collected from parks and playing-fields. In a single year 35,712 milk bottles were collected by dustmen from household dustbins.

So serious is this loss of milk bottles that some 3,000 of the most important distributors and dairy farmers have formed an organisation to recover lost bottles and return them to their rightful owners. At its headquarters 50,000 bottles are received every day of the year for sorting. Among these are milk bottles from every country in the world, which have found their way to England. There have been taken to the depot at least 1,500 bottles from South Africa. According to the Merchandise Marks Act a dairyman who sells milk in bottles belonging to and marked with, the name of another owner can be prosecuted.

A stuffed specimen of the extinct great auk

An egg of the great auk. Perfect specimens fetch over £300

lieved to be 22 specimens in Great Britain, and only about 70 eggs remain in the world. As the bird laid only one egg in a season we can understand how easily it could be exterminated in a few years by greedy and bloodthirsty men, encouraged by vain and fashionable women.

The eggs are pear-shaped and resemble those of the razor-bill in general coloration, being whitish or pale brown, blotched or spotted with dark reddish brown and black. Some exhibit a green tinge. A good specimen has been sold for 315 guineas, and even a cracked and damaged specimen will realise more than £100. In 1934 the skin of a male great auk was sold in London for £525.

west to Scandinavia, the North Sea and Bay of Biscay in the east, and from Greenland and Iceland in the north to Boston and the North of Spain in the south. In its European haunts the bird was last seen and killed at St. Kilda in 1821, and in the Shetlands in 1812. There are reports of the bird having been seen alive as late as 1852 in Newfoundland, but of this there is no real evidence.

The great auk was the only bird found in the Northern Hemisphere which was unable to fly, for the penguins are confined to the Southern Hemisphere. Probably if there had been as much land in the Southern Hemisphere and it had been inhabited by man the penguin also would have been exterminated by now.

The great auk was about the size of a goose, white beneath with a black head and back. Its legs were so far back under its body that when resting it had the appearance of sitting on its tail, when actually it was resting on its legs. The bird was, of course, quite helpless against man, and as its feathers

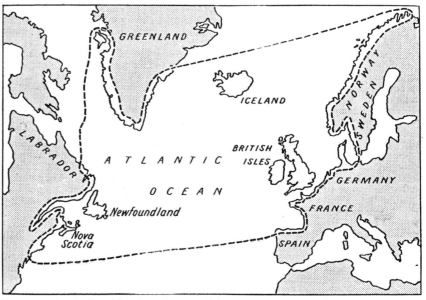

The area within the dotted line shows the range of the great auk before it was exterminated by man

Where is There a Lion Farm?

THERE is a lion farm near Hollywood in America conducted by Mr. Charles Gay, who has about 250 lions, and whenever a lion is wanted for the films it can be supplied from this farm. The lions are trained, and how good their discipline is can be gathered from the fact that there is a roll-call of the lions every day. The lions like to rest

Those who have trained lions tell us that they are much more tractable and reliable than some of the smaller animals popularly regarded as less fierce. The lion when in captivity is generally fed once a day, and the usual allowance is from eight to nine pounds of beef to a meal, exclusive of bones.

What is the Meaning of Bell, Book and Candle?

THIS is a reference to a ceremony in the Catholic Church in the eighth century, known as the greater excommunication. The sentence of excommunication was read, and then a bell was rung, a book closed, and a candle extinguished as symbols. The person was, from that moment, ex-

Lions on a lion farm in California answering to their names as the roll is called

on a kind of trestle bridge with a slanting log at the end, and when the roll is called, each lion as it hears its name rises and walks down the slanting beam.

Many stories are told of the docility of lions and of their attachment to man or child, becoming their companions in both sleep and play and expressing their fondness by fawning or caressing. Mr. Jesse, the naturalist, tells of an old lion that recognised its former master. The lion, when very young, had become the property of an English gentleman, who had treated it kindly and kept it some time with him abroad. Returning to England, he brought it over with him, and not knowing what else to do with it, sent it to the Tower of London, which was at that time the Zoo of London. Here the beast became exceedingly fierce, so that he was regarded by the keeper as untamable. When the gentleman, however, at the end of two or three years, called at the Tower to inquire for his old acquaintance, the animal immediately recognised him with such symptoms of pleasure that he went boldly into the cage and caressed him.

What is on the Unknown Warrior's Grave?

THE inscription on the coffin plate is : " A British Warrior who died in the Great War, 1914–18." On the permanent gravestone of black Belgian marble from a quarry near Namur, unveiled on November 11th, 1921, are the words : " Beneath this stone rests the body of a British Warrior, Unknown by name or rank, brought from France to lie among the most illustrious of the land and buried here on Armistice Day, 11 Nov. 1920, in the presence of His Majesty King George V, his ministers of State, the chiefs of his forces, and a vast concourse of the nation. Thus are commemorated the many multitudes who during the Great War of 1914–1918 gave the most that man can give, life itself for God, for King and Country, for loved ones, home and Empire, for the sacred cause of justice and the freedom of the world. They buried him among the kings because he had done good toward God and toward His house."

Round the four margins of the slab are the four inscriptions : " In Christ shall all be made alive " ; " Unknown and yet well-known, dying and behold we live " ; " The Lord knoweth them that are His " ; and finally, " Greater love hath no man than this."

cluded from the divine ministrations. Shakespeare refers to the ceremony in his play of " King John " : " Bell, book and candle shall not drive me back."

What Are Apparels?

THIS is the old name for the embroidered borders of ecclesiastical garments. They were worked in silk and gold, and often enriched with pearls and precious stones. Many examples of

Apparels, the embroidery at the bottom of an ecclesiastical garment

apparels are to be seen in monumental effigies and brasses. They were very common in the 13th and 14th centuries, but were less used in later times. In modern times, however, they have been revived. They were generally placed round the bottom of the vestment, but are also found on the waists of some.

Where is a Silver Ball Hurled?

AT St. Ives, Cornwall, there is an ancient custom of hurling a silver ball in the streets, this taking place on a day early in February each year. The ball is started off by the Mayor, and is thrown from person to

The Mayor of St. Ives, Cornwall, throwing a silver ball to a crowd of children, a custom that has been carried out for centuries

person till noon. The lucky person who happens to catch the ball just as the clock strikes noon takes it to the Mayor and is rewarded with five shillings.

Do Monkeys Like Ice-Cream?

SIR GARRARD TYRWHITT DRAKE, of Cobtree Manor, Maidstone, tells us that at his private zoo two chimpanzees, Martha, aged five years, and Albert, aged six, are allowed to be fed by the public. Their favourite foods from this source are potato chips and ice-cream. One day in winter he saw them busy, in their covered outdoor open cage, collecting the snow from the ledges outside and eating it. They only returned to their indoor quarters when there was no more ice or snow available. Evidently, therefore, anything cold like ice-cream appeals to the monkey palate.

What Was the Andrée Expedition?

THIS was an Arctic expedition organised by Salomon Andrée, a Swedish engineer, in 1896. He, with two companions, set out from Danes Island on July 11th, 1897, in a balloon to reach the North Pole. They were never seen alive again, and for thirty years their fate was one of the great Arctic mysteries. Then in August, 1930, the bodies of the three men were found on White Island near Franz Josef Land. Their diaries were also re-

covered, and told the story of their ill-fated expedition.

At the beginning of September, 1937, forty years after the expedition set out, a globe of copper thrown from the balloon by Andrée was found on Bastion Island, to the north-west of Spitzbergen, containing a report on the progress of the flight.

Has South Africa a National Anthem?

ACCORDING to General Hertzog, the Prime Minister of the Union, there is no official national anthem in South Africa. " God Save the King," he declared, was regarded as such by many South Africans, but this had never been accepted by Afrikaans-speaking people. He and his fellow Afrikaans-speaking South Africans, however, always received " God Save the King " with the

utmost respect because it was " a solemn invocation to the Almighty for our King." In that character it was played when the Governor-General, his Majesty's representative, ascended the throne at the opening of Parliament, and in that character it would always be played on appropriate occasions.

But " Die Stem Van Suid Afrika," which means " The Voice of South Africa," and which in February, 1938, was played for the first time at the opening of the South African Parliament, was, said General Hertzog, a genuine South African anthem in the fullest sense of the word, sprung from the hearts of Afrikaans-speaking people. Therefore, when it was suggested to him that the time had arrived for " Die Stem " to be given a place at the opening of Parliament he unhesitatingly agreed. He hoped that eventually " Die Stem " would be accepted by English-speaking South Africans as South Africa's national anthem.

How Can a Frozen River Wreck Buildings?

AN example of how buildings along the bank of a river can be wrecked when the river freezes occurred at Niagara early in 1938. After a spell of intensely cold weather the masses of ice carried down by the river and falls froze together, turning the river below the falls into a glacier. But this sheet of ice did not remain at the same level. The pressure from higher up the river raised it more and more, till at last the edges were pushed up on the banks. Nothing could withstand the inexorable pressure, and those buildings near the shore were gradually crushed and wrecked.

The tremendous pressure of the ice and its irresistible force are experienced by ships that get caught in the frozen polar seas. Many a good ship has been crushed by the pressure of the ice all round it.

Buildings wrecked by the pressure of the ice rising in the Niagara River

Who Was "The Favoured Child of Victory"?

THIS was a name given to Marshal Massena, Duke of Rivoli, one of Napoleon's greatest lieutenants. His whole military career in Italy, Switzerland, Germany and Poland was an unbroken series of successes. Then he was sent to Spain and the spell was broken by Wellington, who beat him.

How is a Ventriloquial Doll Worked?

THE head of a ventriloquial doll is quite an elaborate piece of mechanism, as can be seen in the drawing on this page, which explains how it is made to work and look so natural. The head can be turned in any direction, by means of the handle underneath, and there are control keys for moving the eyes, eyebrows and lips. By pressing a key down a series of levers is set working and by their means the eyes or other parts are moved. To make the figure shed real tears a bulb containing water and connected with the eyes by an india-rubber tube is pressed. Of course, it is not enough to possess such a dummy. Great skill and much practice are needed to make it work naturally, and in addition, of course, there must be the ventriloquial talking, so that the operator's lips remain still and the words appear to come from the dummy.

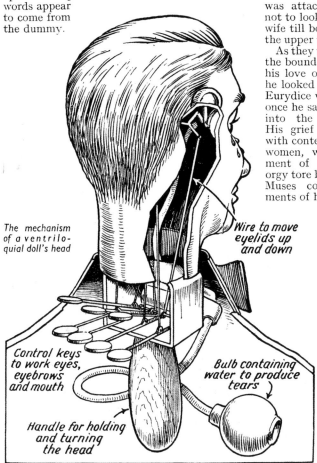

The mechanism of a ventriloquial doll's head

Wire to move eyelids up and down

Control keys to work eyes, eyebrows and mouth

Bulb containing water to produce tears

Handle for holding and turning the head

What is the Story of Orpheus?

THIS mythological personage in the old classical mythology was regarded by the Greeks as the most celebrated of the poets who lived before Homer. Presented with the lyre by Apollo and taught by the Muses how to play it, he enchanted with its music wild beasts, trees and even rocks, so that they moved from their places to follow the sound.

After his return from the expedition of the Argonauts he lived in Thrace, where he married the nymph Eurydice. But when his wife died from a serpent's bite he followed her into the shades of Hades. Here the music of his lyre relieved the torments of the damned, and won back his wife from the inexorable Pluto. The condition, however, was attached that he was not to look upon his restored wife till both had arrived in the upper world.

As they were about to pass the boundary the anxiety of his love overcame him, and he looked round to see that Eurydice was following. At once he saw her caught back into the infernal regions. His grief led him to treat with contempt the Thracian women, who in the excitement of the Bacchanalian orgy tore him to pieces. The Muses collected the fragments of his body and buried them at the foot of Mount Olympus. His head and his lyre were carried by the sea to Lesbos. The astronomers declared that his lyre was placed by Zeus among the stars at the prayer of Apollo and the Muses.

Many poems ascribed to Orpheus were in existence during the period when Greek literature flourished, but most of those existing today are forgeries.

What is a Rottweiler Dog?

THIS is the name of a breed of dog which has been known for generations on the continent of Europe, but was shown for the first time at Cruft's Dog Show in 1937.

Fine examples of the rottweiler breed of dogs

It is a strongly-built animal, active but not too heavy. The body, which is of medium length, is firm and muscular. The tail is short, and is usually carried in line with the back. The head is short but the skull wide, and the ears are pendant. The colour is invariably black, with tan markings on the head, chest and legs, and the coat is short and glossy. The average height is about 25 inches at the shoulder.

The rottweiler originated in the part of Germany that borders on Switzerland, and is used as a drover's dog. It is highly intelligent, and in the days before modern transport, when large herds of unruly cattle were driven for considerable distances, this dog gave valuable assistance to the drovers.

The rottweiler is often used for police and army service, and many are trained to lead the blind. It forms an excellent guard, and is faithful and affectionate to its owner.

What Quantity of Sweets is Eaten in Britain?

THERE are no definite figures of the quantity of sweets consumed in Great Britain, but we can get some idea by the size of the industry. The chocolate and confectionery industry in Great Britain employs upwards of 85,000 insured workers, and according to Sir Francis Terry, President of the Manufacturing Confectioners' Alliance, 35s. worth of its products are sold every second of the day and night, including Sundays. If this estimate is correct, the British are undoubtedly a sweet-eating nation. A hundred years ago most people made their own sweets.

How Does That Plant Catch Insects?

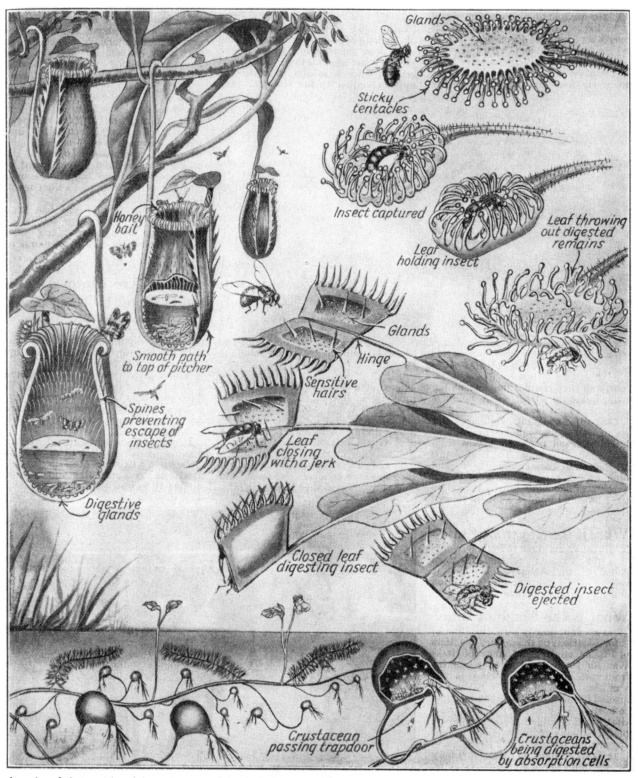

A number of plants catch and devour insects, and the chief of these are shown in the drawings on this page. Some of these are British, like the sundew in the top right-hand corner. This has sticky tendrils that close round and capture any insect that alights on the leaf. Then the leaf absorbs the juices, and afterwards opens and discards the remains. At the bottom of the page is the British bladderwort, a water plant which has no roots, but floats below the surface. Minute crustaceans are caught in small bladders known as eel-traps. The creatures enter by a trap-door, which is a kind of one-way valve that prevents escape. They are then digested, and the nourishment is gradually absorbed by the plant. In the top left-hand corner is the pitcher plant, which grows in the tropics. The end of each leaf is extended into a tendril, with a pitcher at the end more than a foot long. This has a coating of wax inside, and a corrugated margin at the top, with a honey-like substance as bait to attract insects. They crawl in and cannot escape. Finally they are drowned, and the plant draws nourishment from the broth. Beneath the sundew is the Venus fly trap, a North American plant. When an insect alights the leaf closes with a sharp jerk, digests the creature, and then opens wide to throw it out

How Does a Rattlesnake Rattle?

RATTLESNAKES are confined to America, though they have close relations in Asia. These, however, are less deadly than their American kinsfolk, and the only

A rattlesnake with its rattle raised and sounding

difference of opinion. Some have thought it was to attract prey, for it closely resembles the sound made by locusts and other insects on which birds feed; but others believe it is a warning to enemies. Here is what Charles Darwin says on the subject:

"It is admitted that the rattlesnake has a poison fang for its own defence and for the destruction of its prey; but some authors suppose that at the same time it is furnished with a rattle for its own injury, namely to warn its prey. I would almost as soon believe that the cat curls the end of its tail when preparing to spring in order to warn the doomed mouse. It is a much more probable view that the rattlesnake uses its rattle, the cobra expands its frill, and the puff-adder swells, whilst hissing so loudly and harshly, in order to alarm the many birds and beasts which are known to attack even the most venomous species. Snakes act on the same principle which makes a hen ruffle her feathers and expand her wings when a dog approaches her chickens.

Miss Catherine Hopley, an authority on snakes, thinks we may reasonably conclude that the rattlesnake expresses a variety of feelings with its sounding tail, fear being the most predominant one. The Red Indians, she says, recognise its utility as a warning by gratefully abstaining from killing one that rattles. They superstitiously regard it as protective to themselves, if not to the snake, and they in turn carefully protect the reptile.

The sound evidently has a language of its own for when one snake is disturbed and rattles, all the others within hearing take up the chorus. It is also believed that the sexes understand each other through the rattling. "In fact," says Miss Hopley, "to each other and to themselves they have no doubt as many variations in the use of their rattles as any other animal in the expression of its tail.... Those who have most closely observed them have detected a variety of cadences in one and the same rattle. Those also who have carefully watched

rattlesnakes under various circumstances must perceive that timidity is one of the strongest features in this reptile....

"We understand that in the first place it is a substitute for the voice— so far as hissing can be called voice— and that what would cause other excessively nervous, timid, terrified snakes to hiss, causes the rattle to vibrate. It may attract insectivorous birds; it may alarm other timid creatures; it may summon its mate; and, as is well known, it has sympathy with its mate; for a second rattle is almost sure to be sounded and they have been observed to sound in pairs or numbers responsively—and it may be to express anger, fear, and for aught we know pleasure, in a state of liberty and enjoyment, feelings expressed by the tails of other creatures."

At one time rattlesnakes were far more common in North America than they are today, and fierce war was waged upon them by both Indian and white man. In some districts the snakes used to assemble in hundreds and even thousands. George Catlin, the historian of the Red Indians, tells us how he assisted at a hunt at a place known as Rattlesnake Den. There was a knot of them like a huge mat, wound and twisted and interlocked together, with all their heads, like scores of hydras, standing up from the mass. Into this he fired with a shot-gun to rouse them and between five and six hundred were killed with clubs and other weapons. One large rattlesnake was taken alive and was made the means of destroying hundreds in the den. A gunpowder horn with a slow fuse was applied to its tail, and it was allowed to crawl back to the cave, where a loud explosion soon told the tale of the destruction that had taken place.

What Are Bucrania?

THIS word, which is Latin, is the plural of bucranium and means ox-skulls. It is the term used to describe certain sculptured ornaments representing the skulls of oxen, with wreaths of flowers or other arabesque-like ornaments, which were used to adorn the frieze of the entablature in

Bucrania, or sculptured ornaments of the classical period representing ox-skulls

the Ionic and Corinthian orders of architecture. They are also found as part of the decoration of Roman altars. An example of its use as a temple frieze is given in the illustration here.

The device has sometimes been used as part of the ornament of Christian churches, but its employment there is, of course, out of place.

vestige of a rattle is a small horny spine at the end of the tail of one species.

The true rattlesnakes are found from Arizona in the United States to Argentine in South America, and they are easily distinguished by the rattle at the end of the tail. This is a pointed horny appendage consisting of rings which in some instances number twenty or more.

These rings are hollow and are something like quills in substance. They are interlocked with one another and yet are so elastic as to permit of considerable motion. The rings do not grow with any regularity. Sometimes several are added in a single year, while at other times one only is developed. The largest rattles belong to old snakes, but now that so many snakes are killed owing to the advance of civilization, specimens with as many as twenty rings in their rattles are rare. One, however, is said to have been found that had forty-four links. The rattle does not begin to develop till the snake is some months old.

The rattling sound is made by the snake vibrating its tail, so that the horny growth is literally a rattle. As to its purpose there has been much

What is That Kitchen Utensil Used

Dish cover

Oyster opener

Oval pie dish

Cheese scoop

Nut pick

Caddy spoon

Spice box

Colander

Chutney spoon

Whisk

Pudding spoon

Oblong meat dish

Egg poacher

Vegetable scoop

Gravy strainer

Skimmer

Scotch girdle

Ice tongs

Egg whisk

Fish trowel

Icing syringe

Ladle

Orange peeler

Suet chopper

Grape scissors

Pickle fork

Hand bowl

Egg beater

Marrow scoop

Masher

Ice hammer

Sardine tongs

Asparagus tongs

Vegetable mincer

Tin roaster

Stewpan

Dutch oven

Steam cooker

Potato peeler

Basting spoon

Whistling kettle

Tea infuser

Basting ladle

Juice extractor

Fish kettle

Braising pan

Lazy tongs

Mincer

Egg decapitator

Pepper mill

Lemon squeezer

Fish slice

Nutmeg grater

Fish fryer

Vegetable ladle

Lobster pick

Here are 110 articles that are in domestic use. Many of them are familiar in most homes, but some may be less known. Of course, in many cases there are various forms, as, for example, in the case of the egg poacher. Marrow scoops are used now mostly in the kitchen for extracting the marrow from bones, but at one time grilled bones were taken to the table, and the marrow was extracted with a scoop there. Dutch ovens and roasting screens are used little now, as the abolition of the large kitchen range and the introduction of gas and electric cookers have made these objects unnecessary. The egg-preserving pail is, of course, for the storage of eggs in waterglass. The eggs are placed in a wire container, and this is let down into an enamel or galvanised pail containing the liquid waterglass. In the drawing the outside pail has been cut away, to show the wire container. A force cup has a rubber hemisphere and a handle, and is worked up and down over a sink-hole to drive down obstructions

For? Over 100 Familiar Objects

Mayonaise mixer

Salamander

Masher and beater

Revolving icing table

Turbot kettle

Sliding toaster

Check flow cork

Potato masher

Butter cooler

Pastry marker

Apple baker

Fruit Preserver

Measuring jug

Bread grater

Steak tongs

Blowpipe

Steel saucepan brush

Measuring spoons

Lemon squeezer

Bottle jack roasting screen

Swinging toaster

Metal pan scrubber

Soap saver

Cork extractor

Window cleaner

Cinder sifter

Knife sharpener

Cucumber slice

Covered pudding basin

Force cup

Porridge saucepan

Jug mop

Fork cleaner

Asparagus kettle

Saucepan with steamer

Dishcloth holder

Tin opener

Egg preserving pail

Preserving pan

Dish washer

Boiling stove mat

Vegetable press

Puff pan

Caramel cutter

Sponge cake pan

Milk boiler

Stockpot

Coffee mill

Boot drier

Double baking pan

Baking shovel

Boiler stick

Pastry stand

Chip potato cutter

that may have found their way down into the pipe. The boiler stick is of wood, and is for grasping clothes that are boiled in the copper. Many of these implements, such, for instance, as the pastry marker, the grape scissors, the ice tongs, the skimmer, the cheese scoop, the caddy spoon and so on, have been in use for a century or more, while others, like the knife sharpener, the cucumber slice, the lemon squeezer and the tin opener, are of more modern usage. It is astonishing how many useful gadgets are now made to simplify the work of the home. But not many homes are likely to have all of these, though even in small homes the number of useful time-saving devices is on the increase, for with mass production many of these are exceedingly cheap and can be bought for a few pence. The production in large quantities of tinplate and aluminium has enabled many of these articles to be made cheaply, and such objects as the puff pan and the meat dish are punched out at one operation in a press

What is an Archbishop-Bishop?

THE term is used to describe a bishop in the Roman Catholic Church who, while still acting as a bishop of his diocese, has the higher dignity of an Archbishop conferred upon him by the Pope, although he does not rule over a province as does an Archbishop. In February, 1938, the Pope bestowed such a dignity on Dr. Peter Amigo, the Roman Catholic Bishop of Southwark, when the latter celebrated the fiftieth anniversary of his ordination to the priesthood.

Why Was Wellington Called the Iron Duke?

THIS nickname had nothing to do with his character. It was given to him in rather a roundabout way. An iron steamship was launched in the Mersey, at a time when iron ships were a novelty, and it was given the name of the *Duke of Wellington*. The newspapers described it as the iron duke and it was not long before the name was transferred to the Duke himself.

How Are Children Taught to Shop?

AT some schools, like the Middle Park London County Council School at Eltham in Kent, the children have a model store with goods of various kinds all priced, and while some act as salesmen others are buyers. In this way they learn mental arithmetic in a very practical way, and something more than that, for they get to understand much of the art of buying and they do this in a way that interests them intensely.

Do Any Fish Mother Their Young?

CERTAIN parent fish look after their young, but it is rather fathering than mothering; for it is the male fish that is solicitous for the welfare of the offspring. The male stickleback does this, and by gently moving his fins to and fro towards the nest in which they are living ensures that a continuous stream of fresh water containing an adequate supply of oxygen shall reach the young fish. If any danger threatens the family the father stickleback erects his spines and at once attacks the foe.

Another male fish which looks after its young is the geophagus. When the young are hatched out the father follows the family about hither and thither, just as a hen follows her chickens. If one of the young fish ventures too far away, the father at once darts after it, takes it in his mouth and flings it back. It seems curious that the mother appears to take no interest of any kind in her young.

How Does a Primus Stove Work?

ALL those who camp or picnic out know how to use a Primus stove in order to boil a kettle of water quickly, but not everyone knows exactly how the powerful flame of this

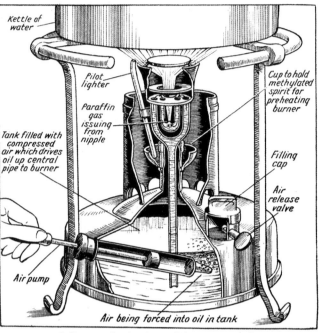

A diagram showing how a Primus stove works

type of stove is obtained. The drawing on this page will help readers to understand the working of the stove, which is wickless and burns paraffin.

The paraffin oil is poured into the reservoir through an opening that has a screw cap. To light the stove a little cup is filled with methylated spirit, and when this is lighted it warms the burner of the stove. When the spirit in the cup has burnt out a small flame remains at the top of a pilot lighter. The air-release valve at the place where the paraffin oil is put into the stove is then closed, and the air pump is given a few strokes. The stove burner itself then catches light from the pilot lighter, a blue flame appearing at the top of the burner.

The pump is then worked once more till a full flame is obtained. What really happens is this. The paraffin tank is filled with compressed air when the pump is worked, and this drives the paraffin oil up the central pipe to the burner. During its circulation through the heated burner the liquid paraffin is converted into gas and issues through the nipple mixed with a proportion of air. The paraffin gas and air mixed together burn and give the exceedingly hot flame which is characteristic of this type of stove.

It is a very ingenious and simple device, and provided the burners are kept perfectly clean, there is no more danger with this kind of stove than there is with an ordinary oil or gas stove.

A model shop in a London school, where children are taught to buy and sell

fessor claims, could be built overhead without interfering with landed property, and the tracks could be brought into the very centres of large cities and compete in speed with air travel. Railway authorities in some European countries have taken a serious interest in this new invention. The illustrations on this page show what the track and car are like.

Above, a model of the new form of rail-car that can travel at 230 miles an hour ; and, on the right, the track banked at a sharp curve

Who Manages the Duchy of Cornwall?

THE estates belonging to the Duchy are managed by a Council which is presided over by the Lord Warden of the Stannaries, the old name of the tin-mining district.

What is the Wiesinger Railway?

IT is a new form of railway invented by Professor Kurt Wiesinger of Zurich, Switzerland, which he claims will change rail transport completely and enable trains to travel in safety at a speed of 230 miles an hour.

The professor's new rail-car including freight weighs about one-fifth of a present-day railroad car, and this lightness at high speeds would be liable in ordinary conditions to lead to derailment. But to prevent this all the wheels of the car as well as the rails of the track are inclined inwards at an angle of about 30 degrees. This makes it impossible for the wheels to jump the rails, and also allows sharp curves to be passed safely at high speed by means of steep banking.

Professor Wiesinger in 1937 built a scale model rail-car, about four feet in length, and laid down a miniature track at Zurich extending for 900 feet His car can be driven like a motor-car or by a propeller, the latter being also used as a brake. Speeds of over 70 miles an hour were reached with this model, corresponding to a speed of 230 miles an hour with a full-size car of this design. This type of railway, the pro-

Are Highly Paid Child Actors Modern?

NO; in 1803 William Henry West Betty, known as the "Young Roscius," who was about eleven years of age, made his début as an actor, was an instant success, and in 56 nights made £34,000. For 13 nights he received nearly £1,000. At Edinburgh, dignitaries of the Church and University, judges and peers vied with each other in doing him honour and offering him presents. When he appeared at Covent Garden, so great was the crowd that the military had to be called out, and many people were seriously injured in the crush to gain admittance.

He was presented to the King and Queen and Princesses, and on one occasion Mr. Pitt, the Prime Minister, adjourned the House of Commons so that members might be in time to witness his performance of "Hamlet" at Drury Lane. Certainly neither Shirley Temple nor Freddie Bartholomew of recent days has had such an honour paid. He went, in 1808, to Cambridge University, where he studied for two years and then returned to the stage.

In a few years Betty made a large fortune, and though he acted on and off through early manhood he had the wisdom to retire with his fortune made in boyhood intact. He died on August 24th, 1874.

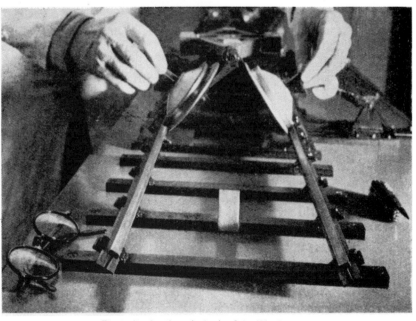

The inclined rails and wheels of the Wiesinger car

Do We See the Sun After It Has Set?

YES, for we never see a heavenly body like the Sun or a star in its exact position, and this is due to the fact that our Earth is surrounded by an atmosphere which bends the rays of light from the Sun or star. The result is that we see the object slightly displaced.

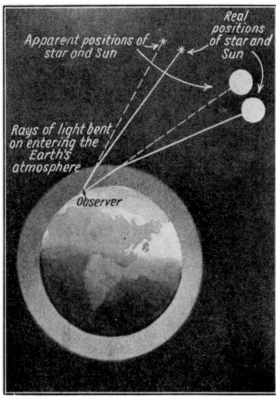

A diagram showing why we can see the Sun after it has sunk below the horizon

The diagram given on this page explains the matter. It shows how the light-rays from Sun and star are bent as they pass through the atmosphere to our eyes. But as we think we always see in a straight line, our imagination makes us believe that the rays have come straight, and so we suppose the position of Sun or star to be at the end of a straight line from our eye to the heavenly body. Thus, even after the Sun has actually passed below the horizon, we still see it. This is entirely due to the action of the atmosphere. If there were no air surrounding the Earth we should not see the Sun once it had actually sunk beneath the horizon.

Who Was Old Hickory?

THIS was a nickname given to Andrew Jackson, President of the United States, who, in a campaign against the Creek Indians in 1813, was so lacking in provisions that he and his men had to live for a considerable time on hickory nuts.

Did Whittington Return on Hearing Bow Bells?

ON Highgate Hill, in the northern suburbs of London, is a stone which bears the inscription " Whittington Stone. Sir Richard Whittington, thrice Lord Mayor of London. 1398, Richard II; 1407, Henry IV; 1420, Henry V; Sheriff in 1396." As a matter of fact, Whittington held the office of Mayor of London (not Lord Mayor, a title that did not exist in his day) four times, for when Adam Bamme, who was elected Mayor in 1396, died after seven months of office, Whittington was appointed Mayor for the remainder of the official year by King Richard II.

The story is told that young Whittington, going away from London, where he had been bound apprentice to a mercer, rested on this spot on Highgate Hill, and there listened to the bells of Bow Church, Cheapside, which, coming across what was then country, seemed to say "Turn again, Whittington. Thrice Mayor of London."

A good many authorities have doubted the authenticity of the story, but Sir Walter Besant in his biography of Whittington says: " It was in the early years of his apprenticeship that he heard that famous carol of Bow Bells which so warmed his heart. For my own part, I see no reason to doubt it at all. I believe in the story, which, however, I read in my own way.

" Why, for instance, should we believe in a poor boy sitting in sadness and dejection upon the slopes of Highgate Hill? Why should the boy be in sadness? He was a strong, active country lad; his master was of his own country and knew his people; he must have been a just and kind man, otherwise Whittington would not afterwards have become his son-in-law; London life was joyous; hope was in the air; the houses of rich men who had made their own way were around him in every one of the narrow streets. Why, instead of despair and misery, I see a Dick Whittington standing with head erect, bright eyes and lithe limbs, alert, high-spirited, brave, ready for any fortune and sure in his own mind of the best; ambitious, too, and self-reliant. What has lusty youth to do with tears?

" Below him, four miles away, he sees the grey walls of London town; beyond the walls, a forest of spires, in every church are the bones of those who died rich after fighting the battle of freedom; their souls are with the just, because they have been good men, and have left money for masses to make all safe. Within the walls are countless treasures of merchandise; within them, too, the most noble and most free of all cities in the world. . . . Then, while he is in this mood, his head full of high thoughts, there comes a message to the boy. It comes with the dash and clang of Bow Bells and cries aloud, 'Whittington, Whittington, Lord Mayor of London.' Ring again, bells, mellowed by the distance, and charged with words so sweet! Turn again, boy; go home to work, that message ringing in thy brain, in patience and in trust."

The Whittington Stone on Highgate Hill, where the famous Mayor of London is said to have rested as a boy and listened to Bow Bells

What is That Indian Weapon Called?

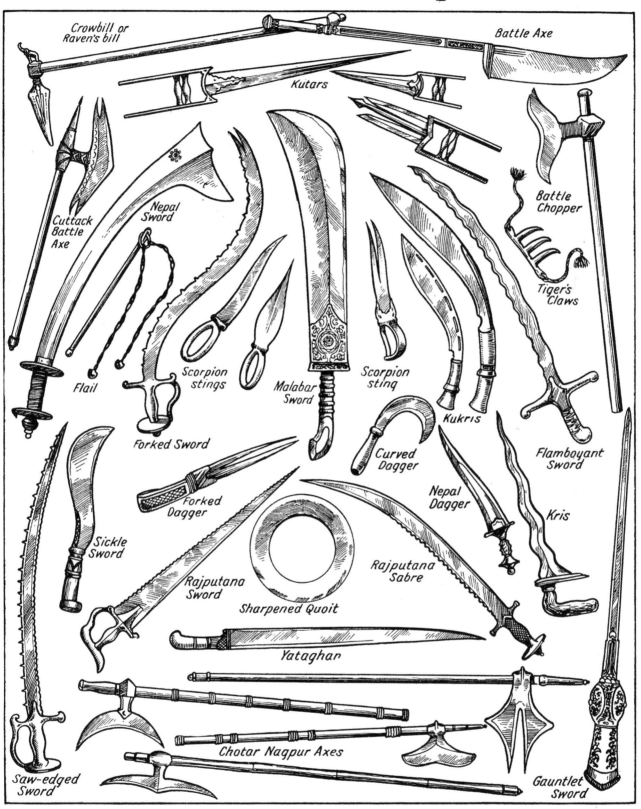

Crowbill or Raven's bill

Battle Axe

Kutars

Cuttack Battle Axe

Nepal Sword

Battle Chopper

Tiger's Claws

Flail

Scorpion stings

Forked Sword

Malabar Sword

Scorpion sting

Kukris

Flamboyant Sword

Curved Dagger

Nepal Dagger

Kris

Sickle Sword

Forked Dagger

Rajputana Sword

Sharpened Quoit

Rajputana Sabre

Yataghan

Chotar Nagpur Axes

Saw-edged Sword

Gauntlet Sword

The native weapons used in India are of various kinds, and some of them are very freakish in appearance. The kutar is held and thrust forward, and sometimes by pressure on the handles two halves of the blade can be opened, revealing a kind of dagger. The scorpion stings, which are daggers that can be concealed along the wrist, are of various forms, some of them having forked points. The forked point is also seen in some of the swords. The blades, both of swords and daggers, take many curious forms. Sometimes they have a double curve, and often the edges of the blades are flamboyant—that is, they are wavy, or have points all along their length. The battle-axes used by the native tribes in the north also vary greatly in the shapes of their blades. The kris, with its wavy blade, is used by the Malays. A gauntlet sword has a handle which completely covers the hand

What is Ski Thursday?

It has nothing to do with skis, long wooden runners for travelling over the snow. The term is short for Skire Thursday, and skire is an Icelandic word meaning clean or pure. The name is given to Maundy Thursday, the day before Good Friday, in allusion to the words of Jesus when he washed his disciples' feet : " Ye are clean but not all," as described in St. John XIII.

How Do the Waves Break on the Shore?

The waves of the sea are caused by the wind blowing on the surface of the water, but as they get to where the beach slopes up, the friction of the ground on the water retards the waves and they become shorter in proportion to their height. The front becomes steeper until at last it topples over and the water is thrown forward as surf. Then the water begins to flow back along the bottom, forming a current or undertow that is often a danger to bathers who are caught by it and held under the water. As the water recedes it takes pebbles and sand with it.

The waves breaking on the shore at Margate

Who Were the Most Famous Boy Calculators?

Jedediah Buxton, born at Elmton, Derbyshire, in 1707, the son of a farm labourer, was a calculating prodigy and in middle life was exhibited in London. As a boy, on hearing a sermon he would tell at once how many words the preacher had used. If any date were given he would calculate in a moment how many seconds had elapsed from that time to the present. Taken to see David Garrick act in " King Richard III," he counted the number of words spoken by the actor. He once calculated how much a farthing would amount to if doubled 140 times, and the answer in pounds had 39 figures. In 1750 he reckoned how many grains of eight different kinds of corn and pulse would cover 200,000 square miles, and how many hairs would make an inch. If he were interrupted he could suspend an intricate calculation for hours or days and then take it up where he left it off.

Zerah Calburn, an American, born at Cabot, in Vermont, on September 1st, 1804, was brought to London when he was eight years old and answered the most complicated arithmetical problems correctly. One was the raising of 8 to the 16th power ; another giving the square root of 106,929 and the cube root of 268,336,125. He would tell in a moment or two how many seconds there are in fifty years. The strange thing was that he had never learned arithmetic, and for the most complicated calculation he never took more than a second or two. As he grew older his mathematical powers vanished.

George Parker Bidder, born in 1806, became a distinguished engineer, was associated with Robert Stephenson in the building of the London and Birmingham Railway, and constructed the Victoria Docks, London. At the age of six he amused himself by counting up to a million, and his powers of dealing with figures were so great that his father, a stonemason, took him from school and exhibited him all over the country as a " calculating phenomenon." Fortunately, friends saw that he was properly educated, and he became a distinguished man, as already indicated.

One other infant prodigy in figures may be mentioned, and that is Nito Mangiamete, a Sicilian, the son of a poor shepherd. When he was eleven he was examined by a group of distinguished scientists on behalf of the Academy of Science in Paris. Asked to give the cube root of 3,796,416 he answered correctly in one minute. He gave the 10th root of 282,475,249 in three minutes.

M. Arago then asked him : " What number has the following proportions : if the cube be added to five times its square, and then 42 times the number, and the number 42 be subtracted from the result the remainder will be 0 ? " Almost before M. Arago had finished his question the boy answered 5.

Which Prince of Wales Was Born With No Skin?

According to an old record, Richard, the son of the Black Prince, afterwards King Richard II, was born without skin and was brought up in the skins of she-goats. There is nothing about this, however, in contemporary documents. It first appears in a book in French and Latin on the Magna Carta, published in 1556. Richard was born of an unhealthy stock, his maternal grandfather being half-witted and his father diseased.

What is Pasteurized Milk?

It is milk that, according to the method suggested by Louis Pasteur, the great French chemist, has been heated to a temperature of from 145 degrees to 150 degrees Fah. for at least half an hour and then immediately cooled to a temperature of not more than 55 degrees. This kills the germs of tuberculosis which find such a ready home and breeding place in milk, and even if the milk came from a tuberculous cow it cannot then communicate the disease to the human being drinking it.

What is Pumice Stone Made Of?

It is a rocky substance ejected from volcanoes which is hard, rough and porous owing to the escape of air when it was in a molten state. The many minute air chambers in it make it lighter than water, so that it will float. Pumice varies in colour, being white, grey, reddish, brown or black. It is used for polishing ivory, wood, marble, metals and glass, and for removing stains from the hands. The dome of the mosque on St. Sophia at Constantinople is built of pumice stone.

Was Hereward the Wake a Real Person?

HEREWARD THE WAKE, the great Saxon hero of William the Conqueror's time, really lived, and he performed remarkable exploits in resisting the Normans, though much that is legendary has in the course of centuries gathered round his name. He is mentioned in Domesday Book as the owner of lands in Lincolnshire. In 1070 he headed a rising of the English in the Isle of Ely, then a swampy region and dangerous to those who did not know its pathways.

Round Hereward gathered many brave men, and so formidable was his opposition that at last William the Conqueror determined himself to crush the rebellion. He besieged the rebels and forced the greater part of them to yield, but Hereward, with a few followers, broke through the Norman ranks and escaped. After this period so much legend has grown round the story of Hereward that it is difficult to disentangle the fact from the fiction.

Hereward is said to have been pardoned by William, but while one account says that he died peacefully, others state that he was slain by private enemies.

How Do We Know Tea Was Pronounced Tay?

WE know that in the time of the poet Alexander Pope, tea must have been pronounced tay, because in

Hereward the Wake escaping from a trap which his Norman enemies had set for him. From a drawing by Charles Kingsley

his "Rape of the Lock" he twice rhymes it with words that have the ay sounds, thus:

> And thou, great Anna, whom three realms obey,
> Dost sometimes counsel take and sometimes tea.

And again, elsewhere in the work:

> Soft yielding minds to water glide away,
> And sip, with myths, their elemental tea.

Who Were the Nereids and the Naiads?

THE Nereids were the fifty daughters of Nereus, the wise old man of the sea, at the bottom of which he dwelt, and Doris, the daughter of Oceanus. The Nereids were the marine nymphs of the Mediterranean, as distinct from the Naiads, who were the nymphs of the fresh water. The nymphs of the great ocean were called Oceanids.

Thetis, the mother of Achilles, was one of the most celebrated of the Nereids, who were lovely divinities and dwelt with their father at the bottom of the sea. They were believed to be propitious to sailors, and were worshipped in seaport towns. They are often represented as half maidens, half fishes.

The Naiads, who dwelt in rivers, lakes, brooks and springs, presided over the latter and inspired those who drank of them. Hence all persons in a state of rapture, like seers, poets and madmen, were said to be caught by these nymphs.

What is a Breeches Buoy?

THIS is the name given to a pair of canvas breeches attached to a lifebuoy slung upon a rope used for life-saving at sea. When a ship is wrecked off a coast and the hurricane or rocky situation prevents a lifeboat going to the rescue, the people on the doomed vessel are often saved by means of the rocket apparatus.

This is a contrivance consisting of a rocket and tube by means of which a thin line is shot from the shore to the ship, the range being about 350 yards. Connection having thus been established, the thin line is used to draw a rope to the ship and make it fast. Then, by means of the breeches buoy, which is hauled to and fro along the hawser, the shipwrecked persons can be brought to shore.

The great advantage of the rocket apparatus is that it is light and mobile. It is kept in readiness at various stations round the coast in a light cart or wagon, and can be taken rapidly to any point where it is needed.

The rocket apparatus was formerly maintained by the Royal National Lifeboat Institution, but in 1855 the British Government took over the system, and there are now some 350 rocket apparatus stations round the coasts of the British Isles. Since 1870 about 13,000 lives have been saved by means of this valuable device.

A rescue by the breeches buoy and lifeline

Which British Bat is That?

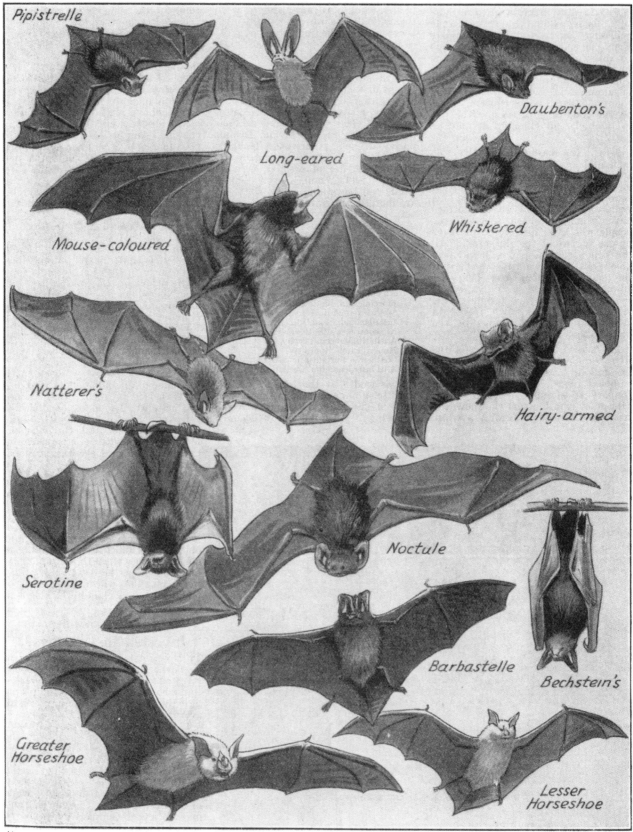

Pipistrelle

Long-eared

Daubenton's

Mouse-coloured

Whiskered

Natterer's

Hairy-armed

Serotine

Noctule

Barbastelle

Bechstein's

Greater Horseshoe

Lesser Horseshoe

Most people who have seen bats flying about as evening falls are unaware that there are thirteen species of bats found in Great Britain. They all feed on insects. The noctule is sometimes called the great bat. It gives out a fetid odour. The pipistrelle is the commonest of all our bats, and it rarely hibernates for more than three months, so that it is seen when others are in hiding. The long-eared bat is also very common. The largest British bat is the mouse-coloured. The barbastelle is rare. The horseshoe bats are found only in the south. Bats are, of course, mammals

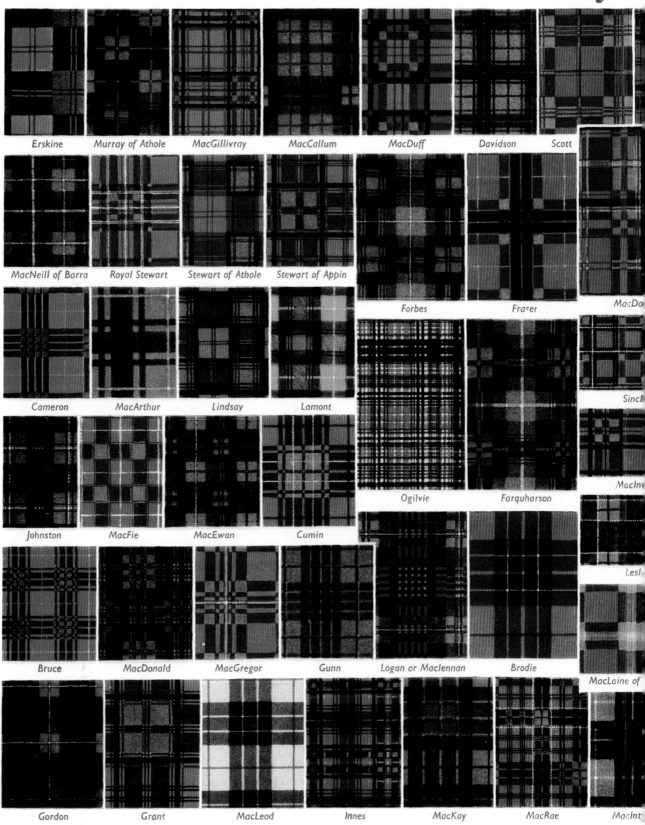

Erskine   Murray of Athole   MacGillivray   MacCallum   MacDuff   Davidson   Scott

MacNeill of Barra   Royal Stewart   Stewart of Athole   Stewart of Appin   Forbes   Fraser   MacDo

Cameron   MacArthur   Lindsay   Lamont   Sincl

Johnston   MacFie   MacEwan   Cumin   Ogilvie   Farquharson   MacIn

Bruce   MacDonald   MacGregor   Gunn   Logan or Maclennan   Brodie   Lesl

Gordon   Grant   MacLeod   Innes   MacKay   MacRae   MacInt

MacLaine of

Although the tartan as a design is not confined to Scotland, but is found in many European countries, it is essentially as a Highland pattern that the tartan is recognised. On this page are 76 of the famous Scottish tartans. Some account of tartan being forbidden is on page 51, and it is a fact that this, more than anything else, is the determining feature of Highland national dress. It must be borne in mind that many of the Scottish clans have from one to five various tartans. There is, for exam worn only by himself and his heir, the dress tar tartan and the mourning tartan. It is ignoranc the correctness of a particular tartan. One of not recognised except by those who have made o

Anemone? Fifty British Species

bellis) ; 16. Waved Muzzlet (Peachia undata) ; 17.
rianthus Lloydii) ; 19. Rosy Anemone (Sagartia rosea) ;
l. Smooth-ribbed Wedge-coral (Sphenotrochus Macan-
3. Cave-dwelling Anemone (Sagartia troglodytes) ; 24.
us Mitchellii) ; 26. Carpet-coral (Phyllangia Americana) ;
adem Pimplet (Bunodes coronata) ; 29. Opelet (Anthea
Tealia crassicornis) ; 31. Sandalled Anemone (Sagartia

sphyrodeta) ; 32. Scarlet-fringed Anemone (Sagartia miniata) ; 33. Ornate Anemone (Sagartia ornata) ; 34.
Arrow Muzzlet (Peachia hastata) ; 35. Gapelet (Stomphia Churchiae) ; 36. Yellow Imperial (Aureliania
heterocera) ; 37. Glaucous Pimplet (Bunodes thallia) ; 38. Parasitic Anemone (Sagartia parasitica) ; 39. Cloak
Anemone (Adamsia palliata) ; 40. Globehorn (Corynactis viridis) ; 41. Warted Corklet (Phellia gausapata) ;
42. Rock Pintlet (Halcampa microps) ; 43. Snowy (Sagartia nivea) ; 44. Plumose (Actinoloba dianthus) ; 45. Crock
(Capnea sanguinea) ; 46. Scarlet-fringe (Sagartia miniata) ; 47. Eyed Anemone (Sagartia coccinea) ; 48. Trans-
lucent (Sagartia pura) ; 49. Marigold Wartlet (Tealia digitata) ; 50. Beadlet (Actinia mesembryanthemum)

What is the Name of That Sea

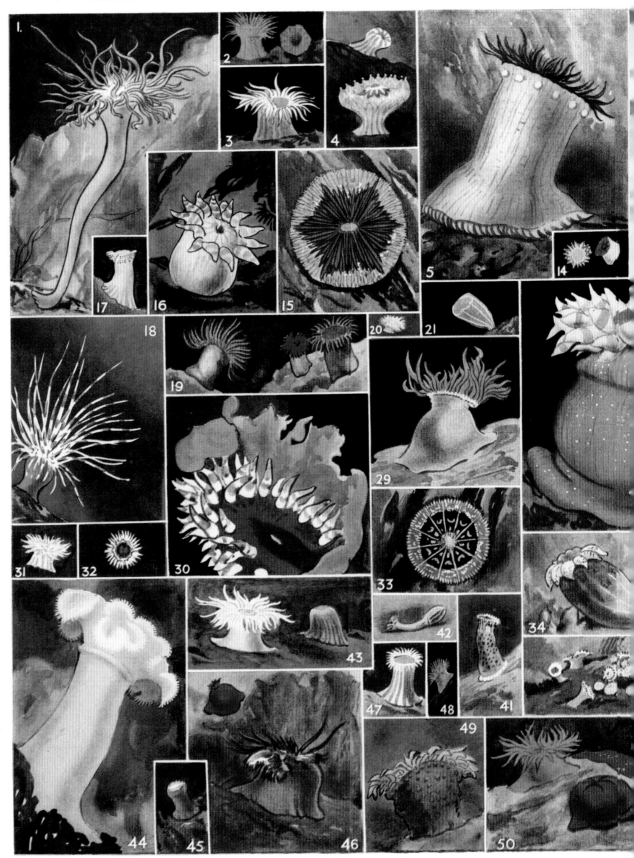

Here are fifty species of sea anemones, those beautiful "flowers of the sea" that are found round the coasts of Great Britain. They can be caught in rock pools at the seaside. Here are their names : 1. Trumplet (Aiptasia couchii) ; 2. Pallid Anemone (Sagartia pallida) ; 3. Orange-disked Anemone (Sagartia venusta) ; 4. Cup-coral (Cyathina Smithii) ; 5. Necklet (Hormathia margaritae) ; 6. Fish-mouth (Sagartia icthystoma) ; 7. Gem Pimplet (Bunodes gemmacea) ; 8. Crimson Imperial (Aureliania augusta) ; 9. Opelet (Anthea cereus, variety Alabastrina) ; 10. Snake-locked Anemone (Sagartia viduata) ; 11. Sandy Creeplet (Zoanthus couchii) ; 12. Gold-spangled Anemone (Sagartia chrysosplenium) ; 13. Red-speckled Pimplet (Bunodes ballii) ; 14. Scarlet star-coral (Balanophyllia regia) ; 15. Daisy (Sagart... Latticed Corklet (Phellia brodricii) ; 18. Vestlet (C... 20. Shetland Cup-coral (Paracyathus thulensis) ; ... drewanus) ; 22. Ringed Deeplet (Bolocera eques ; ... Deeplet (Bolocera tuediae) ; 25. Scarlet Pearlet (Ilyant... 27. Painted Pufflet (Edwardsia callimorpha) ; 28. D... cereus, variety Smaragdina ; 30. Dahlia Wart et ...

Plate X

Six Distinctive Scottish Examples

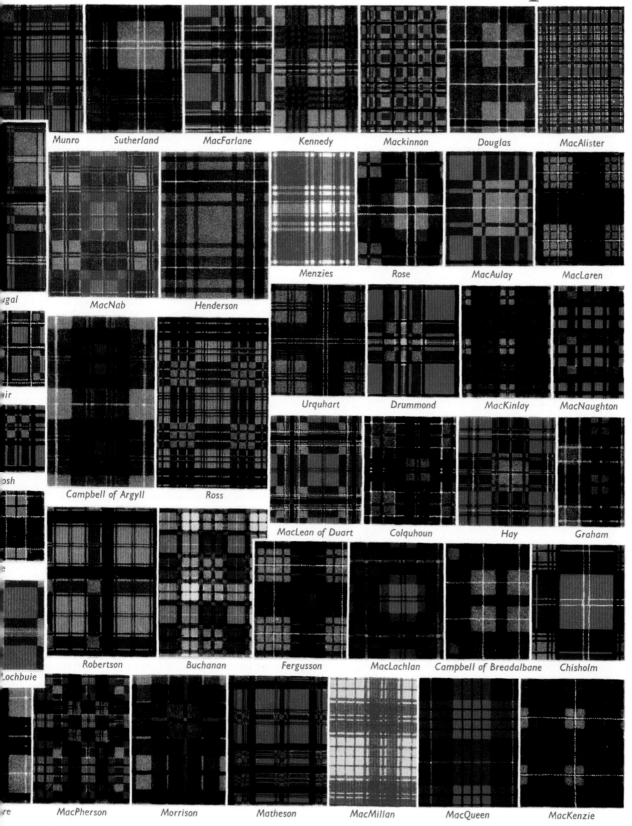

Munro   Sutherland   MacFarlane   Kennedy   Mackinnon   Douglas   MacAlister

Menzies   Rose   MacAulay   MacLaren

ugal   MacNab   Henderson

ir

Urquhart   Drummond   MacKinlay   MacNaughton

osh

Campbell of Argyll   Ross

e

MacLean of Duart   Colquhoun   Hay   Graham

Lochbuie   Robertson   Buchanan   Fergusson   MacLachlan   Campbell of Breadalbane   Chisholm

re   MacPherson   Morrison   Matheson   MacMillan   MacQueen   MacKenzie

le, the common clan tartan, that of the chief, an used for ceremonial occasions, the hunting of this fact that often leads people to dispute these special tartans of a clan is sometimes study of the subject or know the history of the

clan. The Royal Stewarts, for example, have the familiar scarlet tartan given above, but there is also a hunting Stewart tartan in green, and a dress Stewart tartan which has a white background. Where there are various tartans the common clan tartan is the one given here. We have been able to give these reproductions of the tartans through the courtesy of Messrs. W. and A. K. Johnston, the publishers, of Edinburgh and London

Plate IX

What is the Ugli?

This is the name given to a fruit that has only recently been imported into England and sold in the shops. It comes from Jamaica, and in flavour

The new ugli fruit, a cross between the tangerine and the grape-fruit, which began to arrive in London in 1938

is a cross between a tangerine and a grape-fruit. It is as large as the latter, has a yellowish skin, with markings something like those of a piebald horse. There is a pronounced snout. It is, of course, one of the citrous fruits famed for their vitamins.

What Was the Longest Will on Record?

It is said to have been that of Thomas Cubitt, a famous builder of the early part of the 19th century. He laid out and built much of North London, then Tavistock Square, Gordon Square, and Endsleigh Street, Upper Woburn Place, and finally Belgravia, which, when he took it in hand, was a bare, swampy expanse. He built Osborne House for Queen Victoria, and the east front of Buckingham Palace. Cubitt Town, a district of London, is named after his brother, William Cubitt, who was Lord Mayor of London.

The will of Thomas Cubitt covered 386 Chancery folios of 90 words each. It disposed of personal property worth over a million pounds, on which the probate duty was only £15,000, a contrast to what it would have been today.

What is a Cat-o'-Nine-Tails?

The modern cat-o'-nine-tails, used in the English penal system, is a whip consisting of a leather rod, on the end of which are nine lashes of whipcord, each about 33 inches long, with a knot in every foot.

When the cat is to be given the doctor first examines the prisoner to see if he is able to bear the punishment. If he is, the man is then stripped to the waist, and his hands and feet are fastened to a steel device something like a school easel. A screen is placed over the back of his head, to protect the neck, and another screen to protect the lower part of his spine. The strokes are then administered by a warder.

The prison doctor watches as each stroke is administered, and if he finds that the prisoner is fainting, or is in a condition which renders him unfit for further punishment, he stops the flogging.

The prison rule which governs this question reads: "At any time after the infliction of the punishment has commenced, the medical officer may, if he deem it necessary, in order to prevent injury to the prisoner's health, recommend that no further punishment be inflicted, and the governor shall thereupon remit the remainder of the punishment."

How Much May a Pawnbroker Lend?

By law a pawnbroker is not allowed to lend more than £10 on any article, no matter how valuable it may be. If he wants to lend sums larger than this he must take out a licence as a moneylender as well as his pawnbroking licence. In 1907 there were 480 pawnbrokers in London, but ten years previously there were 604.

Why Are Banbury Cakes So Named?

These cakes were named after the town of Banbury in Oxfordshire, where they were made as far back as 1615. The place is still famous for them and what is said to be the original Banbury cake shop is pointed out, though it bears the date 1638. The Oxford Dictionary gives the first reference to Banbury cakes as 1615, a reference appearing at that time in a book called the "English Housewife."

Banbury cakes are made of pastry with a filling consisting of brown sugar, nutmeg, dried currants, candied peel, butter and flour, the whole mixed together. An oval of pastry is cut, the filling spread on it, and then, after the edges of the oval have been brushed with white of egg, a second pastry oval is laid on top, the edges pressed together, the pastry glazed and then baked. There are other recipes for the filling, but this is the one generally used.

The original Banbury cake shop at Banbury

Who Invented the Screw?

No one can say It must have been some man back in the days before history came to be written. The screw is really an inclined plane wound round a cylinder, and it is used today in an immense variety of forms—the wood

A drawing showing how the screw is supposed to have originated in prehistoric times

screw, auger, gimlet, corkscrew, and so on. It seems a very natural and obvious device today, but someone had to think of the idea first. Perhaps it was a twisted branch, with which a hole could be more easily made in the soft ground, that gave some Stone Age man the idea of the screw.

What Was the War of the Spanish Succession?

It was a dynastic war, a striking example of how nations with little or no interest in the family affairs of royal houses could be drawn into a prolonged and destructive war.

Carlos II of Spain had no child and at his death there were four claimants to his throne, the King of France, the Emperor of Germany, the Elector of Bavaria, and the King of Savoy The last two retired and left the field to the others. Louis XIV was a cousin of Carlos and son-in-law of the previous King Philip IV, whose eldest daughter he had married. Carlos had recognised this claim and had bequeathed his crown to Philip of Anjou, the second son of the Dauphin. Louis proclaimed his grandson Philip V of Spain.

But on the ground that Louis XIV had, by the Treaty of the Pyrenees, renounced all claim to the Spanish throne, the Emperor Leopold proclaimed his second son as Carlos III of Spain. War at once resulted and this War of the Spanish Succession lasted for twelve years, England, Holland, Portugal, Savoy, Brandenburg and Germany all joining in to support the imperial nominee. In the end, after many bloody battles including Blenheim, Ramillies, Oude-

narde and Malplaquet, the Treaty of Utrecht was signed, all parties acknowledging the French claimant.

Robert Southey in his poem "The Battle of Blenheim" has well set forth how little interest the common people of any nation had in this dynastic war when he makes old Kaspar say:

" With fire and sword the country round
Was wasted far and wide,
And many a childing mother then,
And new-born infant died.
But things like that, you know, must be
At every famous victory.

" Great praise the Duke of Marlbro' won,
And our good Prince Eugene— "
" Why, 'twas a very wicked thing ! " said little Wilhelmine.
" Nay—nay—my little girl," quoth he.
" It was a famous victory."

A magnified view of the tip of a corkscrew

" And everybody praised the Duke
Who such a fight did win."
" But what good came of it at last ? "
Quoth little Peterkin.
" Why, that I cannot tell," said he,
" But 'twas a famous victory."

What is Mons Meg?

It is an old cannon of great size consisting of bars of hammered iron hooped together. It gets its name from the fact that it was made at Mons in Flanders, and it is now to be seen in Edinburgh Castle.

Can a Star's Heat Be Measured?

The stars are thousands of millions of miles away from us, and appear merely as points of light. Yet the heat they give is appreciable, but it is too small to be measured by an ordinary thermometer. There is, however, a very delicate instrument, known as the thermocouple, or thermopile, which will actually record the heat of a distant star. In this instrument alternate layers of antimony and bismuth are soldered together at their ends, and connected to a moving-coil galvanometer, which is so sensitive that it will record the slightest electric current. The ray of light from the star, falling upon the face of the thermocouple, is sufficient to set up an electric current and deflect the galvanometer needle slightly. Then, by means of a small mirror attached to the galvanometer, the light is reflected across a scale so that the temperature can be read. These thermopiles are so sensitive that even a hand held up some distance away will make the galvanometer move.

The temperature of the star Betelgeuse has been found to be 3,000° Cen.—that is, the exterior temperature—but as Sir Arthur Eddington says, the interior temperature of a star is generally from two to twenty million degrees at the centre. Of course, such temperatures are calculated from the state in which matter must exist in the star's interior, and the condition of the star's interior is understood from the character of the light received from it.

What is the Meaning of "Licked Into Shape"?

The phrase means to mould by rough-and-ready means and is a reference to an old superstition, referred to seriously by Aristotle and Pliny, that a bear's cub is born an amorphous mass and is licked into the shape of a bear by its mother.

Who Was the Warming Pan Hero?

He was the Old Pretender, called by the Jacobites James III, the son of James II by his second wife, Mary of Modena. The story was that Mary never had a living child of her own, but wishing for an heir, had a male child brought to her in a warming pan which she substituted for her own still-born baby. Some colour was given to the story by the fact that James was born at least a month before his time, and at his birth certain persons who should have been present were not there, such as the Princess Anne and the Archbishop of Canterbury. William of Orange openly refers to this son and heir of James as spurious, and it was because of the warming-pan story that he was given the nickname of Pretender. Probably there was no truth in the story, which may have been invented by those who wanted to get rid of the Stuarts.

How is Stonework Made Smooth?

It is smoothed and polished in much the same way as metal-work, by means of rotating wheels and burnishers. As the fine dust which gets into the air as the polisher works would be very harmful if breathed by the workman, he wears a respirator to prevent the dust getting into his lungs.

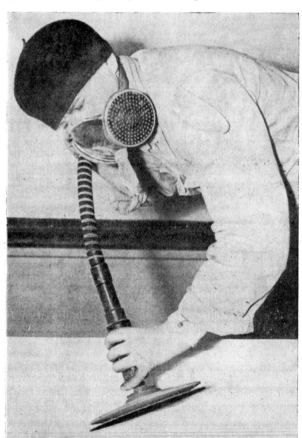

A workman smoothing the stonework with a pneumatic tool. He wears a respirator to prevent the dust getting into his lungs

How Long Have Children Had Dolls?

Children have always played with toys. In the days when toys were not manufactured in numbers and sold in the shops, children made

The King and Queen examining dolls at the British Industries Fair in 1938. These dolls are supposed to represent Princess Elizabeth, Princess Margaret Rose and Prince Edward

their own toys, and one of the earliest of these was the doll. It is a natural toy, for children always like to imitate their elders, and girls, seeing their mothers looking after the baby, have wanted to imitate them, and have used a doll in place of the baby. As scientists would say, it is the child showing its mother instinct.

Dolls were used in the very earliest times, and some of these have come down to us from ancient Egypt and Greece and Rome. Savage children play with dolls, and these toys can be found all over the world.

It does not matter how roughly the doll may be made. The child's imagination adds what may be lacking, and the poor child of the slum, or the African or Eskimo, with a piece of wood dressed up with rags, regards it with as great affection and treats it with as much care as the Mayfair child of rich parents, with

a finely dressed doll worth several guineas.

But the doll is not everywhere confined to children. Among the Bechuanas married women carry a doll with them till they have a child of their own; then the doll is discarded. The same practice is observed among the Basuto women.

Among the American Indians the doll represents the image of a deity, and is regarded as sacred. It is given to a child as part of its religious instruction.

The material of which dolls are made, of course, depends upon what is most easily available. Thus, poor European children will make their dolls of rag, African natives of wood, and Eskimos of bone or ivory. In Japan a common form of child's doll is a shaved willow stick, the shavings being left on the top to represent hair, and the clothes being made of coloured paper. In Korea the little girls make their own dolls out of bamboo, putting grass at the top to represent hair. Curiously enough, they do not paint a face, but often put a little white powder in the place where the face should be. The bamboo stick is dressed in clothes like those worn by women.

Among the people of India, where girls are married while they are still children, elaborately dressed dolls are often among the presents given to a girl at her marriage. Although the Koran forbids the representation of the human figure, dolls as playthings for children are quite common in Mohammedan countries. The children, however, are not often given dolls by their parents, but make them out of folded cloth.

In all three realms of nature there is no substance out of which a doll cannot be made.

How Are Sons Distinguished in Heraldry?

THE different sons of a family are distinguished by having different charges or devices borne upon the paternal arms. These different charges are shown in the illustration on this page. The eldest son, during his father's lifetime, bears on the arms what is known as a label. It is here shown upon a shield.

The charges or devices used in heraldry to distinguish the different sons of a family

The second son has a crescent, the third a mullet, the fourth a martlet, the fifth an annulet, the sixth a fleur-de-lys, the seventh a rose, the eighth a cross moline, and the ninth a double quatrefoil.

These marks are generally placed upon the honour point of the shield, that is, next above the centre, or else in chief, that is, in the upper part of the shield as shown in the first illustration.

Only these nine differences are used in English heraldry, and they not only denote the sons of one family, but also the subordinate degrees of kinship in each house.

Thus, the first son of the first son may charge his label with a label, and the second son with a crescent. The first son of the second son may charge his crescent with a label, and so on.

Who Were Paolo and Francesca?

FRANCESCA DA RIMINI was an Italian lady of the 13th century, daughter of the lord of Rimini and wife of Giovanni Malatesta. She fell in love with her husband's brother Paolo, and both met their deaths at the hand of the husband. The story of their love is told by Dante in his Inferno. Poems and tragedies have often been written round the story and it has also been the subject of painting.

Is a Waterspout Salt Water?

IT will probably be a surprise to many readers to be told that a waterspout at sea consists almost entirely of fresh water. The popular idea is that a whirling wind sucks up the water from the sea and that the waterspout is really composed entirely of salt water.

This, however, is not the case. The waterspout is really a tornado over the sea, but it is generally less violent than a land tornado. A funnel-shaped column of air extends down from a storm cloud to the surface of the sea, and as it whirls round causes an up-draught which cools the air and condenses the moisture.

Water appears to be drawn up from the sea, but this is only an illusion. The sea and spray may rise for a few feet, but no higher. Ships that have run into a waterspout have been drenched not with salt water but with fresh. The waterspout is dangerous only to small boats.

What is the Smallest Baby Ever Born?

THE smallest baby of which there is a properly authenticated record was born at Newcastle-on-Tyne in 1935 and weighed only 13 ounces. In a month he had increased in weight to 4 pounds 10 ounces. In February, 1938, a daughter was born to Mrs. Gwen Bass of Margate which weighed only 14 ounces and measured 8 inches. It was packed in cotton-wool to keep it warm, and was fed with sugared water by means of a fountain-pen filler.

Do Miners Wear Gloves At Work?

THE use of gloves in the mine is steadily increasing, and is causing a considerable reduction in the number of accidents to miners. The report of the Safety in Mines Research Board for 1936 says : " Hand protection is important, because most of the minor accidents involve injury to the hands. The chief difficulty—that of producing at a reasonable cost a sufficiently durable glove which will give suitable protection without hampering the work—has now been largely overcome. It does not take long to become accustomed to the use of gloves, and it has been found that, once the strangeness has passed, many miners actually prefer to work in them."

Safety boots are also now worn by many miners, and, according to the Research Board's report, they have prevented many potential foot injuries. For protection against flying fragments a light spectacle goggle is now worn. Shin-guards also are being increasingly worn by miners at the coal face, and have prevented many leg injuries.

How Do Mongolians Guard Against Dust Storms?

IN Mongolia most of the villages are of the movable type, for the people are nomads, and when a region no longer provides sufficient pasturage and crops they move on to another area. Their houses are made of woven millet stalks and are covered with canvas and then securely tied down to prevent them being blown away by the fierce winds that pass over the country from time to time.

Terrific dust storms occur, but the houses, frail though they look, protect

The movable, dust-proof homes of Mongolian natives.   They are made of woven millet straw

the natives from the dust. Millet canvas, as the double covering is called, is fortunately dust-proof. The dust comes from the Desert of Gobi and is carried by the wind for hundreds of miles. Bitter cold besides dust makes this wind very unpleasant.

When Was the First Flight From a Warship?

THE first flight of an aeroplane from a warship was made in December, 1911, by Lieut. C. R. Sampson, who flew a Short biplane off the bows of H.M.S. *Africa*, lying in Sheerness Harbour. Lieut. Sampson had constructed a runway on the ship for his flight. A few days later Lieut. Sampson and Lieut. Malone repeated the flight, this time with a seaplane fitted with wheels from H.M.S. *Hibernia* when she was steaming into the wind at about ten or twelve knots. The first real aircraft carrier was H.M.S. *Hermes*, which was commissioned in June, 1913, and carried aircraft which flew from runways on forecastle and quarter-deck.

Where Are Cheeses Rolled Downhill?

FOR over 400 years the villagers of Witcombe, in Gloucestershire, have carried out a curious custom on Whit Monday. They roll cheeses down Cooper's Hill, and the local lads run after them to catch them before they reach the bottom. This hill is really grazing common, and the ceremony is said to be carried out in order to preserve the rights of common.

The starting of the cheese-rolling is quite a ceremony. There is a Master of the Ceremonies, who wears a smock and silk hat. He gives the signal, and a cheese is set rolling. The boy who catches it before it reaches the bottom is allowed to keep it, and prizes of 4s. and 3s. are given to those who are nearest to him. Altogether, six races are held, one being for girls only. Sometimes a cheese breaks open in its journey down the hill.

Another Whitsuntide custom, which used to be carried out in the village of St. Briavels in Gloucestershire, was the distribution of pieces of bread and cheese after church on Whit Sunday.

The cheese-rolling ceremony at Witcombe on Whit Monday

Is Singing a Natural Gift?

THERE is some difference of opinion among scientists, but Sir Milsom Rees, the distinguished throat specialist, who has been laryngologist to Covent Garden Theatre for forty years, has definitely stated that singing is not a natural gift. He declares that the vocal cords are not constructed by Nature for singing purposes.

"Singing," he says, "is an acquired accomplishment, into the services of which have been pressed certain organs not intended for it. The same conclusion is suggested by the multitude of troubles that afflict even the best singers. If these be true there is no such thing as a natural singing voice. I have never heard of a leading opera singer, or even a chorus singer at Covent Garden, who had not been taught how to sing."

Is Sand a Menace in Great Britain?

WE know how the sand in regions like those bordering on the Sahara and Gobi deserts is constantly encroaching on the fertile lands and

Houses at Newton, Porthcawl, on the Welsh coast, being overwhelmed by drifting sand dunes

overwhelming them. Underneath the sands of both these deserts are the ruins of what were once flourishing cities in the midst of a thriving civilization. Nothing can withstand the onrush of the relentless sands which are ever burying more and more territory.

Something of the same kind on a much smaller scale is happening in some parts of Great Britain. On the mid-Glamorgan coast, for instance, hundreds of thousands of tons of sand are moving steadily inland and threatening the safety of scores of homes. At Newton, Porthcawl, the ever-moving sand dunes have now almost covered gardens, garages and outbuildings at the rear of some of the houses. Barriers erected to hold back the sand have been overwhelmed, and in some cases the sand is now settling against the backs of the houses. The photograph on this page shows how very real the menace of the sand is.

What Was the Bishop's Bible?

THIS English version of the Scriptures, compiled by Archbishop Parker of Canterbury and a number of bishops, was issued in 1568, and was the official Bible of the Church of England. It is sometimes called Parker's Bible. In general it is simply a revision of the Great Bible of 1539. Its most notable feature is the new version of the Psalms, translated, it is believed, by Thomas Bickley, afterwards Bishop of Chichester. This version is known as "the Treacle Bible," because in Jeremiah VIII, 22, "balm" is translated "treacle."

What Are Those Scissors Used For?

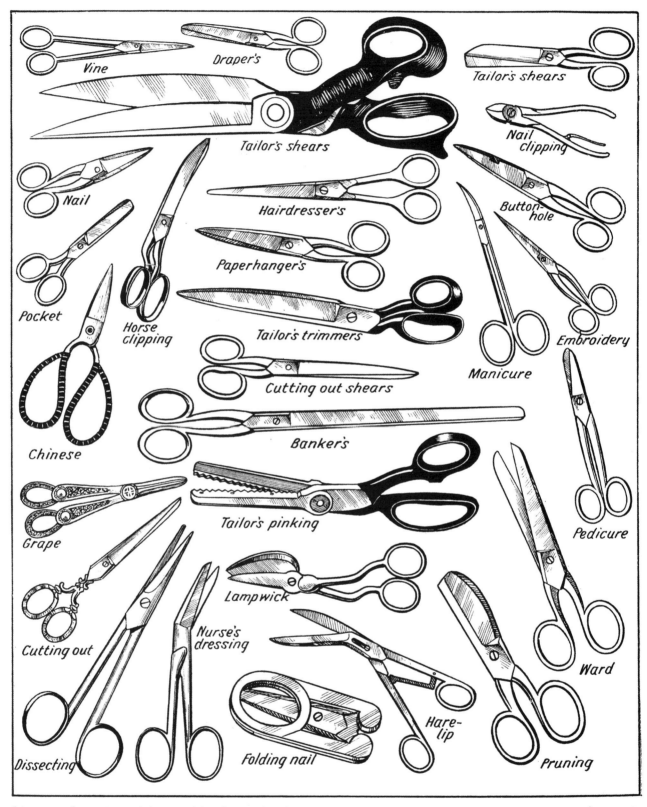

Vine
Draper's
Tailor's shears
Tailor's shears
Nail clipping
Nail
Hairdresser's
Button-hole
Pocket
Paperhanger's
Horse clipping
Tailor's trimmers
Embroidery
Chinese
Cutting out shears
Manicure
Banker's
Grape
Tailor's pinking
Pedicure
Cutting out
Lampwick
Nurse's dressing
Ward
Dissecting
Folding nail
Hare-lip
Pruning

Scissors are of many sizes and shapes, and their form is adapted to the particular use to which they are to be put. Nurses' scissors, for example, are often bent so that they can cut bandages easily. Surgeons use a great variety of scissors, one example of which is given, the dissecting scissors. Bankers' scissors are long and slender, and are used in offices for cutting paper. Tailors' scissors are very large and heavy. They are, of course, used for cutting out the cloth from which suits are made. Vine scissors are used for cutting the bunches of grapes from the vine. The tailors' pinking scissors enable a scalloped edge to be cut. Chinese scissors have the handles bound with thin cane. The lampwick scissors are something like the old snuffers, used in the days of tallow candles, and have a chamber to receive the burnt wick that is cut off. Manicure scissors are, of course, used for the nails, and pedicure scissors, which are heavier in make, are for the feet. Pocket scissors without a case generally have blunt points

Will London's Population Go On Increasing?

FIGURES prepared by Sir Charles Bressey, of the Ministry of Transport, of the recent and estimated future population of London are as follows :

1931	9,500,000
1941	10,350,000
1951	10,750,000
1961	10,700,000
1971	10,700,000

Mr. Frank Pick, Vice-Chairman of the London Passenger Transport Board, has suggested the possibility of a population of 12,000,000 for London. If the population increases to this extent Mr. Pick declares that transport could not keep pace with it. If London develops beyond a limit of twelve miles from Charing Cross, he says, the means of transport on which it depends must prove inadequate.

What is the Heaviest Anchor Made?

THE anchors for large Atlantic liners nowadays often weigh twelve tons, but the new anchor supplied to the *Queen Mary* at the beginning of 1938 has the record weight of fourteen tons. The photograph on this page showing it being hoisted up from the quay-side gives some idea of its enormous size.

The 14-ton anchor of the " Queen Mary " being hoisted on board at Southampton

Why Do Heath Fires Occur in Summer?

THEY occur in summer because then the grass and undergrowth, owing to dry spells, have become very dry, and a lighted cigarette or a burning match will soon set the grass on fire, and in a moment or two a big blaze has been started.

Plants normally, of course, contain an immense amount of water. They are constantly taking up water by the roots and passing it off by their leaves, so that there is a regular stream of water going through the plant. But when the leaves and stems are all dried up by the hot Sun in a time of drought, the plant then has a very small proportion of water in it, and so it is easily combustible.

Further, the hot Sun, shining for hours upon the dry vegetation, raises it very near to its combustion or ignition point. That is why a spark from an engine may start a big fire. The amount of heat poured upon an area when the Sun is shining in its summer strength for hours at a time is enormous. Scientists tell us that the desert of Sahara receives daily in solar energy the equivalent of that from 6,000 million tons of coal.

Why Are Birds Taken Down Coal-Mines?

CAGED linnets are taken down coal-mines for the detection of gas. These birds are much more sensitive to the presence of gas than are men, and so if there is any suspicion of gas

A member of a coal-mine rescue team about to descend a mine with a caged linnet used for detecting gas in the workings

a bird's assistance is obtained, and it shows by becoming unconscious that there is gas present. Steps can then be taken in time to combat the evil.

The coal-mines of Durham and Northumberland have one of the most efficient colliery fire and rescue brigades in the world. It is manned by about fifty trained officers and men, who among them control four stations. At the Crook station in Durham County is an underground gallery where the men can practise the art of life-saving in conditions exactly similar to those which occur in the mines after an explosion or fire. The brigade is equipped with the latest fire-fighting apparatus. Liquid air, which is indispensable in underground rescue work, is actually manufactured at the station, and there is a supply of linnets for the gas detection.

Is a Hog a Sheep?

WHILE the word hog is generally used in common language for the adult domestic swine or pig, it is also the correct term for a young sheep before its first shearing, and as such is used by farmers.

What is an Arabesque?

It is an ornament consisting of a pattern, more or less intricate, composed of stems, foliage, leaves, fruits, scrolls and mathematical figures. It gets its name from the fact that the

An example of the arabesque or moresque in art

Arabs adorned the walls, ceilings and floors of their buildings with such decoration. The reason for making the patterns up of the figures mentioned is that the Mohammedans were forbidden by their Prophet to make representations of men or animals.

The type of decoration known as arabesque was not, however, the invention of the Arabs. It was known to the Greeks and Romans, and was largely employed by them to adorn their architecture, and has been much used since in Christian architecture. Europeans have added to the other forms those of curious and fantastic animals. This decoration is also called moresque, after the Moors.

Is the Ass a Native of Hot or Cold Countries?

In the domesticated condition, asses are now spread over a large part of the warmer regions of the Old World, and are common in many parts of South America; but the ass is essentially a southern animal, partial to hot and dry countries and exceedingly averse to entering water. It has been stated that "the ass, and with it its name, accompanied the progress of the culture of the vine and olive to the north, not crossing the limits of that culture."

Mr. Richard Lydekker says that from the reputed Eastern origin of the West European names of the ass, it has been very generally considered that the animal itself, in its domesticated condition, is likewise of Eastern origin and that it reached Europe by way of Asia Minor and Syria, although its original home may have been north-western Africa, where true wild asses are alone found at the present day.

"Nevertheless," says Mr. Lydekker, "even if domesticated asses were introduced into Europe from the East, it is probable that the wild animal was first tamed in the Mediterranean countries, as we have no evidence that it ever existed to the eastward of the Red Sea. If this view be correct, asses must have reached India from the westward; this being the opinion of Darwin, who unhesitatingly regards all the domesticated breeds as the descendants of the North African wild animal."

The ass is nearly related to the true zebra of southern and south-western Africa, with which it agrees in general form—in the shape of its head, in the length of the ears and in the narrowness of the hoofs. The ass has, however, lost the stripes of its southern cousin, except that one and occasionally a pair of stripes is generally retained on the shoulders and barring often persists on the legs. The ass's unmelodious bray is nearly paralleled by the cry of Grévy's zebra.

No doubt the domesticated breeds have inherited their capacity for existing on the poorest and driest fodder from their wild ancestor, whose food consists of the hard, dry grasses growing in semi-desert districts in North Africa.

In the East the ass is much more generally used for riding and in agriculture than is the case in Europe. Many countries have breeds specially adapted for particular kinds of work. Formerly asses were largely kept in the East for the sake of their milk, which is highly nutritive. Droves of she-asses formed a special part of the possessions of the Biblical patriarchs.

The largest breed of domesticated ass is the Poitou breed of France, which rivals the cart-horse in size and make, and is an ugly-looking animal with an ungainly head, enormous ears, stout limbs and broad hoofs. It is kept almost entirely for the breeding of mules. Spain also has a big breed of asses, believed to be the ancestral stock of the Poitou asses. These also are kept for mule-breeding.

The Poitou ass stands sometimes 16 hands, or 5 ft. 4 ins., at the shoulder, but at the opposite extreme is the little grey Mahratta donkey of western India, which is only half the height of the Poitou breed. Yet it can carry enormous loads. A special characteristic of the domesticated ass in all countries is its surefootedness.

Though the subject of scorn and ridicule in many lands, the ass has had its moment of triumph, as Mr. G. K. Chesterton has pointed out in his poem "The Donkey":

> The tattered outlaw of the earth,
> Of ancient crooked will;
> Starve, scourge, deride me; I am dumb,
> I keep my secret still.
>
> Fools! For I also had my hour;
> One far fierce hour and sweet;
> There was a shout about my ears
> And palms before my feet.

The poet is, of course, referring to the time when Jesus rode in triumph on an ass into Jerusalem on Palm Sunday amid the crowd's plaudits.

What is a Sand Picture?

It is a picture formed by arranging sand of various tints on a sticky background, so that the grains will remain in position. It was a popular form of ornament towards the end of the 18th century and at the beginning of the 19th, and sand pictures are sometimes seen exposed for sale at seaside places where the local sands vary in colour, as at Alum Bay in the Isle of Wight. Some of the results are remarkably clever and give the effect of a painted picture. The older specimen's are sought after by collectors.

Donkeys used for giving children donkey rides at Brighton

What Great Composer's Tomb is Empty?

It is the magnificent tomb erected in 1934 to Franz Josef Haydn, composer of "The Creation," "The Seasons," and hundreds of other works, by Prince Paul Esterhazy in the parish church of Eisenstadt. The composer's headless body lies in the crypt of the same church, while his skull is in a museum at Vienna. The latter has been on exhibition in the museum of the Gesellschaft der Musikfreunde since 1895. The story of how the head came to be separated from the body has been told in the "Daily Telegraph" by Miss Alice Mehler.

"Haydn," she says, "who died on May 31st, 1809, was buried in the Vienna Hundsthurm Cemetery. A night or two later a venal grave-digger disposed of the skull to two strangers. Prince Nicholas Esterhazy obtained permission ten years afterwards for the transference of the body to Eisenstadt, where for many years the composer had been Capellmeister to the prince's grandfather. The disappearance of the skull was then discovered, but was kept secret.

"Police investigations led to the discovery of the culprits, Josef Peter, manager of the Provincial House of Correction, and his friend Rosenberg, secretary in the house of Prince Esterhazy. These two, enthusiastic

Vienna, Prof. Rokitansky, who bequeathed it to the museum of the Gesellschaft der Musikfreunde, the Society of the Friends of Music. The skull was handed over by Prof. Rokitansky's three sons, and the society had to bind itself never to give away the relic without the consent of the city of Vienna.

"Since the erection of the mausoleum negotiations between Prince Esterhazy and the Gesellschaft have been going on for the transference of the skull, which the Prince wishes to be buried with the body. An official of the society tells me that in principle the Gesellschaft would be willing to hand over the skull if the city of Vienna would release them from their obligation, but this has so far not been done. Another impediment : on the rumour of the intention to transfer the skull to Eisenstadt, a grandson of Prof. Rokitansky has threatened an action against the society for disregarding his grandfather's will.

"In the circumstances, then, the Gesellschaft der Musikfreunde is not a free agent. The trunk remains in the crypt and the mausoleum, the most handsome ever built for an Austrian musician, is likely to continue to be a mere cenotaph."

Does the Hudson River Freeze Over?

Yes ; in very severe winters such as New York often experiences, the Hudson River actually freezes right over and all navigation is stopped. When the ice first forms, a passage-way for ships is kept open as long as possible by powerful ice-breakers. But when the weather continues severe the river gradually freezes completely

An ice-breaker making a path for an oil tanker in the icebound Hudson River at New York

from bank to bank, so that it can be crossed on foot some miles above New York as seen in the accompanying photograph.

What is the Longest Delayed Fall?

The longest delayed fall—that is, the longest fall from an aeroplane before opening a parachute—was made on March 4th, 1938, by a French airman who uses the name "James Williams." Jumping from an aeroplane at a height of 5 miles 500 yards, he did not open his parachute till he had fallen 5 miles, making a world record for a delayed drop.

Careful preparations had been made for the fall and the ascent was made from Chartres aerodrome. The descent took 141 seconds. "I pulled the parachute when I was seven seconds from the ground," said the airman. "The parachute spread open at once."

It is doubtful if there is any feat that man could accomplish in cold blood which requires more nerve than one of these delayed falls from an aeroplane.

People walking across the Hudson River when it was frozen over in the winter of 1937-38

believers in the theory that the measurements of a skull afford a clue to the capacities of the owner, had acquired Haydn's head for their scientific experiments. To placate the police Rosenberg handed over the skull of another person, and this was attached by a metal clasp to Haydn's skeleton and buried at Eisenstadt. Years later, however, he presented to Dr. Karl Haller of Vienna Haydn's actual skull.

"Dr. Haller made it over to the director of the Anatomical Institute at

How Does That Nut Grow?

Many people in Great Britain eat nuts of various kinds, without having the faintest idea as to how the nut grows on the tree. Many, for example, do not know that the ordinary walnut, when it grows, has an outer case or covering which is taken off. This is first green and then turns brownish. We eat that outer case only when the nuts are very young, and before the shell forms. Then we pickle the walnuts. Chestnuts and almonds also grow inside an outer case, as shown. Filberts and hazel nuts have a green covering in which they partly rest. The most curious of nuts, however, is the Brazil. The nuts, with their hard shells, when they are growing on the tree are all packed together like the sections of an orange, inside a stout globular shell, which is very hard indeed. Monkey nuts or peanuts ripen underground, as shown. Nuts are, of course, the fruits of the plants

Was Magna Carta Really Important?

In the early years of the present century a well-known historian wrote an article in which he insisted that what had hitherto been cited as a charter of liberty was no such thing, and that Magna Carta had merely extorted liberties from a helpless king for the sole benefit of a

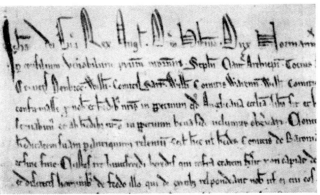

A facsimile of the opening words of Magna Carta, the great charter of English liberties

ruling class. Its claim to be a charter of freedom for the whole nation was, he said, a splendid myth invented by a lawyer, Chief Justice Sir Edward Coke, in the 17th century as a weapon of attack against James I.

But as the Rev. J. S. Whale has said, the undoubted truth which gives to Magna Carta a precious importance today is that " that document signed at Runnymede stands out as a landmark not only because of what it actually was, but because of what it has come to be in the minds of later generations. It embodies not only a fact but a faith. Its real value lies in what it was in 1215, of course, but also in what it came to mean to Pym and Hampden in 1625 and in what it has come to mean to you and me in 1938. The historic fact is more than bare fact ; living men look back to it, believe in it, and make it their own."

Of course, it is true that Magna Carta was extorted from an evil king by powerful barons and that they were thinking of themselves and not of the masses of the people. But despite that fact it was a great charter of liberty, the basis of many liberties in which all eventually participated ; Magna Carta underwent several changes before reaching a final form, but in its original form, among other things it empowered anyone to go away from and come back to the realm unhindered, mitigated the oppressiveness of the Forest laws and banished the royal mercenaries. After various confirmations by later sovereigns it reached its final form in 1225. It released tenants from many oppressions, guaranteed to London and other cities and towns all their ancient franchises, gave merchants full licence to go about buying and selling unfleeced, insured to villeins that their tools and implements should not be

distrained on to pay fines, guaranteed to the community that Courts of Justice should be held in fixed places, and that fines should be proportioned to the offence, and determined that weights and measures should be uniform. But the most famous clauses are those which guarantee justice to all without delay and assure to every freeman security from punishment except after trial by the law of the land and before his peers.

To suggest that a document that guarantees these things is not a charter of liberty is to talk nonsense. Not many years ago, a poor woman in London who owed money to a man had her sewing-machine taken in distraint. The woman went to the magistrate and told him what had happened, and the man, who had infringed Clause 20 of Magna Carta, had to return the machine and pay the woman compensation. Her rights were guaranteed and insured to her by the famous document.

What Does it Cost to Move a Statue?

People often suggest that a statue set up in a public place should be moved to another site, forgetting that the cost of doing this is considerable. When it was suggested that the statue of the Prince Consort, which had long stood at Holborn Circus in London,

should be moved to some other place in the City where it would interfere less with traffic, it was found that the cost of removal would be £900. The London Passenger Transport Board had agreed to make a contribution of £300 towards the expense of removal, and it was practically decided to carry out the work, till the City Corporation discovered that the cost would be at least three times that amount.

What Bishop Ate His Boots?

It was Bishop Stringer of the Yukon, afterwards Archbishop of Rupertsland, who in 1935 died suddenly in a street in Winnipeg. Years before, travelling in an out-of-the-way part of his lonely diocese, and being short of food and in danger of starvation, he took a spare pair of boots which he carried, and stewed them. Then he and a companion gnawed the hide and drank the water in which it had been cooked. This saved them from starvation.

What is a Double Cottenham?

This is the name of a cheese which was a favourite in England at least 250 years ago, and in the second half of the 19th century was eaten by everyone who was anyone at Cambridge. It has been described by an authority as " the queen of all the cheeses," and " as much superior to Stilton as Stilton is to Dutch cheese." It gets its name from the village of Cottenham, about seven miles from Cambridge.

Are Lions Playful?

Yes, like other members of the cat family, lions, especially when they are young, like to frolic and play, and may often be seen indulging in a game at places like Whipsnade and the national game preserves in Africa, where they are free. They romp and have mock battles just like kittens.

Full-grown lions romping on the ground

What Were the "He" and "She" Bibles?

When "King James's Bible"—that is, the so-called Authorised Version—was issued in 1611, two versions were printed, both bearing the same date, and these have come to be known as "the Great He Bible," and "the Great She Bible." The reason for these names is that the translation of Ruth III, 15, reads in one edition "he went," and in the other "she went." But this is not the only discrepancy. There are many other differences in the text, and which of the two versions was the original one is not known. The Bible as we have it printed today is not a copy of either issue, for as the years have gone by many changes have been made, usually improvements.

Are Many More Boys Born Than Girls?

For every 100 girl babies that are born alive, no fewer than 105·6 boys are born. But this ratio of the sexes becomes greatly altered as the males and females grow up. The boys die much more frequently than the girls, and between the ages of 15 and 19 the two sexes are about equal in numbers. Then, among those persons 20 to 24 years old, the females begin to outnumber the males, and then as age succeeds age the female numerical ascendancy increases until among those persons 85 years old or over there are more than twice as many women as men.

As Professor F. A. E. Crew says, "It would appear from these figures alone that to be born is a more dangerous adventure for the male than for the female. . . . The expectation of life at all ages is greater in the case of the female of the species, and the true recipe for longevity is to be born a girl."

Violent deaths remove twice as many males as females from a population in the course of a year; but, apart from this fact, which necessarily distorts the sex ratio among certain age groups, there is no doubt, as Dr. Crew points out, that the whole course of sex mortality in pre-natal life, in infancy and in all subsequent age periods, is consistent with the view that the male in mankind is the inherently weaker sex, more prone to death from diseases of all kinds.

Who Started the National Gallery?

This famous picture-gallery in Trafalgar Square was begun in 1824 by the purchase for the Government of the collection of John Julius Angerstein, an English merchant, philanthropist, and art connoisseur. The present building was opened on April 9th, 1838, and was enlarged in 1860. At one time the Royal Academy Exhibitions were held in this building, but in 1868 these went to Burlington House and have been held there since.

Is Kissing an Ancient Custom?

It is certainly an ancient custom, but it is not a primeval human instinct for in the lower levels of culture it is rarely found and among the red and black races it is unknown. It is also unknown among the yellow races except where they have come under European influences.

The kiss of affection was known in ancient Greece and, as is clear from many references in the Bible, the kiss of respect was common in western Asia. In the Bible we find the kiss as a mark of affection between parents and children (Genesis XXVII, 26), and between members of a family or near connexions (Genesis XXIX, 13). It passed as a salutation between equals in rank (II Samuel XX, 9) and was given as a mark of condescension by a superior (II Samuel XV, 5). Guests also were received with a kiss (Luke VII, 45). These kisses were generally given on the cheek or neck. The kiss was also a token of love (Canticles I, 2) and of homage or submission (Psalm II, 12). Kissing an idol was part of heathen worship (I Kings XIX, 18).

Moslems kiss the black stone at Mecca, and often the hand of a person is kissed, as that of a sovereign by a subject, or of an eastern husband by his wife. In the early Christian church the holy kiss as a salutation and mark of mutual esteem was common (I Corinthians XVI, 20) and the kiss of peace was one of the rites of the Eucharistic service in the primitive church. It was omitted on Good Friday in remembrance of the traitorous kiss of Judas Iscariot.

The ceremonial kiss, especially developed by the Persian kings, was introduced into Greece after the Macedonian conquest and into Rome towards the end of the republic. Later it was adapted to imperial and papal usage. The kiss became a morning salutation in the Roman household, but probably because of abuse was interdicted by Tiberius.

In England in the Middle Ages kissing was common and Erasmus comments approvingly on the custom among English girls. Kissing between men, which survives on the Continent, disappeared in England in the 17th century.

Foot-kissing is of Persian origin, and in Europe is now reserved for the cross-embroidered slipper worn at papal audiences. The Greek and Roman custom of kissing the feet of temple statues survives in Rome where the toe of St. Peter's image is still kissed. From the same source came the practice of kissing the New Testament when taking the oath in a court.

Who Was Mother Shipton?

She was a supposed prophetess of South Wales, whose real name was T. Evan Preece. She is said to have lived in the 16th century and to her are attributed a number of prophecies which are supposed to have come true, among them the deaths of Cardinal Wolsey and Lord Percy. She also made many other prophecies, but a number of the so-called Mother Shipton prophecies were compiled in the 17th and 18th centuries and some were written in the 19th by Charles Hindley, a Brighton bookseller, who died in 1893.

The kiss, which is a very ancient form of greeting, but is not universal

What is a Sand Artist?

IT is a man who models figures or makes high relief pictures on the beach, using only the fine sand there as his medium. When an erect group is to be modelled, the sand must be very fine and wet, so that there may be proper cohesion among the particles. Given these conditions some sand artists can produce truly remarkable

A remarkable group representing the King and Queen and their family made in sand on the beach at Bournemouth

results, like the group of the King and Queen and the little princesses shown in the photograph here, which was taken on the beach at Bournemouth early in March, 1938.

What Was Tyndale's New Testament?

THIS was a translation of the New Testament by William Tyndale, an Oxford scholar, who was eventually strangled and burned as a heretic at Vilvorde in 1536. The first edition of his New Testament was printed at Worms in 1525 in octavo size in an edition of 3,000 copies. In 1534 he issued a revised version of the New Testament with English translations of parts of the Old Testament, but he died without completing an English version of the whole Bible. The translation of Tyndale was condemned by ecclesiastical authorities, but more than forty editions were printed between 1525 and 1566.

What is an Eater of Horseflesh Called?

THE name is hippophagist, and the practice of eating horseflesh is hippophagy. The words are from the Greek. Though practically no horseflesh is eaten in England, on the Continent there are many hippophagists, most countries making use of old horses, that are no further good for draught purposes, in this way.

Can Butter Be Distinguished From Margarine?

MANY people would declare that they could without difficulty distinguish butter from margarine, but whenever tests have been held it has been almost impossible for any person to know from the taste which was which. In 1937 a tasting competition was held in which 250 people were invited to taste white bread, brown bread, biscuits and scones, and say which were spread with butter and which with margarine. Only one person out of the whole 250, a man, was successful in distinguishing correctly. Later, another test was held at the Food and Cookery Institute and thrown open to the public. A reward of £5 was offered to the first person to give the correct solution and £1 to every other successful competitor. Over 600 people entered and the entries were checked by a firm of chartered accountants. Only one person, again a man, succeeded in distinguishing correctly between the butter and margarine. When he was handed his prize he was offered a further £5 if he could repeat the feat, but this time he failed. This proves that the objection which some people profess to margarine on the ground that its taste is inferior to that of butter is based on prejudice and imagination.

Dr. Edwin Slosson, the scientist, tells an amusing story of a university professor of chemistry who suggested to his wife during the Great War that she try margarine, which he had analysed and found to be quite satisfactory. She did not appear to be enthusiastic about the suggestion.

"But women are naturally conservative," says Dr. Slosson, "and wives do not always pay as much attention to the opinions of their husbands as they should even when their husbands are scientists. So he made up his mind to trick her into trying it. He bought a pound of margarine and stole some anatta to colour it. I should explain that he is ordinarily an honest man and never steals unless he has to. This time he had to, for the laws of the State forbid the grocer to sell or give away any colouring matter with margarine, but he keeps a box of anatta capsules on the counter and if customers help themselves he never calls a policeman.

"Well, the chemist came home while his wife was working with the other ladies of the faculty at Red Cross supplies; and, taking out the pat of butter from the ice-box, he tinted and salted and shaped the margarine till it looked and tasted just like what was in the butter-dish. That evening he watched his wife narrowly as she buttered her bread and potatoes, but she did not seem to notice the difference. When dinner was over he asked her if she noticed anything peculiar about the butter. She said she did not. Then he laughed in the harsh and unfeeling way of husbands who get a joke on their wives, and said : 'That's margarine you've been eating.' 'I know it,' his wife replied calmly. 'We've had nothing else in this house for the last three weeks.'"

How Much Did U.S.A. Pay for Alaska?

THE United States bought Alaska from Russia in 1867 for a mere £1,480,000. Since that time the purchased territory has produced £146,000,000 worth of gold and other minerals, and in the adjacent waters

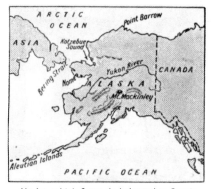

Alaska, which formerly belonged to Russia

more than £200,000,000 worth of fish have been caught.

The salmon industry alone gives employment to 17,500 persons, and its annual income now is £7,000,000, half the total income of the territory.

The national forests of Alaska cover a surface of more than 20,000,000 acres, and yield white spruce and excellent yellow cedar. Coal mining is an increasing industry, and copper is mined near the Copper River. Platinum is found in the Seward and Copper River districts, and tungsten near Seward and Fairbanks.

What is the Name of That Bag?

Nurse's

Lady's hat case

Carry-all

Surgeon's

Square-mouth attaché

Brief

Collar

Modern zip-fastening

Post

Self-closing

Rucksack

Silver mesh

Leather suitcase

Kit

Silk

Fibre suitcase

Tennis ball

Attaché case

Music satchel

School satchel

Lady's handbag

Pouch bag

Monitor

Oxford

Round-frame

Knitting

The bag is certainly an exceedingly useful article, and the variety of purposes for which it is used is indicated by the many shapes and sizes in which it is made. The bag is a later invention for carrying things than the earthenware pot and the basket, but in most civilized countries bags have now largely taken the place of baskets for carrying purposes. Bags are made of a great variety of materials, the strongest of which is, of course, leather. Where bags are needed for hard use, such as travelling-bags, cricket bags and so on, they are generally made of leather. But when these are very large and the leather very thick the bag becomes exceedingly heavy, apart from its contents, and because of this, in recent years travelling-bags and suitcases have been frequently made of a fibrous material which, though strong, is very much lighter than leather, and also has the added advantage of making the bag much cheaper. Some bags, like the Gladstone, have been named after well-known people. The smaller types of bags,

Many Examples in Use Nowadays

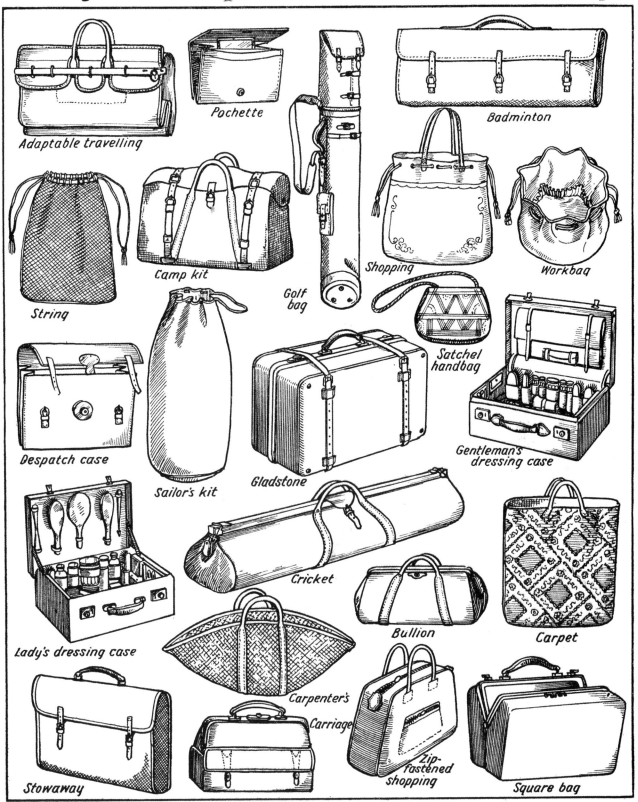

Adaptable travelling

Pochette

Badminton

String

Camp kit

Golf bag

Shopping

Workbag

Despatch case

Sailor's kit

Gladstone

Satchel handbag

Gentleman's dressing case

Lady's dressing case

Cricket

Bullion

Carpet

Stowaway

Carpenter's

Carriage

Zip-fastened shopping

Square bag

like ladies' handbags, are made of such materials as lizard skin, crocodile skin, silk, silver chain-mail and so on. Shopping bags are often of carpet, though they are also made of straw, string and fibre. The carpenter's tool-bag is made of fibre. In recent years the adaptation of the zip fastener to bags has made it much easier to undo the bag. Dressing-cases are, of course, leather bags fitted with various articles such as brushes, combs, bottles and so on. The bags used for carrying sports gear vary with the sport. Golf bags are made with a leather sling for carrying, vertically suspended from the shoulder, this being the easiest method of transport on a golf course. Cricket bags are long and narrow. Sailors' kit-bags are generally made of very stout canvas. Perhaps no bag changes its shape and style so frequently as the lady's handbag. Not only is the form varied, but the colour also is frequently made to match the lady's clothes. In fact it follows the fashion just as clothes do

What Language Did Jesus Speak?

It is not certain, though most modern scholars believe that He used Aramaic, a Semitic language that was spoken in Palestine after the Captivity. Considerably before the time of Christ, Hebrew had ceased to be spoken in Palestine, and its place as the vernacular had been taken by Aramaic, a language in which a few short passages in the books of Ezra, Jeremiah and Daniel in the Old Testament are written.

At the time of Christ, Palestine was really bilingual, Greek as well as Aramaic being spoken to some extent at least. Scholars believe that Jesus had some knowledge of Greek, and from the fact that in three separate instances in the Gospels Aramaic sayings of Jesus have been preserved in that language, it has been contended by some that they were so preserved because they were exceptional. From this it is argued that the customary language used by Jesus was Greek. But the majority of scholars believe that it is clear from evidence of various kinds that Aramaic was the prevailing language of Palestine in the time of Jesus, and that therefore in teaching and preaching to the people He must necessarily have used it. The Rev. James Young sums up the evidence in the words : "There can be no doubt that Aramaic had the supreme honour of being the language in which He gave expression to His imperishable thoughts."

What is a Chronogram?

It is a species of literary device, consisting of an inscription, certain letters of which representing Roman numerals are printed or written in larger size than the others. The words are generally in Latin. Here is an example from a medal of Gustavus Adolphus, the famous King of Sweden : ChrIstVs DVX ergo trIVMphans.

If the numeral letters be extracted and placed in the order of their relative importance we get MDCXVVVII, a clumsy representation of 1627, the year in which Gustavus won the victory commemorated on the medal.

Here is a chronogram in English :

My Day Closed Is In Immortality.

This refers to Queen Elizabeth's death, and the date made up by the large capital letters MDCIII, 1603, is the date of that death.

Does An Insect Prepare for a Dry Season?

No doubt a number of insects living in areas that periodically dry up make some instinctive preparation for the dry season, but perhaps the most remarkable example is that recorded by Sir Edward Poulton, President of the British Association, in 1937. He gives it as an example of a "prophetic instinct," and the insect in question is the maggot of an African fly.

"This maggot," he says, "lives and feeds in soft mud, which during the dry season, when the chrysalis stage has been reached, will be traversed in all directions by wide and deep cracks, in which insectivorous animals can search for prey. But the maggot, while the mud is still soft, prepares for this danger.

By tunnelling spirally up and down it makes a line of weakness which will cause a pillar to separate from the mass when the mud hardens and contracts. It then tunnels into the still soft pillar, and becomes a chrysalis in the centre of its deeper end. However wide the cracks which appear in the mud, the maggot has arranged beforehand that they will not invade its cylinder."

Sir Edward Poulton asks : "How would it be possible to explain these prophetic instincts, adapted not to meet but to avoid future experience, except by the operation of natural selection ? "

Which is the Nameless Finger?

It is the third finger of the right hand.

The various fingers are named as follows : on the right hand, the pointer, the long finger, the nameless finger and the little finger ; on the left hand they are the pointer, the long finger, the ring finger and the little finger.

Do Ships Go Through Magellan Strait Today?

Yes, this is the regular route for ships that pass round the extreme south of America. The passage is both shorter and easier than round Cape Horn. The Strait of Magellan takes a very winding course between the Chilean mainland and the island of Tierra del Fuego. It is 365 miles long, and its width varies from $2\frac{1}{2}$ miles to 17 miles.

It has only one harbour, that of Punta Arenas, about halfway through. This strait was discovered by the Portuguese navigator, Ferdinand Magellan,

A map showing the Strait of Magellan

in the first voyage round the world, and was named after him. A thorough exploration of the strait took place in the ten years between 1826 and 1836.

What is the Biggest Flame Ever Known?

During a total eclipse of the Sun crimson flames are often seen to shoot up from the Sun's surface at a speed of thousands of miles a minute. During an eclipse in 1919 a flame was seen which measured 350,000 miles from end to end, and, as Sir James Jeans has said, could have gulped down the whole Earth like a pill. This great flame was photographed, and immediately after the photograph was taken it took a great leap to a height of 475,000 miles. This is the biggest flame of which there is any record.

A photograph of the Strait of Magellan, which connects the Atlantic and Pacific Oceans. Here it rains on 250 days of each year

Which British Bird's Egg is That?

Woodcock
Cirl Bunting
Starling
Jackdaw
Jay
Tree Sparrow
Reed Bunting
House Sparrow
Moorhen
Spotted Flycatcher
Bullfinch
Goldfinch
Greenfinch
Hawfinch
Chaffinch
Hedge Sparrow
Swallow
Stonechat
Nuthatch
Nightingale
Skylark
Magpie
Yellow-Hammer
Whitethroat
Pied Wagtail
House Martin
Rook
Carrion Crow
Golden Plover
Hooded Crow
Snipe
Redbreast
Willow-Wren
Cuckoo
Nightjar
Kingfisher
Chiffchaff
Wren
Kestrel
Meadow Pipit
Blue Tit
Song-Thrush
Mistle-Thrush
Blackbird
Linnet
Long-tailed Tit
Sparrow-Hawk
S.N

Here are 47 eggs of familiar British wild birds, and from these it will be possible to identify the eggs when seen. Of course, the eggs of the same species may vary somewhat, and that of the cuckoo varies a great deal, resembling to some extent the eggs of the bird in whose nest it is placed

Plate XI

What Type of Aircraft is That?

Armstrong Whitworth "Whitley". Heavy Bomber

Avro "Anson".

Blackburn Dive-bomber Fighter

Fairey "Battle". Medium Bomber

Bristol "Blenheim". Medium Bomber

Gloster "Gladiator". Single-seater Fighter

Handley Page "Harrow". Heavy Bomber

Saunders Roe "London". Coastal Flying Boat

Hawker "Hurricane". Single-seater Fighter

Westland "Lysander".

Short "Singapore" III. Long range Flying Boat

Vickers-Supermarine "Spitfire". Single-seater Fighter

The Royal Air Force possesses the most up-to-date and fastest service machines in the world, and here is a selection of types in use. The Armstrong-Whitworth "Whitley" and Handley Page "Harrow" bombers weigh about 10 tons each, with a maximum speed of about 200 miles per hour. The Hawker "Hurricane" and the Vickers Super-marine "Spitfire" are the latest types of monoplane fighters, with speeds in excess of 300 miles per hour. The Gloster "Gladiator" is a fighter, with four machine-guns, two firing through the air-screw and two fitted under the lower wing. The single-engine Fairey "Battle" and the twin-engine Bristol "Blenheim" are high-speed bombers. The Saunders Roe "London" flying boat is used for coastal reconnaissance, as are the Short "Singapore" flying boat and the Avro "Anson" landplane. The Blackburn fighter known as "Skua I" is a dive bomber fighter. The Westland "Lysander" is a new type of Army Co-operation aircraft

Plate XII

Can Punctuation Alter the Sense?

M OST certainly it can, as in the well-known sentence, " Charles the First walked and talked half an hour after his head was cut off." A semicolon should be placed after the word talked. Another oft-quoted example of how punctuation can alter the sense is the rhyme :

> Every lady in the land
> Has twenty nails on each hand,
> Five and twenty on hands and feet,
> This is true without deceit.

A semicolon should, of course, be

Cutting off the roots of a broccoli before sending it to market

placed in the second line after the word nails, and a comma after five in the third line.

The Tsar Alexander III had written on a petition for pardon, " Pardon impossible ; to be sent to Siberia." The story goes that the tender-hearted Tsarina, seeing this on the Tsar's desk, took up a pen and, striking out the semicolon after impossible, put one before that word. The endorsement then read, " Pardon ; impossible to be sent to Siberia." It is said that the Tsar allowed the alteration to stand.

One of the most expensive blunders in punctuation occurred in an American tariff bill at the end of the 19th century. The misplacement of a comma cost the United States Government about two million dollars. There was a section enumerating what articles should be admitted free of duty.

Among the many articles specified were " All foreign fruit-plants," etc., meaning plants for transplanting, propagation or experiment. The enrolling clerk in copying the bill accidentally changed the hyphen in the compound word fruit-plants to a comma, making it read " All foreign fruit, plants," etc. The consequence was that for a year, until Congress could remedy the blunder, all oranges, lemons, bananas, grapes and other foreign fruits were admitted free of duty.

Some years ago a French will was contested, and the law expenses cost thousands of francs because there was doubt as to whether a certain mark was a blot or an apostrophe. A line in the will read " A chacun d'eux cent milles francs," which means " To each of them a hundred thousand francs," but the legatees maintained that the supposed apostrophe was a small blot owing to the folding of the paper while the ink was still wet, and that what the testator really wrote was, " A chacun deux cent milles francs," " To each two hundred thousand francs." The paper had been folded before the ink was dry and there were other blots, so the court decided that the mark was a blot and not an apostrophe.

Some years ago a Prussian school inspector with the burgomaster arrived on a visit at a school. The burgomaster

A scene in a Cornish broccoli field

was being taken round against his will and was heard to mutter, referring to the inspector, " What is this donkey here again for ? " When the inspector said he proposed to examine the boys in punctuation the testy burgomaster said, " Oh, never mind punctuation ; what do commas and such trifles matter ? "

The inspector told a boy to go and write on the blackboard the sentence : " The burgomaster says the inspector is a donkey." Then he told him to place commas after burgomaster and inspector, making the sentence

read, " The burgomaster, says the inspector, is a donkey." It was a timely lesson to the burgomaster on the importance of punctuation.

What is Broccoli ?

I T is one of the several usual vegetables which by careful selection and breeding have been developed from the insignificant wild cabbage of the countryside. These vegetables are now very varied in their forms. They include the ordinary cabbage ; the savoy, a hardy winter cabbage with closely curled wrinkled leaves ; the curly kale, which has curly leaves ; the brussels sprout, in which a number of miniature cabbages spring from one stem ; the kohl-rabi, a kind of cabbage with a fleshy, turnip-shaped stem ; the cauliflower, a variety with a white, fleshy flower head ; and the broccoli, which puts out numerous sprouts, each like a miniature cauliflower. Sometimes these heads grow large.

No more striking instance can be given of what man can do to improve edible plants than the case of the cabbage. Broccoli is frequently mistaken for the cauliflower. In the United Kingdom it can be obtained in nearly every month of the year. The seeds are sown every month from March to July. Large quantities are grown in Cornwall on the tops of unused tin and copper mines, and the growers are in many cases the out-of-work miners. In West Cornwall alone the income obtained from broccoli is said to exceed half a million sterling a year, and at certain seasons broccoli trains follow one another to London daily. The word broccoli comes from an Italian word meaning " a little splinter "—that is, a sprout.

The broccoli, which is something between a cabbage and a cauliflower

Where Do Restaurants Put Up Their Diners' Names?

THIS is done in Japan. When a Japanese host entertains his guests at a restaurant, his name during the feast is displayed prominently on

Posters exhibited outside a Tokyo restaurant, giving the names of hosts who are entertaining parties inside. This is an old Japanese custom

a large board outside the restaurant. Sometimes a score or more of boards will be seen outside the establishment giving the names of as many customers who are giving dinner parties inside.

Does Tennyson's Cock Tavern Still Exist?

MOST readers of Tennyson know his " Will Waterproof's Lyrical Monologue," which, as the poet himself has stated, was " made at The Cock." It opens :

O plump head waiter at The Cock,
  To which I most resort,
How goes the time ? 'Tis five o'clock,
  Go fetch a pint of port.

The tavern which the poet used to visit stood on the north side of Fleet Street on the site where now stands a branch of the Bank of England. This building was demolished in 1888, but one room of that ancient structure which had survived the Great Fire of London was preserved intact and was embodied in the present Cock Tavern erected on the south side of Fleet Street. It is to be found on the first floor, where are the actual mahogany boxes which Tennyson knew and used.

Old boxes, larded with the steam
  Of thirty thousand dinners,

and there also is the stately old fireplace with which Pepys was familiar.

Should Blackboards Be Coloured?

EXPERIMENTS carried out early in 1938 by the National Institute of Industrial Psychology suggest that blackboards should be superseded by yellow boards. In three different experiments children were found to be able to copy nearly ten per cent more in the same time from a yellow board than from a black one. Not only can time be saved by using a yellow board, but it is believed that the strain of looking at the writing on the board is lessened.

The experiments were carried out to see whether a board with a higher reflection than the blackboard would enable children to copy from it more quickly. A black board, of course, absorbs the light falling upon it. Blue chalk was used for writing on the yellow board, the result, of course, being green writing.

The idea of using a coloured board instead of a black one, however, is not new. At a large junior school at Tibshelf in Derbyshire dark green blackboards have been used since 1908. In 1911 and again in 1924 Mr. Cyril Sheldon of Leeds carried out experiments to test the most legible combination of coloured letters on a coloured board, and white on black, like chalk on a blackboard, proved inferior to nine other combinations. The best result was obtained by black letters on a yellow ground, and the second and third places in 1911 were obtained by green on white, and red on white. In 1924, while black on yellow again obtained first place for legibility, the second and third places were won respectively by maroon on pale buff and black on pale buff. It is possible that as a result of these researches, blackboards may eventually disappear from our schools.

Has Any British Nobleman a Private Army?

YES, the Duke of Atholl has a small army, known as the Atholl Highlanders, which wears a uniform and attends levees at Holyrood Palace and other functions. The duke is the only British subject allowed to maintain a standing army, and he holds this privilege by a royal patent granted to his grandfather by Queen Victoria. The regiment is recognised by the War Office, and so the Uniforms Bill, which forbids the wearing of political uniforms, does not affect the duke's Highlanders.

How Were the First Rectangular Houses Built?

THE earliest houses built above ground were probably round in shape, and when the first rectangular houses were erected the walls did not rise perpendicularly from the ground. Two pairs of bent trees, in form like the lancet-shaped arches of a Gothic church, were fixed in the ground and joined at the top by a straight tree. Then two beams were fastened across at different levels to strengthen the framework and the walls were filled in with wattle-work plastered over with clay or mud, and the roof was thatched with straw or reeds.

Sometimes houses of this inverted boat shape are to be seen today in England. The walls of the room slant together towards the top. They are interesting as marking a stage in the evolution of the modern house with vertical walls from the sloped walls of a round, beehive hut. It was not long before men realised the advantage of having vertical walls, as these give much more room in the house and make it a far more convenient place in which to live.

The triangle house, called Teapot Hall, which stands in a Lincolnshire village

What is the Shortest Letter on Record?

THE shortest letter is sometimes said to be that of a schoolboy to his father, quoted by Lord Birkenhead: "S O S, L.S.D. R.S.V.P." But a shorter letter than this was once written by Victor Hugo, the great French author. A new book of his had just been published and, anxious to know how it was selling, he wrote to his publisher as follows: " ?, Victor Hugo." The publisher, equal to the occasion, replied, " ! "

The Duke of York of the early 19th century, seeking church patronage for a friend, wrote to the Bishop of Cork, " Dear Cork, Please ordain Stanhope, York," to which the bishop replied, " Dear York, Stanhope ordained, Cork." Sir Herbert Beerbohm Tree, the actor and producer, once wrote to a would-be dramatist who had submitted a play, " My Dear Sir, I have read your play. Oh, my dear sir! Yours faithfully, H. Beerbohm Tree." Such brevity, however, is rare; most people are far too discursive in their letters and could say all they need in half the number of words they use.

What is a Mobile Dental Surgery?

THE Nottinghamshire Education Committee has had a motor-van equipped as a dental surgery and this visits the schools in rural areas, so that the scholars can receive proper dental service. When the mobile surgery arrives at a school the children are paraded and examined by the dental surgeon. Those needing special attention enter the van, which has all the latest equipment such as is found in an ordinary dentist's establishment.

Who Was Pastor Niemoeller?

HE was a German Lutheran clergyman who, for his outspoken resistance to the paganism of the Nazi movement in Germany, was first suspended from office, then arrested, and finally, after being in gaol untried from the beginning of July, 1937, to the end of February, 1938, was eventually tried for treason. He was sentenced to seven months' imprisonment and fined, but was at once released, as his long con-finement was reckoned as having liquidated the sentence. But as soon as he was released he was again arrested and sent to a notorious concentration camp, as was stated, for his own protection.

Martin Niemoeller was born in West Prussia in 1893 and in the early years of the Great War was a sub-lieutenant in a German battleship. Then in 1916 he was promoted lieutenant and joined the submarine service. By 1918 he had become a submarine commander and was in charge of a U-boat in the Mediterranean.

The travelling dentist attending to the school-children in a Nottingham village

After the War he left the Navy, married and became a farmer. But being ruined by the collapse of the mark he studied for ordination in the Lutheran Church. At the same time he earned his living at any work he could obtain, and was in turn bank clerk, platelayer, harvester and railway clerk. He was ordained in June, 1924, and becoming pastor of a small church in Berlin's fashionable suburb of Dahlem, was soon known for his outspoken evangelical views. Then when Hitler tried to Nazify the Lutheran Church, Niemoeller became head of an Emergency Union of Pastors, who resisted the pagan ideas, and this landed him in trouble as explained above.

Why is the Bishop of Sodor and Man So Called?

MAN is, of course, the Isle of Man, and the see is now confined to that island. But formerly it comprised also the Hebrides, from which it gets the name Sodor, as a relic of the past. A group of about 30 islands of the Hebrides were once known as the Sudoer or Southern Islands. Magnus, King of Norway in 1098, took possession of the Hebrides and united them to the Isle of Man, under one bishop. In the 14th century England took possession of the Isle of Man. The Hebrides belonged to Norway till 1266. Later the head of the Macdonald's subdued them and called himself " Lord of the Isles."

Children interested in watching a fellow scholar receiving attention in the mobile dental surgery

When Were Twelve-Oared Boats Raced?

THE first twelve-oared boat was built for the London Rowing Club in 1860 and a second boat in 1866. In the latter year the first twelve-oared boat-race took place during the autumn. From that year till 1895 the race was held on the Thames annually. But the boats were uncomfortable and when they needed repairs the cost was considered prohibitive, and after a last race on the Saturday before Christmas in 1898, the boats were condemned and broken up.

Is There a Monument to Tom Thumb?

THERE is a monument to Tom Thumb of the fairy tales—not the so-called Tom Thumb of Barnum's Show, referred to on page 553—in the Children's Park at Budapest, and it is shown in the photograph given here. Tom, dressed in long boots, is shown on top of a pillar that rises out of a hemisphere. He is striding along and looks very perky. This statue of a famous fictitious character in children's literature holds the same place in the juvenile life of Budapest as the celebrated and attractive Peter Pan statue beside the Serpentine in Kensington Gardens has in the child life of London.

Are There Many Natural Dyes?

MOST of the dyes used today are made chemically, and it is this process of manufacturing colours that has given us the immense variety of hues we now possess. There seems no end to the number and fresh shades that are produced almost every week.

But as to natural dyes, Sir William Bragg says: "The number of known and much-used natural dyes is very small. It is to be remembered that they are something more than mere colours. They must be capable of attachment to the material so firmly that sun and rain and wear have little effect upon them; they must be fast to light and to washing and to rubbing. Not many colouring matters can satisfy these conditions. Men have tried great numbers of them, extracting them from plants, from the earth, even from insects and shell-fish. Very few, indeed, have been found of real use. There are indigo and madder, Tyrian purple and woad."

Scarlet is obtained from the cochineal insect; the Romans obtained yellow from the crocus; black is obtained from American logwood and indigo was formerly extracted from various plants.

Do Judges Wear a Special Court Dress?

THE Court dress of judges—that is, the dress in which they attend the King's levees—is quite different from the dress they wear when sitting on the bench or when attending functions in their capacity of judges. At the

Judges of the High Court going to the King's levee in their Court dress

King's Court the judges dress like King's Counsel—that is, they have silk stockings, buckled shoes, knee-breeches cutaway coat and silk gown, with a full-bottomed wig. They have lace frills at the wrist and lace at the neck, as shown in the photograph on this page of judges proceeding to a levee.

Why Does an Offshore Wind Pile Up Shingle?

IT is a curious fact that when the wind is blowing from the shore towards the sea the shingle or pebbles are heaped up on the beach, while a wind blowing towards the shore from the sea results in the shingle or pebbles being swept down again.

The reason for this is not quite clear, but it is believed to be due to the fact that a wind blowing from the shore meets the onrush of the wavecrest, slowing down its progress. The base of the wave, however, not being affected by the wind, continues to move forward, and pushes the beach materials up so that they can accumulate.

A statue of Tom Thumb in the Children's Park at Budapest

Who Was the World's Worst Penman?

He is said to have been Horace Greeley, the famous American newspaper editor and writer. His handwriting was constantly misread, and it is said that one compositor, newly engaged, when he was handed a manuscript of Greeley's exclaimed, " If Belshazzar had seen this writing on the wall, he would have been more terrified than he was."

Another compositor, discharged by Greeley, is said to have taken the letter of dismissal to another newspaper, declaring that it was a testimonial, and as such it was received and the man given a job.

When Mr. M. B. Castle of Sandwich, Illinois, wrote and asked Greeley to lecture before a local association, the great editor wrote back in his illegible scrawl: " Dear Sir,—I am overworked and growing old. I shall be sixty next February third. On the whole, it seems I must decline to lecture henceforth except in this immediate vicinity, if I do at all. I cannot promise to visit Illinois on that errand—certainly not now.—Yours, Horace Greeley."

The committee puzzled long over the letter, came to the conclusion that it was an acceptance, and wrote back to Greeley · " Dear Sir,—Your acceptance to lecture before our association next winter came to hand this morning. Your penmanship not being the plainest, it took some time to translate it, but we succeeded, and would say your time, ' third of February,' and terms ' sixty dollars ' are perfectly satisfactory. As you suggest, we may be able to get you other engagements in the immediate vicinity ; if so, we will advise you.—Yours respectfully. M. B. Castle."

Professor E. S. Morse, an ex-president of the American Academy for the Advancement of Science, was another very bad penman. When he wrote to Mr. T. B. Aldrich, the famous author, he received the following reply : " My Dear Mr. Morse,—It was very pleasant to me to get a letter from you the other day Perhaps I should have found it pleasanter if I had been able to decipher it. I don't think that I mastered anything beyond the date (which I knew) and the signature (which I guessed at). There's a singular and perpetual charm in a letter of yours ; it never grows old ; it never loses its novelty. One can say to one's self every morning, ' There's that letter of Morse's. I haven't read it yet.' I think I'll take another shy at it today and maybe I shall be able in the course of a few days to make out what he means by those ' t's ' that look like ' w's ' and those ' i's ' that haven't any eyebrows.' Other letters are read and thrown away and forgotten ; but yours are kept for ever—unread. One of them will last a reasonable man a lifetime. Admiringly yours, T. B. Aldrich."

The story is told of a university student who handed in to his professor a paper, which he was surprised to receive back the next day with a note scrawled on the margin. He studied this diligently, but was unable to decipher it, so he took the paper back to the professor. " I cannot quite make out what this is that you have written, sir," he said, whereupon the professor snapped out, " That, sir, says that I cannot read your handwriting, it is illegible "

Is Shetland or Greenland Farther South?

It will probably come as a surprise to most people to learn that the extreme south of Greenland is farther south than most of the Shetland Islands. Yet how different are the climates of the two countries. The difference is due to the cold water of

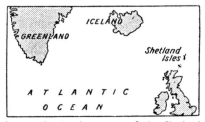

A map showing how some of the Shetland Islands are north of South Greenland

the Arctic current which flows along the coast of Greenland, while the warm Gulf Stream Drift encircles the Shetlands like a scarf.

What is a Punter?

Newspapers often refer in their sporting columns to " the punter." This strange word seems to come from the same source as the word " point," and was used in connection with such games as ombre. The idea of punter, therefore, was originally that of a " pointer," or a man who scored points in some game of chance.

Its meaning was later particularised to signify a small professional gambler, and since the latter part of the 19th century it has been used for anyone who gambles, but particularly on the turf or on football pools.

Are Boats Ever Upset in Bumping Races?

In a bumping race at Oxford or Cambridge, the boat pursuing another merely touches it when it bumps, and the bumped boat is not upset. But on one occasion at Cambridge, when the Corpus boat was head of the river, and the Jesus boat behind, the latter, making a bump, shot right over the stern of the Corpus boat and upset it. The cox of the Corpus boat had the long rudder-lines round his waist, and could not extricate himself. No. 2 in his boat went to his rescue, walking down the tilting boat as it sank at the stern.

The would-be rescuer, however, fainted at the touch of the cold water, and himself went in. The Corpus cox was rescued, and also No. 2, but by some accident the latter was reported to have been drowned, and the Jesus crew sent a wreath in sympathy.

On the next evening, however, No. 2 was back in his place in the Corpus boat, and every man in the crew was wearing part of the Jesus wreath as a buttonhole.

A bump in the Oxford Torpid Races. The pursuing boat's bows have run over the other's side

What Bird Built That Strange Nest?

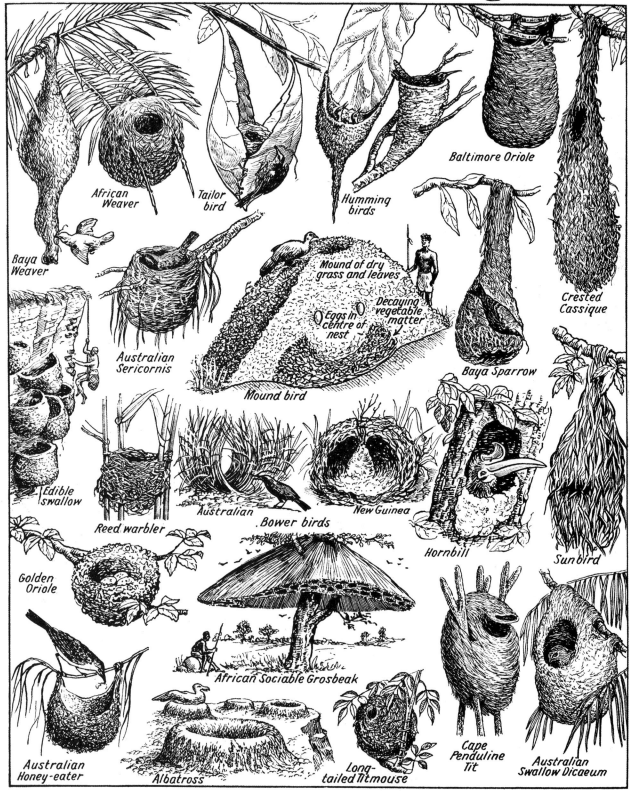

African Weaver

Tailor bird

Humming birds

Baltimore Oriole

Baya Weaver

Australian Sericornis

Mound of dry grass and leaves

Eggs in centre of nest

Decaying vegetable matter

Mound bird

Crested Cassique

Baya Sparrow

Edible swallow

Reed warbler

Australian

Bower birds

New Guinea

Hornbill

Sunbird

Golden Oriole

African Sociable Grosbeak

Australian Honey-eater

Albatross

Long-tailed Titmouse

Cape Penduline Tit

Australian Swallow Dicaeum

As we know, the nests built by British birds are very beautiful structures, but they follow more or less the same form. In different parts of the world, however, birds build some queer nests, and some of the strangest of these are shown in the drawings on this page. The tailor bird, a native of India, actually sews leaves together to form its nest, making holes with its beak, and using vegetable fibre as thread. Many nests, like those of the weaver bird, are beautifully made, and are suspended from the boughs of trees. We have an example of the suspended nest in Britain in the nest of the golden oriole, which is usually hung at the end of some small bough. The mound bird of Australia builds a huge mound and buries its eggs inside. The nest is here shown in section. The bower bird of Australia builds a platform and then into it fixes twigs, so that the tips cross at the top, forming an arched bower. Another bower bird lives in New Guinea. The albatross lays an egg on the bare ground and then scrapes the earth up round it, so as to form a circular wall. The edible swallow's nest, from which bird's-nest soup is made, is built of a kind of gelatine and is attached to cliffs. The female hornbill nests in a hole in a tree, the entrance being plastered up by her mate, who feeds her through a small opening

What is a Slow-Motion Picture ?

THE name "slow-motion picture" is given to a film shown on the screen in such a way that rapid movements, such as diving or running, are slowed down to a snail's pace.

The way in which this interesting operation is brought about is as follows : With an ordinary film 24 pictures are taken per second. But for a slow-motion picture the photographing is speeded up, so that 240 pictures are taken every second. Then, when this film is projected upon the screen at the ordinary rate of 24 pictures a second, the motions are all

Medlars growing on a tree

slowed down so that a movement which in the ordinary way would occupy 2·4 seconds to carry out, now takes 24 seconds.

The moving picture can also be speeded up so as to make motion far more rapid than it really is. In this case the film is taken at the rate of 2·4 pictures per second, and is then projected on the screen at the rate of 24 pictures a second, with the result that everything moves at ten times its usual speed.

Are Volcanoes Good or Evil ?

WHEN a volcano has an eruption and the molten lava or fiery ashes bury a village or destroy a farm it is, of course, an evil. But on the whole volcanoes are good, for they act as useful safety valves for the Earth. When they erupt, great volumes of gas which have formed deep down underground make their escape through the crater of the volcano or through fissures in its side. Were it not for these safety valves there would probably be much more disastrous results, and the type

of earthquake which occurs in volcanic regions would probably be much more widespread.

Altogether there are scattered about the world between three and four hundred mountains that from time to time throw out lava and ashes. There are three classes of volcanoes, those that are more or less continually active, like Vesuvius, Etna and Stromboli, those that are dormant or sleeping like Fujiyama in Japan, and those that are extinct like Snowdon.

At one time the greater part of Wales and of central England was occupied by groups of volcanoes from which copious flows of lava were poured out, and enormous quantities of volcanic dust ejected and spread in every direction.

How quinces appear when growing

What Was Michelangelo's Hoax ?

IT is said that Michelangelo, wearied of hearing modern sculpture contrasted with ancient, to the disparagement of the former, hit upon the plan of burying a modern Cupid, having first knocked off an arm. When it was dug up he had the satisfaction of hearing his former detractors praise it as a genuine antique.

What Are the Slang Names for Policemen ?

IN the early days they were called Peelers, after Sir Robert Peel, who originated the force. The names Robert and Bobby, by which they are sometimes known today, are also from Sir Robert Peel's name. Copper is a name made up from the slang word cop, meaning to catch or capture. Another name often used for a policeman is slop. This originated from what is known as back-slang—that is, the pronouncing of words backwards. Thus police came to be ecilop, which developed into slop. A constable is also often called a blue-bottle, this being a reference to his blue uniform.

What Are the Quince and Medlar ?

THE quince is a tree or shrub belonging to the rose family, and is a near relation of the pear. It was introduced into Britain in 1573, and grows in height from 5 to 20 feet. The pink flowers that form in clusters are something like large wild roses, and are very beautiful, and the golden fruit, which is pear-shaped, is astringent, and is used for making jelly.

The medlar, another member of the rose family, is a hardy tree which is a native of Greece, Persia and Asia Minor. It is sometimes found growing wild in Great Britain, and is also cultivated. The flowers are white and develop into globular green fruits with a depressed top. These fruits have a rather acid flavour. Medlars should be stored in a cool room until brown and on the verge of decomposition ; then they can be used for flavouring purposes and for making jellies.

The core of a medlar is exposed at the blossom end, as if there were not quite enough flesh to reach round the seeds. Medlars are grown in America as curiosities.

What is Egg and Dart Ornament?

IT is a form of decoration frequently met with in classical architecture, carved on the ovolo or convex moulding of an Ionic or composite capital. The decoration varies slightly, and is some-

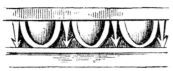

An example of egg and dart moulding

times called "egg and tongue," or "egg and anchor" ornament. It is also called echinus, which means a hedgehog, because of the spiny appearance of the darts.

Was the Authorised Bible Really Authorised?

THERE seems to be no real justification for the description of the 1611 version of the English Bible as "the Authorised Version." A new translation of the Bible into English was decided upon at the Hampton Court Conference of 1604 and 54 learned men were appointed to carry out the work. When the translation was issued copies of the title page bore the words "Appointed to be read in Churches," and from that fact the book has come to be known as "the Authorised Version." But as Professor J. H. Penniman says, "We have no record of any special action of Church or Parliament or King which would justify that title."

How Are Young Seals Enticed by Camera Men?

IT is very difficult to get near enough to young seals to photograph them properly, but by a trick the camera men are able to entice them to the camera. The photographers taking

parent's cry. Sure enough the young seals were deceived and came up to the photographers, who were thus able to catch them for their pictures. In this way some very interesting photographs of seal life in the North Sea were obtained.

How Are Performing Fleas Trained?

A GREAT deal of nonsense is talked about the training of fleas. The acts they carry out are largely the natural movements of the insects, more or less hindered by confinement in miniature harness or carriages, or handicapped by tiny weapons attached to their limbs. Mr. E. A. Butler, who has written much on this insect, says : "The chief difficulty met with in the training of fleas is, it seems, to restrain them from jumping and to induce them to walk in an even and regular manner. One of the methods of overcoming this tendency to sprightliness is to imprison them in circular glass-topped boxes which are kept revolving ; every leap they take brings retribution in the shape of violent collision with the sides of their cell ; and, as they are at the same time dazed, it is believed, by the movement of the box, they seem to get tired of this unpleasant experience and after a while cease leaping and settle down to a steady walk.

"Mr. W. H. Dall, an American entomologist, who once visited an exhibition of performing fleas with the view of determining to what extent the performances were really the result

the greatest amount of intelligence seemed to be exhibited, could be accounted for in other and more natural ways.

"Take, for example, the waltzing, in which the fleas go spinning round in pairs to the sound of a musical-box. Two fleas of equal size and strength are attached to an extremely delicate piece of wire, one at each end ; but as they are fastened in such a way as to face in opposite directions and at right angles to the wire, their struggles produce equal and opposite pulls at the end of the bar, or, in other words, form what in the language of mechanics would be termed "a couple," and therefore necessarily produce, without any intention on their part, a rotary motion.

"To aid in the illusion a small orchestra is added consisting of fleas fastened before tiny models of musical instruments. As they are set upright their legs can only flourish about in the air, suggesting the idea of their performing on the instruments ; and if they should be at all slow to begin their pawings, an attendant stirs them up by running a little barb from a feather across their legs, when, of course, they set to work kicking about vigorously.

"In the duelling performance we have something very similar to the orchestra : two fleas are fastened upright to little wire pillars, and tiny wands in lieu of swords attached to their forelegs ; they are placed opposite one another, but at such a distance that they are just out of one another's reach, except with the 'swords.' As they brandish their legs about in

A baby seal wriggling towards the photographer, whom it mistakes for its mother

their efforts to liberate themselves from their constrained position, it will occasionally happen that their 'swords' will meet and produce the semblance of the clashing of weapons in a combat."

Does Any British Regiment Wear the Shako?

YES, the Highland Light Infantry and the Cameronians or Scottish Rifles both wear the shako as their head-dress. They are the only British regiments to do so, although this particular kind of head-dress was formerly worn by many regiments.

A photographer pretending to be a mother seal to attract the young animals to his camera

pictures of seals on a bank in the North Sea noticed that the mother seals called their offspring by a peculiar cry. So the men imitated the mothers. They lay flat on the sand with their feet twisted together to look like the seal's tail, and then imitated the

of training, and how far, therefore, they indicated any docility in the performers, came to the conclusion that all the movements consisted of struggles on the part of the insects to escape, and that what looked like concerted action, in which, of course,

Were Old Keys Like the Modern?

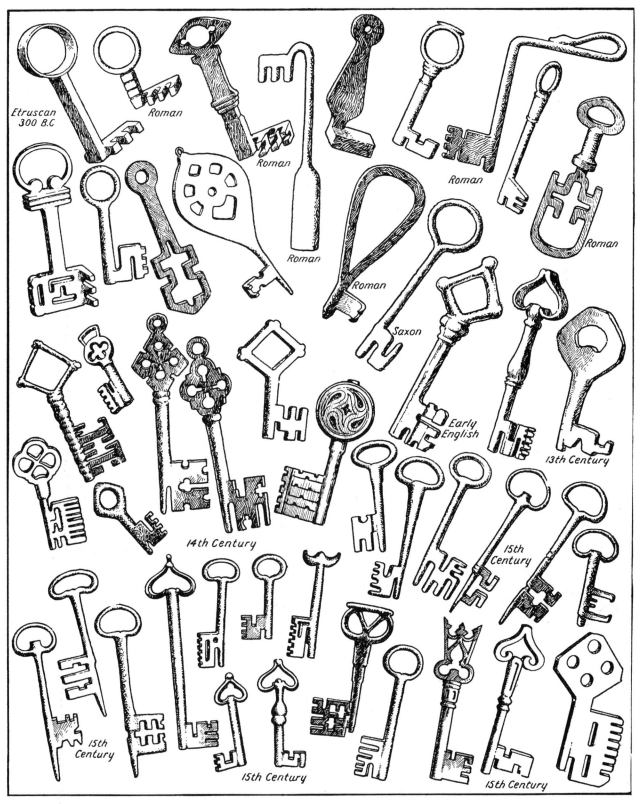

Etruscan 300 B.C
Roman
Roman
Roman
Roman
Roman
Roman
Saxon
Early English
13th Century
14th Century
15th Century
15th Century
15th Century
15th Century

Keys that in principle were the same as the keys we use today have been found dating back hundreds of years before Christ. On this page are given various examples of early keys, and it will be seen that many of these are remarkably like the keys we use today. The Etruscan key, in the top left-hand corner of the drawing, is in the Editor's collection, and is made of bronze. Many of the other keys also, shown here and on the next two pages, are drawn from actual specimens in the Editor's collection. The Romans were very fond of locking things up, and their simplest type of lock had come down from Greek times. The key was pushed through a vertical slot, and after being turned round was hooked into pegs or tumblers, which were raised, and allowed the bolt to be drawn back. The fourth illustration in the top row is a key of this type

Are There Antelopes in India?

YES, and the largest is the nilgai, which has the forelimbs longer than the hind pair. This gives the animal an ungainly appearance. Its tail is tufted, and in both sexes the neck is maned. Only the males are horned. This antelope is unknown in Ceylon.

Another Indian antelope is the chousingha, or four-horned antelope, and it differs from all its relatives in that the male has two pairs of horns, of which the larger is placed far back, while the smaller pair is immediately over the eyes. All the horns are very short, and the front pair are often reduced to mere knobs. Sometimes, indeed, they are quite absent. This antelope, which stands just over two feet at the withers, and an inch and a half higher at the haunches, weighs about 40 pounds. Its general colour is a dull, reddish brown, becoming white underneath the body.

It does not go about in herds, and very rarely are more than two seen together. It haunts the thin forest country, and keeps chiefly to undulating or hilly ground. It is never seen far from water, for it must drink daily. The chousingha is a shy animal, and moves about with a curious jerky motion, whether it is walking or running. It is a great jumper, and can leap more than twice its own height.

An Indian antelope making a great spring at the Edinburgh Zoo

Where is Europe's Largest Mound?

ANYONE using the Bath Road between Marlborough and Calne passes a huge conical mound of turf close to the turning for Avebury. Silbury Hill, as it is called, is the largest

A hostelry at night, taken from an illuminated manuscript of the 15th century. The sleepers are wearing no night clothes except nightcaps

artificial mound in Europe, being about 130 feet high and covering five acres of ground. But who built it and why are problems still awaiting solution.

Two facts have been established, first that the hill is not a burial mound. Shafts have been driven through it from the apex to the base and from the side to the middle without any trace of interment being found. The other fact is that the line of the Roman Road from Winchester to Bath makes a definite bend from its otherwise straight course to avoid the mound, thus proving that Silbury was in existence at the time the road was made. The theory that it was a Norman castle mound is thus ruled out.

Some believe Silbury to have been built by men of the same culture as erected the Great Pyramid of Egypt, and that it was used as a gigantic sundial from which the seasons of the year could be determined

and the right time for planting crops assured. The fact that a double line of stones runs from the hill in the direction of the huge stone circle in Avebury village seems to connect the hill with that wonderful prehistoric monument.

Were Nightgowns Worn in Olden Times?

THERE are plenty of drawings of bedroom scenes in old illuminated manuscripts, and it is clear from these that ordinary healthy people wore no night clothes at all when they went to bed. It is equally clear from drawings showing invalids in bed that they did wear nightgowns.

A sick-room, from an illuminated manuscript of 1470. Here the invalid wears night clothes

The fact that all classes of the community slept without night clothes is shown by a great variety of illustrations during the early centuries. These represent rich as well as poor, and perhaps it was the absence of night clothes that led to the popularity of the feather bed, which would be very warm.

How Many Home Rule Bills Were There?

THERE were two measures to which this name was given. The first Home Rule Bill was introduced into the House of Commons by Mr. Gladstone in 1886, and was defeated on its second reading on June 7th by 341 to 311, a majority of 30. It established an Irish legislature with powers to make laws, but withheld some things from the jurisdiction of the Irish Parliament, such as succession to the Crown, peace and war, the army, navy and militia, foreign and colonial policy, customs and excise, coinage, and posts and telegraphs.

In 1893 a second Home Rule Bill was introduced by Mr. Gladstone, very similar in character, but whereas in the measure of 1886 the Irish members were excluded from the Imperial Parliament, by this Bill they were admitted. The second reading passed the House of Commons with a majority of 43, but the House of Lords rejected it by a majority of 378.

What is a Lipogram?

IT is a form of literary ingenuity in which the author omits from his composition, prose or verse some particular letter or letters of the alphabet. There are ancient Greek lipograms. Here is a modern example, a poem in which each stanza contains every letter of the alphabet except "e."

A jovial swain should not complain
Of any buxom fair
Who mocks his pain and thinks it gain
To quiz his awkward air.

Quixotic boys who look for joys
Quixotic hazards run ;
A lass annoys with trivial toys,
Opposing man for fun.

A jovial swain may rack his brain,
And tax his fancy's might ;
To quiz in vain, for 'tis most plain
That what I say is right.

Massed lava inside the giant crater of Mount Nambagira, an active volcano in the Belgian Congo near the Uganda border

"Notes and Queries" some years ago published a series of five verses, each of which contained only one vowel. Here they are. The first one deals with the Russo-Turkish War, and contains only the vowel "a."

War harms all ranks, all arts, all crafts appal ;
At Mars' harsh blast, arch, rampart, altar fall !
Ah ! hard as adamant, a braggart Tsar
Arms vassal swarms, and fans a fatal war !
Rampant at that bad call, a Vandal band
Harass, and harm, and ransack Wallachland.
A Tartar phalanx Balkan's scarp hath past,
And Allah's standard falls, alas ! at last.

The second verse, called "The Fall of Eve," contains only "e".

Eve, Eden's empress, needs defended be ;
The Serpent greets her when she seeks the tree.
Serene she sees the speckled tempter creep ;
Gentle he seems—perverted schemer deep—
Yet endless pretexts, ever fresh, prefers,
Perverts her senses, revels when she errs,
Sneers when she weeps, regrets, repents she fell,
Then, deep-revenged, reseeks the nether Hell !

The third verse, containing only the vowel "i," is called "The Approach of Evening."

Idling I sit in this mild twilight dim,
Whilst birds, in wild swift vigils, circling skim.
Light winds in sighing sink, till, rising bright,
Night's Virgin pilgrim swims in vivid light.

The "o" verse, called "Incontrovertible Facts," is longer :

No monk too good to rob, or cog, or plot ;
No fool so gross to bolt Scotch collops hot.
From donjon tops no Oronooko rolls,
Logwood, not lotos, floods Oporto's bowls.
Troops of old toss-pots oft to sot consort,
Box tops our schoolboys, too, do flog for sport.
No cool monsoons blow ott on Oxford dons,
Orthodox, jog-trot, book-worn. Solomons !
Bold Ostrogoths of ghosts no horror show,
On London shop-fronts no hop-blossoms grow.
To crocks of gold no Dodo looks for food ;
On soft cloth footstools no old fox doth brood.
Long storm-tost sloops forlorn do work to port.
Rooks do not roost on spoons, nor woodcocks snort ;
Nor dog on snowdrop or on coltsfoot rolls,
Nor common frog concocts long protocols.

The final verse with "u" is "The Same Subject Continued."

Dull humdrum murmurs lull, but hubbub stuns.
Lucullus snuffs up musk, mundungus shuns.
Puss purrs, buds burst, bucks butt, luck turns up trumps ;
But full cups, hurtful, spur up unjust thumps.

It will be agreed that these verses are certainly feats of ingenuity.

Are There Active Volcanoes in Africa ?

YES ; active volcanoes exist in the Great Rift Valley of East Africa, in which lie many of the large lakes of that region, and recently-extinct volcanoes are also found in the same area.

In the Belgian Congo there is an active volcano, Mount Nambagira, situated near the Uganda border. Its crater is two miles wide, a sterile area piled high with masses of cooled lava at the outskirts, becoming more fluid near the centre and having several small openings through which belch clouds of sulphurous smoke. Through some of the openings the sea of molten lava below can be seen.

A view from the rim of the giant crater of Mount Nambagira, looking across the smaller craters

What Gigantic Fraud Was Exposed by a Newspaper?

In 1841 Mr. O'Reilly, "The Times" correspondent in Paris, learnt of a projected fraud on a gigantic scale and exposed it in his newspaper with the result that the bankers of Europe were saved a loss of a million sterling. It was a daring project. Forged letters of credit to the amount mentioned were to have been issued simultaneously on the chief European bankers. As a testimonial of gratitude to the newspaper for its action the bankers raised a fund and established a scholarship at Oxford for boys educated at Christ's Hospital, and another at Cambridge University for boys educated at the City of London School. One of the great services which newspapers perform for the community is the light which they throw on would-be fraud and dishonesty.

Is There a Leaning Tower in England?

The tower of the Temple Church at Bristol leans five feet out of the perpendicular, and the slant is sufficient to be noticeable by the eye. This tower was built in the 14th century and soon began to tilt. It is said to have been in its present position for over six hundred years. It is stated that during the Civil War Cromwell's men stabled their horses in the church.

How Does the Cricket Chirp?

Although few people have seen a cricket, many have heard it make its loud and shrill chirping. This sound is sometimes heard inside the house, when it is produced by the house cricket, and sometimes in the fields, when the field cricket is responsible.

The sound is not made by the mouth, but by the elytra or wing-covers. The way in which the sound is produced has been described by Mr. Westwood, who says the sound is made by the male insect alone. "On the internal margin of the wing-cover, about one-third of its length from the base, a thickened point is observed, from whence several strong veins diverge, forming an angle from this point. The

A handful of crickets. The photograph gives an idea of their size

which, being divided into a number of irregular spaces, have each a distinct vibration, and produce a separate sound, which unitedly forms the

strongest of these veins, which runs towards the base of the left wing-cover, is found on the underside to be regularly notched transversely like a file. When the wing-covers are closed, this oblique bar of the wing-cover lies upon the upper surface of the corresponding part of the right wing-cover, and when a tremulous motion is imparted to the wing-covers this bar rubs against the corresponding bar of the right wing-cover, and thus produces a vibration which is communicated to the other parts of the wing-covers,

stridulation or chirrup so well known."

The sound has been produced artificially by rubbing the wing-cases together in imitation of the movements of the insect.

Both the house and field cricket are alike lovers of moisture. They are great fighters and combat desperately with others of their own kind. They bite fiercely at anything which annoys them.

The field cricket has such an irritable temper that it can be caught by the simple process of pushing a grass stem into its burrow. The angry insect at once seizes the intruding substance firmly with its jaws, and can be pulled out of the hole before it loosens its hold.

While the chirping of the cricket is pleasing to some people, its constant repetition hour after hour can be very irritating. And yet it is exceedingly difficult to rid a house of crickets.

Who Was the "Liberator"?

This was a title, in Spanish El Libertador, conferred by the people of Peru in 1823 on Simon Bolivar, the famous general of the South American colonies in their revolt from Spain. He is known as the Washington of South America, and Bolivia is named after him.

The leaning tower of the Temple Church at Bristol

How Was the Tinder Box Used?

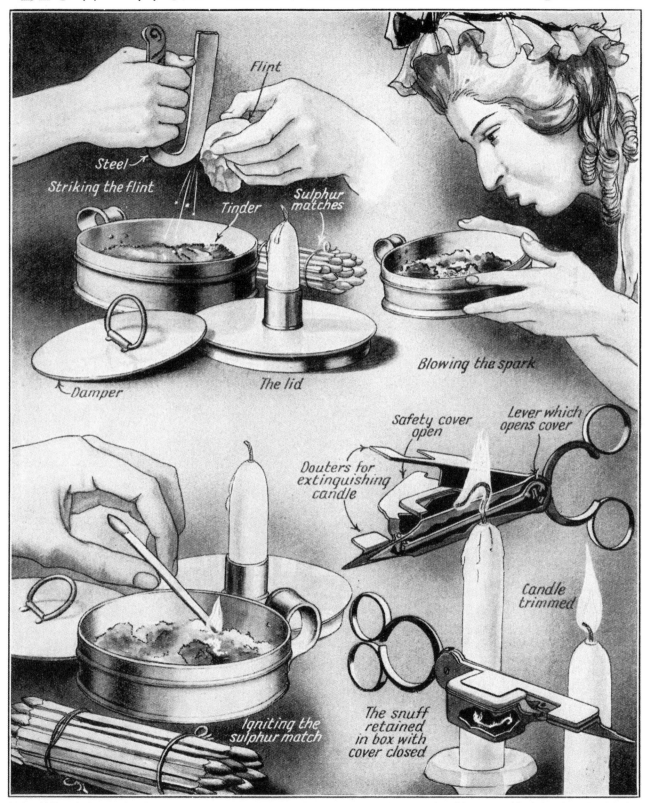

In the old days, before the friction match was invented, a light was obtained by means of a flint and steel kept in a tinder box. Every home had its tinder box, and the tinder consisted of partly burnt linen, which would easily catch light. When a light was wanted the flint was held in the left hand, and the steel, in the right hand, was struck downward with great force on the flint. At each blow the steel broke off some minute fragments of the flint, the friction making these white-hot. The striking was done over the tinder box, and as the blows were struck downward, the sparks flew into the tinder and communicated their heat to that material. The tinder spark was then fanned by being blown upon till there was sufficient fire to light a sulphur match—that is, a strip of wood dipped in sulphur. With the match alight a candle could then be lighted. In the old days the wicks did not burn away completely and had to be snuffed or cut off from time to time in order to keep the candle burning brightly

Who Was Diana of the Ephesians?

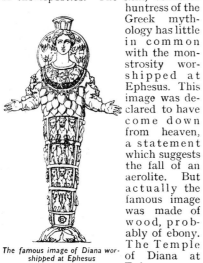

THIS is the goddess referred to in the nineteenth chapter of the Acts of the Apostles. The slim, beautiful huntress of the Greek mythology has little in common with the monstrosity worshipped at Ephesus. This image was declared to have come down from heaven, a statement which suggests the fall of an aerolite. But actually the famous image was made of wood, probably of ebony. The Temple of Diana at Ephesus was regarded as one of the Seven Wonders of the Ancient World. It was 425 feet long and 220 feet wide.

The famous image of Diana worshipped at Ephesus

The silversmiths of Ephesus made a good living by selling little silver shrines of Diana to the many visitors who used to go to her temple from different parts of the world.

What is Chain Verse?

IT is a form of poetic ingenuity in which the last word or words of each line form the opening words of the succeeding line. Its invention is said to be due to the French poet Lasphrise. It is sometimes called concatenation verse. Here are portions of two chain verse poems:

> Wing the course of time with music,
> Music of the grand old days—
> Days when hearts were brave and noble,
> Noble in their simple ways.
> Ways, however rough, yet earnest,
> Earnest to promote the truth—
> Truth that teaches us a lesson,
> Lesson worthy age and youth.
> Youth and age alike may listen—
> Listen, meditate, improve—
> Improve in happiness and glory,
> Glory that shall heavenward move.

and so on for sixty lines.

Here is an example in which several words are repeated:

> The longer life, the more offence;
> The more offence, the greater pain;
> The greater pain, the less defence;
> The less defence, the greater gain.

What Was the First Book Printed in the U.S.A.?

IT is said to have been the Bay Psalm Book, printed at Cambridge, Massachusetts, in 1640. It is a thin volume and possession of a copy is greatly coveted by American bibliophiles. A second edition printed several years later is also very rare and is of considerable value.

What Kind of Animal is the Chinchilla?

THIS animal is best known by its skin, which forms one of the more expensive furs worn by women in winter. The chinchilla is a rather heavily built, squirrel-like rodent, a near relation of the porcupine. It is found in Peru and Chile, and the best skins are exported from Valparaiso and Buenos Aires. It lives high up in the Andes and is subterranean in its habits, living chiefly in holes in the rocks. In olden times the Incas of Peru used chinchilla fur to line their mantles and from the hair they wove a fine cloth.

The chinchilla is nine or ten inches long and in addition the tail is about half the length of the body. The fur, which is about an inch in length, is extremely soft and of a delicate pearly grey colour, mottled with black above and yellowish-white beneath, while the tail is mostly black with lighter bands on the sides. The animals live in companies and may be seen abroad in the daytime. They keep, however, to the shadowed places among the rocks. On the ground they run like mice, but when eating sit up on their hind-quarters like squirrels, grasping their food between their forepaws.

The regions they inhabit are barren,

that it is becoming scarce, and this partly accounts for the high price of its skin.

In 1938 a pair of chinchillas was brought to England with a view of starting a farm for their breeding. The two animals cost £640, and there was difficulty in obtaining them, for in South America, where they are said to be almost extinct, there is a reluctance to part with them at any price.

The first chinchilla to reach London alive was taken to the Zoo at Regent's Park by Captain Beechey of the Royal Navy in 1829. Between that date and the beginning of the present century the Zoo often had specimens, and no fewer than thirty have at different times been born and bred in the gardens in small hutches.

For many years it was impossible to get any specimens at all, but about 1912 an Englishman sent out a collector to Peru to obtain some. With much difficulty he managed to bring back a dozen, and great efforts were made to insure that these should become the foundation of a fur-breeding stock in Kent. Unfortunately the experiment was unsuccessful, but perhaps the new effort will have better fortune.

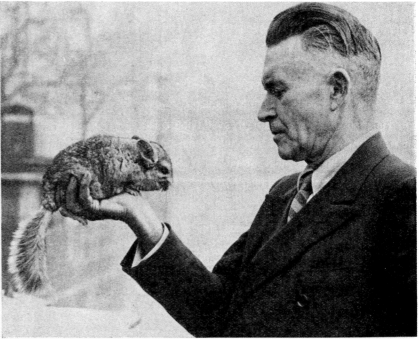

A chinchilla from the Andes of South America, one of several brought to England to start a chinchilla farm

and they dart up and down the almost perpendicular faces of the rocks with a rapidity so great that it is almost impossible for the eye to follow them. The natives hunt them with a species of weasel which they drive into the burrows. A second species of chinchilla has a shorter tail and is known as the short-tailed chinchilla.

In recent years the attractive little animal has been hunted so mercilessly

What is the Odium Theologicum?

IT is the enmity and bitterness caused by religious differences or existing between different sects or schools of theology. No hatreds are so bitter as those arising from religious differences, just as no wars are so fierce as religious wars. There have been many sad examples of this in world history.

What is That Edible Mollusc?

Mussel · Banded Snail · Wood Snail · Periwinkle · Common Snail · Cockle · Limpet · Sea wing · Apple, Vine or Roman Snail · Ear Shell · Red-nose cockle · Trough Shell · Gaper · Piddock or Clam · Oyster · Common Scallop · Whelk · Painted Scallop · Heart Shell or Oxhorn Cockle · Pullet · Setting Sun · Warty Venus · Razor Shell

Many of the molluscs found in Great Britain, either on land or in the coastal waters, are edible, although, curiously enough, many people think that only a few of these, like the oyster, scallop, mussel, cockle, winkle and whelk are suitable for food. There are, however, many British molluscs which are equally nutritious and appetising, although they are seldom if ever seen in the markets, and are used only locally as food. The sea wing, for example, is the largest of our British bivalves, in some specimens the shell being twelve inches long and seven inches wide. As a food this is nearly as good as the scallop. Sea wings, fried in oil or butter with chopped parsley till they are brown, are delicious; or they may be boiled with salt and pepper and vermicelli, when they make a fine soup. Razor shells, of which there are several species round our British coasts, also make a good soup, or they can be stewed in milk. English people do not take kindly to land snails, although they eat plenty of winkles, or periwinkles to give them their full name. Several of our land snails, however, are edible and are reckoned delicacies, the best and largest being the Roman snail

Do All Dragoons Wear Gilt Helmets?

ALL the dragoon regiments in the British Army except two wear gilt metal helmets, but the 5th Royal Inniskilling Dragoon Guards and the

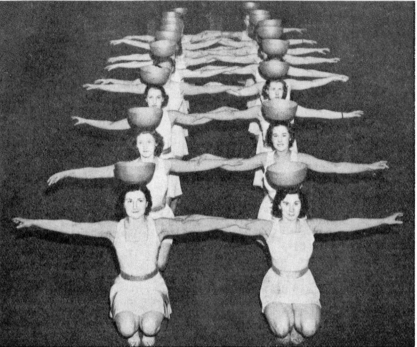

Members of the Women's League of Health and Beauty exercising with bowls balanced on their heads

1st Royal Dragoons have steel helmets. The plumes vary in colour. The 1st King's Dragoon Guards have a red plume, the Queen's Bays and the 1st Royal Dragoons, black; the 3rd Carabineers have a black-and-red plume, the 4th/7th Royal Dragoon Guards have a white plume, and the 5th Royal Inniskilling Dragoon Guards a red-and-white plume. The Royal Scots Greys, the 2nd Dragoons, wear black bearskins with a grenade on the left side as a plume socket, and a white hackle feather 10 inches high.

What Was the Alaskan Boundary Dispute?

IT was a dispute between Canada and the United States about the boundary between the former country and the territory of Alaska which the United States bought from Russia in 1867 for 7,200,000 dollars, or about £1,440,000. The dispute turned on the interpretation to be given to the words in the Russo-British Treaty of 1825 which placed the boundary at " ten marine leagues, or thirty miles from the ocean."

Canada maintained that this meant 30 miles from the main coast-line and did not apply to indentations. The way the dispute was settled formed an excellent object-lesson to the rest of the world. A commission was appointed in January, 1903, which,

according to the treaty, was to be composed of " six impartial jurists of repute." Great Britain appointed Lord Alverstone, the Lord Chief Justice of England, and two Canadian jurists, and some surprise was caused when the United States appointed, not more or less impartial jurists, as specified in the treaty, but two senators who had shown their strong partiality by speeches on the subject, and the United States Secretary for War.

However, the Commission's findings were accepted by both countries. The boundary was fixed along the summits of a range of mountains running parallel to the coast, the disputed area being halved by this plan. The Lynn Canal passed to the United States, but the British claims in the Portland Channel were upheld, two small islands alone being given to the United States.

Who Was the Great Cham of Literature?

THIS was a title conferred on Dr. Samuel Johnson by Tobias Smollett in a letter to John Wilkes, the demagogue, and it became popular. The word cham is an obsolete form of khan, and at the time the phrase was coined men spoke of a far-eastern ruler as " the Great Cham of Tartary." By this they often meant the Emperor of China.

How Do Mannequins Learn to Pose?

THEY are taught at schools, where they are put through various exercises to develop grace and ease of slow movement. One exercise is to stand and walk with books poised on top of the head. When a girl learns to do this she can move and stand without any of those awkward leanings and lurchings that are common to most of us in our efforts to preserve our balance.

A mannequin training to walk gracefully with books balanced on her head

What is the World's Most Accurate Clock?

IT is an electric clock installed at the Royal Observatory, Greenwich, in 1938, which does not vary more than a fraction of a second a year. Hitherto the standard clocks at Greenwich have been pendulum instruments. These are liable to sudden small changes of rate, which are corrected by astronomical observations. In cloudy weather, however, the observations cannot be made, and slight errors may accumulate. Only by keeping a constant watch on the comparison between various standard clocks can this be detected. The new electric clock renders much of this anxious watchfulness unnecessary. The probable margin of error is only one in a hundred million.

Are Any London Streets Playgrounds?

YES, some streets are closed to through traffic so that they may be used by the children of the neighbourhood as playgrounds. Of course, no important thoroughfare is ever closed in this way, and even those that are made into "Play Streets" are open to tradesmen's carts and vans for the delivery of goods.

The provision of such playgrounds in districts where there are no open spaces in which children can play has proved a great boon and the idea is now being extended to some other large cities.

Who Was Ally Sloper?

ALLY SLOPER was the name given to a comic character who figured in cartoons in a weekly illustrated paper of the late 19th century called "Ally Sloper's Half Holiday."

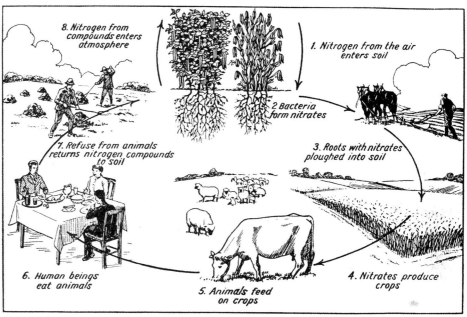

A pictorial representation of the cycle by which nitrogen is taken from the air and, after passing through plants and animals, is returned once more to the atmosphere

He was a grotesque figure with a large nose. In the window of the office of the paper in Shoe Lane was a museum made up of all kinds of ridiculous objects such as old hats, clay pipes, and supposed personal relics of Ally Sloper. There was also an "Ally Sloper Club" for readers of the paper.

What is the Cycle of Nitrogen?

THIS is a term given by scientists to the way in which nitrogen is taken from the air to build up plants and feed animals and human beings. This process goes on as a constant round, hence the name cycle. All plants and animals need nitrogen if they are to thrive. But neither animals nor the majority of plants can use the free nitrogen of the air, of which there is such a vast stock available. The nitrogen must be taken in the form of a compound.

But certain bacteria in the soil are able to take nitrogen from the air which is mixed up with the grains of earth, and then entering the roots of leguminous plants like beans, peas and clovers, combine it with substances in those roots and form nitrates. In this way the leguminous plants gradually enrich the soil, and when another crop is grown on the same soil it thrives because it finds nitrate food stored up in the soil by the previous leguminous crop.

Animals, of course, feed on the crops and human beings eat both animal and plant food, so that they get the nitrogen necessary for the building up of their bodies in a digestible form. The refuse and remains of animals in the soil cause the right kind of bacteria to multiply there, and so a regular nitrogen cycle goes on continuously to the advantage of all.

What is Prince's Metal?

IT is a metal invented by Prince Rupert of Bavaria, nephew of King Charles I and a leader in the Civil War. He was a scientist of some note and this metal called after him is a mixture of copper and zinc.

A London street closed to traffic so that children can use it as a playground

What is That Insect Pest Called?

Pupa — CODLIN MOTH — Caterpillar

WOOLLY APHIS — Winged female

Eggs — LACKEY MOTH

APPLE SAWFLY — Caterpillar

SMALL ERMINE MOTH

APPLE SUCKER — Pupa

larva — ROSE BEETLE — Insect in flight

GOAT MOTH

Larva — APPLE BLOSSOM WEEVIL

CHERRY APHIS — Winged female

CURRANT SHOOT MOTH — Caterpillar

EARWIG — Winged male — Female

DOT MOTH

MAGPIE MOTH

Female — Larval scale — GOOSEBERRY AND CURRANT SCALE

Larva — CHERRY AND PEAR SAWFLY

Chrysalis — CURRANT CLEAR-WINGED MOTH

LAPPET MOTH — Caterpillar

Female scale — Larva — WHITE WOOLLY CURRANT SCALE

IVY RED SPIDER

Cocoon — GOOSEBERRY AND CURRANT SAWFLY

Larva — NUT WEEVIL

VAPOURER MOTH

Larva — Pupa — PEAR MIDGE

SOCIAL PEAR SAWFLY

It has often been said that of all living creatures the insects are the only ones that contest the supremacy of the world with man. In some areas they have so spread disease that they have driven man out. In others, insects like the tsetse fly in Central Africa prevent man keeping domestic animals. In the United States insect pests do damage to the extent of hundreds of millions of pounds every year, and vast sums have to be spent in fighting these pests in order that crops like fruit and cotton may be grown at all. On these pages are shown nearly 50 insect pests that do damage in Great Britain. Many of these pests are familiar in our gardens. Our apple trees often suffer from the codlin moth and woolly aphis, and most gardeners who grow dahlias have to bewail the ravages of the earwig. The winter moth, too, is a great pest, but it can be fought by

194

What Special Damage Does It Do?

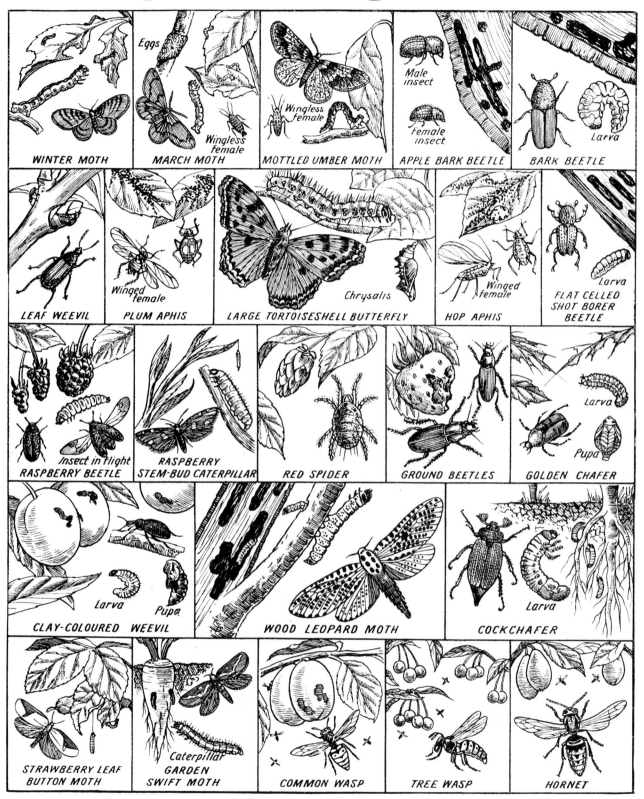

WINTER MOTH

MARCH MOTH — Eggs — Wingless female

MOTTLED UMBER MOTH — Wingless female

APPLE BARK BEETLE — Male insect — Female insect

BARK BEETLE — Larva

LEAF WEEVIL

PLUM APHIS — Winged female

LARGE TORTOISESHELL BUTTERFLY — Chrysalis

HOP APHIS — Winged female

FLAT CELLED SHOT BORER BEETLE — Larva

RASPBERRY BEETLE — Insect in flight

RASPBERRY STEM-BUD CATERPILLAR

RED SPIDER

GROUND BEETLES

GOLDEN CHAFER — Larva — Pupa

CLAY-COLOURED WEEVIL — Larva — Pupa

WOOD LEOPARD MOTH

COCKCHAFER — Larva

STRAWBERRY LEAF BUTTON MOTH

GARDEN SWIFT MOTH — Caterpillar

COMMON WASP

TREE WASP

HORNET

banding the fruit trees with sticky paper. Only the male has wings. The female has to crawl up the trunk, and when she comes to the sticky band she is caught and so cannot go higher and lay her eggs. The cockchafer is, of course, a great enemy. The thick white fleshy grubs do immense damage among the roots of growing plants. Wasps, although they prey on the ripe fruit, also do a certain amount of good by devouring other insects that are pests. Even a beautiful insect like the large tortoiseshell butterfly may become a nuisance at times, although it is not a very serious pest in Great Britain. Sometimes, however, the attack upon the elm, cherry or other trees on which the caterpillar feeds becomes serious. A strong shaking of the branches will often bring the caterpillars down, when they can be destroyed, and the eggs should be watched for carefully and destroyed

How Did "M" Come Into Napoleon's Life?

AMONG many superstitions peculiar to the two Emperors Napoleon is that of regarding the letter M as ominous of good and evil. Perhaps the following catalogue of men, things and events, the names of which begin with M, shows that the two emperors had some cause for considering the letter a momentous one.

Marboeuf was the first to recognise the genius of the great Napoleon at the Military College. Marengo was the first great battle won by General

A great dust storm approaching the town of Clayton in New Mexico

Bonaparte, and Melas made room for him in Italy. Mortier was one of his best generals, Moreau betrayed him and Murat was his great cavalry leader. Marie Louise shared his highest fortunes. Moscow was the abyss of ruin into which he fell. Metternich vanquished him in the field of diplomacy. Six marshals, Massena, Mortier, Marmont, Macdonald, Murat, Moncey, had names beginning with M, and two others had titles with the same initial —Lannes, the Duke of Montebello, and Ney, Prince of Moskowa. Twenty-six generals of divisions under Napoleon had the letter M for their initial. Maret, Duke of Bassano, was his most trusted counsellor. His first battle was that of Montenotte, his last Mont St. Jean, as the French term Waterloo. He won the battles of Millesimo, Mondeir, Montmirail and Montereau. Then came the storming of Montmartre. Milan was the first enemy's capital and Moscow the last, into which he marched victorious. He lost Egypt through Menou and employed Miollis to take Pope Pius VII prisoner. Malet conspired against him; Murat was the first to desert him, then Marmont. Three of his ministers were Maret, Montalivet, and Mollieu; his first chamberlain was Montesquieu. His last halting-place in France was

Malmaison. He surrendered to Captain Maitland of the *Bellerophon*, and his companions in St. Helena were Montholon, and his valet Marchand. His body servants were known as Mamelukes, and his secretary was Meneval.

The same predominance of the letter M has been found in the history of Napoleon III. He was born on April 20th, 1808, which in Corsica is the last day of the feast week of Machreal. His early military instruction was given to him by Moreith of Montélimar. His empress was the Countess Montijo; his greatest friend was Morny. The taking of the Malakoff and the Mamelon-Vert were the greatest feats of the French arms in the Crimean War. He planned his first battle of the Italian campaign at Marengo, although it was not fought until after the engagement of Montebello. At Magenta, MacMahon, for his important services in this battle, was named Duke of Magenta, as Pélissier had for similar merit received the title of Duke of Malakoff.

Napoleon III then made his entry into Milan and drove the Austrians out of Marignano.

After the great victory of Solferino, fought on the banks and in the waters of the Mincio, he turned back before the walls of Mantua. All this was up to the year 1860, after which the letter M has an ominous significance. There was the Mexican adventure with Maximilian, and the vain hopes of the Franco-Prussian War founded on the three M's, Marshal MacMahon, Count Montauban, and the Mitrailleuse. Mayence was to have been the basis for further operations of the French Army, but pushed back first to the Moselle, its doom was sealed on the Maas at Sedan. Then followed the capitulation of Metz, and all the subsequent disasters were due to the strategy and skill of Moltke.

Such compilations are, of course, of no value, being mere coincidences, but one can understand a man with a streak of superstition and fatalism in his make-up taking some notice of the coincidence.

Do Dust Storms in America Bury Buildings?

IN the last year or two, owing to the destruction of so much forest land and repeated droughts there have

The same town a few minutes later, after the dust storm from the Dust Bowl in the states of New Mexico and Oklahoma had struck it. Most of the buildings were covered with sand and dust

been terrific dust storms in certain of the States, and in some cases farms with all their buildings have been absolutely overwhelmed. This has been the case in the so-called Dust Bowl of Oklahoma and New Mexico. In 1938, for example, a dust storm was suddenly seen approaching the town of Clayton in New Mexico, and a few minutes later, after the storm had passed, every building was buried in dust to a depth of several feet, and some of the buildings were covered entirely and disappeared from sight.

What is That Optical Illusion?

Here are some curious optical illusions which make it quite evident that seeing is not always believing. For example, in Nos. 1, 3, 5, 6, 8 and 17 we see lines which are really parallel, but appear to slant because our eyes are distracted by other lines adjacent to them. We can test the parallel lines with a rule or, instead of looking down upon them, we can look along them slantingly, when we shall see that they are parallel. This is particularly striking in the case of the word " file " in No. 17. In Nos. 2, 9 and 10 the triangle, square and circle appear warped, although they are not really so. They are made to look untrue by the other lines that form a background. In No. 7, if we look steadily at the black star for a minute, and then look at the white square at the side, we shall see a white star on a grey background. In No. 15 the middle disk at the bottom appears larger than the one at the top, although both are the same size. The distances between the arrow points in No. 19 are all the same, although they appear to vary so much. In Nos. 11 and 16 the tops and bottoms become reversed if we look for a moment or two. In 13 the two shapes do not appear the same size, although they are. In 14, if we close the right eye and look at the black dot, and then bring the page nearer to our face, the cross will at one time disappear. In 18 the three figures are all really the same height.

Why Does the Peacock Display Its Tail?

WHAT we call the tail of the peacock, the large brilliant display of feathers with the shimmering eyespots, is not really the tail at all, but the tail coverts. These long covert feathers are developed for the courting season and are raised and spread like a great fan, the true tail being raised at the same time to support the brilliant feathers. With the train spread, the wings dropped and the neck thrust forward, the bird presents a very beautiful and striking appearance as he faces the hen, but she invariably appears quite unimpressed.

Many other cock birds display their finery and go through strange antics at the courting season. Among them may be mentioned the turkey cock, the argus pheasant and the birds of paradise.

Different species of birds have their own methods of courtship. The male ostrich, which differs from his greyish brown mate in being black and white, takes up a position facing the hen, drops on his hocks in a squatting attitude, spreads his wings, lowers his tail and, throwing his neck over his back, sways slowly and rhythmically from side to side, swinging his neck from right to left and often shaking his wings. These antics may go on for ten minutes or more at a time and then, suddenly rising to his feet, the cock bird will rush towards the hen with wings outspread, and sometimes repeat the performance at close quarters. The queer evolutions are brought to an end by the bird stamping on the ground. From beginning to end the hen appears to be taking no notice whatsoever of her companion.

What is Invisible Ink?

INVISIBLE ink is a fluid in which a message can be written with a pen and will leave no trace upon the paper. The letter appears as clear as if it had never been touched, but if it be subjected to heat or is treated with some chemical the writing stands out clearly. There are many such fluids that can be used for invisible writing.

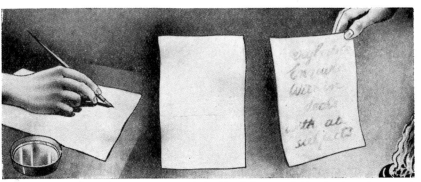

How unseen words written with cobalt chloride become visible when heated

Cobalt chloride, for example, forms a solution that can be used in this way. A weak solution leaves a very pale red tracing on the paper that is all but invisible, but when the paper is heated the writing appears blue and quite distinct.

If words be written with dilute nitrate of silver the writing when dry will be entirely invisible, but if the paper be held over a vessel containing sulphate of ammonia the letters will stand out with the brilliancy of silver. Equal parts of sulphate of copper and sal ammoniac dissolved in water will provide an invisible ink, but the

writing when warmed will turn yellow. A cheap invisible ink may be made by dissolving a fluid ounce of common oil of vitriol in a pint of soft water. The solution should be stirred well and left to cool. Used as a writing fluid the words will be invisible, but if the paper be held to the fire, the writing will turn an indelible black.

There are many other fluids which can be used in a similar way. The application of heat or some other treatment sets up chemical changes which alter the colour of the fluid. All chemicals should be used with care.

What Did the American Civil War Cost?

THE total cost of this war, which lasted from 1861 to 1865, was £1,400,000,000. The Federal expenses were £940,000,000, and the Confederate £460,000,000. The cost in lives was 800,000.

What is the Proposed Reformed Calendar?

THERE is some inconvenience caused by the weeks not corresponding with the months so that any particular date is a day in the week later in each succeeding year, and two days later after a leap year. Thus January 1st was on Tuesday in 1935, on Wednesday in 1936, on Friday in 1937, and on Saturday in 1938.

To get over these difficulties it has been proposed to the League of Nations that a reformed calendar should be brought into operation. The year would have 364 days plus one additional day, known as Year-end Day, which would be at the end of December. In leap years there would be another similar day at the end of June. There would be four quarters in the year of 91 days each, consisting of one month of 31 days followed by two of thirty days. As a result the same date would be on the same day of the week in all the years, every year would begin on a Sunday, every quarter contain the same number of days, and every month the same number of week-days, though not of Sundays.

A peacock at the Whipsnade Zoo displaying its tail covert feathers

Are Photographs Deceptive?

PHOTOGRAPHS are very often deceptive for by varying the angle of the camera and by changed focusing a completely false impression may be given of a scene. Rooms may be made to look much larger than they are, though all the details in the room may be accurate; buildings may be made to look taller or shorter or wider than they really are, and often the surroundings may, by a curious and ingenious placing of the camera while the photograph is being taken, cause a well-known building to appear quite strange and unlike itself. Two good examples of this photographic misrepresentation are to be seen in the accompanying photographs of the London Monument and St. Paul's Cathedral. In the former case the photograph of the Monument is taken looking through a group of daffodils growing on a City roof; and in the case of St. Paul's, the dome was taken with the camera pointing up over a pile of sand that had been unloaded from a river barge.

Are B.B.C. Appeals Successful?

EVERY Sunday evening the B.B.C. allows certain appeals for money to be made to the charitable public under the general title of " The Week's Good Cause." It is interesting to know that these appeals are successful and that considerable sums are obtained for charity in this way. The figures show a progressive increase. In 1930 the amount received was £54,439, and this had increased by 1937 to £139,368. But the previous year, 1936, was the bumper year, when the money subscribed to The Week's Good Cause amounted to £186,144. Some causes attract very large sums. The Christmas Wireless for the Blind appeal in 1937 brought £23,044. In the previous year it was £19,851. The highest sum ever realised as the result of a B.B.C. appeal was £27,408 brought in after Canon H. R. L. Sheppard and Lord Kinnaird had asked over the wireless in January, 1936, for money to assist the Red Cross work in Abyssinia.

In these broadcast appeals men are much more successful than women, and it is thought that most of the money that is given is from women, and women respond more readily to a masculine voice. It is also stated that the poor respond much more generously than the rich. One disadvantage is that people cannot on Sunday get a postal order to send off. By Monday morning their good resolutions have sometimes gone.

Could Beings From Other Planets Live Here?

A FRENCH professor has been describing what would happen if beings anything like ourselves could come to the Earth from other worlds. The conditions here are so different from what they are on the other planets that the visitors would experience serious trouble.

For example, a man from Mars on arriving on the Earth would be unable to endure the excessive amount of oxygen that there is in our atmosphere and would soon be overcome by congestion.

A man from Venus would be stifled by gases to which he was not accustomed, and could not breathe, and an inhabitant from Mercury would find our climate so different from what he was used to that he would shiver, whatever coverings were over him.

A person from Neptune arriving on the Earth, even if he landed in the frozen regions of the Arctic or Antarctic, would find our temperature suffocating and the light blinding. The conditions are not nearly alike on any two of the Sun's family of worlds.

Who Were the Original Nonconformists?

THEY were the two thousand clergymen of the Church of England who in 1662 left the Church rather than conform to the conditions of the Act of Uniformity which enjoined " the unfeigned assent to all and everything contained in the Book of Common Prayer." By this Act all clergymen who refused to comply were to be imprisoned for six months for the first offence, to lose their livings for the second offence, and to be imprisoned for life for the third offence. The name is now loosely applied to all Protestant dissenters— that is, those who decline to accept the doctrine and discipline of the Church of England.

Above is the dome of St. Paul's Cathedral photographed from the bottom of a sand heap unloaded from a barge on the banks of the Thames, and, below, the top of the Monument as seen over daffodils growing on a roof garden

What is a Wind Rose?

IT is a graphic representation of the prevailing winds of a district over a given period, used by meteorologists. The four directions—north, south, east and west—are first drawn as lines from a central point and then other lines are drawn to represent the directions intermediate between these. On the eight lines distances are marked off

July 7th, 1792, between the various factions in the French National Assembly. It is thus described by Sir Walter Scott :

" The deputies of every faction, Royalist, Constitutionalist, Girondist, Jacobin, Orleanist, rushed into each other's arms and mixed tears with the solemn oaths by which they renounced the innovations supposed to be imputed to them. The king was

Who Said "First Catch Your Hare"?

IT is generally believed that these words appear in an old cookery book, known as " Mrs. Glasse's Cookery Book," in the directions for roasting a hare ; and there have been writers who have explained that what Mrs. Glasse really wrote was " first scatch (that is, skin) your hare."

At last it occurred to someone to look up the book itself, and then it was found that the phrase does not occur there at all. What the author wrote was " Take your hare when it is cas'd and make a pudding." Case is an old English verb meaning " skin." The book in question was originally published in 1747 under the title "The Art of Cookery by a Lady." The name of Mrs. Glasse was only added in succeeding editions. The real author, it is suggested, was Dr. John Hill.

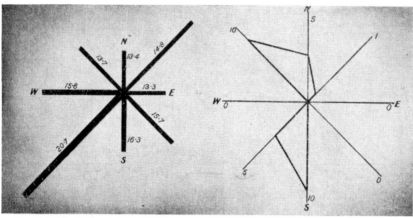

Two examples of the wind rose used by meteorologists

proportionate to the number of times the wind is observed blowing in each direction. In one form of wind rose, shown in the drawing on this page, the distances are connected by straight lines. The figures show the number of times the wind blew from each particular direction. In the example on the left the proportionate length of time during which the wind blew is shown by the length of the lines and the average velocity is indicated by the width.

What is a Palindrome?

A PALINDROME is a word, phrase or sentence that reads the same from either end. The name means " running back again." Here are some examples :

Madam, I'm Adam.
Able was I ere I saw Elba.
Name no one man.
Red root put up to order.
Draw pupil's lip upward.
No, it is opposition.
No, it is opposed ; art sees trade's opposition.
Snug & raw was I ere I saw war & guns.

Some names are palindromes as, for example : Hannah, Otto, Eve, Anna, Ada, Glenelg, Notton, Sillis, Mary Byram. Noxon is not only a palindrome but it reads the same if turned upside down when spelt in capitals.

What is the Meaning of Lamourette's Kiss?

THE phrase means a sudden but short-lived reconciliation, or a reconciliation of policy without abatement of rancour. It was used derisively to describe the reconciliation brought about by the Abbé Lamourette, on

sent for to enjoy this spectacle of concord, so strangely and so unexpectedly renewed. But the feeling though strong, and, it might be, with many overpowering for the moment, was but like oil spilt on the raging sea, or rather like a shot fired across the waves of a torrent, which, though it counteracts them by its momentary impulse, cannot for a second alter their course. The factions, like Le Sage's demons, detested each other the more for having been compelled to embrace."

What Are the Seven Works of Mercy?

THESE are to tend the sick, to feed the hungry, to give drink to the thirsty, to clothe the naked, to house the homeless, to visit the fatherless and afflicted, and to bury the dead. The idea is obtained from St. Matthew's Gospel, chapter xxv, verses 35 and 36.

Where is a Churchyard Wall Made of Tombstones?

THE church of Cricklade in Wiltshire has its boundary wall built up entirely of old tombstones, which are placed side by side and fastened together with iron clamps.

A churchyard at Cricklade, Wiltshire, which is enclosed by a wall made up of old tombstones

What Are the Commonest Misquotations?

AMONG the commonest misquotations, apart from those from the Bible and Shakespeare given on other pages, are the following:

" He who hesitates is lost." This is from Joseph Addison's play " Cato," where it reads, " The woman that deliberates is lost."

" If the mountain will not come to Mahomet, Mahomet must go to the mountain " is from Francis Bacon's Essays and should be, " If the hill will not come to Mahomet, Mahomet will go to the hill."

" Cool as a cucumber " should read " As cold as cucumbers." It is from Beaumont and Fletcher's " Cupid's Revenge."

" One man's meat is another man's poison." This is from Beaumont and Fletcher's " Love's Cure " and should read, " What's one man's poison, signor, is another's meat or drink."

" Boys will be boys " is an adaptation of Isaac Bickerstaffe's " Young fellows will be young fellows," from " Love in a Village."

" The age of chivalry is past " is from Burke's " Reflections on the French Revolution," where it reads, " The age of chivalry is gone."

" Lick it into shape," should be " Lick it into form." It is from Burton's " Anatomy of Melancholy."

" Marriages are made in heaven " should be " Matches are made in heaven," from the same book.

" When in Rome do as Rome does " is misquoted from Burton, who wrote in the " Anatomy," " When they are at Rome they do there as they see done."

" There's many a slip 'twixt the cup and the lip " is Burton's " Many things happen between the cup and the lip."

" At daggers drawn," from Samuel Butler's " Hudibras," should be " At daggers drawing."

" Have an eye to the main chance " is misquoted from " Hudibras," where it reads " Have a care o' th' main chance."

" Genius is an infinite capacity for taking pains " is misquoted from Carlyle's " Frederick the Great," where we read " Genius . . . means the transcendent capacity of taking trouble."

" Possession is nine points of the law " should be " Possession is eleven points in the law " and is from Colley Cibber's " Woman's Wit."

" An Englishman's home is his castle " is a misquotation of Sir Edward Coke's " For a man's house is his castle."

" Water, water everywhere, And not a drop to drink " should be " Water, water, everywhere, Nor any drop to drink." It is from S. T. Coleridge's " The Ancient Mariner."

" Everything comes to him who waits " is from Disraeli's " Tancred," and should be " Everything comes if a man will only wait."

" Little things amuse little minds," from Disraeli's " Sybil," should read " Little things affect little minds."

" Time is the great healer " is misquoted from Disraeli's " Henrietta Temple," where it reads " Time is the great physician."

" It's worse than a crime, it's a blunder." This is not only misquoted but is often erroneously attributed to Talleyrand, whereas it is from Joseph Fouché, who really said " It is more than a crime ; it is a political fault."

" Ask no questions and you'll be told no lies " should read " Ask me no questions and I'll tell you no fibs," from Goldsmith's " She Stoops to Conquer."

" The even tenor of their way " should be " The noiseless tenor of their way." It is from Gray's " Elegy."

" Listeners seldom hear good of themselves " is from Matthew Henry's " Commentary on Ecclesiastes." He wrote, " Hearkeners, we say, seldom hear good of themselves."

" A poet is born, not made " is misquoted from Ben Jonson's lines, " To the Memory of Shakespeare," " For a good poet's made as well as born."

" The daily round, the common task," from John Keble's " The Christian Year," should be " The trivial round, the common task."

" When Greek meets Greek " is a misquotation of Nathaniel Lee's " When Greeks joined Greeks, then was the tug of war."

" Enough to make a saint swear " is misquoted from James Russell Lowell's " Biglow Papers," " It's most enough to make a deacon swear."

" There's more in this than meets the eye " is a misquotation of Milton's lines in " Il Penseroso," " Where more is meant than meets the ear."

" A little knowledge is a dangerous thing " is from Pope's " Essay on Criticism," and should read " A little learning is a dangerous thing."

" Pure as the driven snow " is misquoted from William Shenstone's " The Schoolmistress," " Whiter than the driven snow."

" Laugh and Grow Fat " is from John Taylor's " Title of a Tract," and should be " Laugh and be fat."

" Like master, like man " is from Thomas Tusser's " Five Hundred Points of Good Husbandry," where it reads " Such master, such man."

" Least said is soonest mended " should be " Little said is soonest mended." It is from George Wither's " The Shepherd's Hunting."

The strange saxophone-like instrument used by some natives of India

What is an Indian Saxophone?

THIS name is sometimes humorously given to a queer instrument used in some parts of India. It is made of dried vegetables and bamboo, and is decorated with peacock feathers and coloured pompons. When played by a powerful blower it gives out a sound something like that of the bagpipe.

What Was the Mouse of the Monument?

THIS was a mouse that took up its abode at the London Monument, on Fish Street Hill, in 1846, and remained there for nearly two years. It became so tame that it allowed visitors to handle it and would take its food from their fingers without fear. It used to run about freely during the day, and in winter would sit by the fire in the caretaker's room. Unfortunately, the mouse met its death through an accident, a burning cigar being thrown upon it and injuring it so severely that it died.

Do Tortoises Love the Warmth?

TORTOISES are creatures of the warmer countries of the world and some, like the giant tortoises of the Seychelles and Galapagos Islands, have their native homes almost on the Equator.

Even the tortoises which we keep in our gardens, known as Greek tortoises, come from the warm Mediterranean countries. When winter arrives they bury themselves away from the frost, but we see their love of warmth as soon as the spring weather comes, for then they wake up and bask in the sun. If the weather turns cold again they at once go and bury themselves till warmer weather returns.

At the London Zoo the tortoises from tropical lands have their house kept warm and at an even temperature

Giant tortoises huddled round the central heating apparatus in their house at the London Zoo

by an electric heater. They love to huddle round the heater, from which they are protected by a circular railing, as seen in the photograph on this page.

Who Were the Ladies of Llangollen?

THEY were two Irish ladies, the Hon. Caroline Ponsonby and Lady Eleanor Butler, who, weary of society, withdrew to a property which they had bought near Llangollen and passed their time amid the simple pleasures of the country and in the exercise of charity and hospitality. They refused offers of marriage and remained constant to one another

Three examples of heraldic crests. The first is an eagle's head couped on a chapeau or Cap of Maintenance, next a demi-dragon on a reef, and on the right a cross Bottonné between wings displayed out of a ducal coronet

till death parted them. Lady Butler died in 1829, aged ninety, and Miss Ponsonby in 1831, aged seventy-six. A monument in Llangollen churchyard commemorates their virtues. They were very famous in their lifetime and were visited at their picturesque home, Plas Newydd, by Wordsworth, Scott, Byron, Burke, the Duke of Wellington, and many others. They were, indeed, quite famous national characters.

What is a Crest in Heraldry?

THIS is the name of an ornament surmounting the helmet and the insignia of a coat of arms. The earliest appearance of a crest in England is on the second seal of Richard I, in which the king is represented wearing a cylindrical helmet surmounted by a semicircle of points. These represent what is known as a demi-soleil, or half-sun, and within them is the figure of a lion passant. The crest is often used separately as an ornament or cognizance for plate, liveries and the like. A crest coronet and a crest wreath are a coronet and a wreath to support a crest.

How Long Did the Council of Trent Last?

THIS great council, held at Trent in the Tyrol during the 16th century, first met on December 13th, 1545, and with several prorogations continued till December 4th, 1563. Its object was to correct, confirm and fix the doctrines and discipline of the Roman Catholic Church and to reform the lives of the clergy. It condemned the leading doctrines of the Reformation and published a series of decisions, known as the Tridentine Decrees, which were confirmed by Pope Pius IV and are binding on all members of the Church of Rome. In 1564 Pius published a Tridentine Profession of Faith and in 1566 a Tridentine Catechism was issued which is still in use.

What Was the Palace of Ice?

IT was a building made entirely of blocks of ice and erected by direction of the Empress Anne of Russia in 1739 to celebrate the wedding of Prince Galitzin with a peasant girl. The bride and bridegroom were compelled to spend their wedding night in a room, the walls, the furniture, and even the bed of which were all made of ice, hardly comfortable surroundings in which to pass a honeymoon.

Which of the Finches is That Bird?

Greenfinch · Siskin · Hawfinch · Goldfinch · Linnet · Chaffinch · Brambling · Twite · House Sparrow · Tree Sparrow · Crossbill · Bullfinch · Corn Bunting · Lapland Bunting · Reed Bunting · Yellow Hammer · Snow Bunting · Cirl Bunting · Lesser Redpoll · Mealy Redpoll

The family of birds which zoologists call the Fringillidae includes the finches, the sparrows and the buntings. Here are the members of this family which are found wild in Britain, and from these drawings it will be possible to identify the various birds. The house sparrow and the tree sparrow belong to this family, but the hedge sparrow is not a finch ; it is frequently classed as a warbler, a member of a different family altogether. Some of the birds shown here, like the sparrows, the greenfinch and the bullfinch, are resident and fairly abundant ; but others, like the siskin, brambling, mealy redpoll and crossbill, are irregular migrants. There is another crossbill, the two-barred species, but it is only a very rare straggler to the British Isles

Can Oil Be Obtained From Grapes?

In the Rhineland large quantities of grape-stones are left after the grapes have been crushed for the making of wine. German chemists have long been at work trying to find some way of utilising these stones, and now they have discovered how to obtain oil from grape-stones.

In 1937 no less than 40,000 litres of oil were obtained in this way, and it is expected that with the process in full swing a million litres a year will be produced ; that is, about a million and three-quarter pints.

Since the Great War the Germans, with a shortage of cash to buy goods from other nations, have been busily engaged in finding substitutes and methods of building up products synthetically, and they have been

Which Was the Longest Parliamentary Session?

In the early part of 1881 the House of Commons once sat continuously for 41 hours. The House met on Monday afternoon, January 31st, at 4 o'clock and went on without a break till Wednesday morning, February 2nd, after the clock had struck nine. Mr. Gladstone was Prime Minister at the time and the subject discussed was leave to bring in a Bill for the " Protection to Person and Property " in Ireland. It was a move against the Land League, and the Irish members tried to weary the House by obstruction. The obstruction was stopped by the Speaker forbidding further speeches on the subject. The Bill was then carried by 164 votes to 19. It is not unusual for members of the House of Commons to sit far into the night.

What is the Saying About Knowing and Not Knowing?

It is an old Arabian proverb as follows :

He who knows not and knows not that he knows not ; he is a fool, shun him.
He who knows not and knows that he knows not ; he is simple, teach him.
He who knows and knows not that he knows ; he is asleep, wake him.
He who knows and knows he knows ; he is wise, follow him.

How is the Speed Limit Ensured in Guatemala?

Mr. Joseph H. Jackson in his Travel Sketches in Guatemala, which he calls " Notes on a Drum," tells us that the Guatemalans have provided a very effective way of preventing road-speeding near their capital.

" Thirty-five minutes before you arrive at the outskirts of Guatemala City," he says, " a traffic officer stationed on the highway takes your licence number and telephones ahead. You must not take less than the specified time to get there ; if you do, it is evidence that you have exceeded the speed limit and you are fined."

Do Floods Destroy Bridges?

Yes ; when a river is in flood and the water rushes at great speed, it sometimes undermines the foundations of a bridge and the bridge collapses. This happened to more than one bridge in California during the terrible floods in March, 1938, which did millions of dollars' worth of damage. The photographs on this page show that a bad flood can be as destructive as an air-raid.

The raging waters of the Los Angeles River during the floods of March, 1938, with the wrecked Southern Pacific Railway Bridge

remarkably successful. They have produced wool from fish, cork mats from potato peelings, and petrol from brown coal. Their artificial rubber tires are said to last longer than those made of real rubber.

Who Was the Literary Leather-Dresser?

He was Thomas Dowse, a famous bibliophile of Cambridgeport, Massachusetts, who lived from 1772 to 1856. He was a currier by trade, but in recognition of his scholarly work Harvard conferred on him the degree of LL.D. This was facetiously interpreted by Edward Everett Hale as " Literary Leather-Dresser."

Another bridge at Los Angeles wrecked by the terrible floods of 1938

How Old is the Game of Chess?

THIS fine game appears to have been played for at least fourteen centuries. A game very much like modern chess can be traced back to the 6th century A.D., and is mentioned in Indian and Persian literature at the beginning of the 7th century.

A game of chess in the 14th century, from an illuminated German manuscript. On the right is an early chessboard and chessmen

At one time it was thought the game was much older, but histories tracing it back to Ancient Troy and Egypt are merely fanciful, although some kind of a war game on a board was undoubtedly played in Egypt.

The game seems to have originated in India, whence it travelled to Persia, and the Mohammedan conquerors of the latter country brought it to Europe in the 7th century. It appears to have been played first of all in Italy and Spain, and then made its way through Germany to northern Europe.

It reached England with the Norman Conquest, and by the 13th century it was being played all over western Europe. During succeeding years the game was developed and improved. The queen and bishop, which had previously been weak pieces, were given greater powers, and the operation known as " castling " originated in the 16th century, when the game as played now came into existence.

The Arabs were skilful players as far back as the 9th century, but the great progress of the game was made in the 15th and 16th centuries in Europe, mainly by the Italians. By the 18th century France had taken the lead. Then in the 19th century England was supreme, and since that time various countries have provided champions.

In the 11th century many regarded chess as a form of dice-throwing. Cardinal Damianus, who became Pope Alexander II, was travelling with a Bishop of Florence.

" In the morning," he says, writing to the reigning Pope, " I was informed by my servant that the aforesaid bishop had been playing at the game of chess, which information like an arrow pierced my heart very acutely. ' Was it well,' I asked, ' was it worthy of the character you bear, to spend the evening in the vanity of chess play, and defile the hands and tongue which ought to be the mediator between man and the Deity ? Are you not aware that by the canonical law bishops who are dice players are ordered to be deposed ? '

" He, however, making himself a shield of defence from the difference in the names, said that dice was one thing, and chess another ; consequently that the canon only forbade dice, but that it tacitly allowed chess. To which I replied : ' Chess is not named in the text, but the general term of dice comprehends both games.' "

Beautifully carved chessmen exist dating back to the 12th and 13th centuries. The chess-boards were large, and were sometimes made of precious metals and other rich materials.

Chaucer refers to the game, and Caxton printed his " Boke of Chesse" in 1474, his idea being to publish a moral treatise, and not to furnish his countrymen

Icelandic chessmen of the 12th century

with a book of instructions in the game. James I discouraged the playing of chess as a " philosophical folly."

An attempt to bring it into more notice had been made early in the reign of Elizabeth, under the patronage of Lord Robert Dudley, afterwards the celebrated Earl of Leicester, who liked refinements of this sort.

How Many Varieties of Pet Mice Are There?

AT the National Mice Club Show many varieties of mice are exhibited. They differ greatly in colour and among those described are blue mice, chocolate mice, champagne mice, red mice, fawn mice, silver mice, black mice, multi-coloured mice, and even mice-coloured mice. Of course, there are the usual white mice with or without patches of other colours.

At the Show in 1937 there were about 900 entrants, coming from places as far apart as Cornwall and Scotland. Great Britain is the chief breeding centre for prize mice.

What Was the Agapemone?

THE word means the Abode of Love, and the name was given to an establishment founded in 1848 in Somersetshire by Henry James Price and a Mr. Starkey for a new sect which they organised, called alternatively the Agapemonites, Princeites and Starkey-ites. The object of the abode was stated by its founders to be perpetual joy. Sorrow, sickness and pain were to be banished and all the members were to have no will or design of their own. More than once events at the Somersetshire establishment and at an Agapemonite Church in London led to great popular ferments. As a small sect the Agapemone still exists.

Is the Length of the Day Changing?

IT is probably changing, but very slightly indeed. There are two causes which tend to make the day longer. The effect of the tides is to lessen the speed of the Earth's rotation gradually and that, of course, would lengthen the day. Then the resistance caused by meteorites as they strike the Earth also tends to slow down the speed of rotation and lengthen the day.

But to counteract these tendencies there are others which would make the day shorter. The Earth is slowly shrinking, and as it gets smaller its speed of rotation would be increased and the day become shorter. Also the wearing down of the mountain peaks and ranges by weathering tends to speed up the rotation of the Earth and shorten the day. The one tendency almost balances the other.

Why Are the Morning and Evening Cool?

THE morning and evening of a hot summer day are always cooler than the middle of the day. The reason is that in the middle of the day the Sun's rays are striking us more or less directly, whereas in the morning and evening the rays slant very much. This means that at noon and round about, the same number of rays will be concentrated on a much smaller area than when they strike slantingly, and so each square foot of ground receives much more heat.

Had Shakespeare a Brother?

YES, he had a younger brother, Edmund, who came to London as an actor and he was helped by William. When he died he was buried in what is now Southwark Cathedral, and in the monthly parochial accounts there is an entry : " 1607, December 31st. Edmund Shakespeare, a player, buried in ye Church with a forenoone knell of the great bell, 20s."

It is believed that William defrayed the funeral expenses of his young brother. A portrait of Edmund is to be seen in a memorial window in the Cathedral, together with the figures of Shakespeare and Edmund Spenser.

Do We Know the World is Round?

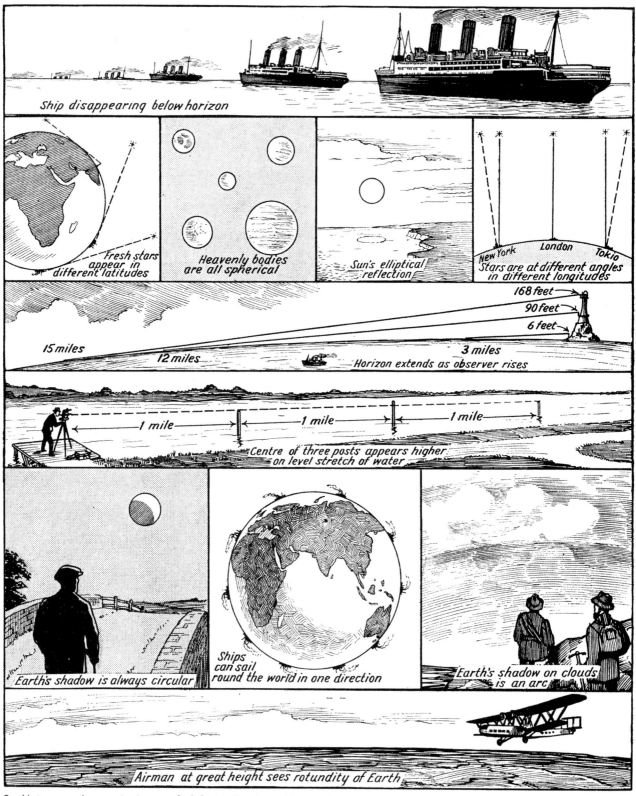

Ship disappearing below horizon

Fresh stars appear in different latitudes

Heavenly bodies are all spherical

Sun's elliptical reflection

Stars are at different angles in different longitudes

New York   London   Tokio

168 feet
90 feet
6 feet

15 miles   12 miles   3 miles   Horizon extends as observer rises

1 mile   1 mile   1 mile

Centre of three posts appears higher on level stretch of water

Earth's shadow is always circular

Ships can sail round the world in one direction

Earth's shadow on clouds is an arc

Airman at great height sees rotundity of Earth

On this page are shown various reasons for believing that the world is round and not flat. If it were flat the hulls of receding ships would be seen last, but actually the funnels and masts disappear last. With a flat world all countries would see the same stars. All other heavenly bodies appear to be round. Careful measurements have shown that the Sun throws a slightly elliptical reflection on the sea. Only on a curved world can the stars appear at different angles to countries in the same latitude. The widening of the horizon as we rise higher is consistent with a round world. The experiment of the three posts on a level stretch of water has been carried out more than once. The middle post appearing higher could only occur on a curved surface. The Earth's shadow cast on the clouds has been seen as an arc, and recently airmen at a height of 72,395 feet have actually seen the curvature of the Earth. The cumulative effect of all this evidence seems to be overwhelming for the belief that the world is round

Were Shakespeare's Plays Successful?

YES, the plays he wrote were very popular and highly successful in his day. They were played before Queen Elizabeth and other distinguished people, and from them and his acting he made an income equal to £1,000 a year in our values. That he saved money was proved by the fact that he returned to his birthplace at Stratford-on-Avon and bought the largest house in the town, known as New Place, put it into proper repair and planted an orchard. He continued to prosper and had a financial interest in more than one London theatre. He spent his time between London and Stratford, and helped his father in his financial difficulties.

What is an Orderly Officer?

HE is the duty officer for the day. Every junior officer in a battalion takes it in turn to act as orderly officer. This means that he goes the rounds, inspects sentries, visits kitchens in barracks, and does similar duties.

Can the Elephant Stretch Its Trunk Horizontally?

YES; this wonderful organ, which combines the offices of nose and hand, can be placed in any position. It can be curled inwards to convey food to the mouth, or outwards to place straw or branches on its back. It can be swung in all directions and it can be stretched out in a perfectly

An elephant stretching out its trunk horizontally to receive a gift

horizontal line. The great mobility of the elephant's trunk is due to the fact that it is supplied with a vast number of muscles. Cuvier estimated the number as about forty thousand. But the trunk is not only exceedingly mobile, it is very strong, and is capable of lifting considerable weights.

What Was the Massacre of Amboyna?

AMBOYNA is one of the chief islands of the Moluccas which, after being settled by the Portuguese in the 16th century, was taken by the Dutch, who laid claim to all the Spice Islands. In 1612 the English East

India Company established a small settlement at Cambello in Amboyna. In the whole island there were only 20 English and 30 Japanese, besides 200 Dutch. The Dutch, being jealous, pretended that the English and Japanese had combined to expel them from the island, whereupon they seized Captain Towerson, with nine other Englishmen, nine Japanese and a Portuguese and, after torturing them, beheaded them. Eventually the Dutch paid £300,000 compensation.

How Did the Cinema Originate?

THE earliest form of moving picture was attained by viewing a series of slightly different drawings through a slit, as they were moved round rapidly. First of all the drawings were made on a disk, and the whole

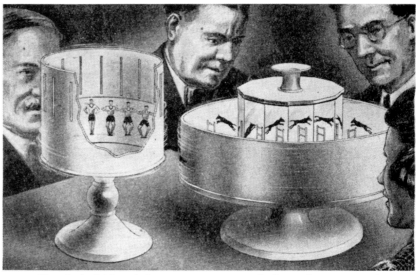

The wheel of life and the praxinoscope, two early forms of cinematograph

rotated, the pictures being viewed through slits in the disk from the other side, while they were reflected in a mirror. This instrument was called a fantascope, or phenakistoscope.

A more convenient form was the zoetrope, or wheel of life, the first apparatus shown in the accompanying drawing. This consisted of a cylinder with slits, in which a strip bearing the pictures was placed. When the cylinder was rotated the person looking through the slits saw the figures moving.

A great improvement on this was the praxinoscope, in which the observer looked into a mirror to see the moving picture. By arranging a series of mirrors round the centre of the instrument, as shown in the drawing, the beholder saw only one moving figure at a time, instead of many, as in the earlier instruments.

All these early forerunners of the cinematograph had forbidding names made up of Greek words.

How Do Bees Fertilize Flowers?

THE body of a bee is covered with hairs and these have tiny spikes on them. When the bee visits a flower to collect nectar, the pollen is caught by the hairs on the bee's body and, of course, when the insect flies away it carries the pollen with it. Then when it visits another flower the pollen is rubbed off, and should that flower be a female blossom it will be fertilised by the pollen which comes from a male flower. In that case the flower will produce seeds.

Can Any Plant Smell?

THE sundew, a little plant that grows in spongy bogs and heaths in England, is able to smell, as well as eat insects.

If a small piece of raw meat be suspended on a wire near the plant,

Sundew leaves reaching out towards a piece of meat which they can smell

the sundew soon becomes aware of its presence. The leaf, which is provided with tentacles that grip an insect and close round it, slowly reaches out towards the meat till at last it grasps this. Photographs have been taken showing how the leaf rises and moves towards the meat, taking over an hour to do so.

Who Was the World's Greatest Genius?

IT is generally agreed that there has never lived another man who was so great and versatile a genius as Leonardo da Vinci. He is known to the general public as a great artist, the painter of the Last Supper and the Mona Lisa. But he was much more than a painter; he was sculptor, architect, engineer and scientist. Indeed, it has been said that there was nothing that Leonardo did not study. He was a geologist before the days of geology, and it is known that he worked, among other things, on the ideas of submarine boats, diving apparatus, poison gas, armoured cars, propulsion by steam, wireless telegraphy and aeroplanes. It is seriously believed by some scientists that in astronomy he anticipated Galileo and Newton, in anatomy Harvey, and in mathematics Einstein. In fact, his manuscripts and rough sketches contain the germs of many if not most of our modern inventions. But it was not merely in the physical sciences that he

was a great thinker on modern lines; he was equally a moralist and was perhaps the first man to describe war as a "bestial frenzy." His invention of war devices was in the interests of freedom and against the plots and plans of dictators. Of Leonardo da Vinci, more than of any other man who has ever lived, may be used Dryden's words:

A man so various that he seem'd to be
Not one but all mankind's epitome.

What Was Canister Shot?

THIS consisted of a metal cylinder containing explosive and small lead or iron balls. It was sometimes called case-shell, and is now obsolete. It was fired from light guns.

Have Eastern Windmills Many Sails?

YES, the windmills used in the east of Europe and in Asia are very different from those seen in England and Holland. They generally have many sails, and in China some of the large windmills have sails that radiate horizontally instead of vertically. Often the vertical sails are in the form of a wheel, and an example will be seen in the photograph given on this page, which shows a windmill in the Italian island of Kos in the Aegean Sea. The sails are of canvas stretched on a frame, and the device has very much the appearance of a dilapidated umbrella.

A strange-looking windmill on the island of Kos in the Aegean Sea

Who Were the Nihilists?

IN the old Tsarist Russia Nihilism was a movement which started originally as an opposition to the social customs of matrimony, parental authority and the tyranny of fashion. In course of time it became a secret political movement whose purpose was to overturn the Government and the existing order of things. Starting in the universities, it spread about 1870 among the working classes, and when the Government tried to suppress the movement it developed into a terrorist organisation and in 1881 caused the assassination of the Tsar Alexander II. Attempts were made on the lives of later tsars and many assassinations resulted. It continued as a movement till the Great War.

Who Invented the Idea of Summer Time?

IT was William Willett, a builder of Chislehurst, Kent, who thought of the idea of providing an extra hour of daylight enjoyment for all, by putting the clocks and watches on one hour in spring and putting them back an hour in the autumn. Willett said: "If people can adjust their watches at sea, day by day, without discomfort, why not on land twice a year?" A writer says: "People rocked with laughter at his silliness." Probably the brilliant idea would never have been tried had not the Great War come, bringing the necessity for economising artificial light. Unfortunately Willett died on March 4th, 1915, rather more than a year before the first Summer Time Act became law on May 17th, 1916.

On August 7th, 1925, the Daylight Saving Act was made permanent and fixed that summer time should begin at 2 o'clock Greenwich mean time on the morning of the day following the third Saturday in April. If, however, that day is Easter Day, then the change is made on the day following the second Saturday. Summer time ends at 2 o'clock Greenwich mean time on the morning of the day next following the first Saturday in October. The Act applies to Great Britain, Northern Ireland, the Channel Islands and the Isle of Man.

A memorial to William Willett has been set up in Pett's Wood, on the south-eastern outskirts of London.

How Far Down Can a Diver Work?

IN the ordinary rubber diving-suit and helmet divers work at depths of over 200 feet, but for great depths like that at which the *Egypt's* gold was recovered, namely over 420 feet, something more is needed owing to the enormous pressure of the water acting on the diver. At 400 feet the pressure on the body is over 150 tons and the diver has to work in what is known as a "shell" diving-suit, so called because the suit is as the shell to the lobster or crab, and takes the whole weight of the water. The shell suits are really huge metal cases and

the diver is unable to use his hands in the ordinary way because they are inside the shell. What he does is to operate mechanical "fingers," with which he can pick up objects, tie knots in a rope, and do a few other things. He can even use an oxy-acetylene torch under water to cut away the metal plates of the sunken ship upon which he is working.

The shell is lowered by a steel cable, while inside the diver breathes air at atmospheric pressure. This means that he can be brought up from the greatest depth to which the shell can descend as fast as the winch will turn. An ordinary diver in a rubber suit breathes compressed air and must gradually pass through a process known as decompression till at last he can breathe ordinary air.

The deep sea diver carries with him his own supply of oxygen compressed in two cylinders behind him, and he regulates the supply by turning on a tap. As he inhales, air enters through a little non-return valve in front of the mouthpiece. The air which he exhales goes into a tube and passes through an absorber containing caustic soda, which extracts the carbon-dioxide. The air then passes out into the interior of the diving-case, where it mixes with oxygen from the cylinders. A telephone enables him to communicate with those above, and a lamp is let down to enable him to see. He also carries a powerful electric torch. The diver when at work wears a suit of thick woollen material to keep him warm.

The shell diving-suits are being constantly

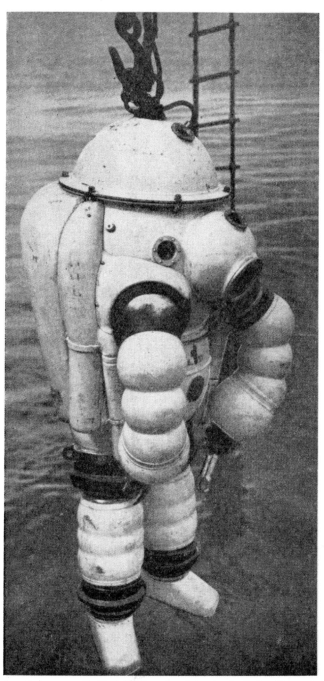

An apparatus used in 1938 for deep-sea diving by the Italian Navy. It enables the diver to work at a depth of 750 feet

improved, and one recently invented by Signor Galeazzi, an Italian, is said to enable divers to descend and work at a depth of 750 feet.

How Long is a Glacier?

GLACIERS vary a good deal in length, but though they are often called rivers of ice, there are no very long glaciers as there are rivers of water. In the mighty Himalayas, where there are thousands of glaciers, none is known longer than sixty miles. In the Alps there are nearly two thousand glaciers, and only one is as long as ten miles. Fewer than forty have a length of five miles, and the great majority are not more than a mile long. Some are only a few hundred feet wide, but one or two are a mile in width, and at the thickest parts these Alpine glaciers are only a few hundred feet deep. In the St. Elias range in Alaska there is a glacier seventy miles long and nearly twenty-five miles wide.

When, as in Greenland, the glacier takes the form of a large field of ice spreading in all directions from its centre and forming a kind of circular glacier it is called an ice-cap or ice-sheet. The ice-cap in Greenland is about a mile thick.

What Was the Most Ridiculous Index Entry?

IT is said that in a law book the index contained an entry, "Best, Mr. Justice, his great mind," and on turning up the page referred to one found the sentence, "Mr. Justice Best said he had a great mind to commit the witness for prevarication." It is sometimes stated that this entry occurs in the index to Binns' "Justice," but it is not there.

Another classical example of the ridiculous in an index is:

> Mill on Liberty,
> Mill on the Floss.

Cross-references are often a source of trouble as in a botany book where, under Birch tree, we read "see Betula," and under Betula "see Birch tree."

In Professor St. George Mivart's "Origin of Human Reason," on the other hand, a trifling story about a cockatoo has no fewer than fifteen entries, as follows:

Absurd tale about a Cockatoo, 136.
Anecdote, absurd one about a Cockatoo, 136.
Bathos and a Cockatoo, 136.
Cockatoo, absurd tale concerning one, 136.
Discourse held with a Cockatoo, 136.
Incredibly absurd tale of a Cockatoo, 136.
Invalid Cockatoo, absurd tale about, 136.
Mr. R—— and tale about a Cockatoo, 136.
Preposterous tale about a Cockatoo, 136.
Questions answered by a Cockatoo, 136.
R——, Mr., and tale about a Cockatoo, 136.
Rational Cockatoo, as asserted, 136.
Tale about a rational Cockatoo, as asserted, 136.
Very absurd tale about a Cockatoo, 136.
Wonderfully foolish tale about a Cockatoo, 136.

This, of course, is indexing gone mad.

How is Cider Made?

CIDER is fermented apple-juice, and its use can be traced back for many centuries in Europe. France is the chief cider-producing country, but much cider is made in England, the counties of Devonshire, Somerset, Gloucestershire, Herefordshire, Kent and Norfolk being noted for their ciders.

The apples used for cider are small in size and are of three kinds, sour, sweet and bitter-sweet. These are generally carefully blended in making the cider. The apples, which grow on standard trees, are allowed to ripen and are then shaken down on the ground and left there or placed under cover till they are ready for milling.

There are two different kinds of cider mills for pulping the apples. In one the fruit is crushed between stone rollers, while in the other it is grated by means of a revolving drum armed with sharp teeth. The apple pulp is known as pomace, and from it the juice is pressed and is allowed to stand in an open vat till any solid matter has risen and formed a scum, which is then skimmed off. The skimming process is known as keeving, and it is continued till the juice is clear, when it is transferred to a fermenting cask. If sweet cider is desired the fermented juice is removed and filtered before the specific gravity falls below 1·025; but for dry cider it is left till the specific gravity falls below 1·015. It is sweet cider that is most popular in England, and this contains less than four per cent. of alcohol. Dry cider may have as much as seven per cent., and this is the variety preferred in France.

Cider has always been popular in the West of England, especially among those who do not care for strong alcoholic liquors.

Who Are the Spiritual Peers?

THEY are 26 Anglican prelates who sit in the House of Lords. The Archbishops of Canterbury and York, and the Bishops of London, Durham and Winchester always have seats.

Driven soil, carried by the wind, in danger of covering the railway lines at Boise City, Oklahoma, in the United States

but the other bishops take vacancies in the order of seniority, as in addition to the five prelates mentioned only 21 others can sit, and there are more bishops than that. Thus, there are always some bishops who have no seats in the House of Lords and consequently take no part in legislation.

Is the World's Soil Deteriorating?

PROFESSOR J. A. SCOTT WATSON has declared that there is distinct evidence of the widespread deterioration of the world's soils, especially in the last sixty or seventy years. During the past sixty years, he said, the consumer had enjoyed the benefit of relatively abundant food at low prices. In part this cheap abundance had been achieved through the progress of farming, but in considerable part it had been obtained at the cost of depleting the fertility of the soils.

Wasteful methods of farming, in the United States and Canada particularly and the cutting down of trees there, have resulted in the fertile soil over large areas being carried away by the wind and the formation of what are known as dust bowls—that is, areas where dust carried often for hundreds of miles has overwhelmed fertile land.

In some districts it would be very difficult to make the land as valuable as it once was, but in other areas the fertility might be restored were it not for the poverty of the farming class, who have no money to expend on the necessary work of supplying fertilisers.

What is St. Anthony's Fire?

IT is an old name for erysipelas, an acute inflammatory disease of the skin, which became an especially destructive pestilence in France and Germany between the years 994 and 1089. It appeared in England in 1011 and 1012. Hugh Capet, the founder of the French Capetian dynasty, died of the complaint.

It was called St. Anthony's Fire because Pope Urban IV in 1089 founded an order of St. Anthony to look after those thus afflicted.

A typical old Gloucester cider mill at work at Bishop's Cleeve

What is That File Used For?

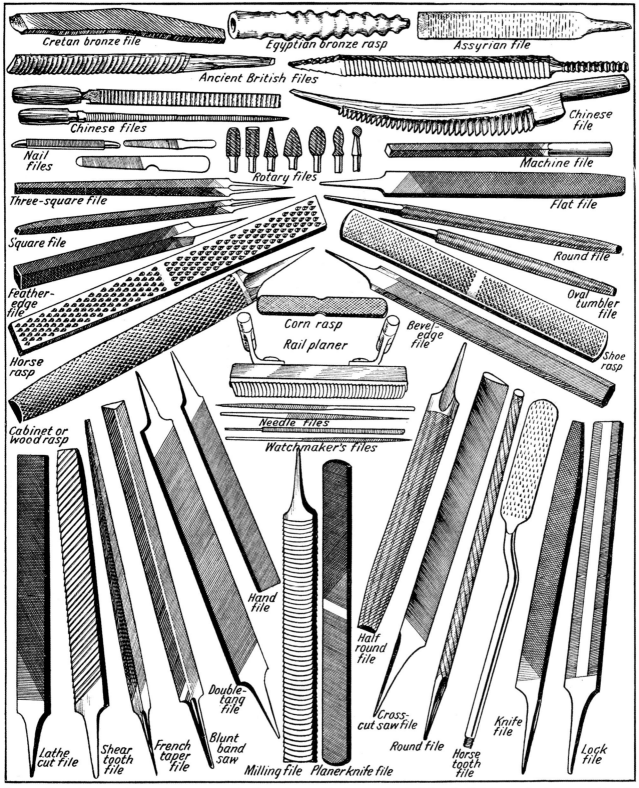

Cretan bronze file

Egyptian bronze rasp

Assyrian file

Ancient British files

Chinese files

Chinese file

Nail files

Rotary files

Machine file

Three-square file

Flat file

Square file

Round file

Feather-edge file

Oval tumbler file

Corn rasp

Rail planer

Bevel-edge file

Horse rasp

Shoe rasp

Cabinet or wood rasp

Needle files

Watchmaker's files

Hand file

Half round file

Lathe cut file

Shear tooth file

French taper file

Blunt band saw

Double-tang file

Cross-cut saw file

Round file

Horse tooth file

Knife file

Lock file

Milling file

Planer knife file

Here are files and rasps used for various purposes. The file can be traced back many centuries before the Christian era, but it is not as old as the saw. In the upper part of this page are some ancient files, and, as can be seen, they closely resemble those made today, though, of course, their workmanship is crude compared with modern tools. The Egyptians, twelve centuries before Christ, made small rasps of bronze, and bronze files have also been dug up in Crete. From the statement in the Book of Proverbs that " iron sharpeneth iron," it has been inferred that there were iron files in King Solomon's time. Files are also mentioned in Homer's Odyssey. The Assyrians, Greeks, Romans, Chinese and Ancient Indians all used files. The making of files and rasps is now a huge industry, in which elaborate machinery is used, although up to comparatively recent times these tools were made by hand. Files are prepared by cutting many lines across the face of a flat piece of iron, to leave points sticking up. In preparing this page the artist received the courteous assistance of Messrs. Buck & Hickman, Limited, the toolmakers, of Whitechapel, London

How Can a Steel Bar Be Magnetised?

A STEEL bar or needle can be magnetised by stroking it with another magnet or two magnets, and some of the methods of stroking are shown in the drawing on this page. In the first method, known as that of single touch, the pole of a single powerful magnet is moved from one end to the other of the bar, and after a time the bar itself becomes a magnet.

In the second and third drawings we see how a bar can be magnetised by stroking it from the middle to one end with one pole of a magnet, and then from the middle to the other end with the opposite pole of the magnet. The middle drawing shows

touching one another by a piece of wood. The two magnets combined are then drawn together backwards and forwards along the whole length of the bar, beginning and ending at the centre.

For magnetising with a horseshoe magnet the method shown in the bottom left-hand drawing is followed. Of course, a bar of steel can be magnetised by coiling wire round it and passing a current through the wire. It is then known as an electro-magnet.

When a bar of steel is transformed into a magnet, it is believed that the molecules, which were previously arranged in a haphazard fashion, become lined up in an orderly and regular way,

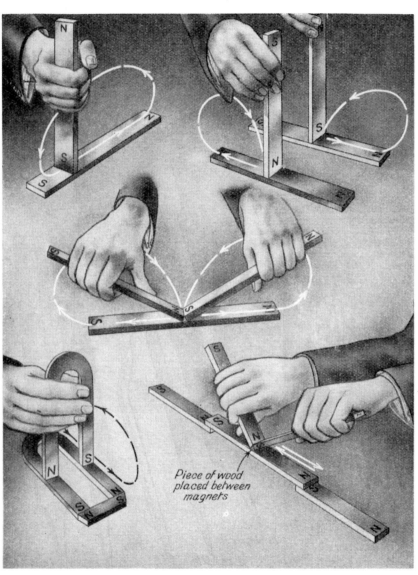

Different ways of making a magnet by using existing magnets

a method of doing this by using two magnets at once. This plan is called that of divided or separate touch.

Another method of using two magnets is to incline them at an angle, as shown in the bottom right-hand drawing, and prevent them from

with all their north poles pointing in one direction, and the south poles in the other. Ampère, the French scientist, suggested that every molecule in a magnet has an electric current circulating round it continuously, and that this makes each molecule a magnet.

Is Mars Inhabited?

No one can, of course, say, but there has been much speculation, chiefly because of certain markings on the planet which have been called canals.

Some astronomers have suggested that these are wholly or in part mere optical illusions, but it is generally agreed that the markings do actually exist. At the poles of Mars there are white caps which are supposed to be either frozen water or carbon dioxide. At certain seasons these melt, and then the so-called canals grow more distinct. This has led to the supposition that they may be channels which fill with water at certain seasons, and, although we do not see the watercourses themselves, a wide band of vegetation of some kind springs into being along their course owing to the seasonal irrigation. Professor Lowell and other astronomers have thought from the fact that the " canals " are so straight that they must be the work of intelligent beings.

Who is Old Nick?

This is a name often used for the Devil. It has an interesting history. Sometimes it is said to be taken from Nicholas or Niccolo Machiavelli, of Florence, the author of a cynical work on government called " The Prince." But this cannot be, as the term existed long before the time of Machiavelli. It is probably taken from the Scandinavian mythology, where Nick or Nikken is a water-wraith or kelpie dwelling in lake or river, and Grimm says the word refers to the evil spirit of the North. The etymology from Nicholas Machiavelli is referred to in Butler's Hudibras :

Nick Machiavel had ne'er a trick
(Though he gives name to our Old Nick).

What Are the Nine Points of the Law?

The nine points of the law which insure success in a lawsuit have been described as a good deal of money, a good deal of patience, a good cause, a good lawyer, a good counsel, good witnesses, a good jury, a good judge, and good luck. It is often said that " possession is nine points of the law."

Why is a Hunter Called a Nimrod?

The name is taken from the name of a Bible character, a son of Cush, who in Genesis x, 8–10 is described as " a mighty hunter before the Lord." The meaning of the name is not known, but some Assyriologists identify Nimrod with Gilgamesh, the principal hero of the ancient Babylonian legends, or " Nimrod Epic " as it is called. Pope says of him that he was a mighty hunter and his prey was man. The name was taken as a nom-de-plume by Charles James Apperley, a famous writer of hunting articles.

What Are the Anglers of the Deep Sea?

Far down in the sea, at a depth of 1,500 feet or more, there is complete darkness, except for the light given by certain luminous creatures. All the fish at these depths are carnivorous—that is, they live on one another, or on prawns and other small creatures that inhabit those regions. The absence of light means that there is no plant life at such depths.

Of course, the pressure of the water at these depths is enormous, and if the fish living there are brought up rapidly they often burst, owing to the removal of the pressure. But when they are caught and brought up slowly they arrive in perfect condition.

Of all the deep-sea fishes known, the strangest and most interesting are the angler fishes. They are so called because the first ray of their dorsal fins is placed on the head, and is modified into a line or bait, which will attract the creatures on which they feed.

colour harmonising with the ground on which they rest, so that they are not seen.

But the anglers of the deep sea are much more grotesque in appearance. They are blackish in colour, and at the end of their fishing-line there is generally a bulb-like swelling that contains a gland, and this has a luminous secretion. Scientists think that the light can be switched on or off at will.

There are sixty known species of these deep-sea anglers. Most of them have enormous mouths in proportion to their size, and they are provided with sharp teeth which can be depressed when their mouths are open,

so that their victims pass inside without trouble. The moment, however, they are in, the teeth become erect, and hold the victim so that there is no escape.

Another extraordinary thing about these creatures is that they can distend their bodies and are able to swallow fishes many times their own size, simply stretching to accommodate them.

Specimens of the Linophryne, shown in the photograph, have been found at the surface of the ocean, swollen out by the large fishes they have swallowed. In all these cases the victim had been seized by the tail, and probably the angler fish was unable to let go as the fish swam upwards.

No doubt the luminous bait is

This deep-sea angler fish, *Gigantactis*, carries a remarkable fishing-line which is four times its own length

moved about to imitate the swimming movement of a small luminous animal. In one genus the line ends in a triangle of hooks, and, as Mr. Regan says, "This fish, with rod, line, bait and hooks, is certainly a Compleat Angler, and should perhaps have been named after Izaak Walton."

In one species, shown in the photograph, the female's husband attaches himself to her head and remains in that position for the rest of his life. If his wife dies, he dies with her, as he is no longer able to feed.

A strange-looking angler fish of the deep sea, *Linophryne*. The attachment on its nose is a luminous lure

There are angler fishes round our coasts, and these lie in wait for their prey at the bottom of the sea, their

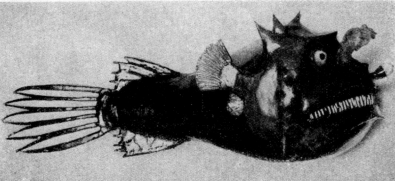

This ugly female angler fish, *Photocorynus*, has her mate permanently affixed to her forehead. He can be seen in front just above the light bulb

Are Turtles Born on Sea or Land?

TURTLES are entirely marine in their habits and only resort to the shore for the purpose of breeding. They select low, sandy coasts, preferably those on uninhabited islands, and after laying their eggs leave them to be incubated by the Sun's heat. The size of the eggs can be seen in the photograph on this page, which shows three young turtles about to

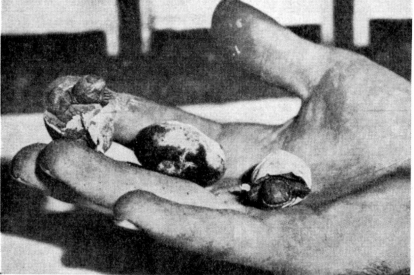

Turtle eggs, from which the young turtles are just emerging

hatch out of eggs held in a man's hand. The young as soon as they are hatched make for the sea, but many fall victims to birds, land crabs and predaceous fish of various kinds.

While tortoises and terrapins have their feet more or less adapted for walking on land, the turtle's feet are converted into very efficient paddles.

How Did the Star Chamber Get Its Name?

THIS court of civil and criminal jurisdiction at Westminster, whose use was so abused by the early Stuart kings, received its name from a star which formed part of the decoration of the chamber in which it met. It had been in existence through many reigns, but in 1641 it was abolished on the ground that " the reasons and motives inducing the erection and continuance of that court do now cease." The Court of Star Chamber was really a judicial committee of the Privy Council, which tried prisoners without a jury and forced them to incriminate themselves. It was set up in Henry VII's reign and gradually became more and more oppressive. Its victims were often subjected to torture and it has been well said that " when the Star Chamber ceased to sit, the use of torture became unknown in England."

Can the Botanist Stop Water Famines?

YES, Professor E. J. Salisbury of London University declares that the botanist could do much in co-operation with the engineer to avert floods and also tragic droughts like that responsible for the American Dust Bowl. Such floods and droughts, said the professor, were " in no small degree capable of regulation by the proper utilisation of plant cover.

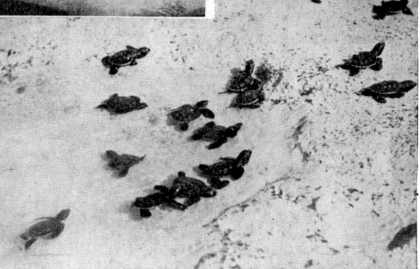

Young Hawksbill turtles that have just been hatched, instinctively making for the sea across the sands. Those on the left have encountered a pool on the way.

Afforestation of the catchment area of the Thames and other rivers would in the long run be perhaps far more effective and less costly as a guarantee against future floods or droughts than grand-scale engineering works, and whilst the former would produce ancillary assets of great value, the latter would not."

It is in many cases the cutting down of woods and forests that has given rise to the frequency of floods. The roots and undergrowth hold the water and prevent it reaching the rivers so rapidly as to cause floods, while in other parts the trees and grass hold the soil and prevent it from being blown away in times of drought.

What is MacFarlane's Lantern?

IT is a name given to the Moon. The MacFarlane clan occupied the fastnesses on the west side of Loch Lomond and used to prey upon the lowlands. Their raids were invariably made by night, and as they chose moonlight nights the Moon came to be called their lantern.

What Was a Fehmgerichte?

THIS was the term given to what are sometimes called the Secret Tribunals of Westphalia. In the 14th and 15th centuries in Germany, when the regular machinery of justice had become demoralised, these secret courts, which had their spies everywhere, summoned people before them, heard evidence and punished those convicted, often with death. Much mystery surrounded their operations, but even princes when summoned to appear dared not disobey. The penalty for non-attendance was death. Their judgments were sure, but no one could discover the executioner. They were really a kind of medieval Ku-Klux-Klan. At first they gave some real protection to the just, but as time went on they became corrupt and demoralized. With the increasing strength of regular governments they gradually disappeared. Sir Walter Scott has given an account of these secret tribunals in his novel "Anne of Gierstein." An alternative spelling is Vehmgerichte.

How Are Animal Voices Described ?

APES gibber, asses bray, beetles drone, bears growl, blackbirds whistle, cats mew, cocks crow, cows low, crows caw, deer bell, dogs bark, doves coo, ducks quack, foxes bark, frogs croak, geese hiss, grasshoppers chirp, hawks scream, hens cackle, horses neigh and whinny, hyenas laugh, jays chatter, lambs bleat, lions roar, magpies chatter, mice squeak, monkeys chatter, nightingales pipe, owls hoot and screech, oxen low, peacocks scream, pigs grunt, rooks caw, sheep baa, stags call, swans cry, tigers growl, turkey-cocks gobble, vultures scream, wolves howl.

Who Were the Muscadins of Paris?

THEY were dudes in the French Revolution who aped London men about town by wearing top-boots with thick soles, knee-breeches, a coat with long tails, a high stiff collar, and a thick cudgel. They even went so far as to imitate a huskiness of voice and a swaggering behaviour which were supposed to be characteristic of John Bull. Byron refers to them in his poem " Don Juan."

Does Flooding Spoil Land?

UNDOUBTEDLY it does. Not only does the soaking of the soil spoil it, but very often the flooding results in the land being covered with matter that does it harm. For example, large masses of clay may be left behind when the water retires. In 1938 when floods occurred in Suffolk some of the lumps of clay left behind on the grazing grounds by the receding waters weighed 5 tons each.

Who Were the Blackfeet ?

THIS was the popular name of the Sihasapa, a tribe of North American Indians of Sioux stock, who are to be distinguished from another tribe belonging to the Algonquin stock, the Siksika, who were also called

King's Counsel leaving the House of Lords after being sworn in

Blackfeet. Probably the name was a reference to the colour of their footwear. A single tribesman is called a Blackfoot and strictly the plural should be, not Blackfeet, but Blackfoots, which are known as moccasins and are made of deer-skin.

What is a K.C. ?

A K.C. or King's Counsel is a barrister appointed by letters patent to be his Majesty's Counsel learned in the law. He is said to be " called within the bar." The bar is a partition running across courts of law, behind which all outer-barristers and members of the public must stand. A King's Counsel in taking that rank is spoken of as "taking silk," because he wears a silk gown as distinct from the stuff gown of an ordinary barrister, renounces the preparation of written pleadings and other chamber practice. He must not be employed against the Crown, without special licence, which is not refused unless the Crown desires to be represented by the individual in the case. The selection of King's Counsel rests in practice with the Lord Chancellor. It is a great honour, but does not necessarily lead to an increased income. Some barristers with a lucrative practice prefer not to take silk when it is offered. Formerly King's Counsel received a small salary attached to the office, but that has been abolished. When the reigning sovereign is a queen these barristers are called Queen's Counsel or Q.C.s.

Who Was Moll Cutpurse ?

THIS was a nickname of Mary Frith, born in London in 1589, who became a notorious thief, pickpocket, bully, forger and fortune-teller. She is said to have been the first Englishwoman to use tobacco. On one occasion she attacked General Fairfax on Hounslow Heath, for which she was sent to Newgate. She escaped by bribery and eventually died of dropsy in the 75th year of her age.

Grazing marshes covered with large masses of clay, which were deposited when the river Alde burst its bank. Some of these masses weighed five tons

Where is That Maze? 32 Examples

Bayeux Cathedral

Hampton Court

Chartres Cathedral

Design by Boeckler

Abbey St. Bertin

Herbal labyrinth by Hill

Wisby Gothland

Sens Cathedral

Design by Commelyn

Design by De Vries

Bourn Church, Cambs.

Design by Mollet

Troy Town, Somerton

De Vries design

De Vries design

Boeckler design

Most people who have visited the sights in and around London have been to the maze at Hampton Court. Large numbers of visitors who make their way into the centre of the maze are unable to get out without help, but there is an unfailing method of getting in and out again. On entering, if a person turns so as to keep his right arm touching the bushes of the hedges, and continues all the time, never taking the right arm away from the bushes, he must eventually get into the centre, and if he continues inside the maze with his right arm still touching the bushes, and walks round and then out, he will eventually find his way out into the open once more. Of course, this method involves going up and down many of the lanes. For instance, on entering one turns to the right, and then comes back along the other side of the first lane, continuing along past the entrance once more. Mazes and labyrinths were very popular in the Middle Ages, both on the Continent and in England. In England they were chiefly cut in the turf or

216

From Different European Countries

Ely Cathedral

Maze by Nesfield

Rheims Cathedral

Boeckler design

Boeckler design

Sneinton

Design by Adam Islip

Theobalds, Herts

St Vitale, Ravenna

Boeckler design

Amiens Cathedral

Ripon

Boeckler design

Boeckler design

Herbal labyrinth by Hill

Lucca Cathedral

made with hedges, like the Hampton Court maze, but on the Continent they were mostly laid out in the tiling of cathedral floors. Similar tiled mazes are found in England, as in Ely Cathedral. Some of the mazes given on these pages still exist, others have disappeared, and others again are known only as designs in books like those by C. A. Boeckler, published in 1664, J. V. de Vries, 1583, and C. Commelyn, 1676. The labyrinth at Bourn Church, Cambridgeshire, is worked in black and red tiles, the centre being occupied by the font, the step of which forms the end of the path. The maze at Sneinton, Nottinghamshire, was called Robin Hood's Race, and its path was 535 yards long, or nearly a third of a mile. It was ploughed up in 1797. The labyrinth at Theobalds, in Hertfordshire, was in the garden, and was destroyed by the Roundheads in 1643. The Troy Town at Somerton, near Banbury in Oxfordshire, is situated in the garden of a farmhouse, and is surrounded by beautiful trees and shrubs

What Was the Peterloo Massacre?

It is the name given to a disturbance that occurred in Manchester on August 16th, 1819. A monster meeting in favour of parliamentary reform was held at St. Peter's Field, in spite of the prohibition of the magistrates. It was presided over by Orator Hunt, who had only just begun to speak when several troops of soldiers, 400 special constables, and the Cheshire and Manchester Yeomanry appeared and charged down upon the crowd, which fled. About a hundred were injured and six were killed. Hunt and nine others were arrested and tried for treasonable conspiracy. Hunt in his defence declared that "the magistrates desired nothing so much as an opportunity of letting loose the bloody butchers of Waterloo upon them," and the conflict came to be known as the Peterloo massacre.

Is the Sloth Slothful?

No, the name suggestive of slow movement is quite a misnomer, for the sloth is an expert climber, full of life, and it can move among the branches of the forest trees at a considerable speed. Its long limbs and its curved claws do not enable it to stand and move easily over the

ground. Probably the name was given to the animal by some who saw it, not in its native element—that is, among the branches of the trees—but on the ground, where it can scarcely move at all. As someone has said : "On the ground the sloth will not take more than thirty steps a day and will not go a mile in a month."

A keeper at the London Zoo supporting a sloth as it hangs upside down

What Was the Ottoman Empire?

This was the name given to the Turkish Dominions before the Great War, and they were so called because the Turkish Empire was founded and ruled by the Ottoman Turks, who obtained their name from Ottoman or Othman, their first Sultan, who reigned from 1288 to 1326. The original home of the Ottoman Turks was in Central Asia, but when they captured Constantinople, now called Istambul, in 1453, they succeeded to the Byzantine Empire. The height of their glory was reached in the 16th

A two-toed sloth hanging from a branch in its native haunts in Central America

century when their dominions extended over the greater part of south-eastern Europe and much of western Asia and northern Africa. The name Ottoman Empire is now dropped and the present capital of Turkey is Angora or Ankara in Asia. As a republic, the old Ottoman Empire has received a new lease of life under Kemal Pasha.

What is Ploughing the Sands?

It is a phrase that means doing at the expense of great time and pains work that will have no tangible result. The phrase was originated by the Earl of Oxford when he was Mr. H. H. Asquith, Home Secretary. Speaking at Birmingham on November 21st, 1894, in connection with the Bill for the Disestablishment of the Church in Wales, which it was freely stated would be thrown out by the House of Lords even if it passed the Commons, Mr. Asquith said, " That is a measure of so much complexity that even if it is

opposed, fairly opposed or discussed fairly and not at unreasonable length, it must occupy a considerable amount of time of the House of Commons. And what is the position ? That we shall be sitting through night after night, week after week, perhaps for a couple of months, discussing seriously and with the endeavour to arrive at a wise and statesmanlike conclusion the best way of settling this difficulty, on the removal of which the hearts of the vast bulk of the Welsh people are set, with the knowledge that all our time, all our labour and all our assiduity is as certain to be thrown away as if you were to plough the sands of the sea-shore, the moment that Bill reaches the Upper Chamber."

What is the Military Chest?

This was originally a strong iron or iron-bound chest in which the payment for the troops was kept, but now the term is applied to military funds generally and to the payment organisation of an army or regiment.

What Was the Muscat Incident?

IN 1862 Great Britain and France agreed to respect the independence of Muscat, but in 1899 the Sultan of Muscat granted a piece of land five miles from Muscat to a French agent

The position of Muscat in Arabia

for a coal depot. On this a fort could have been erected and a naval harbour constructed. The British Government protested and then sent a squadron which threatened to bombard Muscat. The concession was thereupon revoked. The 1862 treaty had made certain stipulations about the alienation of territory which the Sultan had broken, although he was receiving a pension from the Indian Government. Great Britain explained that she had no objection to France having a coaling station in Muscat provided there was no concession.

Who Was Casabianca?

THIS was the name of the captain of a French man-of-war, *L'Orient*, at the battle of Aboukir in 1798. His name was Louis and he was a Corsican by birth. He had with him on the ship his young son Giacomo Jocante, and when the ship was likely to be captured Casabianca, having first secured the safety of his crew, blew up the ship to prevent it falling into the hands of the English. His son, refusing to leave him, perished with his father. Mrs. Hemans wrote a ballad on the subject, modifying the incident, however, and two French poets, Lebrun and Chénier, have also celebrated the event.

What Was the Dun Cow of Dunsmore Heath?

DUNSMORE HEATH is a moorland track in East Warwickshire, and the Dun Cow was a savage beast said to have been slain by Sir Guy, Earl of Warwick, an Anglo-Danish hero of marvellous strength. His exploits include, in addition to the slaughter of the Dun Cow, the killing of a boar of "passing might and strength" at Windsor, and of a dragon with lion's paws, wings, and a hide which no sword could pierce in Northumberland.

The story of the Dun Cow is that it belonged to a giant and was kept on Mitchell Fold, Shropshire. Its milk was inexhaustible, but one day an old woman, who had already filled her pail, wanted to fill her sieve also. This made the cow so angry that she broke loose and went to Dunsmore Heath where she was slain by Sir Guy. Dr. Isaac Taylor says that Dun Cow is a corruption of Dena Gau or Danish settlement, and that Sir Guy's real exploit was a victory over the Danes. At Harwich Castle a huge tusk, probably that of an elephant, is still shown as one of the horns of the Dun Cow.

How Many Oecumenical Councils Have There Been?

THERE were nine eastern councils and twelve western councils of the Church. The eastern were those of Jerusalem, mentioned in the Acts of the Apostles, Nice in 325 and 787, Constantinople in 381, 553, 680, 869, Ephesus in 431 and Chalcedon in 451. The western councils were those of the Lateran in 1123, 1139, 1179, 1215 and 1517; the Synods of Lyon in 1245 and 1274; the Synod of Vienne in Dauphine in 1311; Constance in 1414; Basil in 1431 to 1443; Trent 1545 to 1563; and the Vatican 1869. Of these the Anglican Church recognises only the first six in addition to that of Jerusalem, namely Nice 325, Constantinople 381, Ephesus 431, Chalcedon 451, Constantinople 553, and Constantinople 680.

How Long is a Year on Mars?

THE orbit of the planet Mars being outside that of the Earth is, of course, much greater. Its diameter is half as much again as that of the Earth and at its greatest distance from the Sun the planet is 154,860,000 miles away, while at its nearest it is 128,440,000 miles from the Sun. The Earth's greatest distance from the Sun is 94,524,000 miles, and its least distance 91,406,000 miles. To complete its journey round the Sun Mars takes not 365¼ days as does the Earth, but 687 of our days, so that its year is nearly twice as long as ours. Mars turns on its axis in 24 hours 37 minutes 22·7 seconds, so that its day is only a little longer than that of the Earth. Mars is the only heavenly body beside the Earth and the Moon whose exact period of rotation is known.

How Big Can a Tortoise Grow?

TORTOISES of different species vary enormously in size. While the giant tortoises of the Seychelles and Galapagos Islands have shells sometimes six feet long and weigh over a ton and a half, other species, like the spider tortoise of Madagascar and the Carolina box-tortoise of North America, are only a little over four inches long. Greek tortoises grow to six inches.

A giant tortoise from the Seychelle Islands, weighing over a ton and a half and reputed to be several hundred years old, with a Greek tortoise on its back

Does Any British Railway Employ Sheep-Dogs?

Yes; sheep-dogs are officially employed by the Great Western Railway as gangers on parts of the system in South Wales where sheep from the mountains are liable to stray on the line. Each morning at Talywain, near Pontypool, for instance, Jack, the dog belonging to a ganger,

A sheepdog which accompanies Great Western Railway workers at Talywain in South Wales each morning to clear the line of straying sheep, cows and horses

has to clear the track of lambs, sheep, cows and horses that have strayed on to the line. These railway sheep-dogs are taught to lie down flat in the centre of the track when a train is coming, so that it may pass over them without hurting them.

Who Was the Arbiter Elegentiarum?

This was a title given to Petronius, the director-in-chief of the pleasures and amusements of Nero. He was the author of a volume of Satires, only part of which exists today. In A.D. 66 Nero compelled him to kill himself. The Polish author, Henryk Sienkiewicz, makes Petronius Arbiter one of the vivid characters of his novel "Quo Vadis?"

Beau Nash is often called the Arbiter Elegentiarum of Bath in the 18th century.

Who Was Aeneas?

He was the great Trojan hero in Homer's story of the Iliad. The son of Anchises and Aphrodite or Venus, he was born on Mount Ida. It was not till Achilles attacked him on Mount Ida and drove away his flocks that he took part in the Trojan War, and led the Dardanians, among whom he was brought up, against the Greeks. From that time Aeneas and Hector appeared as the great bulwarks

of the Trojans against the Greeks. The gods loved Aeneas, and on more than one occasion saved him in battle. On the capture of Troy by the Greeks Aeneas carried his father Anchises on his shoulders from the burning city.

Aeneas and his descendants reigned at Troy after the extinction of the house of Priam. According to later stories, after the capture of Troy Aeneas withdrew to Mount Ida, and then crossing over to Europe settled at Latium in Italy, where he became the ancestral hero of the Romans. Virgil's Aeneid describes the wanderings of Aeneas before he reached Latium. Eventually Aeneas fell in battle against the Rutulians. The story of the descent of the Romans from the Trojans through Aeneas has no historical basis.

What is the Story of the Kilkenny Cats?

Dr. Brewer gives the origin of the expression "to fight like Kilkenny cats" as follows. "During the rebellion of Ireland," he says, "Kilkenny was garrisoned by a troop of Hessian soldiers, who amused themselves in barracks by tying two cats together by their tails and throwing them across a clothes-line to fight.

"The officers, hearing of this, resolved to put a stop to the practice. The look-out man, enjoying the sport, did not observe the officer on duty approaching the barracks; but one of the troopers, more quick-sighted, seizing a sword, cut the two tails and the cats made their escape. When the officer inquired the meaning of the two bleeding tails he was told that two cats had fought and devoured each other all but the tails." Another explanation is given on page 549.

What is a Mixed Metaphor?

A metaphor is a figure of speech in which a word or phrase is used to describe something entirely different from the idea which it usually expresses. Examples are "the curtain of night," "the ocean of life," "all Nature smiled." A mixed metaphor is the mixing up in the same sentence or sentences of various entirely different figures of speech of this kind. In its extreme form it is the so-called Irish bull.

In the House of Commons a member once declared that "it only required a spark to let slip the dogs of war." An Irish speaker said, "We will burn all our ships and, with every sail unfurled, steer boldly out into the ocean of freedom." A judge addressing students in Vienna declared "the chariot of the revolution is rolling along and gnashing its teeth as it rolls." Addressing the Emperor William I soon after the proclamation of the German Empire at Versailles a Rhineland mayor said, "No Austria! No Prussia! One only Germany! Such were the words the mouth of your imperial majesty has always had in its eye." It is clear, therefore, that mixed metaphors are uttered by people of many nationalities.

But many poets and distinguished authors are guilty of writing mixed metaphors. Shakespeare himself makes Hamlet say:

Whether 'tis nobler in the mind to suffer
The slings and arrows of outrageous fortune,
Or to take arms against a sea of troubles,
And by opposing end them.

Dr. Johnson made fun of a couplet by Addison:

I bridle in my struggling Muse with pain,
Which longs to launch into a nobler strain.

Dryden speaks of seraphs that

Unguarded leave the sky,
And all dissolved in hallelujahs lie.

Longfellow gets his metaphors mixed in the Psalm of Life:

Lives of great men all remind us
We can make our lives sublime,
And, departing, leave behind us
Footprints on the sands of time.

Footprints that perhaps another,
Sailing o'er life's solemn main,
A forlorn and shipwrecked brother
Seeing, shall take heart again.

Mariners sailing on the main can hardly leave footprints on the sands, and other mariners, forlorn and shipwrecked, could scarcely be "sailing o'er life's solemn main," and while doing so see footprints on the sands.

Macaulay considered the worst mixed metaphor to be the lines of Robert Montgomery:

The soul aspiring, pants its source to mount,
As streams meander level with their fount.

"We take this," he says, "to be, on the whole, the worst similitude in the world. In the first place, no stream meanders, or can possibly meander, level with its fount. In the next place, if streams did meander level with their founts, no two motions can be less like each other than that of meandering level and that of mounting upward."

What Was the Bering Sea Dispute?

It was a dispute between the United States and Great Britain arising out of the rights of seal hunting in the Bering Sea. The matter was submitted to arbitration by the two countries and the award, issued in 1893, decided that the Bering Sea was an open sea,

The position of the Bering Sea

that the United States had no jurisdiction or property in the seals frequenting the islands outside the three-mile limit. Regulations were framed for the future protection of seals.

Was Merlin a Real Person?

No one can say definitely, for a half legendary bard of the 6th century was in course of time confused with an imaginary character of the same name known as the Enchanter. The real Merlin, if there was one, was born between 470 and 480 during the Saxon invasion and, taking the name of Ambrose, became bard to King Arthur. After a disastrous defeat about 560, he is said to have lost his reason, and was found dead on the bank of a river.

The enchanter Merlin, also at Arthur's court, was said to be of miraculous birth and an adept in magic. One version says he was beguiled by the enchantress Ninive, who buried him under a rock from which he could not escape. Another story is that Vivien, the Lady of the Lake, left him spellbound in the tangled branches of a hawthorn bush, where he still sleeps, though sometimes his voice can be heard. Merlin gave a magic mirror to King Ryence which would reveal to him treason and secret plots.

What Was the Orsini Conspiracy?

This was an attempt to assassinate the French Emperor Napoleon III as he drove to the opera with the Empress Eugenie on January 14th, 1858. The carriage had just arrived at the door of the opera house in Paris when a bomb was thrown which exploded and killed twenty people. A second bomb was then thrown, and this killed one of the horses in the Emperor's carriage. A third burst under the carriage itself and the

vehicle was shattered and an aide-de-camp killed. But as though by a miracle the emperor and empress escaped with only slight injuries.

Count Felix Orsini, an Italian, who had organised the plot, was arrested and executed with two accomplices. The French ambassador remonstrated with the British Government for harbouring such villains, the plot having been hatched in London, and Lord Palmerston introduced a Bill into Parliament to punish those who conspired to murder foreign rulers. Fire-eating French colonels cried for war with England and this caused a reaction so that the Bill was lost in the House of Commons by a majority of 19. The life of Napoleon III was attempted six times.

What is a Mop Fair?

It is a statute fair where in former days servants were hired and farm labourers engaged. It possibly gets its name from the fact that the servants carried mops as an indication that they were waiting to be engaged. Carters used to fasten to their hats a piece of whipcord, shepherds a tuft of wool, grooms a sponge, and so on. Sometimes the name was given to a second fair held soon after the statute fair for the benefit of those persons not already engaged.

What is the Common Law?

This term is used in two senses. In one sense it is the ancient unwritten law of the kingdom em-

What is a Metonic Cycle?

It is a cycle of nineteen years, at the end of which the new and full moons occur on the same days again, having in the period passed through all the possible changes. It is named after Meton, an Athenian astronomer of the 5th century B.C., and is the basis of modern European calendars, being used for fixing movable feast days like Easter.

Who Was Steenie?

This was a pet name given by James I to his favourite George Villiers, afterwards Duke of Buckingham, because of his supposed likeness to a beautiful head of St. Stephen at Whitehall. He was also called by the King "my dog Steenie" because the Queen said Villiers must be her watch-dog, and whenever the King was about to make a fool of himself he was to "pull the old sow by the ear."

What is Stoolball?

It is an old English game which is, by some, regarded as the ancestor of cricket. A stool was placed on the ground and defended by a player with his hand against a ball thrown at it by his opponent. Later the defender used a stick. In the present century this old game has been revived, and is often played at girls' schools. In the modern form a wooden bat, shaped like a tennis racket, is used, the ball is of solid rubber, and a wicket is set up

Girls at a Sussex school playing stoolball. It was in this county that the game was revived in 1916

bodied in judicial decisions as opposed to statute law—that is, the law enacted by Parliament. Then the term is also used in the sense of the municipal law of England as opposed to the Roman civil law or other foreign law.

consisting of a square of wood with sides of one foot placed on a pole 4 feet 8 inches above the ground. There are two wickets 16 yards apart. Ten balls go to the over. The game was first revived in 1916 at Brighton.

What British Bird Nests in the Water?

THE great crested grebe builds its nest among the reeds growing in the water, and while sometimes the foundation rests on the bottom, at other times the nest is moored to the surrounding vegetation. The nest

A great crested grebe's nest, photographed at Buscot Park, Berkshire

often appears to be floating on the surface. It is constructed of sedge leaves, reeds, and all kinds of dead water plants heaped together. From three to five white eggs are laid which soon become stained. The grebe likes to build on large sheets of water and it nests on the Norfolk and Suffolk Broads, in Wales and in Yorkshire, Shropshire, Cheshire, Lancashire, Surrey, and several other counties. It is found nesting in April, May and June.

Who Was the Mad King of Bavaria?

HE was Ludwig, or Louis the Second, born in 1845, who devoted himself to art and music rather than to affairs of state. He was the great patron of Wagner. Owing to his prodigal expenditure in building superfluous palaces in all sorts of out-of-the-way places, he was constantly at feud with his ministers and family. He also spent vast sums on performances of Wagner's operas with himself as the only spectator. At last, in June, 1886, he was declared insane and incapable of ruling, and a few days later drowned himself and his physician, who tried to save him, in the Starnberger Lake, near his castle of Berg. He had not only given Wagner a pension but also paid up his debts.

What is Plimsoll's Line?

PLIMSOLL'S line or mark is a line on the hull of a ship showing to what depth the vessel may be legally submerged when loaded. The mark, which is named after Samuel Plimsoll, a Member of Parliament who worked hard to bring about safer and better conditions for the crews of British ships, really consists of several lines. There is a circle with a line through it and a series of straight lines at the side something like the letter E. The first is sometimes called the free-board disk, and all British ships are compelled by law to have this mark. Free-board is the distance from the water-line to the main deck of a ship, and it varies according to climate and place of travel. The Plimsoll mark shows the maximum depth to which the hull of a British ship may be submerged under various conditions.

The horizontal line across the middle of the circle indicates the depth for loading in salt water in summer months—that is, from April to October. Salt water is more buoyant than fresh water, and so a sea-going vessel may be submerged five or six inches more when loading in fresh water. The lines by the side of the disk show not only the fresh-water loading line, but the winter loading line, with a winter North Atlantic loading line and an Indian summer loading line. The ordinary summer loading line is also given with the others at the same level as the line that bisects the disk. Stormy weather is so often encountered in the North Atlantic in winter that ships travelling in that sea are not allowed to submerge so much as for winter travelling in other seas. For summer travelling in the Indian Ocean the summer line is above the ordinary summer line. There is no doubt that many thousands of lives have been saved by the institution of the Plimsoll mark on British ships.

What is a Moon Dial?

A MOON, night or nocturnal dial is an instrument for showing the hour of the night by the shadow cast by the Moon. Such a dial is constructed relative to the Moon's motion, but the irregularity of this motion, due to the Moon's varying speeds at different parts of its orbit, makes such an instrument far from accurate.

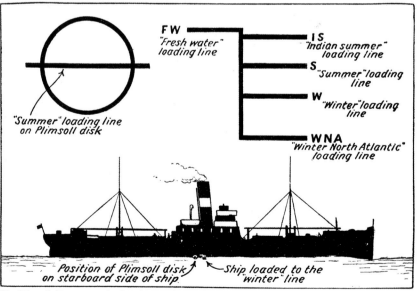

The Plimsoll line, or mark placed on a ship to show to what depth it may be legally submerged when loaded ready for a voyage

Why Has the Monument an Iron Cage on Top?

THIS iron cage which encloses the gallery at the top of the London Monument on Fish Street Hill was placed there in 1842 after Jane Cooper, a servant maid living at Hoxton, had

The railing round the top of the Monument in London, placed there to prevent suicides

committed suicide by jumping from the top into the street. This was the sixth suicide from the Monument. The first was that of John Cradock, a baker, on July 7th, 1788 ; the second Lyon Levi, a Jewish diamond merchant, on January 18th, 1810 ; the third a baker named Leander, later in the same year ; the fourth Margaret Moyes, daughter of a baker in Hemmings Row, on September 11th, 1839 ; the fifth Robert Donaldson Hawes, a boy of fifteen, on October 18th, 1839, and finally Jane Cooper, already referred to, on August 19th, 1842. It is curious that so many of the suicides were connected with the baking trade.

On June 25th, 1750, William Green,

a weaver, whilst reaching over the railing of the balcony to look at a live eagle kept there in a cage, accidentally lost his balance and fell over into the street and was killed.

Have Orchestras Always Had Conductors?

A CONDUCTOR standing in front of the orchestra and beating time with a baton has been known on the Continent for several centuries, but in England it is an institution of comparatively recent date. Sir George Grove says : " In former times the chief musician sat at a pianoforte in the orchestra with the score before him ; but it does not appear that he beat time continuously, or in any way influenced the band, or did more than put in a few chords now and then when the orchestra was going astray, which when heard must have had a very bad effect. The leader it was who kept the band together—or as nearly together as possible—beating time with his bow, stamping, and occasionally tapping on the desk. But as he stood in the middle of the violins, and was therefore out of sight of the majority of the orchestra, he could have had but a very small influence on the other players."

The first baton employed in England was probably used by Spohr at the Philharmonic in 1820, thinks Sir George Grove. It was not till 1846 that we find the announcement "Conductor, Signor Costa," and that, says Grove, was the commencement of the present system.

Originally a long baton was used which was rapped against the floor. Later this gave place to the small conductor's wand of today, 21 or 22 inches long and tapering from three-quarters to three-eighths of an inch in diameter. At a big concert, such as takes place in the Queen's Hall, London, one may see two or even three batons ready on the conductor's desk. This is simply in case one of these fragile implements should get broken during the performance.

What Are Chasseurs?

THESE are lightly equipped soldiers in the French Army, and there are both foot chausseurs and horse chasseurs, known respectively as chasseurs-à-pied and chasseurs-à-cheval. They correspond to the Rifle Brigade and Auxiliary Light Horse of the British Army and to the Jaegers of the German Army.

Should Potatoes Be Cooked in Their Skins?

ALL authorities agree that it is good to cook potatoes in their skins or jackets. Most of the valuable salts of the potato are stored chiefly in the cells under the skin and these are wasted when the potato is peeled before cooking. Not only so, but it is probable that most of the vitamins are also collected chiefly under the skin, and these are wasted when the parings are thrown away.

It is curious that this valuable food plant is a near relative of the deadly nightshade, the most poisonous plant that grows wild in England. The leaves and fruit of the potato plant also are poisonous, but the tubers which we eat are immune. Children have been poisoned through eating the green balls that enclose the seeds of potato plants.

Boys peeling potatoes at a holiday camp

Has St. Paul's Cathedral Two Domes?

YES, there is the outer dome, which is seen from the street, and an inner dome, which can be seen as we look up from the floor of the cathedral. As seen from the outside, it looks as though the stone lantern, with the ball and cross, are supported on the dome, but this is not the case, as the sectional drawing given on this page will show

Was Half the Cullinan Diamond Lost?

IT has often been stated that the great Cullinan diamond, which in its rough state weighed 3,026 carats, was only a fragment of a much larger gem which had been stolen by a native worker and smuggled out of the Premier Mine. A white farmer named Fourie, who afterwards ended his days on the scaffold for the murder of a native chief by poison, heard that

wards, Fourie said he suspected that the native was armed, for he carried an open revolver holster, and he probably had supporters not far away ; in fact, the distant sound of native voices, which carry far on a quiet night, was distinctly audible. ' What is the word you were to say ? ' he asked Fourie, keeping his hand on his holster. 'Bula-la.' ' Yes ; then where is the money ? ' " Fourie indicated the bag. The native asked the two white men to retire a few paces and then brought the lantern closer and thrust his hand deeply into the bag. He instantly discovered the leaden disks and, stepping back, extinguished the lantern by dashing it to the ground and vanished in the darkness. And although Fourie and his assistant gave chase, the native had no difficulty in escaping. Nor was the diamond seen ; nor, indeed, has it ever been seen by a white man, although still much discussed among the natives."

Mr. Chilvers thinks Fourie was far too unimaginative to have made up the story.

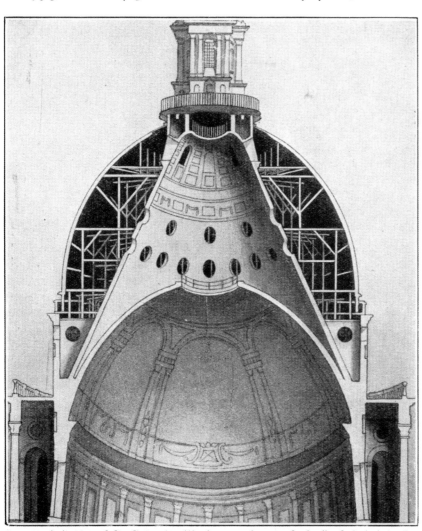

A sectional drawing of Sir Christopher Wren's great dome at St. Paul's Cathedral, London, showing how the stone lantern with its ball and cross are supported on a conical wall between the outer and inner domes

The great weight of this superstructure is supported on a conical wall built between the outer and the inner domes.

What is Midsummer Madness?

OLIVIA in Shakespeare's " Twelfth Night " is made to say to Malvolio, " Why, this is very midsummer madness " (Act III, Scene 4). The reference is to rabies, the disease of dogs at one time supposed to be caused by great heat such as that which often occurs at midsummer.

a Kaffir possessed this other portion of the Cullinan diamond and was prepared to sell it for a thousand pounds in gold. The story told by Fourie was that he drove out at night in a cart with a companion to a place appointed, taking with him not the thousand pounds in gold which was stipulated, but a bag containing leaden disks covered with a hundred sovereigns.

" He reached the meeting-place near a kopje," says Mr. Hedley A. Chilvers in " The Seven Lost Trails of Africa," " and presently the native emerged out of the darkness. He was tall, lightly clad, carried a lantern and seemed nervous. Telling the story after-

Was Shakespeare a Poacher?

ACCORDING to accounts that have come down to us, Shakespeare when quite a young man joined in a midnight poaching expedition to capture some deer in the grounds of Charlcote Manor, about four miles from Stratford-on-Avon. He seems to have been caught in the act and, after being kept in prison all night, was brought before the lord of Charlecote, Sir Thomas Lucy, the next morning. One account says he was whipped and that he was also imprisoned. He was very indignant at his treatment, and obtained his revenge by writing a scurrilous ballad about Sir Thomas Lucy, with punning jokes on his name, and then fixing it to the park gates. The angry knight would seem to have made things so hot for William Shakespeare that the young man had to leave his native home and go to London.

What is the Bag on a Hussar's Busby?

THE uniform of the Hussar originally came from Hungary, and the so-called " bag " or pouch on the right side of the busby was actually used for carrying papers or dispatches. The troopers generally carried their pipes in this bag. It also served as a protection against sword-cuts.

What Was the Nose Tax?

IT was a tax of one ounce of gold on every householder in Ireland exacted by the Danes in the 9th century. It was continued for thirteen years and then a general massacre of the Danes put an end to the tax. It received its curious name owing to the fact that non-payment was punished by the slitting of the defaulter's nose.

What is the Latest Electrical Treatment?

THE latest method of giving electrical treatment is to place the patient inside a kind of cage made of wire and to pass the current round the

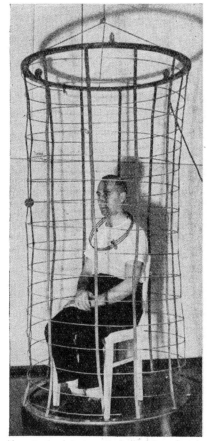

Here is the latest method of giving electric treatment to a patient. He sits in a cage while the current is passed through the wires

wires. This method is said to have more healing qualities than the ultra-violet rays. A small instrument is worn round the neck of the patient which shows a light while the current passes, but ceases to do so immediately the circuit is broken.

What is the Fabian Society?

IT is a society of socialists formed in the 19th century which included some distinguished members, such as Mr. Bernard Shaw. Its objects were set out in one of its tracts as follows : " The Fabian Society aims at the reorganisation of society by the emancipation of land and industrial capital from individual and class ownership ; and the vesting of them in the community for the general benefit." It took its name from that of Quintus Fabius, the Roman general who defeated Hannibal by wariness and caution, and not by violence and defiance. As someone has said, " Fabian tactics lie in stealing inches, not in grasping leagues."

Is the Elephant a Heavy Walker?

No ; as a matter of fact this animal, though looking so heavy and clumsy, is very light on its feet and its tread is so soft that a rider on its back instead of being jolted experiences only a series of regular rollings.

" The reason for this ease of step," says the Rev. J. G. Wood, " may be found in two peculiarities of formation ; one of the joints, and the other of the foot. On examining the legs of the elephant it will be seen that, although there is no pastern, the knee-joint is placed so low that it perfectly supplies its place ; and on dissecting the foot a most beautiful arrangement will be observed. The bones and flesh of the foot should be removed, the interior of the hoof carefully cleared from all vestiges of the soft substances, and, if possible, the hoof slowly dried ; the interior of the hoof will then be found to consist, not of a mere horny cup for the foot, but of a series of horny plates, amounting to many thousands in number, each placed at a little distance from the other, so as to form a most beautiful apparatus of springs."

Mr. Wood tells us that although the elephant is afraid to trust itself on loose ground or precipitous places, yet it can climb rocks which neither horses nor oxen could surmount and which are not very accessible even to men. " Whole herds are sometimes seen ascending exceedingly steep and dangerous eminences, under the guidance of one animal, who serves as their leader. The only rocks which elephants cannot endure are those of a crumbling nature, or where the hard rock is covered with loose soil. In the ascent the trunk is of great service, not so much in affording a means of grasp by which the animal may haul itself up, but in feeling the ground and discovering the most secure footing. The mode by which the elephants descend from the rocks is ingenious and closely resembles that employed by mules in their descent from the Andes. The leading elephant looks out for the best spot for the descent and, having found it, he sits down, just as

a cat or dog sits, with his forefeet stretched out before him and his hind legs gathered under his body. He then slides down the declivity, retarding his progress when necessary by resisting with his forefeet, by which means he can also alter his course if necessary. The entire herd follow this example."

Elephants never tread by accident on a person. Mr. Charles F. Holder quotes an English officer who served in India as follows : " I have myself seen the wife of a mahout—for the followers often take their families with them to camp—give a baby in charge of an elephant while she went on some business, and have been highly amused in observing the sagacity and care of the unwieldy nurse. The child, which like most children did not like to be still in one position, would, as soon as left to itself, begin crawling about, in which exercise it would probably get among the legs of the animal, or entangled in the branches of the tree on which he was feeding ; when the elephant would, in the most tender manner, disengage his charge, either by lifting it out of the way with his trunk, or by removing the impediments to its free progress."

Many instances are on record where a child or older person has suddenly fallen in the path of a marching elephant, but in no case has the animal trodden upon him as a horse might.

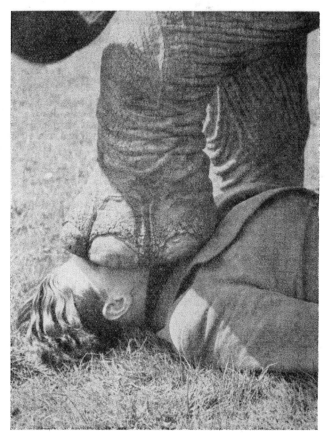

An elephant placing its forefoot on the face of a man without injuring him. The elephant's tread is very light

What is the Helston Floral Dance?

THIS is a quaint, old-fashioned dance which takes place in the streets and houses of Helston in Cornwall on "Furry Day"—that is, May 8th—to a

The floral dance taking place in the streets of Helston, Cornwall

quaint old hornpipe tune. Early in the morning bands perambulate the town, playing the tune and rousing the people. Then the younger inhabitants come out and begin dancing.

The principal dance, however, does not take place till the afternoon. The dancers are all attired in their best clothes, the men wearing tall silk hats and the women summer dresses and large hats. A procession having been formed, a start is made from the Market House at one o'clock. The band plays and the couples dance into and through the nearest house. Leaving by the back door, they return to the street through the next house, and so on in and out of the houses go the musicians and the dancers. This "Furry Dance" has been carried out at Helston for centuries.

What Was the Ligurian Republic?

IT was a state created by Bonaparte in 1797 consisting of Venetia, Genoa and part of Sardinia, with a constitution similar to that of the French Directory. It received its name from Liguria, part of its territory. In 1805 it was annexed to France.

Who Was the Man in the Iron Mask?

HE was a French state prisoner, confined in the Bastille under much secrecy, who died there on November 19th, 1703. His name was never mentioned, but he was buried under that of Marchiali. He always wore a mask of black velvet, erroneously described as of iron, and was treated with a good deal of respect. Various suggestions have been made as to his identity. He is said to have been a natural son of Louis XIV and Mademoiselle de la Vallière. Another suggestion is that he was a twin brother of Louis XIV. Another that he was an elder brother of Louis XIV, the son of Anne of Austria and the Duke of Buckingham. A fourth suggestion is that he was Count Matthioli, a minister of the Duke of Mantua, and that he was imprisoned for treachery. A fifth idea is that he was a soldier of fortune named Marechiel, the head of a band of assassins who intended to kill the French king and his ministers. This was considered the most plausible suggestion till in 1891 the publication of some cipher dispatches of Louis XIV and his minister Louvois appeared, to show that "the man in the iron mask" was General de Bulonde, who raised the siege of Cuneo un-

necessarily and imperilled the success of the campaign. The matter, however, must remain an unsolved mystery in the absence of definite evidence.

What Are Gingerbread Husbands?

THIS was the humorous name given to gingerbread cakes made in the form of men and gilded. They were sold at fairs and fêtes up to the middle of the 19th century.

Where is the Biggest Vine in Britain?

SOME people suppose that the biggest vine in Britain is that at Hampton Court Palace. It grows in a lean-to house at the south end of the palace, 90 feet long. The vine, a black Hamburgh, was planted in 1769 and has a stem 6 feet in circumference at the ground, and the main branch is 114 feet long. At the present time its annual crop of fruit amounts to about 500 bunches of grapes, but in the past it used to yield 1,500 bunches a year, and in 1874 there were 1,750 bunches.

This Hampton Court vine, however, is not the largest in Britain. At Kippen in Stirlingshire is a vine, 45 years old, which in 1937 yielded 1,914 bunches and in some years has produced over 2,000 bunches. Already this vine is the largest known in the world and it is still growing bigger. It is shown in the photograph below.

The largest grape vine in the world at Kippen, Stirlingshire

Has Anyone Been Reprieved After Hanging?

YES, and the man of whom this is true is known as Half-Hanged Smith. He was John Smith, the son of a farmer at Malton, near York. After serving an apprenticeship to a baker in London, and working as a journeyman, he went to sea, and later joined a man-of-war and saw active service.

On being discharged he enlisted as a soldier in the Guards, and then his troubles began. He associated with dissolute companions, and on December 5th, 1705, was charged on four indictments for housebreaking. He was convicted of two of these and sentenced to death.

The sentence was carried out on Christmas Eve, and as Smith went to Tyburn for the execution he performed his devotions and was then hanged.

But after he had been suspended by the neck for about fifteen minutes a reprieve suddenly arrived, and he was thereupon cut down and carried to a neighbouring house, where after bleeding and other treatment he recovered.

He was asked on regaining his senses what his feelings were during the time of hanging, to which he replied that when he was " turned off " he was for some time sensible of great pain, occasioned by the weight of his body.

He felt his spirits in a strange commotion, and they seemed as though they were violently pressing upwards. Then when they had forced their way to his head he seemed, as it were, to see a great blaze of light, which appeared to go out at his eyes with a flash. From that moment he lost all sense of pain in the all-pervading darkness of a merciful oblivion.

After he had been cut down and was coming back to consciousness, said Smith, the blood and spirits seemed to force themselves into their former channels, and by a severe pricking sensation gave him intolerable pain, so that he wished in his agony and exasperation that those who had cut him down could themselves be hanged.

One might have thought that such an experience would have made Smith walk in less dangerous paths, but he soon returned to his former practices. He was tried at the Old Bailey, and owing to some technical difficulty between judge and jury was acquitted. A third time he was indicted, but the prosecutor happening to die before the day of trial, Smith once more secured his liberty, and he eventually died in his bed.

Where is Bank-Note Paper Made?

THE special paper on which the notes of the Bank of England are printed is made at a paper-mill at Laverstoke, a village in Hampshire two miles from Overton. It was established in 1727 and so has been carrying on the industry for over two centuries, the business being handed down from father to son.

The Laverstoke paper-mills in Hampshire, where the paper for Bank of England notes is made

What Does "Good Wine Needs No Bush" Mean?

IT was the custom in olden times for an inn to hang out as a sign a bush or bough of ivy or some other plant. An inn that became noted for its good wine would have plenty of customers and would not find it necessary to hang out a bush or other sign to attract people to its doors.

What Was the Massacre of St. Bartholomew?

IT was on August 24th, 1572, that something like 30,000 French Protestants, or Huguenots as they were called, were suddenly murdered in Paris at the instigation of King Charles IX and his mother, Catherine de Medicis. It was one of the most terrible and disgraceful massacres in history and some place the death-roll as higher than the figure given. Admiral Coligny, the Huguenot leader, was among the slain. Pope Gregory XIII went in state to a grand Te Deum as a public thanksgiving for the brutal and cowardly slaughter, had a medal struck to commemorate the event, and proclaimed the year a year of jubilee.

What Was the Barebones Parliament?

THIS was the nickname given to a Parliament, often called the Little Parliament, summoned by Cromwell and the Council of Officers in 1653 after the expulsion of the Rump Parliament. It derived its name from a prominent member, a leather-seller of Fleet Street called Praise-God Barbon, later corrupted into Barebones. It consisted of 139 members and was called to pave the way for a Parliament on a national basis, but began to make drastic reforms in Law and Church. Thereupon it was suddenly proposed, when only a few members were present, that the Parliament should resign its power into the hands of Cromwell, and this was carried. The Barebones Parliament sat only from July 4th to December 12th, 1653.

Is the Leopard Still Found in Palestine?

YES, this animal, which is several times mentioned in the Bible, is still found wild from time to time in the more rugged and less inhabited parts of the country. Its spotted skin is occasionally to be seen exposed for sale in the cities of Palestine. It is possible that the references to the leopard in the Bible concern three different species, the leopard proper, the ounce, and the well-known cheetah or hunting leopard.

Why is Birdcage Walk So Called?

THIS well-known thoroughfare in London on the south side of St. James's Park, between Buckingham Gate and Storey's Gate, was so named from the aviary established there in the reign of James I, and the decoy made there in the reign of Charles II. In " Amusements of London," by Tom Brown, published in 1700, is a reference to " the Bird-Cage inhabited by wild-fowl; the ducks begging charity, and the black-guard boys robbing their own bellies to relieve them."

How Does a Spider Make Its Web?

Framework completed and first radial spoke being spun

Further spokes being added

Temporary spiral being spun about the centre to steady the framework

Permanent spiral completing the web and signal line to spider's hiding place near by

Magnified view of web showing the sticky globules

The garden spider first throws out a line, which is carried by the breeze and attaches itself to a branch or leaf. This, like all the web, is made up of a number of fine threads, exuded as a fluid from the spinnerets at the rear of the body. When the line has caught on some branch the spider fixes the other end to another branch, and walking out like a tightrope walker drops another line, till at last it has made a framework, as shown at the top of this drawing. Then it makes radial lines, and strengthens these by spinning a number of small circles in the centre where they join. Next the spider weaves a wide spiral, but this is only a temporary affair, to hold the structure together while the real permanent spiral is spun. When this is completed the spider eats up the temporary spiral. The threads have at intervals little globules of a sticky substance on them which holds flies and other insects that fly into the web. If the web becomes damaged by wind, rain, or other cause the spider repairs it

Is the Great Pyramid Larger Than St. Peter's?

THE Great Pyramid of Cheops in Egypt has a square base 760 feet each way, its area being 13 acres, or twice the extent of St. Peter's at

cliffe, Bristol. They were written in an antiquated style on yellow parchment, and deceived Horace Walpole. It was an amazing achievement for so young a boy, but when the forgery was discovered, Walpole and others showed their resentment by leaving

What is Mothering Sunday?

IT is Mid-Lent Sunday, that is, the fourth Sunday in Lent, when it was formerly the custom for people to visit the mother church of a town or district to present offerings. Later the practice was to visit one's parents on this day and give them a present. " Mothering cakes " were made and eaten on the day.

Can Swimming Be Taught on Dry Land?

OF course, the final stages in the teaching of swimming must always be carried out in the water. But recently much has been done in giving preliminary instruction on dry land. In the photographs on this page are shown an apparatus which is used at the City Swimming School in Pilsen, Czechoslovakia, which teaches pupils the motions of swimming before they ever go into the water. This ingenious apparatus is in three sections. The pupil lies on the central part, in a position required for breast-stroke swimming. He places his hands in gloves fixed to the front section of the apparatus, and his feet into straps on the back section.

The apparatus is then set in motion by machinery, causing the pupil automatically to carry out the movements required for the breast-stroke The three sections of the apparatus can be adjusted for persons of all sizes. It has proved very successful and useful in preliminary training and will, no doubt, find its way into swimming establishments in other countries.

The Great Pyramid of Cheops, and the other pyramids, photographed from a British aeroplane. It is difficult to realise that the Great Pyramid covers twice as much area as St. Peter's Cathedral at Rome

Rome. It is equal to the size of Lincoln's Inn Fields in London. Each face of the pyramid is an equilateral triangle laid sloping and meeting at a point. The height is 481 feet, and the angle of the sides 51° 51′.

Professor Banister Fletcher, the distinguished architect, says, " The Pyramids are the most extravagant of all ancient buildings in many ways. The relative return in impressiveness and the higher beauties of the art is comparatively small when compared with the amount of labour, expense and material used in their erection. The finishing and fitting of such large masses of stone is remarkable. Many of the blocks, perfectly squared, polished and fitted, are at least 20 feet long by 6 feet wide. How such masses were quarried, moved and transported by land and water 500 or 600 miles, and finally accurately fixed in splendid masonry by a people unacquainted with iron and destitute of modern appliances is a problem as insoluble as the Sphinx."

poor Chatterton to starve. He lived in a garret in London in great destitution and committed suicide at the age of 18 on August 25th, 1770.

An apparatus which enables the various motions of swimming to be learnt before the pupil actually enters the water

What Were the Rowley Poems?

THEY were a collection of poems written by the youth Thomas Chatterton and attributed by him to a mythical Thomas Rowley, a priest of the 15th century. Young Chatterton, a lad of 16, pretended that he had found the poems in a chest in the muniment room of the Church of St. Mary Red-

What is Stromboli?

STROMBOLI is an island in the Mediterranean Sea, about thirty-five miles north of Sicily, which consists of a volcanic cone rising with a roughly circular outline out of the water to a height of 3,090 feet. For at least two thousand years the island has been in a constant and regular, but not in a violent or dangerous, state of activity. Masses of vapour emerge from the mountain and unite to form a cloud over the top, the outline of this cloud varying according to the direction and force of the wind.

Viewed at night-time, Stromboli is an impressive sight. The mountain, with its cloud of vapour, is visible over an area having a radius of more than a hundred miles, and from time to time a glow of red light makes its appearance, increases gradually in intensity, and then as gradually dies away. After a short interval the same appearance is repeated, and this goes on till dawn renders the phenomenon no longer visible owing to the daylight. The resemblance of Stromboli at night is, indeed, that of a flashing lighthouse on a gigantic scale. The mountain has long been known as " the lighthouse of

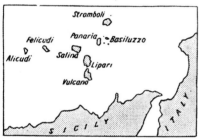

A map showing the Lipari Islands, of which Stromboli is one

the Mediterranean." The intervals between the flashes, however, are irregular, sometimes being only one minute and at other times twenty minutes or more. The duration and intensity of the red glow also vary a good deal.

The island is entirely built up of material ejected from the crater, and resembles the surroundings of an iron furnace with its heaps of cinders and masses of slag. Soundings in the sea all round have shown that the bottom gradually shelves round the shores to a depth of nearly 600 fathoms, so that Stromboli is a great conical mass of cinders and slaggy materials, having a height of over 6,000 feet and a base whose diameter exceeds four miles.

Inside the crater are many fissures and cracks from which issue curling jets of vapour, but there are also several larger openings, varying in number and position at different periods. Sometimes only one aperture is visible ; at other times six or seven. There are three kinds of openings. From some steam is emitted with loud, snorting puffs, like those produced by a locomotive, but far less regular and rhythmical in their succession. From another class of opening masses of molten material well out and steam escapes in considerable quantities. A third class of opening is still more interesting. Within the walls a semi-liquid substance is seen slowly heaving up and down. The agitation increases, and presently a gigantic bubble is formed which bursts violently, throwing up steam and fragments of the scum-like substance. At night the cracks and openings glow, and the liquid matter revealed when the bubble bursts is seen to be white-hot.

In August, 1907, and June, 1921, eruptions of some violence occurred at Stromboli. The island, whose area is five square miles, has a population of 2,600 persons. One might almost have thought that such an island would have remained uninhabited.

Stromboli is only one of a group of volcanic islands north of Sicily, known collectively as the Lipari Islands. The chief island is called Lipari and has a town of the same name, which is a bishop's see. Many of the smaller islands form part of the rim of a gigantic crater. The old classical writers regarded one of the islands—Vulcano, 1,017 feet high, which is intermittently active—as the abode of the fiery god Vulcan, hence its name. And that name has now been given to fiery mountains everywhere.

Boys at an open-air fête carrying beakers made of papier mâché

What is Papier Mâché?

THE words are French and mean pulped paper. The term is used for a material which consists of paper pulp, compressed and moulded into the form of various articles. Different kinds of paper can be pulped together for this purpose and in the coarser kinds of papier mâché earthy matter and glue or resinous matter are often used to bind the material together. The composition is rolled into thick sheets, which are pressed to the required shape and after being dried can be decorated with paint, enamel or inlaid material. Trays, boxes, masks, cups and other articles are made of papier mâché and the material is also used in the printing trade for stereotyping. When the pages of a book or paper are all made up in type, an impression is taken with a sheet of damp papier mâché and this after being dried is used as a mould for casting the metal plates from which the paper or sheets of the book will be printed.

Old papier mâché articles are much sought after by collectors of bygones.

Stromboli, with its cloud of steam, as seen from the sea

Is the Ladybird a Friend of Man?

CERTAINLY the ladybird is one of our greatest friends in the garden and orchard, and it should always be carefully protected. It is the relentless enemy of the aphis or greenfly, which does so much harm. We know this sufficiently well in our English

Three familiar ladybirds, and the larvae of the two-spot ladybird, which is seen flying on the left

rose gardens, but in the fruit orchards of California various kinds of aphides do immense damage, and were it not for the ladybirds they would often destroy entire crops.

Long ago it was known that the ladybird devoured the greenfly, but unfortunately in California the ladybirds appeared a month or two before the greenfly. Some plan was needed to keep back the ladybirds till the greenflies were ready to be devoured. Scientists therefore set to work to find out where the ladybirds hibernated during the cold months of winter. They spent years and took a great deal of trouble over this, and at last they were successful. It was discovered that the ladybirds flew away up into the Rocky Mountains, and there spent the winter.

Arrangements were therefore made to send men on mules up into the snow-clad mountains at the close of the year and collect the sleeping ladybirds by the million. The insects are packed into sacks and brought down to special depots known as State Insectaries. There they are put into cold storage, and so when the Sun begins to get warm outside the ladybirds do not wake up. They are kept sleeping till April or May.

Then, as soon as the scientists learn from the farmers that the greenfly is beginning to appear, they rouse the ladybirds by putting them in a warm place, pack them in batches of about 33,000, and send them in bags to the farmers. The farmer lets them loose in the orchards and the ladybirds, after their long sleep, being very hungry, at once begin devouring the greenfly. This work has been going on now for many years, and has proved a tremendous success.

There are several species of ladybirds in England known by the number of spots which they have. Some have two spots, some seven spots and some more. Some of the ladybirds are red in colour and others yellow, but they are all useful and prey upon the aphis.

But it is in the larval stage that the ladybirds do most of their good work, and the ladybird larva is quite different in appearance from the winged insect. The picture on this page shows what the ladybird larvae are like. They are a dark grey in colour, and many people, seeing these insects, suppose that they are some kind of harmful beetle and destroy them. They should be saved with the utmost care, and will repay any attention they may receive. The Rev. Theodore Wood says of ladybirds: "Their voracity is so great that it would be impossible to over-estimate the value of their services."

What is the Football Association Cup?

IT is a silver trophy competed for annually by football clubs in England that play the Association game. The Cup competition was arranged in 1871, when fifteen clubs, all amateur, entered and the first Final was played at Kennington Oval on March 16th, 1872, between the Wanderers and the Royal Engineers, the former winning by one goal to nil. In 1884 Blackburn Rovers first won the Cup and soon afterwards amateur teams began to drop out of the competition. The Cup has been won six times by Blackburn Rovers and Aston Villa, and five times by the Wanderers.

Under existing rules, drawn up in 1905–6, 64 clubs compete in six rounds. They are the four clubs that have played in the semi-finals of the previous year, 48 leading clubs selected by the authorities of the Football Association, and 12 clubs that have proved victorious in qualifying rounds. These qualifying rounds are played between all the entrants, save the 52 clubs referred to above, and they are grouped in twelve geographical areas, there being one victor in each.

In 1895 the Cup was stolen from a shop window at Birmingham and never recovered. It had been on exhibition following one of Aston

King George VI presenting the Football Association Cup to the captain of Preston North End, the winners in 1938

Who Were the Black Flags?

THEY were bands of Chinese pirates who, during the war in 1883 between the Annamese and the French, opposed the French and proved the bravest and most daring of their foes.

Villa's wins. A second trophy was prepared and this was withdrawn and presented to the late Lord Kinnaird in appreciation of his services as President of the Football Association. The present cup was prepared in the year 1911 and was first won by Bradford City.

Is There a Village Well Worked by Electricity?

At Toys Hill village, near Sevenoaks in Kent, a new electric automatic pump for the use of the villagers was installed early in 1938, and has all

The village well at Toys Hill, Sevenoaks, worked by electricity

the picturesque appearance of an old village well. Previously there was no adequate water supply for the fifty houses and cottages, and the people had, for a long time, to make daily journeys down to a stream and carry their water in pails up a steep hill.

Is Joan of Arc's Day Celebrated in France?

Yes; St. Joan's Day is celebrated throughout the whole of France in May. At Orleans the Maid's standard is displayed before the Town Hall, and in Paris a ceremony is held before the statue of St. Joan in the Place des Pyramides, which the Prime Minister generally attends. Services are held in the churches. It was on May 30th, 1431, that the Maid was condemned to death by the ecclesiastics and burned to death in the market-place at Rouen. Her last words were the name of Jesus thrice repeated. Within a few years the ecclesiastical courts annulled the sentence, and after the lapse of five centuries she was canonised by the Church. A monument to Joan was placed in Winchester Cathedral in 1923.

What Are Bouts Rimés?

Bouts Rimés, or rhyming terminations, is a form of recreation that was popular in France last century and spread to England. At an evening party a number of rhyming words were given and these were to form the end words of lines in a poem which each member present had to make up in a given time. Thus, suppose the words wave, lie, brave, die, were given, three efforts might be as follows:

> Whenever I sail on the wave,
> O'ercome with sea-sickness I lie!
> I can sing of the sea and look brave,
> When I feel it, I feel like to die.

> Dark are the secrets of the gulfing wave,
> Where, wrapped in death, so many heroes lie;
> Yet glorious death's the guerdon of the brave,
> And those who bravely live can bravely die.

> High o'er the ship came on the 'whelming wave—
> One crash! and on her beam I saw her lie!
> Shrieked high the craven, silent stood the brave,
> But hope from all had fled—'twas only left to die.

It was a pleasant exercise for an intelligent gathering, but it is doubtful if at any average party today many of the members would be capable of constructing verses at all, let alone to do so bringing in definite words in a given order.

What Were the Cities of Refuge?

They were cities set apart as sanctuaries to which those who slew a person by accident could flee and remain safe till the death of the High Priest for the time being, when they were immune and could leave their city of refuge. Moses set apart three cities on the east side of Jordan, and Joshua afterwards added three others on the west side. The three on the east were Bezer, Ramoth and Golan, and those on the west Hebron, Shechem and Kedesh. The matter is referred to in Deuteronomy IV, 43, and Joshua xx, 1–8.

Where Are There Wavy Division Lines on Roads?

In some American cities and their approaches the white lines dividing the roads for up and down traffic are made wavy to indicate that at adjacent places, such as hill-crests and junctions, there is need for special care and caution. Los Angeles, in California, for instance, makes use of the wavy line as shown in the photograph on this page. It will be noticed that traffic keeps to the right.

A wavy line on a Los Angeles road which warns motor-car drivers of an approaching hill-crest or other danger point

Who Are the Peculiar People?

THEY are a sect of Protestant Christians who believe that sickness can be cured by prayer and the anointing of the sick with oil as described in the epistle of St. James, chapter v, verses 14 to 15. They do not believe in seeking the assistance of doctors and because of this are sometimes in trouble before the coroner's court when a patient has died without proper medical attention

Will an Iron Axe Float?

AN iron axe will not, of course, float in water as will a cork or a piece of wood. The reason is that the density of the iron is much greater than that of the water, and being so much heavier it sinks to the bottom. The density of cork and wood is less than water and so they float; that is, they are pressed up by the heavier water. But if an axe-head be placed in a bowl of mercury or quicksilver, then it will float as the cork does on water. The reason is that the quicksilver is very much denser than the iron, or, as scientists say, its specific gravity is just over $13\frac{1}{2}$, while that of iron is less than 8. The specific gravity of a solid means its weight compared with an equal bulk of water.

What Are Ground Pearls?

THIS is the name given to a collection of Margarodes or scale insects of the family Coccidae. They are so named from their pearly appearance. The scaly covering often causes the insect to be mistaken for a mollusc. These hard scales or "shells" are

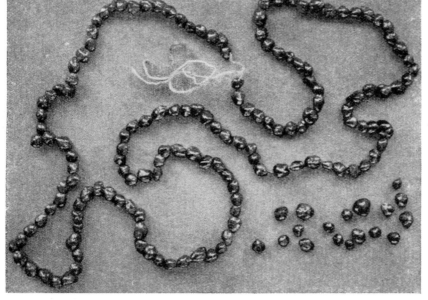

A necklace of ground pearls, which are really formed by a South African scale insect

often strung together to form a bead necklace. Those of a South African species are yellow and look remarkably like amber beads.

What is the Bottom of a Periscope Like?

THE top of a periscope is a narrow tube, which when a submarine is submerged can be seen jutting up out of the water. At the top of the tube is a prism, and a picture of the surrounding view is caught by this as in a mirror and reflected down the tube, through a number of lenses to another prism at the bottom of the tube. The lower prism directs the rays of light at right angles through a kind of telescope in which a number of lenses magnify the view so that an officer looking through the telescope's eyepiece can see an enlarged picture of the scene above. The photograph on this page

An officer at the periscope on the British submarine L 26

shows an officer looking through the eyepiece of the periscope on the British submarine L 26. It will be seen that the bottom of the periscope is quite a formidable-looking apparatus.

By means of the handles which he is grasping the officer can rotate the periscope so that he can obtain a view of what is going on upon the sea above in all directions. Sometimes the periscope is rotated by means of a wheel. Submarines generally have two periscopes, one for steering and one for the use of the commander as he directs operations. On some submarines there are even three periscopes. A lens with sighting scales is engraved with lines which enable a target to be centred for firing. When a periscope is three feet above the surface of the sea, the horizon is at 4,000 yards. When it is two feet up, the horizon is 3,100 yards away, and at one foot it is 2,200 yards distant. The periscope proper is encased in an outer tube for protection.

What is a Corybantic Religion?

THIS means a religion whose outward expression is noisy and emotional. The term was used by the late Professor Huxley of the Salvation Army and its methods. The Army processions, he said, reminded him of the wild behaviour of the ancient Corybantes or devotees of Bacchus. Of course, such a criticism was unfair.

How High Can a Giraffe Reach?

THE giraffe is far and away the tallest of all animals, when it stands erect reaching to a height of 20 feet. It is largely because of this great height that it is so difficult for hunters to approach it, for with large eyes looking out all round at a height of some 19 feet from the ground the animal has a very wide range of view.

It is sometimes said that the giraffe has developed its long neck because its ancestors reached out for the food on the tall trees, and only those which had exceptionally long necks and could reach them were able to survive. But as one writer has said, why the shorter giraffes did not eat the tops of the shorter trees seems very strange. Many of the mimosa trees in the giraffe country are only 14 or 15 feet high. The tree in the giraffe's pen at the Zoological Gardens has to be protected for many feet up from the ground by iron railings, to prevent the animal nibbling the bark and in time killing the tree.

feet from the ground. When thus feeding on the tall trees the giraffe is a graceful-looking animal, but when it drinks or tries to pick up a leaf from the ground it is anything but graceful and has to straddle its legs in a ludicrous fashion to bring its head low enough to reach its goal.

A giraffe feeding on a tree with its head tilted up to form a continuation of the long neck

But the giraffe, which feeds on the tops of the mimosa and other trees, can reach higher than its 19 or 20 feet, for the head is so constructed that it can be raised perpendicularly so as to form a continuation of the long neck. Then the hairy upper lip can be extended to a great distance, and finally the long flexible tongue, which is 18 inches or more long, can be protruded to an astonishing distance to grasp and tear down the leaves on which the animal feeds. Thus a 20-ft. giraffe can reach leaves and branches that are 22 or 23

What is the Roman Notation?

IN the notation used by the Romans I stood for 1, II for 2, III for 3, IIII or IV for 4, V for 5, VI for 6, VII for 7, VIII for 8, IX for 9, X for 10, XI for 11, XII for 12, XIII for 13, XIV for 14, XV for 15, XVI for 16, XVII for 17, XVIII for 18, XIX for 19, XX for 20, and so on. Higher numbers were as follows ; XXX, 30 ; XL, 40 ; L, 50 ; LX, 60 ; LXX, 70 ; LXXX, 80 ; XC, 90 ; C, 100 ; CC, 200 ; CCC, 300 ; CCCC, 400 ; D or IↃ, 500 ; M or CIↃ, 1,000.

Every Ↄ annexed to IↃ increased its value tenfold, thus IↃↃ stood for 5,000, IↃↃↃ for 50,000, and so on. Every C and Ↄ joined to CIↃ increased its value tenfold. Thus CCIↃↃ stood for 10,000, CCCIↃↃↃ for 100,000, and so on. A line drawn over a character increased its value a thousandfold. Thus, while a plain V stood for 5, $\bar{V}$ stood for 5,000 ; $\overline{IX}$ for 9,000, $\bar{C}$ for 100,000.

When any character was followed by one of less or equal value the expression denoted the sum of their value. Thus III stood for 3 ; VI for 6 or 5+1 ; XX for 20 or 10+10 ; LXVII for 67 or 50 + 10 + 5 + 1 + 1. On the other hand, when any character was preceded by one of less value the expression denoted the difference of their values. Thus, IV stood for 4 or 5−1 ; IX for 9 or 10−1 ; XL for 40 or 50−1 ; CD for 400 or 500−100.

Does the Moon Go Round the Earth in a Circle?

No. The Moon's passage round the Earth is an ellipse. When it is nearest to the Earth the Moon is only 221,610 miles away, but at its greatest distance it is 252,970 miles. The mean distance is 238,000 miles.

A giraffe at the London Zoo with its 18-inch tongue protruding to receive a gift of food

Which English Sovereign is That?

William I, 1066 — William II, 1087 — Henry I, 1100 — Stephen, 1135 — Henry II, 1154 — Richard I, 1189 — John, 1199

Henry III, 1216 — Edward I, 1272 — Edward II, 1307 — Edward III, 1327 — Richard II, 1377 — Henry IV, 1399 — Henry V, 1413

Henry VI, 1422 — Edward IV, 1471 — Edward V, 1483 — Richard III, 1483 — Henry VII, 1485 — Henry VIII, 1509 — Edward VI, 1547

Mary I, 1553 — Elizabeth, 1558 — James I, 1603 — Charles I, 1625 — Charles II, 1660 — James II, 1685 — William III, 1688

Mary II, 1688 — Anne, 1702 — George I, 1714 — George II, 1727 — George III, 1760 — George IV, 1820

William IV, 1830 — Victoria, 1837 — Edward VII, 1901 — George V, 1910 — Edward VIII, 1936 — George VI, 1936

On this page are portraits of all the reigning sovereigns of Britain from William the Conqueror to King George VI. As can be seen, there have been only five reigning queens, and one of these, Mary II, reigned jointly with her husband, William III. Lady Jane Grey, who is often called the Nine Days' Queen, was not a true sovereign, but only a usurper. The shortest reigns were those of Edward V, who reigned for only two months, and Edward VIII, who abdicated when he had been on the throne 46 weeks. The dates are those of the actual years when the rulers began to reign

Do Pearl Divers Use Diving Helmets?

THE native pearl divers of Ceylon and other places do not use diving helmets, but often go down under the water with a clip on their noses to prevent the entry of the water.

Recently, however, the pearl divers of Kameran Island, in the Red Sea, have taken to constructing rough diving helmets which consist of old petrol tins, in the side of which a hole is cut and a piece of mica fitted.

By means of these helmets the men are able to look down into the sea before diving, to see if any sharks are about. If they see one they pierce it with a spear which they hold in their right hand.

The helmet as they go under water holds a certain amount of air and enables them to remain down a little longer than they would be able to do

A pearl diver at Kameran Island, in the Red Sea, wearing his diving helmet made from an old petrol tin and a piece of mica

without the apparatus. It really serves as a kind of diving bell.

It is said that the pearl divers of Ceylon and the Persian Gulf, with no apparatus at all, can sometimes remain below the surface of the sea for two minutes at a stretch. This, however, is definitely bad for their lungs and, of course, eventually undermines their health.

What is Black Friday?

IN history it is December 6th, 1745, the day on which the news reached London that Charles Edward, the Young Pretender, with his army had reached Derby.

More recently the name is given to Friday, April 15th, 1921, the day on which the railwaymen and transport workers declined to stop work in support of the miners' national strike, thereby inaugurating a general strike.

What is a Domestic Court?

IT is a court conducted under the Summary Proceedings (Domestic Procedure) Act of 1937 whereby magistrates may hear matrimonial cases—that is, disputes between husband and wife—in private and quite apart from the ordinary police-court procedure and the attendance of the baser type of public who take pleasure in listening to the domestic squabbles of their neighbours. Domestic courts are generally held in the magistrate's private room, with chairs arranged around the table as though for an informal conference. Husbands and wives face each other with or without solicitors, and the only other people in the room besides the magistrates are the conciliation officer, a policewoman, and perhaps a friend or two of the parties. The sympathetic and friendly atmosphere often leads to the healing of a matrimonial breach that might otherwise lead to a permanent separation and the breaking up of the home. Such courts do much good work.

Can Ice Burst a Bomb-Shell?

YES, and for the same reason that it bursts leaden pipes. As water gets colder it contracts, but at 4° Cen. or 39° Fah. it begins once more to expand, and it is this expansion that bursts the water-pipe.

Last century a Major Williams, during a severe winter at Quebec, took an iron bomb-shell, about three-quarters of an inch thick, and filled it with water. After carefully plugging the opening, he left the bomb out of doors on the ground. When the water froze it drove out the plug and hurled it to a distance of 330 feet, and at the same time a cylinder or rod of ice 8½ inches long projected from the opening. The Major then took another bomb-shell and fixed the plug more securely, so that it could not be driven out. The result was that when the water in the bomb froze it burst a crack right round the circumference, and a ring of ice was forced through the rent.

Did Queen Victoria Have a Sister?

SHE had no sister of her own, but had both a step-sister and a step-brother. Her mother, the Duchess of Kent, had before her marriage to the English Duke of Kent, George the Third's son, been married to Emich Charles, Prince of Leiningen-Dachsburg-Hardenburg, a widower twenty-three years her senior. The marriage was happy and there were a son and a daughter. The son was Charles Frederick William Ernest, Queen Victoria's step-brother, and the daughter was Anne Feodorowna Augusta Charlotte Wilhelmina, Queen Victoria's step-sister, who married Prince Ernest Christian Charles of Hohenlohe-Langenburg. Queen Victoria used to correspond with and visit her step-sister.

The pearl diver about to go under the water

What Was the Seven Weeks' War?

IT was the war between Prussia and Austria for German supremacy that lasted from June 8th to July 26th, 1866. Italy was allied to Prussia and Austria was defeated. The most notable battle was that of Sadowa or Koeniggratz on July 3rd, when the Austrian army of 205,000 men lost 40,000. The Prussians lost only 10,000 men. After the war, Prussia became head of the German states and Austria was excluded from Germany. Venice was given up by Austria and added to the newly formed kingdom of Italy.

What is Ambrosia?

THE word means "not mortal," and it is the name given to the substance which, with nectar, formed the food and drink of the Greek gods. It was said to make immortal all who partook of it. Ambrosia was the food and nectar the drink, but some writers like Sappho, the poetess, reverse the terms. Because anything used by the gods must be excellent, the term has come to mean anything delicious to the taste or having a fragrant odour.

Why is the Lion's Tongue Rough?

THE tongue of the lion, like that of all the cat family, is very rough, and if it is looked at closely it will be seen that the tongue is covered all over with hard points, which rise above the softer flesh. These are all directed backwards, and when the animal licks itself the tongue acts as a comb and smooths the fur.

That, however, is not the principal use of the rough tongue. The lion, tiger, leopard, cat or other member of the family is able with the rough tongue to scrape a bone so clean that no flesh is left upon it. It can clean a bone better than a dog.

The tongue is well supplied with muscles that enable it to be shortened, lengthened, or twisted in any direction. The tip can be formed into a kind of spoon, which enables a cat to lap up milk, or a lion to take up water. It also serves the purpose of a kind of hand inside the mouth, directing the food.

It is because of these hard points all over the tongue that a lion licking a human hand will after a time draw blood. It scrapes away the skin.

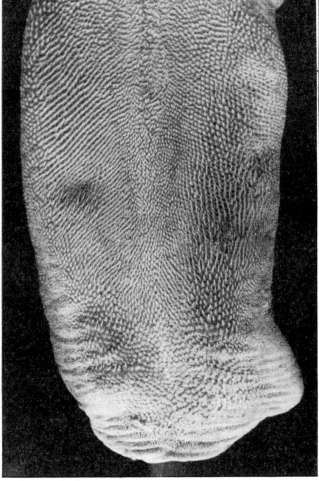

A remarkable photograph of a lion's tongue, showing the rough and pointed projections

What Were the Seven Metals of the Alchemists?

THE old alchemists used the following seven metals in their experiments: Gold, representing Apollo or the Sun; Silver, Diana or the Moon; Quicksilver, representing Mercury; Copper, Venus; Iron, Mars; Tin, Jupiter; and Lead, Saturn.

Zoological students of the University of Miami in Florida, studying marine life at the bottom of the sea

How is the Sea Bed Studied?

FORMERLY very little was known about the bed of the sea. Then a certain amount of information was obtained by scientific expeditions dredging up vegetation and other objects from the sea bed. More recently massive chambers with thick glass windows and searchlights have been let down on to the sea bed from ships, and in these chambers scientists have been able to watch life at the bottom of the sea.

The latest idea for students of zoology and oceanography is to study marine life at the bottom of the sea round the coasts. This they are able to do by dressing in swimming costume and wearing on their heads diving helmets fitted with windows. Air is supplied by a pump from a boat above, and a great deal of real knowledge is obtained by students in this way, without the expense or bother of wearing proper diving clothes. The strong sunlight of Florida enables one to see in deeper water than in England.

What is the Hapsburg Lip?

It consists of a protruding under-jaw, with a heavy lip that does not shut tight. It is said to have come into the Hapsburg family from

Ferdinand I, Emperor of Germany, 1558-64 a striking example of the Hapsburg lip

Cimburgis, a Polish princess who married Kaiser Frederick III, and showed itself in their son Maximilian I. It still persists in the former Spanish royal family. It is also called the Austrian lip and the Cimburgis under-lip.

Was Guy Fawkes a Gentleman?

Most people think of Guy Fawkes as an uneducated ruffian and desperado, but this is very far from being the truth. He was a gentleman of good family, the son of a notary of York, and held the office of Registrar and Advocate of the Consistory Court of the Cathedral Church there. Among his schoolfellows at York was Thomas Morton, afterwards Bishop of Durham.

Contemporary evidence describes Guy Fawkes as "a man of great piety, of exemplary temperance, of mild and cheerful demeanour, an enemy of broils and disputes, a faithful friend, and remarkable for his punctual attendance upon religious observances." His society is said to have been much sought after by those distinguished for nobility and virtue. He had been a Protestant, but had become a Roman Catholic, and it was religious fervour and fanaticism, and not pay, that made him willing to blow up the king and parliament.

What Was the Ban of Empire?

In German history, to be put under the ban of the empire meant to be cut off from society and deprived of all rank, titles, privileges and property. It was a kind of outlawry only declared in extreme cases.

What Are the Oldest Living Things?

They are the giant redwood trees of California, called by botanists *Sequoia gigantea*. These trees, some of which reach a height of 285 feet and a diameter of over 22 feet, are among the greatest wonders of the world. Mr. D. M. Delmas, a native of California, has said of them : " A sense of humility overwhelms you as you gaze upon these massy pillars of Nature's temple, whose tops, lost amid the clouds, seem to support the vault of the blue empyrean. The spell which the mystic light of some venerable cathedral may at times have thrown upon your soul is tame compared to that which binds you here. That was man's place of worship ; this is God's. In the presence of these titanic offspring of Nature, standing before you in the hoar austerity of centuries, how dwarfed seems your being ; how fleeting your existence ! They were here when you were born ; and though you allow your thoughts to go back on the wings of imagination to your remotest ancestry, you realize that they were here when your first forefather had his being. All human work which you have seen or conceived of is recent in comparison. Time has not changed them since Columbus first erected an altar upon this continent, nor since Titus builded the walls of the Flavian amphitheatre, nor since Solomon laid the foundations of the temple at Jerusalem. They were old when Moses led the children of Israel into the promised land, or when Egyptian monarchs piled up the pyramids and bade the Sphinx gaze with eyes of perpetual sadness over the desert sands of the Valley of the Nile."

Some authorities estimate the age of these trees as five thousand years or more. There are several groves of trees all situated on the western slopes of the Sierra Nevadas, the Mariposa Grove, the Calaveras Grove, the Fresno Grove, and so on. This giant species has well been called "the Great Sequoia, king of all the trees." In the case of some fallen specimens, the height in life must have been over four hundred feet—that is, higher than the cross that gleams on St. Paul's Cathedral in London, and the girth was 80 or 90 feet. The largest found had a diameter of 35 feet 8 inches, and a girth of over 100 feet.

The first grove of these giants to be discovered was found by A. T. Dowd in 1852. One of the trees was afterwards cut down, and its size may be gathered from the fact that on its stump 32 persons danced a cotillion, while on it also stood 17 others, including musicians and onlookers. This tree was 302 feet high, and had a circumference of 96 feet. In 1890 the United States Congress set apart 161,597 acres as a Sequoia National Park, and the trees may not be interfered with. " Unsubdued by Time," says Edwin Markham, " the sequoias stand in their places as the oldest watchers of our world."

The name sequoia was given to them in honour of Sequoiah, also called George Guess, an Indian of the Cherokee tribe, who invented an alphabet and taught it to his people.

Giant sequoia trees in the Sequoia National Park, California. A man at the foot of the middle tree appears a mere pigmy

Who Was Cagliostro?

ALESSANDRO DI CAGLIOSTRO was the assumed name of Guiseppe Balsamo, born at Palermo, Sicily, in 1743. He was an Italian charlatan and adventurer, notorious for his impositions in various countries. Among other things he offered everlasting youth to all who would pay for the secret. When he visited England he was imprisoned in the Fleet prison. Being mixed up in Paris in the affair of the Diamond Necklace, he was imprisoned in the Bastille. Afterwards he went to Rome, where he was sentenced to death, but the sentence was commuted to perpetual imprisonment at San Leone, and there he died in 1795.

How Many Kinds of Sundials Are There?

THERE are various kinds of sundials and they are named generally according to the positions they are intended to occupy. When the dial-plane is on the plane of the horizon, the instrument is called a horizontal dial and this is the most usual type. It is generally supported on a pedestal. When the dial plane is perpendicular to the plane of the horizon, the instrument is called a vertical dial and this

A striking example of a ring sundial with the signs of the Zodiac common in Sweden

A ring sundial at Falsterbo, Sweden

type we see frequently on church towers and the walls of buildings. An equinoctial dial is one whose plane is parallel to the equinoctial plane; that is, it is at a slant to the level ground. Dials are named from the position of the dial plane—south dial, north dial, east dial, west dial and polar dial.

Sometimes the dial is drawn on the curved surface of a cylinder and then it is called a cylindrical dial. Another type of sundial is the ring dial, which is often a portable instrument. Recently, however, the ring dial has been revived, especially in Sweden, where it is becoming the practice to erect such dials in the public parks. In these dials the gnomon is a rod, and this casts a shadow on the figures marked inside the ring.

A sundial, of course, unlike a clock, which can be altered, always records Sun Time, and not Summer Time.

What Were the Most Questions a Jury Was Asked?

THE largest number of questions ever asked of a jury was 21,642. This was in a case in May, 1938, the hearing of the evidence at which lasted a week in Paris. Three men were charged on two counts with having forged and discounted 3,607 share certificates. No fewer than 21,642 questions arose in connection with this fraud, and according to French law, each of the questions had to receive a written answer from the jury. To most of the questions the answer was a simple "Yes" or "No." Twelve large books contained the printed questions, and the 21,642 answers, written one by one by the jurymen, were taken into court with them. The jurymen during the long session in which the answers were being written out had a seven-course luncheon and an eight-course dinner. At one o'clock in the morning they sought further refreshment, and when all the answers had been given they went to sleep in beds ranged round the room.

Of course, in an English court the questions would have been reduced to a very small number.

Who Was the Mad Queen?

SHE was Juana or Joanna, wife and afterwards the widow of Philip of Flanders, generally called Philip the Fair of Austria. She was Queen of Castile and very rich, and Henry VII of England proposed to marry her in 1506 so as to secure her fortune. His indecent proposal was rejected. Joanna was the daughter of the famous Ferdinand and Isabella of Spain, and her son was the Emperor Charles V.

Do Blue Eyes Contain Blue Pigment?

WHEN we see the very blue eyes which some people have, we might well be pardoned for supposing that there was some blue pigment, but, as a matter of fact, eyes of all colours have the same colour pigment, and that is black. In brown-eyed people the black pigment is in both the back and front layers of the iris, while in blue-eyed people the pigment particles are in the back layer only.

The particular colour of the eye, varying from blue to black, depends on the number of black pigment cells in the iris. The more cells there are the darker is the colour of the eye. The colour depends partly on the reflection of the light from the iris and partly upon the coloured particles.

What Were the Alfonsine Tablets?

THEY were a series of astronomical tables constructed in 1252 by Isaac Hazan, a Jewish rabbi, who named them in honour of his patron, King Alfonso X of Castile, surnamed "the Wise."

What is the North-East Passage ?

IT is the route for ships along the northern coast of Europe and Asia from the Atlantic to the Pacific Ocean. The first navigator to make the com-

The dotted line on this map shows the north-east passage to the Far East

plete voyage, after it had been attempted again and again for three centuries, was the Swedish explorer Nordenskjöld in 1878-79.

What Are the Curious Facts About the Figure 9 ?

MR. W. GREEN, who died in 1794, was the first to call attention to the curious fact that all through the multiplication table the product of nine comes to nine when the digits are added together ; thus, twice 9 is 18, and 1+8=9 ; six times 9 is 54 ; and 5+4=9, and so on. When we come to eleven times 9 the product is 99, and 9+9=18 but 1+8=9. The same thing happens in large multiplications, thus nine times 2543917 is 22895253 and these digits total 36, and 3+6=9.

Then a Frenchman, M. Maivan, discovered that if you take any row of figures and, reversing their order, subtract one from the other, the result of adding up the digits of the answer is always 9. Here is an example :

$$92543987$$
$$78934529$$

$$13609458$$

The sum of the digits is 36, and 3+6=9.

The same result is obtained if the numbers used are changed to their squares or cubes. Thus, taking 62 and reversing it we get 62−26=36, and 3+6=9. Now take the squares of the two numbers 3844−676=3168. These digits add up to 18, and 1+8=9. The same thing happens with the cubes 238,328−17,576=220,752. The digits total 18, and again 1+8=9.

Who Invented Money Orders ?

THE money order system of the Post Office was invented by an accountant named Gosnell, of Crutched Friars, London, who, however, obtained neither thanks nor recognition. It was in 1791 that he proposed to the Post Office a money order scheme almost identical with that now in use, and also an alternative plan. But the Post Office rejected both on the ground that enabling people to send money was not part of its proper function. In the following year, however, a plan like Gosnell's came into use, but others obtained the credit. Five guineas was the maximum sum which could be sent and the commission was sixpence in the pound, reduced to fourpence a little later. After being worked for six years the accounts showed a loss of £298. Money orders, or money letters, as they were called, were therefore abandoned officially, but a number of individuals ran a money order service and made a profitable business of it. For forty years the money order system was run as a private business, and then, in 1838, the Post Office took it over.

What is a Court Martial ?

IT is a military tribunal held according to the provisions granted in the Army Act of 1881. Normally a court martial takes note only of offences committed by officers, soldiers and sailors. When, however, martial law is formally proclaimed, civilians also may be taken before a court martial for trial. Courts martial are general, district and regimental.

Where is the Cottonian Library ?

IT is in the British Museum. This library was founded by Sir Robert Bruce Cotton, after whom it is named. Cotton, who was born in 1571, was an ardent collector of manuscripts, books, coins and other antiquities, and he was often consulted by such men as Bacon, Ben Jonson, Speed and Camden. Falling out of favour with the Government, his library and collections were placed under seal and he never regained possession, and in 1707 the library was bought by the nation, and when the British Museum was founded in 1753 it was transferred to that institution.

How Does Helium Travel ?

HELIUM gas, when it is sent to a distance for use, is packed like oxygen and other gases in powerful metal cylinders. The gas is greatly compressed, hence the need for very strong containers so that it may not burst them. The United States has almost a monopoly of this gas, which, although not quite so light as hydrogen, is almost equally suitable for filling balloons and airships, and has the enormous advantage that, unlike hydrogen, it is not inflammable. A more recent use of helium is in hospitals, for patients who find it difficult to breathe ordinary air. The helium

How helium gas is packed under pressure in cylinders for transport

is mixed with oxygen and the resulting product is said to be three times easier to breathe than air. It easily diffuses to those parts of the lungs where air is most needed. The United States in 1938 first permitted helium to be supplied for this purpose.

What is That Garden Flower? Types

Love-in-a-Mist · Pansy · Viola · Verbena · Sweet Peas · Convolvulus · Shirley Poppy · Mignonette · Aquilegia · Campanula · Musk · Delphinium · Gaillardia · Polyanthus · Zinnia · Forget-me-not · Scabious · Coreopsis · Chrysanthemum · Lobelia · Wall-flower · Rose · Lupin · Anemone · Phlox · Tiger Lily · Carnati · Crocus · Lily of the Valley · Gladiolus · Begonia · Aubretia · Geranium · Evening Primrose · Madonna Lily · Saxifrage · Larkspur

It is marvellous what man by careful selection and cross-breeding has been able to do with comparatively unattractive wild flowers. All the magnificent blossoms full of rich colour, and many of them enormous in size and attractive in design seen in gardens, have been produced by plant breeders from the wild flowers of the country-side. On this page are given types of most of the families of flowers which we cultivate in our gardens. Of course, only one can be given in each case, and in many flowers, such as the dahlia, aster, lupin, peony, chrysanthemum, poppy and sweet pea, there is an immense variety of colour, as anyone who visits the Chelsea Flower Show or any other large flower exhibition will realise. In the illustration of a rose the artist has chosen a rambler. It is difficult to pick out

Native Ferns of Great Britain

Maidenhair Spleenwort · Royal Fern · Lanceolate Spleenwort · Lady Fern · Limestone Polypody · European Bristle Fern · Adders-tongue · Alpine Bladder · Oblong Woodsia · Holly Fern · Prickly-Toothed Buckler · Alternate Spleenwort · Rigid Buckler · Soft Prickly Shield · Forked Spleenwort · Green Spleenwort · Three-Branched Polypody · Rock Spleenwort · Common Polypody · Prickly Shield Fern · Brittle Bladder · One-Sided Filmy · Bracken · Tunbridge Filmy

al plants vary greatly in size, according to the moisture and fertility of the soil. Some ferns, adder's tongue and hart's tongue, vary from ches. The bracken is a large fern which often overruns a district and destroys other vegetation. It is the most familiar and abundant of all ferns. Some people think there is a distinction between bracken and ferns, but this is a mistake. While all these ferns are native to Great Britain, they also grow wild in other parts of the world, some being found not only in Europe but in America, Africa and Asia

Broad Buckler

Mountain Buckler

Sea Spleenwort

Rue-Leaved Spleenwort

Hard Fern

Black Spl

Mountain Bladder

Marsh Buckler

Hartstongue

Scaly Spleen-wort

Moonwort

True Maiden-hair

Annual Maidenhair

Crested Buckler

Hay-scented Buckler

Little Adderstongue

Male Fern

Mountain Polypody

Parsley Fern

Common Maidenhair Spleenwort

Alpine Polypody

Hard Shie

Alp Wo

HERE are all the ferns that grow native in the British Isles, and from these drawings it will be possible to identify any fern that may be found growing. As can be seen, many of them are rather alike. But there are some differences, and it should be possible with care to identify any particular individual. Some of these ferns, like the royal fern, may grow as tall as 12 feet high, but indivi place in which they are growing and the like the spleenworts, maidenhair, moonwor the more common form with its fronded bra

Plate XIV

Nasturtium · Sweet William · Sweet Sultan · Gentian · Sun-flower · Dianthus · Double Poppy · Geum · Heliotrope · Phlox Drummondi · Michaelmas Daisy · Cornflower · Cyclamen · Cineraria · Iris · Eschscholtzia · Pink · Clarkia · Hollyhock · Candytuft · Stock · Godetia · Primula · Antirrhinum · Hyacinth · Tulip · Peony · Marigold · Clematis · Daffodil · Narcissus · Siberian Wallflower · Calceolaria · Dahlias · Canterbury Bells · Sedum · Aster · Foxglove · Alyssum

any particular class of flower as an outstanding example of what can be done by plant breeding, but perhaps if some are to be named the chrysanthemum and the dahlia are pre-eminent. Chrysanthemums vary in size from a small flower not much bigger than a dandelion, to a large globular blossom the size of a football, and the colours are as varied as the sizes. In the dahlia, too, astonishing varieties of size, colour and form have been obtained. Even in the simpler flowers like the pansy and viola wonders have been performed in producing beautiful varieties of large size. In some flowers, in addition to varieties of form, the scent has been greatly enhanced. This is the case with such flowers as the hyacinth, mignonette, lily of the valley, and the rose

What is a Mezzo-Relievo?

IT is a form of relief sculpture in which the figures stand out in half their real proportions. This is less than in an alto-relievo, or high relief, where the figures project from their background by more than half their thickness and where the heads and limbs are often entirely detached from the background. In a basso-relievo, bas-relief or low relief, the figures or design project but slightly from a flat surface. Mezzo-relievo means middle relief.

How Did Wren Trick the Windsor Councillors?

THE Town Hall in the High Street at Windsor was built partly by Sir Christopher Wren in 1686. When the town councillors found that it had no pillars to support the ceiling they complained to Sir Christopher, who assured them that the chamber was designed that way and that the ceiling was perfectly safe without pillars. The councillors, however, thought they knew better than the great architect and insisted that pillars should be placed in the room. So Wren erected four pillars, as shown in the photograph on this page, and the councillors were satisfied. The ceiling, they realised, was now properly supported.

Some years later, when the chamber was being cleaned, it was found that Sir Christopher had tricked the city fathers after all, for though he had erected the pillars as ordered, he had not carried them up to the ceiling. There was a space between the tops of the columns and the ceiling, which was not therefore supported by them at all. The gap in each case is about an inch.

What Fish is Called "74"?

THIS is a fish found in South African waters which was so named by Captain Alexander Anderson, who died in April, 1938. It was named after the 74 guns of the *Victory*, Nelson's flagship at Trafalgar. Captain Anderson, who founded the fishing industry at Durban and named four species of fish, loved Nelson's ship because a great-aunt of his was born aboard the flagship. The fish called the "74" has a dark black line and other markings which Captain Anderson considered resembled those of the *Victory*.

What Was the Confederation of the Rhine?

A CONFEDERATION of 16 German provinces in 1806 which allied themselves to France. Bavaria and Württemberg had allied themselves to France in 1805 and were rewarded by having their electorates raised to kingdoms In 1806 14 other German princes signed an act of alliance. After the downfall of Napoleon in 1814 the Confederation broke up and the princes then allied themselves against the common enemy.

When Did Shakespeare's Works First Reach U.S.A.?

IT is believed that no copy of Shakespeare's works crossed the Atlantic till the end of the 17th century. In 1723 Harvard University possessed a copy, but it was not till 1750 that a play of Shakespeare's was first acted in America. On March 3rd of that year "Richard the Third" was given at the theatre in Nassau Street, New York, by a company that had already acted in Philadelphia and probably gave a Shakespeare play there.

Why is St. Anthony Shown With a Pig?

THERE are two notable saints named Anthony. One, called "the Great," lived in the 4th century, and is known as the patriarch of the monastic life, because he founded monasteries and ruled his monks with great wisdom. Because of the submissiveness of the animals to him he is regarded as the patron saint of all herdsmen.

St. Anthony of Padua, accompanied by a pig, from a 15th-century glass painting.

It is not, however, this saint who is shown with a pig in painting and sculpture, but St. Anthony of Padua, a native of Lisbon and the friend and companion of St. Francis of Assisi. He was born in 1195 and after being an Augustinian monk for ten years entered the Franciscan Order at the age of 25. He was appointed by St. Francis to instruct the members of the order in theology, but he was chiefly famous as a preacher.

Anthony in the spirit of St. Francis was the friend of all animals, and used to preach to them when men refused to hear him. Because of this he is the patron saint of the lower animals and is shown accompanied by a pig, the lowliest and most despised of the domestic animals. He died at Vercelli near Padua in 1231.

Can Crabs Climb Trees?

ORDINARY crabs, of course, never climb trees, but there is a species known as the robber crab which lives in the islands where the Indian and Pacific Oceans join. It is a large creature and has only its abdomen armoured. Actually it is a relative of our hermit crabs who like to take shelter in disused whelk shells.

The robber crab breathes atmospheric air like ourselves, and not air mixed with water as does its relatives round the British coasts. It lives on coconut and seizes the nuts that have fallen from palm trees, making a hole and scooping out the white nut from the inside. Then it often puts its tail inside the shell as a protection. When no nuts are lying about this crab actually climbs the tall palms to pluck the nuts, and then when these have fallen to the ground he climbs down again and attacks them.

These crabs are very strong and it is said that they can break a man's arm with a nip of their powerful foreclaws. Charles Darwin placed one in a strong tin box, and it ate its way out.

The Town Hall at Windsor with pillars that do not reach the roof

What is the Order of the Golden Fleece?

THIS is an order of chivalry founded in 1430 by Philip III, surnamed the Good, Duke of Burgundy, on the occasion of his marriage with the Infanta Isabella of Portugal. The

A portrait of Charles the Bold, Duke of Burgundy, wearing the collar of the Order of the Golden Fleece

office of Grand Master of the Order passed to the House of Hapsburg in 1477 with the acquisition of the dominions of Burgundy, which included the Netherlands.

After the death of the Emperor Charles V the office was exercised by the Spanish kings, but when the Netherlands were ceded to Austria, the ruler of that land claimed the office. The dispute was never decided, and till the collapse of the thrones of Spain and Austria, the order existed independently in both countries. The symbol of the order, a golden ram, was chosen because wool had long been the staple industry of the Low Countries and the chief source of their wealth.

What is Unearned Increment?

IT is that portion of the increase in value of land which is due, not to anything the owner has done, but to the work of others, such as the making of a road, the building of a railway, the development and growth of a town, and so on. Some maintain that this value added to the land by the work of others than the owner should go, not to the owner, but to the State or the local authority.

Who Was Captain Swing?

THIS was the name assumed by certain persons between 1830 and 1833 who sent threatening letters to those farmers who used threshing machines. The wording of the letters was as follows: " Sir,—If you do not lay by your threshing machine, you will hear from Swing." The gangs went about to damage the machines and could scarcely be prevented by the yeomanry. They practised arson, the incendiary outbreaks being known as " Swing fires."

What Was the Ministry of All the Talents?

IT was an administration formed by Lord Grenville and Charles James Fox after the death of William Pitt in 1806. It was so called because it included so many notable statesmen, but George Canning was not a member of the ministry. It lasted from February 5th, 1806, to March 23rd, 1807, when it was dismissed by George III for attempting to pass a Bill to relieve Roman Catholics and Dissenters in the Army from their disabilities. The Duke of Portland then became Premier.

What Are the Singing Sands?

IN different parts of the world there are sandy areas which, when a person walks over them, give out a musical note or other sound. The late Marquis Curzon made a special study of these, and collected much evidence. In some cases the noise is like the sound of distant drums, at other times like mellow bells, and at other times like the vibrations of a stringed instrument. The sound sometimes lasts for a quarter of an hour at a time.

Lord Curzon tells us that at Kabul the people believe that the sounds of some singing sands in that region are caused by mysterious horsemen in a cave far underground shoeing their horses and beating their drums. The cause of the sounds is not definitely known, but it is believed that they are due, in some cases at any rate, to the rushing in of air to fill vacuums between sand grains as the traveller walks.

Who Were the Anti-Tobacconists?

THEY were a political party in Italy in 1848, when the Austrians, having a monopoly for the sale of tobacco in that country, the Liberals resolved to leave off smoking as a patriotic gesture. A cigar thus became the sign of loyalty to Austrian rule, and non-smoking of disaffection. The Austrians resented the anti-tobacconist movement and supplied their Italian troops with cigars, ordering them to smoke them ostentatiously in the streets. The insult was resented by the Italians, and on March 17th, 1848, the people of Milan rose in revolt and expelled the Austrians. Venice rose next and eventually Garibaldi liberated Italy, making it one united kingdom.

How Long Can a Cock's Tail Grow?

THE long-tailed cocks of Japan sometimes grow enormous feathers in their tails, and an example is given in the photograph on this page. The white cock shown here has a tail that is 25 feet long, one of the longest ever produced.

A Japanese cock exhibited in Tokyo with a tail 25 feet long

What Variety of Cat is That?

Silver Tabby

Wild cat of Scotland

Siamese

Black Persian

White Persian

Blue Persian

Russian

Abyssinian

Black Short-haired Cat

Tabby

Tortoiseshell

Chinchilla

Manx

Here are the principal varieties of cats that are shown at the cat shows and are kept as pets, together with the wild cat of Scotland. Of these, the Persian long-haired breeds are most esteemed as pets. The tailless Manx cat, it is thought, may be of Japanese origin. The Siamese cat, as its name implies, was originally imported from Siam. The breeding of fancy cats is a very lucrative industry. The colour of the eyes is important. Black cats should have orange or amber eyes, white Persians blue eyes, and blue Persians orange eyes. Some other cats have green eyes

What is the Anglo-Saxon Chronicle?

It is an historical document of great importance for the earlier part of English history. It is in the form of annals, beginning with the Christian era and ending at 1154. There are several ancient copies, which vary a great deal, but are all probably copies of one original. It is said to have been begun at the orders of King Alfred the Great.

What is Boat Drill?

Boat drill is a rehearsal on a steamship of what would happen, should it be necessary through collision, fire or other cause, to abandon the vessel. At a given signal the boats are lowered with their crews, just as they would be if the passengers had to take to the boats and leave the ship. Similar drills are held from time to time on the ships for the passengers, who have, at a given signal, to assemble on deck and don their life-belts. The value of such drills is not only to accustom the crew and passengers to what they would have to do in case of emergency, but also to prove from time to time that the life-belts are in their places and the boats and their tackle in working order.

What Are the Chillingham Cattle?

A breed of long-horned cattle, creamy white in colour with red-tipped ears, preserved on the Chillingam estate of the Earl of Tankerville in the North of England, and supposed to be the last remnant of the wild oxen of ancient Britain.

What is the Dance of Death?

This morbid subject was a great favourite with painters and sculptors in the Middle Ages and up to the 16th century. It was originally intended as a moral or allegorical lesson to remind people of the imminence

The crew of the British India liner " Mantola " going through boat drill in the Royal Albert Dock, London. They are obeying the order " Abandon Ship "

and power of death. People of all ranks in life and many callings were shown with Death as a skeleton dancer leading or accosting all mankind.

The best-known Dance of Death is that attributed to Hans Holbein, and published at Lyons in 1538. It was painted by him in fresco at Basle, but the original has long since been destroyed. A famous series of the Dance of Death was painted round the cloister of Old St. Paul's Cathedral in London during the reign of King Henry VI, at the expense of Jenkyn, a carpenter and citizen of London. Many cathedrals and churches had their Dance of Death, either sculptured or painted on the walls.

Do Snakes Ever Feign Death?

Snakes generally do not do this, but there is a species known as the hog-nosed snake, which lives in the southern United States, and which has the remarkable power of shamming death. When it is first alarmed this snake inflates its neck, forms a hood and then hisses loudly. Generally this bluff succeeds, but should it fail, the serpent, which is harmless, becomes completely limp and appears to all intents and purposes lifeless. It allows itself at such times to be handled without making the slightest movement to suggest that it is alive.

What is Riding the Marches?

This is another name for beating the bounds—that is, going round the parish and striking the boundaries with wands in order to draw attention to their position, as described on page 8. March is an old word for a boundary or frontier, and in the old days the frontiers between certain areas were ridden round.

A Chillingham bull, a specimen of the old type of English cattle

Who Was Torquemada?

HE was one of the most bigoted and bloodthirsty villains in history. A Dominican prior, he was instrumental in establishing the Inquisition in Spain and became its first inquisitor-general. His name has, ever since, been a byword for pitiless cruelty. Even the inquisitors under him tried to modify somewhat the horrible tortures he enjoined, and the number of victims who suffered death under his regime is said to have been nine thousand. His earliest victims were Jews, thousands of whom were burned, and he had the chief hand in the banishment of the Jews and Moors from Spain in the reign of Ferdinand and Isabella. Torquemada died in 1498.

What is Palissy Ware?

THIS is pottery made by the famous French potter Bernard Palissy, born about 1510. For 16 years he struggled and experimented to find a way of making enamels, and at last, after breaking up his furniture and tearing up his floors to feed the furnaces, he succeeded.

His most characteristic work consists of dishes or vases with a rough ground upon which are frogs, snakes, lizards and shells. But he also produced much very beautiful work, such as ewers and dishes adorned with classical figures and floral decoration.

Palissy was a Huguenot, and was imprisoned in 1562, but was released and set up his workshop in the Palace

A vase made by Bernard Palissy

of the Tuileries. He was later again arrested as a heretic and imprisoned in the Bastille, where he died. The results of attempts to copy Palissy ware have always fallen short of the originals.

What is the "Ship of Fools"?

IT is a translation by Alexander Barclay in 1508 of a satirical poem by Sebastian Brandt, a Strasbourg lawyer, called "Narrenschiff," which means the "Ship of Fools." This poem, published in 1494, was immensely popular at the time. It has 110 chapters, and tells of a transport ship of this world, laden with fools and bound for Fools' Paradise, which was capsized by Antichrist.

The travellers, tossed by the waves, sought safety in different ways. Some prayed, others scrambled into a crazy boat, and some clung to pieces of wreckage. The sea was strewn with books of an heretical character, and the moral is that the abuse of printing will wreck the Earth. The poem, however, attacks social weaknesses more than religious or moral evils. We read of tradesmen who are not honest, and diners who eat too fast. The English translation of 1508 is interesting as being the first English book in which reference is made to the New World.

Who is Old Fritz?

THIS, in its German form "Der Alte Fritz," is a popular nickname for Frederick the Great of Prussia, and is the name by which he is generally referred to in Germany.

An artistic dish of Bernard Palissy

Why Has a Billy-Goat a Beard?

THE beard in the male goat is probably there for the same reason that the male lion has a beard and mane, and the male fowl a comb.

A billy-goat, with its long beard, being given a bath

Darwin tells us that among animals the beard is generally confined to the males, and that they probably first acquired this feature through sexual selection, and that it was transmitted to their offspring. In other words, just as the fine tail coverts of the peacock are pleasing to the female bird, so in a bygone age the beard of the male animal attracted the females of the species, and so bearded males obtained mates where others failed. They were thus able to raise families and transmit their peculiarity to their offspring.

Among civilised human beings the beard has been a matter of fashion, being popular in some periods and unpopular in others. The male goat, like other male animals, often has formidable horns, and these were, of course, weapons of offence and defence. The animals with powerful horns, and the ability to use them, would survive where weaker animals with small or no horns would die out.

Who Started the Band of Hope?

THIS society for encouraging the total abstinence plea among children under 14 was started at Leeds by the Rev. Jabez Tunnicliffe. Its first president was Canon Morse.

How Do Rabbits Warn Their Fellows of Danger?

WHEN danger threatens a rabbit will warn its fellows by stamping on the ground with its hind feet and by showing the white patches

How a rabbit warns its fellows of danger by stamping on the ground

under its short tail. It is the white patches, looking like tufts of cotton-wool, that have led the Americans to call the rabbit "Molly Cottontail."

What Are Aldine Editions?

THESE are books published by Aldus Manutius, or, to give him his Italian name, Aldo Manuzio, at Venice from 1490 onwards. His son of the same name continued his work, and by 1597 about 908 books had been issued. The printing was fine, and the Aldine mark was an anchor entwined by a dolphin. In the 19th century Pickering, an English publisher, issued an edition of the British poets, which he called the Aldine edition.

Does the Rateable Value of London Increase?

YES ; at the revaluation of 1938 the rateable value of the County of London increased by £933,650 from £60,648,628 in 1937 to £61,582,278. This increase was the largest made in any year since the Valuation (Metropolis) Act was passed in 1869. About 60 per cent. of the increase was accounted for in the City of Westminster, St. Marylebone, Wandsworth, St. Pancras and Fulham. Decreases occurred in Southwark, £2,741 ; Deptford, £384 ; and Shoreditch, £246. This was partly due to a large amount of demolition preparatory to the erection of new dwellings.

Who Was Pope Joan?

SHE is said to have been a female pope who reigned from about 855 to 858, under the name of John VIII. She is said to have been of English descent, although born at Ingelheim or Mainz. Falling in love with a young Benedictine monk, she fled with him in male attire to Athens and after his death went to Rome where, disguised as a man, she rose to the rank of cardinal and was elected to succeed Leo IV on the papal throne. Modern historians regard the story as mythical, but like so many other old-established myths, it survives despite historical evidence to disprove it.

What is a Robin's Pincushion?

THIS is the name given to the curious mossy-looking red growth on a wild rose-tree which is due to the work of a little fly or wasp called by scientists *Rhodites rosae*. The female insect perforates a leaf-bud of the plant with her ovipositor and lays a number of eggs in the wound. With the eggs she probably leaves some irritating substance which causes the plant at the place affected to grow in a very curious way. A bright red mass of tough, wiry fibres develops, and it is the supposed resemblance of this growth to a pincushion that has led to the popular name. The growth is also called a bedeguar, which comes from a Persian word meaning "brought by the wind." It was an old idea that the wind carried these growths to the plant.

If the bedeguar be cut open, a number of little white grubs or larvae will be found inside which have hatched out of the eggs. They vary in number according to the size of the gall. The word gall means a sore place

The rose gall, which is called the Robin's Pincushion and also the bedeguar

or swelling. In due course, if the bedeguar is not interfered with, the grubs will change into little winged wasps that will emerge and start the life-story all over again.

Although the bedeguars or pincushions appear to grow from a twig or stem of the plant, this is apparent only, for actually they originate in a leaf. In some bedeguars there may be only three or four cells containing eggs or grubs, while others may have as many as forty-five. In the latter case the growth is of considerable size. Sometimes quite a number of bedeguars may be seen close together.

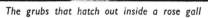

The grubs that hatch out inside a rose gall

What is the Ant-Lion?

This is the name given to the larva of an insect that is not found in Britain but is common in the south of Europe. Other species are found in North America. The perfect winged insect, which resembles a dragon-fly, is about an inch long. The larva is only half this length and is greyish-yellow in colour. Its head has two large mandibles and it has an ingenious way of catching its food which consists of ants and other insects, whose juices its sucks.

Above is the adult winged ant-lion resting on a grass stem, and on the right the larva. Both are shown considerably enlarged

The ant-lion is a slow mover and it could not catch the prey by chasing it, so it constructs a trap. It excavates a funnel-shaped pitfall in the ground and lies in wait at the bottom, generally buried except for the powerful mandibles. Insects crawling near the pitfall slip down the sloping sides as the sand gives way and are seized by the mandibles. Should they recover before they reach the bottom and begin to crawl up the slopes the ant-lion hurls sand upon them by quick jerks of its head, and they are soon thrown to the bottom where they can be seized. After the juices of the victims have been sucked the bodies are hurled out of the pit by a jerk of the ant-lion's head.

It is very interesting to watch this clever insect make its pitfall. It begins at the circumference and gradually narrows and deepens the pit, throwing out the sand with its head as it excavates. If in the course of digging it meets with a stone that it cannot easily remove, it abandons the trap and starts a new one elsewhere. The pit is about two inches deep. The ant-lion larva is capable of existing without food for a long time. Mr. Westwood, the entomologist, had a specimen which lived for six months without any nourishment whatever. This is Nature's provision for a creature whose food supply is precarious.

What Was the First Boat?

Probably man first learnt to travel in or on the water when some flood overtook him and he grasped a floating log to support himself, and found that by moving his legs he could drive the log towards the shore. Then perhaps two or more logs were fastened together with thongs or tough creepers, and so a raft was formed, on which man could float down the stream.

But the first real boat was no doubt a dug-out—that is, a tree-trunk hollowed out so as to make a place in which a man could sit. Dug-out boats are still made by primitive tribes in South America and in Africa. Perhaps the trunk of the first dug-out canoe was hollowed out by means of fire or by a stone adze.

Why Were Americans Called Red Indians?

They were called Indians because when their country was first discovered it was supposed to be the eastern shores of India. The descriptive adjective Red was given because the natives daubed their skins, as well as their canoes, clothes and weapons, with red ochre mixed with grease. It is not known whether this practice had some religious significance or whether the red coating was merely to protect the bare skins from the attacks of mosquitoes which swarm in the woods during the summer.

What Were Bushrangers?

They were lawless robbers who ranged the Australian Bush in early days and preyed upon the farmers and sheep stations. Most of them were escaped convicts, and so bad did this form of brigandage become that in 1815 martial law had to be proclaimed in one district. In New South Wales stringent repressive measures were taken to put down the evil, and in 1880, when the Kelly gang was broken up, this form of crime practically died out.

What Was the Augsburg Confession?

It was a statement of the doctrines of Martin Luther and his followers handed to the Emperor Charles V at the Diet of Augsburg on April 8th, 1530. There were two parts, the first containing 21 articles of faith and doctrine and the second seven articles on disputed points. This Confession does not now represent the theological views of the German Protestants.

The pit made by the ant-lion larva into which its prey tumbles

Is the Turkey Buzzard a Turkey?

No, it is quite a different bird. The turkey is a relation of the domestic fowl and pheasant, while

Turkey   Turkey Buzzard

The turkey and the turkey buzzard, which are entirely different birds

the turkey buzzard, also called the turkey vulture, is a condor, and a near relation of the vultures. The turkey is a native of North America, and was brought to Europe by the Spaniards about 400 years ago. At that time many of the luxuries of life came from Turkey, and so it was supposed that this bird had come from the Orient, and it was called after the country of its supposed origin, Turkey.

Curiously enough, the French when they received it thought it had come from India, and called it *coq d'Inde*, or Indian cock. The turkey buzzard, like all its kin, is a scavenger, and when it finds a dead animal it will not leave it until all but the bones and other hard parts have been eaten.

What is the New Domesday Book?

It is a return compiled by the Local Government Board in 1875 in two volumes, like the old Domesday Book, recording under each county in England and Wales the names and addresses of all owners possessing more than one acre of land in the county, with the size of the holding and its gross rental.

Can Elephants Swim?

Yes, although so ponderous in body, they are excellent swimmers, and if killed while in the water their carcasses will immediately float with one flank high out of the water.

"It is very interesting," says Sir Samuel Baker, "to watch the passage of a large river by a herd of these creatures, who, to a stranger's eye, would appear to be in danger of drowning, although in reality they are merely gambolling in the element, which is their delight. I have seen them cross the Brahmaputra when the channel was about a mile in width. Forty elephants scrambled down the precipitous bank of alluvial deposit and river sand. This, although about 35 feet high, crumbled at once beneath the forefeet of the leading elephant, and many tons detached from the surface quickly formed a steep incline. Squatting upon its hind quarters, and tucking its hinder knees beneath its belly, while it supported its head upon its trunk and outstretched forelegs, it slid and scrambled to the bottom, accompanied by an avalanche of earth and dust, thus forming a good track for the following herd. . . .

"Once within the river the fun began in earnest," continues the writer. "After a march in the hot sun it was delightful to bathe in the deep stream of the Brahmaputra, and the mighty forms splashed and disported themselves, sometimes totally submerged, with the drivers standing ankle-deep upon their hidden backs, which gave them the appearance of walking upon the surface. A tip of the trunk was always above water, and occasionally the animal would protrude the entire head, but only to plunge once more beneath the stream. In this way, swimming at great speed, and at the same time playing along their voyage, the herd crossed the broad river, and we saw their dusky forms glittering in the sunlight as they rose, wetted, from their bath, and waded majestically along the shallows to reach an island, from which they again started upon a similar journey to cross another channel of the river."

Elephants can remain floating for several hours without undue fatigue, but the limit of an elephant's swimming powers depends upon many circumstances, such, for example, as whether it is going with the stream.

What is a Gamekeeper's Larder?

This is the name given to the collection of vermin and predatory birds killed by the gamekeeper and nailed up in some conspicuous place on a tree-trunk or beam. In recent years gamekeepers have shown more intelligence and knowledge in selecting their victims. Formerly many birds which are not really enemies of the game at all used to be slaughtered. For example, on one gamekeeper's larder in Berkshire were seen the remains of twenty-three jays, three white owls and three brown owls, besides crows, sparrow-hawks and kestrels. White or barn owls are not enemies of game, and kestrels attack game very rarely.

The name "larder" is said to be given to the collection of victims because they are left hanging up to decay so as to provide gentles and other grubs for the pheasants.

The gamekeeper's larder, with the vermin he has caught and suspended

What Exactly is the Proletariat?

THE term means the great mass of the wage-earners who are dependent for their support on their daily work and possess neither property nor stable source of income. The word comes from the Latin name for the lowest classes of the community, the people who assist the State only by the production of offspring. Proles is the Latin word for offspring. "The dictatorship of the proletariat" is a phrase much used by Russian Bolsheviks for their system of government by soviets, in which the working classes are supposed to rule. It is a pet word with all Communists, probably because of its high-sounding character.

Who Were the Blanketeers?

THIS was a name given in 1894 to the Coxeyites, a band of 50,000 persons persuaded by "General" Coxey, their leader, to march 700 miles to Washington, with blankets on their backs, to terrorise Congress into finding work for the unemployed.

The name had previously been given to a body of half-starved Manchester operatives who met at St. Peter's Field on March 10th, 1817, each man provided with food and a blanket. Their purpose was to march to London to urge certain reforms upon Parliament, but the authorities were terrified and arrested their leaders.

Why Have London Firemen New Helmets?

THE brass helmets worn by men of the London Fire Brigade were picturesque and smart-looking, but they were not the most suitable headwear, as they needed a great deal of polishing to keep them bright, and they were a source of danger when in contact with live electric wires. It was therefore decided to adopt a new type of helmet, that shown in the photograph, made by Helmets Ltd. of Wheathampstead, who manufacture various types of firemen's helmets.

The new London helmet, known as the "Cromwell," weighs only 26 ounces, as against the 35 ounces of the brass helmet, and it can be cleaned easily and quickly with a wet rag or the application of any domestic wax polish. The body of the helmet is of four-ply natural cork, specially selected

The Colonial type of fireman's helmet

and treated to ensure insulation. It is covered with cotton drill steeped in non-alkaline flame-proof solution, and enamelled with special acid chemical and heat-resisting enamel to withstand a temperature of 350° Fah. without damage. The comb is built up of solid cork incorporated in the helmet, treated and insulated in the same manner as the rest of the helmet. The inside lining is of Pegamoid, the detachable chin-strap of canvas and rubber with bakelite studs, and no metallic substance of any kind is used in the helmet or its fittings. The

helmet is guaranteed to withstand safely a number of very strenuous tests, including the following:

Two rectangular bricks joined together and weighing 14 pounds are dropped four times in succession from a height of 12 feet on a supported helmet without it losing shape or breaking sufficiently to damage a shaped wood supporting-block representing the wearer's head. A stream

The helmet of the National Fire Brigade Association

of water is applied to it for 48 hours, or it is immersed in water for 70 hours without the water penetrating the helmet. Nor is the helmet affected when an electrical current up to 20,000 volts is gradually applied following the water resistance test, or a coal-gas flame under pressure applied at 1,000° Cen. is passed round the helmet in 34 seconds. It will be agreed that such a helmet is a marvel of protection and vastly superior to the old type of helmet.

What is a Planet Hunter?

THIS is the humorous name given to astronomers who make it their special business to discover planetoids or minor planets that have not been seen before. More than a thousand have been discovered, and at a meeting of the Royal Astronomical Society in 1909, a well-known astronomer banteringly suggested that it should be made a legal offence to discover any more minor planets, which shows that even astronomers are not without a sense of humour.

How Much Sugar Do We Eat?

THE quantity of unrefined sugar imported into Britain in a year is over 4,302 million pounds, so that the consumption per head of the population, men, women and children, is about 100 pounds. In addition, 115 million pounds of refined sugar are imported and 1,000 million pounds of molasses. About 130 million pounds of molasses are exported from England every year and 750 million pounds of refined sugar. The home production of beet sugar in England is about 1,100 million pounds.

London firemen in their new helmets. They are taking home the Challenge Cup given in a London Fire Brigade escape competition

How Many Readers Have British Museum Tickets?

THERE are about 15,000 names on the register of readers who possesss tickets for the British Museum Reading Room. Some of these, however, rarely use the room. But, of course, this does not represent the number of people who make use of the Reading Room, for day tickets are used for special purposes. Though the room seats 450, it is used on an average by 750 readers every day. There is an attendant to every ten readers, but, of course, the work of obtaining and checking books is very great, for there are many miles of shelves.

The Reading Room is open from 10 to 6, and some would like to see it kept open later for readers who cannot use it in the day time. The cost of keeping the Room open longer would amount to £2,750 per year for every extra hour.

What is the City of Destruction?

THIS is the name given in his allegory of "The Pilgrim's Progress" by John Bunyan to the city from which Christian set out on his journey to the Celestial City. The City of Destruction stands for this world and the Celestial City for Heaven.

Where Are the Largest Baskets Used?

THE largest baskets in general use are some that are employed in South Africa for loading oilcake, and they are made by the Cardiff Institute for the Blind. These huge baskets hold a ton of oilcake and their size can be seen from the examples in the photograph on this page.

Who Was the Stagirite?

THIS name is often given to the Greek philosopher Aristotle because he was born at Stagira, a city on the coast of Chalcidice in Macedonia, about 43 miles east of Thessalonica. Aristotle was the most famous of all the Greek philosophers and had an enormous influence on the development of philosophy and science in all the centuries before the birth of modern knowledge. He died at Chalcis in Euboea in 322 B.C. Much of his work was lost in after years.

A young elephant at the London Zoo holding a birch broom in his trunk

Can an Elephant Hold a Stick?

YES, by means of its trunk it can hold even a thin stick, and it can use a birch broom by curling its trunk round the handle as shown in the photograph. While the trunk is very powerful and can lift considerable weights, it is so sensitive that with the finger at the end the elephant can pick up a pin from the ground.

What Does the Defence of India Cost?

IN the year 1938–39 the estimated cost was £33,885,000, but in the previous year the cost was £35,407,000, and in 1936–37 £34,087,000. The British soldier in India costs three or four times as much as his Indian comrade. The authorised establishment of British troops in India is 57,000, but in May, 1938, the number was 6,000 below that figure.

How Many Books Did St. Augustine Write?

ST. AUGUSTINE of Hippo, says Mr. George H. Putnam, " was probably the most voluminous writer of the earlier Christian centuries. He was the author of no less than 232 books in addition to many tractates or homilies and innumerable epistles. His literary work was continued even during the siege of Hippo by the Vandals, and he died in Hippo (in 431) in his seventy-sixth year, while the siege was still in progress." Of course, his most famous books were the "Confessions" and "The City of God."

Making baskets at the Cardiff Institute for the Blind, each to hold one ton of oilcake

What Was the Camp of Boulogne ?

I_T was the name given to the vast preparations made in 1802 by Bonaparte, when First Consul of France, for the invasion of England. A camp was formed at Boulogne which became the centre of the preparations. Huge military stores and munitions were gathered and a large number of flat transports built to carry the troops

A peasant woman of Czechoslovakia, with her baby strapped to a board

across the Channel. The presence of the British Fleet made the invasion impossible and nothing came of the preparations.

Where Are Babies Strapped to Boards ?

T_HIS is done in many parts of the world and no doubt originated as a convenient method of carrying a child. We find it not only among the Red Indians of North and South America, but among the peoples of Asia and Polynesia and even in Europe. The photograph on this page shows a peasant woman of Myjava, a village in Czechoslovakia, with her baby strapped to a board.

Among savage or semi-savage people, however, the strapping down of the child on a board has another purpose than that of transport. The heads of the children are bound tightly to the board in order to alter the shape of the skull. The Chinook Indians of the neighbourhood of the Columbia River continued the process till quite recently. " It might be supposed," says Mr. Kane, " that the operation would be attended with great suffer-

ing, but I never heard the infants crying or moaning, although I have seen their eyes seemingly starting out of the sockets from the great pressure ; but on the contrary, when the thongs were loosened and the pads removed, I have noticed them cry until they were replaced. From the apparent dullness of the children whilst under the pressure I should imagine that a state of torpor or insensibility is induced, and that the return to consciousness occasioned by its removal must be naturally followed by a sense of pain."

The Wallamat Indians place the infant soon after birth upon a board to the edges of which are attached little loops of hempen cord or leather ; and other similar cords are passed across the back in a zig-zag manner through these loops, enclosing the child and binding it firmly down. To the upper edge of this board, in which is a depression to receive the back part of the head, another smaller one is attached by hinges of leather, and made to lie obliquely upon the forehead, the force of the pressure being regulated by several strings attached to its edge, which are passed through holes in the board upon which the infant is lying and secured there. Although to Western ideas the strapping of a baby to a flat board seems a strange proceeding, there is not necessarily anything injurious in this. The board may be healthier than a soft bed.

What is it to Grangerise a Book ?

I_T is to add to a book all kinds of things such as newspaper cuttings, illustrations, letters, and so on bearing on the subject-matter of the book. In this way, by adding many illustrations, etc., a single - volume book may be expanded to several volumes. The word is derived from the name of the Rev. J. Granger, who lived in the 18th century and started the practice. The adding of many outside illustrations to a book is often called " extra-illustrating."

Who Was Iphigenia ?

S_HE was the daughter of Agamemnon and Clytemnestra. When Agamemnon had killed a hart in the grove of Artemis or Diana, the angry goddess produced a calm which prevented the Greek Fleet in Aulis from sailing against Troy. On the advice of the seer Calchas, Agamemnon decided to sacrifice Iphigenia to appease the goddess. Artemis, however, put a hart in her place, and then carried her to Tauris, where she became the priestess of the goddess. Later she fled to Greece with her brother Orestes, whom she had saved, carrying off with her the statue of Artemis.

What is Paddle-Board Riding ?

T_HIS is the name given to a form of aquatic sport at Californian seaside resorts. The riders lie or sit on long oval boards that are something like flat canoes and drive themselves along by using their hands as paddles. They face the incoming surf, and a race of paddle-board riders is certainly an exciting sport to watch.

Bathers riding the waves on paddle-boards at Venice, California

Can a Sole Conceal Itself ?

FLAT-FISH like the plaice and sole have the uppermost side, which is exposed to the light shining down through the water, coloured, while the underside is white. The reason for this is that an enemy looking up at the fish from below would see its

and, of course, the greater the supply, the lower the price. In spring mackerel feed largely upon plankton, floating organic life found in the ocean. The plankton that the mackerel eat is made up of small crustaceans, and these in turn feed upon vegetable plankton, such as diatoms, as well as upon lowly animals called infusoria.

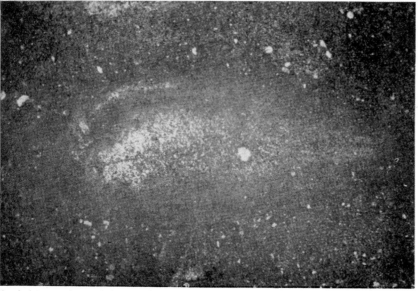

A sole lying on the sandy bottom of the sea. It will be seen that its colour camouflages the fish

body white like the light, while an enemy looking down from above, while the fish is lying on the sea bed, would see its body dark, merging with its surroundings. The fish would not be noticed, and how well it is camouflaged by its upper colouring can be seen by the accompanying photograph which shows a sole lying on the sandy bottom of the sea. Not only is its colour an excellent camouflage, but the fish, when it comes to rest, stirs up a cloud of sand grains, which, settling down, help still further to hide the fish.

Experiments have shown that if such fish be kept in tanks lighted from beneath instead of from above, the underside will, in course of time, cease to be white and become covered with pigment.

Who Said "Think Imperially"?

THIS injunction was given by Mr. Joseph Chamberlain in a speech at the Guildhall on January 20th, 1904. "If I may venture to give you a message now," he said, "I would say, 'Learn to think imperially.'"

Does the Sunlight Affect the Price of Mackerel ?

MR. E. J. ALLEN, the well-known marine biologist, says there is a close connection between sunlight and the price of mackerel. The more sunshine there is in May, the more mackerel there will be at Billingsgate,

The production of these forms of plankton depends largely on the amount of light falling on the sea, and so when there is much sunshine the diatoms and infusoria multiply, the tiny crustaceans have plenty of food, they supply the mackerel, which, having ample sustenance, increase in numbers. Thus plenty of sunlight helps the housewife buying mackerel.

How Many Telephone Calls Are Made Yearly?

IT is stated that the total number of telephone calls in the world every year is now 25,000 million, and that of these half are handled in the United States. In Great Britain the annual number of local calls is 1,881,600,000 and of trunk calls 100,704,000, or nearly 2,000 millions altogether.

What Was Babington's Conspiracy ?

IT was a conspiracy in 1585 to murder Queen Elizabeth and place Mary, Queen of Scots, on the English throne. Pope Pius V had excommunicated Elizabeth and authorised all true Catholics to compass her death. A Jesuit undertook to assassinate her, and he was joined by nearly a dozen other conspirators including Anthony Babington, a young man of fortune, who had become enamoured of the Scottish queen. Babington revealed the plot in a letter to Mary, and this being intercepted, the conspirators were all arrested and executed. It was this conspiracy that sealed Mary's fate.

How Many Young Does a Goat Have ?

THE domesticated goat, of which there are almost innumerable varieties, differing greatly in appearance, breeds naturally once a year in the spring, but with the introduction of foreign blood it is possible to get them to breed at other periods, so that a continuous supply of milk can be obtained all the year round, as in the case of cattle. Generally a domesticated goat has two kids at a birth, though occasionally three or four.

Children playing with the two kids of a nanny-goat

What is a Magic Ring?

IT is a ring which in the old days of superstition was supposed to have some virtue or property that would bring the wearer good or bad luck. Sometimes the magic ring was made of

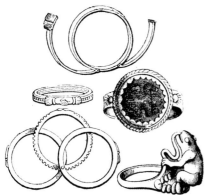

On the right are two magical rings and on the left some gimmal rings

half a dozen metals and ensured the wearer's success in any undertaking on which he chose to embark. Other rings were supposed to render the wearer invisible in danger, to enable him to read the secrets of another's heart, or to ensure him from losing blood when wounded.

Somewhat akin to the magic rings were the gemal or gimmal rings used to unite couples in love. The name means " twin " and the ring is constructed of twin or double hoops, which play one within another, like the links of a chain. Each hoop has one of its sides flat, the other convex ; each is twisted once round and each surmounted by a hand issuing from an embossed fancy-work wrist or sleeve, the hand rising somewhat above the circle and extending in the same direction.

The course of the twist in each hoop is made to correspond with that of its counterpart, so that on bringing together the flat surfaces of the hoops, the latter immediately unite in one ring. A man would put his finger through one of the hoops and his lady-love her's through the other. In this way they were symbolically yoked together. " A yoke," says one writer, " which neither could be said wholly to wear, one half being allotted to the other. In this use of the gimmal may be seen typified a community of interests, mutual forbearance and a participation of authority."

What is the Origin of "Open Sesame"?

THIS phrase, which has come to mean any charm of person or speech which will procure for its possessor an entry into select or exclusive circles, comes from the "Arabian Nights' Entertainments." There, in the tale of Ali Baba and the Forty Thieves, Cassim finds "Open Sesame" to be the magic words at whose utterance the door of the robbers' cave flies open.

Who Was the Man of Ross?

THIS name was given to John Kyrle, a citizen of the town of Ross, in Herefordshire, who lived from 1664 to 1754 and was noted for his great benevolence and public spirit, although his income was never more than £500 a year. The name " Man of Ross " was given to him in his lifetime by a country friend, and it was perpetuated by the poets Pope and Coleridge. Here is Pope's tribute to the Man of Ross :

> But all our praises why should lords engross ?
> Rise, honest muse ! and sing the Man of Ross.
> Pleased Vaga echoes through her winding bounds,
> And rapid Severn hoarse applause resounds.
> Who hung with woods yon mountain's sultry brow ?
> From the dry rock who bade the waters flow ?
> Not to the skies in useless columns tost,
> Or in proud falls magnificently lost,
> But clear and artless, pouring through the plain.
> Health to the sick and solace to the swain.
> Whose causeway parts the vale with shady rows ?
> Whose seats the weary traveller repose ?
> Who taught that heaven-directed spire to rise ?
> " The Man of Ross " each lisping babe replies.

Can One Multiply Products By Themselves 15 Times?

POSSIBLY a person might, but he is hardly likely to do so for the task would take him about a quarter of a century to perform. " Take the number 15," says Mr. William S. Walsh. " Multiply that by itself and you get 225. Now multiply 225 by itself and so on, until fifteen products have been multiplied by themselves in turn. You don't think that is a difficult problem ? Well, you may be a clever mathematician, but it would take you about a quarter of a century to work out this little sum.

The final product called for contains 38,589 figures, the first of which are 1442. Allowing three figures to an inch, the answer would be over 1,070 feet long and require about 500 million figures. At the rate of one a minute, a person working 10 hours a day for 300 days a year would be 28 years about it."

Where Does the Water of the Spring Come From?

WHEN the rain falls from the clouds some of it runs away into streams and rivers, while other water sinks through the soil till it reaches a layer of impervious earth like clay. There it remains unless the clay slopes away in one direction, when the water slowly makes its way down on top of the clay, till at last it finds an outlet where the clay ends in the side of a hill or cliff. This outlet we call a spring.

Spring water is cold because it has been for a long time underground away from the heat of the Sun, and it often tastes pleasant because it has dissolved various kinds of mineral matter. Hard water is always more pleasant to the taste than soft water.

Where Are Birch Brooms Made?

BIRCH brooms, which have been made and used for many centuries, are still manufactured in different parts of England. A notable centre of the industry is Forest Row, Sussex, where something like 75,000 brooms are made every year. The industry has been carried on here for centuries, and among those engaged in it in 1938 was Mr. William Card, eighty years of age, who had worked as a birch broom maker since he was fourteen. Besom is another name for this kind of broom.

Making birch brooms at Forest Row, Sussex, where 75,000 are produced every year

1st Avatar of Vishnu

2nd Avatar

3rd Avatar

4th Avatar

5th Avatar

6th Avatar

7th Avatar

8th Avatar

9th Avatar

10th Avatar

Rama

Ballaji and wife

Witthoba and wife

Krishna

Krishna

The Boy Krishna

Sita

Triveni

Hanuman

Ravana

Ganesa

Kama-deva

Karttikeya

Garuda

Nagnis

Devi

India is undoubtedly the land of idols par excellence. Everything almost is personified and becomes a god, and according to the Reverend E. Osborn Martin, long a missionary in India, there are said to be at present 330,000,000 gods and godlings among the Hindus. As Dr. Monier Williams explains, " There is not an object in Heaven or Earth which a Hindu is not prepared to worship; Sun, Moon and stars; rocks, stocks and stones; trees, shrubs and grass; sea, pools and rivers; his own implements of trade; the animals he finds most useful; the noxious reptiles he fears; men remarkable for any extraordinary qualities—for great valour, sanctity, virtue or even vice; good and evil demons, ghosts and goblins, the spirits of departed ancestors; an infinite number of semi-human and semi-divine existences, inhabitants of the seven upper and the seven lower worlds—each and all come in for a share of divine honours or a tribute of more or less adoration." On these pages are given representations of

God? Some of India's Many Deities

Agni

Surya

Chandra

Indra

Pavana

Kuvera

Kuvera

Yama

Nirritu

Varuna

Narayana

Trimurti

Brahma

Saraswati

Vishnu

Lakshmi

Siva

Siva

Siva

Siva

Siva

Kali

Kali

Kali

some of the more important gods of the Hindu mythology. The great Hindu trinity consists of Brahma, Siva and Vishnu, and according to the sacred books, Vishnu had ten avatars or incarnations, which are represented in the first ten drawings. Kali is the cruel goddess, the fierce and bloody consort of Siva, and is represented in various ways. Krishna is the most celebrated hero of the Indian mythology, and the most popular of all the deities. Hanuman is the celebrated monkey god who assisted Rama, the king of the solar race, who was the seventh incarnation of Vishnu, in his war against Ravana, the demon king of Ceylon. Ganesa, the elephant god, is regarded as the god of wisdom. Krishna is sometimes shown as a boy. Devi, or "the great goddess," is the wife of the god Siva, and daughter of Himavat, that is, the Himalayan Mountains. She is mentioned in the great Indian classic Maha-bharata. Nirritu is a deity personating death. Agni represents fire, one of the most ancient objects of Hindu worship

Is the Daddy-Long-Legs a Pest?

THE daddy-long-legs or crane-fly, the spidery-looking fly with gauze wings, is very familiar to us all, and it looks quite inoffensive. So far as doing any harm to our bodies is concerned, it is harmless, but this

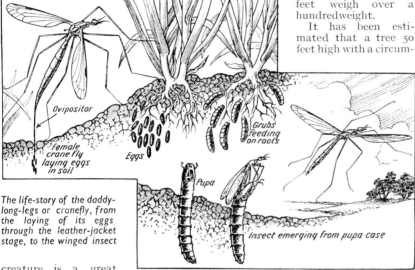

The life-story of the daddy-long-legs or cranefly, from the laying of its eggs through the leather-jacket stage, to the winged insect

Ovipositor / *Female crane fly laying eggs in soil* / *Eggs* / *Grubs feeding on roots* / *Pupa* / *Insect emerging from pupa case*

creature is a great pest and should be killed when seen. The female crane-fly bores a hole in the soil with her ovipositor and lays eggs underground. In course of time little grubs hatch out and these at once start feeding upon the roots of the grass. As a result the grass soon perishes, and woe betide a lawn where the crane-fly lays its eggs.

The grubs or larvae, when full grown, are known as leather-jackets. They are rarely seen, for they remain underground. After a time the larva becomes a pupa and then the imago or winged insect emerges. Just before this happens the pupa raises or works itself half out of the ground by means of spines on its sides. The winged insect escapes and then the life-story starts all over again.

It is, of course, in the leather-jacket stage that the crane-fly is a great pest.

What Are Brassarts?

THIS is a term used in describing plate armour for the metal pieces which protect the upper part of the arms, and connect the shoulder pieces with the elbows, and cover the arm thence to the wrist. The upper part was called the rerebrace, and the lower the vantbrace or vambrace.

How Does Snow Wreck a Tree?

AFTER a very severe snow-storm trees often have their boughs broken off, and telegraph wires and poles are demolished. Snow is such a light substance that we may be excused for wondering how it is that the snow can do so much damage. Of course, if there is not a hard frost the snow soon gets blown from a tree or telegraph wire, and little harm is done, but when there is a frost and the snow is frozen into ice, the weight carried by a tree or a number of telegraph wires is very great. A cubic foot of ice weighs 57½ pounds, or in other words, two cubic feet weigh over a hundredweight.

It has been estimated that a tree 50 feet high with a circumference, including all its branches, of about 60 feet, will carry after a heavy snowstorm as much as 5 tons of snow. In one blizzard in America the weight of snow on eighty telephone wires was 4 tons for each span between the poles, and naturally the strain on the wires when a strong wind was blowing must have been very great.

It is not surprising that the poles were snapped off and the wires torn.

How Are the Mountains of the Moon Measured?

THE shadows of these lunar peaks are cast upon the ground of the Moon, and it is by measuring the shadows that astronomers are able to discover the height of the various mountains on the Moon.

It seems strange, but a scientist can measure the mountains of the Moon much more exactly than he can measure such peaks on the Earth as Mount Everest. Knowing the time of the day and the extent to which the shadows lengthen at that time, the height of the mountain is worked out by mathematics. In proportion to the size of the Moon the mountains there are much taller than those on the Earth. Some of the mountains are found to be 20,000 feet above the plains on which they stand.

Mountains on the Earth on the same scale would be 15 miles high.

Where Are Rope Bridges Most Common?

IN Northern India, especially in the mountainous regions, rope bridges are very common, the difficulty and cost of building more substantial bridges in such districts being prohibitive. In many cases a stout rope is suspended across the river or ravine and some sort of a rope seat is provided on which travellers can be pulled across from one side to the other. Other bridges consist of a stout rope on which the passenger walks, while he steadies himself by holding two lesser ropes placed one on each side for his hands. More pretentious bridges have a footpath of rope and woven balustrades on each side as in the photograph below.

Two types of rope bridge crossing the river Jhelum near Uri, India

What is That Wonder of the Sea?

Looming

A striking example of phosphorescence of the sea

Above is an iceberg, weighing millions of tons, and below, deep sea luminous fishes

Above is a waterspout, and below, a giant squid being drawn from the sea

Here are some wonders of the sea. The first drawing shows a phenomenon which is of the same nature as the mirage of the desert. It is known as looming. Mariners see in the air inverted images of ships. The explanation is that the air in contact with the water is colder and denser than that above, and so the rays are bent and the image of a ship, which may be a long distance away below the horizon, is thrown up in the sky. A person always imagines that bent rays come in a straight line, hence the illusion that the ship is high up. Sometimes there are two images, one seen the right way up. The second illustration shows phosphorescence, in which the sea appears to be illuminated. This is due to myriads of small phosphorescent creatures known as infusorians or protozoa. Each is the size of a pin's head. The third drawing is that of a waterspout, and the fourth that of a giant iceberg. Some icebergs contain hundreds of millions of tons of ice. At the bottom is a giant squid being hauled aboard ship. These strange creatures sometimes have bodies 10 feet long and tentacles 30 feet in length. They weigh as much as half a ton. The last drawing shows some of the curious luminous fishes that are found in the lower depths of the sea. The lights they show are believed to be for the purpose of attracting prey

Plate XV

What is That Strange Appearance?

The Spectre of the Brocken

The Aurora

The " Greasy Ring " Round the Moon

Mock Moons and Haloes

A Circular Halo Round the Moon

Meteors or Shooting Stars

The Zodiacal Light

St. Elmo's Fire

A Lightning Flash

Various strange phenomena are seen from time to time in the sky, and some of these are illustrated on this page. The Spectre of the Brocken is really the throwing of the shadow of a person by the morning Sun on the distant mist of the mountains. The aurora is, of course, an electrical phenomenon seen in the north and south, particularly in the neighbourhood of the magnetic poles. The greasy ring round the Moon is a halo due to the refraction and reflection of the light by minute ice crystals, which form a thin veil of cirro-stratus clouds, very high up. Sometimes there is a circle of light round the Moon, formed by the diffraction of the light as it passes through a cloud made up of minute drops of water. Mock moons and double haloes are caused by the refraction of light through ice crystals high up. Shooting stars are, of course, meteors from Space being burnt up in the air. The Zodiacal light, sometimes seen in England, is a slanting cone of very faint light thought to be a reflection of sunlight on minute particles of matter surrounding the Sun. St. Elmo's Fire is an appearance like tongues of fire due to electric discharges from pointed objects like the masts of ships, the spires of churches, and the branches of trees. It is most often seen at sea. Lightning is, of course, a huge electric spark between electrified clouds or clouds and Earth

Plate XVI

Can a Crab Grow a New Claw?

CRABS and lobsters when periodically changing their clothes, or in other words shedding their carapace, so as to grow a new and bigger one to contain their expanding body, often lose one of their claws. In some way it becomes detached from the body and they then have only one claw. At other times two of these animals

A common shore crab, which has lost a claw in a fight, growing a new limb. This is very small and is seen on the right

may engage in a fierce fight and one of their claws is torn off. Now, when a human being loses a limb, it is gone for ever and he can never grow another. Not so the crab or lobster. The next time he sheds his carapace he begins to grow a new limb. It grows very much as a bud grows into a branch, but for a long time it is much smaller than the limb that it replaces. Only after the crab or lobster has cast its shell three or four times will the new claw attain anything like its full proportions.

What Were "Paul's Walkers"?

THIS name was given in the 17th century to loungers in St. Paul's Cathedral, in London, which was then a regular place of resort as a club might be today. The young gallants met there, and also business men, for the discussion of commercial transactions. Indeed, the interior of the Cathedral was as noisy as any street.

Who Was Xantippe?

XANTIPPE was the wife of the Greek philosopher Socrates, and is said to have been of a peevish and quarrelsome disposition. Her name has become proverbial for bad temper.

What is the Body of a Man Worth?

IN the sense that it is the only means by which the real man can do anything it is worth a great deal, especially in the case of writers, scientists, engineers, and so on. But actually the body regarded as so much material is not worth very much. Mr. C. E. M. Joad, the scientist, and Dr. T. E. Lawson, the eminent physician, have declared that for one man's body all that is needed is a ten-gallon barrel full of water, enough fat for seven bars of soap, carbon for 9,000 lead pencils, phosphorus for 2,200 match-heads, iron for one medium-sized nail, lime enough to whitewash a chicken coop, and small quantities of magnesium and sulphur, the whole lot worth a few shillings. Yet what a marvellous thing that when these materials are put together and occupied by a mind, they can produce a Galileo or a Newton, a Shakespeare or a Shelley, a Napoleon or a Columbus, an Edison or a Marconi.

How Many Rivets Can Be Driven in a Day?

IN the old days when rivets were driven home with the hammer, one riveter striking while the other held the rivet, to drive 400 rivets was considered a good day's work. But with the new pneumatic riveter the speed was greatly expedited and during the War there was a great competition between riveters in England and America to obtain a record. It seems incredible that while at the beginning of the War the record was 836 rivets for a nine-hour day, this was constantly increased till at last in a Belfast yard a workman drove 11,209 rivets in a nine-hour working day.

The use of the pneumatic hammer, or air-gun as it is called, can be learnt in a very short time, and one man who had never driven a rivet in his life went to work in a shipyard and after six weeks' training was able to drive 2,803 rivets in an eight-hour day.

What Are Mother Carey's Chickens?

THIS is a name given by sailors to the stormy petrel. Mother Carey is a corruption of Mater cara or "dear mother," meaning the Virgin Mary. French sailors call these birds "Oiseaux de Notre Dame" or "birds of Our Lady." The stormy petrel is supposed to give warning to sailors of an approaching storm, and it is regarded as very unlucky to kill one of these birds. The legend is that each stormy petrel contains the soul of a dead seaman. Mother Carey's goose is the great fulmar.

How Many Kinds of Lenses Are There?

THE two principal varieties of lenses are the convex and the concave, but there are a number of modifications

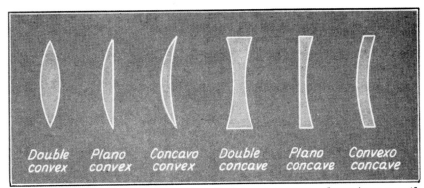

The various types of lenses shown in section, with their correct names. Convex lenses magnify and concave lenses diminish

and these are shown in the diagram on this page, where the different types of lenses are given in section. A convex lens is thicker in the middle than at the edges and magnifies objects viewed through it, while a concave lens is thinner in the middle and diminishes.

What is a Thrush's Anvil ?

THE song-thrush, or throstle as it is often called, feeds on insects of all kinds, earthworms and slugs and snails. The snail-shells are broken by being struck vigorously against a stone, and as the same stone is used again

The anvil of a thrush, with the smashed shells of snails lying about

and again large quantities of newly broken shells are sometimes found lying on and all round it. It is such a stone that is called a thrush's anvil.

An interesting fact is that when the thrushes are in the neighbourhood of the seashore they often seize periwinkles, probably mistaking them for snails, and try to break the shells open in the same way. But these shells are much stronger than those of snails, and despite constant batterings on the stony anvil the thrush is unable to fracture them.

Who Was the Chief God of the Norse Mythology ?

HE was Odin, corresponding to the Anglo-Saxon Woden, and he is the source of all wisdom and the patron of culture and heroes. His father was Bör, his brothers Vilë and Ve, his wife Frigga, and his sons Thor and Balder. His steed was Sleipnir, his attendant wolves Geri and Freki, and he also had two ravens. He held his court at Valhalla, sat on a throne called Hlidskjalf and was surnamed the All-Father. He was ultimately swallowed by the wolf Fenris.

What is Target Ball ?

TARGET ball is a game which is played by sides who have to beat a ball with their hands through holes on a raised board. There are four holes, numbered respectively 1, 2, 3 and 4, and according to the number of the hole that the ball passes through so points are scored. It is a good game for school camps.

How Does the Bee Make Its Wax ?

UNLESS the wax is supplied by the bee-keeper, the bees begin their work in the hive by producing the wax of which their combs are formed.

This wax-making is done by the workers. The abdomen of each is made up of six rings, and under these are eight little pockets in which, by means of certain glands, the bee can make wax from honey.

The wax is produced in a fluid condition and a temperature from 87 degrees to 98 degrees Fahrenheit is necessary. This temperature is made by the bees clustering together. The fluid wax cools into little scales, and these are pushed out of the wax pockets, removed by means of pincers on the hind legs, transferred to the front legs, and then passed to the jaws. The bee now chews up the wax, mixing it with saliva. Then it is attached with other wax to the roof of the hive, and this forms the foundation of the comb.

We build our storehouses upward from the ground. The bee builds them downward from the roof. Architect bees form the wax into hexagonal cells.

Is Homicide Ever Regarded in Law as Justifiable ?

YES, there are in English law several kinds of justifiable homicide. They are the putting of a man to death as the result of a legal sentence, the killing by an officer of justice of a person who assaults or resists him and cannot otherwise be taken ; and the killing of persons for the dispersion of riots or rebellions, assemblies or the prevention of atrocious crimes.

In addition to justifiable homicide the law recognises excusable homicide, which is of two kinds—first by misadventure, and secondly in self-defence. But there is now no practical difference between justifiable and excusable homicide.

It must be understood that the law is very strict in regard to homicide in self-defence. The person who slays another must really prove that he had reason to think his life was in danger.

A game of target ball in progress at a school camp in Glamorganshire

How Are Eastern Bells Rung?

ORIENTAL bells such as those found in China and Japan have no tongue and are sounded by being struck from the outside. In the case of small bells a wooden hammer or mallet is generally used, but the huge

How the great nunnery bell at Kioto, Japan, is rung

temple bells are struck by a log or beam suspended by ropes and swung against the bell by means of a smaller rope suspended from the beam. The photograph on this page of a priestess ringing the great bell of a 12-century-old nunnery at Kioto, Japan, illustrates the method. The bell shown is more than nine hundred years old.

How Big Can a Jellyfish Grow?

THIS depends upon the species, for there are many kinds of jellyfish. We know those that float in the sea round the British coasts which are often about six or seven inches in diameter. But there are some jellyfish found off the coast of Greenland that are so small that a wineglass of water could hold three thousand of them. At the other extreme is a species found in the Arabian Sea which grows to enormous proportions. A specimen found on the shore near Bombay is said to have weighed several tons. Yet the creature had no bones or shell, and in the course of nine months it disappeared altogether into the air.

Does a Stone Fall Perpendicularly Down a Shaft?

NO, for when it is released at the top of the shaft it has the speed at which the surface of the Earth is rotating, and it keeps this speed as it falls. The result is that when it strikes the bottom of the shaft it is moving a little faster than the Earth at that point, and so it strikes the bottom a little in advance of the point at which it would have fallen if the Earth had been stationary. This is one of the proofs of the Earth's rotation.

Scientists have found after many experiments that a body falling 520 feet down a shaft deviates more than an inch to the east, and, of course, the deeper the shaft in which the experiment is carried out, the more will the stone deviate. Many experiments of this kind have been carried out by scientists.

Who Were the Black Friars?

THEY were the Dominicans or Preaching Friars and were so called in England because of the colour of their dress, as distinct from the White Friars or Carmelites and Grey Friars or Franciscans. The Dominicans were founded in 1216 and first appeared in England in 1221. The Franciscans or Mendicant Friars were authorised by the Pope in 1210 and formally ratified in 1223. They first entered England in 1224. The Orders, of course, flourish today.

Which Part of Our Skin is Most Sensitive?

THE skin is not equally sensitive everywhere. The fingers are more sensitive to touch than the toes. When the two points of a pair of compasses touch our finger-tips they can be detected separately if only a twelfth of an inch apart. On the under-lip the two points to be detected must be a sixth of an inch apart, and on the tip of the nose a quarter of an inch. In the palm of the hand they must be half an inch apart, and on the back of the hand an inch apart, otherwise we could not recognise that there were two points. At the back of the neck they must be opened two inches.

The most sensitive part is the tongue, and there the two points of the compasses can be detected when they are one-twentieth of an inch apart.

Do Monkeys Play With Their Young?

YES; monkeys, both in the wild state and in captivity may often be seen playing with their young, and when the children try to get away the parents will often pull them back by grabbing their tails.

A mother monkey in the Berlin Zoo trying to keep her child out of mischief

Can the Fox Be Tamed?

YES, foxes are often tamed and become the pets of their owners, but they must be taken very young or be born in captivity. It is nevertheless a fact that, though they are brought up in company with domestic

An inquisitive fox looks out for danger

dogs and are treated kindly, they generally remain suspicious, sly and timid, though there have been examples to the contrary.

The fox is a queer animal and, though it preys on poultry and rabbits, will sometimes behave towards these in a friendly manner. Cases are on record where a fox has lived with rabbits in a warren and never touched them—certainly an exhibition of self-control which is astonishing.

The cunning of the fox is proverbial, and it shows this in captivity as well as in the wild state. A fox which was kept in a yard was confined by a chain that allowed him a fair range for walking. One evening in the autumn a farm wagon, returning from the field with a load of corn, passed near the shelter of the fox, and an ear of corn dropped from the pile.

The fox went out, took the corn, and carried it quickly back into his home. What he wanted with the corn no one could understand, but the next morning he was seen to come out of his shelter and nibble off some of the grains from the ear, scattering them about in view of the poultry which were in the yard.

In due course the chickens went up to the corn, and while they were eating it out sprang the fox and seized one of them, taking it back into his shelter,

where he made a meal of it. This looks remarkably like reasoning on the part of the fox.

Another story which seems to show reasoning power tells how a badger was seen moving leisurely along the bank of a river in Scotland, when a fox came out and walked just in the rear of the badger. Then suddenly the fox leapt into the water, and soon afterwards a pack of hounds at full speed came up. They had been pursuing the fox, which by this time was far off, floating down the stream, while the luckless badger was torn to pieces by the dogs.

Some foxes kept in captivity in the country have run off at the mating season, but have returned to their masters later and behaved as though they had never revisited their native haunts.

What is the Lindisfarne Manuscript?

IT is a manuscript containing the four Gospels in Latin with certain prefatory matter by St. Jerome, written about the year A.D. 700 in the island of Lindisfarne, now called Holy Island, off the coast of Northumberland, by Bishop Eadfrith. It is a very beautiful manuscript, with coloured patterns adorning some of its pages, and is written on a very stout parchment. The MS. contains later notes in the Northumbrian dialect. The work is now in the British Museum.

Does Rain Fall Up or Down?

THIS may seem a foolish question, for, as we know, the rain always comes down wherever we may be. But if a person were on another planet and could, with some super-telescope, see what was going on on the Earth, he might see rain falling down on England and at the same time falling up on Australia. Down and up are only relative terms. If while standing in London we could look right through the Earth and see people in Melbourne or Sydney, they would appear to be walking upside-down and the rain would be falling up. It is the attraction of the Earth that holds us all to the Earth wherever we may be.

Why Does a Plant Need Water?

IT needs water in the first place because more than three-quarters of the weigh of an average plant

Six young fox cubs caught in a wood near Londonderry which are being tamed by their owner

consists of water. It is giving off water all the time, and so a constant supply of water is needed to prevent the plant withering. Then large quantities of water must pass through the plant continuously in order that the food solution in the soil may be carried to the leaves. This water travels up through the roots and, after yielding its nourishment, passes off into the air through the leaves. Experiments carried out by scientists show that for each ton of dry grain produced from the soil, from 300 to 500 tons of water must have been taken in from the soil by the plants that produce the grain.

Why Are Geese Eaten at Michaelmas?

AN old legend says that St. Martin, being tormented by a goose, killed and ate the bird. Apparently he dined too well for he died from the repast, and ever afterwards good Christians sacrificed the goose on St. Martin's Day. But St. Martin's Day is November 11th, and not Michaelmas, and so this explanation does not fit.

Probably the geese were eaten at this season because it was a time of year when stubble geese were at their best. Dr. Brewer says tenants formerly presented their landlords with a goose at Michaelmas to keep in their good graces. It was a popular saying, " If you eat goose on Michaelmas Day you will never want money all the year round." Ploughmen indulged in a goose harvest home which fell about Michaelmas.

Which Was the Augustan Age of England?

THIS name is given to the reign of Queen Anne, from 1702 to 1714. It is also called the Silver Age in contrast with the Golden Age which was that of Elizabeth. Anne's reign included some part of the lives of Sir Isaac Newton, John Ray, the father of English botany, Sir Christopher Wren, Addison, Defoe, Pope, Gay, and John Churchill, Duke of Marlborough.

What Was the Lutestring Administration?

IT was that formed by Lord Rockingham in 1765 following the Grenville Administration. It was clear that the ministry could not last long, and Charles Townshend, himself Paymaster of the Forces in it, said, " It is a mere lutestring administration," the reference being to lutestring, a corruption of lustrin, a summer silk unfit for winter wear.

Are Dandelions Good to Eat?

IT is surprising that the dandelion is not made more use of for culinary purposes. The young leaves, when freshly gathered, make an excellent addition to the salad, and the roots when ground and roasted make a good substitute for coffee. Indeed, for people who are very liable to suffer from indigestion, doctors often recommend dandelion coffee in place of other drinks.

Can a Man Steal His Own Dog?

ACCORDING to a case which came before the Grimsby justices some years ago, apparently a man can be charged with stealing his own dog. In this case the animal was found wandering, and a boy took it to the police-station, where it was placed in the kennels. Later, the owner climbed the railings and removed his dog from the kennels. But the police maintained that while the dog was in the kennels it was legally the property of the Chief Constable. It was suggested that the owner had removed his dog in the way described because he did not want to pay the police charges for its recovery, and so he was actually charged with stealing his own property. The magistrates, however, dismissed the case.

How Many Princes of Wales Have There Been?

THERE have been altogether nineteen, counting from Edward, afterwards King Edward II, the first Prince of Wales in our modern sense, who was created in 1301, to the Prince, afterwards King Edward VIII, created in 1910. Among these nineteen Princes of Wales there have been six Edwards, four Georges, three Henries, two named Charles, and one each named Richard, Arthur, Frederick and Albert.

What Was the Aulic Council?

IT was the supreme tribunal of the German Empire and was called the Aulic or Court tribunal because it always followed the Imperial Court. It was instituted in 1501 and often interfered in military affairs, as when in Napoleon's time it cramped the strategy of the Austrian Archduke Charles. It was suppressed in 1806.

What Was the Bloody Assize?

IT was the infamous Assize held by the notorious Judge Jeffreys in the West after the collapse of the Monmouth Rebellion in 1685. Some 300 persons were condemned to death, others were whipped or imprisoned, and more than a thousand were sent to the American plantations as slaves, because they had taken some part in the uprising, although most of them were simple folk who had been led away. Jeffreys bullied the jury into bringing in verdicts of guilty and threatened the witnesses.

Why is Land Ploughed?

THE farmer ploughs his land to prepare it for the crops, and the reason for doing this is to break up the soil so as to expose a fresh layer to the air, sun and rain, and also to lay open insect pests to the attacks of the birds. The need for ploughing has been recognised for thousands of years and has been practised in all parts of the world.

A field when ploughed is divided into sections of equal length, separated by furrows that vary in width according to the lightness or heaviness of the soil. Skilled ploughmen always make their furrows straight. At first land was ploughed by pulling through the soil an implement something like

Ploughmen at work near Calver in Derbyshire

a large hoe. Later horses were used, but for many centuries there was little change in the character of the plough. In 1850 steam ploughs were introduced, and in the present century tractors for ploughing have become common.

Which Was Wesley's First Chapel?

THE first chapel built by John Wesley, the 200th anniversary of whose conversion was celebrated on May 24th, 1938, was erected at Bristol in 1739 and was known as the New Room in the Horse Fair. Wesley rebuilt and enlarged this chapel in 1748.

Sixty years later it was acquired for the use of the Welsh Calvinistic

John Wesley's first chapel, still to be seen at Broadmead, Bristol

Methodist Church, and in 1929 it was repurchased and restored by private benefaction and given to the Wesleyan Methodist Church, being reopened for worship on February 13th, 1930. It is now called Broadmead Chapel.

In the courtyard of the chapel stands a statue of Wesley on horseback. It was in this way that he travelled all over England preaching the Gospel. Inside the church is a double-decker pulpit, as can be seen in the lower photograph. It was from the upper pulpit that Wesley used to preach. Such pulpits were formerly common.

Should Cinema Be Spelt With a K?

THERE are many intellectual snobs who love to spell this word with a K and pronounce it accordingly, but this is quite incorrect. While the word is ultimately derived from the two Greek words which mean " motion writing," it did not come into the English language from the Greek but from the French. Cinema is really an abbreviation of the French word *cinematographe*, and it should be pronounced " sinema " and not " kinema."

Which Planet is Most Like the Earth?

ASTRONOMERS tell us that it is undoubtedly Venus. This is the brightest and most beautiful of all the planets, and it circles round the Sun inside the Earth's orbit and next to our globe. In size and density and physical condition it is like a twin sister of the Earth. Its diameter is only 300 miles less than the Earth's, and its mass or weight is about four-fifths of that of the Earth. It is surrounded by an atmosphere as dense as that which surrounds the Earth, and astronomers believe that the physical conditions on the surface of Venus are more like those on the Earth than can be found on any other of the planets.

Professor E. B. Frost, of Yerkes Observatory, says that living beings are much more likely to exist on Venus than on Mars. Venus, revolving round the Sun inside the Earth's orbit, presents phases like those of the Moon. So far as we know, this planet has no satellite or moon. Actually Venus receives from the Sun almost exactly double the heat and light that are received by the Earth.

Who Said Italy Was Only a Geographical Idea?

IT was Prince Metternich who, during the Austrian dominion in Italy, used this expression to denote that in the policy of the Austrian empire Italy was not a state or a people with any rights that ought to be respected. He would be surprised if he could return to Europe and see Italy and Austria today.

Is Human Hair Very Strong?

YES, for such a slender thread human hair is very strong indeed. Four hairs will sustain a weight of a pound, and Eastern potentates have sometimes had a thick rope made of women's hair when they wanted one that should be particularly strong. The hair is also very elastic, and will stretch to an additional third of its length. Unlike flesh, hair when it is dead does not easily decay.

Can a Sheet of Paper Cut Through Wood?

THIS seemingly difficult task is not at all difficult if the sheet of paper is circular in form and is whirling round at a great speed. Speed has the effect of stiffening the paper till it

Inside Wesley's Chapel at Broadmead, showing the double-decker pulpit

becomes as rigid as a disk of steel, and then if a block of wood be placed against it the paper will cut through the wood like a circular saw.

What is the Proboscis Monkey?

IT is the queerest-looking of all the monkeys, and is so named because of its enormous nose, which gives the animal the appearance of being deformed. Mr. Richard Lydekker, the scientist, says: " It is very difficult to

The proboscis monkey, with its queer-looking nose

imagine of what possible advantage it can be to its owner."

The proboscis monkey is a native of Borneo, and this strange development of the nose is regarded as one of the proofs indicating the great antiquity of that island and the long period during which it has been isolated from other lands.

The strange animal first became known to Europe in 1781, when Baron Wurmb, the Dutch Governor of Batavia, described it. Later on, actual specimens were sent to Europe, and at first it was supposed that there were two different species, in which the size of the monkeys varied. Later knowledge, however, showed that the supposed distinct species were really the male and female of the same animal.

The head and body of the male monkey measures about 30 inches, and the tail 27 inches. The general colour is yellowish, the head and upper parts of the body being chestnut. The under parts are lighter.

The large naked face is surrounded by a hairy frame. The proboscis monkey is generally found in large troupes, which assemble in the morning and evening on the banks of rivers and streams, where they may be seen sitting on the branches of some large tree, or leaping from branch to branch. The natives declare that they hold their long noses when jumping, but European observation does not confirm this and it seems hardly likely to be a fact.

Which is the Deepest Ocean?

THE Pacific is, so far as soundings show, the deepest of the oceans. Off Mindanao in the Philippines a part has been found with a depth of 35,410 feet or nearly seven miles. That means that if Mount Everest were stood on the bottom of the ocean it would quite disappear, and would have more than a mile of water above it. Everest is only 29,140 feet high or just over 5½ miles. Another part of the Pacific is 32,089 feet deep.

The deepest sounding yet obtained in the Atlantic is 27,962 feet in the Porto Rico Trench. Here Everest would peep above the waters. The greatest depth in the Indian Ocean is the Sunda Trench, 22,968 feet, and in the Arctic Ocean 13,200 feet. The average depth of the Pacific is about 11,790 feet, and of the Atlantic 4,920 feet. Of the whole of the seas of the Earth the average depth is 11,472 feet. As a contrast with these great depths it may be mentioned that the deepest part of the North Sea is off the Skaggerak, 1,998 feet; but in most parts of the North Sea, if St. Paul's Cathedral were stood on the sea bed, the golden cross would be above the water.

Who is Gil Blas?

HE is the hero of a novel by the French writer Le Sage published in part in 1715 and completed in 1735. In it the hero tells the story of his life. He is described as timid but audacious, well-disposed but easily led astray, shrewd but easily gulled by those who played upon his vanity, and good-natured without moral principle. Smollett translated the book into English.

Is Anything Really Large or Small?

NOTHING can be described absolutely and without qualification as large or small. The size of a thing is entirely a question of relativity. A football is large compared with a pea, but it is very small compared with the Earth. On the other hand, the Earth is very small compared with the Milky Way. St. Paul's is a big building, but here again it is a mere speck compared with Mount Everest, and Mount Everest compared with the size of the Earth is hardly noticeable.

There is no such thing as absolute size or absolute speed. A thing is large or small and fast or slow only when compared with something else.

How Large Can a Hen's Egg Be?

THE average weight for a hen's egg is just over two ounces, but many, of course, are much smaller, and many larger. From time to time extraordinarily large eggs are laid by hens, and a specimen is shown being held in the right hand of the girl in the photograph.

This egg was laid by a cross between a Rhode Island Red and a Wyandotte. The bird was a pullet, and the egg weighed 6½ ounces. Its size can be compared with a normal egg, which the girl is holding in her left hand.

The large egg shown was laid at Rotherfield in Sussex, but it is not a record, for some time earlier a hen kept on a farm in Kent laid an egg that weighed 8 ounces.

The egg on the left of the photograph weighs 6½ ounces, about three times that of the normal egg on the right

What is a Magnum of Wine?

A MAGNUM, from the Latin word *magnus*, great, is a large bottle that holds two quarts. The term is generally used of a magnum of port, claret or champagne.

What Makes the Face Mobile?

THE human face is very mobile—that is, the various parts can be moved so as to give different expressions. Among English people the face is much less expressive of inward thoughts than it is among such Continental peoples as those of France and Italy. Of the people of those lands it has been said that they allow their faces to show what they feel and think, just as a child does.

The mobility of the face is due to

Some individuals have a much greater power of moving their faces than others. It is said that the burglar and murderer Charles Peace, who escaped capture so long, had the most marvellous power of changing not only the expression of his face, but its very appearance, so that he seemed different people at different times, without any need of adding outside disguises.

Some comedians also have a wonderful power of changing their faces, so as to make people laugh. Some can even bring their lower lips over their noses.

These two photographs showing the same man are a striking example of how elastic the skin may be, and how mobile the features are in some people

the fact that the skin is very elastic, and that, underneath, it is furnished with a great number of small but remarkable muscles. These muscles have various uses. They enable us to open and shut the mouth, to move it about, to raise the eyebrows, wrinkle the forehead, and screw up the eyes. Some people can even move their ears.

All the muscles under the skin of the face are governed by a single pair of nerves, called the facial nerves, one for each side of the face. They are closely connected with the brain, and thus a great deal of what happens in the brain affects them, and may show its signs in the face by movements of the muscles which these nerves control.

But it is not only when we are thinking that the face changes, but also when we feel. Thus, we can very often see that a person is feeling glad or grieved by watching the expression of his face.

What Were the Locofocos?

THIS name, derived from the Latin *loco-foci*, meaning "in place of fire," was the name given to lucifer matches in America during the eighteen-thirties. But the name was afterwards transferred to a political party, the Ultra-Radicals, because during an excited meeting at Tammany Hall, New York, when the candles were blown out in the hope of breaking up the gathering, they were quickly relighted with lucifer matches or locofocos. The meeting was continued and the Radicals had their way.

What is a Miller's Eye?

IT is the name given to a lump of unleavened flour found in a loaf of bread and forming a more or less hard lump. It is so called because it is white and in shape is supposed to be round like an eye.

How Did the Sea Become Salt?

PROBABLY the sea has always been salt, for when the oceans were first condensed out of gases and vapour that enveloped the planet there was, no doubt, mixed with these gases salt vapours which would be carried down by the condensing water into the primeval ocean.

But the sea has been getting salter and salter. The rivers as they run in their beds dissolve a certain amount of various salts and carry these in solution to the sea. At the same time the Sun is evaporating water too, leaving behind the mineral matter, with the result that the ocean must be ever getting salter. Oceanographers tell us that the sea on an average contains about 3½ per cent. of dissolved mineral matter. The salt, however, is not all common salt or sodium chloride. There are various other substances. The idea that the water of rivers and lakes is quite fresh is not correct. These also contain salts but, of course, to a much less extent than the sea water.

Who Were the Cordeliers?

THIS name was given to a political club which during the French Revolution held its meetings in the Convent of the Cordeliers in Paris. Its principles were far in advance of those of the Jacobins, whose rivals the Cordeliers were, and among its members were included Danton, Marat, Camille Desmoulins, Hébert and other extremists. The Cordeliers were the first to demand the abolition of the monarchy. They were nicknamed the Pandemonium and later changed their name to the "Society of the Rights of Man," but it is as the Cordeliers that they are best known in history. Most of the leaders were eventually put to death.

How Old Are Band-Saws?

THE band-saw is not so old as the circular saw, for while the latter was invented in 1770, the band-saw was first patented in 1808. The inventor in both cases was an Englishman. It was William Newberry of London who took out the first patent for a band-saw, but some archaeologists have declared that the band-saw was known to the Ancients. If so, its use was lost through the ages till the beginning of the 19th century.

Who Were the Albigenses?

THEY were religious reformers of the 11th to the 13th centuries, declared heretics by the Pope Alexander III, who excommunicated them in 1179. A quarter of a century later Pope Innocent III organised a crusade against them. Revolting barbarities were practised and it is said that 60,000 men, women and little children were massacred. Another crusade against them was set on foot in the year 1209.

What Exactly is a Beadle ?

A BEADLE was formerly a subordinate parish officer chosen and appointed by the vestry whose business was to attend the vestry, to give notice of its meetings to the parishioners, and to execute its orders generally. He acted for the vestry in the relief of the poor and kept order in church. Nowadays the office

The beadle of All Hallows, Barking-by-the-Tower, in the City of London, leading the procession for the beating of the bounds

of beadle is obsolete, except in certain parishes like those of the City of London, where he still dresses in an old-fashioned uniform, wears a cocked or three-cornered hat, carries a staff, and heads such processions as those that go round the parish to beat the bounds, as described on page 5.

The doorkeeper of certain institutions is known as a beadle, and the church officer and attendant of a church minister in Scotland has the same title. The bearer of the mace in public processions in universities is called the bedell, spelt in that old-fashioned way. The name beadle means a messenger or herald.

Who Was Grace Darling ?

SHE was the daughter of William Darling, keeper of the Longstone lighthouse on the Farne Islands, and on September 7th, 1838, helped her father to save the lives of nine of the crew of the steamer *Forfarshire*, which had run ashore in a gale. Grace rowed out with her father to a rock on which the nine men had taken refuge. For this she was awarded a gold medal by the Royal Humane Society, and a public subscription was got up for her. She became a national heroine, but on October 20th, 1842, when she was only 27, she died of consumption.

Can Silver Be Prevented From Tarnishing ?

A RECENT discovery has shown that if silver, after being given a chemical bath, be dipped in a solution of rhodium, it is freed indefinitely from tarnishing. The rhodium is unaffected by heat and does not crack or chip. Rhodium is generally found in platinum, and before its use in treating silver was discovered it was practically useless. Most of the rhodium used comes from Ontario.

How Much Milk is Drunk in England ?

THE total quantity of milk sold for liquid consumption in Great Britain during the month of July, 1937, was 50,499,151 gallons, a record consumption, and exceeding the corresponding month of the previous year by 3,209,372 gallons. Of the increase, half a million gallons is accounted for by the daily milk drink taken by workers in 4,000 workshops. July, 1937, was the first time on record that the monthly consumption of milk has exceeded fifty million gallons. The total production of milk during the month was 84,521,177 gallons, which was a decrease of 2,783,715 gallons over the previous July. Milk manufactured into dairy produce accounted for 34,022,026 gallons. The bulk of the increase in milk drunk is attributed to the advertising campaign with its milk bars and its "Drink More Milk" slogans.

How Many Do the British Railways Employ ?

THE number of people of all ranks and offices employed on the British railways is 580,766, of whom 558,033 are males and 22,733 females. The average salary of the salaried classes is £4 11s. 9d. per week, and of the wages class about £3 5s. per week.

Do Stoats Drive Away Rats ?

YES, a single stoat will clear a set of farm buildings or a house of rats. It not only goes into their burrows but chases them along roofs and gutters. Mr. Alfred E. Pease tells how his home, Pinchinthorpe House, at Guisborough, in Yorkshire, where there was a plague of rats, the animals swarming everywhere, was cleared entirely of the pests in six weeks by a stoat. The stoat also drove away the mice which had previously been common there.

What is the Wedged Rock of Antrim ?

AT Grey Man's Path on Fairhead, in County Antrim, there is a rock which has become detached from the main cliff and has fallen in a sloping position across a gap, as shown in the photograph. The name Greyman's Path was given because of the bridge formed by this rock.

The wedged rock which forms the Grey Man's Path in County Antrim

How Do American Soldiers Learn to Climb?

AMERICAN soldiers trained at the American Army Signal Corps School at Fort Monmouth, New Jersey, are taught to climb rapidly up any tree, or telegraph or telephone

American soldiers of the Army Signal Corps School at Fort Monmouth, New Jersey, learning to climb a tall telegraph pole

pole. The method of climbing is shown in the accompanying photograph. Attached to the waist-belt of each man is a strap which encircles the tree, and then with climbing irons on the feet the man can go up a bare trunk or a pole very rapidly. He simply walks up, the climbing irons catching in the timber, and the leather strap preventing him from falling outwards. The strap is, of course, moved up as the feet rise.

Must M.P.s Take the Oath?

ALL Members of Parliament must take the oath of allegiance, except those who, for conscientious reasons, prefer to make an affirmation. Members of the Society of Friends do the latter, and also occasionally a member who professes no religious belief.

Who Founded the Foundling Hospital?

IT was a kindly mariner and shipwright, Captain Coram, who on his journeys to and from Rotherhithe was distressed to see so many half-clad, half-starving infants left in the streets by heartless parents. In 1741 he opened a house for foundlings in Hatton Garden with accommodation for twenty. In 1745 a new site of 55 acres was obtained in Lamb's Conduit Fields, and a spacious building erected. A basket was hung outside the gate and an advertisement announced that all children under the age of two months tendered for admission would be received. On the first day of general reception, June 2nd, 1756, 117 children were deposited. Later the age was extended to twelve months and wagons brought children from all parts of the country.

Handel gave an organ to the chapel of the hospital, and often conducted at performances of the "Messiah" given in aid of the funds. In June, 1926, the Foundling Hospital left London for temporary premises at Redhill, and in 1935 moved to a fine new home erected at Berkhamsted. Coram was one of the greatest friends of children that England has produced.

How Long Did It Take to Sail From New Zealand?

THE time varied a great deal according to the ship and kind of weather encountered. In 1898, for instance, the *Invercargill* took 121 days from Wellington to London, but the record for a fast passage by a sailing ship was 63 days by the *Otaki* of the New Zealand Shipping Company in 1877.

Who Were the Furies of the Guillotine?

THEY were a body of women who, during the Reign of Terror, were more ferocious than any other of the revolutionaries. They were called tricoteuses or knitters, because they used to attend the sittings of the convention, the trials and the executions, knitting and shrieking out their bloodthirsty demands for the death sentence. With the fall of the Jacobins in 1794 they disappeared.

What Are the Nicknames of the United States?

HERE are the various states with their recognised abbreviations and the nicknames by which they are often called in America. Thus, Alabama is the Cotton State, Lizard State and Yallerhammer State. Four states have no abbreviations.

State	Abbreviation	Nicknames
Alabama	Ala.	Cotton, Lizard, Yallerhammers
Arizona	Ariz.	Baby, Sunset, Apache
Arkansas	Ark.	Bear, Bowie
California	Cal.	Golden, El Dorado
Colorado	Col.	Centennial, Silver
Connecticut	Conn.	Constitution, Nutmeg
Delaware	Del.	Diamond, Blue Hen's Chickens
District of Columbia	D.C.	This is not a state
Florida	Fla.	Everglade, Land of Flowers
Georgia	Ga.	Empire State of the South, Cracker, Buzzard
Idaho	—	Gem
Illinois	Ill.	Sucker, Prairie
Indiana	Ind.	Hoosier
Iowa	—	Hawkeye
Kansas	Kan.	Sunflower, Jayhawk
Kentucky	Ky.	Blue Grass, Corn-Cracker, Dark and Bloody Ground
Louisiana	La.	Pelican, Creole
Maine	Me.	Pine Tree, Old Dirigo
Maryland	Md.	Old Line, Cockade
Massachusetts	Mass.	Bay, Old Colony
Michigan	Mich.	Wolverine, Auto
Minnesota	Minn.	Gopher, North Star
Mississippi	Miss.	Bayou, Eagle, Magnolia
Missouri	Mo.	Ozark, Iron Mountain, Show Me
Montana	Mont.	Stub Toe, Bonanza, Treasure
Nebraska	Neb.	Antelope, Black Water, Cornhusker
Nevada	Nev.	Silver, Sage Brush
New Hampshire	N.H.	Granite
New Jersey	N.J.	Jersey Blue, Garden, Mosquito
New Mexico	N.M.	Sunshine, Spanish
New York	N.Y.	Empire, Excelsior
North Carolina	N.C.	Old North, Turpentine, Tar Heel
North Dakota	N.D.	Flickertail, Sioux
Ohio	—	Buckeye
Oklahoma	Okla	Sooner
Oregon	Ore.	Beaver, Web-Foot
Pennsylvania	Pa.	Keystone, Steel, Coal
Rhode Island	R.I.	Little Rhody, Plantation
South Carolina	S.C.	Palmetto
South Dakota	S.D.	Sunshine, Coyote
Tennessee	Tenn.	Volunteer, Hog-and-Hominy
Texas	Tex.	Lone Star, Beef
Utah	—	Deseret, Beehive, Mormon
Vermont	Vt.	Green Mountain
Virginia	Va.	Old Dominion, Mother
Washington	Wash.	Evergreen, Chinook
West Virginia	W. Va.	Panhandle, Mountain
Wisconsin	Wis.	Badger, Copper
Wyoming	Wyo.	Equality

Where is the Longest Straight Railway?

IT is in Australia, where for 328 miles across the Nullabor Plain the Transcontinental Railway runs in a dead straight line. The level of this stretch, however, is not dead straight. Throughout this 328 miles the railway does not cross a single river and there is not a tree within sight of the trains.

Who Were the Guelphs and Ghibellines?

THESE were the two parties who contended for mastery and kept Europe at war in the 12th century. The Guelphs were the dukes of Bavaria and they contended for mastery with the house of Hohenstauffen, who provided several German emperors in the Middle Ages. Starting as a mere German feud, the conflict spread and developed into a contest between the civil and spiritual powers. The Guelphs were the Pope's party and laboured to set the Pope above crowned princes. The civil or imperial party were called Ghibellines from Waiblingen, an estate in Franconia belonging to the Hohenstauffen family. The words Guelph and Ghibelline were first used as battle-cries in 1138 when Guelph, the brother of Henry the Proud, was defeated by Conrad of Hohenstauffen at Weinsberg.

After the reign of the Emperor Henry VII in 1313 the terms changed their meaning. The Ghibellines became the name of the Italian rebels. The emperors had continually tried to disturb the government of the Italian states, and so Ghibelline came to be a name for any rebel, insurgent or disturber of a state. The insurgents in turn retorted by calling the government party Guelphs. The names were dropped at the end of the 15th century. It is interesting to remember that the British royal family is descended from the Guelphs.

What is the Biggest Electric Lamp?

THE biggest electric filament lamp is one of a hundred thousand watts that was made in America, and its immense size can be seen in the photograph where a woman is inside the glass bulb and holds an ordinary 60-watt lamp for comparison.

This huge lamp, which was made not for use but for exhibition purposes, would give a light so bright that it could be picked out by an observer

What is Laissez Faire?

THIS is the term used for a policy in industry and commerce of " let alone." It originated in France, where Jean Colbert, the famous French statesman of the 17th century, in order to foster certain industries made various orders regulating them. When the vine-growers complained Colbert asked some merchants what he could do to give relief. They replied " Laissez faire, laissez-passer," which freely interpreted means, " Don't interfere with our mode of manufacture; don't stop the introduction of foreign imports."

The term "laissez faire," or "let alone," became very popular in England at the time of the industrial revolution and afterwards, when manufacturers wanted no interference by the State in the way of regulating hours or wages or insistence on healthy conditions in the factories. The result of "laissez faire," was the most abominable sweating of men, women and little children, starvation wages, and deadly conditions in the factories. All that has now been changed, thanks chiefly to the fine pioneer work of the great Lord Shaftesbury.

What Are the Cardinal Virtues?

THESE are fortitude, justice, prudence and temperance. On these all the other virtues are supposed to hang. The word cardinal is, from a Latin word meaning the hinge of a door.

The biggest electric filament lamp ever made. The woman is inside the bulb. She is holding an ordinary 60-watt lamp for purposes of comparison

What is the Bottom Drawer?

ENGLISH girls who are thinking of getting married begin to collect a number of things that will be useful in their homes—clothing, linen and so on. This collection is called the " bottom drawer," because the articles are generally stored in the bottom drawer of the chest of drawers in their bedroom. This drawer is used because it is often deeper than the other drawers.

In Canada a girl engaged to be married who is thus collecting articles for her home speaks not of her bottom drawer but of her " hope chest."

on the Moon looking through a powerful telescope and it is said that the heat of it would be about half the temperature of the Sun's atmosphere, burning everything that came close to it. The glass bulb has walls a quarter of an inch thick, and is capable of resisting a crushing strain of 40,000 pounds induced by the vacuum inside. The tungsten filaments of this great lamp are as thick as a fountain pen.

Does a Pelican Feed Its Young With Blood?

THIS is a very old legend, which some people still believe, but there is no foundation whatever for it.

What is the Origin of the Domestic Fowl?

THE numerous breeds of domestic fowls vary enormously in size, colour and outward form, but they have all come from one wild species, the red jungle fowl of northern India. This bird, known to scientists as *Gallus bankiva*, is found not only in India, but throughout south-east Asia and in the Philippines. Charles Darwin found in carrying out experiments that the domestic fowl, no matter what its breed, had a tendency to revert to the form of the jungle fowl when crossed. In colour the jungle fowl resembles the English red game fowl.

How Did the Locomotive Develop?

Puffing Billy, 1813

Locomotion Nº1, 1826

Royal George, 1827

Agenoria, 1829

Rocket, 1829

Invicta, 1830

Northumbrian, 1830

Wilberforce, 1832

Samson, 1833

Atlas, 1834

North Star, 1837

Hector, 1839

Great Western, 1846

Bloomer, 1850

The illustrations on these pages, though giving, of course, only a selection of locomotives from the early 19th century almost to the present time, will convey some idea of the changes that have taken place in the railway engine. The real pioneer of the locomotive was a curious engine built in 1803 by Richard Trevithick. It had huge gear wheels, but it travelled with smooth wheels on smooth rails. This proved that a rack rail and cogwheel were not necessary to carry a locomotive along. Nevertheless, that clumsy device was used after Trevithick had shown that it was quite unnecessary. With "Puffing Billy," built by William Hedley in 1813 for use at a colliery, the real story of the locomotive begins. This remarkable engine of early times actually ran till 1872. George Stephenson, the father of the modern railway, built one or two engines for colliery use before constructing "Locomotion No. I" for use on the Stockton and Darlington Railway. His "Rocket," built in 1829 for the Liverpool and Manchester Railway,

Its Evolution Through a Century

Problem 1859

Kirkley's Express 1864

Tank Engine 1870

Express engine 1874

Brighton Express 1882

Great Eastern Express 1895

Caledonian Express 1886

Midland Express 1896

Great Western Express 1896

London, Brighton and South Coast Express 1896

Great Central Express 1903

Caledonian Express 1906

London and North Eastern Express 1922

King Class, Great Western 1927

was a great triumph. It beat various rivals and established the true principles of the locomotive that was to transform travel throughout the world. With this engine George Stephenson firmly established his reputation as the greatest of railway engineers. From the time of the " Rocket " to the present, when streamlined express locomotives are coming more and more into use all over the world, the story of the railway engine has been one of steady progress in size, power and efficiency. Till the development of the streamlined engine in recent times, an example of which is given in the colour plate number II, the general form of the railway engine remained very much the same. Just as in early days England was the pioneer of the locomotive, so ever since she has taken a leading part in new developments, and this is as true today as ever it was. Of course, the British locomotive cannot be classed in size and power with the huge machines that are employed in countries like America, where vast distances have to be covered

Do Rubber Soles Protect From Lightning?

No, they are no real protection at all. Professor Lowe says: "It would be easier to put out the kitchen fire with a hundredth part of a drop of water than to get protection in such a way. Lightning travels so fast and so powerfully that it would soon overcome such slight resistance."

Who Was George Sand?

This was the pen-name taken by a Frenchwoman, Mademoiselle Armandine Dupin, who after marriage became Baroness Dudevant. Although she had two children her married life was not happy and she set off for Paris in search of an independent life. She began to write in collaboration with Jules Sandeau, and then started as a novelist and dramatist on her own account. She adopted revolutionary views and took part in politics. She was a prolific writer and many of her novels appeared serially. She was not a very pleasant character.

Why Does the Big Drummer Wear an Apron?

The man who carries the big drum in a military band wears an apron either of leather or of leopard skin, the reason for this being to protect his uniform from damage by the drum.

Corporal Clarke of the Irish Guards Band, the tallest drummer in the British Army, wearing his leather apron

Are Any Monkeys Civil Servants?

In the sense that they are employed in Government service, two apes engaged in regular work at the Singapore Botanic Gardens may almost be described as civil servants. These apes, named Jambul and Puteh, have been trained to collect botanical specimens from high trees in the Malayan jungle. They are of the pigtailed or coconut species, and have been honoured by special mention in the annual Government report of the Botanic Gardens.

When working in the forest a botanical monkey is tied to a string,

The big-drum player of Newport Market Army Bands School at Orpington, Kent, wearing his leopard-skin apron

and the more one speaks to them using the same words, the more, they understand. After some practice in the jungle they do not have to climb every tree, but by a series of shouts and jerks on the string, and pointing and slapping of trunks, they can be induced to tree their strings and leap from bough to bough, so that they can visit numerous trees before they are obliged to come down for a drink of water. Further, the more practice they get, the more they understand what is wanted, and they drop down any arresting objects, such as opening buds, flowers, fruits and galls, which are invisible from below. Indeed, to work with a clever berok in the jungle is like fishing in the tree-tops."

Berok is the Malay name for this species of monkey, which has been used for centuries to pick coconuts, and even mangoes and other fruits.

Many monkeys show a high order of intelligence. When food was placed on a table out of the reach of a small rhesus monkey kept on a chain, the animal would drag a box to the table, mount it, and so obtain the booty.

180 feet long, which is wound on a wooden frame like a fishing-line. Instructions are given in Malay, of which the monkeys understand twelve words, and the intelligence they show while working in tall trees quite out of sight of their masters is amazing. "It will be obvious," says Mr. E. L. H. Corner, the acting director of the Gardens, "that these monkeys delight in what they are doing,

Who Was the Great Duke?

This name is given to the famous Duke of Wellington, Napoleon's conqueror, whose prestige throughout Europe was unprecedented. Tennyson used this expression in his "Ode on the Death of the Duke of Wellington" which begins, "Bury the Great Duke with an empire's lamentation."

Who Were Cromwell's Ironsides?

This name was given to a body of a thousand men raised by Cromwell in the Eastern Counties to fight for the Parliament against King Charles I. They were all strongly religious men, for Cromwell had told Hampden that the one weapon which could meet and turn the chivalry of the Cavaliers was religious enthusiasm. The regiment proved irresistible in fight and so was nick-named Ironsides. The name was later applied to all Cromwell's army.

When & Where Was That Bell Used?

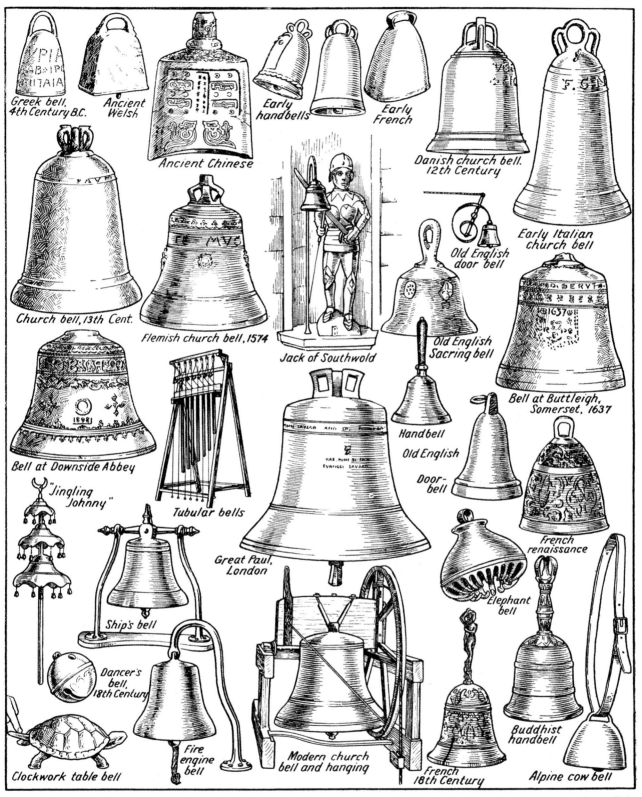

Greek bell, 4th Century B.C.

Ancient Welsh

Ancient Chinese

Early handbells

Early French

Danish church bell, 12th Century

Early Italian church bell

Church bell, 13th Cent.

Flemish church bell, 1574

Jack of Southwold

Old English door bell

Old English Sacring bell

Bell at Buttleigh, Somerset, 1637

Bell at Downside Abbey

"Jingling Johnny"

Tubular bells

Great Paul, London

Handbell Old English

Door-bell

French renaissance

Elephant bell

Ship's bell

Dancer's bell, 18th Century

Clockwork table bell

Fire engine bell

Modern church bell and hanging

French 18th Century

Buddhist handbell

Alpine cow bell

It is believed by some that the earliest musical instrument ever made was the bell, and legend says that Jubal, described in the Bible as "the father of all such as handle the harp and organ," caught the first suggestion of musical sound from the ring of his brother Tubal Cain's hammer on the anvil. It was probably some such sound that gave the idea for the bell. Certainly it is a very ancient instrument. Bells have been found in both Europe and Asia dating back to hundreds of years before Christ. On this page are given various types of bells from ancient times down to the present. Most Oriental bells have no swinging tongue inside, but are rung by being struck on the outside with a hammer. On page 259 is a photograph showing a huge Japanese bell being rung by swinging a log against it. The drawings show the various changes in shape of European bells. In the case of the modern church bell at the bottom, the hanging or device enabling the bell to turn right over is given

What Was the French Fury?

It was a treacherous attack on Antwerp by about 4,000 French soldiers under the Duke of Anjou, who had recently been raised to the sovereignty of the Netherlands. The Duke assembled his soldiers in the city, ostensibly for a review, but actually for the purpose of seizing the place. At a given signal the French fell on the burghers, who repelled the attack, killed about half the French and made prisoners of the remainder. Thus the biters were bit and the French became victims of the Fury they had planned.

What is the Latest Method of Getting Tanned?

Modern methods are used even in sun-bathing and getting the skin tanned. In 1938 a method said to produce a quick sun-tan was introduced and is shown in the photograph on this page. A highly-polished shield that fits round the body reflects the sun's rays on to the skin, and even when there is not much sunshine produces a tan. Whether such methods are really healthful, however, is doubtful. The bathers wear dark glasses to protect the eyes from the glare.

What Was Dynamite Saturday?

It was Saturday, January 24th, 1885, when Irish Fenians did great damage by dynamite explosions at the Houses of Parliament and the Tower of London. The Law Courts and other public buildings escaped because they were so well guarded.

What is a Fresco Painting?

The word means "fresh," and fresco painting is the art of painting on freshly spread plaster before it dries. Fresco painting is generally done on walls and ceilings. Mineral pigments are used, as vegetable pigments are

Bathing girls on the front at Hastings using reflectors to increase the rate at which their faces are being tanned

not suitable. The pigments are ground with clean water and rendered so thin that they can be worked easily with the brush. Lime and milk are added to some, the pigments uniting with the lime and becoming exceedingly durable.

The ground on which the painting is done after standing a night is unfit for painting, and so only a sufficient quantity for one day is prepared. On this account fresco painting is difficult, because it cannot be retouched. Fresco painting became important in Italy in the 16th century.

It is quite wrong to call any wall painting, such as the ancient paintings that are sometimes found on old churches, frescoes. These are more accurately called distemper paintings, and are quite distinct in style from pure frescoes. The art of fresco painting was known to the ancients, and was subsequently revived in the 16th century.

What is the Lion of Lucerne?

It is a great crouching lion hewn out of the sandstone rock in a park outside the city walls at Lucerne, and commemorates the bravery of the 800 Swiss Guards who fell at Paris in 1792 while defending the Palace of the Tuileries and King Louis XVI against the revolutionary mob. The sculpture, 28 feet long and 18 feet high, is the work of Thorwaldsen, the Danish sculptor.

What is a Messuage?

This name, which often appears in leases, means a house with its outbuildings, orchard, curtilage or courtyard, and garden.

The famous Lion of Lucerne, sculptured by the Scandinavian artist Thorwaldsen. It was unveiled in 1821 in commemoration of the Swiss Guards who perished at the Tuileries in 1792

Do London Elephants Bathe?

THE elephants at the London Zoo have a daily bathe and thoroughly enjoy this in the summer season. They go right down into the water of the bathing-pool and squirt water from their trunks over their bodies. No elephant is happy that cannot occasionally go right down into the water.

Who Are the Chief Enemies of the Earthworms?

IT is sad to relate that they have many human enemies, although worms confer nothing but benefits on human beings by making their cultivated lands more fertile. Birds, of course, are always on the look-out for worms, and if they can get hold of the end of a worm will drag it out of the ground. If a bird catches a worm by the tail when it is disappearing into its burrow, it cannot drag the entire creature out of the hole, but will nip off the tail end. The worm in that case is able to grow a new tail without difficulty. Even if a gardener with his spade cuts a worm in two, the mutilated creature is able to grow a new end for each extremity.

When worms venture near the water they are often caught and devoured by their relatives the leeches, and they often fall victims to the hedgehog and the mole. One of their chief human enemies is, of course, the angler, who digs them up for bait.

What Sportsman Has Killed the Most Animals?

THIS doubtful distinction may belong to the late Lord Ripon, formerly Lord de Grey. The Duke of Portland gives us the following list of the game he killed between 1867 and 1900, a total altogether of 370,728. The list includes 2 rhinoceroses, 11 tigers, 12 buffaloes, 19 samburs, 97 pigs, 186 deer, 382 red deer, 56,460 grouse, 97,759 partridges, 142,343 pheasants, 2,218 woodcock, 2,769 snipe, 1,612 wild duck, 94 black game, 45 capercailzie, 27,686 hares, 29,858 rabbits, and 9,175 other creatures.

What Was the Council of the Ancients?

IT was a body consisting of 250 members whose function was to elect Directors to rule France at the end of the 18th century and to ratify or reject the resolutions of another body, the Council of the Five Hundred. Members of the Council of the Ancients had to be at least forty years old, married or widowers, and to have been householders for fifteen years. The members of the Council of Five Hundred had to be thirty years of age and to have been householders for ten years. They sat in the palace of the Tuileries.

How Much Bread Does 100 lb. of Wheat Make?

A HUNDRED pounds of wheat, when milled, produces 70 pounds of flour, and that produces 91 pounds of bread. A hundred pounds of flour produces 130 pounds of bread. The difference in weight between the flour and the bread is made up by moisture and potatoes mixed in the dough.

An elephant at the London Zoo giving himself a cool shower-bath with the aid of his trunk

What Was the Capon Tree?

IT was an oak, no longer existing, on which six followers of Prince Charles Edward, the Young Pretender, were hanged on October 21st, 1746. They were Colonel James Innes, Peter Lindsey, Ronald Macdonald, Thomas Park, Peter Taylor and Michael Delard. It was called the Capon Tree because under it the judges and their retinue ate a meal of capons on their way from Newcastle to Carlisle.

How Much Damage is Done by Fires in Britain?

THE amount varies from year to year. Sometimes, as in 1931, it is less than eight millions, or to be exact, £7,945,000; and sometimes, as in 1929, over eleven millions, or £11,784,000. Generally it is about nine million pounds. In some years about 800 people lose their lives in fires in different parts of the country.

An elephant at the Zoo enjoying a rest in his bathing-pool

How Does That Plant Go to Sleep?

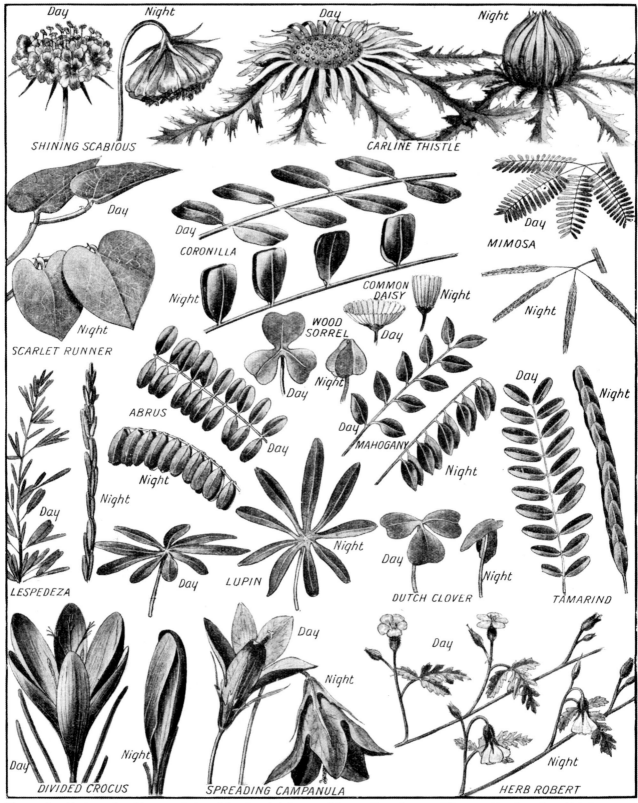

Like ourselves plants may be said to go to sleep at night, when their leaves and flowers often take up a different position from that which they assume in the daytime. Just as we lie down and curl ourselves up to keep warm, so the leaves and flowers of many plants close up at night to protect themselves from the cold. In plants like the clover the leaves droop, just as we nod forward if we go to sleep sitting up. It has been found that when some leaves on a plant are prevented from folding at night, they suffer from the cold. Only the folded leaves escape, the others dying. But it is not only to keep out the cold that leaves fold together, for many tropical plants also fold their leaves at night. In the same way flowers close their petals or droop. Here are a number of plants awake and asleep, and, as can be seen, many of them are common British wild plants of the countryside

Where Was Excalibur Thrown?

THE famous sword of King Arthur, which was called Excalibur, was thrown at the King's command into a mere or lake by Sir Bedivere. The

Dozmare Pool, near Bodmin, into which King Arthur's sword Excalibur is said to have been thrown

knight, hoping to save the sword, attached his girdle to it so as to draw it out again, but as the sword reached the water it was seized by a mysterious hand that came up out of the water. Tennyson in his "Idylls of the King" has described the scene thus:

Then quickly rose Sir Bedivere and ran,
And, leaping down the ridges lightly, plunged
Among the bulrush beds, and clutch'd the sword,
And strongly wheel'd and threw it. The great brand
Made lightnings in the splendour of the moon,
And flashing round and round, and whirl'd in an arch,
Shot like a streamer of the northern morn,
Seen where the moving isles of winter shock
By night, with noises of the Northern Sea.
So flash'd and fell the brand Excalibur:
But ere he dipt the surface, rose an arm
Clothed in white samite, mystic, wonderful,
And caught him by the hilt, and brandish'd him
Three times, and drew him under in the mere.

The place where this occurred, and the mere across which the dying Arthur passed in a barge to Avalon, is by ancient tradition said to be Dozmare or Dosmery Pool, just over nine miles from Bodmin. The tarn lies 890 feet above sea-level and measures a mile in circuit. It was once believed to be bottomless.

What Was the Crimean War About?

IN 1852 the French Emperor Napoleon III demanded that the protection of the Holy Places in Palestine should be restored to the Latin Church according to a treaty of 1740 called the "Charter of the Latins." The Greek Church, supported by Russia, had in course of time ousted the Latins from the trust. Turkey was quite indifferent

to the religious question, but fearing to offend either France or Russia, changed her policy according to the pressure brought to bear on her by one or other of these countries. At last, threatened by Russia, Turkey declared war on the Tsar in October, 1853, and supported by England, France and Sardinia, continued the war till 1855, when Russia sued for peace. The peace treaty was signed on March 30th, 1856.

Who Was Imprisoned in an Iron Cage?

THE victim is said to have been a Bishop of Verdun who, in the 15th century, invented as a punishment the iron cage, too small to allow the person confined inside to stand upright or lie at full length. He was the first to be shut up in one, and Cardinal La Balue, who had recommended the idea to King Louis XI, was also himself eventually confined in one for ten years.

What is the Bronze Used For Pence?

WE speak of coppers, but, of course, our pennies, halfpennies and farthings are made not of copper, but of bronze. The metal used is an alloy of copper, 95 parts of copper, 4 of tin and 1 of zinc being used in every 100 parts of coinage metal. Alternatively the composition may be $95\frac{1}{2}$ parts of copper, 3 parts of tin and $1\frac{1}{2}$ of zinc. The legal weight of a penny is one-third of an avoirdupois ounce; of a halfpenny, one-fifth of an ounce; and of a farthing, one-tenth of an ounce. A halfpenny is one inch in diameter.

What is a Master in Lunacy?

HE is a judicial officer appointed by the Lord Chancellor to conduct inquiries into the state of mind of persons alleged to be lunatics. The inquiries usually take place before a jury. A Master in Lunacy can make an order as to the administration of the estate of a lunatic.

What is a Clay Pigeon?

IT is a disk of clay or other composition which is shot up into the air from a spring trap to form a target for a man with a gun, and is the method of shooting practised at many local gun clubs. In 1893 an Inanimate Bird Shooting Association was formed in England, and in 1903 it was renamed the Clay Bird Shooting Association. Similar organisations exist in France, Belgium, Holland and other European countries; and in Canada and the United States. Clay

The man who fires the clay pigeons at a shooting tournament sitting in his shot-proof box. He is about to shoot a pigeon into the air

bird shooting has formed one of the events at some of the Olympic Games. The clay disks can be thrown so as to come direct towards the gun or fly off at a right or left angle.

Where Do People Go About on Stilts?

THE inhabitants of the Landes or waste lands of southern France in order to traverse the sands and marshes have to walk on stilts from four to six feet high, supporting them-

Yugoslavia, for example, sent a Sokol contingent to the Prague Congress of 1938.

The Sokols were founded over 75 years ago as the result of Garibaldi's exploits in Italy, and the movement had for its object the obtaining of Czech independence from Austria.

Shepherds of the Landes in south-western France on their stilts

selves by a pole which serves as a walking-stick. The number of people who do this, however, is declining, for there are fewer marshes than there used to be and many roads have been constructed in the Landes district.

This region is a triangular plateau 150 to 200 feet above the sea and bounded by the Atlantic and the valleys of the Garonne and the Adour. On the side next to the sea the region is 120 miles long with a maximum width of 60 miles. It covers altogether an area of about 2,300 square miles. The sand dunes used to invade the country inland, advancing at the rate of about twenty yards a year, but the attack has been arrested by the planting of sea-pine trees.

What is a Sokol?

SOKOL is a Czech word meaning "falcon," and a Sokol is the name given to an organisation or society in Czechoslovakia whose members are associated for purposes of physical training and education. Both the societies and the members are known as Sokols and huge congresses of Sokols are held in Prague every six years when members attend from all parts of the country and give demonstrations which for size and skill perhaps surpass anything else of the kind to be seen in Europe. Czechoslovakia now has nearly a million Sokols, and the movement has spread to other Slav nations.

That came as a result of the Great War, but the Sokol movement is stronger than ever today in face of the German menace.

The Sokols wear red shirts, but the red is not that of the Communists, but the Garibaldi red of freedom. The perfection of the mass-gymnastic displays given by the Sokols is unsurpassed in Europe or elsewhere.

How Many English Kings Were Deposed?

SINCE the Conquest five kings have been deposed, namely : Edward II in 1327, Richard II in 1399, Henry VI in 1460, Charles I in 1649, and James II in 1688. The deposition of the last-named is sometimes described as his "abdication," but, of course, he always claimed to be king up to his death so did not abdicate.

What Plant Travels Regularly?

THERE is a plant found on the Steppes of northern Asia, known as the plantago, which frequently travels. The seed sprouts and develops into a compact plant and then produces buds, flowers and fruits in the ordinary way. But as the fruits begin to ripen the stems of the plant curve downward and outward and this gives a wrench to the roots. The soil at this season is very dry and cracked, and so directly a strong wind blows the plantago is uprooted and rolled along the ground. As it travels the seeds drop out and these spread over a large area where they have a better chance of getting nourishment. The plant often travels over many miles in this way.

What is a Nautical Fender?

IT is a stout mass of rope hung over the side of a ship to take the pressure when the vessel is going alongside another ship or a wharf or pier. Sometimes the fender is partly made of timber or cork. Tugs that tow vessels in and out of docks are often surrounded by fenders, like the one shown in the photograph below. Notice the particularly large fender made fast to the bows.

A new steamship launched at Birkenhead being towed by a tug that has fenders all round it

What is a Wash Tally?

IT is a device that was in use in Stuart times by which the careful housewife kept a check upon the household linen to avoid loss or theft. The tally was about six inches long and five inches deep, and had on its face a number of disks. Each had a circular

An ancient wash tally, and the way it was used

opening, and the disk could be turned round, showing through the circular opening figures written on the board beneath. Each disk represented some article of wear, and there were labels such as "ruffs," "cuffs," "sockes," "napkins," "sheets," "towells," "capps," and so on.

The housewife sorting up her laundry for the maids put these various classes of articles in piles, and then turned the disk round so as to mark the number sent to the wash. One of these washing tallies is still to be seen preserved at Haddon Hall.

What is Earthshine?

WHEN the first lunar crescent is seen soon after the date of the New Moon, the dark part of our satellite, within the horns of the crescent, is seen on a clear night to be illuminated very faintly. It has a pale reddish colour and this is known as earthshine. It is a very good name, for the faint illumination is really the Sun's light which shines upon the Earth reflected back by the Earth upon the dark surface of the Moon.

At such a time people often speak of the phenomenon as "The Old Moon in the New Moon's arms."

Astronomers tell us that the earth-shine by which the Moon is faintly illuminated is from fifteen to twenty times as strong as the moonshine of the Full Moon. The reddish colour is due to the Sun's light having passed twice through the Earth's atmosphere, thereby acquiring a sunset tinge.

Who Was the Maid of Saragossa?

SHE was a young girl named Agustina, or Augustina, who fought with great heroism against the French in defence of Saragossa, when that city was besieged in 1808 and 1809. She survived the war and died at Ceuta in 1857.

What Are Laodiceans?

THIS is a name given to people who sit on the fence and take neither one side nor the other in a religious or political dispute. The name is a reference to the members of the Church of Laodicea, described in Revelation III, 16, who were blamed because they were "neither hot nor cold."

What Were the Statutes of Labourers?

THESE were Acts passed in the reign of Edward III after the Black Death had carried off about half the population of England. There was in consequence a great scarcity of labour, and able-bodied labourers were required under pain of imprisonment to work at the wages current before the Plague. Employers who offered more were liable to be fined. The statutes were only repealed as obsolete in 1863.

Who Was Nike?

NIKE in the Greek mythology is the goddess of victory, and was called by the Romans Victoria. She is represented in ancient art as a winged maiden, generally just alighting from flight, carrying in one hand a palm branch, and in the other a garland or a fillet, both hands being outstretched. Sometimes, however, she holds a herald's staff.

She was particularly associated with Athene and Zeus, and the golden and ivory statues of Athene at Athens and of Zeus at Olympia each held a winged Nike in its hand. Coins struck in commemoration of a victory frequently had a figure of Nike impressed upon them. One of the most celebrated statues of Nike in existence is the work of Paeonius. It was ordered by the Messinians to commemorate the victory over the Athenians at Sphacteria. A cast of this statue is to be seen in the British Museum.

What is Armageddon?

ARMAGEDDON is a mountain district of Palestine, and the name means "the mount of Megiddo," which is an ancient town in the Plain of Jezreel at the foot of Mount Carmel. In the Book of Revelation Armageddon is the scene of a great battle between the forces of good and evil (chapter XVI, verse 16). In popular usage the term is applied to any very great battle or campaign involving enormous slaughter.

What is the Origin of Kissing the Pope's Toe?

MATTHEW of Westminster says that it was formerly the custom to kiss the Pope's hand, but that in the 8th century a certain woman not only kissed but squeezed the hand. The Pope, seeing the danger to which he was exposed, cut off the hand and in future was compelled to offer his foot, a practice that continued ever after.

Is the Suez or Panama Canal the Longer?

THE Suez Canal is double the length of the Panama Canal. The latter is 50·72 miles long, while the Suez is just over 104½ miles long. The Suez Canal has no locks, but the Panama is a lock type of canal, in which there are locks to take the ships up from one ocean and down to the other. At one point vessels going through the Panama Canal reach the Gatun Lake, the surface of which is 85 feet above sea-level.

What is the Malthusian Doctrine?

IT is that population increases in a geometrical, and the means of subsistence in an arithmetical, ratio, and that if no check be put upon the increase of population many must starve or be ill-fed. Malthus suggested that something must be done to check the increase of population, otherwise all the land would not suffice to feed its inhabitants. Malthus, who died near Bath in 1834, was a pioneer in this line of thought.

How Do Goats Fight?

THE goat fights with its head and, having a very thick skull, is able to give and take severe blows. The males have horns, and these also are exceedingly powerful. A Persian wild goat which in taking a great leap among the rocks missed its footing, saved itself by alighting on its horns. Goats when fighting rush at one another, their skulls and horns coming into collision. They can also stand stationary and push very hard with their foreheads.

Can the Width of a Star Be Measured?

THE stars, even when seen through the greatest telescope, namely the 100-inch reflector at Mount Wilson Observatory in California, appear only as points of light. But by a wonderful instrument invented by Professor A. A. Michelsen, and called the interferometer, the width of one or two of the larger stars has actually been measured.

This instrument is very complicated, but the principle on which it works is that thin lines of light from each of the two halves of the disc of a star are received by small flat mirrors near the ends of a great beam 20 feet long, and these rays are then reflected parallel to the beam to a second pair of mirrors near the middle of the beam, and these throw the light down the tube to a large mirror from which they are reflected into an eye-piece.

The two pencils of light from the two halves of the star interfere with one another, hence the name of the instrument. They form a series of bright and dark fringes, and by a series of intricate calculations based on the amount of interference and the distance between the mirrors on the great arm, the diameter of the star can be measured.

Betelgeuse, the bright orange-coloured star in the constellation Orion has been found to measure 250 million miles across, or about 300 times the diameter of our Sun. Antares,

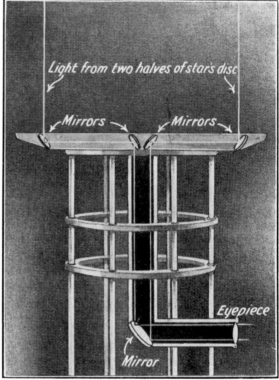

A drawing which shows the principle of the interferometer, the instrument which enables astronomers to measure the width of some stars

the chief star in the constellation of the Scorpion has a diameter of about 400 million miles. These giant stars, however, though so much vaster than our Sun in size, are made up of matter less dense than that of the Sun. In other words, their mass is not in proportion to their size. Indeed, the stars at different stages of their existence vary enormously.

Where is the World's Biggest Gas-Burner?

THE ordinary gas-burner used in a house for domestic purposes is a very small affair. But in some manufacturing processes exceedingly large burners are brought into use. What is said to be the biggest gas-burner in the world is employed in a sugar refinery at Johnstown, Colorado. It is used in maintaining a kiln at the very high temperature of 2,750° Fah. This giant burner is 14 feet long, has a nozzle opening 15 inches in diameter, and consumes 50 cubic feet of natural gas an hour.

What is a Rotta?

IT is a musical instrument like the ancient Asiatic lyre, and is sometimes called the cithara Teutonica. It was pre-eminently a German instrument, but the Continental nations may have adopted it from the Celtic races of Britain. In old illuminated manuscripts King David is often shown playing the rotta.

A goat trying its strength against the head of its young owner

Fights between goats are often very fierce, and despite their thick skulls and horns they often damage one another badly. A human being attacked by a powerful male goat would have a very bad time, for apart from its strength the impetus in charging is very great.

What is That Can Used For?

Hot water can

Billy can

Oil can

Nursery milk can

Jointless dairy can

Milk can

Watering cans

Seamless oil can

Oil feeding can

Painter's can

Cycle oil can

Funnel-shaped filling can

Lathe drip oil can

Fireman's drinking can

Direct pump oil can

Forced feed oil can

Bench oil cans

Direct pump oil cans

100-gallon water can

Mess can

Workman's tea can

Locomotive oiling can

Bait cans

Billposter's can

There are all sorts of cans, and most of the types in use today are shown in the drawings above. Cans are made of various metals. Generally they are of tinplate, that is, iron sheet metal covered with a coating of tin. At other times they are made of brass or copper, and sometimes they are of steel, while large cans like the hundred-gallon water can are made of galvanised iron. One great advantage of the use of metals like tinplate for the making of cans is that the vessel is much lighter than it would be if made of thick iron. Bait cans are, of course, used by anglers, and billposter's cans carry the paste. Oiling cans are of many shapes and sizes, and of these several varieties are found among the drawings above

What is That Marine Object?

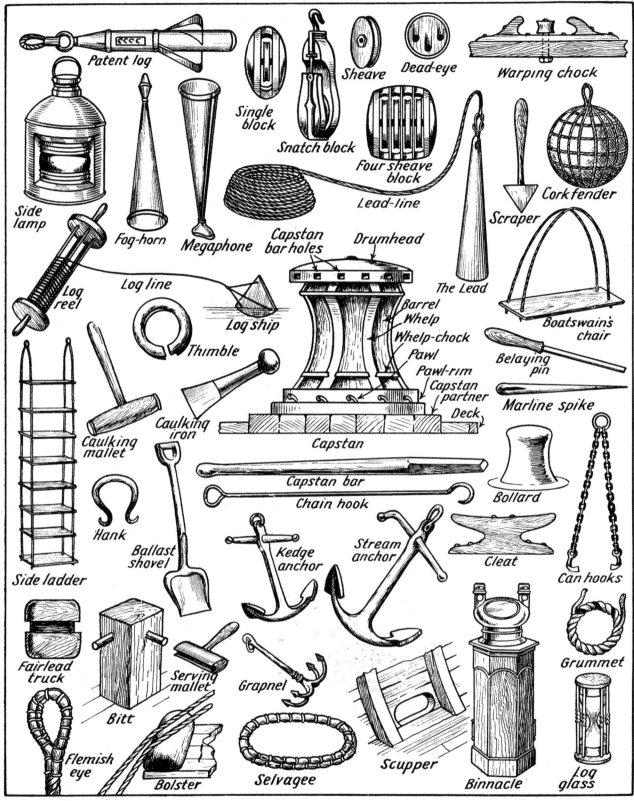

Patent log · Sheave · Dead-eye · Warping chock · Single block · Snatch block · Four sheave block · Lead-line · Cork fender · Scraper · Side lamp · Fog-horn · Megaphone · Capstan bar holes · Drumhead · The Lead · Boatswain's chair · Log reel · Log line · Log ship · Thimble · Barrel · Whelp · Whelp-chock · Pawl · Pawl-rim · Capstan partner · Deck · Belaying pin · Marline spike · Caulking iron · Caulking mallet · Capstan · Capstan bar · Chain hook · Bollard · Side ladder · Hank · Ballast shovel · Kedge anchor · Stream anchor · Cleat · Can hooks · Fairlead truck · Serving mallet · Grapnel · Bitt · Grummet · Flemish eye · Bolster · Selvagee · Scupper · Binnacle · Log glass

Here are various objects connected with ships, together with their names. The log is an apparatus for ascertaining speed. Blocks are iron or wooden shells containing one or more sheaves or pulleys. The lead is used for ascertaining depths. The cork fender is to protect the ship chafing against the quayside. The foghorn and megaphone are for amplifying the voice. The bosun's chair is a light swing seat suspended by a line for working on the stays and elsewhere. A thimble is a ring of thin metal with a grooved outer edge, so as to fit within an eye-splice. A caulking iron is for filling the seams of the deck with oakum and pitch. A belaying pin is of wood or iron, and is used for making gear fast to. A marling or marline-spike is used for unravelling rope and knots. A hank is a ring of wood or iron attached to the edge of a gib, and running on a stay. Bitts and bollards are for making fast heavy ropes. A fairlead truck is for letting ropes run through steadily. A grummet or grommet is an eyelet of rope. The capstan is a cylinder round which is wound the rope when raising heavy weights, and the capstan bar is inserted in a hole for turning the capstan

What is Joie de Vivre ?

THIS expression in French, which means literally " joy of living," is used to describe a feeling of healthy enjoyment of life. It was first used in English literature in 1901 by Lucas Malet in her novel " The History of Sir Richard Calmady," where she spoke of " the hungry all-compelling *joie de vivre* which is begotten whensoever youth thus seeks and finds youth." Four years later E. F. Benson

What Was the Good Parliament ?

IT was a Parliament that met in 1376 in the reign of Edward III and was so called because of its firm opposition to the illegal government of the Crown and Council. Its speaker was Sir Peter de la Marc, and it denounced the mismanagement of the French war, the oppressive taxation, and the behaviour of John of Gaunt,

The young bees appear as small white grubs and these are at once fed by worker bees acting as nurses. The nurses produce from glands in their bodies a kind of bee milk, which is called chyle. The word comes from the Greek and means " cheese," and it is made from ordinary honey.

After about three days the fluid supplied to the little grubs is changed and a richer form of bee milk is given. On this diet the grub grows rapidly, changes its skin several times and then, when it is fully-grown, it is sealed up in the cell with wax, and itself spins a cocoon of silk in which it changes into a nymph, a kind of chrysalis. After various changes take place, it becomes a perfect worker bee, and with its sharp jaws cuts a hole in the wax door when, assisted by the nurse bees, it comes out and is soon ready for work.

A group of happy girls jumping at their health exercises, a good example of joie de vivre

used the expression, and then it was adopted by newspaper journalists, and we find it in such references as " the *joie de vivre* of Blackpool Beach." Curiously enough, although the expression is given in the supplement to the " New English Dictionary," it does not appear in French dictionaries.

What is the Hottest Place in the World ?

THE highest shade temperature ever recorded is 134 degrees Fahrenheit, and that was on July 10th, 1913, at a place called Greenland Ranch, in the Death Valley of Southern California. The name Greenland was given not as a joke, but because of the green alfalfa which thrives there. A shade temperature of 154 degrees Fahrenheit has been reported from the Sahara, but this was not properly authenticated like the other.

The Death Valley is nowhere near the Equator, where we might expect the highest temperature, but is north of the 36th degree of latitude on a level with Gibraltar. The Death Valley, however, is a very dry area with masses of rock exposed all round and with little air movement and these factors increase the sun's effect.

Duke of Lancaster. It exposed many abuses, drove the King's mistress, Alice Perrers, from Court, and denounced the gross aggressions of the Pope, who received from the taxes five times as much as the King.

When Were Most British Sovereigns Alive at Once ?

ON December 25th, 1684, seven British sovereigns were all alive, and also Richard Cromwell, who for a time had been sovereign in all but name. They were Richard Cromwell, born October 4th, 1626, died 1712; Charles II, born May 29th, 1630, died 1685; James II, born October 14th, 1633, died 1701; William III, born November 4th, 1650, died 1702; Queen Mary II, born April 30th, 1662, died 1694; Queen Anne, born February 6th, 1665, died 1714; George I, born March 28th, 1660, died 1727; George II, born October 30th, 1683, died 1760.

What is Bee Milk ?

THIS is the name sometimes given to a substance produced by the nurse bees that look after the young insects when they hatch out in the cells from the eggs laid by the queen.

Where is Your Centre of Gravity ?

IN an adult human being the centre of gravity is situated near the last lumbar vertebra. But in young children it is much higher up, and that is why they are more or less top-heavy and tumble over so easily. The proportions of the human body change as a child grows older.

What Was the Forbidden Fruit ?

THE fruit which Adam and Eve were forbidden to take is not more definitely specified in the Old Testament, but tradition has made it the apple. Mohammedan doctors, however, declare that it was the banana or Indian fig. Probably the suggestion that it was the fig is due to the story telling how Adam and Eve made themselves clothing of fig leaves.

Which Country Has Most Pigs ?

CHINA is far ahead of all other countries with about 70 millions, and the United States comes next with about 40 millions. Then follows Germany with 26 millions, and Russia with 17½ millions. England with Wales has 3,800,000 pigs, and the Irish Free State, popularly supposed to be the land of the pig par excellence, has only 1,088,000. Northern Ireland has 520,000. Scotland has 236,000.

Which is the Largest Flying Bird ?

MR. E. G. BOULENGER of the London Zoo says that the largest flying bird is the great bustard, which weighs 40 pounds. The condor, which has a 10-foot wing span and is the largest bird of prey, tips the scales at only 24 pounds. The ostrich may weigh 260 pounds or nearly 2½ hundredweights, which just balances 120,000 humming-birds. A king penguin weighs just over 20 pounds.

How Are Rock Terraces and Pinnacles Formed?

THE terraces of rock seen in the Canyon of the Colorado and similar places are due to erosion, that is, the wearing away of the rock, partly by the river and partly by the weather. Sometimes in past ages a mass of hard rock already partly weathered has been overwhelmed by a deposit of softer material. Then millions of years later when weathering occurs the softer material is worn away while

Cedar Breaks in Southern Utah, U.S.A., which is said to be the world's most outstanding example of erosion at work. The harder rocks can be seen projecting as the softer rock is worn away

the harder rock remains as terraces and pinnacles, as shown in the photograph on this page.

How Far Down is a Stormy Sea Felt?

EXPERIMENT has proved that stormy waves create a violent disturbance in the water down to a depth of 150 feet beneath their troughs. Sand at this depth has been swept up to the surface during a storm.

Who Invented Algebra?

THE earliest work on algebra, which Sir Isaac Newton described as "universal arithmetic," was a Greek treatise by Diophantus of Alexandria, written in the 5th century of the Christian era. Europeans obtained their first knowledge of algebra from the Arabs, who probably derived their information from the Hindus. The earliest Arabian writer on algebra is Mohammed Ben Musa, who wrote in the early part of the 9th century. Many improvements were made as the centuries went by, and Thomas Harriott, an eminent English mathematician, born in 1560, first used small letters instead of capitals.

Why Are City Roads Always Rising?

TOWNS always have a tendency to attain higher levels, and we may have noticed that in the older parts of our big cities and towns, when we enter a very old shop or house we frequently have to step down into it from the street level. Such buildings were not, of course, originally built in this position, but the roadway has imperceptibly grown higher and higher in the course of the centuries, each repair in the past raising the surface a trifle higher.

In London, for example, the gradual growth upwards of the roadways has approximated to nearly a foot in a hundred years. The reason is that in the old days, when the roadway was repaired, fresh material was added without the removal of the old surface, and this gradually raised the level. Nowadays the method of road construction in cities and towns requires the removal of old surfaces, and this, with the great wear and tear of the present age, will tend to keep roadways at their present level.

Which is the Oldest Fibre Plant?

LINEN is the oldest fibre of which we have any record and the early Egyptian mummies are wrapped in linen cloths. Linen is, of course, made from the fibre of flax, and carved on the tombs of Ancient Egypt we find pictures of the flax plant growing. No one knows where this plant came from originally, but it probably grew wild in Assyria and in the Nile Valley. Nowadays it is not really a wild plant at all. It is cultivated in many countries, and where in England it is found growing wild it has escaped from some plantation.

Linen was an article of luxury in olden times, and in the Bible we find references to wealthy people being clothed in "purple and fine linen." The lake-dwellers of Switzerland who lived in the Stone Age grew flax for its fibre and wove linen cloth.

Should Dancers' Shoes Be Blocked With Wood?

THOUGH there are some who have tried this, the greatest authorities on dancing are agreed that it is harmful and incorrect. Madame Adeline Genée, President of the Royal Academy of Dancing, which is incorporated by Royal Charter, says that toe-dancing, or as it is correctly termed "dancing on pointes," is an outcome of certain exercises in connection with ballet dancing. The strengthening of the pointes is achieved by constant and correct practice of various specified exercises set forth in the syllabus of the Royal Academy of Dancing and other acknowledged societies concerned with the art of the ballet. Madame Genée, one of the greatest exponents of the art, says that she herself was not permitted to do pointe-work till she had served two years' apprenticeship, and she has never worn blocked shoes.

What is an Amphora?

AMONG the Greeks and Romans this was a large earthenware vessel with a handle on each side of the neck, and ending in a point. Amphorae were used for holding various forms of produce, but chiefly wine, oil and honey, and they were placed side by side in an upright position in the cellars of houses. They were stuck in the ground to keep them upright. Sometimes they were used as coffins. It is interesting to notice on some of the amphorae in the British Museum that the name of the maker and place of manufacture are stamped upon them.

Who Was Cerberus?

IN the Greek mythology he was the dog which kept watch at the entrance to the Nether World. He is described as a monster that sprang from Typhaon and Echidna. While some poets represent him with 50 or 100 heads, the later classical writers describe him as having only three heads, with the tail of a serpent, and serpents round his neck. His den was placed on the farther side of the river Styx, at the spot where Charon landed the shades of the departed. Cerberus fawned on those who entered Hades, but showed his teeth to those who went out.

How Can Cats Be Kept From a Garden?

IT has been suggested that the best plan is to put a few jars containing a little liquid ammonia in the garden. The cats do not like the smell of ammonia, and it is said that the garden can be kept entirely free by this means.

Are Coracles Used Today?

THE coracle, which is a primitive fishing-boat made of wicker or laths covered with skins or leather, was used by the Ancient Britons. It

A salmon fisherman on the River Dee sitting in a coracle, the type of boat that was used by the Ancient Britons two thousand years ago

is still to be seen in the Hebrides, in the west of Ireland and in some parts of Wales. It is a light, almost circular, boat and the basket-work frame is tarred to preserve it. It holds only one person, and is used by fishermen. The man fishes with one hand while with the other he directs the boat by a paddle.

Which Continent Has the Largest Irrigated Area?

THERE is more artificial irrigation in Asia than in any other part of the world. This continent, which covers over 16½ million square miles, has 140,754,000 acres irrigated. Next comes North America, covering more than 8½ million square miles, with 26,834,000 acres irrigated. Europe covers 3,723,081 square miles, and its irrigated area is 14,800,000 acres. Africa, with over 11½ million square miles, has 10,310,000 irrigated acres. South America, with more than 7 million square miles, has 6,613,000 acres irrigated. Oceania, with 3,307,940 square miles, has 1,270,000 acres of irrigated land. Thus with a total of over 50,600,000 square miles, the world has 200,531,000 acres of irrigated land.

Who Was the Wisest Fool in Christendom?

THIS was a name given to James I by Sully, the French statesman. James was a student with considerable

learning and also a prolific writer and ready in retort, but his ordinary conversation had little dignity. The Hon. Clive Bigham sums up his character in the words : " Witty, canny, and amusing, a cheery buffoon, vain of his scholarship and position, yet unable to appraise the dignity of either, James was as good a judge of books as he was a bad one of men. . . . Crafty and timorous, an advocate of peace at any price, with a curious lack of vision and understanding, he brought the English monarchy into contempt at a time when its critics were serious, strenuous and increasing."

Are Many Objects Left in London Buses?

THE number of objects of one kind and another left behind in the buses, tramcars and underground trains of the London Passenger Transport Board is astonishing. In 1937 the total number of objects left by passengers was 348,477, of which only 112,068, or not quite one-third, were claimed.

Here is a list of some of the objects : 112,977 umbrellas, 49,999 pairs of gloves, 19,798 single gloves, 33,611 pieces of clothing, 25,949 attaché cases, 24,660 books, 24,158 parcels, 5,805 pairs of spectacles, 5,278 keys, 4,005 pipes, 2,037 different pieces of foodstuff.

Every minute and a half throughout the day somebody leaves something behind in a tube train, bus or tramcar, and every five minutes an umbrella is left.

Some of the things forgotten by passengers are curious, and one wonders how they can be left. They include motor-bicycles, steel helmets, fur coats and pistols.

After six months, if an article is not claimed, the London Passenger Transport Board becomes its legal owner. It is sent with other goods to a public auction held on the 3rd of every month. Fifty per cent. of the proceeds go to the company, and the other fifty per cent. to the staff fund. But even stranger than the leaving behind of these articles is the fact that so many people do not take the trouble to go back for them.

Some of the enormous number of miscellaneous articles left daily in London trains, trams and buses

What Was the Battle of Marathon?

THIS was one of the decisive battles of the world and was fought in September, 490 B.C., between the Greeks under Miltiades and the Persians under Datis and Artaphernes. There were only 11,000 Greeks against 100,000 Persians, but thanks to the clever tactics of Miltiades the Greeks won a great victory. They lost only 192 men, while the Persians lost 6,400. This victory ended the menace of a Persian invasion of Greece. Marathon is a plain in Attica, 18 miles north-east of Athens, and lies between Mount Pentelicus and the sea. A conical mound covering the Athenian dead marks the central point of the battle.

Can Man Resist the Sea's Inroads?

CERTAINLY he can, but the cost of doing so is very heavy in material and labour. Where there is a large town on the coast, a strong sea-wall is built, often with protecting groynes jutting out into the sea, and these are kept in good repair. Sometimes, as at Pakefield, near Lowestoft, the waves are so fierce that they smash even the stone barrier, but funds are available in a large town for repairing the damage.

It is where there are no large towns with adequate rates for building and repairing sea-walls that the sea has its way and eats away the coast. It is doing this round various parts of the British coasts. Nothing but constant vigilance can keep out the sea where it is trying to advance on the land. The ravages of one stormy night may undo the work of years

Who Was the Angelic Doctor?

THIS was a name given to Thomas Aquinas, the great scholastic philosopher of the Middle Ages, be-

An apprentice who has served his time being " passed out " according to an ancient custom

cause, it is said, he discussed many knotty points in connection with the being and nature of angels. His followers were called Thomists. Thomas Aquinas, or Thomas Aquino was born near Aquino in Italy about 1225 and died at Fossa Nuova in 1274.

What is the "Passing Out" of an Apprentice?

AN apprentice is said to " pass out " or to be " passed out " when he has completed his time, and in the old days there was a quaint ceremony to mark the event, which is still observed in some old firms in the City of London. The apprentice is stood on his head and held in that position while pieces of metal are banged with hammers, after which all are provided with beer or ale paid for by the apprentice. He is then free to work as a journeyman.

What Was the Missouri Compromise?

THIS was an agreement with reference to the extension of slavery embodied in a Bill passed by the American Congress on March 2nd, 1820, and in an Act of Congress passed in the following year admitting Missouri to the Union. It was declared that in all the territory ceded to the United States by France and known as Louisiana north of 36° 30" north latitude, excepting Missouri, slavery should be prohibited for ever. Only on this condition was it agreed to admit Missouri as a state.

What is the Difference Between High and Low Mass?

LOW mass is the service said by the priest throughout without music, while at high mass there is music and incense and a full ceremonial. The mass is really the celebration of the eucharist, and the name comes from the Latin words of dismissal at the end of the service, *missa est.*

Huge seas pounding the sea-wall at Blackpool

What is Hemp?

HEMP is the name given to various kinds of plants producing fibre, such as Sisal hemp, Manila hemp and Bowstring hemp, but the true hemp is the bast fibre of the plant which botanists call *Cannabis sativa*, a native of western Asia and a near relative of the stinging-nettle. It is a plant about nine feet high, and it is grown not only for its fibre but for resin, the oil contained in the seed, and the seed itself. The fibre is very tough, elastic and durable, and is used for making rope and cordage, and for weaving into sail-cloth, canvas and tarpaulin.

The chief hemp-growing countries are Russia, Italy, Austria, Hungary, Turkey, China, Japan and the United States, and the product is known commercially according to its source as Italian, Russian, Hungarian and so on. The finest hemp is grown in Italy. The Russians use hemp oil in their lamps, and the residue of the seeds after the oil has been extracted is

Gathering the hemp harvest in Italy

made into cakes for cattle food. Hemp seed is also used for cage-bird food.

The fields where hemp is grown need plenty of manure. When the tops of the plants begin to turn yellow, the crop is ready for harvesting, and the male plants, which yield the best fibre, are always cut before the female. The stems are gathered in bundles and placed on trestles to dry. Then they are retted or soaked in water, and after being dried in the open air or in bread ovens the external bark is removed and the fibre extracted.

What is Roger's Blast?

THIS is the name given in English rural districts to a kind of whirlwind that sometimes carries hay or straw up to a great height and then lets it drop back to earth.

Which Country Has Most Sheep?

THE latest statistics give the total number in the Commonwealth of Australia as 113 millions. In India sheep and goats together number 98 millions, and in Russia the sheep with the goats 61 millions. In the Argentine and Uruguay there are 55 million sheep, and in the United States 52,200,000. The Union of South Africa has 35 millions, and New Zealand 28,650,000. In England and Wales there are 16,630,000, in China 15 millions. Iran has 14,500,000, Turkey 10,750,000, and Scotland 7,600,000.

What is the Greasy Ring Round the Moon?

THIS familiar phenomenon is caused by the refraction and reflection of the light of the Moon by minute ice crystals high up in the air. When the Greasy Ring is visible, as in the illustration facing page 621, the sky is generally covered with a thin veil of cirro-stratus or alto-stratus clouds. These, which are very high up, are composed of minute ice crystals.

What is a "Black Widow"?

THIS is the name given to a very poisonous South African spider, specimens of which have been seen in the London Zoo. With the exception of a North American Black Widow it is the most venomous spider that has ever been sent to England, and the Zoo authorities gave orders that if London should be bombed from the air the Black Widows were to be destroyed immediately so that there might be no chance of their getting loose. The Black Widow spider in the Zoo laid several batches of eggs from which young spiders hatched out.

Why Does Our Hair Crackle When We Comb It?

IF we comb our hair rapidly when it is very dry with a vulcanite comb we hear a crackling sound, and if we do this in the dark it is often possible

Electric sparks caused by combing the hair with a vulcanite comb

to see a shower of sparks coming from the hair.

What happens is that the combing generates electricity. Electrons are taken out of the atoms of the comb and added to other atoms of the hair, and it is the passing of these electrons that causes the apparent sparks that we see in the dark. The crackling is really a thunderstorm on a small scale.

What is a Hanging Valley?

THIS is one of the results of glacial erosion. A main valley may be eroded by glacial action to a depth of a hundred feet, while a tributary valley running into it is not lowered. The lower end of the latter will thus be a hundred feet above the main valley when the ice disappears. Such a valley is called a hanging valley. Many examples are to be seen in regions which were recently glaciated, as in the Western Mountains of North America.

What Does the Term "Lub-Dup" Mean?

"LUB" and "dup" are terms which doctors use to describe the sounds made by the heart-beats as the blood is pumped through the body. The first sound "lub" is low-pitched and prolonged, while the second sound "dup" is high and sharp. If we listen to the beating of the heart through a stethoscope we shall hear these sounds distinctly: lub-dup, pause; lub-dup, pause; and so on. The sounds are made as the walls of the heart move to and fro during its pumping work.

Who Was the Man of December?

THIS is a nickname given to the Emperor Napoleon III, because he became President of France on December 11th, 1848, made his *coup d'état* on December 2nd, 1851, and became Emperor on December 2nd, 1852.

What Breed of Pig Is That?

Here are the various breeds of pigs which are seen on British farms. The pig, as a food animal, has been enormously improved by careful breeding during the past century, and no variety of pig has made a greater advance in public favour than the Large White. It is particularly suitable for bacon. Its white colour is an asset, for according to bacon-curers, bacon from white pigs sells at a higher price than that from dark animals. This is due to fancy, but the Large White furnishes a greater proportion of lean to fat meat than any other breed, and that pleases the public. A large white boar weighs as much as half a ton. The Large Black is one of the oldest breeds in the country. Pigs are very economical animals to keep

What is a Noise Meter?

It is a scientific apparatus used to measure the intensity of loudness of a noise and increases in noise. There are two distinct kinds of noise meters. In one kind, known as the subjective noise meter, the loudness of a noise as heard by the ear is matched with a reference tone as heard in a telephone earpiece held tightly against one ear. In the other type, known as the objective noise meter, the idea is to be able to measure every type of sound and noise on a scale of phons, the phon being the unit for indicating increases in loudness.

What is Timber?

Most people would say that the word was synonymous with wood, but this is not the case. Though in a loose way any wood and growing trees are spoken of as timber, the word actually means wood cut up and prepared for building purposes. The word timber originally meant a dwelling, and is allied to the Latin word *domus*, which means a house. Only trees which are suitable and ripe to form building material can rightly be called timber, and the word is misused when applied to conifers.

Are Monkeys Good Jumpers?

Yes; living as most of them do among trees or rocks they have acquired the habit of making great leaps from bough to bough or rock to rock. In some parts of the East Indies monkeys have been trained to gather fruit from tall trees, and they pass from tree to tree over long distances without ever descending. Even at the London Zoo the monkeys can often be seen making remarkable leaps on Monkey Hill.

Why Does Water Splash When Thrown?

Water pouring from a tap or emerging from a hose or squirt remains in one stream, but when thrown from a pail it divides up and

How the water shot from a pail takes the form of a sheet as it falls

splashes about. Why is its behaviour different in the two cases? Well, in the case of the tap and the hose, the water emerges with force from a comparatively small opening, and, all the drops being shot out in one direction, they cohere and the water remains a united stream. When, however, the water is hurled from a pail or bowl, it is shot out with less force and with a jerky motion which causes the drops and molecules of which it is composed to spread out, and thus the water gets splashed in different directions. The photograph on this page will show the behaviour of the water when being shot out of a pail. It first takes the form of a sheet and then divides up.

Who Was Lord Dundreary?

He was a character in Tom Taylor's play "Our American Cousin," and represents a good-natured, indolent, empty-headed swell with long side-whiskers which came to be known as "Dundreary whiskers."

Where is Poets' Corner?

This is the popular name given to the south end of the east aisle of the transept of Westminster Abbey, and to the south end of the central aisle, because of the great number of poets' monuments there. They include those of Chaucer, Spenser, Addison, Campbell, Dryden, Gay, Goldsmith, Gray, Ben Jonson, Longfellow, Milton, Shakespeare and others.

What is the Blue Boy?

It is a painting by Thomas Gainsborough of a boy wearing a 16th-century costume of blue satin, with a landscape in the background. The boy, who is shown as a full-length portrait, was Master Jonathan Buttall, the son of an ironmonger of Soho. The Blue Boy grew up and succeeded to the business, carrying on till 1796.

A monkey at the London Zoo making a great leap on Monkey Hill

What Was the Vinegar Offered to Jesus?

THE vinegar referred to in the Gospels as having been offered in a soaked sponge to Jesus while He was hanging on the Cross was not the same as the vinegar used by us as a table condiment. It was really a light

A photograph showing something of the development of the bathing costume from the 'eighties of last century to the present day

wine which turned sour much more rapidly than modern wines. It was a favourite drink of the soldiers of that time, and the offering of this to the sufferer was probably an act of mercy.

What is Maiden Castle?

IT is an extensive prehistoric earthwork at Dorchester where for several years past elaborate excavations have been made, revealing a great deal about the life of men in the Stone Age. The earliest inhabitants of the district lived there before 2000 B.C., practised agriculture and had herds of cattle and sheep. In the 4th century B.C. immigrants from the Continent built the first Maiden Castle. It was elaborately defended. There were two gateways with ramparts, and a defensive ditch of exceptional depth and steepness.

Then later more ambitious defences were built, with a high stone rampart. An armoury has been found with 5,000 sling stones. The people lived in circular houses with storage pits and cooking pits for baking. After the Roman Conquest the defences were demolished. Many of the stones from the rampart have in course of time been taken away for the building of cottages.

Maiden Castle is one of the most extensive earthworks ever discovered anywhere.

How Far Has Bathing Dress Changed?

BATHING costume has changed more, perhaps, during the past half-century or so than ordinary dress, and the accompanying photograph, which shows actual bathing dresses of various years between 1880 and today, will make this clear. Almost down to the Great War the costume worn by women when bathing clothed and concealed their bodies almost as much as a winter walking dress. Farther back still, in the 1860's, the bathing dress was still more voluminous and hideous, but about 1862 the first attempts were made to render it less unattractive.

Mr. C. Willett Cunnington in his exhaustive work on " English Women's Clothing in the Nineteenth Century " says : " Hitherto it had been a shapeless loose gown like a flannel chemise, in which the fair sex were adequately concealed from prying masculine eyes, but now inspection was positively invited. Very pretty costumes are made : trousers long and straight to the ankle in the shape of knickerbockers, and a long, half-fitting *casaque* ; or else a blouse-tunic with trousers ; these are made in flannel or rep, black with blue or red worsted braid."

Four years later we were told " The Zouave-Marine swimming costume, a body and trousers cut in one, secures perfect liberty of action and does not expose the figure." It was made of stout brown holland or dark blue serge, with scarlet braid trimming. In 1868, to make a bathing costume five yards of flannel or serge were required. The trousers reached to the ankles, the tunic to the knees, and the trimming was black braid.

In 1870 woman's bathing dress consisted of a basque bodice and drawers fastened below the knee with scarlet ribbon, short skirts and puffed sleeves. The description of a bathing costume four years later is : " Made with a tunic and worn with a waistbelt and deep sailor collar not opened at the throat if you wish to preserve the whiteness of your neck. Buttons down the front. The drawers should button on each side, but a string should be added for

Buried skeletons found on a battlefield of A.D. 40 during the excavations at Maiden Castle near Dorchester

safety, and they should be gathered just above the ankle."

By 1880 bathing costume was getting chic. Here is the description: "A loose blouse of dark blue serge, elbow sleeves and collar, wide drawers a few inches above the ankle, all trimmed with wide braid, and a red woollen sash." The next year some daring women had no sleeves at all to their bathing dresses, and in 1882 the description is: "Belted tunic and drawers, loose below the knee; no sleeves, but an epaulette." The last-named feature was no doubt a tribute to Mrs. Grundy. In 1886 the bathing costume was made of stockinet in one piece with a detachable short skirt or tunic over knickerbockers, and the warning was added in the fashion

A young elephant being landed at the Royal Albert Docks on its arrival from India. (See below)

notes: "Care should be taken lest they reveal the figure when wet."

By 1889 and 1890 women had apparently become rather nervous, and bathing costumes had trousers to the ankles once more and tunics gathered at the waist. In 1892 we read among the fashion notes: "An American lady is surprised that English bathers do not wear black stockings as worn in the U.S.A. for mixed bathing. You have no idea how decent they make the whole proceedings."

The wearers of those demure costumes would be amazed if they could see the more daring bathing dresses of today. Of course, the approach to freedom and sanity came with the Great War.

What is Reticulated Porcelain?

THE word "reticulated" means "like a net," and the term applied to porcelain indicates a style of Oriental work in which the outer side of vases is entirely cut out in geometric patterns, sometimes in circles, at other times honeycombed, the whole being superimposed on a second vase of the same general form.

What is the New York Elevated?

THIS is a series of railway tracks in New York corresponding to the underground railways of London, but instead of running in tunnels the trains run on a continuous bridge or viaduct supported on iron columns. The general height is about on a level with the first-floor windows of the houses, but at some places it is much higher, rising to 65 feet above the pavement. The stations occur at every five blocks of buildings in some sections, and are never at any part more than half a mile apart. Passengers ascend from the street by staircases, and at one time about 200 million passengers were carried annually.

But with the development of other forms of transport the Elevated Railway, or "L" as it was popularly called, fell on evil days, and in July, 1938, New York City had accumulated tax claims totalling more than eight million dollars, or £1,600,000. It was expected that if the property was seized on account of these unpaid taxes the elevated railways would be torn down. They had served the city for over sixty years.

How Are Elephants Taken on Board Ship?

THEY are slung on board with a stout wide belt under their bodies, and are disembarked in the same way, as shown in the photograph above of an elephant from India being landed at the Royal Albert Dock in London.

When Was an Ox Roasted on the Thames?

THIS was done on several occasions during great frosts which caused the ice to be continuous from bank to bank. Fairs were held, and various amusements were conducted on the ice. One of these great frosts when an ox was roasted was in the winter of 1683–84, and others in the winters of 1715–16, and 1739–40. During the great frost of 1789 a pig was roasted on the Thames, and in that of 1813–14 a sheep.

Has Metal Ever Been Melted By a Burning-Glass?

YES, about 1800 an Englishman named Parker made a burning-glass so big that when it concentrated the Sun's rays upon gold, silver, copper, iron or steel, it melted the metal. This huge burning-glass cost £700, and it is said that it was afterwards taken to Peking, but what happened to it then is not known.

What Are the Horses of St. Mark?

THESE are four horses of gilt bronze taken by the Venetians from the Hippodrome at Constantinople and erected over the west porch of the Church of St. Mark at Venice. The date and artist are unknown, but Augustus took them from Alexandria and set them on a triumphal arch in Rome. After several removals Constantine carried them off to Constantinople. When Bonaparte captured Venice in 1797 he removed the bronze horses to Paris, but in 1815 after his fall they were returned to Venice and replaced once more on the Church of St. Mark.

What is Erastianism?

IT is the name given to that idea of the Church which regards it as under the control of the civil power. The word comes from the name of Thomas Erastus, a physician of Baden in the 16th century, who taught that the Church is not a divine but a civil institution, subordinate to and dependent upon the civil power.

What Was an Olympiad?

THE era of the Olympiads, which began on July 1st, 776 B.C., was a system of dates adopted by the ancient Greeks. An Olympiad was a period of four years intervening between two consecutive celebrations of the Olympic Games. They were first used for chronological purposes when Choroebos won the foot-race, the principal event before the introduction of chariot-races. By this system of dating, events were said to have happened on the first, second or fourth year of such-and-such an Olympiad.

What is a Public or Common Nuisance?

In his Book of English Law Dr. Edward Jenks says: "It includes the obstruction of highways and navigable rivers, the non-repair of highways, the polution of public waters, the allowing of buildings to become a source of danger, the emission of loud and distracting noises or poisonous fumes,

An enlarged photograph of a house spider killing a bluebottle fly

the exposing to public contact of persons known to be suffering from contagious disease, the exposing to sale of adulterated or unwholesome food, and the keeping of an unlicensed tavern or other place of entertainment requiring a licence."

Who Was Horatius Cocles?

He was a legendary Roman hero who with two companions became famous by defending a bridge over the Tiber against an army of Etruscans, as described in one of Lord Macaulay's "Lays of Ancient Rome."

John Haring, who defended a dyke against a thousand Spaniards till all the men under the Governor Sonoy, who had been put to flight, had made their escape, is called the "Horatius Cocles of the Horn." He afterwards threw himself into the sea and escaped.

Alexandre Davy Dumas, son of Dumas the elder, the novelist, is called the "Horatius Cocles of the Tyrol" because in 1798, while in

Doumouriez's army, he defended alone at Brixen the passage of a bridge on which depended the success of the French Army.

How Does the Spider Kill the Fly?

When the fly is caught in the web, the spider hurries up and generally binds the victim round with threads to prevent escape. "Spiders, like cats," says Mr. Edward C. Ash in his account of the British spiders, "frequently play with their victims. After damaging the fly sufficiently to prevent any escape, they will allow it to wander off, only to be caught and carried back again, just as it felt free. In good time it is trussed up and eaten."

Spiders when capturing prey, adds Mr. Ash, only use poison in cases of strict emergency when other less drastic methods of control have failed. The falces or jaws without the poison are a sufficiently drastic weapon and cause serious injuries in the tender parts of the victims. "The quantity and power of the poison depends not only on the species but largely on the temper of the individual. The more angry or excited, the more poison produced. When an insect is poisoned by a spider, the insect is paralysed, the poison works off, the insect recovers. Spiders are conscious of this fact, and hence, even after using their poison, tie their victims most securely so as to prevent any chance of escape when they shall recover."

What is the Kraken?

It is a mythical sea-monster which is said to have appeared at times off the coast of Norway. A description of it was written in the first half of the 18th century by Pontoppidan. It is generally spoken of as a great sea-serpent, and possibly a giant octopus may have been the origin of the legend.

Scandinavian sailors often speak of having seen it and mistaken it for an island. The name means tree-trunk or stump.

Is the Earth Moving Towards a Point in the Sky?

Yes, the Earth with all the solar system to which it belongs is travelling through Space towards a point in the constellation of the Lyre. In that constellation there is a star of the first magnitude named Vega, and it is towards this point that the whole solar system is moving.

Vega is about 163 million million miles from the Earth, and its light takes 26 years to reach us. It is the brightest star in the northern sky. We are travelling towards this point at about 44,000 miles an hour, or over a million miles a day. But when we get to where Vega is now, that star will, of course, have moved from its present position.

What is a Corbel?

It is a projecting stone or piece of timber supporting a weight of some kind. Corbels are used in many situations, and are carved and moulded in a variety of ways. Sometimes they have the shape of a head. Any construction which is carried by corbels so as to stand beyond the face of a wall is said to be corbelled. When a row of corbels supports a parapet or cornice, the whole structure is called a corbel table.

The fronts of many old houses are examples of corbelling, each story jutting out beyond the one below, so that when the streets are narrow and the gables high the top stories of the houses approach so near to one another as almost to touch. Such houses were characteristic of London before the Great Fire. The term corbel steps, sometimes called corbie steps, refers to steps up the sides of a gable, such as are frequently found in old houses in Flanders, Holland and some parts of Germany.

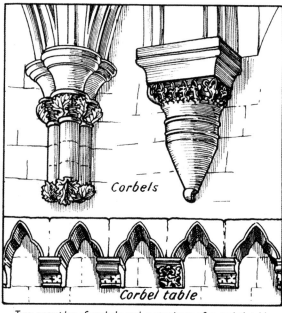

Two examples of corbels and a specimen of a corbel table

When Was That Helmet Worn?

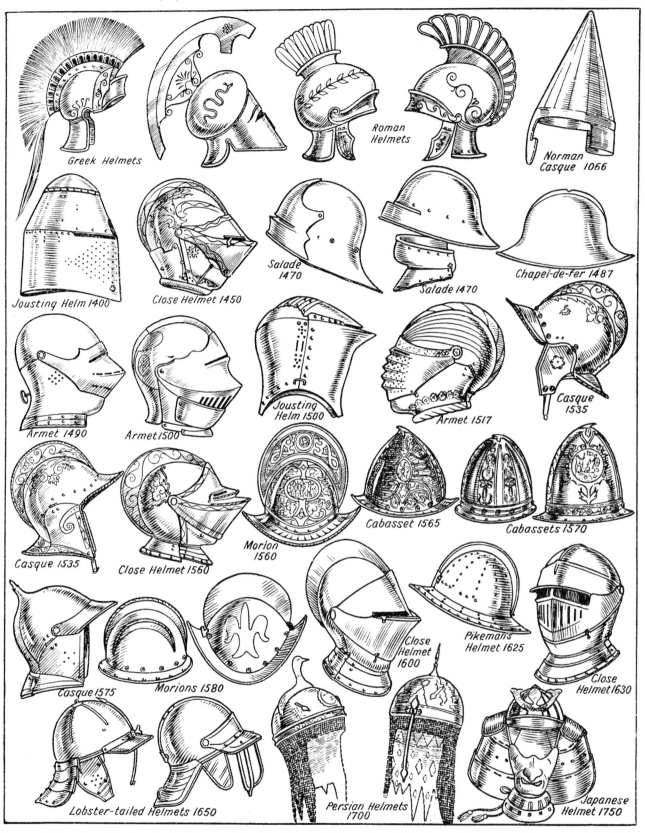

Greek Helmets

Roman Helmets

Norman Casque 1066

Jousting Helm 1400

Close Helmet 1450

Salade 1470

Salade 1470

Chapel-de-fer 1487

Armet 1490

Armet 1500

Jousting Helm 1500

Armet 1517

Casque 1535

Casque 1535

Close Helmet 1560

Morion 1560

Cabasset 1565

Cabassets 1570

Casque 1575

Morions 1580

Close Helmet 1600

Pikeman's Helmet 1625

Close Helmet 1630

Lobster-tailed Helmets 1650

Persian Helmets 1700

Japanese Helmet 1750

Here are 32 drawings which show the development of the helmet through 25 centuries. The helmets of the Greeks and Romans reached a high pitch of artistic beauty, and then came the Dark Ages, in which the helmet was made almost entirely for use. But as time went on its form became more attractive, and often it was beautifully decorated, either by chasing the steel or by damascening it with gold and silver. Jousting helms and close helmets used in tilting completely enclosed the head, with only small slits through which the warrior could see. Indeed, sometimes he tilted without being able to see at all. The salade was a light helmet, and with it was worn a beaver or bavier to protect the chin. The armet came into use about the middle of the 15th century. Morions and cabassets were familiar types of helmets in the 16th century and the "lobster-tail" followed

291

What Are The Horny Objects on the Beach?

THE horny objects found on the beach round the British coasts and often called by children "mermaids' purses" or "pixies' purses," are of different shapes. The one with long coiled tendons attached to the ends is the egg-case of the dog-fish, a close relative of the shark. When dry the horny substance looks like amber. The strings are used for fastening the

The shell of the egg consists of a horn-like substance, feeling to the touch like a sheet of moistened leather. This horny substance is called keitene. It is analogous to the substance which forms the horny wings of beetles.

"The two ends of the egg differ in appearance : one end is permanently soldered up ; at the other the two sheets of horn-like material are so arranged that when the young fish inside is about to be born they will give way and allow the young fish to struggle out."

Sometimes after a severe storm one of these egg-cases will be thrown up on the shore, and when it is opened a small live skate is to be seen inside about to be born. As soon as the fish is hatched the empty shell floats away on the water.

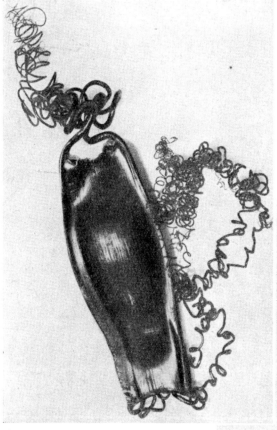

Above, the egg-case of the common dog-fish, and, on the right, a skate's egg-case

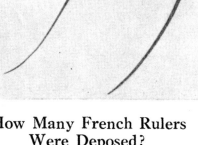

case to seaweed, thus anchoring it, and they are like the tendrils of a vine. As Mr. Frank Buckland, the naturalist says: "It is a very curious circumstance that Nature seems to have used the same kind of ligature to fasten up the branches of a plant and to anchor the egg of a fish." The tendrils of the egg of the dog-fish or nursehound are, when only slightly stretched, ten inches long. It was at the Brighton Aquarium that the dog-fish was first seen attaching its egg to the seaweed by the strings.

The other horny substance, somewhat similar in appearance, shown in the second photograph on this page is the egg-case of a skate. "Each egg," says Frank Buckland, "is of an oblong shape and may be likened to a hand-barrow, for from each corner there project two horn-like processes. The total length, not including the horns, is eight inches ; breadth three inches.

How Many French Rulers Were Deposed?

FIVE : Louis XVI in 1793 ; Napoleon I, twice deposed, in 1814 and in 1815 ; Charles X in 1830, and Louis-Philippe in 1848, both euphemistically said to have abdicated ; and finally, Napoleon III in 1872.

What is a Speleologist?

A SPELEOLOGIST is one who engages in speleology, the science of studying caves. The name is from the Latin word for a cave, "spelaeum," and seems to have first come into use in 1895, though as far back as 1839 a person who frequented caves was described by the adjective "spelaean."

In July, 1938, the third annual conference of the British Speleological Association was held at Giggleswick and expeditions were made to the caves and potholes of Yorkshire.

Who Lived at Gadshill?

GADSHILL PLACE was for long the home of Charles Dickens, the novelist, and there he died. Gadshill is three miles north-west of Rochester on the road to Gravesend, and is noted as the place where Sir John Falstaff and three of his knavish companions attacked a party of travellers, robbing them of their purses as described in Shakespeare's "King Henry IV," First Part (Act II, Scene 2). Gadshill, one of the thieves, is a character in the play. There is a Falstaff Inn at the place.

What Was Hampton Court Conference?

IT was a conference held at Hampton Court Palace in January, 1604, to see if a settlement could be arrived at between the bishop's party and the Puritans. James I presided, and according to his own account he peppered the commissioners soundly. The conference lasted several days, and eventually its decisions were adverse to the Puritans. Its chief result was a few slight alterations in the Book of Common Prayer. An important indirect result of the conference was the revision of the English Bible.

Which is the Granite City?

THIS is a name given to Aberdeen since the beginning of the 19th century when it was largely rebuilt and many fine structures of granite erected. New Hampshire in the United States is called the Granite State because of the abundant granite it contains.

What is Ithuriel's Spear?

IT is the spear carried by the Angel Ithuriel, the slightest touch of which exposes deceit. Ithuriel in Milton's "Paradise Lost" is one of the angels commissioned by Gabriel to search for Satan, who had entered Paradise to tempt Eve.

Can Monkeys Enjoy the Cinema?

In August, 1938, two of the Zoo chimpanzees, Jackie and Peter, were taken to see a film called "Monkey Into Man," in which apes appeared.

monkey, he imitated the motions. Peter showed more interest than Jackie, but he grew tired earlier.

One correspondent tells us that

A herd of camels at Oodnadatta in Central Australia

The special correspondent of the "Daily Telegraph" says: "Both apes reacted well during the experiment, but it was difficult to decide how much they could distinguish on the screen, and whether the interest they showed was stimulated simply by the effect of sound combined with movement on the screen.

"At first, when close-ups of men and women speakers were shown they seemed worried. They looked at the screen and then turned round to stare at the projector. But when chimpanzees appeared on the screen, and their voices were heard, both Jackie and Peter were impressed. They sat still and watched with interest.

"The climax came when their colleague in the Monkey House—the chimpanzee Jimmie—was shown and heard in his famous kicking turn. Accompanied by music, he beat a tattoo with his feet on the door of his den. Jackie then got off his seat, moved forwards, and sat on the floor, gazing intently at the screen. Peter not only got up, but went right up to the screen and stood swaying from side to side to the rhythm of the music.

"Later, when this part of the film was shown again without sound, the apes showed less interest, though they still watched. A close-up of their keeper and the sound of his voice had no effect on them, nor did they register any emotion when gorillas, penguins, small birds and turtles were shown. Yet all monkeys and apes demonstrate against live tortoises."

When the end of another Zoo film, "Behind the Scenes at the London Zoo," was shown, Peter showed much interest. When he saw chimpanzees eating and the chattering of a capuchin

when Mok, the now defunct male gorilla, was shown jumping at the audience, Peter retired hastily.

What Was the Amphictyonic League?

In Greek history this term is used to describe a league of tribes inhabiting neighbouring territories and drawn together for mutual protection. There were several such leagues at different times, but the most famous

was that of Delphi. It consisted of twelve tribes and its representatives met twice a year, alternately at Delphi and Thermopylae. It exercised authority over the famous oracle of the Pythian Apollo at Delphi and over the surrounding country. It was a kind of league of nations of early days. It was named from Amphictyon, son of Deucalion, its supposed founder.

Has Australia Any Camels?

Of course, there are no wild camels in Australia; indeed, there are no wild camels anywhere, for this animal, both in the one-humped Arabian species and the two-humped Bactrian kind, is now entirely a domestic animal. But there are thousands of camels in the more arid parts of Australia. Till the coming of the motor-car, communication across the waterless plains was generally possible only by camel trains.

In early days much of the exploration of the arid interior was accomplished by means of camels. These animals were first used by the Burke and Wills expedition of 1860–61, which crossed the continent by a route to the east of Lake Eyre. Several expeditions which failed with horses for transport afterwards succeeded with camel trains. At the present time there are large herds of Arabian camels in Central Australia.

What Are the Arundel Marbles?

They are gems of Grecian sculpture collected by Sir William Petty at the instance of the Earl of Arundel and presented to the University of Oxford in 1667.

Two of the London Zoo's chimpanzees watching a cinema performance in which monkeys appeared on the screen

Why Do We Cook Our Food?

WE do not cook all foods. Salads, fruits and some other foods are eaten raw; but we cook most of our food for several reasons. In the first place, it is generally rendered more palatable. Then cooked food is often more digestible, and, further, when it is cooked it becomes sterilised by the heat and so will keep for a longer period. Cooking does not destroy all bacteria, but it kills many. Animal foods, however, which we almost invariably cook, become less digestible after the process, although indirectly the cooking may help in this way; for by making the food more attractive and palatable the cooking calls forth a better flow of gastric juice, the fluid in our body which digests the food.

Where Are Storks' Nests Made to Order?

DANISH farmers always like to have a stork nesting on their roofs as the bird is supposed to bring good luck. Recently, for some reason, the storks have not been building as freely as formerly, and so ready-made nests are provided for them. A co-operative factory exists in Jutland where the nests are manufactured for sale to the farmers. Storks are also becoming less common in Germany, though the reason for this is not known.

Building a stork's nest at a nest factory in Denmark

Who Invented Spectacles?

SPECTACLES were unknown to the Ancients, and it is generally supposed that they were invented by Alexander de Spina, a monk of Florence

Girls at Lowestoft repairing a drift-net. The cork floats can be seen

in Italy about 1285. Others think he merely rendered their use more common, and that they were invented by Salvino Armati, a Florentine, who died in 1317. On the tomb of Armati in Florence is an inscription in Latin, which translated reads: "Here lies Salvino Degli Armati, inventor of spectacles. May God pardon his sins." It has been stated by some authorities that spectacles were invented by Roger Bacon about 1280, but there is little evidence of this.

What is a Mugwump?

THIS word from the Algonquin language, one of the Red Indian tongues, means a person who holds himself aloof from and superior to party politics. In the native tongue it means one who thinks independently, and it was first used in modern times of independent members of the Re-publican Party. Later it came to have a contemptuous meaning. In Eliot's translation of the Bible into the Red Indian tongue the word centurion in the Book of Acts is rendered "mugwump."

How Are Drift Nets Kept Floating?

THE huge drift-nets kept floating for fish just below the surface of the sea are maintained in position by means of a row of cork floats. The specific gravity of cork is about ·22, that is, it is only one-fifth the weight of the water it displaces, and so it has power to support another weight beside itself.

How Many Tins of Food are Eaten in Britain?

IT is said that about 1,600 million tins of food are eaten in Great Britain every year, and that these contain 350 different kinds of food. Experts state that the whole of the people of England could be fed for a year with 15,000 million tins of food.

How Could a Man Take Up His Bed and Walk With It?

THE paralytic who was told by Jesus to take up his bed and go to his house, and did so, did not have such a formidable task to perform as would be the case if a similar command were given in England. The bed consisted merely of a mattress which could be rolled up and carried easily.

Are Many Rabbits Imported for Food?

BELGIUM sends about 1,250 tons of fresh rabbits every year, but the amount of frozen rabbits coming from Australia is sometimes over 20,000 tons, while from other countries about 10,000 tons of frozen and canned rabbits are received.

What Were the Bills of Mortality?

THESE were records of burials and baptisms kept in London by the Company of Parish Clerks, but they were not accurate, as only baptisms and burials in parish churches and burying-grounds were registered, and there were many dissenters in London. The name "Bills of Mortality" was later extended to mean the district covered by the returns and so certain events were described as taking place "within the Bills of Mortality." The area included, in addition to the City of London, the parishes of Bethnal Green, Bermondsey and Hackney, but did not cover the extensions of London in the west, such as Marylebone and St. Pancras.

How Do Army Chaplains Rank?

THE Chaplain-General, who is always a clergyman of the Established Church of England, is head of the Ecclesiastical Department of the Army and ranks with a Major-General. A chaplain of the first class ranks with a colonel, of the second class with a lieutenant-colonel, of the third class with a major, and of the fourth class with a captain.

What is a Porters' Rest?

IN the old days, when much of the carrying of goods was done by porters, platforms were placed here and there in the streets on which the porters could support their burdens for a minute or two while they rested. One such porters' rest is still to be seen in Piccadilly, London, opposite the Cavalry Club. It was placed there in 1861 and even today one may sometimes see a boy or man resting a load upon it while he stands for a few moments before continuing his journey.

Who Was Endymion?

IN the classical mythology he was a youth noted for his beauty and his perpetual sleep. As he slept on Mount Latmus in Caria, Selene or the Moon saw him and had her cold heart

A condor of the Andes with its wings spread out

warmed by his beauty. She came down to him and kissed him. Some stories explain his eternal sleep as being caused by Selene, who sent him to sleep so that she might kiss him without his knowledge. Other stories say Zeus gave him his expressed wish for eternal sleep.

Can Condors be Shot on the Wing?

THIS is not an easy feat to perform, for at a distance of 30 or 40 yards a charge of buckshot produces no effect. Hunters, however, sometimes draw the birds within reach by tying up a dog and concealing themselves behind a rock close by. Soon the whining or barking of the dog has the desired effect. Condors are drawn to the spot; they pass and repass in majestic flight, and curiosity brings them nearer and nearer, until at last they may pass within a few yards of the hiding huntsmen.

Condors are great fliers, their wing-spread being as much as nine feet. They soar at lofty heights in graceful circles, and Charles Darwin says he is sure they do this only for pleasure. Sometimes, however, they may be watching a dying animal, or a puma devouring its prey.

"If the condors glide down, and then suddenly all rise together," says Darwin, "the Chileno knows that it is the puma which, watching the carcass, has sprung out to drive away the robbers."

With regard to the habits of the condor, Mr. Whymper, the famous climber of the Andes, says, "On the few occasions upon which we were approached by condors in a menacing manner, we became aware of their presence from their shadows being cast upon us by a nearly vertical Sun. They never came near when the Sun was concealed, and if they hovered in our neighbourhood, they always kept the Sun at their backs."

The old porters' rest still standing in Piccadilly, London

How Do Self-Changing Gears Work?

I n a circular self-changing gear-box, as shown in the drawing on this page, there are four sets of epicyclic gears, three sets being used for forward speeds and the fourth set for reverse. Epicyclic means a circle whose centre moves round the circumference of another and larger circle.

The forward speed is obtained by the direct drive clutch shown on the left of the drawing. Each of the four sets of gears consists of a central sun wheel, a set of planet pinions and an internal toothed ring or annulus. The sizes of the wheels differ in each case, in order to obtain the different speeds.

The sun wheels for the first and second gears only are fixed to the engine shaft, while the planet pinions for the first and reverse gears are fixed to the back-axle shaft by brackets. For the top gear or direct drive the clutch engages the last drum on the left and all the gears are locked together and rotate as a solid mass at engine speed.

On the outside of each drum and gear train is a band brake which, when applied—and only one can be applied at one time—causes the drive to be transmitted by that particular gear train. The drawing shows the brake of the first gear drum applied, by means that will be explained later.

Now that particular sun wheel is being driven direct by the engine and therefore will carry the planet pinions and their bracket round in the same direction, but at a reduced speed, because the internal toothed ring is held stationary by the band brake.

Since the planet bracket is fixed to the back-axle shaft it will revolve that shaft at about one-fourth of the engine shaft rate, thus giving first speed or " low."

All the other gears and the reverse are obtained in the same manner when the respective toothed rings are held stationary by their band brakes. We must remember that only one brake can be applied at one time. Whatever speed is required some of the gears are always running idle. When the first gear is in operation, as shown in the drawing, the drive is transmitted by the portions that are shaded.

All these operations are performed at will by the driver. When, for example, he wants to change gear he pre-selects the one required by a little lever on the steering-wheel, as shown in the top left-hand of the drawing. The lever actuates cams which select the gear required and move an arm ready for applying the

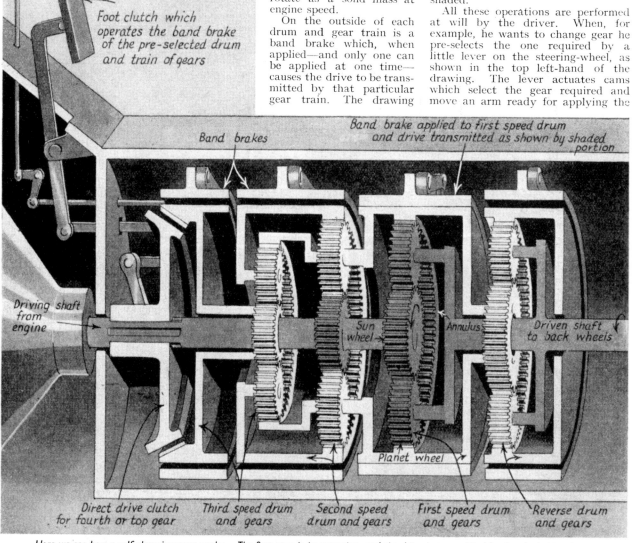

Selector arm on steering wheel which pre-selects the train of gears required by means of rods and cams

Foot clutch which operates the band brake of the pre-selected drum and train of gears

Band brakes

Band brake applied to first speed drum and drive transmitted as shown by shaded portion

Driving shaft from engine

Sun wheel

Annulus

Driven shaft to back wheels

Planet wheel

Direct drive clutch for fourth or top gear

Third speed drum and gears

Second speed drum and gears

First speed drum and gears

Reverse drum and gears

Here we see how a self-changing gear works. The first gear is in operation, and the drive is transmitted by the shaded portions band brake. When the driver is ready he depresses and releases the clutch, which then actually applies the already selected band brake.

The system is fool-proof and it is quite impossible to jam the gears as they are always in mesh. This type of gear is being increasingly used on modern cars, buses, coaches, and even on army tanks. It entirely abolishes the old terrors of gear-changing.

What Were the Phoenix Park Murders?

On May 6th, 1882, Lord Frederick Cavendish, the newly-appointed Secretary for Ireland, and Mr. Thomas Burke, the Under-Secretary, were walking in Phoenix Park, Dublin, when they were attacked by a gang of ruffians in the employ of the Irish Land League and stabbed to death. James Carey, one of the gang, turned Queen's evidence, and it was found that 21 persons were implicated in the cowardly murder. Five men were hanged. Carey, to escape the vengeance of the Irish Invincibles, secretly shipped for South Africa under the name of Power, but spies discovered his plan. He was followed and shot before the vessel reached its destination.

What is a Quixotic Person?

A person to whom this description is given is one who is full of generous and chivalrous instincts, but who has little or no common sense. The name is derived from the hero of Cervantes' famous Spanish novel "Don Quixote." He was a knight-errant filled with ideals of chivalry but who attempted ridiculously impossible tasks, such as tilting at a windmill in the belief that it was the foe of some fair lady. The novel was written to caricature in a kindly way the decayed chivalry of the Middle Ages.

What is a Barbican?

A barbican was in medieval military architecture an outwork placed in front of a fortified castle or other military post. Often it was built at the entrance to a bridge or town, and generally took the form of

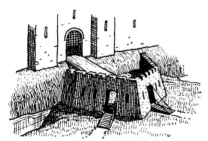

A barbican protecting the front of a castle

a tower or towers, sometimes quite large and strong. The word was also used for a narrow vertical opening through which arrows might be shot.

A bartizan was a small watch-tower made to project from the top of a tower or wall, generally where there was an angle. City gates were often furnished with bartizans. They were originally built of wood, but from the 11th century onwards were made of masonry, and so formed part of the main structure.

What is it to be In the Arms of Morpheus?

It is to be asleep and dreaming. In the later Roman poets Morpheus is the god of sleep and the god of dreams. The name means the fashioner or moulder and was given because he shaped or formed one's dreams.

The Fascist and Nazi standards carried when Mussolini and Hitler attended the German army manoeuvres in 1937

What Are the Fascist and Nazi Symbols?

The Fascists of Italy use a representation of the ancient fasces carried by the lictors before the superior magistrates at Rome, this being only one manifestation of their love of aping anything connected with the ancient empire of the Caesars.

The fasces were bundles of birch or elm rods bound together by a red thong and containing in the middle an axe, the iron of which projected. The lictors carried them on their left shoulders and they were regarded as a symbol of authority. When an inferior magistrate met one higher in rank, his lictors lowered their fasces. It is from the fasces that the modern Fascists of Italy take their name.

The symbol of the Nazis of Germany is the swastika, an equal armed cross with the extremities bent uniformly at right angles. It was adopted by Herr Hitler as a symbol for his party, because it is primarily an Aryan sun-symbol, found at Troy and in India,

and he and his colleagues have a passion for anything which they think is essentially and exclusively Aryan. The swastika is believed to be the oldest of all Aryan symbols.

Mr. Thomas Wilson, the greatest authority on this symbol, says: " The first appearance of the swastika was apparently in the Orient, precisely in what country it is impossible to say, but probably in central and south-eastern Asia among the forerunners or predecessors of the Brahmins and Buddhists. At all events, a religious and symbolic signification was attributed to it by the earliest known peoples of these localities."

It is first found in the Bronze Age, and wherever it originated it had spread in a few centuries over India, Europe, Asia Minor, Egypt, Persia, China, Japan, Tibet and North and South America. It has not been found among the aborigines of Australia or New Zealand.

How Did the Aeroplane Develop?

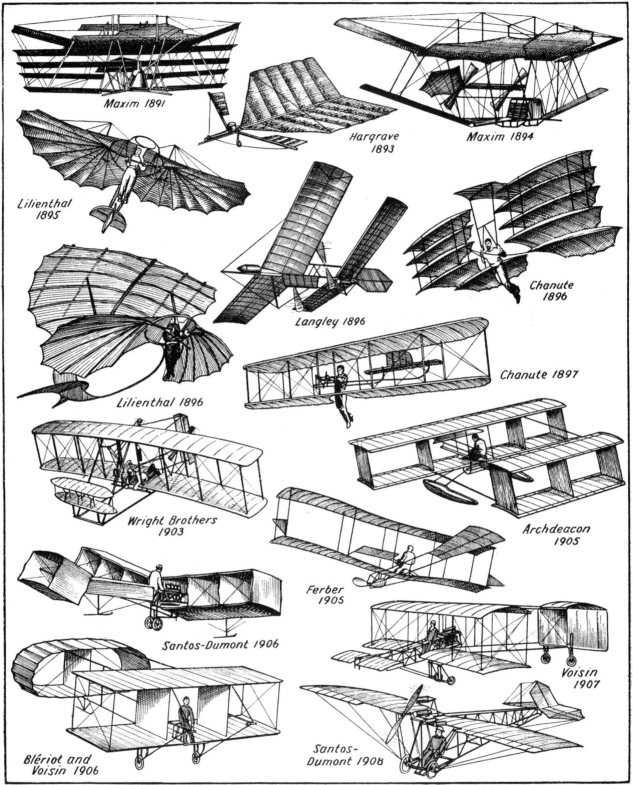

Maxim 1891

Hargrave 1893

Maxim 1894

Lilienthal 1895

Langley 1896

Chanute 1896

Lilienthal 1896

Chanute 1897

Wright Brothers 1903

Archdeacon 1905

Santos-Dumont 1906

Ferber 1905

Voisin 1907

Blériot and Voisin 1906

Santos-Dumont 1908

The aeroplane, which is really a power-driven kite, has made marvellous strides in the last fifty years, and the drawings on these two pages will show some of the stages through which it has passed before reaching the state of perfection which we see today. Enormous credit is due to the early pioneers, who not only spent their money, but risked their lives in order to show the way in which men could travel through the air. Many pioneers were killed, and those men, although they were full of vision and enthusiasm, and really believed in the possibilities of aerial flight, would be astonished if they could see the wonderful air liners which travel regularly over world routes today. These modern aeroplanes weigh many tons, and yet rise with the greatest of ease and look like birds as they travel at 200 miles an hour or more, far above the ground, and sometimes above the clouds. The mistake of the earliest pioneers was, of course, in supposing that men could fly like a bird by flapping wings up and down, instead of

Stages Over Nearly Fifty Years

A.V.Roe's Triplane 1909

Blériot's Monoplane 1909

Farman 1910

Levavasseur Antoinette Monoplane 1910

Paulhan 1910

Avro Biplane 1914

De Havilland Moth 1925

Vickers Vimy 1919

Junkers Monoplane 1928

Flying Boat 1931

Dornier DO-X 1934

De Havilland Air Liner 1937

Handley Page Air Liner 1934

Composite aircraft 1938

gliding through the air like a kite or a straw hat blown from the head of its wearer. It was really the invention of the internal-combustion engine which made flying possible. Without this device it is doubtful if aerial travel would ever have become very practical. The great power developed by the petrol engine and the comparatively small weight of fuel that has to be carried has made the modern aeroplane possible. What will happen to all the aircraft as well as to the motor vehicles in the world should the supply of oil ever run out, as some authorities prophesy, it is difficult to say. Of course, petrol can be prepared from coal, but it would be much more costly, unless some new method of manufacture were devised. It is interesting in looking at the pictures above to notice how the biplane gave place to the monoplane, and the monoplane later was superseded by the biplane, while at a still later stage the monoplane came into its own again, and is now very efficient and is among the fastest of machines

What is Aquaplaning?

THIS is the name given to a new form of sport on the water which is certainly very exciting and needs a good deal of nerve and stout muscles.

The aquaplane is a board to the front of which are attached ropes that can be held like reins by a person standing upright on the board. The plane is also attached by a long rope to a speedboat. The speedboat then travels off at a rapid rate, dragging the aquaplane after it, while the rider stands on the board, holding the reins so steady himself and keep the plane level as it rushes over the water at a rate of sixty miles an hour or more.

It needs some practice to get into an upright position on the board as the speedboat starts off. The method is to kneel on the aquaplane, as shown in the first photograph, and grasp the rope reins. Then, as the boat gets up speed and the board travels faster and faster and rises in front, the rider gets up on his feet as shown in the second photograph. The lower photograph shows the traveller moving at over sixty miles an hour.

A swimmer mounting an aquaplane

What is the Most Distant Nebula Photographed?

THE great 100-inch telescope at Mount Wilson Observatory in California enables distant stars and nebulae to be photographed that are quite invisible to the naked eye. A long exposure enables these faint bodies in outlying space to affect the sensitive plate.

The latest triumph of the astronomers with this great telescope is to photograph the spectra of nebulae so far away that they are 30,000 times fainter than the faintest star visible to the unaided eye. It is calculated that these nebulae are 80 million light-years distant from the Earth. This means that they are something like 470 million million miles away. To photograph these nebulae an exposure of 60 hours is given.

Dr. M. L. Humason of the Mount Wilson Observatory, who is responsible for this triumph of photography, found a faint cluster of nebulae in the constellation of the Great Bear, which is probably one of the most remote clusters known at the present time. The spectroscope showed that it was running away from the Earth

at the rate of 26,000 miles a second. This means over 93½ million miles an hour, or 2,246,400,000 miles a day.

Do Cows Eat Buttercups?

NO, they avoid them, for from the point of view of pasturage the buttercup is a useless weed. But generally where buttercups grow the soil is good, and so there is a rich crop of luscious grass. A cow will eat the grass all round a buttercup, leaving the plant severely alone.

What Were Fleet Marriages?

THESE were clandestine or irregular marriages performed in the 17th and 18th centuries within the purlieus of the Fleet Prison in London. Sometimes they took place in the prison chapel, at other times in rooms of the prison, and at other times in taverns just outside. They were performed by disreputable parsons who lived in or about the prison and were not under the jurisdiction of the Bishop of London. They became a very great scandal and were at last declared illegal by Lord Chancellor Hardwicke's Act, which came into operation on March 26th, 1754. On the day before such marriages became illegal, 217 were celebrated in the prison and entered in one of the prison registers.

The swimmer holding the reins and rising on his feet

Sometimes there were thirty marriages a day, and in the four months ending February 12th, 1705, no fewer than 2,954 were carried out.

Strangely enough, there was much opposition to the abolition of the Fleet marriages on the part of the mob, which paraded the streets and declared that their liberties were being taken away in the interests of the rich.

Why Do Some Chimneys Have a Cowl?

A COWL is put on to prevent the smoke being driven down the chimney into the room when a fire is

Three different types of chimney cowls

burning in the grate. This occurs generally when the wind is in a certain direction. But it has to be deflected down the chimney, and usually some tall object, such as a tree or an adjacent wall or roof, does this. By putting on a cowl the wind is deflected, so that the smoke is carried away instead of going down the chimney. Cowls are of various kinds. Sometimes they rotate, creating a draught; at other times they turn round so that the opening is away from the wind, and at other times they slant so that the wind which would go down the chimney is thrown off all round.

Where are Bats Protected?

IN some parts of the United States infested by mosquitoes it is unlawful to kill a bat, and notices to this effect are posted up. Not only so, but municipal bat rests are erected in some parts of Texas, so that the bats may have a proper shelter. It has been estimated that one bat will eat as many as 250 mosquitoes in a single night's hunting.

The aquaplane with its rider drawn through the water at high speed by a motor-boat

How Many Policemen Are There in Great Britain?

In England and Wales there are altogether 58,303 police, and in Scotland 6,512. The English police are administered by the Home Office and those of Scotland by the Scottish Office. The biggest individual force is, of course, the London Metropolitan Police, which has a strength of 19,384, of whom 15,644 are constables, 2,791 sergeants, 914 inspectors, and 35 superintendents. There are in this force 244 horses. The City of London Police, a separate body, has 982 constables, 125 sergeants, 17 sub-inspectors, 25 inspectors, 8 chief inspectors, 3 superintendents, and an assistant commissioner, under a commissioner. Northern Ireland has a police force numbering 2,798. Special constables are extra. The City of London area has 2,233 of all ranks, and the Metropolitan Police area 8,782.

Where is There an Inn Fire Over 100 Years Old?

At the Warren House Inn on the Exeter-Princetown road, Dartmoor, there is a fire in the bar parlour that has been burning continuously without a moment's break for nearly 140 years. It has never been allowed to expire since the year 1800, and it has long been thought that if it did go out bad luck would visit the inn.

The curious thing is that the inn was originally on the other side of the road. But it was pulled down and another inn built opposite. When this was done the fire and fireplace were carried bodily across the highway to their new resting-place so that the embers should not die.

The Warren House Inn, on the Exeter-Princetown road in Devon, where a fire has been burning in the bar parlour for over 130 years

How Many Wives Did Mohammed Have?

There were ten in all. The first was Kadidja, a rich widow of the tribe of Koreish, who had already been twice married and was forty years old. For 25 years she remained his only wife and it was after her death that he married the nine others, all of whom survived him. They were Ayesha, daughter of his chief supporter Abu-Bekr, who was only nine on her wedding-day. She was the youngest and favourite wife; Sauda, a widow and nurse to his daughter Fatima; Hafsa, a widow of 28 with a son; Zeinab, wife of Zaid, who was divorced in order that the prophet might marry her; Barra, a captive, whose father and husband were slain in a battle with Mohammed; Rehana, a Jewish captive; Safiya, whose betrothed was put to death; Omm Habiba, a widow; and Maimuna, a widow of 51 who survived all the others. In addition Mohammed had ten or fifteen concubines, by one of whom he had a son who died when he was only fifteen months old.

What is a Papaw?

This is the name given to the fruit of an evergreen tree, called both papaw and papaya, which grows in tropical America. The tree is of palm-

Papaws, the fruits of the papaya tree, growing in a conservatory in Chicago. These are the first that have ever been produced outside the tree's native home in tropical lands

like appearance, crowned with large seven-lobed leaves and clusters of yellow flowers. From the latter there results a large yellow fruit with pulpy flesh and a thick rind. It is eaten both raw, as a fruit, and boiled as a vegetable. It is also pickled and preserved.

All parts of the plant contain a milky juice, a substance called papain, something like pepsin. A digestive medicine is made from this.

In the papaya tree the male and female flowers are often on separate trees. In 1938 Mr. August Koch, a famous horticulturist of Chicago, succeeded for the first time in making the papaya tree produce fruit outside its native home. He says that he played the role of a bee, and carried the pollen from the male to the female tree, with the result that the female tree bore fruit.

What is a Genius Loci?

This was the name given by the ancients to the guardian deity of a place, but the term is now often used to describe such things as the local atmosphere or some character.

Has England at Any Time Returned Colonies?

YES, on a number of occasions territories taken during a war have been handed back to their former owner. A notable case is that of the Dutch East Indies, which England occupied during the Napoleonic Wars.

The famous exploration ship "Discovery I" anchored in the Thames off the Victoria Embankment

This seizure, however, was done, not as a conquest, but as a trusteeship during the Napoleonic usurpation. As soon as Napoleon had been defeated and finally disposed of at St. Helena the colonies were returned to Holland —Java in 1816 and Malacca in 1818. Later Malacca was returned to England in exchange for Bencoolen, and the Dutch were left with undisturbed sway over Sumatra which is still one of their valuable colonies.

How Does a Gun Differ From a Howitzer?

A GUN is aimed directly at the target, whereas a howitzer throws a shell up so that it will come down more or less vertically upon the target. A 60-pounder field howitzer hurls a five-inch shell to a distance of 15,000 yards, or nearly nine miles.

What is the Ship "Discovery I"?

THE *Discovery* was a vessel built at Dundee in 1900 for use in Polar exploration, and was launched there in the following year. She was built of oak and teak, as these were said to stand up to the strain and weight of the ice far better than any metal, which would crumple under identical pressure. The sides were 26 inches thick.

The first voyage of this now famous ship was in 1901–4, when she went on the Antarctic Expedition under Captain Scott. She got frozen in the ice there and dynamite had to be used to get her free.

From 1905 and for many years she traded between West India Dock and James Bay in Canada. She saw War service and in 1916 went to the aid of the stranded members of the Shackleton Expedition.

In 1923 the *Discovery* went on a three-year voyage for oceanographical and meteorological purposes, and her last sailing for scientific work was to Kerguelen Island. In one expedition alone she discovered seven uncharted regions.

She is of 485 tons' register, 172 feet in length, and lay idle from 1931 till 1938 at the East India Dock. Then she was presented by the Australian Government to the Boy Scouts' organisation for the use of its sea scouts. She is now moored in the Thames off the Temple. It is fitting that this ship, which embodies so much of Britain's spirit, should rest in the Empire's capital.

Who Were the Chief Saxon Gods?

THE chief gods of our Anglo-Saxon forefathers were Odin or Woden, the father of the gods, to whom Wednesday is dedicated; Frea, the mother of the gods, to whom Friday is dedicated; Hertha the Earth; Tuesco, to whom Tuesday is consecrated; and Thor, to whom Thursday is dedicated.

What is Colour-Blindness?

IT is a defect of the vision which makes the sufferer incapable of distinguishing between certain colours. There are three varieties of colour-blindness. The most common is known as the red-green variety, in which the person cannot distinguish between the colours red and green. Rather more than seven per cent. of the population in Great Britain is colour-blind in this way. In a country like China, where thousands were examined, the percentage was about 6 per cent.

A second form of colour-blindness is known as blue-yellow blindness, though it is sometimes called violet blindness. In this type the ability to see blue and yellow is affected, but the ability to distinguish between red and green is not affected.

The third type of colour-blindness is much rarer, only eighty cases having been recorded so far. This is total colour-blindness, or achromatopsia, in which no colour can be distinguished, and the spectrum with its violet, indigo, blue, green, yellow, orange and red is merely a colourless band, differing only in luminosity. As Dr. Mary Collins says, "Red may appear black; orange, dark grey; yellow, light grey, and so on." To such a monochromat, as scientists call him— that is, a one-colour person—bright light is always extremely dazzling. In fact, ordinary illumination is sometimes unbearable, but in dim illumination he can see ordinary objects fairly accurately.

What is a Mule?

IT is a cross or hybrid between the horse and the ass. A mule is, properly, the offspring of an ass-stallion and a mare. The name given to the offspring of a she-ass and a horse is hinny. This word is derived from a Greek word imitative of the neigh or whinny of a horse. Mule is from the Greek word for a he-ass.

What English Author Forecast the Suez Canal?

IN the second part of his "Tamburlaine the Great," written in 1587, Christopher Marlowe forecast the Suez Canal and the short route to India. Tamburlaine, about to die, calls for a map that he may see how much of the world is left for him to conquer and may explain his plans to his sons so that they can complete his work. Placing his finger on the map he says:

Here I began to march toward Persia,
Along Armenia and the Caspian Sea,
And thence into Bithynia, where I took
The Turk and his great empress prisoners.
Then marched I into Egypt and Arabia,
And here, not far from Alexandria,
Whereas the Terrene and the Red Sea meet,
Being distant less than full a hundred leagues,
I meant to cut a channel to them both,
That men might quickly sail to India.

It was certainly a remarkable forecast of what was to be done three centuries later.

How is a Cinema Cartoon Made?

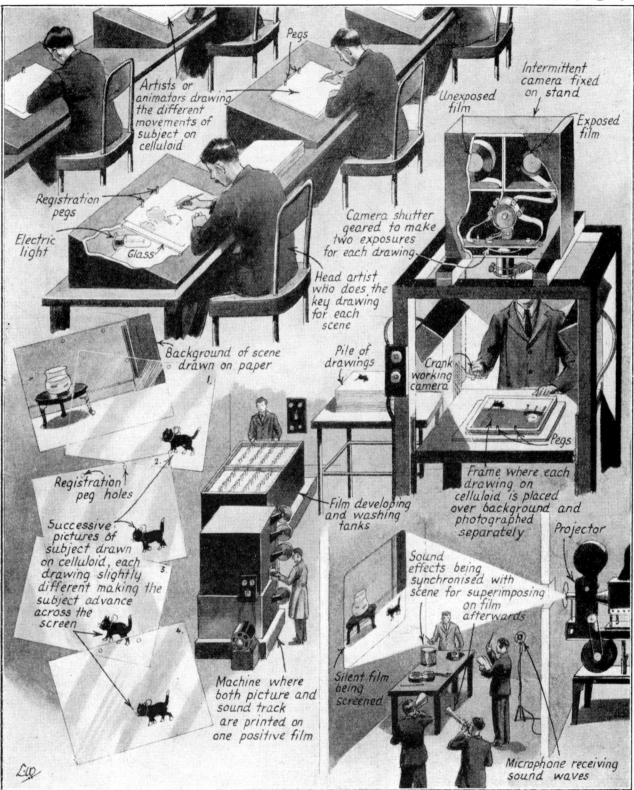

These drawings show how a coloured cartoon like "Micky Mouse" or a "Silly Symphony," so popular on the screen, is made. A creative artist prepares a series of key drawings showing the main movements of the figures, and these are handed to a large staff of artists known as animators, who draw on celluloid sheets a big series of variations in the movements. The celluloid sheets are then taken to the camera room and photographed on a previously drawn background. Two exposures are made of each drawing, so that in the film the drawings may be in pairs. The film is developed and a positive printed from it, and then it is thrown by a projector on a screen and the necessary sounds are made and synchronised with the film. The sound is superimposed on the picture film, and in the cinema 24 pictures run through every second, so that in a film lasting 15 minutes 21,600 pictures are seen. There are secrets in producing these films, including the way in which the characters are made to dodge behind the scenery

What Was the Coercion Act?

WHEN agrarian outrages took place in County Westmeath in 1871, an Act of Parliament was passed authorising the arrest and detention of suspected persons. The Coercion Act of 1881 extended the provisions of this Act to the whole of Ireland till September, 1882. The Irish members obstructed the passage of the Bill, and there were long sittings, lasting in one case to 41 hours. The Bill became law on March 2nd, 1881.

What Was the Fashoda Incident?

A FEW days after the battle of Omdurman in 1898 a small French force under the command of Major Marchand entered Fashoda on the White Nile and raised the French flag. Lord Salisbury, the British Prime Minister, thereupon pointed out that, " by the military events of the past week all the territories which were subject to the Khalifa passed by right of conquest to the British and Egyptian Governments."

Great Britain asked that Marchand should be recalled, but the French tried to make this conditional on a settlement of territorial questions in dispute, which would give France part of the left bank of the Nile.

Relations became strained, and military and naval preparations were made by both countries, but on November 4th Lord Salisbury announced that the French Government had come to the conclusion " that the occupation of Fashoda was of no sort of value to the French Republic." The French evacuated Fashoda in December, and thereupon the British and Egyptian flags were hoisted there.

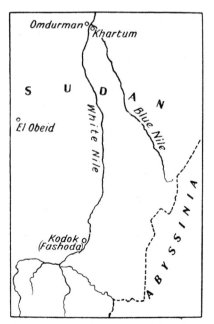

A map showing the position of Fashoda on the White Nile

Which Regiment Wears Badges Back and Front?

BOTH battalions of the Gloucestershire Regiment, formerly the 28th and 61st Regiments of Foot, wear the regimental badge in front and at

The 2nd Battalion Gloucestershire Regiment formed up back to back for inspection

the back of the cap. This distinction was bestowed on the old 28th regiment to mark its bravery at the battle of Alexandria in 1801. The troops were attacked by the French cavalry while in line, and, there being no time to form square, the Colonel ordered the rear rank to " Right about face." They did so, and succeeded in beating off the French horse, 7,000 in number. The badge is the Sphinx superscribed " Egypt."

Because of the incident described the regiment is known as " The Rightabouts," and is also sometimes called " The Fore and Aft." Other nicknames are " The Old Braggs," from the name of the Colonel, 1734 to 1751; " The Slashers," possibly from their gallantry at the battle of White Plains and the passage of the Bronx River in America in 1777; " The Whitewashers," a name given to the old 61st during the Indian Mutiny, from their white facings; the " Brass Before and Brass Behind; " and the " Silver-Tailed Dandies," a name said to be given because the officers wore lace-coated long skirts after other regiments had adopted the short coat.

After the disaster in the Khyber Pass in 1842, the 28th regiment, then in Australia, embarked for India and the transport grounded on a coral reef in Torres Strait. This is now marked on the maps " The Slashers' Reef."

What is a Yankee?

THIS term, used by Europeans for any native-born white citizen of the United States, was originally applied only to citizens of New England. By extension it was later given to other Americans. The Confederates

The badge on the back of the cap of the Gloucestershire Regiment in commemoration of the battle of Alexandria

in the American Civil War called Federal soldiers Yankees. The term is supposed to be a variation of Yengees or Yaunghees, a name given by the Massachusetts Indians to the English colonists. It is supposed to be a native corruption of the English word " English " or, as some think, of the French word " Anglais."

Who Was the Baker of Augsburg?

THE story is told that during the Thirty Years War in Europe, when the city was besieged and the people inside starving, a baker flung the last loaf of bread over the walls

The effigy of the brave baker of Augsburg

into the face of the attacking and equally hungry enemy, with the taunt that the town still had plenty of food and could hold out.

The ruse broke the morale of the enemy, who raised the siege, and a grateful city ordered that an effigy of the baker should stand for ever outside the house where he had lived. There the effigy stands today to be seen by all who visit Augsburg.

What is a Sun Clinic?

IT is an institution where children or older people can sunbathe or receive benefit from ultra-violet rays produced by a special kind of apparatus known as a centrosol lamp. There is a solarium where the children's naked bodies can be exposed to natural sunshine in fine weather, but when the sky is overcast and there is no natural sunshine, they then sit round a centrosol lamp and receive in a short time similar benefits to a longer exposure to real sunshine.

There are various kinds of ultra-violet rays and some of these produce sunburn. They are also beneficial in the treatment of certain diseases, especially rickets, but even healthy people, if they sit without clothes in the sunshine or in ultra-violet rays from a lamp, receive great benefit. The ultra-violet light, whether from the sunshine or artificially produced by a lamp, causes many chemical actions. It is thought by some people that these rays are a preventive of the common cold. But that has never been definitely proved.

Ultra-violet rays are essential for the proper growth of children and for the health of all. They are stopped by ordinary window glass, and so closed windows shut them off. Special glass is now made which lets them through, but it is expensive to fit in an ordinary house and so it is cheaper to open the windows and let the sunshine, including the ultra-violet rays, enter the room unimpeded. In smoky cities, to get enough of these rays it is necessary that we should be out of doors for even longer than if we were in the country.

How Many Sets of Teeth Have Salmon?

LORD DESBOROUGH told the Salmon and Trout Association in February, 1938, that it had now been definitely settled by Dr. Tchernavin that a salmon had two sets of teeth— one set for sea-feeding dropped out shortly after coming into fresh water, and the other, a set of curved teeth which grew in fresh water, came to their greatest development in the kelt stage and then decayed and dropped out to make room for a new set of sea-feeding teeth. The object of the kelt teeth is a mystery for salmon are not known to feed in fresh water.

What Was the Caduceus?

IT was originally a white wand carried by Roman officers when they went to treat for peace. It was also regarded as a herald's staff. It consisted of three shoots, one of which formed the handle, the other two being intertwined at the top in a knot. Later their place was taken by two serpents and the caduceus assumed the form which we generally recognise today in the hands of Hermes or Mercury, who carried it and was said with it to give sleep to whomsoever he chose. It has two wings at the top to indicate speed, Mercury in the old classical mythology being the messenger of the Gods

The caduceus

When Was the First Aerial Post?

THE first aeroplane mail service in England was established in September, 1911, when a London to Windsor Coronation Post by air was organised to celebrate the event. That, however, was not the first aerial post in the world. During an exhibition at Allahabad, in India, in February of the same year, a mail-carrying flight was established, the first in the history of aviation. Both were organised under Government supervision.

The first letter ever carried by aeroplane is said to have been one sent by Captain (now Commander Sir Walter) Windham on August 10th, 1909. This letter was sent across the Channel from France to England.

Children gathered round a centrosol lamp at the Islington Sun Clinic. The light from this lamp gives artificial sunshine to the children's bodies

Are the Bricks For Tall Chimneys Shaped?

NOT generally. In most cases they are ordinary rectangular bricks, but if the diameter of the tall chimney is small, the builder knocks off a little on each side of the brick to give it a slightly wedge-shaped form. For expensive ornamental circular chimneys the bricks would be shaped.

Where Do Trains Run Through the Streets?

IN Weymouth the Channel Islands boat express train passes through the streets from Weymouth Junction to the quayside, with a flagman on the

On the left a boat train is seen passing through the Weymouth streets on its way to the quayside

front of the engine, sounding a bell to warn people to keep out of the way. It is a strange sight for an English town in the 20th century, and suggests the pioneer days of trains.

Who Was the Cock of the North?

THIS is a nickname given to George, fifth Duke of Gordon, who died in 1836. He raised the Gordon Highlanders in 1795, and is given the name "Cock of the North" on a monument erected to his honour at Fochabers in Aberdeenshire. Cock of the North is also a popular name given to the brambling or mountain finch.

What Are Quicksands?

A QUICKSAND is a movable sand-bank in a sea, river or lake which readily swallows any heavy body placed upon it. It consists of a large mass of loose or moving sand mixed with water or gas, and when formed on the sea coast is dangerous to ships. The captain of the vessel on which St. Paul travelled was fearful that his ship would " fall into the quicksands." (See Acts XXVII, 17.)

Dr. J. C. Owens, in a paper which he read before the British Association, explained how quicksands are formed and he demonstrated experimentally that the condition can be brought about by allowing water to flow upwards through the sand. Since, he says, a grain of siliceous sand of one-fiftieth of an inch in diameter settles through water at the rate of little more than 0·2 of a foot per second, a very slight velocity of current is capable of lifting the grains out of contact and keeping them separated by layers of water, so that they will not bear weight. In Nature, says Dr. Owens, quicksands are due to springs rising under beds of sand.

But another authority, Mr. C. Carus-Wilson, has shown that there are also quicksands in which there is no upward current of water. They are produced, he says, by the inclusion of gas in wet sand. Such quicksands are found in Morecambe Bay, where cockles and other organisms may decompose and produce gas.

At the Royal Institution Mr. C. E. S. Phillips demonstrated the effect of gas being mixed with sand. He had two vessels containing sand, and while to one he added only water, in the other he placed with the water a little carbonate and hydrochloric acid. When he pressed the point of his finger in the vessel containing only water and sand it penetrated a short distance and was then stopped by the resistance of the material. In the other vessel, where carbon dioxide gas was being generated and was mixed with the sand, the inserted finger went down without resistance.

Mr. Vaughan Cornish thinks that the inclusion of ordinary air often makes wet sands unable to bear a load, thus becoming quicksands.

What Are the Harmattan and Khamsin?

THESE are the names of two winds which blow in the desert regions of North Africa. The harmattan is a hot, dusty east wind blowing in the western Sahara during December, January, and February, and the khamsin is a hot wind from the desert in Egypt. It blows for from twenty to fifty days a year, generally from the south or south-east. " Harmattan " is an Arabic name for the wind, and " khamsin " is also an Arabic word meaning " fifty," a reference to the period over which the wind may blow.

The boat train passing through a Weymouth street, with the flagman on the front of the engine to warn pedestrians

Where Are Streets Paved With Flowers?

At Genzano, a town near Rome, on the eighth day after the Feast of Corpus Christi a flower festival is held in which the main street is completely paved with flowers, as seen in

The streets of Genzano near Rome paved with flowers following the feast of Corpus Christi

the photograph on this page. The flowers are arranged in designs that are chiefly of a religious character. At the end of the street is a church, and outside this an altar is erected and mass is celebrated. The festival ends with fireworks and merry-making.

Has a Horse Ever Chosen a King?

It is said that after the death of Cambyses, King of Persia, when the pretender Smerdis had been defeated and killed, a council of the chief men was called to determine on a successor, and that these agreed to meet at sunrise on the following morning, each seated on horseback, and he whose horse neighed first was to be king. The groom of Darius Hystaspes thereupon took a mare to the spot and showed it to his master's horse, which on the following morning neighed as soon as it came to the place. Thus Darius was chosen as king by his horse.

Has Japan Altered Her Spelling?

Yes; in 1938 the Japanese Diet decided on drastic alterations in the spelling of Japanese words in Roman characters. Such spelling is known as Romaji. The new spelling of this word is Romazi, although its pronunciation remains unchanged.

The new spelling affects not only scholars, but ordinary travellers, for all station and ships' names are being changed, and tourists who return to Japan for a second visit will find difficulty in recognising the names they knew before. Thus Chosen, the Japanese name for Korea, has become Tyosen, and Mount Fuji is now Mount Huzi.

The Japanese themselves do not need the Roman spelling, so the reason for the change, which can only confuse foreigners, is difficult to understand.

Japanese words are ordinarily written in Chinese characters, and in addition the Japanese have invented fifty simple characters to represent sounds used in their speech.

In the new spelling Tokio becomes Toukiyou, Kobe is Kaube, and Osaka, Ohosaka.

What is Grahame's Dyke?

This is a popular name given to the Wall of Antonine, between the Firths of Forth and Clyde, erected in A.D. 139 on the site of a line of forts built by Agricola in A.D. 81 to keep out the northern barbarians.

What Elephant is Called Alice?

This is an elephant, said to be 152 years old, which is now travelling with a circus in Australia. The elephant was originally in the London Zoo, being bought by the Zoological Society in 1865. King Edward VII as a boy rode on her at the Zoo, and the Editor of this book well remembers having a ride on the back of Alice when he was a small boy.

She was in the London Zoo at the same time as the famous Jumbo, and was popularly described as " Jumbo's wife." After Jumbo was sold to Barnum it is said that Alice fretted, and she too was sold in 1886 to an American circus. Later she was taken to Australia, where she has lived ever since, travelling from place to place, and this photograph was taken in Sydney. Alice is said to weigh nearly four tons. She must have been born at the time of the French Revolution.

Alice, the elephant once in the London Zoo, that is now travelling with a circus in Australia. She is said to be in her 153rd year

Where is the Trusty Servant Inn?

THIS is the name of an inn at Minstead, Hampshire, a hamlet in the New Forest near the Rufus Stone described on page 1062. Its name is taken from an original painting that now hangs in Winchester College, and dates back to the 16th century. This may seem strange as the figure of the Trusty Servant in the picture is wearing Georgian costume. The explanation is that when George the Third visited the College in 1778, the figure was repainted and given the Windsor

The sign of the Trusty Servant Inn at Minstead in Hampshire

uniform of the period. In the coat of arms at the top left-hand side are the mottoes " Honi soit qui mal y pense " and " Manners makyth man."

A verse below the painting explains the title of the Trusty Servant and is attributed to Christopher Johnson.

How Soon Will a Person Starve to Death?

IF he is deprived of all foods, liquid and solid, a person will die in a little over a week. But a very small quantity of food or water will prolong life considerably. Death generally occurs when the body has lost two-fifths of its weight. The fat almost disappears, the blood loses three-quarters of its weight, the pancreas and liver more than half, the muscles and stomach two-fifths, the skin and kidneys one-third, the bones one-sixth, and the nervous system only one-fiftieth. Resting and being allowed to take water, men have lived over 40 days without other food.

Why is a Canvas for Portraits Called a Kit-Cat?

THIS size of canvas, 28 or 29 inches by 36 inches, was the size adopted by Sir Godfrey Kneller for painting the portraits of members of the Kit-Cat Club. They were shown not quite three-quarter length, and were painted this size so that the picture might fit the walls of Tonson's Villa at Barn Elms, where they met. Portrait canvases of this size have been called kit-cat ever since.

The Kit-Cat Club was an association of politicians and literary men who favoured the Protestant Succession. It was established in 1703 and included among its members Addison, Steele, Walpole, Marlborough, and other staunch Whigs. It was dissolved about 1720. The club took its name from Christopher Cat, a pastry-cook, who kept the " Cat and Fiddle " in Fleet Street, where he supplied them with his special mutton pies.

When Was English First Used in the Law Courts?

IT was by an Act of Edward III passed in 1362 that the English language was ordered to be used in all courts of law. The sovereign, however, still uses Norman French instead of English in giving the royal assent to Acts passed by both Houses of Parliament.

Are Deer Good Swimmers?

YES, the red deer are excellent swimmers, and they like the water. They often go to muddy ponds and roll over and over in the slime till they are covered with it ; then they stand up and shake themselves like dogs. When pursued by hounds they will often go into a lake or river and lie down with only the tips of their noses held above the surface for breathing. They are thus hidden from sight. Mr. Fred Goss tells us that a fisherman was once astounded to find that his net had become entangled with a stag, which thereupon started swimming across the river, taking the fisherman with it.

What is the Oldest Business Company in the World?

IT is said to be the company known as the Stora Kopparbergs Bergslags Aktiebolag. This company owns and runs a paper-mill in Sweden, but it is said to have existed since the 13th century. The earliest documents which it possesses are dated 1288.

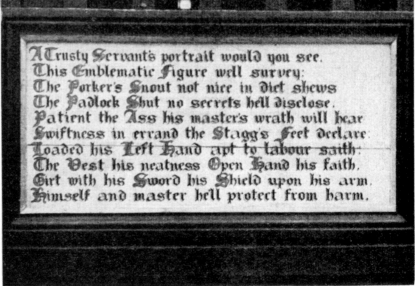

A Trusty Servant's portrait would you see.
This Emblematic Figure well survey:
The Porker's Snout not nice in Diet shews
The Padlock Shut no secrets hell disclose.
Patient the Ass his master's wrath will bear
Swiftness in errand the Stagg's Feet declare:
Loaded his Left Hand apt to labour saith:
The Vest his neatness Open Hand his faith.
Girt with his Sword his Shield upon his arm.
Himself and master hell protect from harm.

The inscription which explains the sign of the Trusty Servant

Where Was Mussolini Born?

BENITO MUSSOLINI, the Italian dictator, was born on July 29th, 1883, in the little village of Predappio in the province of Forli. The house, which is still standing, is an unpretentious peasant home and in June, 1938, it was visited by the King of Italy in company with Mussolini,

The modest house at Predappio in Italy where Mussolini was born on July 29th, 1883

who showed his royal visitor the room where, as the Duce has related, he used to sleep with his brother " on an iron bedstead made by our father and having for a mattress a sackful of maize leaves. At one side of the bed was the cupboard for the bread, and close. by the fireplace, always empty." Mussolini became, before he was twenty, a school-teacher, and then a revolutionary and socialistic journalist. He advocated strikes and was imprisoned for opposing the war in Tripoli. During the Great War he urged that Italy should throw in her lot with the Allies, and when she did so he at once joined up and was wounded in March, 1917. Then after the War was over he founded his Fascist organisation, which grew steadily and under his forceful direction broke the general strike of August 1st, 1922. After declaring his allegiance to the monarchy he organised the famous march on Rome. The Fascist columns entered the capital on October 27th, 1922, and triumphed after clashes with the Communists. The same day the king sent for him to conduct the Government and ever since he has been in power and overshadowed the monarch.

Who Was Hudibras?

HE was the hero of a satirical poem of the same name by Samuel Butler, published in the years 1663

to 1678. It was directed against the Puritans, and its hero, a Presbyterian country justice, accompanied by his clerk, an Independent, ranged the country like Don Quixote endeavouring to correct abuses and repress superstition. It has been described by Hazlitt as "the greatest single production of wit of this period." It contains every variety of drollery and satire, and these are crowded together into almost every page of the work. It is astonishing how many familiar quotations came from Hudibras. It is written in a doggerel eight-syllable rhyming verse which has come to be known as Hudibrastic verse.

How Many Bridges Cross the Thames in London?

EXCLUSIVE of railway bridges, of which there are several, fifteen bridges cross the Thames in the County of London. From east to west they are Tower Bridge, London, Southwark, Blackfriars, Waterloo, Hungerford, Westminster, Lambeth, Vauxhall, Chelsea, Albert, Battersea, Wandsworth, Putney and Hammersmith. London Bridge is the only one with a long history. The second to be erected was Westminster Bridge, built between 1739 and 1750. Next came Blackfriars Bridge, begun in 1760 and finished in 1770.

When Was the Royal Assent Last Refused to a Bill?

IN the old days the Royal Assent did not follow automatically on a Bill passing both Houses of Parliament. Assent might be refused and the form of words used was, " Le Roy s'avisera," " The King will consider." The power of refusal was last exercised in 1707 when Queen Anne refused to assent to a Scottish Militia Bill.

How Did the " Cutty Sark " Get Its Name?

THE compound word " cutty-sark " means a short chemise, and is a Scottish expression. It occurs in Robert Burns's poem "Tam o' Shanter," where Tam, seeing the witches dance, one wearing a short garment, roars " Weel done, Cutty Sark ! " The ship known as the *Cutty Sark* is said originally to have carried as a figurehead a female figure representing the witch of Burns's poem.

The figurehead of the " Cutty Sark," which explains the curious name of the vessel

Have Shoes Ever Been Shortened by Law?

YES; after the introduction of the long pointed shoes with upturned toes into England from Poland in the fourteenth century, shoes were

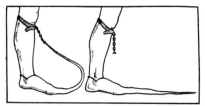

The long-toed cracowes shown in two positions

made longer and longer, till at last they were so long that the toes had to be fastened to the knee These shoes were called cracowes from the name of the city of Cracow, whence they originally spread all over Europe. The fashion became so ridiculous that at last a law was passed limiting their length.

How Many Kinds of Lightning Are There?

THERE are three kinds of lightning, one being known as forked lightning, which was formerly supposed to take the form of a zigzag line of fire between two clouds, or between the

Then there is what is known as sheet lightning, seen on or near the horizon. This is really the reflection on the clouds of distant flashes of fork lightning from a storm many miles away. Finally there is the very rare globe or ball lightning, which takes the form of an incandescent ball moving slowly along in an erratic course and often finally exploding. Little is known about this form of lightning.

How Long is a Cubit?

THIS measure has varied very much at different times and in different countries. In ancient Egypt there were two cubits, the natural cubit, or small cubit, of 6 palms or 24 fingers, equal to 18 inches, and the royal cubit, of 7 palms or 28 fingers, equal to 21 inches. The Greek cubit was equal to about $18\frac{1}{4}$ inches, and the Roman to nearly $17\frac{1}{2}$ inches. Among the Hebrews the cubit was the length of the arm from the elbow to the tips of the fingers, and measured about $17\frac{2}{3}$ inches. This measurement is said

Why Does a Cycle-Racer Lean Out of the Side-Car?

A MOTOR-CYCLIST gets up a very high speed, and, as we know, the tendency of a moving body is to go on

A motor-cycle and side-car turning at a hairpin bend

in a straight line. When he turns a corner, therefore, with a side-car, owing to this tendency to go forward in a straight line the inner wheel is raised off the ground, and unless extra weight be put upon it to keep the cycle down, the car will go over on its side and crash badly.

To stop this, the passenger in the side-car leans out horizontally, throwing the full force of his weight over to the side towards which the cycle is turning in order to keep the inner wheel on the ground. It is only by acting as shown in the photograph that the occupant of the car can prevent the whole machine going over when it turns a corner on the track at high speed.

What is a Ship's Log?

THE word has two meanings. In the first place, it is an apparatus used to measure and record the speed of a ship through the water. It received this name because originally the apparatus consisted of a wooden log attached to a knotted cord thrown out and reeled in at intervals.

Log is also used as short for log-book, a record or journal kept on board ship of the chief events of the voyage, including the results of reading the log. No doubt originally the log was merely a record of speed, and was afterwards extended to include other items of interest.

A remarkable photograph showing the wavy character of lightning during a storm over London in June, 1937

clouds and the Earth. Instantaneous photography, however, has shown that the angular and zigzag form is an optical illusion, and that the lightning really travels in a wavy line, something like the course of a river

to have been obtained from the Egyptians. In the New Testament the cubit is supposed to be one of $17\frac{1}{2}$ inches. Different authorities, however, vary in their estimates of this measure.

Why Do Spectacles Help Our Sight?

WHEN we need spectacles it is because our eyes are defective, and the curved lenses of the spectacles, by altering the direction of the light

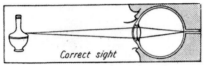

Correct sight
Rays meeting exactly on the retina

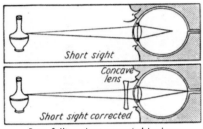

Short sight
Short sight corrected
Rays falling short extended by lens

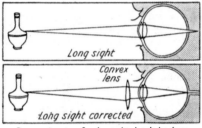

Long sight
Long sight corrected
Rays going too far brought back by lens

rays that pass into our eyes, set right the difficulties.

For example, if we are short-sighted our eyeball has become lengthened and the rays of light, instead of being focused upon the retina or curtain at the back of the eye, are focused before they reach the retina. The result is that no clear image is formed. Similarly, in a long-sighted person the eyeball has become shortened, with the result that the rays, instead of being focused on the retina, have their focus behind it, and again no clear image is formed.

The diagrams given here will show how the curved lenses of the spectacles placed in front of the eye alter the direction of the rays, so that they are focused exactly on the retina, and then clear vision is obtained.

There are, of course, many defects of the vision, but in most cases spectacles with the right kind of lenses can remedy the defect. We have only to notice how many of the people we meet wear spectacles to realise how many individuals have defective sight. Though we do not often give the matter a thought, spectacles are among the greatest boons that have ever been invented.

Can a Whale Drown?

CERTAINLY it can, just as we or any other air-breathing creature can be drowned if our heads remain too long under water. The whale can, of course, remain beneath the surface longer than we can, but it has to come up at regular intervals to exhale stale air from its lungs and inhale fresh air.

Some time ago a whale was sighted by a German tug near the mouth of the Elbe. A wire hawser and a chain cable were with difficulty passed round the animal's tail and the tug then steamed with the whale into Cuxhaven Harbour. The whale was suspended by the tail with its head under water, and in a short time it had been drowned.

Did Dame Partington Really Live?

THIS character is said to have lived in a cottage at Sidmouth, in Devon. When in November, 1824, a great gale drove the waves into her house, she tried with a mop to stay the progress of the water. But, finally, she had to take refuge in the upper part of her house.

The great wit, Sydney Smith, afterwards compared the House of Lords rejecting the Reform Bill to Mrs. Partington trying to stay the waves

How Can a Photograph Be Wirelessed?

THE photograph is placed on a revolving drum, and as this turns round a light is focused upon it through lenses and a prism. As the drum rotates it is moved slowly to one side by a screw motion, and so the beam of light traces out a fine spiral of 130 lines on every inch strip of picture. This beam of light is broken up by a revolving disc known as a scanning disc, which has perforations near the edge.

The beam is interrupted 1,300 times per second, and is thus broken up into a series of dots of light, which are reflected from the photograph through another prism to a photo-electric cell. Naturally the intensity of the light varies with the light and shade of the photograph.

The photo-electric cell converts the light rays into electric impulses, and these are amplified and sent out by wireless on a carrier current from the transmitting station. At the receiving station the electric current, which is weak, is picked up by an aerial, and after being amplified is passed on to an oscillograph mirror.

Light from a lamp is directed upon this mirror, and the light impulses are reflected through a slit, the amount of light varying according to the strength of the impulses received by the mirror. The mirror is oscillated by the amplified aerial current, and the rays received by it are reflected on to a receiving drum, which has sensitised photographic paper arranged round it. It revolves in a darkened chamber, and the photograph being transmitted is built up spot by spot by the light from the mirror. The result when this is developed and printed is shown in the accompanying photograph of the arrival of airmen at Melbourne.

How a photograph sent half across the world by wireless is received. The photograph shows Mr. Lincoln Ellsworth arriving at Melbourne after his dramatic rescue by Discovery II, with his companion, Mr. Hollick Kenyon, when they had been missing for two months on their Antarctic flight

INDEX

Openhand knot

LIST OF COLOUR PLATES

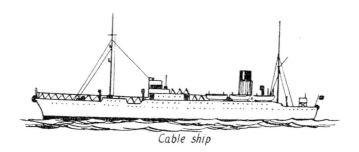

Cable ship